The HELLENISTIC WORLD
and the Coming of ROME

VOLUME I

The
HELLENISTIC
WORLD *and*

Erich S. Gruen

the Coming of ROME
VOLUME · I

UNIVERSITY OF CALIFORNIA PRESS

Berkeley   Los Angeles   London

University of California Press
Berkeley and Los Angeles, California
University of California Press, Ltd.
London, England
© 1984 by
The Regents of the University of California
Printed in the United States of America
1 2 3 4 5 6 7 8 9

Library of Congress Cataloging in Publication Data

Gruen, Erich S.
  The Hellenistic world and the coming of Rome.

  Bibliography: p.
  Includes index.
  1. Rome—History—Republic, 265–30 B.C.
2. Greece—History—281–146 B.C.   3. Hellenism.
4. Imperialism.   I. Title.
DG241.2.G78   1984   937'.02   82–8581
ISBN 0–520–04569–6 (2 vols.)   AACR2

DISCIPULIS MEIS

Preface

This work has been long in gestation and formulation. Grappling with the problems and analysis of its subject occupied a considerable portion of the past decade. Time available for actual composition during that period was scarce. Hence I am the more grateful for certain benefactions that significantly facilitated the process of writing. A Humanities Research Fellowship from the University of California at Berkeley afforded a welcome respite from normal duties. The hospitable and challenging atmosphere of the Institute for Advanced Study at Princeton fostered the early stages of this study. And a large part of the text was drafted in Oxford, where I enjoyed the handsome generosity of Merton College as Visiting Fellow.

Colleagues, friends, and students who have contributed directly or indirectly to the evolution of this book are far too numerous to cite in a list of acknowledgments. I have derived much benefit from invitations to present some of the material at lectures, seminars, and conferences—and from the vigorous response that those presentations provoked. Several draft chapters received the scrutiny of scholars whose incisive comments prodded me into improvements. In this regard I note especially the kindness of S. M. Burstein, E. Gabba, C. Habicht, B. A. Marshall, H. B. Mattingly, and F. W. Walbank. (They should not, of course, be presumed guilty of concurrence with the conclusions.) No less important are the criticisms, dissent, and (occasional) agreement expressed by my students over the years. Their stimulation has been of inestimable value. A particular debt is owed to my research assistants, G. Chiranky, N. Rosenstein, and J. Scholten, who considerably lightened the burdens of compiling references and keeping abreast of bibliography. And I register with fond admiration my thanks to Pericles Georges, student, friend, and copy editor.

The composition of this book has often tried the patience but never encountered the resistance of my family. Their forebearance has earned the deepest gratitude.

Berkeley, California   E. S. G.
August 22, 1982

Contents

Introduction

The expansion of Rome into the world of the Greeks holds persistent fascination for scholars and students. Reasons are obvious enough. The clash and intermingling of the two peoples eventually created that amalgam which formed the dual culture of classical antiquity. The peculiar mix that resulted grew from complex beginnings, elusive and enigmatic: a repeated inducement to research. The earliest stages of intercourse between Roman West and Hellenic East, the commencement of that long and fertile relationship, retain an abiding attraction.

This book investigates the nature of Roman expansion in the East against the background of Greek society and institutions. The period under scrutiny comprises much of the third and second centuries B.C., the era of Rome's initial movement overseas and of Greek adaptation to the authority of the western power. A broad geographical area falls within our scope: Greece proper, Macedonia, Illyria, Thrace, the Aegean, Asia Minor, Palestine, and Egypt. An attempt is made to see this pivotal time in its own terms, not as prelude or preparation for the future imperial administration of the East. The first steps of Roman infiltration into the Hellenic world had their own dynamic. A principal goal of this study is to understand that process, the setting in which it occurred, and the concepts that guided it.

V

Origins, motives, and consequences of the expansion have provoked inquirers for over a century, and increasingly so in recent years. Approaches diverge and solutions differ. But one fundamental question has governed debate from the start: how does one account for Roman subjugation of the Hellenistic world? The question derives from antiquity; Polybius posed it. The Achaean statesman and historian lived through the age of Rome's penetration into the Greek East, witnessed the phenomenon from both sides, and employed the topic to structure his history. A desire to uncover the wellsprings of Roman expansionism, its manifestations, and the reasons for its success impelled Polybius to his project.

One looks to Polybius in vain, however, for definitive answers. Ambiguities and inconsistencies lurk in his pages, leaving unsolved the central puzzles of how Rome achieved her dominion, through what stages, and to what ends. Questions arise also as to how far the process stemmed from deliberation and how far from an innate dynamic. Nor is it clear what mixture of condemnation, approbation, and suspended judgment the historian applies. Experience induced Polybius to modify and revise conclusions over the course of time. But he held firm to his basic conviction: a belief in the aggrandizing character of Rome's expansion and her overriding push toward world dominion.[1]

Polybian analysis stands at the root of all modern discussion. Some find it simplistic and one-sided, the general thesis contradicted by interpretations of particular events, or indeed refuted by the facts recorded by Polybius himself. Some reduce it to a belief in mere aggressive impulses, others see a more subtle recognition of complex motives. Still others embrace the analysis as consistent theory and a genuine understanding of Roman aggrandizement.[2] Caution needs to be applied. Polybius' perspective is invaluable but slanted. As a Greek who both suffered through and benefited from Roman movement into Hellenic lands, he could hardly develop a sense of detachment from the subject. His involvement generated insights—but also partisanship. The judgments of Polybius cannot serve as the starting point for recovering truth. They command respect, yet invite dissent.

The question of Roman "imperialism" is Polybius' question in

---

1. See the fuller examination below, pp. 343–351.

2. M. Holleaux developed at length the argument that Polybius' view of Rome's imperialist strivings is at variance with his assessment of the reasons for individual wars; *Rome, la Grèce, et les monarchies hellénistiques* (Paris, 1921); reinforced and brought up to date by F. W. Walbank, *JRS* 53 (1963): 1–13. The inconsistency is denied by P. S. Derow, *JRS* 69 (1979): 1–15; W. H. Harris, *War and Imperialism in Republican Rome* (Oxford, 1979), 107–117. For P. Veyne, *MEFRA* 87 (1975): 790–804, Polybius mistakenly views Roman imperialism as a mere will to power. D. Musti, *Polibio e l'imperialismo romano* (Naples, 1978), 57–64, 88–132, rightly criticizes Veyne's reductionism. He redresses the balance, however, by ascribing to Polybius rather more attention to economics than his text allows.

origin. His circumstances naturally prompted it. And all subsequent investigation has kept that question to the forefront. As a consequence, scholarship on the topic has a troubling, one-sided quality. Studies almost invariably concentrate on the vantage-point of Rome, the object being to explain her actions and intentions, and to outline the spread of her authority over Hellas. That approach inescapably promotes the idea that Rome exported her system and practices within Italy to the East, foisting them upon a submissive or subdued people.

A different line of inquiry is pursued here, with a different perspective. The setting can be as important as the actors. Greek institutions, Greek patterns of behavior, and the presuppositions of Greek international society provide an indispensable backdrop. The principal question takes on a reverse aspect: what were the circumstances that Romans encountered in the East and how did they adjust to them?

V

Polybius gave the lead. And moderns continue to labor with his aim in mind, to explain Roman "imperialism." The subject has inherent appeal and contemporary implications. Yet its very contemporaneity carries the risk of distortion: the pejorative character of the term "imperialism" beclouds and bedevils analysis.

The term itself is a modern one, unknown to antiquity. Indeed, it is a late-comer even in the modern world. "Imperialism" began to gain currency in the mid-nineteenth century, bearing a negative connotation, and principally with reference to the empires of Napoleon I and Napoleon III. Its meaning, however, had at first a narrow and not particularly informative range. It denoted the aggressive policy of an emperor, hence a usage that combined the notions of "Caesarism" and "militarism"—nearly equivalent, in fact, to "Bonapartism."[3] Not until the later nineteenth century did the term start to acquire a different and more familiar definition, with reference to a policy of expansionism, to embrace extension of national power abroad, regardless of the type of government which implemented it. The colonial holdings of Great Britain provided the impetus for a controversy that swirled about the Disraeli government in the 1870s, aggravated in particular by the campaign to have Queen Victoria declared the "Empress of India." "Imperialism" thus emerged as an anti-Disraeli catchword. Political sloganeering gave it publicity. As late as 1878 Disraeli's

3. Cf. D. Flach, *HZ* 222 (1976): 4–12.

Colonial Secretary, Lord Carnarvon, could claim that "imperialism, as such, is a newly coined word to me." Rightly so, in that its usage had hitherto been associated with continental despotism. The broader meaning soon took hold. Liberal critics of the Disraeli government denounced "imperialism," but would not renounce empire. Hence, the terminology received redefinition on both sides of the political fence. "True" and "false imperialism" became bandied about: a moral trusteeship of backward peoples as against mere territorial aggrandizement.[4] The word received its molding in the political debates of late nineteenth century England.

In transition from sloganeering to theorizing a chief stimulus came from the Boer War. It generated one of the most influential and enduring works on the subject, J. A. Hobson's *Imperialism: A Study*, published in 1902. Although the ideas had been adumbrated earlier, the war sharpened and articulated them. Hobson's analysis turned attention vigorously upon the economic aspects of overseas expansion. His fierce criticism of British policy traced it to the accumulation of surplus capital in the hands of the few. Domestic "underconsumption" created a demand for foreign markets and overseas investment which brought, in turn, the militarism and aggrandizement characteristic of "imperialism."[5] The emphasis on economic motives and consequences then received a different twist from Lenin. In his celebrated formulation, imperialism constituted the most advanced stage of capitalism. The ascendancy of cartels and monopolies on a worldwide basis intensified the exploitation of workers, but also presaged collapse of the system.[6] Thus, imperialism, which for Hobson was a pernicious prop for capitalism, became in Lenin's hands the manifestation of capitalism's extreme form and the potential agent of its own destruction. On either view, monetary greed and the economic advantages of expansion take central place in the course of imperialism, an association that has weighed heavily on all subsequent speculation.[7]

4. See the thorough treatment of R. Koebner and H. D. Schmidt, *Imperialism* (Cambridge, 1964), 107–165; the statement by Carnarvon in *Fortnightly Review* 24 (1878): 760.

5. J. A. Hobson, *Imperialism: A Study* (3rd ed., London, 1938), first published in 1902. The assertion of Koebner and Schmidt, *Imperialism*, 221, that this theory "was a clear product of Marxist thought" is inaccurate; see T. Kemp, *Theories of Imperialism* (London, 1967), 30–39.

6. V. I. Lenin, *Imperialism, The Highest Stage of Capitalism* (New York, 1939), first published in 1917.

7. Kemp, *Theories of Imperialism*, 152–171, correctly argues that Marxist-Leninist thought does not require "annexation" as an indispensable accompaniment of imperialism.

An alternative thesis has wielded comparable influence. Joseph Schumpeter wrote his famed study, *The Sociology of Imperialisms*, shortly after Lenin's work, but independent of it and probably in ignorance of it. Schumpeter, in any case, took an altogether different line. Imperialism, in his conception, stemmed not from calculation of gain or material benefits but from an atavistic drive for power: "imperialism is the objectless disposition on the part of the state to forceful expansion without limit." Psychological factors come into play, nationalistic self-assertion, instinctive belligerency, the "dark powers of the subconscious."[8] In similar fashion, Leninist theory was confronted directly by Raymond Aron, who characterized economic interests as either pretext or secondary consequence of imperial expansion. The root of imperialism rests in a "national will to power"—even when unrecognized by its protagonists.[9]

Debate swings between the two poles. Imperialist strivings can be analyzed either as rational policy, with definable objects, notably material gain, or as inchoate impulses, an urge to extend power and control over others.

V

Or else one may reject both. Attention centered at an early stage upon the character of Roman expansion as a natural object for scrutiny and comparison. Theodor Mommsen, as so often, set the lines of discussion. Writing in the mid-nineteenth century, before the term "imperialism" had come into vogue, Mommsen did not use the neologism but addressed the issue. He vigorously denied Roman aggression, whether rational or impulsive. In his view, the increase of Roman dominions stemmed from a dread of powerful neighbors. Rome's offensive actions had defensive aims. Roman conquests were reluctant and unplanned, constrained by outside pressures rather than willed for purposes of aggrandizement.[10] Mommsenian pronouncements exercised potent influence on later generations, and the line he pursued still retains its force. The thesis gained elaboration in the early twentieth century, when explicit debate on "imperialism" spilled over from the modern to the ancient world. Tenney Frank entitled his work *Roman Imperialism* in 1914, but argued that Rome's policies in the initial decades of involvement with the East were "anti-imperialistic." He analyzed Roman behavior in terms of philhellenic

8. J. Schumpeter, "The Sociology of Imperialism," in *Imperialism and Social Classes*, ed. B. Hoselitz (New York, 1955), 3–98; first published in 1919.

9. R. Aron, *Paix et guerre entre les nations* (Paris, 1962), 243–281.

10. T. Mommsen, *Römische Geschichte* I (Berlin, 1903), first published in 1854.

sentiments and an eagerness to receive acceptance among Aegean powers through championing Greek liberty.[11] The tenacious logic of Maurice Holleaux gave the thesis its most compelling formulation. Holleaux expounded at length and with rigorous consistency the view that Rome lacked any serious interest in the Hellenic world until the end of the third century. She entered that world only for reasons of security, fearful of attack and driven to conquest out of groundless alarm. Holleaux rejected categorically the ascription of "imperialism" or "militarism" to Roman motives: an incentive for self-protection rather than a compulsion toward dominance characterized Rome's movement to the East.[12]

Harsher verdicts too gained articulation in the early twentieth century. Guglielmo Ferrero's extensive study located the origins of Roman expansionism in the third century and saw progressive brutality and heedless aggression in the second and first centuries. Rational motives were secondary at best; only the will to power and ascendancy mattered.[13] A parallel judgment issued from the pen of one of the true giants among Roman historians, Gaetano De Sanctis. Writing at almost the same time as Holleaux, he arrived at opposite conclusions. For De Sanctis, Rome's undertaking of wars in the East gravely altered the course of her history. Militarism took over, an insatiable passion for conquest and control that robbed the state of moral authority and presaged its ultimate demise.[14]

In other analyses, calculation rather than mere power lust served to explain Roman expansionism. Debates on modern European history had their repercussions on the question of Rome. The economic element naturally drew attention from the beginning of the twentieth century. Gaston Colin in 1905 postulated the pressures of mercantile and financial enterprises on Roman decisions to move abroad.[15] The mutual effects of overseas expansion, increased emphasis on business interests, and the rise of a commercial class found expression in Rostovtzeff's classic work on Roman social and economic history.[16]

The main lines of interpretation were thus laid down early in this century. Variations on the themes or combinations of them continue to be played. So, for example, the important work of Ernst Badian stresses both Rome's reluctance to occupy and administer for-

11. T. Frank, *Roman Imperialism* (New York, 1914), 138–189.
12. Holleaux, *Rome, la Grèce, passim.*
13. G. Ferrero, *Grandezza e decadenza di Roma* I (Milan, 1907).
14. G. De Sanctis, *Storia dei Romani* IV : 1 (Florence, 1969), first published in 1923.
15. G. Colin, *Rome e la Grèce de 200 à 146 avant Jésus Christ* (Paris, 1905).
16. M. I. Rostovtzeff, *A Social and Economic History of the Roman Empire* (2nd ed., Oxford, 1957), 6–23; first edition published in 1926.

eign lands and her determination to dominate them. She achieved this dual purpose through transferring her domestic traditions of patronage and clientage to the stage of international relations, a form of "hegemonial imperialism." [17] The heritage of Mommsen and Holleaux remains pervasive. A long line of scholars has embraced the thesis, in one form or another, of Rome's "accidental" imperialism, an obsession with security that entailed repeated extension of frontiers. British experience provided the analogy of an empire acquired in "a fit of absence of mind." [18] For Paul Veyne, in a recent essay, Roman imperialism was an almost unconscious, machine-like routine, aimed not at conquest but at the security afforded by eliminating all rivals—a species of isolationism. [19] By contrast, deliberate calculation, in particular the calculation of economic benefits, has its champions as well, in increasing numbers. Italian scholars led the way in this generation, at first with concentration upon mercantile influences; more recently they have argued with greater sophistication and on a broader front that Roman imperialism aimed at the enrichment of all social classes through the emoluments of war, tribute, exploitation of resources, and slavery. [20] The latest formulation, that of William Harris, sees a coalescence of various aggressive motives: the belligerency and militarism cultivated by the Roman system, the grasping after material gains that came with conquest and empire, the compulsive drive for expansion and world supremacy, a national habit of resort to arms. [21]

V

The concept of "imperialism" arose in political circumstances and was appropriated for scholarly debate. Its manipulation has not

17. E. Badian, *Foreign Clientelae, 264–70 B.C.* (Oxford, 1958); *Roman Imperialism in the Late Republic* (Oxford, 1968), 1–15; R. Werner, *ANRW*, I: 1 (1972), 501–563, in his survey of the subject, goes further along these lines and detects a movement from indirect "hegemony" to a pragmatic "imperialism."

18. The celebrated quip comes from J. Seeley, *The Expansion of England* (London, 1883), 8; cited repeatedly as comparison between the Roman and British imperial acquisitions; e.g. E. T. Salmon, *The Nemesis of Empire* (London, 1974), 1–28. For those who have adopted some variant or another of the Mommsen/Holleaux approach, see the list in Werner, *ANRW* I: 1 (1972), 503–504, n. 12.

19. P. Veyne, *MEFRA* 87 (1975):793–855.

20. The mercantile aspect is emphasized to excess by F. Cassola, *I gruppi politici romani nel IIIe secolo a. C.* (Trieste, 1962). See now the treatments of L. Perelli, *Imperialismo, capitalismo, e rivoluzione culturale nella prima meta del IIe secolo a. C.* (Turin, 1975); Musti, *Polibio e l'imperialismo romano*; cf. Harris, *AHR* 76 (1971): 1371–1385.

21. Harris, *War and Imperialism, passim*; cf. J. A. North, *JRS* 71 (1981): 1–9. A brief summary of various views now in G. Brizzi, *I sistemi informativi dei Romani* (Wiesbaden, 1982), 151–161.

necessarily brought us closer to the truth. The negative ring of the term can prejudice rather than facilitate understanding. Definitions tend to be arbitrary, and thus unilluminating.

A definition of "imperialism," however, is beside the point. The present study moves along a different path. Roman "imperialism" is not its subject. Rather, it is the Roman experience in Hellas and the Hellenic experience under the impact of Rome. Neither approbation nor condemnation motivates the quest, but an effort at explanation. The Hellenic context of Roman behavior receives emphasis—and the continuities of the Hellenic world that persisted even after the coming of Rome.

This book does not, of course, profess to answer (or even offer answers for) all questions related to so large and complex a topic. Cultural interconnections between Hellenic and Roman societies, for example, demand volumes unto themselves. They can receive but peripheral and scattered treatment here. Rome's experience with the western Greeks, in particular the Hellenic communities of Campania, south Italy, and Sicily, is also touched on only briefly. The importance of that experience in forming impressions on both sides should not be underestimated. But information on it is too sparse and limited to allow anything beyond speculative inference. Roman movement across the Adriatic, the impressions delivered, and the reactions encountered form the subject of this study. Circumstances and implications differed markedly from the process of expansion in Italy. For similar reasons, this study does not explore the juridical relations and administrative arrangements that marked Rome's network of associations with Latin and Italian communities prior to the turn eastward. The testimony is ambiguous, confused, and late, the arrangements do not amount to a discernible system, and Roman concern for Italy always held a place that set it apart from affairs abroad. The focus of this inquiry, with all its omissions and deficiencies, is on the adaptations of the two peoples to the novel situation of Roman presence in the Hellenic East.

V

This work falls into three parts. Part I analyzes the institutional conventions that helped to shape the political and diplomatic confrontation of East and West. Part II seeks to interpret some of the presuppositions and expectations that Romans and Greeks brought to their encounters and to discern the understandings that arose from them. Part III comprises the narrative portion, organized by regions; it reconstructs the early history of Roman penetration into the Hel-

lenic East in light of the structures and attitudes outlined in Parts I
and II.

The five chapters of Part I inspect the principles, practices, and
institutions, both formal and informal, that marked interstate associations in the third and second centuries. Chapter 1 examines the role
played by formal treaties in defining Roman-Greek relations, the
models on which they were based, and the mixture of symbolic and
substantive meaning that they carried. The second chapter turns to
the diplomatic category of "friendship," traces the development of
this Hellenic institution, and tests the proposition that Rome cultivated it as a device to convert "friends" into dependencies. A parallel
investigation occurs in the third chapter, which treats the traditional
Greek method of resolving disputes by interstate arbitration and the
consequences of its adaptation by the Romans. Chapter 4 sets the
Roman claim to champion Hellenic "freedom and autonomy" in the
context of Hellenistic propaganda conventions. The "patron-client"
model receives scrutiny in Chapter 5: that chapter asks to what extent
this concept grew out of Roman domestic practice and to what extent
it served as a Hellenic means of exploiting Rome's power. Each of
these studies challenges the common assumption that Rome molded
the Greek world to her own purposes. They underscore instead the
Hellenic structures within which the interrelationships developed.

Part II moves from institutions to attitudes and motivation. The
sixth chapter ponders the making of "eastern policy" in Rome and
questions the idea that it was fashioned by men with specialized
knowledge, connections, and commitments to the Hellenic East.
Chapter 7 addresses the issue of how far Roman attitudes toward
Greek culture translated themselves into national policy toward Hellas. An effort is made in the eighth chapter to ascertain when and for
what reasons Rome first began to rationalize overseas expansion,
thus to determine the concept's effect as an impetus to empire. The
material advantages of empire form the subject of Chapter 9: what
role did they play as either stimulus or consequence of "imperialism"
in the East? The tenth chapter then explores the broad range of Greek
reactions to Roman expansion in order to help define the meaning
and intentions of that expansion. These chapters of Part II avoid simple and unilinear answers. Roman attitudes were diverse, shifting,
and often inconsistent, a curious mixture of attraction, indifference,
and disdain. For the Greeks, no steady image of Rome took hold;
rather, a sequence of blurred and changing images emerged, which
created a variety of emotions and produced a highly complex relationship between the peoples.

Eight narrative chapters in Part III follow the Roman experience in different theaters of the Greek world. The examination is ordered geographically, comprising studies of Roman relations with Illyria, Macedonia, Greece proper, Asia Minor, the Seleucid kingdom, and Ptolemaic Egypt. Analyses of events bring certain findings into focus. Rome's attention to the East was unsteady and intermittent. Informal rather than formal relationships predominated. Romans showed themselves adept at Hellenistic posturing, thus readily stepping into the roles of "liberators" and "benefactors." Greeks in turn became skilled at utilizing Roman power and authority, and at enlisting Roman collaboration (or at least reputation) for their own ends.

The age of "Roman imperialism," when surveyed from a Greek vantage-point, discloses a surprising amount of continuity with the Hellenistic past. Traditional rivalries repeated themselves, local and regional concerns prevailed, old patterns recurred. The energy of the Hellenic world survived the coming of Rome.

· *Part* 1 ·

The Instruments of Diplomacy

· *Chapter 1* ·

Alliances and Entanglements

As the diplomatic instrument *par excellence*, the treaty of alliance springs first to mind. It formalizes and gives concrete expression to interstate relationships, putting on public show the engagements entered into by communities and nations. The public character of alliance agreements in antiquity in itself compelled adherence or, at least, made violations conspicuous. In the lands of the Mediterranean such agreements were ubiquitous. The συμμαχία has a long history in the Greek experience, and the *foedus* dates back to the early days of Rome. The time of overlapping and intersection holds the center of attention here. Our investigation begins with a probe of the role played by formal association in defining the relationship of Rome and the states of Hellenistic Greece.

A principal question will occupy us at the outset and suggest a thesis for consideration: to what extent did Rome undertake official commitments in the Greek East, on what models, and to what ends? The issue, too often approached on juridical lines, has to be treated in its historical dimension. No standard pattern emerged already mature at the beginning—if ever. Particular engagements, called forth by special circumstances, altered and modified in the course of time, varying from place to place, and dependent upon the motives and demands of the participants, complicate the diplomatic scene immeasurably. Yet careful scrutiny can discern patterns, at least on a broad level, and throw important light on Roman attitudes toward Hellas.

The Problem

Rome's diplomatic contacts in the East begin in the third century B.C. Her experience with treaties of alliance, however, goes back much earlier. The ties between Rome and Italian communities would seem to supply the obvious model for formalized relationships with Greeks. Do they in fact? Here we enter slippery terrain indeed. The terms of these *foedera* rarely come to light, except as vague generalities or as isolated stipulations.

Scholarship has discerned a neat dichotomy: all treaties are classifiable as *foedera aequa* or *foedera iniqua*.[1] Hence, a lengthy battle rages in the literature over which form predominated in Rome's associations with her *socii*.[2] The debate is misguided and the distinction unhelpful—if not bogus. The phrase *foedus iniquum* appears but once in the ancient authors and then clearly without technical significance.[3] *Foedus aequum* may be found more often. But it has no stronger claim as a technical term. Cicero never employs it, though he twice applies the superlative construction, *aequissimum*: obviously a rhetorical flourish, not a legal definition.[4] Livian usage offers a few examples, but they contain their own ambiguity. At times the phrase carries a meaning of "treaty on an equal footing."[5] Elsewhere it seems to signify no more than a "fair" or "just" agreement.[6] Or the word *foedus* occurs in a context with some substantive or adjectival form of *aequus*,

1. See the classic treatise of E. Täubler, *Imperium Romanum* (Leipzig, 1913) I:2–6 and *passim*. Still adopted by W. Dahlheim, *Struktur und Entwicklung des römischen Völkerrechtes im 3. und 2. Jahrhundert v. Chr.* (Munich, 1968), 119–121; *Gewalt und Herrschaft: Das provinziale Herrschaftssystem der römischen Republik* (Berlin, 1977), 177. Cf. A. N. Sherwin-White, *The Roman Citizenship* (2nd ed., Oxford, 1973), 119–125, who states even "because of this schematic character there is nothing to be gained by surveying the history . . . of the federation of allies."

2. E.g. Sherwin-White, *Roman Citizenship*, 120–125; A. J. Toynbee, *Hannibal's Legacy* (Oxford, 1967) I:261–263; W. V. Harris, *Rome in Etruria and Umbria* (Oxford, 1971), 101–107: *foedus iniquum* predominates; E. Badian, *Foreign Clientelae*, 25–28; Dahlheim, *Struktur und Entwicklung*, 119–121: *foedus aequum* predominates.

3. Livy, 35.46.10. Rightly pointed out by Badian, *Foreign Clientelae*, 26—who, however, accepts the concept and the institution; cf. *idem*, *RivFilol* 100 (1972): 94; H. Galsterer, *Herrschaft und Verwaltung in republikanischen Italien* (Munich, 1976), 101–103.

4. Cic. *Pro Balbo*, 46: *foedus omnium foederum sanctissimum atque aequissimum* (on the treaty with Camerinum); *Pro Archia*, 6: *civitas aequissimo iure ac foedere* (on Heraclea—whose treaty he elsewhere describes as *prope singulare foedus*; *Pro Balbo*, 50).

5. Cf. Livy, 9.4.4, 28.45.20, 34.57.8, 42.25.11.

6. Cf. Livy, 8.4.2: *sub umbra foederis aequi*; 23.5.9: *quod foedus aequum dedistis, quod leges vestras, quod . . . civitatem nostram magnae parti vestrum dedimus*; 39.37.13: *specie, inquis, aequum est foedus*.

but not modified by it.[7] When Livy once draws a contrast, it stands between "an equal treaty" and one which places the contracting partner in the power of Rome.[8] That makes a meager sum of examples, dwarfed by innumerable instances in which *foedus* appears without such modifiers. More important, no ancient source attests the dichotomy of *foedus aequum* and *foedus iniquum*. As a criterion of classification it is best abandoned.

A variety of conditions, stipulations, and agreements marked Roman alliances with the communities of Italy. Concrete information on any individual pact is wanting. Military obligations of some form certainly supplied a feature common to all treaties. A *formula togatorum* governed the call-up of allied troops, based on the several *foedera*, but adjustable in practice and administered by Rome. The obligation is clear—and the dependency. Rome declared the wars and summoned the *socii* who mustered their forces at the behest of Roman officials.[9]

Did such compacts provide a model for Rome's agreements with Greek states? In the Hellenistic world, mutual defense pacts requiring the contracting parties to assist one another in the event of attack were common and numerous. Epigraphic documents disclose a standard and relatively unchanging formula: if any power brings war on one of the partners to the treaty, the other will come to his aid.[10]

7. Cf. Livy, 8.4.3: *si foedus, si societas aequatio iuris est;* 24.1.9: *ut foedus extemplo aequis legibus fieret;* 28.34.7: *cum quo nec foedere nec aequis legibus iungeretur amicitia;* 39.37.10: *si foedus ratum est, si societas et amicitia ex aequo observatur.*

8. Livy, 9.20.8: *impetravere* (the Teates Apuli) *ut foedus daretur neque ut aequo tamen foedere sed ut in dicione populi Romani essent.* Cf. 4.30.1, 8.2.13. And see Proculus, *Dig.* 49.15.7.1: *sive in aequo foedere in amicitiam venit sive foedere comprehensum est, ut is populus alterius populi maiestatem comiter conservaret.* The last is, of course, a jurist's definition, after the establishment of the Roman Empire, and not necessarily applicable to the period in which Rome was constructing her network of alliances in Italy.

9. E.g. Polyb. 1.16.2, 3.107.12–14, 6.21.4, 6.26.3–9, 12.5.2; *FIRA*, I, no. 8, lines 21, 50; Livy, 22.57.10, 26.39.5, 27.9.2–3, 27.10.3–4, 29.15, 34.56.5–6, 35.16.3, 35.16.8, 41.8.7–8. On the *formula togatorum*, see P. A. Brunt, *Italian Manpower, 225 B.C.–A.D. 14* (Oxford, 1971), 545–548.

10. E.g. *IG*, IX.1², 85 = H. H. Schmitt, *Die Staatsverträge des Altertums* (Munich, 1969), no. 463, lines 14–15 (Aetolia and Boeotia ca. 292); *IC*, II, 17, 1 = Schmitt, *Staatsverträge*, no. 468, lines 9–14 (Magas of Cyrene and Oreioi, 280–250); Schmitt, *Staatsverträge*, no. 561, lines 5–11 (Rhodes and Telos, early third century); *IG*, II², 687 = Schmitt, *Staatsverträge*, no. 476, lines 74–81 (Athens and Sparta ca. 266); *Syll.*³ 421A = Schmitt, *Staatsverträge*, no. 480, lines 27–40 (Aetolia and Acarnania ca. 263); *Syll.*³ 581 = *IC*. III, 3, 3a = Schmitt, *Staatsverträge*, no. 551, lines 12–22 (Rhodes and Hierapytna ca. 201); P. Ducrey, *BCH* 94 (1970): 639, A, lines 9–29 (Pergamum and Malla ca. 200); *ZPE* 17 (1975): 101–102, lines 15–21, 35–36 = P. Frisch, *Die Inschriften von Ilion* (Bonn, 1975), no. 45 (Antiochus III and Lysimacheia ca. 196); *Syll.*³ 633, lines 40–44 (Miletus and Heraclea, early second century). The formula, in fact, goes back well beyond the

Whether analogous reciprocal commitments existed in Rome's treaties with the Italians is quite uncertain. Dionysius of Halicarnassus specifies them for the *foedus Cassianum* between Rome and the Latins, ostensibly in the early fifth century.[11] But both the date and the authenticity of those terms are in dispute.[12] It would be hazardous to assume that individual treaties with Italian cities followed the pattern of the *foedus Cassianum*. Whatever their formal character one can hardly doubt that, in practice, the obligations went in one direction: support for the wars of Rome.

When inscriptions eventually detail Roman *foedera* with eastern states, however, their bilateral nature is fixed. Such documents stretch from the mid-second century to the Augustan era. And wherever the text survives in sufficient clarity, it underlines mutual commitments, including military assistance guaranteed by each side to the other in the event of attack. Those provisions appear already in Rome's treaty with Cibyra, possibly before the mid-second century.[13] Comparable ones occur in the pacts with Maronea (probably after 146), Callatis (after 146), Methymna (after 129), Astypalaea (105), and Mytilene (25).[14] All are plainly analogous to the formulas in Greek treaties with whose practices, by this time, Rome will have been quite familiar. They also parallel the Italian compacts in at least one central regard: obligations are explicitly spelled out in written agreements permanently binding on the signatories.

The important historical question must now be faced. None of the epigraphical treaties between Rome and eastern states can be confidently placed before 167, and all but one are definitely later.[15] Pydna

---

Hellenistic era. Numerous examples can be cited for fifth- and fourth-century Greece; see P. Graetzel, *De Pactionum Inter Graecas Civitates Factarum Ad Bellum Pacemque Pertinentium Appellationibus Formulis Ratione* (Halle, 1885), 52–57.

11. Dion. Hal. 6.95.

12. Cf. H. Horn, *Foederati* (Frankfurt, 1930), 87–97; R. Werner, *Der Beginn der römischen Republik* (Munich, 1963), 443–463; A. Alföldi, *Early Rome and the Latins* (Ann Arbor, 1963), 111–117; K. E. Petzold, *ANRW* I:1 (1972), 364–411; E. Ferenczy, *RIDA* 22 (1975): 223–232; Galsterer, *Herrschaft und Verwaltung*, 84–87.

13. *OGIS*, 762. Actually, only Cibyra's obligation is fully extant (lines 3–5), but the missing prior portion of the stone unquestionably recorded a similar commitment on Rome's part. On its date, see below, Appendix I.

14. For Maronea, see *BCH* 102 (1978): 724–726: *Arch Delt* 28 (1973): 464; Callatis: *ILLRP*, II, no. 516; Methymna: *Syll.*[3] 693, lines 10–17; Astypalaea: *IGRR*, IV, 1028 = R. S. Sherk, *Roman Documents from the Greek East* (Baltimore, 1969), no. 16B, lines 40–44; Mytilene: *Syll.*[3] 764 = Sherk, *RDGE*, no. 26d, lines 12–16. Similar provisions in Rome's treaty with the Jews of 161; 1 Macc. 8:24–28; Josephus, *Ant.* 12.417–418. On all this, see below, Appendix I.

15. Cibyra is the only possible exception and the placement of her treaty before 167 is most dubious; see below, Appendix I. The first treaty with Aetolia, of course, comes in 212 or 211, but that falls in a different category; see below pp. 17–20.

marked a great divide for Rome's role in the Hellenistic world; arrangements made after the fall of Macedonia in 168 have their own logic, a new departure that may bear little relation to previous policy. We need to push the inquiry much further back. Did treaty commitments define Rome's early engagements with states of the Greek East? What provided the diplomatic context: Italian experience or Hellenistic precedent?

Early Diplomatic Arrangements

Roman incursions into Illyria during the later part of the third century supply the natural starting point. Military forces crossed the Adriatic for the first time, setting a pattern for conflict, negotiation, and the entanglements of diplomacy. The evidence does not contain treaties of alliance. Roman armies crushed the Illyrian queen Teuta in 229/8; a decade later they captured the island of Pharus and expelled the dynast Demetrius. Rome's involvement in Illyrian affairs deepened; the opportunities for formal compacts multiplied. Yet the Republic studiously avoided contracting formal obligations. The peace treaty with Teuta imposed a war indemnity, reduced her holdings, and limited her future movements. Unlike agreements which followed Roman victories in Italy, however, it did not constitute a *societas*.[16] Greek coastal communities and islands, as well as tribes in the interior, namely Corcyra, Apollonia, Epidamnus, Issa, the Parthini, and the Atintates, gave themselves into Roman protection during the First Illyrian War and were accepted as *amici*. None asked for or obtained an alliance.[17] At the conclusion of the Second Illyrian War, the Roman commander busied himself with "organizing" Illyria as seemed suitable.[18] The cities and areas for which Rome had taken responsibility, so our sources state, came "under her authority"—a far cry from συμμαχία.[19] The Illyrian ventures did not create contractual obligations.

In 212 or 211 Rome did conclude a military alliance with Aetolia. The partners proposed to combine operations against Philip V, the

16. Polyb. 2.12.3; Appian, *Ill.* 7; cf. Dio, fr. 49.

17. Polyb. 2.11.5–12, 2.12.2. Demetrius of Pharus was apparently also an *amicus* until his ill-fated endeavors of 220/19: Polyb. 2.11.17, 3.16.2, 3.16.4; Dio, fr. 53; Appian, *Ill.* 8. Corcyra and Apollonia, in Appian's terminology, were "left free": *Ill.* 8. Polybius speaks of surrender into Roman πίστις and of φιλία, but no συμμαχία.

18. Polyb. 3.19.12: πάντα διατάξας κατὰ τὴν αὑτοῦ προαίρεσιν.

19. Polyb. 3.16.3: τὰς ὑπὸ Ῥωμαίους ταττομένας; 7.9.13–14 (the oath of Hannibal): μηδ᾽ εἶναι Ῥωμαίους κυρίους Κερκυραίων μηδ᾽ Ἀπολλωνιατῶν, etc. . . . οἵ εἰσιν ἐν τῷ κοινῷ τῶν Ῥωμαίων; Appian, *Ill.* 7: Ῥωμαίων ὑπηκόους εἶναι.

so-called "First Macedonian War"; a limited goal was envisaged, not a permanent commitment. That seems clear from the terms of the agreement: they specify a particular enemy, Philip and his allies, with detailed arrangements for the fighting of the war and stipulations for a future peace treaty.[20] Nothing suggests that they designed an enduring arrangement. Aetolia, in fact, broke the alliance—at least in Roman eyes—by coming to terms with the Macedonians independently in 206; and when Rome made war on Philip a second time she had to begin negotiations with Aetolia anew in 199.[21] After Philip's defeat at Cynoscephalae, the Aetolians, naturally enough, appealed to their former treaty with Rome, hoping to take advantage of its favorable terms to secure territorial acquisitions. The Romans rejected the claim outright. From their vantage point, the treaty of 212/11 was a mere temporary alliance.[22]

Eminent scholars, to be sure, have held that the Roman-Aetolian pact intended an enduring partnership. An abstract argument advances the idea: Rome never concluded any alliances except on a permanent basis; hence, the conditions expressed in our sources are simply *Spezialbestimmungen*, to be distinguished from the *Grundvertrag*.[23] This distinction is fictive, the reconstruction on which it rests inconclusive and unsatisfactory. Analogies with Roman treaties of the later second century risk anachronism, for we know too little of Rome's prior diplomatic practices. In fact, she was not averse to concluding pacts that looked to a specific situation rather than to a general alliance. Her agreement with Carthage in 278 outlined particular

20. *SEG*, 13, 382 = *IG*, IX 1², 241 = Schmitt, *Staatsverträge*, no. 536 = L. Moretti, *Iscrizioni storiche ellenistiche* (Florence, 1975), no. 87; Livy, 26.24.8–13. The top of the stone is missing. But τούτους πάντας in line 2 is certainly an allusion to particular foes specified in the agreement; cf. also lines 4–5: τούτων τῶν ἐθνῶν. The fact is confirmed by Polybius, who gives a list of Philip's allies, the targets of Rome's alliance with Aetolia: Polyb. 9.38.5, 11.5.4.

21. Livy, 31.28.3–31.32.5; cf. Livy, 31.46.5. See, especially, Livy, 31.31.20 (speech of the Roman legate): *vobis restituendi vos in amicitiam societatemque nostram fortuna oblata est*. Cf. Appian, *Mac.* 4: ἠξίουν (the Aetolians) τε αὖθις ἐς τοὺς Ῥωμαίων συμμάχους ἐγγραφῆναι.

22. Polyb. 18.38.7–9, 18.47.8, 18.48.7; Livy, 33.13.9–12, 33.34.7, 33.49.8.

23. So Täubler, *Imperium Romanum*, 4–6, 210–214. Followed by M. Holleaux, *Rome, la Grèce*, 237; J. A. O. Larsen, *CP* 30 (1935): 199–200; F. W. Walbank, *Philip V of Macedon* (Cambridge, 1940), 82–84; G. A. Lehmann, *Untersuchungen zur historischen Glaubwürdigkeit des Polybios* (Münster, 1967), 366–369. The view is challenged by A. Heuss, *Die völkerrechtlichen Grundlagen der römischen Aussenpolitik in republikanischer Zeit* (Leipzig, 1933), 37–44; K.-E. Petzold, *Die Eröffnung des zweiten römisch-makedonischen Krieges* (Berlin, 1940), 14–16; Dahlheim, *Struktur und Entwicklung*, 206–207; M. R. Cimma, *Reges socii et amici populi romani* (Milan, 1976), 100–107—but none with adequate argumentation.

stipulations for the war against Pyrrhus.[24] And a treaty with Hiero of Syracuse in 263/2 fixed a fifteen-year time limit.[25]

The matter should be approached from a different angle. Roman practice may not be the appropriate guide. The compact with Aetolia came at a time when the Republic was engaged in a death-struggle with Hannibal, who had recently added Philip V to his list of allies.[26] Circumstances impelled Rome actively to seek Aetolian cooperation and to enlist aid in her increasingly serious plight.[27] The provisions of the treaty, heavily weighted in favor of Aetolia, show that Rome could hardly have dictated the terms.[28] It is *Aetolian* practice that is pertinent here. Some revealing instances bear notice. In the mid-third century the League concluded an agreement with Alexander II of Epirus, with the expressed purpose of subduing and partitioning Acarnania.[29] At about the same time came an alliance with Antigonus Gonatas, who aimed to dismember the Achaean League.[30] And in 220 Aetolia

24. Polyb. 3.25.1–5. The disputed interpretation of these clauses is not here to the point; cf. Walbank, *A Historical Commentary on Polybius* I (Oxford, 1957), 349–351; Toynbee, *Hannibal's Legacy*, I: 544–549.

25. Diod. 23.4.1—renewed at the end of that time and made permanent; Zon. 8.16.2. The time limit is rejected on *a priori* grounds by Täubler, *Imperium Romanum*, 91–92; so also Walbank, *Commentary* I: 69. But see Dahlheim, *Struktur und Entwicklung*, 131–136.

26. Polyb. 7.9.

27. Polyb. 5.105.8: Ῥωμαῖοι πρὸς τοὺς Ἕλληνας (ἐπρέσβευον) δεδιότες τὴν τοῦ Φιλίππου τόλμαν, καὶ προορώμενοι μὴ συνεπίθηται τοῖς τότε περιεστῶσιν αὐτοὺς καιροῖς; Livy, 25.23.9: *Aetolorum . . . amicitiam adfectantibus Romanis*; 26.24.1–8; Justin, 29.4.5. The contrary indications in Polybius appear in a speech rebuking the Aetolians, not to be taken as an accurate reflection of the historical circumstances; Polyb. 9.37.4, 9.37.8, 9.37.10; cf. 20.11.7; and see Holleaux, *Rome, la Grèce*, 201–202.

28. Parallels with earlier Greek treaties are pointed to by Täubler, *Imperium Romanum*, 430–432. Principal responsibility for the war is delegated to the Aetolians, the Romans to assist them; Livy, 26.24.10; cf. 27.30.2, 29.12.4; Appian, *Mac.* 3.1. But see Livy, 26.26.1. Division of the war profits also finds good Greek precedents; see, especially, the treaty between Malla and Lyttos a few years earlier; *IC*, I, 19, 1 = Schmitt, *Staatsverträge*, no. 511, lines 4–8; other examples in Α. Aymard, *Études d'histoire ancienne* (Paris, 1967), 501–503; cf. V. Ilari, *Guerra e diritto nel mondo antico. Parte prima: Guerra e diritto nel mondo greco-ellenistico fino al III secolo* (Milan, 1980), 294–296. The practice was not, however, foreign to Rome; a similar clause occurs in her second treaty with Carthage: Polyb. 3.24.5. The custom was probably widespread in antiquity: Aymard, *op. cit.*, 499–512. Greek criticism of the Aetolian treaty was directed not at the terms themselves, but at the fact that Aetolia had linked herself with the Romans, the βάρβαροι, against fellow Greeks: Polyb. 9.37–39, 11.5; so, rightly, Dahlheim, *Struktur und Entwicklung*, 191–192.

29. Polyb. 2.45.1, 9.34.7, 9.38.9; Justin, 28.1.1. The exact date is unknown; cf. Walbank, *Commentary* I: 239–240; N. G. L. Hammond, *Epirus* (Oxford, 1967), 589–590; P. Cabanes, *L'Épire de la mort de Pyrrhos à la conquête romaine* (Paris, 1976), 61–62, 91–93.

30. Polyb. 2.43.9–10, 2.45.1, 9.34.6, 9.38.9.

secured the cooperation of the Illyrian prince Scerdilaidas, contracting for a division of spoils in return for a joint venture against Achaea.[31] Clearly the practice of framing an alliance for limited and specified goals was a familiar one to the Aetolians, and to Greeks elsewhere.[32] Such engagements supply the proper context for the League's treaty with Rome. It was not designed as a permanent alliance.

A clause in the treaty permitted other states to link themselves to the participants, with the same rights of *amicitia*.[33] Some certainly did join, to take part in the war against Philip: Sparta, Elis, Messene, and Pergamum. Their involvement, however, derived from explicit alliances with Aetolia.[34] Did Rome enter into any formal commitments? From the Roman vantage-point, *amicitia* with those states would be presumed to endure beyond conclusion of the war. It does not follow that the agreements instituted lasting alliances. Collaboration with Attalus of Pergamum is designated by Polybius as κοινοπραγία and, in Livy's phraseology, an *amicitia* inaugurated through waging war in tandem against Philip.[35] Nabis of Sparta, to be sure, referred in 195 to his *vetustissimum foedus* with Rome. And both Elis and Messene were called Roman σύμμαχοι in 197.[36] Phraseology can mislead. The facts belie permanent mutual defense pacts. Nabis in 201 initiated a war on the Messenians, who evidently had no claim on Roman succor.[37] Indeed Rome happily received Nabis into *amicitia* once more in 197, even though he had framed an agreement with Philip in the meantime.[38] Objections to Nabis' behavior came only in 195 when Flamininus endeavored to drum up support for a war against him—and the complaint then alleged violation of *amicitia et societas*.[39] Rome, who

31. Polyb. 4.16.9–10, 4.29.5–6.

32. Note the alliance between Rhodes and Prusias I of Bithynia in 220, aimed specifically at Byzantium; Polyb. 4.49.4; cf. 3.2.5. The division of responsibility on land and sea marks a close parallel to the Roman-Aetolian treaty; Livy, 26.24.10.

33. Livy, 26.24.9: *eodem iure amicitiae*.

34. Polyb. 9.30.6, 9.31.1–4, 10.25.3, 16.13.3; Livy, 31.46.3; cf. Horn, *Foederati*, 24–25. Cimma, *Reges socii*, 67–68, 103–104, misreads Livy, 31.46.3, as referring to an alliance between Rome and Attalus.

35. Polyb. 16.25.4; Livy, 29.11.2: *cum Attalo rege propter commune adversus Philippum bellum coeptam amicitiam esse.* Note also Livy, 29.11.1: *nullasdum in Asia socias civitates habebat populus Romanus* (205).

36. Nabis' claim: Livy, 34.31.5—accepted, in essence, by Flamininus, who states that Messene entered Roman *amicitia* on the same footing; Livy, 34.32.16: *nam et Messenen, uno atque eodem iure foederis quo et Lacedaemonem in amicitiam nostram acceptam.* Elis and Messene as Roman σύμμαχοι: Polyb. 18.42.7.

37. Polyb. 16.13.3; Livy, 34.32.16.

38. Livy, 32.38.2–4, 32.39.1–10, 34.32.17–19.

39. Livy, 34.31.5–6, 34.32.14–20. See the discussion of Dahlheim, *Struktur und Entwicklung*, 221–229, refuting Larsen's view, that these were permanent alliances, in

had linked herself to Aetolia for circumscribed purposes, had no more reason—indeed less—to undertake binding commitments in the Peloponnese or in Asia Minor.

The peace of Phoenice ended hostilities between Rome and Macedonia in 205. The above-mentioned states, and others too, if Livy is to be trusted, signed the peace treaty as *adscripti* on the Roman side. Whence derives this institution? Its roots lie firmly in the Hellenistic world, once again rendering irrelevant a search into the Roman mentality. Parallel instances from Greek interstate relations are easily cited.[40] The Romans had themselves experienced this feature of Hellenic diplomacy before: Pyrrhus in 275 offered peace and an alliance, provided that Tarentum be included as a signatory to the treaty.[41] The inclusion of *adscripti*, states which had engaged on one side or the other in the war or were interested parties in the peace, entailed no obligations on the principal contractors. Those states which joined Rome in signing the pact did not thereby have any formal claims on her protection and support. Rome emerged from the peace of Phoenice without military alliances or fixed commitments in Greece.[42]

The Second Macedonian War found several Greek states ranged

CP 30 (1935): 210–212 and *CP* 32 (1937): 16–17. Relevant bibliography in Dahlheim, *loc. cit.*

40. Livy, 29.12.14. The authenticity of the individual signatories is much debated, but may be left aside here. Greek parallels were discerned by E. Bickermann, *Philologus* 87 (1932): 278–285; *RevPhil* 61 (1935): 66–67. As examples, Athens and Philip II in 340 (Aesch. 3.69); Ptolemy IV and Antiochus III in 219/18 (Polyb. 5.67.12), Miletus and Magnesia ca. 196 (*Syll.*³ 588, lines 58–60); several states of Asia Minor in 180/79 (Polyb. 25.2.12–13). And one may notice the effort of Lampsacus to attach herself to the peace treaty of 196 between Rome and Macedonia; *Syll.*³ 591, lines 64–66.

41. Appian, *Samn.* 10.1.

42. The annalistic account, which has *sociae urbes ex Graecia* complaining to Rome in 203 about attacks by Philip *adversus foedus*, is not to be taken seriously: Livy, 30.26.2–4, 30.42.2–10, 31.1.9; cf. Appian, *Mac.* 3.2. Nothing of this appears in Polybius, nor even in Livy's recital of events directly leading to the Second Macedonian War. The story is wholly accepted by U. Bredehorn, *Senatsakten in der republikanischen Annalistik* (Marburg, 1968), 100–123, who regards it as based on authentic senatorial records; cf. J. P. V. D. Balsdon, *CQ* 47 (1953): 162–164; B. Ferro, *Le origini della II guerra macedonica* (Palermo, 1960), 5–34; rejected altogether by Petzold, *Die Eröffnung*, 44–47. Annalistic exuberance warrants little faith. Elsewhere, even Philip's victims in Thrace, the Aegean, and the Hellespont are described as *sociae urbes* (Livy, 31.31.2–4)! The account is either sheer fabrication or the places referred to are Illyrian. Cf. Polyb. 18.1.14—which does not imply that these areas are protected under the peace of Phoenice, or even that they are linked to Rome. Notice Polybius' παραδοῦναι, mistranslated by Livy as *restituenda . . . loca*: 32.33.3; see Walbank, *Commentary* II (1967), 551. For bibliography on these questions, see J. Briscoe, *A Commentary on Livy, Books XXXI–XXXIII* (Oxford, 1973), 54–55.

on the side of Rome against Philip. None entered into official treaty relationships. When representatives from Athens, Pergamum, and Rhodes arrived at Rome in 201, they appealed for help but not on the basis of any prior commitments.[43] Roman envoys at Athens, in turn, helped to urge the Athenians into war by stressing its advantages—a practical rather than a legal argument.[44] The Pergamene claim on Rome based itself simply on collaboration in the previous war against Philip.[45] As for Rhodes, the evidence is decisive: the island framed no formal alliance for another generation.[46] Aetolia was induced to join the coalition in 199 when the prospects seemed propitious. She came in without a *foedus*, merely a revival of *societas et amicitia*.[47] The Achaean League voted a *societas* with Rhodes and Pergamum in 198, but a formal union with Rome had to await ratification by the *populus Romanus*. Two years later Achaean envoys were still seeking such an alliance and were put off by the senate.[48] Boeotia entered the war in 197, on the same footing as Achaea, i.e. without a treaty of alliance.[49] Wartime cooperation, it is plain, did not entail binding engagements for the future.[50]

A peace treaty, of course, followed Philip's defeat in 197/6.[51] Is there any reason to believe that mutual defense pacts came on the heels of that treaty? Roman legates actually invited Philip to seek a συμμαχία with Rome in order to still fears that he might collaborate with Antiochus III of Syria.[52] The outcome of that effort is nowhere

43. Livy, 31.1.10–31.2.2.

44. Polyb. 16.25.4, 16.26.5–6; cf. Livy, 34.23.3.

45. Polyb. 16.25.4

46. Polyb. 30.5.6–8, 30.23.3; Livy, 45.25.9.

47. Livy, 31.40.9–31.41.1; cf. 31.31.20. After the war, in fact, the Aetolians kept making reference to their *earlier* agreement with Rome, the compact of 212/11: Polyb. 18.38.7, 18.47.8, 18.48.7; Livy, 33.13.9, 33.34.7, 33.49.8, 34.23.7.

48. Livy, 32.23.1–2; Appian, *Mac.* 7; Polyb. 18.42.6–7.

49. Livy, 33.2.6, 33.2.9. Cf. Livy, 42.12.5: *Boeotorum gentem . . . numquam ad scribendum amicitiae foedus adduci potuisse.*

50. One such wartime pact may be alluded to in Tacitus' mention of a *foedus* concluded between Rome and Byzantium; *Ann.* 12.62. He dates it to the war against "pseudo-Philip": hence, ostensibly, ca. 148; so H. Furneaux, *The Annals of Tacitus* II (Oxford, 1907), 139–140; E. Koestermann, *Tacitus, Annalen* III (Heidelberg, 1967), 215–216. But the order of events in this chapter would seem to place the *foedus* before the Syrian War; so "pseudo-Philip" may be a mistake for Philip himself; see the arguments of W. Henze, *De Civitatibus Liberis* (Berlin, 1892), 62–63; followed by R. Bernhardt, *Imperium und Eleutheria* (Hamburg, 1971), 72–73; E. Grzybek, *MH* 37 (1980): 50–59. Certainly an alliance against Andriscus would be difficult to square with the evidence of Diod. 32.15.6. But if it does come ca. 200, it can hardly be regarded as a formal συμμαχία. No reference to it exists anywhere outside this passage—and here it appears in a speech of the Byzantines seeking Roman favor and stressing distant services for Rome.

51. Sources and discussion in Walbank, *Commentary* II:609–612.

52. Polyb. 18.48.3–5; Livy, 33.35.2–7. An erroneous interpretation in Cimma,

reported; it can be confidently asserted, however, that Philip never got his συμμαχία.[53] Achaea, as already mentioned, endeavored to obtain a συμμαχία in 196 but failed to get it.[54] A similar rebuff was accorded to Antiochus III. Three times the king asked for a *foedus sociale*, in 195, in 193, and again in 193—and three times he was turned down.[55] It hardly looks as if Rome welcomed formal alliances.[56]

The repeated reluctance should suffice to refute hypotheses, often put forth, that Rome concluded *foedera* with Epirus and Acarnania.[57] For Epirus we have reference to a συμμαχία only in 170, and the term need not have technical significance even then.[58] It is enough to point out that in 191 the Epirotes were simply Roman *amici*.[59] The same unquestionably holds for Acarnania. Livy describes her

---

Reges socii, 66–67, who considers only Livy's language and ignores the Polybian passage which lies behind it.

53. The issue is discussed in full in Gruen, *CSCA* 6 (1973): 123–136. Accepted now by Walbank, *Commentary* III (1979), 275. Most telling is Polyb. 25.3.1, which speaks of the renewal of φιλία in 179; cf. Livy, 40.58.9: *amicitiam paternam renovandam*; Diod. 29.30.

54. Polyb. 18.42.6–7.

55. 195: Livy, 34.25.2; 193: Livy, 34.57–59; Diod. 28.15; Appian, *Syr.* 6; later in 193: Appian, *Syr.* 12; cf. Livy, 35.15–16; see Badian, *Studies in Greek and Roman History* (New York, 1964), 138, n. 78.

56. Lampsacus in late 197 asked to be included in the peace treaty and received some promises: *Syll.*[3] 591, lines 30–36, 64–76. On the chronology, see Schmitt, *Untersuchungen zur Geschichte Antiochos' des Grossen und seiner Zeit* (Wiesbaden, 1964), 289–295. Fear of Antiochus is generally taken as the motive—though the Syrian king is nowhere alluded to in the inscription! That Lampsacus was, in fact, named in the treaty is most doubtful. Certainly she was not given an alliance—indeed not even *amicitia* for another quarter of a century: Livy, 43.6.9–10. All this was rightly seen by Bickermann, *Philologus* 87 (1932): 291–299. Yet he did not balk at including Abrupolis, a Thracian princeling, as one of Rome's allies, either through the peace of 197/6 or the (postulated) alliance with Philip: *op. cit.*, 287–291. This is quite false. The only evidence is Roman propaganda at the time of the Third Macedonian War, seeking pretexts for the war on Perseus: *Syll.*[3] 643 = Sherk, *RDGE*, no. 40, lines 15–17; Livy, 42.13.5, 42.40.5; Appian, *Mac.* 11.2; Paus. 7.10.6; cf. Diod. 29.33. And the same consideration which excludes Lampsacus as a Roman ally holds against Abrupolis: Philip subdued the Lampsacenes some time in the 180s, without any objection on the part of Rome; Livy, 43.6.7; similarly, Perseus expelled Abrupolis in 179, but Rome offered only retrospective complaints, nearly a decade later: Polyb. 22.18.2–3; cf. Livy, 42.41.10–11; Diod. 29.33; Appian, *Mac.* 11.6. On Abrupolis, see P. Meloni, *Perseo e la fine della monarchia macedone* (Rome, 1953), 63–64.

57. E.g., B. Niese, *Geschichte der griechischen und makedonischen Staaten seit der Schlacht bei Chaeronea* (Gotha, 1883–1903), II: 653–654; Holleaux, *Études d'épigraphique et d'histoire grecques* (Paris, 1957), V: 134; Walbank, *Philip V*, 182; Hammond, *Epirus*, 621.

58. Polyb. 27.15.12: πραττομένου δὲ τοῦ πολέμου τὰ κατὰ τὴν συμμαχίαν ἐβούλετο δίκαια ποιεῖν 'Ρωμαίοις. On the ambiguity of συμμαχία, see Horn, *Foederati*, 10–12.

59. Livy, 36.35.8–9: *in amicitia pristina*. They had, in fact, felt free to negotiate with Antiochus: Polyb. 20.3; Livy, 36.5.

relationship with the Romans as a *societas*—which proved to be shaky indeed during the Syrian war. When Rome had occasion to rebuke the Acarnanians twenty years later she did not charge them with violation of a treaty.[60] Tacitus characterizes Athens as an allied city bound to Rome with a *foedus*, the earliest reference to that relationship—and it applies to the time of Tiberius! The conjecture that her *foedus* belongs ca. 196 lacks all foundation; that is a most unlikely time for it.[61] No alliances are attested in the aftermath of peace with Philip, and certainly none was sought by the senate. Similarly, the defeat of Nabis in 195 brought a peace treaty and imposed terms on the vanquished Spartans, but not any *foedus*.[62]

We may forego examining the events of Rome's wars against Aetolia and Antiochus of 191–189. Suffice it to say that the Greek states that cooperated with Rome did so through calculations of expediency and advantage. Nowhere is there record of participation based on treaty commitments; nor any suggestion that formal alliances took shape in the course of those wars.[63] The situation at Chalcis serves as appropriate illustration. A Roman mission to the city in 192 had gained its adherence via political upheaval: the expulsion of traders who leaned to Aetolia.[64] The Chalcidians subsequently resisted Aetolian importunations, not by citing formal obligations but by pointing to Rome's valor in war and generosity in peace. No state in Greece, they maintained, had bound itself to Rome by an unjust

60. Livy, 36.12, 42.38.3–4. Reference to Epirotes and Acarnanians as *socii* in Livy, 35.27.11 applies to their relationship with Achaea, not to Rome; so Larsen, *CP* 30 (1935): 202, n. 47; *contra*: Aymard, *Les premiers rapports de Rome et de la confédération achaienne* (Bordeaux and Paris, 1938), 310–311, n. 16. Formal alliances for Epirus and Acarnania are rightly rejected by S. I. Oost, *Roman Policy in Epirus and Acarnania in the Age of the Roman Conquest of Greece* (Dallas, 1954), 55–56. Cabanes, *L'Épire*, 276–278, accepts the Acarnanian alliance, but not the Epirote.

61. Tac. *Ann.* 2.53. The *foedus* is put ca. 196 by Horn, *Foederati*, 65–67, G. De Sanctis, *Storia dei Romani* (Florence, 1964), IV:3, 80–81, n. 6a, and by S. Accame, *Il dominio romano in Grecia dalla Guerra Acaica ad Augusto* (Rome, 1946), 101—without argument. Rightly rejected by Heuss, *Völkerrechtliche Grundlagen*, 33–34, n. 2. No hint of an alliance in 192 when some Athenians leaned to the side of Antiochus: Livy, 35.50.4. The assertion of Bernhardt, *Imperium und Eleutheria*, 86, that it comes no later than 167 also lacks any basis.

62. Livy, 34.35, 34.40.2–7.

63. The assistance offered by Ptolemy and by Philip was volunteered: Livy, 36.4.1–4, 37.3.10; cf. also the forces provided by Achaea, based on a specific vote of the assembly: Livy, 35.50.2–3. When Rome solicited support for the war from Achaeans, Athenians, Chalcidians, and Thessalians, she acted very gingerly indeed; she could make no appeal to alliances: Livy, 35.31. Similarly, Aetolian appeals to various states insisted that their backing would not involve any infringements of obligations to Rome: Livy, 35.46–50.

64. Livy, 35.31.3, 35.37.4.

foedus that limited its freedom of choice.[65] The Roman determination to stay free of entangling alliances holds good through the 190s.

To sum up the discussion so far. For more than a generation Rome had been involved intermittently and increasingly in Hellenistic contests: two major wars (against Philip and Antiochus) and four lesser ones (the Illyrian wars, the First Macedonian War, and the conflict with Nabis). Numerous opportunities—and several invitations—for permanent compacts had presented themselves. None saw fruition. That is hardly coincidence. Rome framed only a single formal alliance, that with the Aetolians in 212/11, but for particular ends and of limited duration. There were *amici* and *socii*, a convenient, loose, and elastic designation; but no *civitates foederatae*.[66] Nor did Rome attempt in any way to transfer her structured system of Italian alliances to the Hellenistic world. Mutual defense agreements specifying the requirement of military aid are unknown for this period.[67] Insofar as she engaged in official diplomatic dealings, Rome relied on Greek models rather than Italian, witness the pact of 212/11, firmly based on Aetolian practice, or the peace of Phoenice with its *adscripti*, a Greek institution. The Romans clearly shunned in the Hellenistic world the types of commitment to which they had subscribed in Italy.

Treaties with Aetolia and Achaea

Circumstances engendered a noticeable change after Rome brought Aetolia and Antiochus to their knees. The strict avoidance of the *foedus sociale* hitherto practiced now gave way to a different diplomatic posture. Its manifestation brings to light an important Roman

---

65. Livy, 35.38.5–6: *Romanorum maxime respectus civitates movit, et virtutem nuper in bello et in victoria iustitiam benignitatemque expertas*; 35.46.10: *nullam enim civitatem se in Graecia nosse quae . . . foedere iniquo adligata quas nolit leges patiatur.* Chalcis' relationship with Rome is described as *societas*: Livy, 35.38.2, 35.38.4. But that is simply a synonym for *amicitia*, as is clear from Livy, 35.46.5, 35.46.7, 35.46.12–13. An even looser usage in Livy, 35.37.4: *eorum qui Romanae societatis erant*—"those (Chalcidians) who favored Rome."

66. The imprecision with which the terms *socius* and *societas* are employed is well known; cf. Horn, *Foederati*, 9–12; Heuss, *Völkerrechtliche Grundlagen*, 26–27, n.1. There is no warrant for the statement of L. E. Matthaei, *CQ* 1 (1907): 188, that "it may be taken for granted without discussion that all *socii* were *foederati*," a conclusion refuted by her own findings; *op. cit.*, 184–187. The recent effort of S. Calderone, *Miscellanea Manni* (1980), II:363–375, to find a formal and consistent distinction between *amicitia* (an agreement to refrain from hostilities) and *societas* (a military alliance) is vitiated by his failure to examine the historical circumstances to which Livy's language refers.

67. Notice that in 191 the senate had to give its consul separate authorization to accept any forces volunteered from states outside Italy; Livy, 36.1.8.

adjustment to the power politics of the Hellenistic world. The change requires careful scrutiny. We need to investigate what form it took and what meaning it had.

The first firmly datable and permanent alliance between Rome and a Greek state comes in 189: the treaty with Aetolia. On the face of it this represents a sharp break with previous policy. How sharp, in fact? The agreement set out forthrightly the lines for a lasting relationship. Rome would tolerate no further difficulties from Aetolia. The latter had been, in Roman eyes, a faithless partner during the First Macedonian War, a dissatisfied and troublesome ally in the Second, and a recalcitrant foe in the latest conflagration. Informal or temporary agreements had led to dispute and military conflict. A mere peace treaty would not satisfy Roman senators who were fed up with Aetolia.[68] Her obligations would have to be conspicuously affirmed in the pact. And so they were: the initial clauses of the document required Aetolia to keep faith with the empire and majesty of Rome, to aid in no way those hostile to Rome, to count Rome's enemies as her enemies, and to make war on whomever Rome shall make war.[69] There are no time limits here. Framers of the association intended it to be a permanent one. Aetolia was committed, at least in theory. But to what had Rome bound herself? Quite simply, nothing. The treaty is altogether one-sided. Reciprocal clauses do not appear in the text; Rome obliged herself neither to assist the Aetolians in any undertaking nor to defend them in the event of attack. In this central regard Roman policy stayed unchanged.

The treaty claims interest also for a different reason. In modern formulations it serves as the very model of the *foedus iniquum*, the *Klientelvertrag*, the compact which underlines dependency and reduces Rome's ally to the status of a client.[70] The idea needs reconsideration. *Foedus iniquum*, as already noted, nowhere appears in our sources as a technical term. Nor is there any Latin equivalent of *Klientelvertrag*. Immediate demands imposed on the defeated foe, such as indemnity payments, surrender of prisoners and hostages, yielding of territorial claims, are not to the point.[71] The only concrete and enduring duty was "to have the same enemies as Rome and to wage war

68. For senatorial anger, cf., especially, Livy, 37.1.4, 37.49, 38.8.7–10, 38.10.3; Polyb. 21.31.1–4; Diod. 29.9.

69. Polyb. 21.32.2–4; Livy, 38.11.2–3.

70. The notion is repeated again and again; e.g., Täubler, *Imperium Romanum*, 3–6, 62–66; Horn, *Foederati*, 28–31; Sherwin-White, *Roman Citizenship*, 120–123, 184; H. Gundel, *Historia* 12 (1963): 289–290; Dahlheim, *Struktur und Entwicklung*, 38–39, 201–202; R. A. Bauman, *Acta Juridica* (1976): 20; Walbank, *Commentary* III: 131–132; cf. Badian, *Foreign Clientelae*, 84–87: "its purpose . . . was to establish a legalized *clientela*."

71. Such were, of course, demanded of the Aetolians: Polyb. 21.32.5–15; Livy, 38.11.4–9.

against them together with the Romans." This condition had been insisted on by the senate from the outset of negotiations and adhered to through a series of diplomatic wrangles.[72] The phrase "having the same friends and enemies" has, for many, carried the clearest mark of subordination, the absence of an independent foreign policy. Hence, a "client-treaty."

Is it so? In fact, the phraseology occurs with regularity, neither new nor, by any means, peculiarly Roman. One encounters it repeatedly in treaties between Greek states, where there is no question of dependency. A host of Hellenistic examples stand in the background.[73] Once again, failure to focus on the Greek diplomatic context has misconstrued circumstances and motivation. "Having the same friends and enemies" was simply a standard formula, not a novel tactic invented by Roman policy makers. The Achaean League, in the course of war in 192, voted to have the same friends and enemies as Rome, a declaration that certainly did not entail a *foedus iniquum*, nor any official *foedus* at all.[74]

Of course the treaty between Rome and Aetolia emphasized their inequality. The superior partner was undisguised. No Hellenistic state would have found that unprecedented or unusual. Ample evidence, primarily epigraphic, shows the "same friends and enemies" clause or a variant thereof and the requirement of assistance in offensive wars in treaties between obviously unequal partners. The *diadochoi* of Alexander engaged in such compacts. So, in 304 Antigonus Monophthalmus obtained the agreement of Rhodes to support him in all wars—so long as they were not directed against Ptolemy.[75] Two years later, the newly formed Hellenic League contracted to have the same friends and enemies as Monophthalmus and Demetrius Poliorcetes.[76] A treaty of 278 obliged the Galatians to make no alliances without the approval of Nicomedes I of Bithynia, to be friends with

72. Polyb. 21.2.4, 21.4.12–13; Livy, 37.1.5, 37.6.7, 37.49.4, 38.8.10; Diod. 29.9.

73. E.g. Magas of Cyrene and the Oreioi between 280 and 250: IC, II, 17, 1 = Schmitt, *Staatsverträge*, no. 468, lines 8–9: τὸν αὐτὸν φίλον κηχθρὸν ἐξῆν; Polyrrhenia and Phalasarna in western Crete before 275: IC, II, 11, 1 = Schmitt, *Staatsverträge*, no. 471, line 4: φίλον καὶ ἐχθρὸν τὸν αὐτὸν ἦμεν; Rhodes and Telos in the early third century; Schmitt, *Staatsverträge*, no. 561, lines 3–5: τοὺς αὐτοὺς φίλο[υς ἦμεν Τηλίοι]ς οἱ κα καὶ 'Ροδί[οις]; Gortyn and Lappa, early second century: IC, IV, 269–270, lines 6–7: τὸν αὐτὸν φίλον κηχθρὸν ἐξην τοῦ Γορτυνίοις; Miletus and Heraclea, early second century: Syll.³ 633, lines 35–37: εἰς ἅπαντα τὸν χρόνον τὸν αὐτὸν ἐχθρὸν καὶ φίλον; Hierapytna and Lyttos, early second century: IC, III, 3, 3B, lines 15–16, 21–22; Rhodes and Crete in 168: Polyb. 29.10.6.

74. Livy, 35.50.2. Cf. 35.46.13, on Chalcis. Notice the same declaration a century and a half later made by Rhodes who had already had a *foedus* with Rome for more than a hundred years: Cic. *Ad Fam.* 12.15.2.

75. Diod. 20.99.3; Plut. *Dem.* 22.8.

76. IG, IV², 1, 68 = ISE, no. 44 = Schmitt, *Staatsverträge*, no. 446, I, line 10.

his friends, and enemies of those hostile to him.[77] Two partially preserved alliances of Antigonus Doson ca. 225, with Eleutherna and Hierapytna, follow the same pattern: the cities engaged to make war against whomever Doson makes war.[78] Olus made a similar commitment to Rhodes in a treaty ca. 201: to choose the same allies and friends as Rhodes, to make war on no one without Rhodian consent, to assist the Rhodians to the limits of her power, to consider any foe of Rhodes her own enemy.[79] The Roman treaty with Aetolia fits snugly into that tradition, a Hellenistic pattern rather than a peculiarly Roman device.

The clause created no controversy. That fact needs stress and is generally overlooked. Harsh conditions demanded by Rome and unacceptable to Aetolia had delayed a peace for almost two years. In the winter of 191/0 the senate offered two alternatives: either unconditional surrender or a pact requiring payment of a thousand talents and consent to "have the same friends and enemies as Rome." The Aetolians asked for clarification of the first alternative; they had earlier had a taste of full *deditio* when the Roman consul ordered Aetolian envoys to be thrown into chains. The senate rebuffed their request and talks broke off.[80] In the spring of 190 the Aetolians asked for peace again and were presented with the same set of alternatives by L. Scipio. Despite the sinking of their military fortunes, they still found both options intolerable: unconditional *deditio* might expose them to personal violence, and an indemnity of 1,000 talents reached far beyond their capacity. They pleaded with the Romans either to

77. Memnon, *FGH*, 3B, 434 F 11, 2: τῆς γνώμης τοῦ Νικομήδου χωρὶς μηδενὶ συμμαχεῖν τῶν πρὸς αὐτοὺς διαπρεσβευομένων ἀλλ᾽ εἶναι φίλους μὲν τοῖς φίλοις πολεμίοις δὲ τοῖς οὐ φιλοῦσι.

78. Condition of the two stones makes restoration of the relevant parts uncertain, but plausible. *IC*, II, 12, 20 = Schmitt, *Staatsverträge*, no. 501, lines 1–2: [τοὺς Ἐλευθερναίους ποιεῖν τὸν] πόλεμον πρὸς οὓς ἂν [βασιλεὺς Ἀντίγονος πολεμῇ]ι; *IC*, III, 3, 1a = Schmitt, *Staatsverträge*, no. 502, line 11: [πρὸς ο]ὓς ἂν πολεμῆι Ἀντίγονος [. . .].

79. Schmitt, *Staatsverträge*, no. 552, a, lines 20–21, 24–25, 29–31. Unfortunately, the treaty between Philip V and Lysimacheia of ca. 202 is too imperfectly preserved to give the relevant clauses: Schmitt, *Staatsverträge*, no. 549. But see no. 549, a, lines 7–9.

80. Polyb. 21.2.3–6; Livy, 37.1.5–6. For the earlier episode, a notorious dispute between the consul and Aetolia's representative on the implications of *deditio*, see Polyb. 20.9–10; Livy, 36.27–29. The confusion has been endlessly discussed, a welter of ambiguity. Whether a genuine distinction exists between *deditio* and *deditio in fidem* and how far the divergence between Polybius' and Livy's accounts reflect differences in Greek and Roman understandings of *fides* need not be discussed here. Among recent works, see S. Calderone, Πίστις-*Fides* (Messina, 1964), 37–51, 61–84; Dahlheim, *Struktur und Entwicklung*, 33–39; W. Flurl, *Deditio in Fidem* (Munich, 1969), 26–106; Walbank, *Commentary* III:79–81. J. Briscoe, *A Commentary on Livy, Books XXXIV–XXXVII* (Oxford, 1981), 259–265 [hereafter cited as Briscoe, *Commentary*, II]. And see now Gruen, *Athenaeum* 60 (1982): 50–68.

give some guarantees if the first alternative were adopted or reduce the indemnity to make the second acceptable. All they got was a temporary truce to permit another Aetolian mission to Rome.[81] That mission was evidently kept waiting a long time, finally heard in the winter of 190/89, then presented with the same impossible alternatives and rudely dismissed.[82] No change in the terms came even in the fall of 189 when Aetolia showed herself ready to accept almost anything.[83] At last, the mediation of Athens and Rhodes induced Rome to soften her demands. She no longer insisted on unconditional surrender and she reduced the indemnity to 200 talents, plus another 300 to be paid over a six-year period. On such terms the agreement swiftly went into effect.[84] A noteworthy fact stands out in all this: never once did the "same friends and enemies" clause come under dispute. Through the long series of abortive negotiations Aetolian reluctance derived from fear of *deditio* and inability to pay an excessive indemnity. The requirement of entering an offensive alliance under Roman leadership caused no difficulty. A familiar Hellenistic formula, it got ready acceptance and incorporation into the peace as a matter of course.

Another feature of the treaty emphasized Aetolian inferiority: the opening lines, the so-called "*maiestas* clause." Aetolia had to respect the empire and majesty of Rome.[85] Those lines have become paradigmatic in modern works as a signal of the "unequal treaty."[86] A legalistic analysis, however, may be inappropriate here. The phrase has no Hellenistic precedents, nor any Roman ones either. Did the Aetolian treaty itself then set a precedent, to be employed in future agreements between unequal partners? An unlikely proposition: the formula does not reappear in any later compact between Rome and a Greek state.[87] In fact only one other example exists altogether: a treaty

---

81. Polyb. 21.4–5; Livy, 37.6.4–37.7.6.

82. Livy, 37.49; Diod. 29.9.

83. Livy, 38.8.1–38.9.2.

84. Polyb. 21.29.9–21.31.16; Livy, 38.9.8–38.11.1.

85. Polyb. 21.32.2: ὁ δῆμος ὁ τῶν Αἰτωλῶν τὴν ἀρχὴν καὶ τὴν δυναστείαν τοῦ δήμου τῶν Ῥωμαίων (διαφυλασσέτω?); Livy, 38.11.2: *imperium maiestatemque populi Romani gens Aetolorum conservanto sine dolo malo.* The last three words are often considered technical Roman phraseology. In fact, one finds them already in Herodotus, 1.69.2: φίλος τε θέλων γενέσθαι καὶ σύμμαχος ἄνευ τε δόλου καὶ ἀπάτης. Still another instance of the Hellenic background behind Roman treaties in Greece.

86. See above, n. 70.

87. Täubler, to be sure, claimed to find it in two treaties of the Augustan era, with Cnidus and Mytilene; *Imperium Romanum*, 64–65, 450–451. But the conjecture depends entirely upon restoration in the epigraphic texts. So, with Mytilene: Täubler, *op. cit.*, 64: ὁ [δῆμ]ο[ς ὁ]Μυτιληνείων ἄρχη[ν καὶ δυναστείαν τοῦ δήμου τοῦ Ῥωμαίων δια]φυλασσέτω. But other alternatives are equally possible; cf. Sherk, *RDGE*, no. 26d, lines 1–2: ὁ

with the Spanish community of Gades in 78. Cicero reports the relevant clause: *maiestatem populi Romani comiter conservanto.*[88] To be sure, it was not an isolated instance in Cicero's day—though evidently infrequent even then. The orator points out that not all treaties included such a phrase and, with regard to the word *conservanto*, that it appeared more commonly in *leges* than in *foedera.*[89] Where else the clause came into play we simply cannot tell. Perhaps only in the last century of the Republic or, so far as our evidence goes, only in treaties with western communities. That it did not become standard in the East can be stated with confidence. The peace treaty with Antiochus in 188, reported in detail by Polybius and intended to establish a permanent relationship, had nothing of the kind.[90] When Rome crushed Macedonia and abolished her monarchy in 167, she imposed numerous restrictions but also declared the Macedonians "free" and avoided any statement about "observing the majesty of Rome."[91] The extant epigraphical treaties from the later second century and beyond confirm the picture. They are explicitly bilateral pacts, at least in form, and make no use of the *maiestas* clause. Such a clause, of course, would be an overt acknowledgment of inequality between the partners.[92] Hence Rome required it of Aetolia, as explicit renunciation of her former faithlessness and treachery. But it clearly did not become a standard instrument of Roman policy. Nor can it be employed, in juristic fashion, as designating a category of Roman *foedera*.

[δῆμ]ο[ς ὁ] Μυτιληναίων ἀρχὴ[ν καὶ ἐπικράτειαν ἣν μέχρι νῦν ἔσχεν] φυλασσέτω, and the bibliography cited on p. 146. The treaty with Cnidus is hopelessly fragmentary and Täubler's reconstruction altogether hypothetical: 450–451. And even Täubler has to admit that these are not pure *foedera iniqua*. The Mytilenaean pact is clearly bilateral: lines 3–16. Hence, he resorts to a category of "*Mischform.*" The less said about this sort of classifying, the better. The arguments of Bauman, *Acta Juridica* (1976): 22–24, for fourth- and third-century usage of the *maiestas* treaty, are speculative.

88. Cic. *Pro Balbo*, 35. An agreement with Gades was initially framed in 206; Cic. *Pro Balbo*, 34; cf. Livy, 28.37.10, 32.2.5. But this seems an informal arrangement made in the field during the Hannibalic war; it was not given official status by the senate until 78; cf. Livy, *Per.* 28: *amicitia facta . . . cum Gaditanis*; Strabo, 3.1.8 (C 140). There is no reason to believe that the *maiestas* clause was part of the pact in 206, as Gundel, *Historia* 12 (1963): 292; Bauman, *Acta Juridica* (1976): 22; more cautiously, Horn, *Foederati*, 43–47; Badian, *Foreign Clientelae*, 118–119. Whether any significance lies in the difference between *conservato sine dolo malo* and *comiter conservanto* cannot be discerned. The discussion by Bauman, *Acta Juridica* (1976): 25–26, is inconclusive.

89. Cic. *Pro Balbo*, 35–36: *non est in omnibus foederibus . . . 'conservanto' quo magis in legibus quam in foederibus uti solemus.*

90. Polyb. 21.42; Livy, 38.38.

91. Livy, 45.29.4–14.

92. So Cic. *Pro Balbo*, 36: *cum alterius populi maiestas . . . foederis sanctione defenditur.* Echoed by Proculus a century later, *Dig.* 49.15.7.1: *ut is populus alterius populi maie-*

Further, one may ask, what practical consequences did the Aetolian treaty have? Rome had committed herself to nothing. Aetolia,
for her part, had contracted to fight in Rome's wars.[93] How seriously
or literally was that intended? The idea of Aetolian troops enlisted for
Roman wars in Spain or northern Italy is, of course, absurd. More
likely, the clause guaranteed support for future conflicts in Greece.
Aetolia, to be sure, was expected to refrain from further hostilities
against Rome. But what of offensive aid? Nearly two decades passed
before the next Roman war in the East. And when it came (the contest
with Perseus), Rome never cited the treaty in soliciting Aetolian cooperation. A senatorial embassy arrived in Aetolia during the fall of 172
and stayed until after the elections when the legates satisfied themselves that the results had returned a man who would favor Rome's
cause. The implication seems clear: Aetolia's leanings would depend
on her leadership; no sign betrays that she was bound by a solemn
pact.[94] After war broke out, the League did indeed send a cavalry
squadron to the Roman consul.[95] Other Aetolian auxiliaries, however,
perhaps mercenaries, fought in the ranks of Perseus, without, to our
knowledge, any official protest from Rome.[96] A second Roman legation to Aetolia in 170 comported itself with considerable restraint. The
legates asked for a number of hostages, at the instigation of certain
Aetolian politicians eager to get rid of their rivals. When the assembly vociferously rejected that request, the Romans dropped it and
departed—hardly an indication of Aetolian obeisance to Rome's *maiestas*.[97] Allegedly pro-Macedonian elements in the state suffered punishment after the war, of course, as everywhere in Greece.[98] Yet the
treaty itself is absent from the record, whether as authority for recruiting aid or as justification for penalizing defectors. In the Achaean War
of 147/6 Aetolian forces never mobilized, so far as our evidence goes.
A Roman legate spent some time in Naupactus; but no recruitment
took place and no appeal to treaty obligations.[99]

The notion that Aetolia lacked an independent foreign policy
after 189 also goes too far. She recovered her influence (or some of
it) in the Amphictyonic League by 178, as an inscription happens to

statem comiter conservaret; hoc enim adicitur, ut intellegatur alterum populum superiorem esse.
Cf. in general, Gundel, *Historia* 12 (1963): 289–297.

93. Polyb. 21.32.4: καὶ ἐὰν πολεμῶσιν πρός τινας Ῥωμαῖοι, πολεμείτω πρὸς
αὐτοὺς ὁ δῆμος ὁ τῶν Αἰτωλῶν; Livy, 38.11.3: *hostes eosdem habeto quos populus Romanus,
armaque in eos ferto, bellumque pariter gerito.*

94. Livy, 42.38.2.   95. Livy, 42.55.9.   96. Livy, 42.51.9.
97. Polyb. 28.4.1–13; Livy, 43.17.5–6.
98. Polyb. 30.13.4–5, 30.13.11; Livy, 45.28.6–7, 45.31.1–2, 45.31.5–9.
99. Polyb. 38.13.9.

reveal.[100] Cordial relations with Macedonia revived at about the same time.[101] When debt problems stirred serious internal difficulties in the 170s, Aetolia felt free to seek arbitration from both Macedonia and Rome.[102] She did not have to consult the Roman senate to authorize her conduct of foreign affairs.

One can hardly avoid the conclusion that the treaty of 189 constituted more form than substance. Aetolia was punished for her recalcitrance and perfidy. The Republic had insisted on a conspicuous sign of repentance: thus, the *maiestas* clause and an enduring commitment to share Rome's friends and enemies. Aetolia would provide an example to deter future uprisings. The senate never seriously considered actual use of Aetolian forces in their wars; nor did they intend to dictate Aetolia's foreign policy. Rome had herself refrained from entering into any obligations. The treaty served to underline Aetolian humiliation rather than to erect a cornerstone of Roman diplomacy.

That the Aetolian treaty set no precedent emerges clearly from the pact with Antiochus which followed on its heels in 188. Apart from the particular stipulations imposed on the conquered, the peace of Apamea shows an altogether different form. It created or meant to create a permanent relationship, but it was not an alliance at all; it was rather an *amicitia* contingent upon Antiochus' fulfillment of the specified conditions.[103] The framers omitted any *maiestas* clause and even passed over military obligations. Rome and Antiochus did pledge to refrain from assistance to enemies of the other; that much, at least, would be expected of *amici*.[104] But they made no undertaking to aid one another in the event of attack, let alone to participate in an offensive war. The treaty, in fact, gave Antiochus the right to defend his kingdom against assault even from states covered by its terms—though he could not expect Roman assistance.[105] The *amicitia* would be "for all time." Once again we must bring to the fore a central and

100. *Syll.*³ 636: representatives listed from the Ainiani, Locrians, and Dorians, areas under Aetolian control; cf. P. Roussel, *BCH* 56 (1932): 24–31; G. Daux, *Delphes au II*ᵉ *et au I*ᵉʳ *siècle* (Paris, 1936), 307–311; A. Giovannini, *Ancient Macedonia*, 1 (1970): 147–154.

101. Livy, 41.24.10.

102. Livy, 41.25.1–6, 41.27.4, 42.2.2, 42.4.5, 42.5.7, 42.5.10–12, 42.12.7, 42.40.7, 42.42.4; Appian, *Mac.* 11.1, 11.7; Diod. 29.33; see Gruen, *AJAH* 1 (1976): 35–36.

103. Polyb. 21.43.1: φιλίαν ὑπάρχειν Ἀντιόχῳ καὶ Ῥωμαίοις εἰς ἅπαντα τὸν χρόνον ποιοῦντι τὰ κατὰ τὰς συνθήκας; Livy, 38.38.2: *amicitia regi Antiocho cum populo Romano his legibus et condicionibus esto.*

104. Polyb. 21.43.2–3; Livy, 38.38.2–3.

105. Polyb. 21.43.24: ἂν δέ τινες τῶν πόλεων ἢ τῶν ἐθνῶν, πρὸς ἃ γέγραπται μὴ πολεμεῖν Ἀντίοχον, πρότεροι ἐκφέρωσι πόλεμον, ἐξέστω πολεμεῖν Ἀντιόχῳ; cf. 21.42.4. Livy wrongly designates these states as Roman, *socii*: 38.38.16.

obvious point, so obvious that it is too easily ignored. The "friendship for all time" is a standard Greek formula, long familiar and conventional in the East, not one drawn from the Roman diplomatic vocabulary. Instances aplenty confirm the fact.[106] Rome adopted an institution that would suit her ends. The treaty with Antiochus seemed to promise an enduring peace, while it kept Rome free of demands binding upon her. The Republic plainly made use of Hellenistic categories rather than shackle herself with Italian-style alliances.[107]

Nonetheless, the aftermath of the Aetolian and Syrian wars had elicited a new diplomatic posture. Rome was now (after 189) prepared to enter into permanent agreements with certain Greek powers. What did that mean? It misconceives the attitude to characterize it as a sharp turn toward more active interest or involvement in Hellenistic affairs. The contrary is more likely to be true. With the defeat of Aetolia and Antiochus (and the territorial arrangements consequent upon the Peace of Apamea), Rome could anticipate a more settled situation, no longer requiring her intervention. Lasting pacts with major powers that desired them would reinforce the atmosphere of concord and stability.

Few powers could serve that purpose. Pergamum and Rhodes qualified, but they preferred to avoid a treaty of alliance; Rome would certainly not impose it on them. The Achaean League, by contrast, had sought one for some years. It is no coincidence that she received it at about this very time.

The date of the Achaean treaty goes unreported in the extant

106. Among Hellenistic examples, see Prusias and Byzantium in 220, Polyb. 4.52.6: εἶναι Προυσίᾳ καὶ βυζαντίοις εἰρήνην καὶ φιλίαν εἰς τὸν ἄπαντα χρόνον; Aetolia and Mytilene in the later third century, IG, XII, 2, 15, lines 16–18; cf. lines 25–26: περὶ τᾶς οἰκηιότατος καὶ τᾶς φιλίας, ὡς κε διομέν[ωσι ε]ἰς τὸν πάντα χρόνον; Miletus and Magnesia in 196, Syll.³ 588, lines 28 29, 39 40: εἶναι εἰ̣ς̣ ἄπαντα τὸ[ν χρ]όνον εἰρήνην καὶ φιλίαν Μάγνησι καὶ Μιλησίοις; Eumenes II and thirty Cretan cities in 183, Syll.³ 627 = IC, IV, 179, lines 1–2; various powers in Asia Minor in 179, Polyb. 25.2.3: εἰρήνην ὑπάρχειν Εὐμένει καὶ Προυσίᾳ καὶ Ἀριαράθῃ πρὸς Φαρνάκην καὶ Μιθριδάτην εἰς τὸν πάντα χρόνον.

107. Nor should it be seen as itself a stereotype of the *Freundschaftsvertrag*; as Täubler, *Imperium Romanum*, 47–54. In fact, it is the only example of the "category" that he can cite; see the criticism by Horn, *Foederati*, 74–76, and Heuss, *Völkerrechtliche Grundlagen*, 13–18. If models be sought, they can be found not only in the Greek instances cited above, but in Rome's own treaties with Carthage which established *amicitia* subject to the fulfillment of certain conditions: Polyb. 1.62.8, 3.22.4, 3.24.3; Appian, *Sic.* 2.1–2; Heuss, *op. cit.* 17–18. The discussions of this pact by A. Polacek, *Listy Filologické* 92 (1969): 1–18, and *RIDA* 18 (1971): 591–621, offer nothing new. Full bibliography in Walbank, *Commentary* III: 156–162. Add E. Paltiel, *Antichthon* 13 (1979): 30–41, who reaches the illogical conclusion that some clauses were binding on Antiochus alone, others on his successors as well.

testimony and has engendered lengthy dispute. Rehearsal of that debate would be pointless here.[108] The Achaeans actively solicited an alliance in 197/6, but Rome turned aside the request.[109] Silence prevails thereafter through the 190s. The Achaean vote in 192 to have the same friends and enemies as Rome implies the absence of a formal *foedus* at that time.[110] And the harsh words of Flamininus in 191, that Rome had not fought at Thermopylae for the sake of the Achaeans, suggests that they still had no official alliance.[111] The Achaean forces sent against Antiochus in 190 depended on an accord with Eumenes of Pergamum, not any pact with Rome.[112] The first undisputed reference to a συμμαχία comes in 183 when Achaean representatives asked for its renewal.[113] A date not long after the Aetolian and Antiochene treaties would seem suitable.[114]

Chronological problems are difficult enough. The terms create even greater difficulty. Our sources nowhere specify them. Moderns generally apply the designation *foedus aequum*. That, as we have seen, is almost certainly not a technical phrase anyway. With regard to the Achaean pact, it appears only once, in a speech, where the remarks plainly do not carry technical significance.[115] Only indirect evidence bears on the provisions, and not much of that. Was this a mutual defense agreement in which each party bound itself to assist the other?

In the winter of 183/2 an Achaean legation came before the Roman senate to ask for support in putting down the Messenian revolt, "in accordance with the alliance." They added, however, the polite

108. Among the more important discussions, see Täubler, *Imperium Romanum*, 219–228; Holleaux, *Études* V:121–140; Horn, *Foederati*, 31–34; Larsen, *CP* 30 (1935): 212–214; Aymard, *Premiers rapports*, 261–267; Badian, *JRS* 42 (1952): 76–80. Nothing new is added by A. M. Castellani, *ContIstFilClass* 1 (1963): 84–86; Lehmann, *Untersuchungen*, 233, n. 80; Dahlheim, *Struktur und Entwicklung*, 261–262, n. 8; R. M. Errington, *Philopoemen* (Oxford, 1969), 114–115; Briscoe, *Commentary*, II, 215.

109. Polyb. 18.42.6–7.   110. Livy, 35.50.1–2.   111. Livy, 36.32.2.

112. Polyb. 21.3b; cf. Livy, 32.23.1, 37.20.

113. Polyb. 23.4.12. The speech of Lycortas in 184, if accurately reported by Livy, indicates the existence of the *foedus* by that time; Livy, 39.37.10: *si foedus ratum est, si societas et amicitia ex aequo*. No explicit chronology can be ferreted out of Polyb. 24.11–13.

114. That the senate in 187/6 could send a formal request to both Aetolia and Achaea to aid in restoration of the Boeotian fugitive Zeuxippus may imply that the treaty had already been concluded; Polyb. 22.4.9.

115. The speech of Lycortas in 184: Livy, 39.37.13: *specie, inquis, aequum est foedus*; cf. 39.37.10, quoted above, n. 113. The rhetorical character of these words is clear, for Lycortas goes on to ask that Rome not put her enemies on the same footing, *in aequo*, with her friends, and employs the identical phrase to describe Achaea's enrollment of Sparta into her confederacy; Livy, 39.37.14–15. Similarly nontechnical is Polyb. 24.10.9: κατὰ ποσὸν ἰσολογίαν ἔχειν πρὸς Ῥωμαίους; cf. 30.31.16.

qualification: "if it is possible." If not, they requested that Rome at least see to it that no arms or supplies from Italy should reach the Messenian rebels.[116] One may reasonably infer that justification for the request could be found in the treaty: an agreement to aid one another in case of attack by a third party and to prevent any assistance to enemies of either signatory.[117] By the same token, it follows that the pact contained a loophole, reflected in the Achaean remark "if it is possible." Once more, the Greek background is decisive here. Qualifications of this sort find their pattern in Hellenistic treaties that often temper military commitments with the proviso κατὰ τὸ δυνατόν.[118] From the Roman vantage-point it supplied a convenient escape clause if the *patres* preferred not to authorize any forces. In fact, they firmly declined the Achaean request for aid. Pretexts came readily to hand: a Roman envoy had earlier endeavored in vain to prevent the Achaean declaration of war on Messene, and the senate could argue anyway that secession within the Achaean League did not fulfill the conditions of external attack. Hence the mutual defense obligation was inapplicable.[119] Achaea went on to fight the war alone and successfully subjugated Messene, while Rome kept aloof. When the outcome became known, however, the *patres* announced that they had lived up to what they considered their part of the bargain: no material assistance had been permitted from Italy to Messene.[120] The facts appear to add up to the following: Rome and Achaea had contracted not to assist any power making war on the other, a provision paralleled in the peace of Apamea; as for mutual defense, qualified wording or tacit understanding left Rome free to honor or decline appeals as she saw fit.

Demands on Achaea, deriving from the *foedus*, were probably

116. Polyb. 23.9.12: τῶν δ᾽ Ἀχαιῶν παρακαλούντων, εἰ μὲν δυνατόν ἐστιν, βοήθειαν αὐτοῖς πέμψαι κατὰ τὴν συμμαχίαν ἐπὶ τοὺς Μεσσηνίους, εἰ δὲ μή, προνοηθῆναι ἵνα μηθεὶς τῶν ἐξ Ἰταλίας μήθ᾽ ὅπλα μήτε σῖτον εἰς τὴν Μεσσήνην εἰσαγάγῃ.

117. So Täubler, *Imperium Romanum*, 221; Horn, *Foederati*, 32; Aymard, *Premiers rapports*, 268–269. The latter provision, in any case, appears also in the treaty with Antiochus: Polyb. 21.42.2–3; Livy, 38.38.2–3.

118. E.g. Rhodes and Telos, early third century: Schmitt, *Staatsverträge*, no. 561, lines 5–11; Gortyn and Lappa, second century: *IC*, IV, 269–270, lines 7–15; Antigonus Doson and Hierapytna ca. 227: *IC*, III, 3, 1A = Schmitt, *Staatsverträge*, no. 502, line 33; Rhodes and Hierapytna in 201: *Syll.*³ 581 = *IC*, III, 3, 3A = Schmitt, *Staatsverträge*, no. 551, lines 12–22, 64–66; also perhaps Athens and Sparta ca. 266: *Syll.*³ 434 = Schmitt, *Staatsverträge*, no. 476, lines 74–81—though the phrase is restored there.

119. That appears to have been the senatorial argument, somewhat graphically expressed by Polybius: 23.9.12–13. For the previous effort to prevent war, see Polyb. 24.9.12; cf. 23.9.8.

120. Polyb. 23.17.3.

no more stringent. Rome surely did not call up—nor ever expected to call up—Achaean forces, under this treaty, for wars in the West.[121] In eastern campaigns she could hope for the League's support. But the treaty did not spell out the terms of such support. A Roman delegation to Greece in 172 asked for Achaea's backing in the war against Perseus. Since the Romans needed to voice a special plea, the *foedus* evidently did not come into automatic operation. The League announced readiness to cooperate, indeed expressed indignation that Rome should have had any doubts, given Achaea's services during the Macedonian and Syrian wars, but no one made reference to any duties contained in the *foedus*.[122] On the basis of this declaration Rome could now apply for Achaean contingents, and she received a limited number in 172 and 171.[123] The commitment, however, was far from absolute. Polybius reports a remarkable debate among Achaean politicians in 170/69, a debate in which he himself took part. The discussion revolved around Achaea's role in the war. Participants voiced various viewpoints: the League should maintain neutrality and supply assistance to neither Rome nor Perseus; or politicians who catered to Rome in defiance of Achaean laws should be squelched; or it was best to wait upon events and decide actions in accordance with circumstances. Conspicuous by its absence is any allusion to the *foedus*. Such a discussion could hardly have taken place if the treaty enjoined Achaean participation in the war.[124] In 169 the League at last voted to commit its entire forces to the Roman cause—a voluntary act, not dictated by a compact nor even requested by Rome. Indeed, the Roman consul Q. Philippus politely declined those troops as no longer necessary.[125] When another Roman legate did make request for five thousand men, Philippus advised the League to ignore it; the as-

---

121. To be sure, an Achaean contingent did fight under Cn. Domitius against the Gauls, as revealed by an inscription honoring the contingent's commander. The decree is dated to 192 by L. Moretti, *RivFilol* 93 (1965): 278–283; *ISE*, no. 60—and connected with the campaigns of Ahenobarbus, consul in that year: Livy, 35.22.3–4, 35.40.2–4. That is certainly wrong. The inscription belongs to 122, the time of Roman incursions into Gaul under another Cn. Domitius Ahenobarbus (sources in T. R. S. Broughton, *The Magistrates of the Roman Republic* [New York, 1951], I:516)—and a time after the League's crushing defeat at Roman hands. Moretti's hypothesis is decisively refuted by T. Schwertfeger, *Der Achaiische Bund von 146 bis 27 v. Chr.* (Munich, 1974), 27–40.

122. Livy, 42.37.7–8.

123. Polyb. 27.2.11–12; Livy, 42.44.7–8, 42.55.10.

124. Polyb. 28.6. Of course, this was a private colloquy, in the circle of Lycortas and Polybius, not a public debate. But the omission of any consideration of the treaty is no less striking for that. Even the κατὰ τὸ δύνατον loophole, which might have been invoked, is omitted.

125. Polyb. 28.12.1–6, 28.13.1–5, 29.24.2.

sembly duly refrained from taking action.[126] Of course, Achaean
shilly-shallying in the war can be ascribed, in large part, to doubts in
high circles of its justice or its advantages. Nonetheless, the behavior
of the League—and of Roman officials—rules out any definitive commitments contained in a treaty. The *foedus* was never at issue.[127]

As for the rest of its terms, little need—or can—be said. An
Achaean measure, on the books by 185, forbade the summoning of an
ecclesia except on matters of war and alliance, or upon written request
from the Roman senate.[128] The latter clause stood apart from the
foedus as a separate piece of legislation passed by the Achaeans. Yet it
obviously presupposes the treaty. *Prima facie*, the enactment accords a
significant privilege to Rome, a *quid pro quo*, so it is often adjudged,
for the granting of a *foedus*.[129] That interpretation may miss its real significance. The kings of Macedonia, at the time of their alliance with
Achaea in the late third century, had enjoyed a similar privilege of
summoning the assembly into session, and had not always exercised
it to Achaean taste.[130] Further, on at least two occasions, in 191 and
189, Roman commanders had curtly ordered meetings of the Achaeans on their own authority.[131] It is a plausible inference that the new
measure aimed to prevent such peremptory interference in Achaean
affairs. That, in any case, appears to have been its effect. Roman officials did again endeavor to summon sessions of the League, but were
rebuffed when they could not present senatorial instructions. And
the Achaean stance went unchallenged by the senate.[132]

Pausanias—and he alone—attests one other clause: deputations

126. Polyb. 28.13.7–13.

127. Nor is there any reason to believe that Achaean auxiliaries who served in
the war against Andriscus were there in answer to treaty obligations: Livy, *Per.* 50. It
might be added that nowhere in all the information on the fateful Achaean War of
147/6 is there any reference to the *foedus* or a violation thereof: Polyb. 38.9–18; Paus.
7.11–16. The nearest we come to it is Stratius' remark that the Romans were φίλοι and
σύμμαχοι: Polyb. 38.13.5. Other references are simply to Achaean πίστις or φιλία:
Polyb. 38.9.8, 38.12.8; and to their revolt as unjust, impious, and ungrateful: Polyb.
38.13.8; Paus. 7.14.3, 7.15.1–2. Polybius' own verdict, πάντων ἀσεβεστάτοις καὶ παρα-
νομωτάτοις ἐπιβαλλόμενος (38.13.8) will hardly be read as an allusion to the treaty.

128. Polyb. 22.10.11–12, 22.12.5–7, 23.5.14–17; Paus. 7.9.1; Livy, 39.33.7.

129. Cf. Larsen, *CP* 30 (1935): 208, 213; Aymard, *Premiers rapports*, 269–271.

130. Polyb. 4.85.3, 5.1.6–7.

131. Livy, 36.31.10, 38.32.3. The passages have gone unnoticed in this connection. They demonstrate that the measure requiring written senatorial instructions to
summon an *ecclesia* was not yet on the books by 189—and by implication, perhaps, that
the *foedus* was not yet in existence.

132. See sources cited above, n. 128. The law was perhaps not unwelcome to the
senate, which could thereby exercise an additional check upon its own legates; so Errington, *Philopoemen*, 174.

to Rome had to be authorized by the League as a whole and could not be sent individually by any constituent member.[133] Scholars have generally dismissed the report as erroneous and have accused Pausanias of his customary ineptitude.[134] Whatever the truth of the matter, individual states in the League, notably the Spartans, did send embassies to Rome with some regularity and without provoking any official objections.[135] Hence, the provision, if contained in the treaty, had merely *pro forma* value and was ignored with impunity.

Tangible effects of the *foedus* between Rome and Achaea largely escape detection. That itself is a telling piece of testimony. One will not read the consequences in specific provisions of the agreement. As with the Aetolian and Antiochene treaties, the fact of a permanent relationship, officially established, was more important than the inscribed terms. Rome remained free to turn down Achaean importunation when she found it inconvenient; and the Achaeans were unconstrained by obligations arising out of the pact. The *foedus* provided a showpiece rather than a basis for action or a call to duty.

Alliances with Aetolia and Achaea and *amicitia* "forever" with Antiochus converge in time and purpose. In the postwar world of 188 they delivered a sense of abiding settlement. Confidence and security could return to the states of the Greek East; Rome could return to the concerns of the West.

Alliances With Rhodians and Jews

In the aftermath of Apamea Rome pulled back again from the Hellenic world. A proper settlement and a stable concord best suited her purposes, circumstances that would not require her reentry by force. To that end Rome restricted the Syrian kingdom in territorial extent and allowed her *amici* Pergamum and Rhodes to obtain an overlordship in western Anatolia. To that end also she consented to the formal agreements examined above: a permanent $\phi\iota\lambda\iota\alpha$ with Antiochus the Great, a one-sided *foedus* with Aetolia, and an alliance with the Achaean League. The pacts served to underline Hellenistic stability, not to facilitate Rome's expansion.[136]

133. Paus. 7.9.4; cf. 7.12.5.
134. So, e.g., Täubler, *Imperium Romanum*, 224–225; Larsen, *CP* 30 (1935): 208; Aymard, *Premiers rapports*, 269, n. 9; Badian, *JRS* 42 (1952): 78, n. 23; defended by Horn, *Foederati*, 32–33; Errington, *Philopoemen*, 282–283.
135. E.g. Polyb. 22.3.1, 22.11.6–8, 23.1.6, 23.4.1–5, 23.6.1, 23.9.1, 23.9.11, 23.18.4–5, 24.1.1–5, 24.10.2.
136. It follows that Rome would find no advantage in concluding alliances with petty states and communities who might trouble her with grievances and claims on

Two decades passed without forcible intervention. Then came the Third Macedonian War, a contest that shook the Republic and its leadership. They wanted nothing of the kind again. After the defeat of Perseus in 168, the atmosphere changed profoundly. So did Rome's attitude. The partition of Macedonia and the pronounced coolness toward Rome's principal friends, Pergamum, Rhodes, and Syria, are its chief signs. The events need not be detailed here. Formal treaties become discernible in increased numbers, but with very different purposes. The senate, seriously disturbed by the diplomatic breakdown manifested in the Third Macedonian War and the unexpected difficulty of that conflict, moved in a new direction. The policy of relying on a balance maintained by various powers—a balance that had not proved durable—received a sharp setback. The *foedera* which came in the decades subsequent to Pydna illustrate the change in attitude. Rome no longer considered it fruitful to bolster the status of major powers in Hellas. She concentrated her favors on minor powers, with whom there would be no question or pretense of equality.

The treaty with Rhodes comes first after Pydna. It affords a prime example. The island republic had collaborated with Rome successfully and to her advantage for more than a generation without securing or indeed ever seeking a formal συμμαχία.[137] But Rhodes had come under suspicion for her tepid support in the war against Perseus and her efforts at mediation. The island then fell victim to Rome's severe turn in policy. Rhodians accused of Macedonian sympathies were rooted out, Lycia and Caria were detached from Rhodian control, the cities of Caunus and Stratonicea received their independence, Delos became a free port, thereby heavily damaging Rhodian economy, and the senate even threatened a declaration of war.[138] Rhodes' policy makers, now stunned and desperate, actively solicited a *foedus* with Rome. The reason is quite plain. not to obtain a military alliance, let alone to achieve any parity, but simply as an overt token of Roman favor and a gesture to relieve Rhodian fears of destruction.[139] Three times in 167 and 166 envoys from Rhodes appeared before the senate pleading for an alliance; and three times they were

---

their neighbors. A few such agreements have been placed in this period. But the chronology generates no confidence; see below, Appendix I.

137. Polyb. 30.5.6–8.

138. See the discussion in Gruen, *CQ* 25 (1975): 58–81, with full references.

139. This is clear in Polyb. 30.5.9–10: βουλόμενοι ταύτης τῆς τιμῆς τυχεῖν παρὰ Ῥωμαίων, οὐ καταπειγόμενοι συμμαχίας οὐδ᾽ ἀγωνιῶντες ἁπλῶς οὐδένα κατὰ τὸ παρὸν πλὴν αὐτῶν τῶν Ῥωμαίων, ἀλλὰ βουλόμενοι κατὰ τὴν ὑπέρθεσιν τῆς ἐπιβολῆς ἀφαιρεῖσθαι τὰς ὑπονοίας τῶν δυσχερές τι διανοουμένων περὶ τῆς πόλεως; Livy, 45.25.10. So also Polyb. 30.31.17: ἵνα γένηται τοῦτο συμφανὲς ἅπασιν ὅτι τὴν μὲν ὀργὴν ἀποτέθεισθε τὴν πρὸς Ῥοδίους.

turned away empty-handed.[140] Only on the fourth such attempt, in 164 or 163, when the island's representatives expressed abject humiliation, confirmed the execution of numerous suspected leaders, and received the endorsement of some Roman statesmen, did the senate consent to an alliance.[141] The agreement came when Rhodes had abandoned all claims to being a significant power. It represented an act of clemency, not the conclusion of a meaningful pact.

A considerable amount of unnecessary ink has been spilled on the question of whether this was a *foedus aequum* or a *foedus iniquum*.[142] As noted already, that distinction is a modern one, unattested in the language of Roman official diplomacy. The sources are silent on the terms imposed by the treaty of 164. We know only that it established a σνμμαχία.[143] More than a century later, in 51, the parties renewed their *foedus*, and the Rhodians swore to have the same enemies as Rome.[144] Then in 48, the agreement, affirmed once more by Julius Caesar, incorporated stipulations that neither state would make war on the other and each would assist the other in military operations.[145] None of these conditions is especially surprising or unusual in a σνμμαχία. Yet scholars have ensnared themselves in difficulties of their own making. The "same friends and enemies" clause has been taken as emblematic of the *foedus iniquum*; but the mutual military obligations seem to signify an "equal treaty." So, some have argued, the renewal of the treaty in 51 is fictitious, an invention by an untrustworthy source: the *foedus* was *aequum* from the start and acknowledged again in that form by Caesar in 48.[146] Or, alternatively, the pact was *iniquum* at the outset, reconfirmed as such in 51, but then transformed into a *foedus aequum* by Caesar, in acknowledgment of Rhodian services during the civil war.[147] The whole argument rests on overlegalistic hypotheses, in no way grounded in the evidence. As we

140. Polyb. 30.5.4–10, 30.21.1, 30.23.2–3; Livy, 45.25.7–10; Dio, 20.68.2–3; Zon. 9.24.

141. Polyb. 30.31; Livy, *Per.* 46; Zon. 9.24.

142. D. Magie, *Roman Rule in Asia Minor* (Princeton, 1950), I:110, II:957, n. 70, oddly denies that it was even a formal treaty. He sees it simply as "the usual relationship of *amicitia et societas.*" That is inadmissible, as shown by Polyb. 30.5.6–8. Rhodes had earlier been an *amicus et socius*; now she needed an official alliance, Polyb. 30.31.17: συνθέσθαι τὴν συμμαχίαν, and she got it: Polyb. 30.31.20; Livy, *Per.* 46. So, rightly, Schmitt, *Rom und Rhodos* (Munich, 1957), 169, n. 1.

143. Polyb. 30.31.20: ἐποιήσαντο τὴν πρὸς Ῥωμαίους συμμαχίαν; Livy, *Per.* 46: *societas cum Rhodiis deprecantibus iuncta est.*

144. Cic. *Ad Fam.* 12.15.2: *foedere quoque, quod cum his, M. Marcello, Ser. Sulpicio consulibus, renovatum erat, quo iuraverant Rhodii, eosdem hostes se habituros, quos S.P.Q.R.*

145. Appian, *BC*, 4.66, 4.68, 4.70.

146. Thus Täubler, *Imperium Romanum*, 207–210; followed by Horn, *Foederati*, 62–64, and Accame, *Il dominio*, 99–101.

147. Such is the conclusion of Schmitt, *Rom und Rhodos*, 168–171, 181–185.

have seen, "having the same friends and enemies" is a standard Hellenistic formula, used between equal or unequal partners, not a Roman creation designating a particular type of treaty.[148] And the military clauses in Caesar's renewal, known only from speeches constructed by Appian, offer just vague expressions, perfectly plausible but hardly indicative of a technical treaty form.

If one abandons the artificial legal subtleties introduced by moderns, the picture becomes simpler and clearer. The συμμαχία of 164/3 may well have embraced phrases like "having the same friends and enemies" and contained bilateral arrangements on military assistance. Its significance, however, lay elsewhere than in such formalities. As with the Aetolian treaty of 189, Rome could expect Rhodian support in eastern wars, if called upon, though no automatic obligation existed. Rhodes stayed out of the Macedonian and Achaean wars of the 140s. Two generations later she fought against Mithridates—in self-defense.[149] The island then supplied forces for Roman commanders, at their request, for that conflict.[150] The treaty does not seem to have been invoked as such; Rome, in fact, praised and rewarded the Rhodians for their cooperation—a cooperation she evidently had no right to take for granted.[151] Nor did the pact, in practice, give Rhodes any concrete claims on the Romans. When Calynda in 163 asked for Rhodian assistance in her revolt against Caunus, the Rhodians complied and occupied the city, only subsequently requesting and receiving the senate's sanction.[152] More telling still is the Rhodian-Cretan war of the mid-150s. Whatever its origins, Rhodes was on her own. She did not—and doubtless could not—expect that her συμμαχία would bring Roman support. Indeed when Cretan victories induced Rhodes to seek help, she bypassed Rome and went to the Achaean League.[153] Only after Achaea declined to become involved did the desperate

148. See above pp. 26–27. It was certainly not unfamiliar to Rhodes, who used it in a treaty of 201, when she was the superior partner; Schmitt, *Staatsverträge*, no. 552a, lines 20–21. There is no warrant for dismissing the explicit reference to a renewal in 51—perhaps in connection with Cicero's campaign in Cilicia: Cic. *Ad Att.* 5.11.4.

149. Appian, *Mithr.* 22, 24–27; Memnon, *FGH* 3B, 434 F 22, 8; Diod. 37.28; Livy, *Per.* 78; Cic. *Verr.* 2.2.159.

150. Appian, *Mithr.* 33, 56; Plut. *Luc.* 3.8–10. Other sources and discussion in Magie, *RRAM* I:218–219, II:1104, n. 40.

151. Cic. *Brutus*, 312; *Ad Q. Fr.* 1.1.33. According to Appian, *Mithr.* 61, the Rhodians were now (in 84!) enrolled as Rome's φίλοι. Rhodes subsequently supplied aid for Roman commanders in the East for Cotta against Heraclea Pontica in 70; Memnon, *FGH* 3B, 434, F 50, 6–7; for Pompey in the 60s: Appian, *BC*, 2.71; Florus, 3.6.8; for Cicero in 51: Cic. *Ad Att.* 5.11.4.

152. Polyb. 31.4–5.

153. Polyb. 33.16; cf. 33.13.2. On the plight of the Rhodians, see Polyb. 33.17; Diod. 31.38, 31.43–45; Trogus, *Prol.* 35; cf. Polyb. 33.4; and see *Syll.*³ 570—with M. Segre, *RivFilol* 11 (1933): 379–392.

Rhodians send representatives to Rome. The senate confined its response to the appointment of a commission, with instructions to mediate the conflict.[154] Quite obviously, the συμμαχία neither intended active military collaboration nor imposed firm obligations upon the partners.[155] It had a symbolic rather than a pragmatic purpose: a gesture of Roman indulgence toward an inferior power.

The symbolic character stands out in another Roman treaty, the pact with the Jews in 161. That document has generated surprise and puzzlement among scholars; it has even induced some to brand it as fictitious. The surprise, however, depends on an erroneous assumption: that the treaty's terms were to be taken seriously or interpreted literally. They were not.

Rome's first recorded contact with the Jews came in 164. A letter from Roman envoys on their way to Antioch professed willingness to treat with the Syrian king on behalf of the Jews.[156] The episode occurs in the midst of the Maccabaean rebellion. Rome's concern for the matter, however, was distant and brief. The letter, obviously solicited by the Jews, gave only a polite nod in the direction of Jewish interests. It had no discernible impact upon their struggle against the overlordship of the Seleucids.[157]

Three years of confused and intermittent warfare followed.[158] In the interim, Demetrius I, a hostage in Rome since 178, escaped and seized power in Syria, probably sometime in 162.[159] Under his aegis conflicts in Judaea resumed, as the Syrians endeavored to establish control through the hellenizing high priest Alcimus. Successful re-

154. Polyb. 33.15.3–4.

155. It goes without saying that Rhodes could engage in other alliances without the sanction or the involvement of Rome. So, e.g., an alliance with Ceramus in the mid-second century; C. Michel, *Recueil d'inscriptions grecques* (Brussels, 1900), no. 458; cf. L. Robert, *Villes d'Asie Mineure* (Paris, 1935), 60–61; Magie, *RRAM* I:110, II:957, n. 71. Rhodes also furnished ships for Attalus II's war against Prusias II: Polyb. 33.13.1–2. And Priene asked for a Rhodian alliance, though apparently without success: Polyb. 33.6.7. None of this would affect relations with Rome. Note, e.g., senatorial favor to Rhodian envoys ca. 100 B.C.: *JRS* 64 (1974): 203, lines 12–13, 16–18.

156. 2 Macc. 11.34–38.

157. A fuller analysis of the letter and its meaning in Appendix II.

158. 1 Macc. 5–7; 2 Macc. 13–15; Jos. *Ant.* 12.327–413. An agreement with Antiochus V falls somewhere in this period, perhaps early 163, and brought a temporary peace: 2 Macc. 11:22–26; cf. 1 Macc. 6:55–61, Jos. *Ant.* 12.379–382. But hostilities were resumed once Demetrius I took the throne: 1 Macc. 7:5ff; 2 Macc. 14:1ff; Jos. *Ant.* 12.389ff.

159. The story of his escape is graphically recounted by Polyb. 31.12–15, cf. 33.19; Appian, *Syr.* 47; Zon. 9.25; Livy, *Per.* 46; 1 Macc. 7:1–4; 2 Macc. 14:1–2; Jos. *Ant.* 12.389–390. See R. Laqueur, *Hermes* 65 (1930): 129–166. On the chronology see the discussions of H. Volkmann, *Klio* 19 (1925): 386–389; F. M. Abel, *Les livres de Maccabées* (Paris, 1949), 128–129; Walbank, *Commentary*, III:478.

sistance by the Maccabees culminated in a striking victory over Syrian forces and the death of Demetrius' general.[160] At this point, in 161, if we may believe our sources, Judas Maccabaeus sent envoys to Rome and persuaded the senate to conclude a treaty of alliance.[161]

The authenticity of the pact has sometimes been denied. Unnecessarily so. No clear motive for a forgery is discernible. The fact that the treaty failed to bring concrete advantages to the Jews argues for its genuineness rather than the reverse. A forger would hardly have invented a document in such circumstances. As we have seen again and again, Roman alliances whose terms bear little resemblance to their consequences are quite common. The form of this treaty contains close parallels to several other Roman pacts, including some preserved on stone. It was not a Jewish invention.[162]

The text presents some peculiarities—not surprisingly, since what we have is probably a third-level composition: a Greek translation of the Hebrew version of a treaty originally inscribed in Greek. But the standard form prevails, the form of a mutual defense alliance. The Jews engage to support Rome or her allies if they come under

160. 1 Macc. 7:5–50; 2 Macc. 14:3–15.37; Jos. *Ant.* 12.391–412.

161. 1 Macc. 8. The account in Josephus is largely derivative; *Ant.* 12.414–419, cf. *BJ*, 1.38—though he may have used another source as well; J.-D. Gauger, *Beiträge zur jüdischen Apologetik* (Köln-Bonn, 1977), 229–239. But the mission is alluded to also in 2 Macc. 4:11, an independent source. And Josephus elsewhere records a letter of C. Fannius, C.f. to Cos, asking for safe-conduct for Jewish emissaries who had recently obtained decrees from the senate; *Ant.* 14.233. That is probably the Roman consul of 161, thus further confirming the date; cf. Niese, *Orientalische Studien Theodor Nöldeke* (1906), II:817–824. Finally, the pact is given brief notice by Justin and placed in the reign of Demetrius: 36.3.9: *amicitia Romanorum petita . . . libertatem acceperunt*—erroneously dated to the time of Antiochus VII by Dahlheim, *Struktur und Entwicklung*, 101, n. 67. Gauger, *Beiträge*, 263–273, squeezes far too much out of this text, a cornerstone for his argument that Rome awarded no treaty, just an acknowledgment of Jewish liberty. The interpretation will not stand in the face of our other evidence.

162. The last point is decisively made by Täubler, *Imperium Romanum*, 239–254, who gives parallels particularly from the Cibyran, Methymnaean, and Astypalaean treaties, with references to earlier literature. Objections by H. Willrich, *Urkundenfälschung in der hellenistisch-jüdischen Literatur* (Göttingen, 1924), 45–49, are indecisive. A recent reaffirmation of the alliance's authenticity by D. Timpe, *Chiron* 4 (1974): 133–152. Most important bibliography in E. Schürer, *The History of the Jewish People in the Age of Jesus Christ (175 B.C.–A.D. 135)* (rev. ed. by G. Vermes and F. Millar, Edinburgh, 1973), I:171–172, n. 33; and Gauger, *Beiträge*, 156–161. For Gauger, the treaty, as we have it, has been interpolated into the text of 1 Maccabees—a "compilation" based not on inspection of a document, but on the author's "recollection"; *op. cit.*, 187–193, 239–241. The so-called treaty is merely Jewish propaganda, on this view; the Jews got no treaty in 161, not even φιλία until after 143: *op. cit.*, 273–278, 311–328. The reconstruction pushes hypercriticism to an extreme. In the most recent formulation, T. Fischer holds that the treaty was proposed but not ratified: *Seleukiden und Makkabäer* (Bochum, 1980), 104–129; *Gymnasium* 88 (1981): 139–144.

attack and to withhold any material aid to those who war upon them. The Romans undertake parallel obligations.[163] The customary loophole also reappears: implementation of the terms will take effect only if circumstances permit. That is a familiar condition, found also in the Achaean treaty and in Hellenistic documents, as well as in subsequent agreements between Rome and Greek states.[164] The senate, as usual, refrained from bargaining away its freedom of action.[165]

Why should Rome have consented to such a treaty at all? The usual answer is that the senate hoped thereby to weaken the regime of Demetrius I by fomenting difficulties and encouraging rebels.[166] After all, Demetrius had illicitly escaped from Italy and usurped the throne of Syria without Roman approval.[167] When the Median satrap Timarchus revolted against the throne in 161, he obtained a senatorial decree in his favor.[168] And a rider to the Jewish treaty directed itself expressly to Demetrius: the senate announced that if he oppressed

163. 1 Macc. 8:24–28. Some have argued that the form itself is one-sided, all in Rome's favor, rather than equal and bilateral. See 1 Macc. 8:26 and 28: καὶ τοῖς πολεμοῦσιν οὐ δώσουσιν οὐδὲ ἐπαρκέσουσι σῖτον, ὅπλα, ἀργύριον, πλοῖα . . . καὶ τοῖς συμμαχοῦσιν. οὐ δοθήσεται σῖτος, ὅπλα, ἀργύριον, πλοῖα. On this theory, the Romans are referred to by both verbs and released from material obligations; the Jews are responsible for the costs of war whether they send contingents to Rome or receive them. But this is quite impossible, and adequately refuted by Täubler, *Imperium Romanum*, 245–247, with citations. No comparable stipulations can be found in any other Roman treaty. And it is unlikely in the extreme that such one-sided terms would be spelled out in a compact, especially one inscribed on bronze tablets and displayed in both Rome and Jerusalem: 1 Macc. 8:22; Jos. *Ant.* 12.416. The phrase ὡς ἔδοξεν Ῥώμῃ denotes only that the alliance was approved by the senate, not that it was dictated in Rome's favor. It was probably not in the official text anyway; Täubler, *op. cit.*, 243; Abel, *Les livres des Maccabées*, 156; Gauger, *Beiträge*, 211–216. The bilateral character of the treaty is plainly conveyed by Jos. *Ant.* 12.417–418.

164. 1 Macc. 8:25 and 27: ὡς ἂν ὁ καιρὸς ὑπογράφῃ αὐτοῖς . . . ὡς ἂν αὐτοῖς ὁ καιρὸς ὑπογράφῃ. On the Achaean treaty and Hellenistic parallels, see above pp. 34–35. The formula appears also in Rome's treaties with Cibyra and Methymna: OGIS, 762, line 5; *Syll.*³ 693, lines 12–15. Josephus gives it in the more customary Greek form, κατὰ τὸ δυνατόν: *Ant.* 12.418.

165. It is possible that this limitation was underlined in the peculiar clause applied to the Jews, φυλάξονται τὰ φυλάγματα αὐτῶν οὐθὲν λαβόντες: 1 Macc. 8:26; cf. Abel, *Les livres des Maccabées*, 156. A Semitic formulation perhaps; but it cannot be regarded as a clumsy translation of *sine dolo malo*, as Täubler, *Imperium Romanum*, 241; followed by J. C. Dancy, *A Commentary on I Maccabees* (Oxford, 1954), 130. For that phrase is plainly rendered in 1 Macc. 8:28: καὶ οὐ μετὰ δόλου. One may compare the irony implicit in Justin's formulation: *facile tunc Romanis de alieno largientibus*: 36.3.9.

166. E.g. Badian, *Foreign Clientelae*, 108; T. Liebmann-Frankfort, *AntClass* 38 (1969): 114–120; Briscoe, *Historia* 18 (1969): 53; E. Will, *ANRW* I:1 (1972), 625–626.

167. He had tried twice before to secure his release but had been turned down by the senate; Polyb. 31.2.1–7, 31.11.4–12; Appian, *Syr.* 46–47; Zon. 9.25.

168. Diod. 31.27a; cf. Volkmann, *Klio* 19 (1925): 392–394.

the Jews further he would face a war with Rome.[169] All this appears to hang together and to form a consistent picture. Or does it?

As so often, one must be wary of interpreting events as if Rome seized the initiative and actively implemented an eastern policy. In fact, the evidence, taken as a whole, reveals a remarkable passivity on the part of the senate. Demetrius' activities in Asia ran into no resistance from Rome. Senatorial envoys gave approving reports, the *patres* made innocuous statements, Timarchus received paper support without tangible assistance. Rebels against the Seleucids would have to fight their own battles.[170]

The Jews fall into that category. If the Roman senate did, indeed, add a rider to the treaty warning Demetrius off and threatening war —itself a dubious proposition—that announcement proved to be empty and hollow.[171] Demetrius proceeded immediately to renew campaigning in Judaea, defeating the rebels and bringing about the death of Judas Maccabaeus.[172] The Romans played no role, indeed offered no protest. Demetrius could operate with impunity; relations with Rome were unimpaired. Nothing here suggests a patterned policy designed to weaken the Syrian kingdom.

Inquiry restricted to Rome's machinations goes amiss. The treaty came on Jewish request, not Roman impulse. For the Maccabees some international recognition might be a valuable element in their struggle. To the senate, the alliance carried no concrete implications. Its provisions were routine and conventional, not intended for literal interpretation. One could hardly expect Jewish forces (let alone ships!) to be summoned to Rome's aid. Nor was there much likelihood that the *patres* would take up arms in a Jewish cause. After Pydna the treaty form had become little more than a ceremonial announcement of Roman beneficence. Arguments on juridical grounds against the alliance's authenticity are consequently beside the point.[173] From the angle of the senate, the Jews, like Timarchus, could claim independent status—but they would have to maintain it themselves.

The treaty doubtless endured, though without practical effect.

169. 1 Macc. 8:31–32.

170. For discussion of these matters, see Gruen, *Chiron* 6 (1976): 83–86.

171. Josephus, it might be noted, does not include the Roman threat in his account of the treaty. For Abel, *Les livres des Maccabées*, 157, it derived from one of the Jewish envoys paraphrasing an oral response by the senate.

172. 1 Macc. 9:1–27; Jos. *Ant.* 12.420–434. That this came before the return of Jewish envoys from Rome is often stated: e.g., Volkmann, *Klio*, 19 (1925), 399; Schürer, *History of the Jewish People* I:173; J. Goldstein, *I Maccabees* (New York, 1976), 368; cf. 1 Macc. 9:3. But the chronology is uncertain.

173. I.e., that Rome could not have entered relations with a state that was under the suzerainty of another power; so Willrich, *Urkundenfälschung*, 45–49. Täubler, *Impe-*

Our sources preserve notice of subsequent "renewals" or of friendly exchanges between Rome and the Jews. Some of the notices carry dubious value. Repeated Roman protestations on behalf of the Jews sound increasingly hollow.[174] Even if one accepts all the diplomatic transactions as genuine, however, they give no greater force to the treaty. An unmistakable pattern recurs: strong senatorial statements without a trace of implementation.

Throughout Jewish history in this period, one confronts persistent discrepancy between Roman assertions in the documents and the absence of Rome from the historical narrative. That can hardly be coincidental. The alliance with the Jews in 161 announced Roman benevolence as a ceremonial convention, not a plan for military action. Judas Maccabaeus had inaugurated relations and the senate complied. Rome framed the official compact, however, with the Jewish people, rather than with an individual leader.[175] Hence, Judas' successors could appeal to the treaty again and again, either to bolster their prestige or to give pause to their enemies. Four or five times during the next half-century there were renewals or reassertions of the pact, courteous responses and friendly representations from Rome. But no one dreamed of enforcing terms to the letter. The Jews were on their own.

The Later Alliances and Their Meaning

After Pydna Rome had nothing further to prove in the East. She had established her military superiority beyond challenge, and she felt no compulsion to institute a formal hegemony. Provincial organization would be unnecessary and too burdensome. Macedonia, humbled and harmless, was simply "left free." Potential troublemakers in Greece found themselves transported to Italy. Coolness or anger toward Pergamum, Rhodes, and Syria sufficed to render them negligible, so far as Rome was concerned. The senate now showed a willingness to grant alliances—when they came on meek petition from minor principalities. The treaties with Rhodes and with the Jews belong quite clearly in that category. They were ceremonial pacts, adopting the language of formal alliance and mutual defense, without the substantive reality. Several such agreements appear on record

---

rium Romanum, 249–251, gets around this by claiming that Demetrius did not get formal recognition until 160. But that too is legalistic and superfluous.

174. The evidence on these exchanges is explored below, Appendix III.

175. 1 Macc. 8:23–30: τὸ ἔθνος τῶν Ἰουδαίων; Jos. *Ant.* 12.417–418; cf. A. Giovannini and H. Müller, *MH* 28 (1971): 168–170; Goldstein, *I Maccabees*, 357–359.

during the next century and more. In every case they involved inconsequential states and cities. None could offer serious aid to Rome and none would receive it. These are mere marks of favor or indulgence. They cost Rome nothing but the price of a bronze tablet.

Designation of a foreign state as φίλος καὶ σύμμαχος does not prove the existence of a treaty. It was an honorific title applied loosely to denote amicable relationship. The phrase occurs with increasing frequency from the middle of the second century. As example, the testament of Ptolemy Euergetes in 155 appeals to his φιλία καὶ συμμαχία with Rome, to which appeal, however, no substantive aid was forthcoming.[176] Mithridates Philopator of Pontus, perhaps ruler during the 150s, has the title "friend and ally" in a bilingual dedication on the Capitoline.[177] He may well have sought Roman recognition in the years after Pydna. The same appellation is displayed by the Lycians and by various minor cities, a source of some pride and security, but of little consequence to Rome: Melitaea, Narthacium, Hierapytna, Priene, Samos, Tabae, Athens, Stratonicea.[178] Whether each or any of them could claim a formal alliance is uncertain—and dubious.

Some states, however, definitely did receive *foedera*. Their

176. *SEG*, IX, 7, lines 19–23. Surely not a formal treaty; cf. W. Otto, *AbhMünch* 11 (1934): 104, n. 5, 108, n. 2.

177. *OGIS*, 375; more recently edited in *ILLRP*, I, no. 180 and Moretti, *IGUR*, no. 9: [*Rex Metradates Pilopator et Pil*]*adelpus regis Metradati f.* [*populum Romanum amicitiae e*]*t* societatis ergo quae iam [inter ipsum et Romanos optin]et; [βασιλεὺς Μιθριδάτης Φιλ]οπάτωρ καὶ Φιλάδελφος [βασιλέως Μιθριδάτ]ου τὸν δῆμον τὸν ['Ρωμαίων φίλον καὶ] σύμμαχον αὐτοῦ; cf. Appian, *Mithr.* 10. The date is controversial. T. Mommsen, long ago, put it in the time of Sulla, postulating an unknown Mithridates Philopator; *ZeitschrNum* 15 (1887): 207–219; the argument for that date restated and strengthened by A. Degrassi, *BullCommArchCom* 74 (1951–2): 19–47. Others identify the king with the known Mithridates IV Philopator of the mid-second century; T. Reinach, *L'histoire par les monnaies* (Paris, 1902), 129; Magie, *Buckler Studies* (1939), 176, n. 1; *RRAM* II:954–955, n. 67; Larsen, *CP* 51 (1956): 157–159; R. Mellor, *ΘΕΑ ΡΩΜΗ: The Worship of the Goddess Roma in the Greek World* (Göttingen, 1975), 203–206; *Chiron* 8 (1978): 325–327; A. W. Lintott, *ZPE* 30 (1978): 141–144.

178. The Lycians: *ILLRP*, I, no. 175. Melitaea and Narthacium ca. 140: *Syll.*³ 674 = Sherk, *RDGE*, no. 9, lines 16–19, 40–42, 60–61. Hierapytna in 112: *IC*, III, 4, 10 = Sherk, *RDGE*, no. 14, lines 2–3. Priene ca. 140: *IvPriene*, 531 = *Syll.*³ 679, IIb = Sherk, *RDGE*, no. 7, lines 41–44; *IvPriene*, 40 = Sherk, *RDGE*, no. 10A, lines 2–3. Samos in 135: *Syll.*³ 688 = *IvPriene*, 41 = Sherk, *RDGE*, no. 10B, line 5. Athens in 112: *Syll.*³ 705 = Sherk, *RDGE*, no. 15, lines 8–9, 55–56. Stratonicea in 81: *OGIS*, 441 = Sherk, *RDGE*, no. 18, lines 45, 69–72. Tabae: Moretti, *IGUR*, no. 10. Four other states whose names are not preserved made dedications in Rome and are described as "friends and allies": Moretti, *IGUR*, nos. 7, 13, 17, 19. Literary sources also designate various kings as φίλοι καὶ σύμμαχοι more regularly after 167; references in P. C. Sands, *The Client Princes of the Roman Empire under the Republic* (Cambridge, 1908), 12–40. Sands rightly shows that these titles are not based on official alliances—but wrongly ascribes them to "treaties" of friendship.

identity helps define the meaning and implications of treaty relationships in the world of late Hellenistic diplomacy. The cities and
communities which bound themselves to Rome carried little weight,
indeed in most instances no weight at all, in international affairs. Selection of such partners exposes from the outset the flimsy substance
of these associations.

The city of Cibyra in Phrygia could boast a full-fledged alliance
with Rome. An inscription preserves it, recording solemn guarantees
pledged by both parties to come to one another's defense in times of
danger and assault. Controversy surrounds the date, incapable of definitive solution. A time after 167 seems most likely.[179] In any case, the
assurances of armed support and the implications of equality between the two states make sense only as formal proprieties.

Carian Alabanda also established a relationship with the Republic, as another document happens to reveal. Again the chronological context is missing and speculation fails to fill the gap. It may
come as late as the Mithridatic wars. Alabanda had a φιλία and
sought a συμμαχία. She may never have got it; certainly she never
received any tangible benefits traceable to it.[180]

A single literary reference discloses an alliance that none would
otherwise suspect: between Rome and the city of Heraclea Pontica.
The two states had at best a distant connection, never pressed into
service. Yet all the formalities were observed: bronze tablets in both
Rome and Heraclea displayed terms of the agreement. To postulate
strategic or economic considerations would give this pact far more
than its due. It had publicity value for Heraclea, a mere exchange of
pleasantries in the eyes of Rome.[181]

Rome entered into alliance with the distant Thracian town of
Maronea some time after the Third Macedonian War and quite possibly after 146. Again no implementation of the accord survives on record. Indeed, the very existence of the relationship is known only
through a recent epigraphical discovery. Despite the vast differences
in power and authority between the two states, the documentary formulas speak of equal and reciprocal obligations.[182] More remote still

179. OGIS, 762. For the discussion of the date and for bibliography, see below,
Appendix I.

180. The relevant text is published in BCH 10 (1886): 299–306; REG 11 (1898):
258–266. On its nature and implications, see Appendix I.

181. The evidence in Memnon, FGH 3B, 434 F 18. See further, Appendix I, on the
chronology. That the treaties with Cibyra and Heraclea were concluded to facilitate future military operations in Asia, as Bernhardt, Imperium und Eleutheria, 72–73—who
puts them both ca. 187—is far-fetched conjecture. If so, why those two towns of all
places?

182. BCH 102 (1978): 724–726 and fig. 176; Arch Delt 28 (1973): 464. See below,
Appendix I.

was the Greek town of Callatis on the shores of the Black Sea. She too could claim an alliance with mighty Rome, duly registered on a Latin inscription, the only preserved treaty with a Greek state in that language. The agreement, so far as its fragments allow reconstruction, exhibits the customary formulaic expressions and authorizes the creation of copies in both cities. Conjectures on the date range from the 140s to the 70s B.C., a matter not subject to resolution. The very existence of such a pact, however, with an out-of-the-way and insignificant town, known only by chance preservation, shows how widespread were these alliances—and how empty.[183]

Two other treaties stem from the period around Aristonicus' revolt in Asia, in the late 130s or the 120s. Rome entered into sworn agreements with Methymna on the island of Lesbos and with an unnamed city within the borders of the former Attalid kingdom in western Asia Minor. The texts repeat with variations the formulas found elsewhere, including prescriptions for public display on bronze tablets. At Methymna the preserved portions enjoin the partners to bring armed assistance to one another in a defensive war, if the situation permits. The phraseology has a familiar ring: the customary escape clause, long a common feature of Hellenistic treaties and now standard terminology in compacts with Rome.[184]

One may imagine a stream of Greek embassies to the senate during the years that followed Roman subjugation of Macedonia and provincialization of Asia. Numerous states scrambled to seek token alliances as a mark of prestige, claimed either through some services performed or through general declarations of loyalty. One such embassy finds note in an Epidaurian document of ca. 112, honoring an ambassador who had gone to Rome ὑπὲρ φιλίας καὶ συμμαχίας. The request was granted. There was no reason to withhold agreement. Epidaurus, a harmless Argolid town, now became an ally of Rome, her *foedus* to be set up in bronze. A few years later Astypalaea in the Aegean gained similar distinction: a comprehensive treaty of alliance with the Republic, its terms almost completely preserved, with all the conventional guarantees of mutual protection. In 94 Thyrreum in Acarnania, a town of small significance to Rome, joined the ranks of those communities which could put on show a formal pact with the western power.[185]

---

183. Text of the treaty printed conveniently in *ILLRP*, II, no. 516. See below, Appendix I.

184. The Methymna treaty: *Syll.*[3] 693. The pact with the Attalid city: *Syll.*[3] 694. This latter is not a text of the treaty itself but a resolution of the city making reference to it. For more detailed discussion of both, see below, Appendix I.

185. Epidaurus: *IG*, IV², 1, 63. Astypalaea: *IGRR*, IV, 1028 = Sherk, *RDGE*, no. 16B. Thyrreum: *Syll.*[3] 732. Further on these treaties in Appendix I.

Finally, we know of three treaties dating to the end of the Republic and the early years of Augustus.[186] Nothing has changed. Aphrodisias obtained a sworn alliance with Rome, as attested by a letter of Octavian to the city and reconfirmed by a *senatus consultum* from the triumviral period, though the text of the treaty is no longer extant. Alliance with a minor city as prize for loyalty or service stands by this time in a more-than-century old tradition. Rome consented to a comparable arrangement at about this time with Cnidus in Caria: a permanent συμμαχία. The text survives only in fragments, but enough exists to show that its form and substance parallel the better preserved documents. Once more a community without importance on the international scene received Roman benefaction in the form of a *foedus*. The last item in this series is Rome's treaty with Lesbian Mytilene, dated to 25 B.C. The inscription that records it, incomplete and mutilated though it be, reveals a mutual defense pact of the usual form: bilateral in nature, its characteristics familiar from treaties over the past century and a half.[187]

Accidents of transmission alone have furnished these texts. It is a safe assumption that others, perhaps numerous others, existed, some of which may still come to light. A pattern seems established: Rome consents more readily to treaties of alliance after 167, and the number of such treaties rises noticeably in the later second century, after the subjugation of Greece and the provincialization of Asia—i.e. at the very time when such agreements lose all meaning as vehicles for real military cooperation. The Republic framed pacts with weakened powers or petty states, with insignificant cities, remote towns, or even communities inside the confines of a Roman province. The terms, where known, are repetitive and tralatician, providing for an armed collaboration that was barely conceivable and expressing an equal partnership that no one could mistake for the reality. The grants had a purely honorific character, signaling Roman benevolence, and couched in a formal phraseology whose effect was symbolic rather than concrete.[188] We may comfortably abandon the subtle disputations of scholars who find a distinction between treaties ratified by the Roman people and those authorized only by the senate, the latter

186. One may safely exclude the arrangement made with Ptolemy Auletes in 59, though Cicero does speak of a *foedus* concluded on the Capitol: *Pro Rab. Post.* 6. Ptolemy in fact simply received recognition as a *socius et amicus* by the senate and people; Caes. *BC*, 3.107; Cic. *Pro Sest.* 57; Suet. *Iul.* 11, 54; Dio, 39.12.1. Similarly, the φιλία καὶ συμμαχία with Issa, attested in 56, need not betoken an alliance; Sherk, *RDGE*, no. 24, with bibliography.

187. Aphrodisias: *OGIS*, 453–455; *FIRA*, I, no. 38 = Sherk, *RDGE*, no. 28 = J. Reynolds, *Aphrodisias and Rome* (London, 1982), 42–43, no. 6. Cnidus: Ἀθηνᾶ 11 (1899): 283–284. Mytilene: Sherk, *RDGE*, no. 26d. See also Appendix I.

188. Cf. the remarks of Dahlheim, *Gewalt und Herrschaft*, 178–186.

being more easily renounced and hence used to keep states in line.[189] This cynical hypothesis misconceives the matter. Alliances with harmless and distant peoples took effect as gestures only, as the distribution of favor and prestige. They provided an index of amicable association rather than an agency of control or of a Machiavellian design.

One last point, easily overlooked, needs stress: treaties with Rome by no means preempted the field of Hellenistic diplomacy. Greek states continued to frame pacts with one another, following patterns that extended back for generations. Examples occur after Pydna as before, indeed after 146 and even into the first century.[190] The practice went on unhindered by the Republic. Hellenic institutions did not vanish with the coming of Rome.

Ⅴ

Roman policy underwent numerous vicissitudes in the course of two centuries of involvement with the East. Treaty relationships form but a small and limited part of that involvement. They never served as a principal apparatus for expansion or imperialism. Hence the juridical and legalistic analyses common in modern works have largely obscured the historical questions. Nonetheless, the *foedera*, or absence thereof, shed important light on changing Roman attitudes and altered associations with the Hellenistic world.

The initial phases of Roman engagement in the East show a

189. On this controversy, see, especially, the discussions of Mommsen, *Römisches Staatsrecht* (Leipzig, 1887), III:340–345, 1170–1173; Täubler, *Imperium Romanum*, 99–157, 351–372; Horn, *Foederati*, 76–82; Heuss, *Klio* 27 (1934): 45–53, 244–250; Accame, *Il dominio*, 75–101. A singularly pointless debate. It can hardly be denied that, from a theoretical standpoint, the legitimacy of a treaty depended upon vote of the people: Polyb. 1.62.8–1.63.1, 6.14.11, 21.30.16; Livy, 32.23.2, 37.19.2; Cic. *Pro Balbo*, 34; Sallust, *Iug.* 39. And there are clear instances in which agreements were concluded by the people or by the senate and people, e.g., with Philip in 205: Livy, 29.12.15; with Carthage in 201: Livy, 30.44.13, cf. 30.43.2; with Philip in 197: Polyb. 18.42.2–3; Livy, 33.24.4; with the Aetolians in 189: Polyb. 21.32.1; with Antiochus in 188: Polyb. 21.17.5, 21.17.9, 21.24.2; Livy, 37.45.14, 37.55.3. See also Caes. *BC*, 3.107.2: *quod et lege et senatus consulto societas erat facta*. Of course, popular sanction was usually a rubber stamp. But despite the arguments of Täubler and Accame, there is no definitive instance of an eastern treaty framed by the senate alone. The main exhibit is the Jewish alliance, with its repeated phrase ὡς ἔδοξε 'Ρώμῃ: 1 Macc. 8:26 and 28; cf. Jos. *Ant.* 12.416–417. But the existence of a senatorial decree—if indeed it be such—does not exclude further action by the assembly. Nor do the *senatus consulta*, appended to or mentioned by the epigraphical pacts, prove that the senate acted without reference to the people. One may note that Antonius' letter to Aphrodisias mentions both a δόγμα and a ὅρκιον; Sherk, *RDGE*, no. 28A, lines 24–27.

190. Observe, e.g., the treaty between Sardis and Ephesus in the 90s; *OGIS*, 437 = Sherk, *RDGE*, no. 47. Other examples in Dahlheim, *Gewalt und Herrschaft*, 199, n. 69.

pointed reluctance to draw up formal compacts. The model of Roman alliances in Italy is inapplicable. On the contrary, Rome sternly avoided commitments that might bind her beyond the immediate occasion. Only the Aetolian treaty of 212/11 produced an official agreement, but this would hold just for the duration of a specific conflict. The terms of that alliance and of the peace of Phoenice that followed derived largely from Hellenistic practice. The senate rested content with Greek conventions. The *patres* had no interest in transporting the Italian system to the East, let alone in establishing *foedera aequa* or *foedera iniqua*, categories fabricated by moderns and inappropriate even in Italy. Relationships instituted during the first four decades of Rome's presence in the East were either informal or impermanent.

The change comes immediately after the Aetolian and Syrian wars. In these years Rome concluded three treaties with major powers, Aetolia, Syria, and Achaea, treaties meant to be of enduring impact. Their form, for the most part, again reproduced Greek usages. Their purpose, however, was largely symbolic rather than substantive. Aetolia was obliged to "honor Rome's majesty." That provision would dramatize her disavowal of previous hostility and promise a lasting concord. Similarly, the permanent agreements with Syria and Achaea advertised a harmonious balance in the Hellenistic world. They aimed not to provide for military cooperation nor to facilitate Roman expansion; rather to create a situation from which Rome could comfortably stay aloof.

These intentions, of course, eventually went awry. Expenses, casualties, and dangers encountered in the Third Macedonian War dictated a redirection of policy. The senate set about to weaken and humble previously potent states. A balance provided by major powers no longer seemed safe. After 167 Rome consented more readily and more frequently to treaties of alliance. The numbers increased further, so far as our documentation goes, after 146 and the crushing of Greece and Macedonia. In every instance, the pacts tied Rome to states, like Rhodes, that had lost their international standing or that had never had it, like the Jews, or with petty communities tucked away in distant corners and part of larger entities. The modern assertion that "use of the treaty in Roman foreign policy fell into disfavor and was eventually abandoned" is puzzling and paradoxical.[191] In fact, the reverse holds. Formal alliances are few before 167, as Rome endeavored to minimize her commitments in the Hellenistic sphere. After that

191. The quotation is from Sherk, *RDGE*, 97. Similar pronouncements by Sherwin-White, *Roman Citizenship*, 183–186, who states that the absence of the *maiestas* clause in later treaties shows "something like contempt for the Greeks." See also Badian, *Foreign Clientelae*, 113–114: "The year 146 . . . sees the end of proper international relations."

date she employed the formal treaty with growing regularity—at a time when it lost all substantive value.

The later alliances, couched in terms long traditional in the Greek world, that echoed mutual defense pacts between equal partners corresponded to no contemporary reality. Rome tolerated these polite exchanges and "equal" agreements. They were mere gestures of benevolence, their literal provisions never to be implemented or invoked. The Republic rarely, if ever, took the initiative in these arrangements. Nor did she conceive any "system" of *civitates foederatae*. Where inequality was there in fact, it was unnecessary to express it on stone or bronze. Bilateral treaties became common at precisely the time when they carried no practical significance. In this sense, Rome's policy, despite various vicissitudes, remained consistent: the evasion of commitments that would restrict or command her activities.

Chapter 2

Φιλία-Amicitia:
The Informal Connection

Informal associations predominated in Roman links with Hellas. They are discerned with clarity throughout the era of Rome's growing involvement in the East. In particular, one institution stands out: φιλία or amicitia. The term appears again and again in our sources, sometimes in conjunction with συμμαχία (societas), sometimes alone. Greek states in ever-increasing numbers could claim to be amici of Rome, from minor cities to federal leagues to Hellenistic monarchies.

A central issue needs to be confronted. The official treaty, as we have seen, played but a small and insignificant role in the story of Rome's eastern adventures. Was it then amicitia which subtly and gradually transformed Greece into a dependency of the Italian colossus? Such is the verdict conveyed with near unanimity by modern scholarship. The very informality of international "friendship," so it is claimed, gave it an elastic character which Rome could manipulate to her own ends. It was a convenient mechanism fostered by the senate to get round the rigid requirements of the fetiales: Rome could employ the concept to justify intervention or to avoid it when she preferred to leave her "friends" in the lurch.[1] On this view, amicitia was soon converted into a relationship between the strong and the weak; it signified not so much collaboration as inferiority and subjection. By the second century amicitia was simply a euphemism for clientship.[2] In short, the

1. Cf., e.g., Badian, Foreign Clientelae, 60–61, 68, 111; Dahlheim, Struktur und Entwicklung, 227–229, 252–254, 258–259.

2. So Sands, Client Princes, 10–11, 44–48; Matthaei, CQ 1 (1907): 182, 187, 203–204; Fr. de Martino, Storia della costituzione romana (2nd ed., Naples, 1973), II:33; Badian, Foreign Clientelae, 12–13, 68; D. Timpe, Hermes 90 (1962): 351–352; Dahlheim, Struktur und Entwicklung, 265–274; Gewalt und Herrschaft, 198–206; Cimma, Reges socii et amici, 146–156; I. E. M. Edlund, Klio 59 (1977): 129–136.

device served as a cynical instrument, a means to establish and expand Roman supremacy, a principal channel of Roman imperialism.[3]

This interpretation needs more serious inquiry than it has received. Did Rome, in fact, shape the concept of diplomatic friendship into a tool for promoting her international ascendancy? The institution of *amicitia* has engendered much discussion from a juridical vantage-point. Rehearsal of the debates would be to little purpose here. It can be stated with confidence that *amicitia* represented an informal and extralegal relationship, not requiring a treaty, a pact, or any official engagements.[4] No fixed formula, no determined pattern existed. *Amicitia* could be entered into in a variety of ways. Military cooperation, with or without a *foedus*, made the partners *amici*.[5] A state that sought Roman assistance and was accepted into *fides* would henceforth be adjudged an *amicus*.[6] Even former enemies, once defeated in war and agreeing to terms, would take on the new status: peace treaties resulted in *amicitiae*.[7] Further, almost any diplomatic intercourse, any friendly exchanges between states, could create the relationship.[8] The title φίλος or φίλος καί σύμμαχος frequently signified no more than a courteous appellation, a token of amicable—or simply non-hostile—dealings.[9] To see in these multifarious arrangements, generally loose and unconnected, created in various ways and under diverse circumstances, a deliberate scheme to promote Roman supremacy is difficult indeed—and probably quite unnecessary.

Amicitia in Roman Foreign Policy

Rome's initial military activity across the Adriatic came in the course of the First Illyrian War, 229/8. The results included establishment of φιλία with states and tribes on or near the Dalmatian coast. The Corcyreans, under occupation by Demetrius of Pharus, welcomed

3. See, most recently, D. Kienast, *ZSS* 85 (1968): 335–340, 352–357, 366–367; K.-H. Ziegler, *ANRW* I:2 (1972), 88.
4. The matter may be regarded as settled by the arguments of Heuss, *Völkerrechtliche Grundlagen*, 12–59, demolishing Täubler's notion of the "Freundschaftsvertrag." See also Dahlheim, *Struktur und Entwicklung*, 136–146. A modified revival of the older view in de Martino, *Storia della costituzione romana* II:29–35; Cimma, *Reges socii et amici*, 23–32, 80–99, 168–185.
5. E.g., Polyb. 21.20.1–4, 21.23.11–12; Livy, 26.24.8–9.
6. E.g., Polyb. 2.11.5–6, 3.26.6.
7. E.g., Polyb. 1.62.8, 21.42.1; Appian, *Ill.* 7.
8. E.g., Appian, *Sic.* 1; Livy, 32.8.13, 33.20.8, 37.25.8; in general, see Heuss, *Völkerrechtliche Grundlagen*, 46, 53–59.
9. E.g., *IG*, XI, 4, 756; *Syll.*[3] 674 = Sherk, *RDGE*, no. 9, lines 21, 47; *Syll.*[3] 679 = *IvPriene*, 531 = Sherk, *RDGE*, no. 7, line 54; Livy, 42.19.8.

Roman troops and, with the consent of Demetrius, put themselves into Rome's *fides*. They were accepted into φιλία.[10] Apollonia followed suit and then Epidamnus.[11] After Roman forces moved into the interior, the tribes of the Parthini and the Atintani sent envoys to declare their obeisance. The action resembled submission by a foe more than cooperation by a friendly power. But the result was the same: acceptance into Roman φιλία.[12] At this time, or perhaps earlier, the island of Issa was also taken under the umbrella of Rome's πίστις.[13] Once the war was over and a peace treaty signed, the conquered Illyrian kingdom—provided that it maintained the conditions imposed—would be accounted a φίλος as well.[14] The collaborator Demetrius profited from his participation in the Roman cause and evidently took his place among the *amici*.[15] Clearly the term *amicus* applied to different associations inaugurated in a variety of ways: it could designate states which joined in Rome's military effort, those which promoted her interests, those which yielded to her power, and those which came to terms after the conflict. *Amicitia*, then, did not denote a special relationship defined by acknowledged duties and requiring particular preliminaries. A Roman mission subsequently made the rounds of several Greek states to announce the results and justify the war. Whether these contacts too produced *amicitiae* is unclear but, given the loose usage, the term would be appropriate enough.[16]

10. Polyb. 2.11.5–6. Polybius' comment is: αὐτοί τε σφᾶς ὁμοθυμαδὸν ἔδωκαν παρακληθέντες εἰς τὴν τῶν Ῥωμαίων πίστιν. Whether this means that the Corcyreans were urged into cooperation by the Romans or were "encouraging one another" is a matter of dispute; see the note on this, with reference to earlier opinions by Walbank, *Commentary* I:162. The former may be preferable, on the analogy of Polyb. 18.38.5: παρακαλοῦντος [Flamininus] σφᾶς εἰς τὴν Ῥωμαίων πίστιν; cf. Livy, 33.13.8: *vocati in amicitiam*—passages not cited by Walbank. Cf. Polyb. 3.100.3: εἰς φιλίαν προυκαλεῖτο [Hannibal] καὶ πίστεις ἐδίδου. But even if Rome took the initiative, this need mean no more than that her commander encouraged the Corcyraeans to choose Rome's side in the Illyrian conflict and to trust to her friendship. There is no reason to claim that Corcyra, without Roman prodding, could not have understood the meaning of Roman *fides* and *deditio*, as Walbank, *loc. cit.* The original encouragement, in fact, came from Demetrius of Pharus: Polyb. 2.11.4.

11. Polyb. 2.11.8–10. Cf. Appian, *Ill.* 7, who refers to Epidamnus being brought ἐς φιλίαν. With reference to Corcyra elsewhere, the same author designates her as Ῥωμαίοις συνεμάχει: Appian, *Mac.* 1. Not to be taken as a loose or ignorant designation. Collaboration in war was equivalent to φιλία.

12. Polyb. 2.11.11; cf. Appian, *Ill.* 8.

13. Polyb. 2.11.12. The event is placed earlier by Dio, fr. 49.1; Zon. 8.19; cf. Appian, *Ill.* 7.

14. See Appian, *Ill.* 7: Πίννην δὲ τὴν ἄλλην Ἄγρωνος ἀρχὴν ἔχειν καὶ φίλον εἶναι Ῥωμαίοις.

15. As is implied by Polyb. 2.11.17, 3.16.2, 3.16.4. And note, especially, Dio, fr. 53, who describes his activities a decade later as τῇ τῶν Ῥωμαίων φιλίᾳ ἀποχρώμενος.

16. Polyb. 2.12.4–8, records the missions but says nothing about φιλία. Accord-

Is this new network of relationships a deliberate prelude to Roman control of the Adriatic's eastern shore? The result is customarily described as installation of a "protectorate," or even as the creation of "dependents." In this view, *amici* are already budding *clientes*, and much labor has been expended in identifying geographically the Roman "zone" of influence.[17] Yet it is not easy to see what a "protectorate" is supposed to amount to. And it would be rash to elicit Roman intentions out of subsequent results.[18] Rome's *amici*, if Appian is to be believed, were described as ὑπήκοοι. But that phrase does not appear in Polybius. After peace was concluded in 228, even Appian asserts that the Greek cities were "left free."[19] The fact is that Roman forces were promptly withdrawn, and no state was made subject to garrisons or tribute. On a later occasion, when Demetrius of Pharus began to expand his power, Polybius accuses him of attacking Illyrian cities τὰς ὑπὸ Ῥωμαίους ταττομένας.[20] The charge need not be taken at face value. It rests on a pro-Roman version, justifying the Second Illyrian War, and is hardly an accurate description of the cities' legal or actual status.[21] Hannibal's treaty with Philip V in 215 depicts the Romans as κύριοι over various Greek states and Illyrian tribes; and certain, presumably Illyrian, territories are designated as ἐν τῷ κοινῷ τῶν Ῥωμαίων.[22] These phrases too possess no technical significance; they are propaganda points to legitimize recovery of the areas by Philip

---

ing to Zon. 8.19, the Romans entered into φιλία with Athens and were even accorded Athenian citizenship. The passage is open to doubt, perhaps part of the later exaggeration of Rome's connection with Athens. But there would be nothing surprising about a vague φιλία established by friendly diplomatic contact; cf. Appian, *Mac.* 4.2. And see H. Bengtson, *Die Inschriften von Labranda und die Politik des Antigonos Doson* (Munich, 1971), 33–37.

17. Among the more important discussions, see Holleaux, *Rome, la Grèce,* 104–112; Badian, *Studies,* 6–9; Hammond, *JRS* 58 (1968): 7–9, who asserts even that "Rome's dependents . . . were to be her dependents for good and not free agents." Cf. Cabanes, *L'Epire,* 221–222. Dahlheim, *Struktur und Entwicklung,* 54–55, n. 9, rightly wonders what the juridical meaning of "protectorate" would be—but does not question the fact. The only serious doubts are expressed by Petzold, *Historia* 20 (1971): 206, 220–221, without sufficient elaboration.

18. That Rome was not, at this point, worried about Macedonia can hardly be questioned; see Badian, *Studies,* 11–16; H. Dell, *CP* 62 (1967): 94–103. Hammond's remark, *JRS* 58 (1968): 9–10, n. 34, that Rome's diplomatic disregard of Macedonia reveals that fear, hostility, and interest were present, goes well beyond the evidence.

19. Appian, *Ill.* 7–8. The word ὑπήκοοι, if it has any serious import here, can only refer to the status of communities during the war. Appian's own account shows that it does not describe relations with Rome after the peace treaty.

20. Polyb. 3.16.3.

21. So, rightly, Badian, *Studies,* 14–15.

22. Polyb. 7.9.13–14. In fact, ἐν τῷ κοινῷ τῶν Ῥωμαίων may well refer to Italy anyway and hence be irrelevant to the question; see Walbank, *Commentary* II:56.

and by Demetrius of Pharus.[23] None can count as evidence for actual Roman control in Illyria or its environs. The notion of direct dependence is clearly unwarranted, and even the term "protectorate" suggests a firmer policy than the sources would allow. Rome evacuated her troops as swiftly after the Second Illyrian War as after the First. Those ventures were demonstrations that she could retaliate against disruption of Italian shipping in the Adriatic and would not countenance the emergence of too strong a power in the area. Were there larger ambitions, to be achieved through manipulation of *amici* and their conversion into stepping-stones for empire? The answer is best sought not in the future but in the past. It would be well to inquire what meaning *amicitia* is likely to have had in the later part of the third century.

A basic assumption needs to be reexamined: was "friendship," as a form of international diplomacy, a Roman idea? The term φιλία or *amicitia*, to be sure, occurs in our literary sources on relations between Rome and various peoples of Italy. As a polite way of referring to friendly intercourse the word was certainly not unknown. Whether it was a recognized diplomatic concept, however, is another matter. On this score the sources are largely silent.

Not much can be made of material in Dionysius of Halicarnassus on the distant and legendary epochs before the creation of the Roman Republic. The language employed seems striking—rather suspiciously so. An Etruscan king seeks to conclude hostilities and sends envoys περὶ φιλίας to the son of Aeneas. Wars are ended between Ancus Marcius and the Volsci, between Tarquinius Priscus and the Sabines, between Rome and Lars Porsenna, on the basis of agreements bringing εἰρήνη καὶ φιλία.[24] This is quite clearly the language of a much later era, very common in Dionysius' own day and, as we shall see, characteristic of international agreements in the Greek world. No one can take it seriously as authentic evidence for seventh- and sixth-century Italy.

Similar portrayals can be found, though rarely, in the course of Roman dealings with Italian communities in the early Republic. So, in 394, we are told, after a peace treaty, φιλία was instituted between Rome and the Falisci.[25] An *amicitia*, of some form, linked Rome and

23. Demetrius is explicitly mentioned in this connection; Polyb. 7.9.14. Nor is any technical force to be given to Apollonia's plea in 214; Livy, 24.40.7: *nuntiantes in obsidione sese, quod deficere ab Romanis nollent.*

24. Dion. Hal. 1.65.5 = Victor, *Or. gen. Rom.* 15.4; Dion. Hal. 3.41.5, 3.66.3, 5.34.4. Other evidence on these pacts collected by V. Ferrenbach, *Die amici populi Romani republikanischer Zeit* (Diss. Strassburg, 1895), 3–4, 7–8, a sober catalogue without much effort to question the validity of the material.

25. Dio, fr. 24.3; cf. Plut. *Cam.* 10.8. Little weight can be placed on this. Other

Caere from ca. 390.[26] In 308, after Roman victory in Umbria, the conquered peoples made their submission; the cooperative Ocriculani, by contrast, were received *sponsione in amicitiam*.[27] But none of these instances can serve as precedents or background for Roman *amicitiae* in Illyria or for any associations established beyond Italian shores. As we have seen, the relationships contracted in the homeland, however they were initiated, resulted in formal *foedera* with fixed obligations and lasting commitments. One may profitably cite the example of the Campanians who appealed to Rome for assistance against their foes in 393 and asked for *auxilium in praesens* but *amicitiam in perpetuum*.[28] At first sight, that appears a good model for future international "friendships." Not so. The Livian account shows plainly what a permanent *amicitia* meant to Campania—and to Rome: a *foedus*.[29] It was not from such institutions that the development of extra-Italian arrangements took its origin.

A different place might seem the obvious one to look for precedents: the contacts between Rome and Carthage. The various pacts between these powers, as transmitted by Polybius, all begin with the same formula: "there shall be φιλία on the following conditions. . . ."[30] Whether these arrangements go back to the beginning of the Republic is an issue we can happily avoid here.[31] The more pertinent question is whether they follow Roman or Carthaginian practice. If the series begins as early as the sixth century, it is difficult indeed to imagine the imposition of Roman categories upon the more powerful partner. And even if the first pact dates to 348, as some scholars maintain, it is unlikely that Rome held the whip hand or took the initiative. At that time she was doubtless seeking Carthaginian support in a prospective conflict with the Latins. One may conclude

---

evidence on the event makes no mention of a φιλία; Diod. 14.98.5; Livy, 5.27.15, 7.38.1; cf. Ferrenbach, *Amici*, 9–10.

26. Livy, 7.20.5; cf. 5.50.2–3; Val. Max. 1.1.10. Again the expression ought not to be pressed. Livy refers to *hospitium publicum*, other sources to the awarding of *civitas sine suffragio*. A much discussed matter; cf. M. Sordi, *I rapporti romano-ceriti e l'origine della civitas sine suffragio* (Rome, 1960), 25–52; Toynbee, *Hannibal's Legacy* I:410–424; Harris, *Rome in Etruria and Umbria*, 45–47; M. Humbert, *MEFRA* 84 (1972): 231–268.

27. Livy, 9.41.20; cf. 9.5.2.

28. Livy, 7.30.1.

29. As is clear from the speech of the Campanians, Livy, 7.30.4: *neque enim foedere Samnitium, ne qua nova iungeretis foedera, cautum est.* Cf. Livy, 10.3.1: *eodem anno cum Vestinis petentibus amicitiam ictum est foedus.*

30. Polyb. 1.62.8, 3.22.4, 3.24.3. Note also a clause in the treaty of 241; Polyb. 3.27.4: μηδὲ προσλαμβάνειν εἰς φιλίαν τοὺς ἀλλήλων συμμάχους. And observe Diod. 23.2 on events of 264: Carthage sent representatives to the consul περὶ φιλίας.

31. A massive bibliography up to 1963 in Werner, *Beginn der röm. Rep.*, 304–306. Most recently, see Petzold, *ANRW* I:1 (1972), 364–411.

with some confidence that the treaties were drafted along Carthaginian lines.[32] Most revealing are two parallel clauses in the second treaty. Carthage shall not bring into Roman harbors any captives from states with which Rome has εἰρήνη ἔγγραπτος. And Rome shall do no injury to places with which Carthage has εἰρήνη καὶ φιλία. The contrast between Roman *foedera* and Carthaginian φιλία is plain.[33] Hence, no reason to see the concept of φιλία as drawn from Roman diplomatic experience. Carthage, on the other hand, made use of the idea—and not just *vis-à-vis* Rome. One may note the Carthaginian treaty with Philip of Macedonia in 215, a document demonstrably based on Semitic practices with which Carthage was familiar. The parties contract an oath περὶ φιλίας καὶ εὐνοίας καλῆς. Further, the Carthaginians refer to peoples in Italy, Gaul, and Liguria with whom they possessed φιλία, by contrast with those cities and nations directly under their control. And, if victory is to be obtained, Carthage envisions even a new φιλία with Rome, one that will comprise Philip as well.[34]

To be sure, it can be argued that Rome learned the principle from Carthage and then adapted it for her eastern adventures. The treaty framed after the First Illyrian War, at least in Appian's formulation, has a prelude analogous to that of the Carthaginian pacts: Pinnes is to be a φίλος of Rome, on condition that. . . .[35] But the same cannot have served as a model for the *amicitiae* with Corcyra, Apollonia, and Epidamnus, nor with the Parthini and Atintani. No conditions were imposed on those relationships and no treaties underlined them. Indeed, the Roman φιλία with Carthage, reiterated on several occa-

32. Strong argument to this effect conveyed by Täubler, *Imperium Romanum*, 263–264. But he is doubtful about the φιλία clause, in view of Polyb. 1.62.8: a preliminary draft of the treaty in 241 and framed at Roman dictation; so also, Walbank, *Commentary* I: 341. That is unnecessary skepticism. The tralatician character of successive treaties, at least in their formulaic phrases, is common enough. And there had been three or more agreements between Rome and Carthage prior to this one. Adoption of the earlier language would be logical. Cf., on the treaty in 278, Polyb. 3.25.2: τὰ μὲν ἄλλα τηροῦσι πάντα κατὰ τὰς ὑπαρχούσας ὁμολογίας. It is surely much less plausible to imagine that Polybius inserted the φιλία clause into the earlier treaties on the basis of a draft agreement of 241, itself never implemented in that form! Cf. the criticisms of Täubler, *loc. cit.*, on different grounds, by Heuss, *Völkerrechtliche Grundlagen*, 16–18; also Dahlheim, *Struktur und Entwicklung*, 147–148, n. 61. That the form of the treaty was dictated by Carthage is recognized also by Werner, *Beginn der röm. Rep.*, 347–348, who sees it as influenced by Greek practice.

33. Polyb. 3.24.6–8. Cf. the discussion, with different purposes, by Werner, *Beginn der röm. Rep.*, 356–368.

34. Polyb. 7.9.4, 7.9.6, 7.9.12. The Semitic background to some of this phraseology is deftly pointed out by Bickermann, *TAPA* 75 (1944): 96–97; *AJP* 73 (1952): 8–9. Notice also Carthage's offer to bring the Lucanians *in amicitiam* in 212; Livy, 25.16.7.

35. Appian, *Ill.* 7.

sions, was each time expressly inserted in a written pact sealed with solemn oaths and preserved on bronze tablets.[36] Not with such solemnities did Rome acquire her *amici* in the East. *Amicitia* might be the consequence of a peace treaty that concluded hostilities; it was not itself a formal agreement. The roots of Rome's relationships across the Adriatic must be sought elsewhere.

The most natural avenue of investigation is surely that of Rome's prior diplomatic contacts with Greek states. The record is muddied by unreliable sources and dubious episodes. But enough authentic material survives to provide some solid conclusions. And the relationship of φιλία or *amicitia* crops up again and again.

Little evidence exists on the first official arrangement with a Greek power: King Alexander the Molossian. Alexander arrived on Italian shores ca. 332, in response to an appeal from Tarentum against the Lucanians and Bruttians. The course of his adventures brought him as far as Paestum, where an agreement was entered into with Rome. Its nature is obscure, its results minimal. Livy's terminology is clearly imprecise: he speaks simply of the framing of a *pax*. Yet there had been no conflict between Rome and Alexander.[37] Somewhat fuller information occurs in Justin, who describes the arrangement as *amicitia* and *foedus*. The purpose is unspecified and the language not to be pressed. Both parties had common foes in the Samnites, a probable explanation for their conjunction. But one will hardly imagine a permanent *foedus*, which would suit the interests of neither. An *ad hoc* collaboration seems more likely. And the initiative almost certainly came from Alexander. As Justin's account shows, the agreement with Rome was but one of several contracted by the Epirote.[38] If *amicitia* is the proper characterization, it seems to be a Greek import.

A half-century later another, and more formidable, Epirote prince invaded the mainland of Italy. This time there was direct conflict with Rome, fierce and bloody fighting. A lull between major battles also saw negotiations. Their precise content varies in the sources and is disputed by moderns. Details do not concern us.[39] What is clear is that the impetus for a settlement—apart from return of prisoners—

---

36. Polyb. 3.25.6–3.26.1. Polybius' term is συνθῆκαι; and cf. Livy, 7.27.2: *foedus ictum, cum amicitiam ac societatem petentes venissent*; 9.43.26: *cum Carthaginiensibus foedus tertio renovatum*.

37. Livy, 8.17.9–10: *Alexander . . . pacem cum Romanis fecit*. The account is rejected entirely by L. Braccesi, *RendIstLomb* 108 (1974): 196–202.

38. Justin, 12.2.12: *cum Metapontinis et Poediculis et Romanis foedus amicitiamque fecit*; cf. W. Hoffman, *Rom und die Griechische Welt im 4. Jahrhundert* (Leipzig, 1934), 17–21; Dahlheim, *Struktur und Entwicklung*, 125–127; E. Manni, *Studi Salentini* 14 (1962): 344–352; M. Liberanome, *AttiAccadTorino* 104 (1970): 79–95.

39. In particular, the vexed question of whether there was one or two sets of

came from Pyrrhus, and at a time when he appeared to have the upper hand. The offer was in the form of a φιλία. Sources disagree as to whether this would be combined with an alliance or simply with a peace treaty. But φιλία was the central concept.[40] How sincere were these proposals and what the wily Pyrrhus had in mind need not here be conjectured. Rome, of course, rejected the terms, a famous tale seized upon by our sources to underline Roman fortitude and glory in a dark hour. The idea of φιλία as a diplomatic instrument, however—and that is the point at issue—had again been brought to Italy by a Greek.

Diplomatic relations between Rome and the Ptolemaic monarchy of Egypt began in the year 273. The matter has roused long scholarly controversy. But no reason exists to doubt the contact itself. Rome's recent successes against Pyrrhus—who abandoned Italy only two years before—had certainly come to the attention of the Hellenistic world. The Ptolemies sent a mission to Rome and received one in return. A friendly interchange and little more. Sources report the result in various terms, thus supplying ammunition for scholarly bickering, most of it unnecessary. The Livian *periocha* characterizes the agreement as a *societas*.[41] None will account that as a formal alliance, which is unthinkable. The term *societas*, if it derives from Livy, need not mean "alliance" anyway, and a military relationship is surely not intended here.[42] Dio presents a vague formulation: "Ptolemy made an agreement."[43] The vagueness is appropriate and ought not be subjected to subtle speculation. In fact, this was an *amicitia*, without obligations or commitments other than to remain on cordial terms. The

---

negotiations, on which see the exhaustive discussion of P. Lévêque, *Pyrrhos* (Paris, 1957), 341–370, 406–409, with full bibliography. The matter at issue here is not touched upon.

40. Plut. *Pyrrh.* 18.2: τὴν φιλίαν καὶ τὰς διαλύσεις; 18.4: τοῦ Πύρρου . . . φιλίαν ἑαυτῷ καὶ τοῖς Ταραντίνοις ἀδείαν . . . αἰτουμένου; 20.4: ὁ Πύρρος . . . ὠρέγετο φιλίαν ἀντὶ πολέμου; Appian, *Samn.* 10.1: ἐδίδου [Pyrrhus' envoy] δ' αὐτοῖς εἰρήνην καὶ φιλίαν καὶ συμμαχίαν πρὸς Πύρρον; Dion. Hal. 19.9.3: εἰρήνην ἐπαγγέλλομαι παρέξειν καὶ φίλος ἔσεσθαι καὶ ἐφ' οὓς . . . πολέμους . . . βοηθήσειν; Zon. 8.4: ἀξιοῖ τοῖς φίλοις καὶ τοῖς συμμάχοις ὑμῶν ἐγγραφῆναι. Other evidence on the negotiations conveniently collected in Schmitt, *Staatsverträge*, no. 467.

41. Livy, *Per.* 14: *cum Ptolemaeo Aegypti rege societas iuncta est.*

42. The case is argued—at needless length—by Holleaux, *Rome, la Grèce*, 60–83, with reference to earlier discussions. See also Manni, *RivFilol* 27 (1949): 79–87; Dahlheim, *Struktur und Entwicklung*, 141–146. Cimma, *Reges socii et amici*, 33–37, argues unconvincingly for a formal compact. Eutropius, 3.1, asserts that, after the First Punic War, Rome offered military assistance to Egypt against the Syrian monarchy. Almost certainly fictitious—among other things Eutropius has the name of the Syrian king wrong. But even if correct, it would not entail a formal συμμαχία, as Holleaux believes; *op. cit.*, 75–77. Rather a polite offer of aid, just as politely declined by Ptolemy.

43. Dio, fr. 41 = Zon. 8.6.11: ὁμολογίαν ἐποιήσατο.

phrase *φιλία-amicitia*—and nothing more—appears explicitly in the accounts of Appian and Eutropius.[44] Friendly relations proceeded apace, with no compromise of independent action on either side. The Ptolemies maintained a strict neutrality in both Punic Wars, despite requests for intervention by the enemies of Rome.[45] This, however, did not prevent Rome from sending a request to Egypt for grain during the trying period of the Hannibalic conflict. And Roman envoys, with due proprieties, renewed the *amicitia*.[46] During the First Macedonian War, Egyptians were active in seeking a resolution of the hostilities. Thus, their foreign policy remained unfettered, friendly to Rome but primarily concerned with peace.[47] What prompted the initial contact in 273 is beyond conjecture: commercial considerations have been suggested, or a united front against Pyrrhus and other powers, or fear of an accord between Carthage and Syria.[48] No more need be assumed than a simple exchange of courtesies prompted by Rome's reputation won in the Pyrrhic wars. That was enough to establish *amicitia*. The relationship, with no strings attached and no limitations upon the foreign policies of either state, endured. And, it should be noted once again, the arrangement was concluded on the initiative of the Greek power.[49]

One need not pause long over two questionable and disputed episodes involving Rome and Greek states in the third century. First, envoys from Apollonia arrived in Rome ca. 266 and were roughly

44. Appian, *Sic.* 1: τῷ [Ptolemy] δ᾽ ἦν ἐς τε Ῥωμαίους καὶ Καρχηδονίους φιλία; Eutropius, 2.15: *legati Alexandrini a Ptolemaeo missi Romam venere et a Romanis amicitiam, quam petierant, obtinuerunt*. Succinctly presented by Ferrenbach, *Amici*, 18. Holleaux's long-winded discussion arrives at essentially the same answer. But his assertion that, because there was no treaty, the Ptolemies were not among Rome's *amici* is unintelligible; *Rome, la Grèce*, 75.

45. On the First Punic War, Appian, *Sic.* 1; on the Second, Livy, 24.26.1; Polyb. 7.2.2: there is no reason to doubt either report.

46. The request for grain in Polyb. 9.11a; the renewal of *amicitia* in Livy, 27.4.10. Both probably refer to the same occasion; Holleaux, *Rome, la Grèce*, 66–70; cf. Heuss, *Völkerrechtliche Grundlagen*, 28, n. 2.

47. Livy, 27.30.4, 27.30.10, 27.30.12, 28.7.13–14; Polyb. 11.4.1; Appian, *Mac.* 3. This activity by a neutral power was in no way hostile to Rome, as suggested by Holleaux, *Rome, la Grèce*, 73–75; so, rightly, Manni, *RivFilol* 27 (1949): 92–94. And see now W. Huss, *Untersuchungen zur Aussenpolitik Ptolemaios IV* (Munich, 1976), 163–172. Nor was the projected marriage alliance with Philip of Macedonia in 203 an anti-Roman move: Polyb. 15.25.13. At the same time Egypt's rulers appointed an envoy to Rome to maintain relations: Polyb. 15.25.14.

48. A summary of various views in Holleaux, *Rome, la Grèce*, 61–63; Manni *RivFilol*: 27 (1949), 79–87. More recently, L. H. Neatby, *TAPA* 81 (1950): 89–98; E. Will, *Histoire politique du monde hellénistique* (Nancy, 1967), I:173–175; H. Heinen, *ANRW* I:1 (1972), 633–637; Cimma, *Reges socii et amici*, 33–37.

49. That is clear from Eutrop. 2.15, quoted above, n. 44; cf. Dio, fr. 41 = Zon. 8.6.11. Other evidence in Dion. Hal. 20.14.1–2; Val. Max. 4.3.9.

treated by two young senators; whereupon, the senate, to make amends, expelled the offenders and turned them over to Apollonia.[50] No more is known and no more should be made of it. The event itself need not be dismissed as fictitious. Rome's expansion to Brundisium is enough to explain Apollonian interest. The seaborne trade with southern Italy was a vital concern for Greek states on the Illyrian coast. And the first approach, once more, comes from the Greek side. But there is nothing to suggest even the framing of an *amicitia*, let alone any grandiose Roman schemes. Apollonia, as we have seen, became an *amicus* during the First Illyrian War. Earlier contacts had not gone even this far.[51] The other episode is more dubious still and probably apocryphal. Justin—and he alone—recounts the tale of an Acarnanian appeal to Rome for aid against Aetolia ca. 237. A Roman diplomatic mission duly appeared in Aetolia, only to be dismissed with sarcasm and scorn.[52] The story deserves little credence, on several grounds. It cannot, in any case, be used to show Roman interest in the East, much less the establishment of any diplomatic relations.[53]

Equally controversial is a purported association between Rome and the Seleucid monarchy during the second half of the third century. But here, at least, the term *amicitia* appears in the evidence. Only one source reports it, and that in a very late context. Suetonius, in his life of Claudius, states that this emperor produced an old letter in Greek recording a Roman promise of *amicitia et societas* to Seleucus if he should dispense Ilium from tribute.[54] The Seleucus concerned here is probably Seleucus II, so the agreement, if such it be, falls between 247 and 226.[55] Its authenticity has been assailed again and again, and the evidence on which it rests is admittedly rather thin; yet a loose relationship of *amicitia* would itself not be incongruous. Rome had been prepared to enter into such an arrangement with the Ptolemies: why not with the Seleucids? Neither one cost her anything in the way of duties or infringement of autonomy. Here, as in the other occasions noted above, the request for an association came from

50. Val. Max. 6.6.5; Dio, fr. 42; Zon. 8.7; Livy, *Per.* 15.

51. See the sober account in Holleaux, *Rome, la Grèce*, 1–5, refuting the exaggerated claims of previous historians: endorsed most recently by P. Cabanes, *L'Épire*, 83–85, with reference to the literature. Ferrenbach's assertion of a "Freundschaftsvertrag" is without basis or argument; *Amici*, 18–19.

52. Justin, 28.1.5–28.2.14.

53. So, rightly, Holleaux, *Rome, la Grèce*, 5–22, who devotes more space than the tale deserves. Not all of his arguments are equally weighty—but they withstand the efforts of Manni, *PP* 11 (1956): 179–190 and F. P. Rizzo, *Studi ellenistico-romani* (Palermo, 1974), 65–82, to defend the authenticity of Justin's account. An overblown interpretation by D. Golan, *RivStorAnt* 1 (1971): 93–98.

54. Suet. *Claud.* 25.3: *recitata vetere epistula Graeca senatus populique Romani Seleuco regi amicitiam et societatem ita demum pollicentis.*

55. Cf. Holleaux, *Rome, la Grèce*, 47; Rizzo, *Studi ellenistico-romani*, 85–87.

abroad, rather than from Rome.[56] Connection with Ilium may be suspect, but does not discredit the whole. There is further evidence. In 193 Antiochus III is referred to by the senate as a *socius et amicus* of the Roman people. That this does not signify a formal pact is certain; Antiochus himself had to seek one later in the 190s. But *amicitia* between the two powers is attested more than once. And it may go back to the initial accords with Seleucus.[57]

An analogous relationship, vague in extent and undefined in its obligations, existed with a Greek community in the West, the city of Massilia. How far back it went is uncertain. In 197 or 196 the Massiliotes could be described as φίλοι καὶ σύμμαχοι of Rome, an association that was evidently (by that time) of long standing.[58] Literary tradition records that Massilia, in the early fourth century, helped to bail Rome out after the Gallic invasion by paying off the Gauls.[59] Another story has Rome send a thank offering to Delphi after the conquest of Veii, an offering placed in the Massiliote treasury there.[60] Whether any formal ties ensued (assuming that the tradition preserved, at least, a kernel of fact) is quite uncertain. Justin's statement that the two states entered a *foedus aequo iure* is not to be taken seriously. The same author earlier reports a *foedus* dated to the founding of the city![61]

56. As is clear from the phrase *amicitiam et societatem demum pollicentis*; noted by Holleaux, *Rome, la Grèce*, 48, n. 3.

57. Livy, 32.8.13, 32.8.16, 33.20.8, 34.57.11. On Antiochus' efforts to obtain an alliance, see Livy, 34.25.2, 34.57; Diod. 28.15.2; Appian, *Syr.* 6. On relations between Rome and Antiochus in the 190s, see Holleaux, *Études* V:156–179; Badian, *Studies*, 112–139. It is possible, of course, that the *amicitia* dates only to 200 when Roman envoys were allegedly sent to Syria and Egypt; cf. Polyb. 16.27.5, 16.34.2; Livy, 31.2.3–4, 31.18.1; Appian, *Mac.* 4; Justin, 30.3.3f; 31.1. But what they accomplished there (if anything) is quite uncertain, and no evidence that they concluded an *amicitia* with Antiochus. Holleaux's extensive arguments against Suetonius' story, *Rome, la Grèce*, 46–60, succeed only in refuting the idea of a "treaty" of *amicitia*. But, as we have seen again and again, *societas* need not imply a formal pact and *amicitia* certainly need not rest on a treaty. Most recent discussion, in support of Suetonius' story, by Rizzo, *Studi ellenistico-romani*, 83–88.

58. *Syll.*³ 591, lines 27, 53–54, 59–60. The Lampsacene envoy honored in this decree sought privileges for his city by using Massiliotes as intermediaries. Clearly Massilia was reckoned as a firm friend of Rome by this time.

59. Cic. *Pro Font.* 13; Justin, 43.5.8–9.

60. Appian, *Ital.* 8.1; Diod. 14.93.4. Connections between Rome and Delphi at this time are doubted by Hoffman, *Rom und die griechische Welt*, 129–131; defended by R. M. Ogilvie, *A Commentary on Livy, Books 1–5* (Oxford, 1965), 660–661.

61. Justin, 43.5.3; cf. 43.3.4. On the treaty after the Gallic invasion, 43.5.10: *immunitas illis decreta . . . et foedus aequo iure percussum*. What sort of *immunitas* Rome could offer in 386 is hard to imagine. Efforts to make historical sense out of this information are singularly unsuccessful; cf. N. J. de Witt, *TAPA* 71 (1940): 605–615; G. Nenci, *RivStudLig* 24 (1958): 24–97; C. Ebel, *Transalpine Gaul: The Emergence of a Roman Province* (Leiden, 1976), 9–15. Salutary skepticism in Werner, *Beginn der röm. Rep.*, 363–365, n. 3, who provides a bibliography of the subject.

It is only on the Hannibalic War that we possess reliable data with regard to cooperation between Rome and Massilia, and no mention of a treaty of alliance.[62] Common interest against the Gauls no doubt brought the two states together. The links were afterwards reinforced when both had reason to fear Carthaginian expansion in areas of mutual concern. But the relationship, as it appears most commonly in the sources, was surely that of *amicitia*.[63] Such a bond could, of course, be translated into military action when both found it profitable, as in the Second Punic War, thereby strengthening the mutual amity. No clear evidence on who inaugurated it exists. But if any truth lies in the tradition of Massiliote *beneficia* in the fourth century, the first move seems to have come from the Greek city.

The loose ties so far discussed rarely issued and were not expected to issue in active joint ventures. Mere mutual recognition as cordial diplomatic interchange could constitute the extent of the link, at least at the outset. That is hardly surprising in the third century, and in reference to contacts with relatively remote powers. But there were more concrete and more immediate consequences in Sicily. Here explicit evidence survives on two states that contracted *amicitia* with Rome, and on the circumstances which called it forth.

The first case may be dealt with swiftly. As is well known, Messana, hard pressed by the Syracusans, appealed for aid to Rome (and to Carthage) in 264. Some doubts ensued but ended in a decision to send armed assistance. The people of Messana, so Polybius asserts, were accepted by Rome into φιλία.[64] On the surface then, here is another Greek city taking the initiative and Rome acquiescing in φιλία. But here the parallel ends. Rome not only dispatched military forces but, at some time thereafter, framed an official *foedus*, with obligations

---

62. Note the vague formulation of Polyb. 3.95.7: κεκοινωνήκασι ῾Ρωμαίοις πραγμάτων καὶ Μασσαλιῶται, πολλάκις μὲν καὶ μετὰ ταῦτα, μάλιστα δὲ κατὰ τὸν ᾽Αννιβιακὸν πόλεμον. Cf. also the Sosylus fragment on military collaboration at the Ebro; *FGH* 2B, 176 F 1. These passages in no way justify the prevailing view that a *foedus* was in operation; as, e.g., Walbank, *Commentary* I:169; G. V. Sumner, *HSCP* 72 (1968): 208; Dahlheim, *Struktur und Entwicklung*, 140, with bibliography. Dahlheim's assertion that renewal of the συμμαχιά in 196 (*Syll.*³ 591, lines 53–54) proves a "formal alliance" is unwarranted. It was simply a conventional greeting, performed in the course of Massilia's intervention for the Lampsacenes. Nor should Livy's implied reference to Massilia as among Rome's *socii* in 218 be taken to signify a *foedus*: Livy, 21.20.8. Elsewhere they are reckoned simply as having an *amicitia*: Livy, 34.9.10.

63. Cf. Strabo, 4.1.5 (C 180); Livy, 34.9.10; Florus, 1.37.3; Justin, 43.3.4; Oros. 5.15.25.

64. Polyb. 3.26.6: Μαμερτίνους προσέλαβον εἰς τὴν φιλίαν. Such is Polybius' description in an aside—his account of the Carthaginian treaties. When he discusses the appeal of Messana in its own context, he refers only to a "handing over" of the city, a request for aid, and a Roman decision to give aid: Polyb. 1.10.2: παραδιδόντες τὴν πόλιν καὶ δεόμενοι βοηθήσειν; 1.11.2: ἔκριναν βοηθεῖν.

explicitly spelled out.[65] Obviously the case does not belong among those previously discussed. An explanation is ready at hand. Messana was under the control not of Sicilian Greeks but of Italians: the Mamertini, mercenaries from Campania who had exercised power in the city for almost a generation. Rome quite naturally extended to Messana the same arrangements long in force in the Italian peninsula. If the first contact might be described as φιλία, from the Roman vantage-point it could only take shape as a *foedus*.

Of greater pertinence is the initial Roman association with Syracuse, a genuine Greek community. It was against king Hiero of Syracuse that Rome first trained her arms in Sicily. But not for long. Roman successes and the arrival of more legions induced Hiero to think better of his opposition and to offer terms in 263. The proposition, as Polybius presents it, is typically Greek: an offer of "peace and friendship." Rome willingly accepted the φιλία.[66] A peace treaty followed, in which Hiero bound himself to return prisoners, to pay an indemnity, and to supply resources for the Roman army in Sicily when necessary; Rome in turn acknowledged the king's authority in Syracuse and in other Sicilian cities subject to him.[67] That the two were now bound in alliance on the model of the Italian *foedera* is nowhere stated and quite implausible. There would, of course, be cooperation in Sicily for the duration of the Carthaginian war. Its limited aims were implicit in the life of the agreement: it was to terminate after fifteen years.[68] And, even at that, Hiero was expected to do little more than supply material resources and provide a safe harbor for the Roman fleet.[69] Fifteen years elapsed, the war still raged, and Roman aims in Sicily had expanded. Hiero's continued friendship, as the senate

65. Cic. *Verr.* 2.5.50–52; cf. 2.3.13, 2.4.26, 2.5.58; Florus, 1.18.3; Plut. *Pomp.* 10.2. Discussion in Horn, *Foederati*, 39–43; Berve, *Hieron II, AbhMunch* 47 (1959), 20–24. A brief *résumé* in Schmitt, *Staatsverträge*, no. 478.

66. Polyb. 1.16.5–8: διεπέμπετο πρὸς τοὺς στρατηγούς, ὑπὲρ εἰρήνης καὶ φιλίας ποιούμενος τοὺς λόγους. οἱ δὲ Ῥωμαῖοι . . . προσεδέξαντο τὴν φιλίαν.

67. Polyb. 1.16.9–10; Diod. 23.4.1; cf. Zon. 8.9; Livy, *Per.* 16; Eutrop. 2.19; Oros. 5.7.3.

68. Diod. 23.4.1: συνέθεντο εἰρήνην ἐπ' ἔτη πεντεκαίδεκα.

69. Polyb. 1.16.10, 1.18.10–11, 1.52.6–8; Diod. 23.9.5, 24.1.4, 24.1.7–9. Even this assistance often appears to be voluntary; cf. Diod. 24.1.4; Zon. 8.10—and see Polyb. 7.5.7. Only one notice of Syracusan ships actually involved in an engagement: Zon. 8.14.7. Syracusan assistance in the war—and nothing more—is implied by Polybius' phrase Ῥωμαῖοι μὲν ὡς φίλοις καὶ συμμάχοις ἐχρῶντο τοῖς Συρακοσίοις: 1.16.9. It does not establish the existence of a *foedus aequum* with mutual obligations, as advocated by Dahlheim, *Struktur und Entwicklung*, 129–131. So also Täubler, *Imperium Romanum*, 91–92; A. Schenk Graf von Stauffenberg, *König Hieron der Zweite von Syrakus* (Stuttgart, 1933), 40–46; Walbank, *Commentary* I:68–69; Berve, *Hiero*, 36–38; D. Roussel, *Les Siciliens entre les romains et les carthaginois* (Paris, 1970), 89–90. Nor is there any reason to speak of a "*foedus amicitiae*," as Cimma, *Reges socii et amici*, 37–41.

recognized, would be invaluable. Hence the relationship was put on a permanent basis. But it was still a φιλία.[70] So it is described unanimously by our sources.[71] Hiero remained a fully autonomous monarch, who kept his own counsel, even with regard to the Carthaginians after the First Punic War.[72] He upheld what could be expected of an *amicitia*. Rome was unwilling or uninterested in imposing upon him a *foedus* of the Italian variety.[73]

A summary is here appropriate. *Amicitia* as a feature of international diplomacy had been brought to Rome's attention well before her adventures in Illyria. It could accompany an agreement of military collaboration for specific purposes, as contracted with Alexander the Molossian. Alternatively, it could be brought into being by a peace treaty, like that with Hiero or as proposed by Pyrrhus, or merely through diplomatic interchange with mutual benefactions, as with Massilia, Egypt, and perhaps with Seleucus and with Apollonia.[74] But

70. Zon. 8.16.2: οἱ Ῥωμαῖοι φιλίαν αἴδιον πρὸς Ἱέρωνα διεπράξαντο. Cf. Naevius, *Bell. Pun.* 47, Vahlen.

71. Polyb. 1.83.3; Dio, fr. 43.1 = Zon. 8.8; Paus. 6.12.3; *Vir. Ill.* 37.5. No more is to be inferred from the conventional formula φίλος καὶ σύμμαχος in Appian, *Sic.* 2.2 and Plut. *Marc.* 8.11. Livy, as is his wont, occasionally employs the loose term *socius* or *societas*: 22.37.4, 24.6.4. But his meaning is clear from 24.28.6: *quinquaginta annis feliciter expertam amicitiam*; cf. 22.37.10, 24.4.5. Polybius' oft-repeated word συνθῆκαι refers to the peace treaty—and not to any permanent alliance: 1.16.9, 1.17.1, 7.3.1, 7.3.4, 7.5.1, 7.5.3, 7.5.7.

72. Cf. Polyb. 1.83.1–3. Of course, once the Second Punic War broke out, Hiero sided with Rome and gave active assistance: Polyb. 3.75.7; Livy, 22.37, 22.56.6–8. But nothing suggests that this was dictated by terms of a treaty.

73. A similar conclusion (arrived at independently) now in A. M. Eckstein, *Chiron* 10 (1980): 183–203. Specific attestation of *amicitia* with other Sicilian cities is lacking. But cf. the general (and, of course, rhetorical) statement of Cic. *Verr.* 2.2.2: *omnium nationum exterarum princeps Sicilia se ad amicitiam fidemque populi Romani applicavit . . . sola fuit ea fide benevolentiaque erga populum Romanum ut civitates eius insulae, quae semel in amicitiam nostram venissent, numquam postea deficerent, pleraeque autem et maxime illustres in amicitia perpetuo manerent.*

74. Possibly also with Rhodes, if one is to trust Polybius' remark that the island shared in Roman enterprises for one hundred forty years before 167, without a formal alliance: Polyb. 30.5.6. No need to rehearse the lengthy controversy over that notice. Holleaux, *Rome, la Grèce*, 30–46, found a date of ca. 306 for the beginning of Roman-Rhodian relations utterly incredible and reduced the "one hundred forty" to "forty." The early date, however, received a powerful defense by Schmitt, *Rom und Rhodos*, 1–49; accepted by Cassola, *I gruppi politici* 41–45; but see the remarks of J. Bleicken, *Gnomon*, 31 (1959), 440–441. A useful review of scholarly arguments by Walbank, *Commentary* III: 423–426, who leaves the matter open. An informal contact, corresponding to *amicitia*, toward the end of the fourth century is not itself unreasonable, though difficult to reconcile with Polybius' own remarks. Whatever the truth of the matter, even Schmitt acknowledges that the initiators of the relationship must have been the Rhodians: *op. cit.*, 47–48. Some relationship between Rome and Rhodes is attested in a fragmentary inscription to be published by Vassa Kontorini, whose personal communication is here gratefully acknowledged. The document indicates an exchange of embas-

one consistent feature stands out: wherever evidence permits or demands conclusion, the φιλία is proffered by Greeks.[75] Long experience in Italy accustomed Rome to the *foedus*. *Amicitia* was not forged by her diplomats.

Philia in Hellenic Diplomacy

It is the Greek background that needs investigation, a more promising line of inquiry too often obscured by the customary Rome-centered approach. Testimony on φιλία as a term of diplomatic discourse in Hellenistic Greece is, in fact, substantial, though it has aroused little curiosity.[76] Observation from the Roman viewpoint stands the history of the phenomenon on its head. Well before the advent of Rome, the Greek practice had its own dynamic and a long development.

The expression φίλοι καὶ σύμμαχοι to designate partners in a military alliance was, of course, very common throughout Greece and throughout Greek history. φιλία alone could also serve as a shorthand expression for a collaborative agreement involving partnership in war.[77] It has been recognized that even the term συμμαχία could be applied loosely to cover cooperative enterprises not based on a formal treaty of alliance.[78] Hence, when Livy employs without discrimination

---

sies and a request for a joint embassy to a third party. Circumstances are unknown—perhaps during the preliminaries to the 2nd Macedonian war; cf. Polyb. 16.35.2.

75. Excluded here are the Carthaginian treaties, which possessed a different and more formal character. But, as shown above, the φιλία incorporated in them was a Carthaginian, not a Roman idea. And that too may have been influenced by Greek practice. Cf. Diod. 16.67.1.

76. Noted briefly in passing by P. Klose, *Die völkerrechtliche Ordnung der hellenistischen Staatenwelt in der Zeit von 280 bis 168 v. Chr.* (Munich, 1972), 140–141—who proceeds to explain it in terms of Roman *amicitia*! Heuss, who did so much to illuminate the latter in his *Völkerrechtliche Grundlagen*, has nothing to say of the former in his *Stadt und Herrscher des Hellenismus, Klio Beiheft* 39 (1937). Similarly, Cimma, in her long book, makes but one allusion to the Greek background and stresses only the Roman model: *Reges socii et amici*, 177, 338–340. The matter receives no discussion in the most recent study by Ilari, *Guerra e diritto*.

77. E.g., the φιλία between Antigonus and Polyperchon in 315; Diod. 19.60.1, 19.61.1. Also the sworn φιλία between Ptolemy and Demetrius, perhaps ca. 309; Suda, s.v. Δημήτριος; cf. Schmitt, *Staatsverträge*, no. 433; more recent discussion by J. Seibert, *Untersuchungen zur Geschichte Ptolemaios I* (Munich, 1969), 180–183, who prefers a date of 298/7. And note the οἰκειότης καὶ φιλία between Argos and Athens recorded in an Athenian decree of the mid-third century; IG, II², 774 = ISE, no. 23, lines 25–27.

78. E.g., Diod. 19.77.3; OGIS, 221, = Welles, RC, no. 10–13 = Ivllion, no. 33, lines 46, 58, 72; Polyb. 5.68.7; cf. Heuss, *Staat und Herrscher*, 137, 178–179; see also Kienast, ZSS 85 (1968): 345–348. Note particularly the cynical comment of Polyb.

the terms *amici, socii,* and *amici et socii,* he is not guilty of imprecision or ignorance. The overlapping character of this phraseology is firmly rooted in Greek as well as Roman practice.

But it is not military alliances with which we are here primarily concerned. The notion of φιλία, as a mode of international relations, even without its frequent concomitant συμμαχία, is ubiquitous in Hellenistic documents and literature.

A familiar feature of Greek diplomacy is the institution of *isopoliteia*: the offer of equal citizenship rights between states, either through mutual agreement or through exchange of individual decrees.[79] Examples of such agreements or decrees are numerous, and the term φιλία crops up in several cases. An *isopoliteia* might establish a φιλία or, more commonly, renew one already in existence. So, the pact between Miletus and Cyzicus ca. 330 records a pledge that the two cities are to be friends for all time κατὰ τὰ πάτρια.[80] Near the end of the fourth century, a Milesian decree, in response to a request from Phygela, renewed the *isopoliteia* between them—together with their φιλία.[81] A more thoroughgoing agreement linked Smyrna and Magnesia on Sipylus shortly after 243: a *sympoliteia* which politically absorbed the latter through extension of Smyrnaean citizenship. But the arrangement is described in our text as the establishment of φιλία.[82] At about the same time and under the urging of Aetolia, Messenia agreed to an *isopoliteia* with the Arcadian town of Phigaleia. The agreement, however, would be void unless Phigaleia should abide by her φιλία with Messene and Aetolia.[83] A colony too could obtain privileges of *isopoliteia* from its mother city, as Kios did from Miletus ca. 228. The Milesian decree includes reference to the maintenance of φιλία by Kios toward the *demos* of Miletus.[84] In the 220s or thereabouts, the island of Keos issued a decree awarding *isopoliteia* to Nau-

---

15.24.4: πάντες οἱ βασιλεῖς κατὰ τὰς πρώτας ἀρχὰς . . . φίλους προσαγορεύουσι καὶ συμμάχους τοὺς κοινωνήσαντας σφίσι τῶν αὐτῶν ἐλπίδων.

79. On the institution in general, see J. Oehler, *RE* IX:2.2227–2231, "isopoliteia." And, now, W. Gawantka, *Isopolitie* (Munich, 1975), *passim*.

80. *Milet,* I, 3, 137 = Schmitt, *Staasverträge,* no. 409, lines 11–13: τὰς μὲν πόλεις φίλας εἶναι ἐς τὸν ἄπαντα χρόνον κατὰ τὰ πάτρια.

81. *Milet,* I, 3, 142 = Schmitt, *Staatsverträge,* no. 453, lines 3–4, 11–13: ἀναveούμενοι τὴν [φιλί]αν καὶ τὴν πολιτείαν τὴν ὑπάρχουσαν . . . ὅπως δὲ ἡ φιλία καὶ ἡ [ο]ἰκειότης ἡ ὑπάρχουσα Φυγαλεῦσι καὶ Μιλησίοις διαμένηι τὸν ἀεὶ χρόνον.

82. *OGIS,* 229 = Schmitt, *Staatsverträge,* no. 492, lines 34–35: ἐπὶ τοῖσδε συνέθεντο τὴμ φιλίαν Σμυρναῖ[οί] τε καὶ οἱ ἐμ Μαγνησίαι; cf. lines 20–22, 92–93.

83. *Syll.*³ 472 = Schmitt, *Staatsverträge,* no. 495, lines 19–21: [εἰ δέ κα μὴ ἐν]μένωντι οἱ Φιαλέες ἐν ταῖ φιλ[ίαι τᾶι πὸτ τὼς Μ]εσσανίως καὶ Αἰτωλώς, ἄκυρος ἔ[σστω ἅδε ἁ ὁμολο]γία; cf. lines 24–26. On the date, see Schmitt, *ad loc.* Cf. P. Gauthier, *Symbola* (Nancy, 1972), 366–368.

84. *Milet,* I, 3, 141, line 8.

pactus, in response to a similar one from Naupactus. The exchange evidently inaugurated or confirmed a φιλία. So it is termed in two other documents, one of the Aetolians and one of Naupactus, both alluding to preservation of the existing friendship.[85] Similarly, Seleucia (Tralleis) offered *isopoliteia* to Miletus ca. 212, noting in justification that the Milesians had long been φίλοι καὶ οἰκεῖοι. The claim is acknowledged by Miletus, whose reciprocal decree underlines friendly relations with Seleucia from the past.[86] A close parallel exists in the exchange of *isopoliteia* between Miletus and Mylasa ca. 209. Both states refer repeatedly to the arrangement as the culmination of a longstanding φιλία καὶ οἰκειότης.[87] Finally, the recently published inscription from Teos discloses, among other things, that state's grant of *isopoliteia* to three cities in Syria. And the grant is accompanied by renewal of the φιλία that stood among them ca. 204.[88] The varied ways in which φιλία is referred to in these epigraphical documents shows that it is not a mere conventional formula. In the Hellenistic world φιλία was a recognized category of international relationship.

The term appears also in another type of document common in Hellas, the *asylia* agreement; i.e., the guarantee of inviolability to a shrine, place, or city.[89] Several Aetolian decrees provide illustration. The privilege was assured by Aetolia to Keos ca. 223 in the decree mentioned above, after assertions of the maintenance of friendship.[90] Other extant resolutions from Aetolia give similar rights to Mytilene, to Magnesia on the Maeander, and to Teos in the last decades of the third century. In each instance the *asylia*-guarantees were accompanied by renewal of φιλία and οἰκειότης and promises to perpetuate

85. *Syll.*[3] 522, I–II = Schmitt, *Staatsverträge*, no. 508, I–II, lines 1–2, 11–12: ποτὶ τοὺς [Κε]ίους τὰν φιλίαν τὰν ὑπάρχουσαν διαφυλάσσειν. Mutual exchange of *isopoliteia* recorded in *Syll.*[3] 522, III = Schmitt, *Staatsverträge*, no. 508, III.

86. *Milet*, I, 3, 143 = Schmitt, *Staatsverträge*, no. 537, lines 46–47 (the Seleucian decree): ἐπειδὴ Μιλήτιοι φίλοι καὶ οἰκεῖοι ὑπάρχοντες διὰ προγόνων πρότερον; lines 1–3 (the Milesian decree): π[ερὶ τῶν πρότερον ὑπαρχόντων ταῖς πόλεσιν ἀμφοτέραις] πρὸς αὐτὰς φιλανθρ[ώπων . . . Σελευκεῖς διὰ προγόνων ο]ἰκείως χρώμενοι τῶι δήμ[ωι τῶι Μιλησίων. Similar language in a Chian decree acknowledging and reciprocating one from Aetolia: *Syll.*[3] 443 = *SEG*, XVIII, 245 = *FDelphes*, III, 3, 214 = *ISE*, no. 78, lines 3–4. And in Miletus' grant of *isopoliteia* to Istria: *SEG*, II, 450 = *ISE*, no. 127.

87. Milet, I, 3, 146 = Schmitt, *Staatsverträge*, no. 539, lines 63–64: Μυλασεῖς φαίνωνται τὴν τε οἰκειότητα καὶ τὴν φιλίαν τὴν ὑπάρχουσαν ταῖς πόλεσιν ἀμφοτέραις ἐπαύξοντες; also lines 2, 6–7, 60, 83.

88. P. Herrmann, *Anatolia* 9 (1965): 40, lines 99–100: [τὴ]ν προυπάρχουσαν τοῖς [. . . .]οις πρὸς αὐτοὺς ἀνανεωσόμεθα φιλίαν.

89. On this institution, see E. Schlesinger, *Die griechische Asylie* (Giessen, 1933), passim; Berneker, *RE* IX:A2, Supplb., 1441–1479, "Asylie"; W. Ziegler, *Symbolai und Asylia* (Diss. Bonn, 1975), 66–101.

90. *Syll.*[3] 522, I = Schmitt, *Staatsverträge*, no. 508, I, lines 1–2; see above, n. 85. Cf. Ziegler, *Symbolai und Asylia*, 198–202.

them.[91] One might note also another document, not an *asylia* decree, but an undertaking by the Acarnanian League to accept financial and administrative responsibility for a religious shrine and festival at Anactorium in 216. The people of Anactorium are described in the decree as συγγενεῖς καὶ φίλοι.[92]

Agreements between states to provide guidelines or machinery for judicial disputes, *symbola*, might contain references to φιλία as well.[93] Such an arrangement between Miletus and Sardis ca. 330 was preceded by a request from the latter to enter into φιλία—a proposition duly accepted by the Milesians.[94] The language here is worthy of mark: acceptance of a proffered φιλία is clearly not an invention of Rome. Further, we may consider a decree of Cnossus from the mid-third century, reviving judicial agreements with Miletus and asserting the maintenance of a traditional φιλία καὶ εὐνοία.[95] Once more not a mere formality: the words καθάπερ δικαιόν ἐστιν imply an acknowledged, if unwritten, obligation.

Peace treaties too could inaugurate a φιλία. Examples from the era of Alexander's successors come to attention. Antigonus Monophthalmus forced the Carian ruler Asander to accept terms in 313, and to pledge that he would henceforth be a "firm friend."[96] In the next year Antigonus' son Demetrius Poliorcetes called off his attack on the Nabataeans when they asked to be recognized as "friends for all time."[97] Some years later Seleucus I entered into a similar compact with the Indian prince Androcottus. Friendship and familial union were established at the close of hostilities.[98] Analogous formulations were still to be found in 220 when Byzantium and Prusias I of Bithynia brought their conflict to an end. The preface to their treaty announced

91. For Mytilene: *IG*, IX, 1², 189, lines 1–2; *IG*, XII, 2, 15, lines 16–17, 25–26; Magnesia: *Syll.*³ 554 = *IG*, IX, 1², 4c, lines 6–11; Teos: *Syll.*³ 563 = *IG*, IX, 1², 192, lines 3–8: τὰν τε οἰκειότητα κὰι τὰν φιλίαν ἀνενεοῦντο . . . ποτὶ τοὺς Τηίους τὰν φιλίαν κὰι οἰκειότητα τὰν ὑπάρχουσαν διαφυλάσσειν; cf. Ziegler, *Symbolai und Asylia*, 219–224.

92. Habicht, *Hermes* 85 (1957): 87–89 = Schmitt, *Staatsverträge*, no. 523, lines 57–58. On συγγενεία, see Musti, *AnnPisa* 32 (1963): 225–239.

93. On *symbola* generally, see Gauthier, *Symbola, passim*; Ziegler, *Symbolai und Asylia*, 18–65.

94. *Milet*, I, 3, 135 = Schmitt, *Staatsverträge*, no. 407, lines 3–5: δέχεσθαι τὴν φιλίην, ἣν ἐπαγγέλλοντι Σαρδινοὶ Μιλησίοις.

95. *IC*, I, 8, 6 = Schmitt, *Staatsverträge*, no. 482, I, lines 11–15: ὑπολαμβάνομεν γὰρ ὑμῖν πάντα τὰ φιλάνθρωπα γίνεσθαι παρ' ἡμῶν καὶ διαφυλάξομεν τὰμ φιλίαν καὶ τὰν εὔνοιαν τὰν ὑπάρχουσαν ἐκ τῶν πρότερον χρόνων πρὸς ἀλλήλους καθάπερ δίκαιόν ἐστιν.

96. Diod. 19.75.1: βέβαιος ὢν φίλος Ἀντιγόνῳ. The pledge was broken shortly thereafter: Diod. 19.75.2. But that is not to the point.

97. Diod. 19.97.4: φίλους νομίζειν Ναβαταίους εἰς τὸν λοιπὸν χρόνον.

98. Appian, *Syr.* 55: φιλίαν αὐτῷ κὰι κῆδος συνέθετο.

a "permanent peace and friendship."[99] The treaty between Syria and Egypt after the Fourth Syrian War apparently produced a relationship that, whatever the political realities, was termed a "friendship."[100] φιλία was evidently a common companion of Greek peace agreements—or a characterization of their outcome.[101] Hence it is no surprise that offers of peace to Rome by Pyrrhus and by Hiero should be accompanied by proposals of φιλία. The combination was customary and natural.

A looser usage was also indulged. States engaged in diplomatic intercourse for a variety of purposes might refer to one another as "friends" or "friends and kinsmen," simply a courtesy signalling relations of amity.[102] One can find this formulation in decrees honoring foreign judges, i.e., arbiters sent from abroad to cities which requested outside mediation. The honorific resolution commonly praised not only the arbiter but the state that dispatched him: a sign of φιλία.[103] The same formality might appear in any honorific decree on behalf of an individual from another state. So Delos lavishes praise on the

99. Polyb. 4.52.6: εἰρήνην καὶ φιλίαν εἰς τὸν ἅπαντα χρόνον.

100. Egyptian envoys in 203 went to Antiochus III, asking him not to violate the treaty and to observe the φιλία: Polyb. 15.25.13.

101. Cf. also Plut. *Pelop.* 29.6: Thebes rejects an offer of εἰρήνη καὶ φιλία from Alexander of Pherae in 367. The peace between the Aetolian and Acarnanian leagues, perhaps ca. 263, brought not only φιλία but a full fledged συμμαχιά: *Syll.*³ 421A = Schmitt, *Staatsverträge*, no. 480, lines 3–5. And see the general statement put in the mouth of Antiochus III by Livy: peace treaties, whether between conqueror and conquered or between equals in war, served to create *amicitiae*: Livy, 34.57.7–8.

102. An early example in Priene's attesting to her συγγενεία καὶ φιλία with Athens ca. 326: *IvPriene*, 5, lines 5ff. The Rhodians indeed enjoyed φιλία πρὸς πάντας τοὺς δυνάστας in the late fourth century: Diod. 20.81.4. A reference to συγγενεία or οἰκειότης, of course, would usually signify a real or imagined ethnic connection.

103. See, e.g., the exchange of decrees by Magnesia and Priene in the late third century following successful arbitration by judges from Priene. The cities affirmed mutual φιλία and οἰκειότης; *IvPriene*, 61, lines 4–6 (Magnesian decree): Πριηνεῖς διατηροῦ[ν]τ[ες τὴν οἰκειότ]ητα καὶ τὴν φιλίαν τὴν ὑπάρχουσαν τοῖς πόλεσι πρὸς ἀλ-λ[ήλας ἐκ π]αλαιῶν χρόνων; lines 32–33 (reply of Priene): Μάγνητες οἰκεῖυ[ι τ]ε [ὄντες ἡμῶν καὶ φίλ]ο[ι]. A similar formula employed by Mytilene in praising an arbiter from Erythrae of the early second century; *IG*, XII, Suppl. 43–44, no. 137 = H. Engelmann and R. Merkelbach, *Die Inschriften von Erythrai und Klazomenai* (Bonn, 1972), I, no. 122, lines 16–17. See also a document of Bargylia honoring a Tean judge and exhorting Teos to maintain φιλία in the mid-third century: *Syll.*³ 426, lines 35–37: παρακαλοῦσιν τὸν δῆμον τὸν Τηίων εἰς [τε] τὸν λοιπὸν χρόνον διαφυλάσσειν τὴμ φιλίαν τὴν [ὑπ]άρχουσαν ταῖς πόλεσι πρὸς ἀλλήλας. Cf. the fragmentary documents from Iasus; G. P. Caratelli, *Annuario* 45–46 (1967–68): 461–462, no. 18, line 2; no. 19, lines 6–7; new text of the latter in Y. Garlan, *BCH* 98 (1974): 116–118. A new inscription from Colophon: P. Frisch, *ZPE* 13 (1974): 112–116, lines 4–5. A recently discovered decree of the Thessalian League sends an arbiter to Teos, referring to the Teans as συγγενεῖς καὶ φίλοι: *AthAnnArch* 5 (1972): 277, lines 1–3.

Macedonian Admetus, ca. 240–230, for services to the island and its sanctuary. By virtue of those services, Thessalonica is adjudged a friend of Delos.[104] In a similar category are public announcements granting recognition of religious shrines and festivals. A whole series of such documents was addressed to Magnesia ca. 207 from several cities, which gave formal recognition to the establishment of a new festival. Most included polite references to the people of Magnesia as φιλοί καὶ οἰκεῖοι or συγγενεῖς.[105] Chios, probably in 246, accepted an Aetolian request to participate in a festival celebrating Aetolia's defeat of the Gauls, with due reference to a φιλία between them.[106] And one other example: a Delian decree of the late third or early second century, giving Cyzicus the privilege of setting up a stele in the sanctuary, calls the Cyzicenes friends of Delos.[107]

These courteous exchanges show that the term φιλία was often employed in a vague and ill-defined fashion, as little more than an expression of cordial relations. But there can be no doubt that it elsewhere has more concrete implications as a form of diplomatic association. As we have seen, it could be linked with specific agreements: *isopoliteia, asylia, symbola,* or peace treaties. More significantly, we know of compacts whose explicit purpose was to institute or renew φιλία. Two widely spaced examples will suffice as illustration. An exchange of decrees between Argos and Pallantium ca. 317 not only asserted renewal of their friendship but authorized its inscription on a public stele.[108] A century or so later, under the auspices of the Epirote confederacy, the Aterargoi and Pergamioi reestablished their old φιλία.[109] There is no point here in tracing such compacts back beyond the Hellenistic age. But one item is worth attention. An agreement between Amyntas of Macedonia and Chalcidice ca. 393 required both partners to contract no φιλία with other states unless it be done jointly.[110] The implication is plain: a covenant of φιλία was a recog-

104. *IG,* XI, 4, 665 = Dürrbach, *Choix,* no. 49, II, lines 19–20: τὸν δῆμον τὸν Θεσσαλονικέων ὄντα φίλο[ν] καὶ οἰκεῖον.

105. *Syll.*³ 557, lines 35–36; 558, lines 3–4; 559, lines 22–23, 30, 51–52; 560, lines 3–4, 21–22; 562, lines 9–10, 26–29.

106. *Syll.*³ 402, lines 2, 11–12: μεμνημένος τῆς τε οἰκειότητος καὶ φιλίας τῆς ὑπαρχούσης αὐτῶι πρὸς [Αἰτωλούς]. Most recent edition in G. Nachtergael, *Les Galates en Grèce et les Sôtéria de Delphes* (Brussels, 1975), 436–440.

107. *Syll.*³ 1158, lines 12–13, 17–18: φίλ[οι] ὄντες τοῦ δήμου τοῦ Δηλίων . . . Δηλίους φίλους ὄντας τῆς πόλεως αὐτῶν.

108. *SEG,* XI, 1084 = *ISE,* no. 52 = Schmitt, *Staatsverträge,* no. 419, lines 5–8, 11–13, 32–34.

109. *SEG,* XV, 411 = Schmitt, *Staatsverträge,* no. 568 = *ISE,* no. 120, lines 8–12, 14; cf. *SEG,* XXVI, 719.

110. *Syll.*³ 135, lines 20–24.

nized diplomatic instrument. Though it might be accompanied by, it was not identical with, a συμμαχία.[111] The practice of certifying φιλία between Greek states through an official arrangement continued well into the second century and well after Rome's initial involvement in the East.[112] Clearly it was an established and longstanding institution.

One final matter deserves remark in this connection. The φιλία, though bilateral in character by definition, need not be (indeed often was not) a pact between equal powers. Not that it was cloak for aggression or aggrandizement—though it could be that too.[113] It was, rather, a conventional way of expressing favor or even signifying protection by a great power for a weaker one. This is obvious enough in several instances and almost explicitly spelled out in some. A dedication at Olympia by the city of Byzantium in 302 honors the Macedonian kings Antigonus and Demetrius. Byzantium announces that in gratitude to her benefactors she will be a πόλις φίλα to the end of time.[114] In the 240s or 230s Smyrna proclaimed her loyal maintenance of εὔνοια καὶ φιλία to Seleucus II and offered sympoliteia to the inhabitants of Magnesia on condition that they profess the same loyalty.[115] In these years, the people of Aradus and other Phoenicians (if the language of Strabo be trusted) are termed both subjects and φίλοι of the Syrian kings.[116] An Attic decree of 236/5 honors a Macedonian officer of Demetrius II for maintaining φιλία toward the Athenians.[117] In 218 Philip V promised a variety of privileges to Elis in return for her φιλία.[118] And, near the end of the third century, the little island of Ios praised and honored Rhodes as protectress of the Nesiotic League; at the behest of the stronger power, she reasserted her φιλία καὶ συμφωνία toward the Rhodians.[119] The examples require no multiplication.

111. Note Philip II's offer to Athens in 359. He was prepared συμμαχίαν ποιεῖσθαι καὶ τὴν πατρικὴν φιλίαν ἀνανεοῦσθαι: Dem. 23.121. A similar distinction between "renewing a φιλία," and "making a συμμαχία" in a decree of the late third century: IG, XII, Suppl. 96, 8 = Schmitt, Staatsverträge, no. 566, line 3—if the restorations be correct.

112. E.g., Achaea and Syria in 188: Polyb. 22.7.4, 22.9.13—wrongly called συμμαχία by Diod. 29.17; Teos and Tyre ca. 126: BCH 49 (1925): 306 = SEG, IV, 601, lines 3–4, 8–11.

113. Such at least is implied by Polyb. 15.24.4, quoted above, n. 78.

114. Syll.³ 349, lines 3–4: ὅτι ἁ πόλις ὧν τε εὐεργέτηται[ι χάριν αὐ]τοῖς ἔ[χ]ουσα φίλ[α ἔσται εἰ]ς τ[ὸ]ν ὑπόλοιπον χρόν[ον].

115. OGIS, 229 = Schmitt, Staatsverträge, no. 492, passim; note, e.g., lines 3, 13–19, 22–24, 37–39, 61–67, 89–98.

116. Strabo, 16.2.14 (C 754): οἱ δ' οὖν Ἀράδιοι μετὰ τῶν ἄλλων Φοινίκων ὑπήκοουν τῶν Συριακῶν βασιλέων, ἅτε φίλων.

117. BCH 54 (1930): 268–282 = ISE, no. 25, lines 2–6.

118. Polyb. 4.84.4–5.

119. IG, XII, Suppl., 96, 8 = Schmitt, Staatsverträge, no. 566, lines 3–4: [ἀνανε-

The concept of φιλία as relationship between a major power and her adherents was familiar in Greece long before the arrival of Rome.

Φιλία/Amicitia:
The Early Stages

It is time to return to our starting point. When a Roman fleet sailed across the Adriatic to engage the Illyrians in 229, some Greek cities and Illyrian tribes entered into *amicitia*. And, after the war, the defeated Illyrian kingdom also became a Roman *amicus*. There is no evidence and no reason to see this development as a contrived plan by Rome to employ *amicitia* as a springboard for suzerainty or a device to guarantee control. Still less is it to be regarded as an outgrowth of private relations between individuals or families in Rome, personal *clientela* transferred to the international scene. The fact is that, at least before the late third century, *amicitia* was not a Roman diplomatic instrument. Rome encountered it in dealings with Carthage and with certain Greek states and monarchs, but in no way converted it to her own purposes. On the other hand, as we have seen, φιλία was a very familiar and widespread institution among Greeks throughout the Hellenistic period, and even earlier. There can be little question that the *amicitiae* which emerged in the Illyrian wars reflected Greek practice, not Roman policy.

The communities of Corcyra, Apollonia, and Epidamnus, possessed longstanding commercial connections with the Greeks of southern Italy, and naturally welcomed Rome's assistance against Illyrian marauders. *Amicitia* would be an obvious vehicle whereby to summon that assistance again, should it be required. The Parthini and Atintani yielded to Roman might and opted for *amicitia* to assure survival. And the peace treaty, as a matter of course, converted the former enemy into an *amicus*. None of this involved explicit obligations; nor did it entail dependency and clientage. We are not in the presence of an instrument of imperialism.

It is equally erroneous to maintain that Rome manipulated the institution to serve her ends in the last decades of the third century.[120]

ὠσασθαι τὸν δῆμον τὸν Ἰητῶν τ}ὴμ φιλίαν καὶ τὴμ συμφωνίαν τὴμ πρὸς Ῥ[οδίους ὑπάρχουσαν] . . . καθὰ καὶ [Ῥ]όδιοι παρακαλοῦσιν. The stone may also have recorded contraction of an alliance, but its mutilated character prevents secure reconstruction.

120. At least not in the East. Northern Italy, of course, was a different matter—and of much greater importance to Rome. It is interesting that the diplomatic categories encountered in the Illyrian War were applied very shortly thereafter to the Gauls. In 224 legionary forces compelled the Boii to accept Roman πίστις, and in 223 the Anares were admitted into φιλία: Polyb. 2.31.9, 2.32.2.

When she sought assistance against Philip V, who had joined Hannibal against her, Rome did not bid her Greek *amici* to take up arms as if
they were vassal states. On the contrary: effective opposition to Philip
required a concrete συμμαχία, the pact with Aetolia in 212 or 211, a
formal treaty of alliance, albeit one which was designed only for the
duration of the war.[121] The συμμαχία, of course, created an *amicitia*
with Aetolia, as any Greek wartime alliance would. And it also solicited the adherence of other states whose involvement on the Roman
side would make them *amici* as well.[122] In fact, the Greek states that
chose to participate, Pergamum, Sparta, Elis, and Messene, did so by
virtue of prior alliances with Aetolia.[123] The only previous "friends" of
Rome who engaged Philip were the Illyrian chieftains Scerdilaidas
and his son Pleuratus—and they had their own reasons.[124] Cooperation in the war instituted a de facto *amicitia*, a φιλία καὶ συμμαχία in
the sense long familiar to the Greeks. Whether Pergamum and the
Peloponnesian allies of Aetolia signed separate alliances with Rome (a
matter of intense scholarly dispute) is quite immaterial. The alliances,
if such there were, were contracted for the particular conflict. But the
informal *amicitia* would be held to endure even after that conflict was
decided. So, Pergamum, Sparta, Elis, and Messene are termed Roman *amici* at the end of the third century, a relationship inaugurated
in the First Macedonian War.[125]

The relevant point, however, is that *amicitia* is essentially a description of the relationship, not a tool which allowed Rome to make
claims or lay obligations upon her φίλοι. That is plain enough from
the events of the war itself. In 208 Attalus withdrew Pergamene forces
from the contest and returned to Asia Minor to see to his own kingdom.[126] After the battle of Mantinea in the following year, Sparta too
dropped out of the war; and the same was doubtless true of Messene
and Elis.[127] Rome had no grounds to enforce their continued participation. Nor did their withdrawal mean a breaking of relations. As we

---

121. See above pp. 17–20.

122. Livy, 26.24.9: *eodem iure amicitiae*.

123. Polyb. 9.30.6, 9.31.1–4, 10.25.3, 16.13.3; Livy, 31.46.3; see above p. 20.

124. Polyb. 10.41.4; Livy, 26.24.9, 27.30.13, 27.33.3, 28.5.7.

125. For Pergamum, see Polyb. 21.20.3: μετασχὼν τῆς ὑμετέρας φιλίας καὶ συμμαχίας; Livy, 29.11.1–2: *cum Attalo rege propter commune adversus Philippum bellum coeptam amicitiam esse*; cf. Polyb. 16.25.4; Livy, 37.53.7–9; Appian, *Mac.* 4.2; Strabo, 13.4.2
(C 624). On Sparta, Elis, and Messene, see Polyb. 18.42.7; Livy, 34.32.16; cf. 34.31.5,
34.31.19, 34.32.1–3.

126. Livy, 28.7.10.

127. On the battle of Mantinea, Polyb. 11.11–18; Plut. *Phil.* 10.1–8. Sparta's subsequent inactivity: Polyb. 13.6.1. The withdrawal of Messene and Elis may be safely
assumed. We hear of no further activity in the Peloponnese; cf. Holleaux, *Rome, la
Grèce*, 262–263.

have seen, those states were still reckoned as Roman *amici* after the war.[128] But they were fully autonomous entities, in no sense under a Roman protectorate or a system of clientage. The peace of Phoenice in 205 establishes the fact, if proof be needed. Under its terms, the Parthini were conceded to Rome, as were three towns in Illyria. But the Greek states that fought against Philip were in an entirely different category. They signed the peace as *adscripti* on the Roman side, a good Hellenistic practice: they were independent powers with an interest in the peace terms.[129]

Rome gave no guarantees to her *amici* under the peace of Phoenice, and received none from them. Nothing of the kind was expected. The treaty conceded Philip's hold on the Atintani, though they had been accepted into $\phi\iota\lambda\iota\alpha$ in 229, and evidently acknowledged his seizure of territory from Pleuratus, another Roman *amicus*. But no one accused Rome of violating her *fides* or abandoning her "protectorate." *Amicitia* did not produce a protectorate.[130] After the peace Rome's Hellenic "friends" went their own way. Their relationship with the western power was inert and remote. So, for example, Sparta attacked Rome's *amicus* Messene in 201 and even made terms with Philip in 198/7 when Rome was at war with him. Yet the senate revived, without hesitation, the *amicitia* with Sparta in 197.[131] *Amicitia* was a presumption of cordiality, not an imposition of duties.[132]

The origins of the Second Macedonian War may be passed over here. One central item, however, needs discussion in this context. Scholarship reckons the event as a watershed in the history of *ami-*

128. Of course, Rome's own active involvement effectively ceased after 208—under pressure of the Hannibalic conflict: Livy, 29.12.1, 31.31.19. But she certainly expected (or at least hoped) that her "friends" would carry on the fight against Philip.

129. Livy, 29.12.13–14; cf. Appian, *Mac.* 3.2; and see above p. 21. Whether Athens and Ilium, included here by Livy, were genuine *adscripti* has long been disputed, but is unimportant for our purposes. There is no good reason to deny any of the others. The staggering bibliography on this question is registered by Dahlheim, *Struktur und Entwicklung*, 210–211, n. 75, 219–221, n. 99; Schmitt, *Staatsverträge*, no. 543, pp. 283–284. Add C. Habicht, *Studien zur Geschichte Athens in hellenistischer Zeit* (Göttingen, 1982), 138–142.

130. Badian, *Foreign Clientelae*, 60, recognizes the elasticity of the concept but gratuitously charges Rome with cynical disregard of her *amici*. The ancients did not so consider it.

131. The war on Messene: Polyb. 16.13.3; the agreement with Philip: Livy, 32.38.2–4, 34.32.16–19; the renewal of *amicitia* with Rome: Livy, 32.39.1–10. Rome did not complain of Spartan transgressions until later, when she sought justification for a war: Livy, 34.32.14–20.

132. Note, for instance, Rome's request for grain from Egypt during the Hannibalic war: Polyb. 9.11a. At perhaps the same time she renewed her *amicitia* with the Ptolemies: Livy, 27.4.10. But that *amicitia* did not entitle her to expect cooperation. Egypt, in fact, remained neutral, not only in the Hannibalic conflict but also in the eastern war, where she played the role of mediator; see above n. 47.

citia. Rome, it is argued, now refashioned the concept to circumvent fetial law, to justify further intervention in the East, and to transform Greece into a protectorate. Rome's friends could provide grounds for expansion. *Amici* were placed on the same plane as *socii*, creating an overlapping institution of *amicitia et societas* designed to further the goals of Roman policy makers.[133] That analysis needs to be reassessed.

First, from the Greek vantage-point: is there any reason to believe that the states that sought Roman assistance against Philip appealed to an *amicitia* relationship? The sources record embassies to the senate from Aetolia, Attalus, Rhodes, Athens, and Egypt. Of these, only Attalus could plead an active prior collaboration, by his services in the First Macedonian War. Naturally the king availed himself of that argument. But nothing suggests that he cited the existing *amicitia* as an obligation, legal or moral, which authorized Roman intervention.[134] The other appellants had not even this circumstance to utilize. Aetolia, if Appian be trusted, came to reinstitute Roman favor, a favor she had lost when making a unilateral peace with Philip in 206.[135] As for Rhodes, Athens, and Egypt, none had participated in the First Macedonian War and all had actively sought to bring it to a close.[136] Rhodes complained of Philip's aggressions in Asia Minor, Athens of his invasion of Attica. Neither had an *amicitia* with Rome, or, at least, neither appealed to one.[137] The Egyptian mission, even if it be genuine and not an annalistic fiction, is irrelevant. The envoys

---

133. So, most fully, Dahlheim, *Struktur und Entwicklung*, 248–259, with literature cited there. Note, especially, T. Frank, *Roman Imperialism* (New York, 1914), 146–147; Badian, *Foreign Clientelae*, 66–69; cf. de Martino, *Storia della costituzione romana* II: 33.

134. Attalus' reference to his κοινοπραγία appears only in Polyb. 16.25.4, in the context of his meeting with Roman representatives at Athens. It is an expression of relief that Rome was mindful of his services and prepared for war on Philip. A pleasant surprise for Attalus—not a fulfillment of any obligation: ἐχρημάτισε τοῖς ἐκ τῆς Ῥώμης πρεσβευταῖς, θεωρῶν δ᾽ αὐτοὺς καὶ τῆς προγεγενημένης κοινοπραγίας μνημονεύοντας καὶ πρὸς τὸν κατὰ τοῦ Φιλίππου πόλεμον ἑτοίμους ὄντας περιχαρὴς ἦν. The evidence on Attalus' mission to Rome does not mention even this argument, let alone any appeal to the *amicitia*; just complaints about Philip's incursions: Livy, 31.2.1, 31.3.1; Appian, *Mac.* 4.1; Justin, 30.3.5.

135. Appian, *Mac.* 4.2; cf. Livy, 31.29.4. The event itself may not be authentic; for discussion, see Badian, *Latomus* 17 (1958): 208–211.

136. Livy, 27.30, 28.7.13–15; Polyb. 11.4–6; Appian, *Mac.* 3.

137. The Rhodian complaints: Livy, 31.2.1; Appian, *Mac.* 4.2; cf. Polyb. 16.24.3; Justin, 30.3.5; the Athenian missions: Livy, 31.1.9, 31.5.6, 31.14.3; cf. Appian, *Mac.* 4.1; Paus. 1.36.6, 7.7.7–8. Even if Rhodes had entered into *amicitia* ca. 306 (for which see above, n. 74) that arrangement plainly played no role here. A Rhodian decision to hold to her φιλία, in fact, took place only after the fall of Abydus in late 200 and after war was a certainty: Polyb. 16.35.1–2. As for Athens, whether or not she was among the *adscripti* at Phoenice, no appeal to that fact was offered in justification. And there is more than an argument from silence. Philip, who had attacked Attica, nonetheless warned Rome against violating the Phoenice agreement! Polyb. 16.34.7.

announced an Athenian request for aid and stated their readiness to act if Rome should desire it; the senate politely declined.[138] Nothing in the foregoing items, whether taken individually or collectively, suggests that Roman aid was expected by virtue of any *amicitiae*. The institution was too loose to engender any such expectation—as the Greeks well knew.

The more important question, however, involves Roman intentions. Did the senate consciously expand and pervert the idea of *amicitia* to justify aggression? It is, of course, true that the annalistic tradition legitimized Rome's venture against Philip as a noble crusade in defense of the Greeks. However, the Livian passages that enshrine this tradition consistently refer to those for whom Rome took up arms as her *socii*.[139] That is obvious distortion and contrived apologia, as few would now deny. But it is dubious methodology, at the very least, to argue from the devices of later apologists to the psychology of contemporary Romans. Did the senate in 200 clothe *amici* in the garb of allies to placate the *fetiales* and trumpet Rome's cause to the world? The evidence of Polybius tells a different story.

Whatever motivated Rome to intervene against Philip, her public claim was not one of acting on behalf of those with whom she had prior connections. In the first message delivered to the Macedonians in Attica, Roman envoys urged Philip "to make war on none of the Greeks." They added that his quarrels with Attalus should be submitted to an arbitral board.[140] The subsequent demands at Abydus were not very different. The Romans asked Philip to let arbiters decide the question of damages owed to both Attalus and Rhodes. He was to keep his hands off the possessions of Ptolemy. And a repetition of the general ultimatum: Philip should "make war on none of the Greeks."[141] What does this mean? Attalus was indeed an *amicus* of Rome; so was Egypt; and perhaps even Rhodes. But Rome made no mention of *amicitia* as justification for her demands on Philip. Still less was she subtly converting her *amici* into *amici et socii*. In the case of Rhodes, her

138. Livy, 31.9.1–5. That Athens did seek assistance from Egypt is supported by Paus. 1.36.5; cf. Moretti, *ISE*, no. 33. But Livy's depiction of the Athenians as Roman *socii* is clearly false and the whole account dubious; cf. H. Winkler, *Rom und Ägypten im 2. Jahrhundert v. Chr.* (Leipzig, 1933), 19–20. An Egyptian appeal for Roman aid is given only by Justin, 30.2.8—a story of little value; cf. Winkler, *op. cit.*, 16–19.

139. Livy, 30.26.2–4, 30.42.2–10, 31.1.9, 31.3.1, 31.5.8–9, 31.6.1, 31.9.1–4. Cf. Justin, 30.3.6: *titulo ferendi sociis auxilii bellum adversus Philippum decernitur.*

140. Polyb. 16.27.2: Ῥωμαῖοι παρακαλοῦσι τὸν βασιλέα τῶν μὲν Ἑλλήνων μηδενὶ πολεμεῖν, τῶν δὲ γεγονότων εἰς Ἄτταλον ἀδικημάτων δίκας ὑπέχειν ἐν ἴσῳ κριτηρίῳ.

141. Polyb. 16.34.3: μήτε τῶν Ἑλλήνων μηδενὶ πολεμεῖν μήτε τοῖς Πτολεμαίου πράγμασιν ἐπιβάλλειν τὰς χεῖρας, περὶ δὲ τῶν εἰς Ἄτταλον καὶ Ῥοδίους ἀδικημάτων δίκας ὑποσχεῖν. Livy, 31.18.1–2.

assertion of adherence to φιλία did not come until *after* the Abydus declaration.[142] We need not spin webs about crafty and prescient manipulations by Roman diplomats. The truth is simpler. By underlining wrongs done to Attalus and Rhodes, Rome merely called attention to Philip's most prominent victims and chief opponents. The warning about Ptolemy's possessions referred plainly to Philip's acquisitions in Thrace and his designs on the Aegean and Asia Minor. Deeper meanings should not be read into the statements. The call for arbitration is itself revealing: a standard Hellenic practice, but one almost unknown to Roman diplomacy. We may be confident that it did not spring from senatorial circles unaided by Greek counsel.[143] Further and more significant: Rome singled out Pergamum, Rhodes, and Egypt, as was logical, but did not confine her attentions to them. When Philip balked at the demands, Rome's spokesmen at Abydus retorted by airing the grievances of Athens, Cius, and Abydus herself, the latter two of whom, at least, were no *amici* of Rome.[144] *Amicitia* is not here at issue. Rome asked Philip to refrain from war on all Greeks. A grandiose propaganda gesture, appropriate and fruitful. It won her much support in the coming war. But the gesture is in no way connected with the claims of *amicitia*.[145]

The states that solicited Rome's participation in the Second Macedonian War naturally became her *amici*, if they were not so already: Athens, Attalus, and Rhodes. In addition, those who joined her side during the course of the conflict would fall into the same category, as was customary. It is significant, however, that Rome did not consider a prior *amicitia* as grounds for coercing or requiring assistance in the war. During the first campaigning season in the fall of 200, Pleuratus, an old *amicus*, and Amynander and Bato, new ones, voluntarily

142. Polyb. 16.35.1–2. A point glossed over by Dahlheim, *Struktur und Entwicklung*, 255–257. And he has no satisfactory explanation for the inclusion of Ptolemy's claims at Abydus. The suggestion that envoys from Alexandria met with the Romans to press their claims (*op. cit.*, 257) is unfounded speculation. Rome's legation was still scheduled to go to Alexandria: Polyb. 16.27.5, 16.34.2.

143. Arbitration as a means of settling interstate disputes in Greece had a long and continuous history; see, e.g., E. Sonne, *De Arbitris externis, quos Graeci adhibuerunt ad lites componendas* (Diss. Göttingen, 1888); A. Raeder, *L'arbitrage international chez les Hellènes* (Christiana, 1912); M. N. Tod, *International Arbitration among the Greeks* (Oxford, 1913); A. Steinwenter, *Die Streitbeendigung durch Urteil, Schiedsspruch, und Vergleich* (Munich, 1925). A full and recent collection of instances down to 338 B.C. by L. Piccirilli, *Gli arbitrati interstatali greci* I (Pisa, 1973). The Romans had previously scorned the practice; see Matthaei, *CQ* 2 (1908): 241–264. And, in connection with this episode, cf. Bickermann, *RevPhil* 61 (1935): 76–79.

144. Polyb. 16.34.5; cf. Livy, 31.18.2.

145. The formulation of Appian, *Mac.* 4.2 is clearly erroneous: Φίλιππον δὲ μηδὲν ἐς 'Ροδίους ἢ 'Αθηναίους ἢ "Ατταλον ἢ ἐς ἄλλον τινὰ 'Ρωμαίων φίλον ἁμαρτάνειν—and finds no warrant in Polybius' text. Cf. Petzold, *Die Eröffnung*, 73–74.

offered aid. Rome accepted with pleasure. She had not demanded help from Pleuratus, despite their longstanding *amicitia*, any more than she had from the Athamanians and Dardani with whom there was no previous connection. The ancient account draws no distinction.[146] In the case of other states, indecisive or neutral, Roman agents actively solicited support. Those who consented, of course, became *amici*, but without undertaking concrete obligations beyond the war itself. So the Romans offered to Aetolia the opportunity of reinstatement into *amicitia et societas*, an offer accepted in 199.[147] After the war, the status of *amicitia* was presumed to continue.[148] Similarly with the Achaeans in 198. They agreed to join the war and even sought the comfort of a formal treaty. Rome declined the latter; binding commitments were not her aim.[149] In 197 Rome came to an agreement with Nabis of Sparta, who had expressed willingness to betray Philip. Hence a revival of *amicitia*, but one tied explicitly to terms of assistance in the present conflict.[150] Support for the war, not long-term association, was its principal purpose. Roman commanders consistently asked Greeks to rely on their *fides*—tantamount to an offer of *amicitia*.[151] Even in wartime, however, Rome did not profess to control her *amici*. When Attalus in 198 asked leave to withdraw his forces in order to protect his own kingdom, the senate delivered a significant response: Rome always regarded the forces of others who gave her assistance as being entirely at their own disposal.[152] A far cry from *amicitia* as a tool of imperialism.

The conclusion of the war brought new *amicitiae*. When Philip signed the peace treaty he naturally became a φίλος, in accordance with Greek custom.[153] Contacts with other states in the course of the postwar settlement, favors granted, or decisions rendered could inaugurate an informal *amicitia*. Details on specific cases are wanting. But evidence is clear enough from later occasions that prompted communities to "renew" their *amicitiae*. So, for example, Delos, probably

146. Livy, 31.28.1–2.

147. Livy, 31.31.20: *et vobis restituendi vos in amicitiam societatemque nostram fortuna oblata est*; 31.40.7–31.41.1.

148. Livy, 36.3.8–10.

149. Livy, 32.23.1–2; Polyb. 18.42.6–7; see above pp. 22–23. Boeotia entered into the war on the same terms as Achaea: Livy, 33.2.6, 33.2.9.

150. Livy, 32.39.10: *de condicionibus amicitiae coeptum agi est*; cf. 34.31.5.

151. Cf. Polyb. 18.38.5: παρακαλοῦντος σφᾶς εἰς τὴν 'Ρωμαίων πίστιν. Rendered by Livy, 33.13.8 as *vocati in amicitiam*.

152. Livy, 32.8.14: *semper populum Romanum alienis rebus arbitrio alieno usum; et principium et finem in potestatem ipsorum, qui ope sua velint adiutos Romanos, esse.*

153. Diod. 31.8.1. The fact is clear from Perseus' renewal of his father's φιλία in 179: Polyb. 25.3.1; Livy, 40.58.8; Diod. 29.30; Zon. 9.22; cf. Livy, 39.28.14, 42.25.1, 42.25.12; Appian, *Mac.* 11.5; Plut. *Flam.* 14.2; Gruen, *CSCA* 6 (1973): 123–136.

around 192, sent a delegation to reaffirm οἰκειότης καὶ φιλία, in typical Greek fashion. Contact no doubt first came during or immediately after the Second Macedonian War.[154] Similarly, an inscription from ca. 140 records missions from the Thessalian towns of Melitea and Narthacium in connection with a boundary dispute. Both legations refer to the time when they were first accepted into Roman φιλία—evidently in 196 when Flamininus and the senatorial commissioners established certain regulations.[155] Plainly such associations were of the vaguest sort, conventional expressions of cordiality and no more. Of special interest is an inscription from Lampsacus, which describes that city's efforts to be included in the peace treaty with Philip. The Lampsacene envoys claim συγγενεία and φιλία with Rome.[156] Quite obviously this is an exaggerated plea for favor and protection. Rome did not accept the Lampsacenes into *amicitia* for another quarter-century.[157] The claim, however, shows just how loosely these terms could be applied—and what little meaning they had outside the military context. For the Greeks, φιλία could be guaranteed in a formal covenant. And the Lampsacene request reflects that practice. They ask not just to be included in the treaty with Philip but in any φιλίαι or sworn agreements which Rome might make with other states.[158] That there would be such formal compacts in the future was a natural Greek assumption. But Rome had no plans of so committing herself.

Though the number of *amicitiae* increased in the 190s, the bonds do not appear to have become tighter. *Amicitia* is attested between Rome and Antiochus III during that decade.[159] Whether this derived from the purported third-century contact with Seleucus II or from diplomatic contact in 200 is immaterial. The relationship certainly did not involve active collaboration, and indeed very little real cordiality. Antiochus' chief rivals, the Ptolemies, were also *amici* of Rome, an *amicitia* that went back three quarters of a century. The sources report a series of embassies, some of them probably spurious, back and forth between Rome and Alexandria at the end of the third and beginning of the second centuries.[160] None of them implies that Rome was

154. *IG*, XI, 4, 756 = Dürrbach, *Choix*, no. 65, lines 2–3.

155. *Syll.*³ 674 = Sherk, *RDGE*, no. 9, lines 21, 47–54.

156. *Syll.*³ 591, lines 18–26, 30–31, 53–56, 59–63.

157. Livy, 43.6.9.

158. *Syll.*³ 591, lines 32–33: ἐὰν πρός τινας φιλίαν ἢ ὅρκια ποῆται. Desideri, *StudClassOrient* 19–20 (1970–71): 501–506, oddly believes that the Lampsacenes fulfilled their purposes simply by an implicit inclusion among Greek cities declared free.

159. Livy, 32.8.13, 33.20.8, 34.57.11.

160. Polyb. 15.25.14 (203); Livy, 31.2.3–4; Appian, *Mac.* 4.2; Justin, 30.3.3 (200); Livy, 31.9.1–5 (200); Polyb. 18.49.3; Livy, 33.39.1, 33.41.2–3; Justin, 31.1.2–3; Appian, *Syr.* 2–3; cf. 38 (196). The famous tale that M. Lepidus was installed as *tutor* for the young Ptolemy in 200 is worthless and generally rejected: Val. Max. 6.6.1; Justin,

prepared to act in the interests of Egypt. To be sure, Roman envoys at Lysimacheia in 196 asked Antiochus to withdraw from cities that had once belonged to the Ptolemies.[161] But the request has nothing to do with *amicitia*. It belongs to a series of demands leveled at Antiochus, including the evacuation of Philip's former holdings, withdrawal from Europe, and noninterference with the autonomous cities of Asia Minor. There is no suggestion that Ptolemy is to recover his possessions. On the contrary. The point of the demands is that Antiochus has wrongly occupied areas for whose liberty Romans had toiled in the Second Macedonian War.[162] They announced the whole program for public consumption, a propaganda move, as in 200.[163] When Rome negotiated again with Antiochus three years later, the claims of Ptolemy are nowhere in evidence.[164]

Peacetime relations with *amici*, it is plain, were nebulous and had little impact on policy. What about wartime? Few would venture to suggest that Rome went to war with Antiochus on behalf of her "friends." Nor did she employ them even as a screen or pretext. The propaganda line dwelled on the liberty of all Greeks, a line echoed by Antiochus as well, for his own purposes. The logic of their pronouncements drove them into conflict, not the obligations or the opportunities of *amicitia*.[165] But the question can be put differently. Had the accumulation of *amici* since 200 also brought a firmer grip on their activities? That is, could Rome in 192—any more than she could in 200—expect automatic military assistance by virtue of *amicitia*?

The answer is clearly no. Philip V, an *amicus* of Rome since 196, was wooed by Antiochus and his allies. Unsuccessfully, as it turned out. But the king wavered for some time before choosing Rome's side. A personal affront by Antiochus decided him, so the sources have it. Certainly it was not the *amicitia*.[166] And even after active cooperation during the campaign of 191 (with unsatisfactory results for the king) Philip's loyalty could not be taken for granted, let alone comman-

30.2.8, 30.3.4, 31.1–3; Tac. *Ann.* 2.67. On Roman-Egyptian relations in this period, see Winkler, *Rom und Aegypten*, 9–25; Manni, *RivFilol* 27 (1949): 95–103; Heine, *ANRW* I: 1 (1972), 644–651.

161. Polyb. 18.50.5–6; Livy, 33.39.4; Appian, *Syr.* 3.

162. That is clear from Polybius' account: 18.50.5–9; Livy, 33.39.4–7. Misinterpreted by Appian, *Syr.* 3. The version of Justin, 31.1.2–3 is a distortion, based on his belief in Roman tutelage of Ptolemy.

163. The same demands had been proclaimed at the Isthmus in the spring of 196: Polyb. 18.47.1–2; Livy, 33.34.2–4.

164. Livy, 34.57–59: Diod. 28.15; Appian, *Syr.* 6.

165. On the propaganda, see the previous two notes. The background to the war is admirably discussed by Badian, *Studies*, 112–139.

166. Livy, 36.8.3–6; Appian, *Syr.* 16. An alternative tale in Livy, 36.4.1–4, has Philip volunteer aid which Rome courteously declined; it is probably fictitious. In either case, it is plain that Rome did not requisition support on the basis of her *amicitia*.

deered. When the Scipios sought to march through Philip's territory on the way to Asia, they had to deal with him most delicately: an embassy went to obtain the Macedonian king's permission.[167] *Amicitia* did not guarantee so much as a safe passage. The same conclusion emerges from the evidence on Rome's effort to gain Achaean support in 192. Flamininus' speech to the Achaeans ridiculed Antiochus' boasts of strength, underlined the advantages of cooperation with Rome, and warned of the consequences of remaining neutral. Not a word about moral obligations implicit in *amicitia*.[168] Individual interests of state determined decisions. Pergamum and Rhodes fought Antiochus, of course; their own immediate spheres of influence were at stake. Egypt, on the other hand, stayed out of the conflict. Roman prodding was unnecessary for the Pergamenes and Rhodians and unattempted on the Egyptians.[169] Antiochus and his allies the Aetolians felt free to solicit support from among Rome's own *amici*. Rebuff came in most places. The answers from Chalcis and Thyrreum seem significant: those cities refused to contract a new alliance without Roman authorization.[170] In both instances, however, the decisions derived from a calculation of interest, not from the bonds of *amicitia*.[171] Those bonds, far from enforcing subjection to Rome's will, were perfectly consistent with neutrality—and even with formal links to Antiochus. So, at least, the Aetolians argued at Chalcis and Achaea. Their arguments went unchallenged.[172] The Chalcidians refused a *societas*; but, in standard Greek fashion, they would welcome an *amicitia* with both sides.[173] Adherence to Rome, in fact, both at Chalcis and at Athens, did not come until after civil upheaval and political expulsions.[174] *Amicitia* itself produced no mobilization. Nor did Rome employ it as a means of coercion.

As Rome's military fortunes rose in the Syrian War, various cities

---

167. Livy, 37.7.8–14.

168. Livy, 35.49. The grounds for expecting Achaean aid, in fact, rested on knowledge of the League's hostility to Nabis: Livy, 35.31.2.

169. A dubious tale in Livy has Ptolemy volunteer assistance in 191 and be turned down: 36.4.1–3. A year later he presented himself again as ready to conform to any wishes of the senate; no reply is recorded: Livy, 37.3.9–11. Whatever one makes of this evidence, it is clear that Rome made no demands on Egypt.

170. Livy, 35.46.13: *ne societatem quidem ullam pacisci nisi ex auctoritate Romanorum* (Chalcis); Livy, 36.12.8 (Thyrreum).

171. Cf. Livy, 36.12.7: *detecta Medione fraus cautiores, non timidiores Thyrrenses fecit.*

172. Livy, 35.46.5–7: *Aetoli magnopere suadere ut salva Romanorum amicitia regem quoque adsumerent socium et amicum . . . nihil autem utilius Graeciae civitatibus esse quam utramque complecti amicitiam;* 35.48.8–9: *nihil postulare ab Achaeis, in quo fides eorum adversus Romanos, priores socios atque amicos, laedatur . . . pacem utrique parti, quod medios deceat amicos, optent.*

173. Livy, 35.46.12: *amicitiam regis non aspernari nec ipsorum Aetolorum.*

174. Livy, 35.37.4, 35.50.4.

and kings naturally moved to her side out of self-interest. The consequent relationship was, of course, described as "acceptance into φιλία." So Prusias of Bithynia, reassured by a letter of the Scipios that Rome was not out to topple kings, embraced Roman friendship in 190.[175] The defeat of Antiochus brought Magnesia on the Maeander into *amicitia* with Rome.[176] Manlius Vulso's campaign in 189 induced several towns, formerly hostile, to save themselves by becoming *amici*.[177] The Galatians humbled themselves enough to inquire on what conditions they might acquire φιλία.[178] Antiochus' erstwhile ally Ariarathes of Cappadocia yielded and was received by Manlius into friendship—upon payment of three hundred talents.[179] All these arrangements, if such they may be termed, fall into the conventional categories of φιλία created by cooperation in war or by cessation of hostilities. Roman practice is not here dominant; rather, the common traditions of the Hellenistic world.[180]

Φιλία/*Amicitia* After Apamea

The treaty of Apamea announced friendship for all time between Rome and Antiochus.[181] The document has been described as the "highpoint of Roman diplomacy," the climax of her gradual fashioning of *amicitia* relations into a protectorate.[182] In view of our discussion, that kind of language may be safely set aside. Peace treaties providing for permanent friendship were standard in Greece.[183] Rome contented herself with adopting those formulas. Nor was this the first

175. Livy, 37.25.8, 37.25.14; cf. Polyb. 21.11.12; Appian, *Syr.* 23.

176. *Syll.*³ 679 = *IvPriene*, 531 = Sherk, *RDGE*, no. 7, line 54: ὅτε εἰς τὴν φιλίαν τοῦ δήμου τῶν Ῥωμαίων παρεγένετο. Probably 190; cf. Tac. *Ann.* 3.62.

177. Polyb. 21.34.13; Livy, 35.14.4–14 (Cibyra); Polyb. 21.35.4; Livy, 38.15.6 (Termessus and Aspendus).

178. Polyb. 21.40.3; Livy, 38.37.5.

179. Polyb. 21.40.4–5, 21.44; Livy, 38.37.5, 38.39.6; cf. Appian, *Mac.* 11.4; Strabo, 12.2.11 (C 540).

180. Eumenes' speech to the senate in 189, expressing claims on territory, underlines fidelity to his φιλία with Rome. But the point of his address is not that the institution as such entitled him to anything; it was only his active services in the war which justified rewards: Polyb. 21.20–21; Livy, 37.53. Cf. especially Polyb. 21.21.11: πολλῷ κάλλιον τὸ τοῖς ἀληθινοῖς φίλοις τὰς ἁρμοζούσας χάριτας ἀποδιδόναι. Note too that the Rhodian speech in reply makes no mention of their φιλία—except to say that it is consistent with offering frank advice: Polyb. 21.23.11–12.

181. Polyb. 21.43.1; Livy, 38.38.2; Diod. 31.8.1; Appian, *Syr.* 38.

182. Dahlheim, *Struktur und Entwicklung*, 267: "Höhepunkt der römischen Vertragspolitik." An echo of Täubler, *Imperium Romanum*, 444–445. Similarly, T. Liebmann-Frankfort, *La frontière orientale dans la politique extérieure de la République romaine* (Brussels, 1969), 64.

183. See above pp. 32–33.

time. The treaty with Philip after the Second Macedonian War almost certainly contained the same or similar heading.[184] An overlooked item needs stress. When Antiochus realized the game was up, he sent to inquire about terms. Polybius' description is apt: the king asked on what conditions he could make a φιλία.[185] The form of the treaty brought no startling innovation or diplomatic coup. Nor did it establish Rome as formal protectress of her *amici* everywhere. Nothing of the kind appears in our text. Antiochus is forbidden to make war on inhabitants of the islands and of Europe.[186] The clause encompasses at once both more and less than the sum of Roman *amici*. Rome did not claim *amicitia* with all the islands of the Aegean, let alone with the whole of Europe. The provision, of course, simply speaks to the fears of those against whom Antiochus' expeditions had been directed in the late 190s. Asia Minor, on the other hand, where Rome *did* have *amici*, goes unmentioned in this prohibition. The reason is obvious enough. Important chunks of that territory were to be turned over to Eumenes and Rhodes. They, and not Rome, would provide protection.

From one other clause large inferences have been drawn. If Antiochus should be attacked by any of those states on whom he is forbidden to make war, he may defend himself, but must submit the disputes to arbitration.[187] This feature is often taken as the capstone of the document: Rome has set herself up as supreme arbiter of Hellenistic quarrels.[188] An altogether unwarranted conclusion. The clause makes no mention of Rome as adjudicator. Its purpose is to prevent military solutions that might stimulate Antiochus to new adventures or reacquisition of territory.[189] Hence the treaty-makers required

184. Not explicitly reported. But Philip became an *amicus* as a result of it. And it is well to remember that we have no text of the treaty, only Polybius' summary of the *senatus consultum* which was to guide Roman commissioners, Polyb. 18.44.2: ἡ δὲ τὰ συνέχοντα τοῦ δόγματος ταῦτα.

185. Polyb. 21.41.3: ἦλθε δὲ καὶ παρ᾽ Ἀντιόχου Μουσαῖος καὶ παρὰ τῶν Γαλατῶν πρεσβευταί, βουλόμενοι μαθεῖν ἐπὶ τίσιν αὐτοὺς δεῖ ποιεῖσθαι τὴν φιλίαν; cf. Livy, 38.37.5; also Polyb. 3.11.9.

186. Polyb. 21.43.4; Livy, 38.38.3.

187. Polyb. 21.43.24–26: περὶ δὲ τῶν ἀδικημάτων τῶν πρὸς ἀλλήλους γινομένων εἰς κρίσιν προκαλείσθωσαν; garbled by Livy, 38.38.16–17: *controversias inter se iure ac iudicio disceptanto, aut, si utrique placebit, bello.*

188. E.g., Täubler, *Imperium Romanum*, 443–445; Dahlheim, *Struktur und Entwicklung*, 266–267; *Gewalt und Herrschaft*, 202–203; Polacek, *RIDA* 18 (1971): 608–609; Cimma, *Reges socii et amici*, 132–133.

189. That is clearly the meaning of the restrictions placed on Antiochus here; he cannot bring under his rule or accept into φιλία any state which made war on him: Polyb. 21.43.25: τῶν δὲ ἐθνῶν καὶ πόλεων τούτων μὴ ἐχέτω τὴν κυρίαν αὐτὸς μηδ᾽ εἰς φιλίαν προσαγέσθω; Livy, 38.38.16. The reference, of course, is to potential reconquests. It was not meant to prohibit φιλία with independent states. A year later Antiochus' successor Seleucus was free to renew his φιλία with the Achaean League: Polyb. 22.7.4, 22.9.13.

arbitration, presumably before a neutral party. Such provisions occur frequently in Greek interstate compacts.[190] Again the practice is firmly imbedded in Greece; it is neither a Roman invention nor a stepping-stone for empire.

The victory over Antiochus removed all doubt of Rome's military superiority. None (it must have seemed) would venture to challenge her legions again. It causes no surprise to find various states eager to be acknowledged as *amici* or to refer to themselves as such. Examples abound in the generation or so after Apamea. One ought not hastily conclude that *amicitia* had become a firmer engagement with mutual obligations, nor that those who expressed friendship had become subservient dependents. The institution was as flexible as ever. The occasions that called forth renewal (by now almost all are renewals) continued to be varied and without fixed patterns.

Monarchs might renew paternal φιλία with Rome upon accession to the throne. Perseus of Macedonia did so in 179; and Ariarathes V of Cappadocia in 163.[191] But there was no necessity about it, as some have thought.[192] Those two supply the only clear examples. Other kings, though friends of Rome, could forego such missions at the inception of their rule. They signified little more than courtesies; certainly not signs of obeisance.[193]

In most instances the missions came on other business: to seek favors or gain advantages. A wide variety of issues prompted them. Renewal of *amicitia* was often just an accompanying gesture. So, in 173, envoys of Antiochus IV came to Rome to ask indulgence for tardiness in paying indemnities owed under the treaty of Apamea. In compensation they had brought the whole of the sum due and more besides. Request to renew *amicitia* was clearly a formality; it had been

190. See, e.g., *Syll.*[3] 464, lines 10–13 (Athens and Boeotia ca. 250); *IC*, III, 3, 4, lines 58–71 (Hierapytna and Priassus, early second century); *Syll.*[3] 633, lines 79–88 (Miletus and Heraclea, early second century). The convention goes back at least as far as the fifth century: Thuc. 4.118.8, 5.18.4, 5.79.1, 5.79.4.

191. On Perseus: Polyb. 25.3.1; Livy, 40.58.8, 42.25.1, 42.25.12; Diod. 29.30; Zon. 9.22; Appian, *Mac.* 11.5; on Ariarathes: Polyb. 31.3.3, 31.8.8; Livy, *Per.* 46; Diod. 31.19.8; Zon. 9.24. For E. Paltiel, *Antichthon* 13 (1979): 38–40, Perseus renewed *amicitia* but later concluded a formal written treaty. That is to misread the texts. Livy's references to a *foedus* denote the peace treaty originally sworn with Philip: Gruen, *CSCA* 6 (1973): 135.

192. Rightly shown by Heuss, *Völkerrechtliche Grundlagen*, 46–53. The assertion of Cimma, *Reges socii et amici*, 92, that this was established and regular practice is entirely without basis.

193. In Perseus' case, it was an obvious matter of prudence: to dispel any doubts of Rome's friendship after the death of his brother Demetrius, a favorite at Rome. For Ariarathes, the renewal was comforting but provided no guarantees. Three years later he was still anxiously seeking signs of Roman friendship and sent more envoys: Polyb. 31.32.3, 32.1.1–3; Diod. 31.28.

established "for all time" at Apamea anyway.[194] An embassy from Egypt came in 170, partly to mediate in the Third Macedonian War, mostly to rebut any arguments made by the representatives of Syria; renewal of φιλία was a polite introduction.[195] It played the same role in a Rhodian visit to Rome in 169; the visit's chief purpose was to obtain grain from Sicily.[196] In 167 Prusias appeared before the senate in person to renew his friendship, to congratulate Rome for her victory over Perseus, but primarily to seek territorial acquisitions in Asia Minor.[197] Nervousness for his newly gained crown, secured through surreptitious escape from Rome, induced Demetrius of Syria to send gifts and seek favor in 161 or 160.[198] And in 152 Attalus II sent a young prince of the Pergamene house to reaffirm the family's φιλία. The motive is unstated. But the timing unmistakably suggests gratitude for Roman help in settling the recent war with Bithynia.[199] Clearly, any number of reasons might call forth such embassies; reference to *amicitia* was usually just an attendant ceremony.

In wartime, of course, it could have more pointed meaning: an affirmation of adherence to the Roman cause. Several examples occur in the Third Macedonian War. On the eve of the conflict deputations from several Thracian peoples arrived in Rome to offer support. Their position on the Macedonian flank, of course, stimulated the move. The senate willingly obliged by accepting them into *amicitia*.[200] Civil upheaval at Thebes in 172/1 brought that city onto Rome's side. The senate's representatives suggested a legation to "renew *amicitia*."[201] Lampsacus abandoned the cause of Perseus in 170, professed firm loyalty to Rome, and asked to be received into friendship.[202] Envoys

---

194. Livy, 42.6.8–10; cf. 42.26.7–8, 45.13.2; Polyb. 33.18.7; Appian, *Mac.* 11.4

195. Polyb. 28.1.7–8; Diod. 30.2; cf. Justin, 34.2.8.

196. Polyb. 28.2.2, 28.2.5, 28.16.7.

197. Livy, 45.44.4–9; cf. Polyb. 30.18, 33.12.5.

198. A request for *amicitia* is not overtly mentioned but implicit in the negotiations: Polyb. 31.33.4–5, 32.2.1; Diod. 31.29–30; Appian, *Syr.* 47; Zon. 9.25. And see, especially, Polyb. 32.3.13: τεύξεται τῶν φιλανθρώπων, ἐὰν τὸ ἱκανὸν ποιῇ τῇ συγκλήτῳ.

199. Polyb. 33.18.2; cf. *IvPergamum*, 224, lines 17–21. On the peace settlement with Prusias, see Polyb. 33.13.5–10; Appian, *Mithr.* 3.

200. Livy, 42.19.6–7.

201. Livy, 42.44.5; cf. Polyb. 27.2.6. Thisbae, on the other hand, opted for Perseus. But a party therein preferred Rome and was later rewarded for remaining ἐν τῆι φιλίαι τῆι ἡμετέραι; *Syll.*[3] 646 = Sherk, *RDGE*, no. 2, lines 7–8; cf. 22, 36–37.

202. Livy, 43.6.7–10; cf. Bernhardt, *Imperium und Eleutheria*, 83–85, n. 182. The text asserts that Lampsacus was then enrolled *in sociorum formulam*. This need not mean, as is customarily assumed, that there was a formal list of *amici*—whether identical with or separate from a list of *socii*; as, e.g., Sands, *Client Princes*, 40–42; Badian, *Foreign Clientelae*, 12; Marshall, *AJP* 89 (1968): 54, n. 35; Kienast, *ZSS* 85 (1968): 343–348. There is no other evidence for official enrollment of states on a list—only for individuals, as a reward for services; Livy, 44.16.7; Sherk, *RDGE*, no. 22, line 12 (in the Latin

from Alabanda came bearing gifts at the same time and, apparently, for the same purpose.[203] A year later Pamphylia dispatched ambassadors to the senate, offering a crown and requesting renewal of *amicitia*. Given the context, this too was doubtless an expression of loyalty in the course of the war.[204]

On other occasions we hear of φιλία only incidentally, as a passing reference in decrees or actions concerned with different matters. A treaty between Pharnaces of Pontus and Chersonnesus, perhaps from the early second century, includes a clause stating that both partners are to adhere to their φιλία with Rome.[205] The city of Oropus issued a decree, ca. 151, honoring an Achaean statesman for aid in her dispute with Athens: the Oropians take pride in being in the φιλία and πίστις of Rome.[206] After 146 examples multiply. It is unnecessary to catalogue the numerous references to φίλοι or φίλοι καὶ σύμμαχοι or renewals of φιλία by embassies who had come on varied items of business.[207] In that period, of course, Rome's authority in the Mediterranean was unquestioned and most of her *amici* were, in fact, dependents. But that does not mean that the term itself signified relations between superiors and inferiors—nor, indeed, that it had ever

---

text), line 25 (in the Greek text); *Syll.*[3] 747 = Sherk, *RDGE*, no. 23, lines 17–18; cf. *OGIS*, 438, lines 3–4; *OGIS*, 439, lines 1–2; *IGRR*, IV, 291, lines 1–2; Jos. *Ant.* 14.194.

203. The mission is given in Livy, 43.6.5–6. Nothing is said there explicitly about renewing *amicitia*. But an inscription which may date to 170 does record renewal of οἰκείοτης καὶ φιλία at a time of serious difficulties: *BCH* 10 (1886): 299–306 = *REG* 11 (1898): 258–266, lines 12–15, 18–21. For discussion of this document, see below, Appendix I.

204. Livy, 44.14.3–4. The *amicitia* had presumably been initiated in 189; cf. Livy, 38.15.6, 38.39.17.

205. *IPE*, I[2], 402, lines 3–5, 25–28. Usually dated to 180/79; cf. E. H. Minns, *Scythians and Greeks* (Cambridge, 1913), 518, 646; Rostovtzeff, *CAH* IX:218; Walbank, *Commentary* III:20. The date is justifiably, if not altogether decisively, challenged by S. M. Burstein, *AJAH* 5 (1980): 1–12, who proposes 155. The term plainly has no official connotation here. According to Appian, *Mithr.* 10, Mithridates V, whose reign began in the 150s, was the first Pontic monarch to enter into φιλία with Rome.

206. *Syll.*[3] 675, lines 11–12, 21–22; cf. *Syll.*[3] 747 = Sherk, *RDGE*, no. 23, lines 50–51.

207. A partial list above p. 47, n. 178. Note too the decree of 129 from a Pergamene city, affirming the maintenance of εὔνοια καὶ φιλία "from the start": *Syll.*[3] 694, lines 12–13. A Galatian king has become φίλος καὶ σύμμαχος of Rome before the end of the second century: Diod. 34/35.36. In the late Republic Rome could refer to her *amici* as a conglomerate: e.g., *FIRA*, I, no. 8, lines 75, 79; Sherk, *RDGE*, no. 22, lines 19–20; *OGIS*, 437 = Sherk, *RDGE*, no. 47, lines 4–5, 28–29; *OGIS*, 438, lines 2–4; *OGIS*, 439, lines 1–3; *IGRR*, IV, 291, lines 1–2. And see the recently discovered document from Cnidus of ca. 100: *JRS* 64 (1974): 201, lines 8–9; 202, lines 17–19, 33–34; 204, lines 23–24. Even in the 80s when Sulla rewarded Asian cities that had opposed Mithridates VI, he is said to have inscribed them as φίλοι: Appian, *Mithr.* 61; cf. *OGIS*, 441 = Sherk, *RDGE*, no. 18, lines 36–38; *IGRR*, I, 63.

been employed as a device to reduce communities to subservience.[208]

It remains to ask whether after Apamea Rome reckoned *amicitia* as sufficient ground whereby to demand support in a military venture. The answer must again be negative. As we have seen, even states with formal treaties of alliance were not thereby obliged to render military aid. Rome forebore from requiring support from Achaea *ex foedere* in the war against Perseus; nor did she constrain Rhodes to fight on her side in wars subsequent to their *foedus* of 164.[209] *Amici* can hardly have been under a more rigid coercion in this sphere than *socii*. In the months that preceded the Third Macedonian War, Rome engaged in furious diplomatic activity, in order to test the opinions of Greeks everywhere. There is little point in investigating the numerous embassies recorded in our evidence, some of them duplicates or fabrications.[210] Nowhere is there any indication that Rome commandeered forces simply by virtue of *amicitiae*. A delegation, so we are told, went to Egypt early in the proceedings to renew *amicitia*, and, no doubt, to sound out the regime's inclinations.[211] Offers of help came.[212] But Egypt was in fact too preoccupied with the contest over Coele Syria, played no part in the war, and even sought to mediate.[213] That course caused no breach in the *amicitia*.[214] Offers came from Antiochus IV as well, but his eyes too were trained on Coele Syria, and the resulting conflict with Ptolemy kept him effectively out of the war.[215] Missions went to Crete and Rhodes, instructed to renew friendship and discern attitudes. The response was positive but the support lukewarm and wavering.[216] Roman envoys visited cities and leagues all over mainland Greece in late 172. They cajoled, encouraged, and exhorted. No doubt an exercise of prudence: there was concern about the widespread appeal of Perseus. But not once, in our evidence, did the envoys maintain that any state owed Rome support because of *amicitia*.[217] Even in Aetolia, a state bound to Rome by a rigorous treaty,

208. When Parthia sought Roman *amicitia* in 92, it was certainly not as a prospective client: Livy, *Per.* 70; Plut. *Sulla*, 5.4.

209. See above pp. 35–37, 41–42.

210. On the events generally, see Meloni, *Perseo*, 166–202.

211. Livy, 42.6.4; cf. 42.17.1, 42.26.7; Appian, *Mac.* 11.4.

212. Livy, 42.29.7.

213. Polyb. 28.1.7–8; Diod. 30.2. In practical terms, the Egyptians did no more than send some grain to the Roman army in Chalcis; *OGIS*, 760; cf. O. Mørkholm, *Antiochus IV of Syria* (Gyldendal, 1966), 91.

214. Cf. Livy, 44.19.10, 45.44.13.

215. Livy, 42.6.6–9, 42.26.7, 42.29.5–6; cf. Appian, *Mac.* 11.4.

216. Crete: Livy, 42.19.8, 42.35.6–7, 43.7.1–4; Rhodes: Polyb. 27.3; Livy, 42.45.1–7; a false version in Livy, 42.26.8–9.

217. Livy, 42.37.3–42.38.7. In Thebes, as we have seen, renewal of *amicitia* was requested by Rome's representatives after the city had chosen her side; Livy, 42.44.5.

the ambassadors awaited the results of an election before feeling confident of assistance.[218] From other quarters help was volunteered without the prodding of *amicitia*-compacts. The Thracians proffered aid, though they had not previously been *amici*.[219] Ariarathes brought promises to Rome, but for his own reasons: he had a marriage alliance with Perseus' chief foe, Eumenes of Pergamum.[220] Prusias, despite his *amicitia* with Rome, preferred neutrality—or token support.[221] Yet he was honored by the senate after the war.[222] Most interesting is Livy's language concerning king Genthius of Illyria. The instructions of the Roman envoy were to persuade Genthius to cooperate—if the king paid regard to his *amicitia* with Rome.[223] As is plain, the relationship was far from a mechanism with which to exercise control.

Nor do the preliminaries of the Third Macedonian War suggest that Rome, even then, was propping up her *amici* as pretext for mobilization. To be sure, there is some propaganda about Perseus' attacks on Roman "allies." It amounts to little. Perseus was charged with expelling from his kingdom a Thracian princeling named Abrupolis, allegedly a *socius et amicus* of Rome.[224] Whatever the nature of this association, Rome's championing of Abrupolis was an afterthought, and a long delayed one at that. The prince was expelled in 179; Rome issued no complaints for several years, content indeed to renew *amicitia* with Perseus in the meantime.[225] Apart from that, there is only the charge that Perseus gave asylum to the assassins of Arthetaurus, an Illyrian chieftain described as a φίλος καὶ σύμμαχος of Rome.[226] The date of this deed is uncertain; it too may have come several years before offi-

---

Acarnania was asked to support the cause in order to make amends for past hostilities, not to live up to an *amicitia*: Livy, 42.38.3–4.

218. Livy, 42.38.2.

219. Livy, 42.19.6.

220. Livy, 42.29.4; cf. 42.19.3–6; Appian, *Mac.* 11.4.

221. Livy, 42.29.3; Appian, *Mithr.* 2; cf. Livy, 44.10.12, 44.14.5–7, 44.24.3.

222. Polyb. 30.18; Livy, 45.44; Diod. 31.15.

223. Livy, 42.37.2: *quem si aliquem respectum amicitiae cum populo Romano habere cerneret, retentare aut etiam ad belli societatem perlicere iussus*; cf. Livy, 42.45.8; Val. Max. 3.3.2. Even earlier Rome had treated Genthius with the utmost delicacy: Livy, 42.26.2–6. The king kept his own counsel: Livy, 42.29.11; cf. 42.48.8—and eventually sided with Perseus: Livy, 44.23.2–9, 44.29.6.

224. Livy, 42.13.5, 42.40.5, 42.41.10; Diod. 29.33; Appian, *Mac.* 11.2, 11.6; Paus. 7.10.6. Abrupolis may have entered into *amicitia* in 197/6, covered by the peace treaty with Philip—according to restorations in the famous Delphic inscription of 171 or 170: *FDelphes*, III, 4, 75 = *Syll.*³ 643 = Sherk, *RDGE*, no. 40, lines 15–17: ['Αβρούπ]ολιν δέ, ὃν ἡμεῖς περιελάβομεν [ταῖς πρὸς Φίλιππον συνθήκαις ἐξέβ]αλεν ἐκ τῆς βασιλείας.

225. Appian, *Mac.* 11.6; cf. Polyb. 22.18.2–3; Livy, 42.41.10–11; Diod. 29.33. Pausanias' version, that the attack on Abrupolis was the real cause of the Third Macedonian War is, of course, absurd: Paus. 7.10.6–7.

226. Livy, 42.13.6, 42.40.5, 42.41.5–8; Appian, *Mac.* 11.2, 11.6.

cial protest was registered. In any case, it was not for such reasons or with such excuses that Rome went to war. The list of indictments against Perseus was long. Their chief emphasis lay on the growth of Perseus' power and resources, the extent of his preparations, the increase of his influence in the Greek world, his burning hostility to Rome. Alleged interference with Rome's friends was a secondary matter.[227] It is well to remember that these accusations were first levelled by Eumenes in order to draw Rome into war, rather than conceived by the senate to use *amicitia* as a cover for intervention.

Scholarly emphasis on the Roman standpoint has obscured a noteworthy fact. Not only was φιλία a Greek institution in which the Romans participated rather than one which they created. It should also be pointed out that the Greeks continued to frame compacts of φιλία with one another, along traditional lines, throughout the second century, and quite independent of any Roman influence or involvement.

A few examples will suffice. The treaty of peace that ended hostilities between Miletus and Magnesia in 196 instituted εἰρήνη καὶ φιλία for all time, in the footsteps of a long tradition of such pacts.[228] A few years later, Miletus and Heraclea, after earlier unpleasantries, concluded an *isopoliteia* agreement and a defensive alliance. The Milesian decree that records it designates the people of Heraclea as φίλοι, in customary fashion.[229] Teos and Magnesia reaffirmed their prior φιλία in decrees dating to the first half of the second century.[230]

Nor were these practices confined to relatively minor states out of the mainstream of the great powers. In 187 Seleucus IV, the new monarch of Syria, sent envoys to the Achaean League to renew his φιλία. Clearly such ceremonial expressions of friendship at the beginning of a reign were not directed to Rome alone.[231] In the 170s Perseus

---

227. Livy, 42.11–13, 42.40; Appian, *Mac.* 11.1–2; cf. Polyb. 22.18.

228. *Syll.*[3] 588, lines 4–5, 28–29, 39–40.

229. *Syll.*[3] 633, lines 11–12. The inscription has usually been dated to 180/79 or 173/2. More recent investigations and (as yet unpublished) finds suggest an earlier date; see A. Peschlow-Bindokat, *ArchAnz* (1977): 95; bibliography in Robert, *BCH* 102 (1978): 509–510.

230. *IvMagnesia*, 97, lines 12–13, 22–23, 64, 72–73. Other examples from the second century: *IvMagnesia*, 20, lines 7, 11 (Magnesia and the Cretan *koinon*); *IC*, I, 5, 53, line 2 (Cretan Arcadia and Teos); *IC*, I, 6, 2, line 19 (Biannos and Teos); *IC*, I, 19, 2, lines 1–2 (Malla and Teos); *IC*, II, 1, 2B, lines 4–15 (Allaria and Paros); *IC*, III, 3, 3C, lines 2–3 (Hierapytna and Magnesia); *IC*, III, 3, 4, lines 9–10 (Hierapytna and Priansos); Michel, *Recueil*, no. 62, line 2 (Teos and Crannians).

231. Polyb. 22.7.4, 22.9.13; cf. Diod. 29.17. In these same years Ptolemy and Eumenes also sought renewals of their associations with Achaea. But in both cases these were genuine alliances, not mere *amicitiae*. Polybius consistently uses the term συμμαχία in connection with their agreements, while employing φιλία for that of Seleucus. For Eumenes, Polyb. 21.3b, 22.7.3, 22.7.8–9; cf. Livy, 32.23.1, 37.20; for Ptolemy, Polyb. 22.3.5–6, 22.7.1–2, 22.9.1–12.

entered into a relationship of *amicitia* with the island of Rhodes; evidently it was an informal cordiality, embracing cooperation but not military aid. It neither violated nor compromised Rhodes' *amicitia* with Rome.[232] A more official pact was concluded by Perseus with Boeotia ca. 173: an inscribed treaty displayed in various parts of Greece. But this too, apparently, was an *amicitia*, arranged by formal agreement in the Greek tradition.[233] So, signed covenants, as well as looser relations of amity, continued to be a feature of Hellenistic diplomacy in the second century. And the term φιλία still covered a variety of diplomatic dealings. A marriage alliance between royal families would create φιλία, like the prospective one between the houses of Cappadocia and Syria in the 160s,[234] or that between Syria and Egypt in 150.[235] Restoration of Spartan exiles under the auspices of certain Achaean politicians was celebrated by the exiles as reestablishment of their old φιλία.[236] Rival claimants for the Syrian throne in 152 sought the support of the Jews, each offering concessions in the hopes of φιλία.[237] Employment of the concept to signify interstate relations among Greeks persisted well beyond 146. It had not simply been absorbed into a Roman system.[238]

V

The history of *amicitia* as a feature of foreign diplomacy has too long been written from a Roman standpoint. The ultimate fall of Greece under the western power must not be allowed to cloud our vision of the beginnings and development of relations between them. It is tempting but delusive to regard *amicitia* as a Roman device carefully nurtured and molded to provide grounds for intervention and a

232. Livy, 44.14.9: *cum pax inter Macedones Romanosque esset, sibi amicitiam cum rege Perseo coeptam;* cf. Polyb. 25.4.9–10, 27.4.3–10; Appian, *Mac.* 11.2; Livy, 42.46.1–6.

233. Called a συμμαχία by Polyb. 27.1.8; cf. Appian, *Mac.* 11.7. But in this case that is probably an imprecise designation. Livy expressly refers to it as *amicitiae foedus*: 42.12.5–6. And Perseus' speech underlines the fact: Livy, 42.42.4: *cum Boeotis amicitiam fecimus.* Elsewhere it is termed loosely a *societas*: Livy, 42.38.5, 42.40.6, 42.43.5, 42.46.7.

234. Diod. 31.28.

235. 1 Macc. 10:54.

236. *Syll.*[3] 634, line 4: εἰς τὰν ἐξ ἀρχᾶς ἐ[οῦσαν] φιλ[ίαν ἀποκ]αταστάσαντα; cf. Polyb. 24.10.15.

237. 1 Macc. 10:6, 10:16–20, 10:23, 10:26.

238. Cf., e.g., an arbitral decision on disputes between Hierapytna and Itane in Crete ca. 112 which endeavored to restore φιλία: *Syll.*[3] 685 = *IC*, III, 4, 9, lines 16–17, 33–35, 44, 120; renewal of φιλία between Teos and Tyre ca. 126: *BCH* 49 (1925): 306 = *SEG*, IV, 601, lines 3–4, 8–11; renewal of φιλία between Hermione and Asine, perhaps in the later second century: *Syll.*[3] 1051, lines 1–9; treaties and *isopoliteia* agreements tying Olus to Lato and Lyttus ca. 115–110: *IC*, I, 16, 5, lines 3–4; *IC*, I, 18, 9a, line 8.

means for control. It is too easy to ascribe to cunning foresight and cynical maneuvers the results that we discern at the end but which need not have been planned from the beginning.

In fact, φιλία was a solid Greek institution, established and ubiquitous long before the coming of Rome. It could be grounded on an inscribed compact; it could attend arbitral agreements, isopoliteia, asylia, peace treaties, royal marriages, or military alliances; it could apply to an equal partnership or a relation between greater and lesser powers; it could signify firm cooperation or slack bonds of amity.

The development of Roman authority in Italy was marked by an accumulation of foedera, with explicit terms and sworn obligations. Carthaginians and Greeks brought φιλία to Rome's attention as an element of international accords. Until the late third century it appears but sporadically and insignificantly in her diplomatic relations, and always on the initiative of other powers. When the senate began to embrace it on a regular basis, the process signified a desire to minimize rather than facilitate Rome's overseas involvement. Amicitia did not serve to justify her wars or to bend her religious requirements in the interests of foreign adventures. Roman propaganda moved in other directions—proclamations of Greek freedom and autonomy, resistance to aggressors—rather than the discharge of moral obligations toward amici. Rome did not summon up assistance from Greeks by citing duties incumbent upon them by that relationship. Aid for Roman wars in the East was volunteered or declined, solicited but not commandeered. Even in the years when Rome's military superiority eliminated any serious challenges, φιλία continued to be a viable Hellenic institution, defining relations between and among Greeks, and independent of Roman direction.[239] It was never an implement fashioned or reforged by senatorial diplomats to convert Greece into a compliant appendage of Rome's dominions.

239. The Greek practice was, it seems, openly acknowledged by Rome. Cf. the senate's response to a Lycian complaint about Rhodian oppression in 177. The message stated that Lycia had been awarded to Rhodes by the peace of Apamea οὐκ ἐν δωρεᾷ, τὸ δὲ πλεῖον ὡς φίλοι καὶ σύμμαχοι: Polyb. 25.4.5; cf. Heuss, Stadt und Herrscher, 185–186. Livy's version puts a starkly pro-Roman tone on this, 41.6.12: Lycios ita sub Rhodiorum simul imperio et tutela esse ut in dicione populi Romani civitates sociae sint. But it is quite arbitrary and implausible to take that as a genuine report of the senate's decision derived from the acta, as does Schmitt, Rom und Rhodos, 122–127; Bernhardt, Imperium und Eleutheria, 81–82, n. 181.

· *Chapter 3* ·

Adjudication and Arbitration

The Greeks were litigious people. Personal and private disputes had their counterparts in quarrels at the interstate level. Rival claims on territory clashed; ill-defined boundaries stimulated ambitions and embroiled cities in dissension. The character of their squabbles had changed little by the later Hellenistic period. But one thing had changed. Roman power loomed as mightier and more prestigious than any authority that emanated from the Hellenic East. An increasingly common phenomenon marks the diplomatic history of the second century: embassies and delegations from Greek states beat a steady path to Rome, laying disagreements and controversies before the senate, asking for resolution of disputes and settlement of contesting claims. The phenomenon, to all appearances, bid fair to transform the Roman senate into an international tribunal.[1] It will repay detailed investigation. Did Rome provoke and encourage this behavior as a means of emphasizing Greek insubordination? Did she capitalize upon it to establish herself as supreme arbiter of the Hellenic world?

Interstate Arbitration in Hellas

A basic fact must be insisted upon at the outset. Interstate arbitration was a Greek institution, deeply rooted in Hellenic history. Examples date back to the eighth century, and indeed well beyond if

1. Cf., most recently, P. Veyne, *MEFRA* 87 (1975): 811: "Rome contrôlait la Grèce en ce sens qu'elle y arbitrait tous les conflits et qu'elle pouvait y interdire toute modification à la carte politique telle qu'elle l'avait établie et garantie." Similarly, G. Cle-

one delves into the realm of mythology.[2] It was plainly a most ancient feature of Greek diplomacy. Under normal procedures, disputing states sought out a third party to arbitrate, either a powerful prince, individuals of special repute, or (the most usual practice) another city. Arbitrating *poleis* in turn would appoint either a small committee or a large body of citizens to render judgment. So regular was the resort to arbitration that states often bound themselves in treaties to submit any differences to a third party, whether specified in advance or to be selected by lot from cities mutually agreed upon. Among the issues brought before arbitral tribunals, territorial conflicts comprised the heavy majority: rights of possession, demarcation of frontiers, control of sanctuaries, and the like. Less frequent but no less important were suits arising out of alleged violations of agreements between states, damages sustained, and financial obligations due.[3] Arbitration was a fixture on the Greek international scene.

If the surviving evidence, mostly epigraphical, be any guide, interstate arbitration saw ever increasing use through the Hellenistic period, an obvious sign of success and acceptability. The practice flourished in the third century, well before Rome appeared on the Greek horizon. Member cities of a league might have disputes adjudicated by league representatives.[4] Or, more commonly, a neutral state delivered the decision, called upon by mutual agreement between the contending parties.[5]

---

mente, *Athenaeum* 54 (1976): 343: "il mondo ellenistico ricorse a Roma come all' arbitrato naturale delle sue dispute, fornendo a questa gli strumenti necessari per attuare uno stretto controllo sulle situazioni locali . . . il Senato fu il vero centro della diplomazia internazionale, e usò tutti i suoi strumenti." So also, Cimma, *Reges socii et amici*, 132, 145; Dahlheim, *Gewalt und Herrschaft*, 202–203.

2. An up-to-date collection of instances to 338 B.C., both historical and legendary, in Piccirilli, *Arbitrati greci* with full texts, commentaries, and bibliography.

3. See the lengthy and still valuable discussion by Tod, 53–168. Other useful, though aging, treatments: Sonne, *De arbitris externis* (1888); A. Raeder, *L'Arbitrage international* (1912); V. Martin, *La vie internationale dans la Grèce des cités (VIe–IVe s. av. J.-C.)* (Paris, 1940), 487–576; I. Calabi, *Ricerche sui rapporti fra le poleis* (Florence, 1943), 91–124. A valuable bibliographic summary in A. J. Marshall, *ANRW* II:13 (1980), 627–628, 633–636. The institution overlaps with but is not identical with the ἔκκλητος πόλις— which might be summoned to judge disputes within a city or between citizens of different communities, as well as interstate quarrels; cf. Gauthier, *Symbola*, 308–338. "Foreign judges" were requested regularly in the Hellenistic era to settle cases of private or civil litigation; see the bibliographical compilation of Marshall, *ANRW* II:13 (1980), 636–640.

4. As Boeotia established the boundary between Acraephia and Capae; *IG*, VII, 2792 = Tod, *Arbitration*, no. XVII—some time in the third century. Megarian judges, ca. 242, settled a dispute between Corinth and Epidaurus at behest of the Achaean League: *Syll.*[3] 471.

5. E.g., Thebes rendering judgment between Halae and Boumelita in 263: *FDelphes*, III, 1, 362; Elis between Phanoteus and Stiris, first half of the third century:

Hellenistic princes, of course, could play a decisive role in settling or exacerbating the rifts among Greek states—when they chose. Philip II of Macedonia had set the example long before. He offered more than once to lay his disagreements before a board of arbitration, only to be thwarted by (not unjustified) Athenian mistrust.[6] After Chaeronea he made sure to conduct his own arbitration. A tribunal was instituted, drawn in principle from "all the Greeks"; but, though the tribunal may have rendered formal verdicts, Philip's voice was the determining one. A series of disputes between Sparta and her neighbors illustrates it: the arbitrators delivered the decision, Philip dictated it.[7] The principle of objective arbitration, however, remained intact. In the footsteps of Philip and Alexander, the *diadochoi* adjudicated interstate disputes brought before them.[8] A letter of Lysimachus of 283/2 provides the clearest example: he heard long-winded arguments from representatives of Priene and Samos on a territorial claim, reproving the former for misleading statements, and announced his judgment to the people of Samos.[9] Antigonus too heard rival claims for possession of land, such as the old contest between Sparta and Messenia, and even regulated the Locrian tribute of maidens to Ilium.[10] Later in the century, a series of documents discloses the long and complex dispute over the shrine of Labraunda, involving priests, a royal official, and the city of Mylasa, a dispute adjudicated at various times by Seleucus II, Antigonus Doson, and Philip V.[11] And, near

G. Klaffenbach, *Glotta* 48 (1970): 204–205; Cassandreia in disputes among various cities: *IG*, IX, 2, *addenda*, p. xi = *FDelphes*, III, 4, 351; Mantineia between Argos and Achaea in 240: Plut. *Arat.* 25.4–5.

6. Ps.-Dem. 7.7–8, 7.36, 7.41, 12.11, 12.14; Aesch. 3.83.

7. The tribunal of the Greeks: Polyb. 9.33.11–12; *Syll.*[3] 665, lines 19–20: αἵ τ᾽ ἐν τοῖ[ς] Ἕλλησιν καὶ συμμάχοις γεγενημένοι πρότερον [κ]ρ[ί]σεις; cf. Livy, 38.34.8. Philip as the source of authority: Polyb. 9.28.7; Paus. 2.20.1, 7.11.2; Tac. *Ann.* 4.43.1–3; cf. Strabo, 8.4.6 (C 361). See on this, most recently, Piccirilli, *Arbitrati greci*, 222–229, with bibliography.

8. Cf. the clause in Antigonus Monophthalmus' letter to Teos of ca. 303, which authorizes new law codes for the synoecism of Teos and Lebedus and, in the event of disagreement, reserves arbitration for himself or for a neutral city to be designated by him: *Syll.*[3] 344 = Welles, *RC*, no. 3, lines 49–52.

9. *OGIS*, 13 = Welles, *RC*, no. 7. The case had also been brought to Demetrius Poliorcetes and then raised again on numerous occasions from the time of Antiochus II to that of Philip V; several monarchs named on the inscription which records Rhodes' arbitration of the 190s: *IvPriene*, 37, lines 76–77, 95–96, 125–154—only the first part reproduced in *Syll.*[3] 599.

10. Sparta and Messenia: Tac. *Ann.* 4.43; Locris: Aelian, fr. 47, Herscher, II, p. 205; cf. A. Wilhelm, *JOAI* 14 (1911): 186–188; Momigliano, *CQ* 39 (1945): 49–53. The Antigonus in question may be Monophthalmus, Gonatas, or Doson.

11. The documents assembled and commented on by J. Crampa, *Labraunda* (Lund, 1969), III, 1; especially, nos. 1, 5, 6, 7.

the end of the third century, Ptolemy (Philopator or Epiphanes) appears as arbitrator, chosen to resolve the dissension between Gortyn and Cnossus and to bring their conflict to an end.[12] The kings, so far as our evidence suggests, consented to arbitrate when appealed to, rather than usurping the prerogative on their own initiative. They recognized the principle and adhered to it. The fact emerges clearly in two partially preserved treaties of alliance between Antigonus Doson and Cretan cities, one with Eleutherna, one with Hierapytna: in both instances the documents specify that any failure to meet obligations under the treaties should be considered by an independent arbitrating city.[13] Doson, at least for official purposes, did not reserve final judgment for himself. Outside arbitration by a third party held a central place in the Greek concept of international justice.

The Roman Experience

In Rome, by contrast, that concept was virtually unknown. One may, to be sure, turn up a few allusions to it among the shadowy legends of early Roman history. Warring cities in the vicinity of Rome at the time of Numa Pompilius allegedly sought out Romans to settle their quarrels and engaged Numa as arbitrator. In the contests that embroiled Rome with the Tarquinii, the Romans turned to Lars Porsenna to mediate differences. So, at least, we are told. Quite apart from the dubious validity of these tales, the author who conveys them, Dionysius of Halicarnassus, was himself a Greek, writing in an age when Roman experience had been colored by long exposure to the ways of Hellas. Dionysius retails another story that (whatever truth lies therein) confirms the direction of influence: Servius Tullius organized an arbitrating tribunal drawn from the Roman senate and the Latin League, using as inspiration the model of Greek Amphictyonic assemblies.[14]

The history of the Republic down to the second century shows

12. *IC*, IV, 176, lines 26–29; cf. *IC*, I, 8, 9. The date is uncertain. Most recent discussion, opting for 200 or a little later, by Huss, *Untersuchungen*, 149–152. Cf. also Antiochus III's reconciliation of the Aradians on the mainland with those on the island in 218; Polyb. 5.68.7.

13. Eleutherna: *IC*, II, 12, 20 = Schmitt, *Staatsverträge*, no. 501, lines 17–22; Hierapytna: *IC*, III, 3, 1A = Schmitt, *Staatsverträge*, no. 502, lines 22–25. On the dating—to the reign of Doson rather than Gonatas—see Schmitt, *loc. cit.*

14. Numa Pompilius: Dion. Hal. 2.76.3; Lars Porsenna: Dion Hal. 5.32.2; Plut. *Publ.* 18.1; *Mor.* 250b; Zon. 7.12; Servius Tullius: Dion. Hal. 4.25–26. The value of this evidence is rightly questioned by E. de Ruggiero, *L'arbitrato pubblico presso i Romani* (Rome, 1898), 59; Matthaei, *CQ* 2 (1908): 246–247.

only a very few instances—and they are questionable—relevant to arbitration. In 446, the Latin towns of Aricia and Ardea appealed to Rome for judgment on a territorial dispute that had caused much bloodshed; the Roman people, in tribal assembly, deftly cut the knot and awarded the territory to themselves! A dubious tale, quite unique at so early a period, and, in any case, hardly illustrative of impartial decision by a neutral party.[15] Livy's narrative of the Second Samnite War includes a Roman offer in 327 to have differences submitted to common *socii et amici* for arbitration, an offer rudely dismissed by the Samnites, thus provoking hostilities.[16] The episode transparently serves the purpose of emphasizing Samnite guilt. Six years later, a Samnite spokesman pleaded for a judgment on his nation's cause but gained no satisfaction; his speech provokes the prelude to the calamity of the Caudine Forks in 321.[17] Both occasions sit ill with the rest of the Livian narrative, which omits any reference to scorned arbitration. They serve to justify Rome's entrance into war in the first instance and to explain the disaster she suffered in the second. In all likelihood, they represent later insertions by writers familiar with arbitral practices, whether themselves Greek or writing for Greek readers.[18]

Authentic Roman encounters with interstate arbitration in the fourth and third centuries derived from dealings with the Hellenic states of southern Italy. So, in 320 Tarentum presented herself as willing to arbitrate differences between Rome and the Samnites. And forty years later, Pyrrhus offered to resolve the conflict pitting Rome against the Italian Greeks. These proposals, coming as they did from Hellenes, are doubtless genuine, whatever motives lay behind them. It is noteworthy that on both occasions Rome peremptorily rejected the propositions.[19] When Ptolemy Philadelphus, appealed to by the Carthaginians, endeavored to reconcile the antagonists of the First Punic War, his efforts met with failure, almost certainly the result of Roman recalcitrance.[20] If there be any truth to the story, reported only by Dio-Zonaras, that the Roman legate "C. Claudius" proposed arbitration between Carthage and Messana on the eve of the First Punic

---

15. Livy, 3.71–72; cf. 4.1.4, 4.7.4–6, 4.11.2–7; Dion. Hal. 11.52. Authority of this sort exercised by the Roman populace, rather than the senate, is enough to cast serious doubt on the story; cf. Mommsen, *Staatsrecht* III:325; de Ruggiero, *L'arbitrato*, 109–110, n. 3.

16. Livy, 8.23.8.

17. Livy, 9.1.7.

18. See the cogent analysis of Matthaei, *CQ* 2 (1908): 248–253.

19. Tarentum: Livy, 9.14.1–16; Pyrrhus: Plut. *Pyrrh.* 16.3–4.

20. Appian, *Sic.* 1.

War, the suggestion may have been prompted by south Italian or Sicilian Greeks. Nothing, in any case, came of it, and the tradition is unsupported elsewhere: perhaps another subsequent insertion to help legitimize the undertaking of war.[21] The practice of arbitration simply did not form part of Rome's diplomatic arsenal in the third century.[22] When, for the first time in our records, the senate actually sent an arbiter to rule on a territorial dispute between two Italian cities, in the early second century, the setting was Greek Campania, the contest between Naples and Nola.[23] The Hellenic character of the institution plainly predominates.

Arbitration in Roman-Greek Affairs

This background allows better comprehension of the main issue: the role of arbitration in Roman dealings with Greeks overseas. No sign of it emerges in the Illyrian Wars or in the First Macedonian War. Its absence is unsurprising in view of Rome's slight acquaintance with, or rejection of, the practice hitherto. It comes to the surface only in the second and major engagement with Philip V. And the evidence confirms decisively what has been argued above.

Roman envoys in Greece in the summer of 200 announced the terms on which Rome would stay her hand against Philip: he must

21. Dio, fr. 43.5–6, 43.5.10; Zon. 8.8–9. See the discussion of Matthaei, *CQ* 2 (1908): 256–258.

22. References to mediators sent by Rome to Africa to reconcile Carthage and her rebellious mercenaries ca. 239 (Appian, *Lib.* 5; *Sic.* 2.3; Zon. 8.17) find no support in Polyb. 1.83.11; cf. Matthaei, *CQ* 2 (1908): 254–256. The presence of Roman "arbitrators" in Saguntum ca. 221 was called forth by an internal Saguntine struggle, not an instance of interstate arbitration: Polyb. 3.15.7, 3.30.2. The relation of this affair to Saguntum's quarrel with the Torboletae or Turdetani is obscure; cf. Polyb. 3.15.8. But Saguntum's appeal to Rome in that affair, according to Livy, 21.6.1–2, was an appeal for military aid, not for adjudication. Appian, *Iber.* 10–11, puts it rather differently: Hannibal invited the Torboletae and Saguntines to present their differences to him for judgment; the Saguntines, for their part, preferred to have Rome arbitrate the affair. Even this version, however, tells us nothing of the Roman attitude toward arbitration. When the senate came to debate the matter, Saguntum was already under siege and the issue was one of sending assistance, not of rendering decision: Appian, *Iber.* 11.

23. Cic. *De Off.* 1.33; Val. Max. 7.3.4. The precise date is unknown, but Valerius Maximus identifies the arbiter, Q. Fabius Labeo, as the consul of 183. Although Cicero is unsure about the identity of the man, there is no reason to question the story itself; cf. de Ruggiero, *L'arbitrato*, 276–279. Roman arbitration between cities in Italy becomes more common later in the century. E.g. between Pisa and Luna (or Luca?) in 168: Livy, 45.13.10–11; between Ateste and Vicetia in 135: *CIL*, V, 2490 = *ILLRP*, I, no. 477; between Genua and the Viturii in 117: *CIL*, V, 7749 = *ILLRP*, II, 517.

make war on no Greeks and must submit to an impartial tribunal for judgment on wrongs committed against Attalus.[24] Later in the year, they delivered a slightly expanded set of demands to the king in person at Abydus: he was to refrain from warring on Greeks, keep his hands off Ptolemy's possessions, and accept arbitration on injuries inflicted upon Attalus and Rhodes.[25] There can be little doubt, in light of what we have already seen, that the suggestion of recourse to a "fair tribunal" stemmed from the Greek allies of Rome. Attalus had insisted on it in the first instance, and Roman envoys had visited Rhodes in the meantime, which explains the addition of that island's grievances in the second set of demands.[26] Rome had no intrinsic commitment to the principle.

Nor did she even fully understand it. The fact is plain enough from subsequent events. At the Aous conference of 198 Flamininus demanded the withdrawal of Philip's garrisons from the places he had occupied, the restoration of property to those whose fields and cities he had ravaged, and the establishment of impartial arbitration to assess all other damages.[27] On the last point Philip responded in appropriate Greek fashion: he would indeed accept arbitration from a neutral state to determine the justice of complaints from those who claimed losses in war.[28] Here Flamininus suddenly drew back. He had not expected (or perhaps even desired) compliance. And he evidently misinterpreted Philip's reply. To Flamininus the king seemed to envisage adjudication on the general question of war guilt. The Roman would have none of that: Philip was at fault, as everyone knew, and

24. Polyb. 16.27.2: τῶν μὲν Ἑλλήνων μηδενὶ πολεμεῖν, τῶν δὲ γεγονότων εἰς Ἄτταλον ἀδικημάτων δίκας ὑπέχειν ἐν ἴσῳ κριτηρίῳ.

25. Polyb. 16.34.3: μήτε τῶν Ἑλλήνων μηδενὶ πολεμεῖν μήτε τοῖς Πτολεμαίου πράγμασιν ἐπιβάλλειν τὰς χεῖρας, περὶ δὲ τῶν εἰς Ἄτταλον καὶ Ῥοδίους ἀδικημάτων δίκας ὑποσχεῖν.

26. The visit to Rhodes is recorded by Polyb. 16.34.2. That the appeal to arbitration was an idea of the Greeks was recognized long ago by Bickermann, *RevPhil* 61 (1935): 76–79, though his notion that this was incorporated in the peace of Phoenice is quite unnecessary and unlikely.

27. Livy, 32.10.3: *praesidia ex civitatibus rex deduceret; eis quorum agros urbesque populatus esset, redderet res quae comparent; ceterorum aequo arbitrio aestimatio fieret.* The assertion of Matthaei, *CQ* 2 (1908): 261, that this was a call for *recuperatores* is without foundation. J.-H. Michel, *Le monde grec, hommages à Claire Preaux* (Brussels, 1975), 508–512, interestingly compares the distinction between possessions to be returned and assessment of damages to similar distinctions drawn in a series of Aetolian *asylia* decrees of the later third century: *Syll.*³ 522 = Schmitt, *Staatsverträge*, no. 508I, lines 5–8; *Syll.*³ 554 = *IG*, IX, 1², 4C, lines 15–19; *IG*, IX, 1², 189, lines 6–11; *Syll.*³ 563 = *IG*, IX, 1², 192, lines 12–15; also in an agreement between Gortyn and Lato: *IC*, I, 16, 1 = Schmitt, *Staatsverträge*, no. 569, lines 7–9.

28. Livy, 32.10.5: *si quas quererentur belli clades eae civitates, cum quibus bellatum foret, arbitrio quo vellent populorum, cum quibus pax utrisque fuisset, se usurum.*

there was no need for arbiter or judge.[29] Negotiations ended. As the episode reveals, Rome's understanding of Greek arbitral practices was less than perfect.

The Romans had duly conveyed the demand, as their Greek allies requested. Philip construed it properly. He made reference to it again in the parley at Nicaea in 197: a fair arbiter, he asserted, would demand restitution from Rhodes and Attalus rather than from him.[30] But by then it had become part of a jest. Rome, as Flamininus had already made clear, did not in fact seriously consider the proposition of a neutral party passing on matters of any importance. After a private colloquy with Flamininus, Philip pronounced himself ready to submit all matters to the senate. Rome's Hellenic allies consented with understandable reluctance, suspicion, and even feelings of betrayal. The issue of arbitration had been shelved.[31] After Cynoscephalae there was no longer any question about it. Any items still unresolved would be settled by Rome.[32] Territorial claims and all other details the senate left to its representatives, the *decem legati*.[33] Impartial arbitration, a Greek not a Roman concept, played no role.

The idea had yet to make a discernible impression upon Rome. When senatorial representatives met with Antiochus III at Lysimacheia in 196, they heard the complaints of Lampsacus and Smyrna against the king. Antiochus was justifiably indignant. He would not be put in the position of seeming to plead a case before the Romans. Instead he offered an appropriate alternative: arbitration by a neutral party, namely the Rhodians. For Greeks that would be a conventional avenue to decision. Rome's envoys, however, were unprepared for and nonplussed by the suggestion. The conference came to an abrupt halt.[34] Differences between the Roman and Greek approaches

29. Livy, 32.10.6: *consul nihil ad id quidem arbitrio aut iudice opus esse dicere: cui enim non apparere ab eo, qui prior arma intulisset, iniuriam ortam, nec Philippum ab ullis bello lacessitum priorem vim omnibus fecisse?* Briscoe's comment is off the mark: "it is clear that Rome regards the amount of damages as the only question available for arbitration, while Philip's offer concerns arbitration on the merits of his case;" *Commentary*, 186–187. In fact, Philip consented to arbitration on damages—which the consul wrongly took to mean judgment on the merits of his case.

30. Polyb. 18.6.1: πρὸς δὲ Ῥοδίους καὶ πρὸς Ἄτταλον ἐν μὲν ἴσῳ κριτῇ δικαιότερον ἂν νομισθείη τούτους ἡμῖν ἀποδιδόναι τὰς αἰχμαλώτους ναῦς καὶ τοὺς ἄνδρας ἤπερ ἡμᾶς τούτοις.

31. Polyb. 18.9.4–18.10.2; Livy, 32.36.3–8.

32. Polyb. 18.38.2, 18.39.5; Livy, 33.11.3, 33.13.3–4, 33.13.14.

33. Polyb. 18.42.7, 18.47.6–13; Livy, 33.34.5–11.

34. Polyb. 18.52.3–5: δυσχεράνας ὁ βασιλεὺς ἐπὶ τῷ δοκεῖν λόγον ὑπέχειν ἐπὶ Ῥωμαίων τοῖς πρὸς αὐτὸν ἀμφισβητοῦσι . . . οὐ γὰρ ἐπὶ Ῥωμαίων, ἀλλ᾽ ἐπὶ Ῥοδίων ὑμῖν εὐδοκῶ διακριθῆναι περὶ τῶν ἀντιλεγομένων. This part of the verbal exchange is interestingly omitted by Livy, 33.39–40. Walbank overlooks the matter: *Commentary* II:623.

manifested themselves again four years later. Aetolian hostility to Rome verged on an open break at a meeting of the League assembly in 192. Flamininus was there and proposed a means for settlement: the Aetolians could debate their case or make a plea, but either way the matter should come before the Roman senate. The assembly took a different course. It summoned Antiochus as arbiter between Aetolia and Rome. As the authors of the resolution well knew, this was a direct challenge—and unacceptable to the westerner.[35]

When conflict was brewing or war raged, Rome showed no interest in the Greek principle of arbitration. Matters took on a different aspect after the establishment of peace. The defeat of Antiochus and the Aetolians relieved Roman concern and made possible her withdrawal. As so often, Rome now found the Hellenic convention acceptable and convenient. The peace of Apamea supplies illuminating proof. In one of the concluding clauses of that treaty it is stipulated that future disagreements and complaints between Antiochus and rival cities or peoples should be presented for arbitration.[36] The modern view that Rome saw herself as arbiter of these conflicts is entirely baseless. The clause stands in a long tradition of Hellenic treaties that enjoined arbitration on subsequent disputes. It underlined the westerner's intention to withdraw, not to expand authority. Rome endorsed the Greek concept and even enshrined it in her own settlement.[37] The fact is demonstrable. Rome's proconsul Cn. Manlius Vulso and the *decem legati*, of course, arranged the major postwar dispositions in Asia Minor. That was the prerogative of the victor. On conflicting interests with regard to land titles, money, or other claims, however, the Romans resigned judgment to arbiters agreed upon by the disputants—the Greek procedure.[38]

35. Livy, 35.33.5 (Flamininus): *si quid tamen aequi se habere arbitrarentur, quanto esse satius Romam mittere legatos, seu disceptare seu rogare senatum mallent*; Livy, 35.33.8 (the Aetolians): *quo accerseretur Antiochus ad liberandam Graeciam disceptandumque inter Aetolos et Romanos*; cf. Livy, 35.45.3.

36. Polyb. 21.43.24–26: περὶ δὲ τῶν ἀδικημάτων τῶν πρὸς ἀλλήλους γινομένων εἰς κρίσιν προσκαλείσθωσαν. Livy, 38.38.16–17, translates in confused fashion: *controversias inter se iure ac iudicio disceptanto, aut, si utrisque placebit, bello*.

37. For references to modern literature and further discussion, see above pp. 87–88.

38. Polyb. 21.46.1: τοῖς μὲν περὶ χώρας ἢ χρημάτων ἢ τινος ἑτέρου διαφερομένοις πόλεις ἀπέδωκαν ὁμολογουμένας ἀμφοτέροις, ἐν αἷς διακριθήσονται περὶ τῶν ἀμφισβητουμένων. Omitted by Livy, 38.39.5–17. Manlius did hear and judge a territorial contest between Samos and Priene, age-old disputants: *IvPriene*, 40–41 = Sherk, *RDGE*, no. 10A, lines 4–5; no. 10B, lines 6–7. Similarly, Rome's commander in Greece, M'. Acilius Glabrio, authorized the Delphic priests to fix the boundaries of their sacred land in 191/0: *Syll.*[3] 826E, col. III, lines 37–38; 827C, lines 5–6; 827D, lines 6–7. But the latter instance took place in the immediate aftermath of Thermopylae and Antiochus'

No direct evidence attests to a similar provision in the treaty with Philip in 196. We do not possess a record of its precise terms. But indirect testimony is suggestive. In 184/3 Thessalians, Perrhaebians, Athamanians, Epirotes, and Illyrians brought a battery of complaints against Philip, charging that they could get no satisfaction from the tribunals to judge territorial and property disputes κατὰ τὸ σύμβο-λον. The king, so they alleged, had subverted the courts and corrupted the arbiters.[39] As is obvious, these are Greek tribunals, arranged through interstate agreements, *symbola*, and possibly authorized by the peace treaty of 196. With victory secure, Rome was quite content to have Greeks regulate their customary arbitral proceedings.

The Antiochene war, however, had markedly altered the shape of international politics. After Rome's awesome display of power, Greeks could hardly fail to believe that she would continue to exercise authority, or, at least, that they could make use of that authority. It was only natural that Hellenic states would begin to turn to the senate for arbitration of matters that had previously been adjudicated by Greeks. What must now be asked is how far Rome welcomed the opportunity or manipulated the institution to tighten control over the eastern world.

In fact, the occasions on which the senate responded meaningfully to such requests during the next half-century or so were remarkably few. The *patres* would, at times, take the trouble of dispatching a legate to investigate. L. Scipio, if Valerius Antias is to be believed, went as envoy to the East in 186 to resolve disagreements between Eumenes and Antiochus.[40] The report carries little authority: unattested elsewhere, not endorsed by Livy, and a product of the tangled tales surrounding the trials of the Scipios. Some have connected it with another notice of a dispute between the two kings: the question of which one had title to Pamphylia as consequence of the treaty of Apamea, a question referred by Manlius to the senate in 188.[41] If L. Scipio were indeed sent out to examine the merits of that controversy, however, the senate was a very long time in taking action. And

---

evacuation of Greece; the former was part of the peace settlement administered by Manlius and the *decem legati*. Neither one indicates a Roman interest in arbitrating future disputes. Flamininus may have made comparable arrangements in 196, together with senatorial representatives. But the one piece of evidence, on the contest between Narthacium and Melitea, states that the determination was made according to Thessalian statutes instituted by Flamininus and the *legati*—not that Romans rendered the decision: *Syll.*[3] 674 = Sherk, *RDGE*, no. 9, lines 48–53, 63–65.

39. Polyb. 23.1.2, 23.1.10–13. A hypothetical and unconvincing interpretation by Gauthier, *Symbola*, 340–342.

40. Livy, 39.22.10.

41. Polyb. 21.45.11; Livy, 38.39.17.

any outcome of the mission escapes record.[42] Other embassies stand on firmer evidence. But there are not many of them. Ap. Claudius headed a delegation to Crete in 184, where he settled a property conflict between Cnossus and Gortyn. The Polybian account of this mission is only a fragment, and the issues are unclear, though one may note that the Romans made reference to a joint tribunal, κοινοδίκιον, evidently to leave further decisions in the hands of the Cretans.[43] Debt problems wracked parts of central and northern Greece in the mid-170s, produced turmoil and bloodshed in Thessaly, Perrhaebia, and Aetolia, and spread even to Crete. Appeals came to the senate. Roman commissioners endeavored to effect settlements among conflicting interests in each area, though not without great difficulty and with but temporary success.[44] The warring factions did not seek Roman arbitration alone. Aetolians looked to Perseus as well for a settlement; and in Perrhaebia an arbiter from Gyrton came to resolve conflict.[45] A comparable situation arose in Macedonia in 163: civil strife prompted the dispatch of a Roman embassy to look into the affair. What, if anything, was accomplished goes unreported.[46] So also in Epirus, where rival factions from Phoenice asked for Roman arbitration in 157/6. The best they could get from the senate was a promise that envoys to Illyria (on business unspecified) would make a stop in Epirus.[47] In sum, the evidence shows a rather inactive record. The senate occasionally bestirred itself to commission individuals as arbiters, but they rarely achieved decisive or enduring results.

Definitive decisions by the *patres* in procedures resembling arbitration were rarer still. They awarded to Athens control over Delos, Lemnos, and the land of the Haliartians in 167/6, an allocation in the aftermath of the Third Macedonian War that was more political than judicial.[48] The new arrangement itself provoked quarrels in later years, giving more cause for senatorial hearings. A *senatus consultum* of 164 instructed Athens to reopen the Serapeum on Delos after its priest had complained to Rome.[49] That ruling simply restored an earlier situa-

---

42. de Ruggiero, *L'arbitrato*, 238–240, assumes the connection, does not notice the time-lapse, and accepts the authority of Valerius Antias.

43. Polyb. 22.15. The term κοινοδίκιον appears elsewhere in Cretan documents: *IC*, IV, 197, line 24; *IC*, III, 3, 4, line 59; cf. H. van Effenterre, *La Crète et le monde grec de Platon à Polybe* (Paris, 1948), 142–148; M. Guarducci, *RivFilol* 28 (1950): 148–154; Walbank, *Commentary* III: 202: either a mixed arbitral tribunal or a federal court.

44. Aetolia: Livy, 41.25.1–6, 41.27.4, 42.2.2, 42.4.5, 42.5.10–12; Thessaly and Perrhaebia: Livy, 42.5.7–10, 42.13.9; cf. Appian, *Mac.* 11.1; Diod. 29.33; see Gruen, *AJAH* 1 (1976): 35–36, 39–40; Crete: Livy, 41.25.7.

45. Aetolia and Perseus: Livy, 42.12.7, 42.40.7, 42.42.4; Appian, *Mac.* 11.1, 11.7; Perrhaebia: *IG*, IX, 2, 1230; cf. D. Asheri, *StudClassOrient* 18 (1969): 67–68.

46. Polyb. 31.2.12; cf. 31.17.2.   47. Polyb. 32.14.   48. Polyb. 30.20.

49. *Syll.*[3] 664 = *IdeDélos*, 1510 = Sherk, *RDGE*, no. 5.

tion. Many of the Delians who had evacuated the island upon Athenian occupation had meanwhile settled in Achaea. There followed complex legal problems, as the ex-Delians, now Achaean citizens, made claims against the Athenian government under the σύμβολον in effect between Athens and Achaea. Athens refused to recognize the jurisdiction. As a consequence, rival embassies appeared in Rome from Athens, and from Achaea on behalf of the Delians, ca. 159. The senate passed judgment, but of a minimalist sort, a mere endorsement of Achaean dispensations.[50] Similarly, around 140, the *patres* ruled on behalf of Narthacium against Melitea, a ruling that followed the lines laid out by previous Greek arbiters from Samos, Colophon, and Magnesia.[51] Apart from these perfunctory interventions, there is little that can be characterized as the rendering of verdicts.[52]

Far more common and more exemplary of senatorial attitude was a different sort of behavior. When appealed to for decision the *patres* would customarily find another way out: a prompt delegation of the matter to Greek arbiters. Their disposition to evade responsibility manifested itself in 184, one of the many occasions when senators were subjected to the tiresome recriminations leveled by Spartans and Achaeans against one another. A Roman commission ruled that henceforth "foreign courts," i.e. neutral arbiters, should hear all capital cases and the rest would come under jurisdiction of the Achaean League.[53] Rome's purpose, quite clearly, was to divest herself of further trouble on this score. But the parade of embassies kept coming. The senate, in turn, persisted in referring complainants to Hellenic

50. Polyb. 32.7.

51. *Syll.*³ 674 = Sherk, *RDGE*, no. 9. The earlier ruling by Greek arbiters is partially preserved; see *Arch Eph* (1927–1928): 119–127.

52. Abdera, represented by Tean patrons, pleaded a cause before the senate against representatives of king Cotys of Thrace in this period. Territorial rights were at issue. But the inscription which honors the Tean spokesmen at length says nothing of any decision: *Syll.*³ 656; cf. Robert, *BCH* 59 (1935): 507–513. At Athenian request, the senate reduced a fine imposed upon Athens by Sicyon in an arbitral proceeding in 155, but declined to alter the decision: Paus. 7.11.5; cf. Polyb. 33.2; see the discussion in Gruen, *JHS* 96 (1976): 51–53. An honorary decree of the early second century discloses a mission to Rome for hearing on a dispute between Larisa Cremaste and Pteleum, again without indication of result, if any: *IG*, IX, 2, 520. Q. Metellus Macedonicus levied fines on Thebes for unwarranted invasion of Phocis, Euboea, and Amphissa in 147. But this came in the aftermath of his war with Andriscus and in his capacity as victorious *imperator*, not as arbitral decision referred to Rome: Paus. 7.14.6–7.

53. Paus. 7.9.5: περὶ δὲ τῇ ἑκάστου ψυχῇ ξενικά σφισι διδόασιν εἶναι δικαστήρια, ὅσα δὲ ἄλλα ἐγκλήματα, λαμβάνειν τε αὐτοὺς καὶ ἐν τῷ Ἀχαικῷ ὑπέχειν τὰς κρίσεις. Pausanias' account seems a confused version, with added details, of what appears in Polyb. 23.4. But there is no reason to doubt this particular Roman decision, a perfectly characteristic one. It was reiterated, in similar terms, a generation later: Paus. 7.12.4.

tribunals. Dispute between Ambracia and Athamania was delegated to Corcyra; between Sparta and Megalopolis to the Achaeans; between Oropus and Athens to Sicyon; between Magnesia and Priene to Mylasa; between Sparta and Messenia to Miletus; between Hierapytna and Itanus to Magnesia.[54] Senatorial reluctance to take an active role can hardly be clearer. One last circumstance underscores it most unambiguously. In 135 representatives from Samos and Priene reopened a longstanding territorial controversy before the senate. Priene cited an award in her favor by Rhodian arbiters during the 190s; Samos, however, could point to a redrawing of boundaries by Cn. Manlius Vulso and the *decem legati* after the Antiochene war. The *patres*, after hearing both arguments, found for Priene, pointedly overturning the arrangements of Rome's own commissioners of a half-century before: they confirmed instead the decision of Rhodes.[55] A few years later, the Rhodians themselves considered submitting a boundary dispute with Stratonicea to Rome—then changed their minds and turned instead to Bargylia as a more reliable arbiter.[56] The senate, wherever possible, elected to withdraw in favor of Hellenic judges.[57]

54. Ambracia and Athamania (perhaps 175–160): *SEG*, III, 451 = Sherk, *RDGE*, no. 4 = *ISE*, no. 91; (A date ca. 140 is proposed by Mattingly, *NC* 4 (1969): 102–104); cf. *IG*, IX, 1, 690; Holleaux, *Études* V:433–447. Sparta and Megalopolis (164): Polyb. 31.1.6–7; Paus. 7.11.1–3; *Syll.*[3] 665; cf. Gruen, *JHS* 96 (1976): 50–51. Oropus and Athens (ca. 159): Paus. 7.11.4–5; Plut. *Cato*, 22.1; cf. *Syll.*[3] 675. Magnesia and Priene (ca. 175–160): *IvPriene*, 531 = *Syll.*[3] 679. Sparta and Messenia (ca. 140): *Syll.* 683; Tac. *Ann.* 4.43—in this instance Rome was willing to turn over decision to a neutral party even though there had been a ruling by her own consul L. Mummius after the Achaean war in 146. Hierapytna and Itanus (ca. 140 and again in 112): *Syll.*[3] 685 = *IC*, III, 4, 9, lines 9–11, 18–21; *IC*, III, 4, 10 = Sherk, *RDGE*, no. 14, lines 22–25; a recent discussion by S. Spyridakis, *Ptolemaic Itanos and Hellenistic Crete* (Berkeley and Los Angeles, 1970), 55–65—with confused chronology. The senate was still delegating such decisions in the early first century; see *IvPriene*, 111, 120: disputes between Priene and Miletus referred to Erythrae and to Sardis. C. Nicolet, *Rome et la conquête du monde méditerranéen* II (Paris, 1978), 893, wrongly regards this Roman practice as exceptional. It is missed altogether by Marshall, *ANRW* II:13 (1980), 641–661. Senatorial instructions to the arbitrating states show some parallels with formulas drawn from Roman civil law; cf. Passerini, *Athenaeum* 15 (1937): 26–52; Marshall, *ANRW* II:13 (1980), 648–650. But the convention of choosing a neutral arbiter is certainly Greek.

55. *IvPriene*, 40–41 = Sherk, *RDGE*, no. 10A–B. See, especially, no. 10B, lines 10–12: ἡμῖν οὐκ εὐχ[ερ]ές ‹εἶναι› ἐστιν μεταθεῖναι ἅ ὁ δῆμος ὁ Ῥοδίων ἑκατέρων θελόντων κέκρι[κε κ]αὶ ὁρ[ισμὸν] πεποίηται τοῦ μ[ὴ] τούτωι τῶι κρίματι καὶ τού[τοις τοῖς ὁρίοις] ἐμμείνωσιν· τ[ούτ]ωι τε τῶι κρίματι καὶ τού[τοις τοῖς ὁρίοις ἐμμένει]ν ἔδοξεν. For the Rhodian decision, see *IvPriene*, 37 = *Syll.*[3] 599.

56. *MemAcadInscr* 37 (1903): 327–328, 334–335 = Holleaux, *Études* II:194–195.

57. This seems to have held for individuals as well. When the Macedonians called upon Scipio Aemilianus to resolve their internal *stasis* in 151, the Roman declined, preferring to go off to the Spanish wars: Polyb. 35.4.10–12.

As a result, the institution, in the form that the Greeks had long employed it, i.e. submission to a neutral state or city in Hellas, continued to flourish in the second century. Indeed, by contrast with the few and standoffish decisions of Rome, examples of Greek arbitration abound—as never before.[58] We need but refer to some representative instances. The aforementioned ruling by Rhodes between Samos and Priene, probably in the 190s, was registered in a lengthy and well-preserved document.[59] When the Roman senate failed to take action in legal controversies between Boeotia and Achaea in the 180s, a settlement was effected by Megara.[60] Rhodian judges pronounced on a boundary dispute between Delphi and Amphissa in 180, and on an Achaean quarrel involving honors for Eumenes in the 170s.[61] In this period, Patrae gave judgment in a case that divided Turia and Megalopolis.[62] The issue of Sparta's voting rights in the Delphic Amphictyony was debated by Dorian and Spartan spokesmen in 161/0 and adjudicated by arbiters from Lamia.[63] Miletus and Rhodes sent representatives to resolve the territorial claims of Hermione and Epidaurus some time in the first half of the second century.[64] Pergamenes settled controversies between Pitane and Mytilene in the middle of the century.[65] Achaea heard the rival claims of Oropus and Athens ca. 151.[66] A representative of Larisa heard those of Phthiotic Thebes and Halus at about that same time.[67] And so on. The practice continued even after 146, unaffected by the results of the Achaean war.[68] Hellenistic

58. Tod counted between forty and fifty occasions known from epigraphic testimony, more than half a century ago: *Arbitration*, 181. Numerous others have come to light since: e.g. Corinthian arbitration of a dispute involving Elis, perhaps with regard to boundary questions in the early second century: N. Robertson, *Hesperia* 45 (1976): 253–266; and a reconciliation between Lemnos and Clazomenae after military conflict, brought about by arbiters from Cnidus, some time in the first half of the second century: Herrmann, *IstMitt* 29 (1979): 250–251. The full collection in vol. II of Piccirilli's *Arbitrati greci* is awaited.

59. *IvPriene*, 37 = *Syll.*[3] 599; cf. Tod, *Arbitration*, 135–140.

60. Polyb. 22.4.11–17; cf. *IG*, VII, 21; Asheri, *StudClassOrient* 18 (1969): 61–62.

61. Delphi and Amphissa: *Syll.*[3] 614. Honors for Eumenes: Polyb. 28.7.8–10; cf. Holleaux, *Études* I:441–443; Walbank, *Commentary* III:335–336.

62. *SEG*, XI, 972 = *ISE*, no. 51.

63. *Syll.*[3] 668; cf. Daux, *Delphes*, 329–335, 679–681.

64. *SEG*, XI, 377 = *ISE*, no. 43.

65. *OGIS*, 335 = *IvPergamon*, 245.

66. *Syll.*[3] 675; cf. Paus. 7.11.7–8; Gruen, *JHS* 96 (1976): 51–53.

67. *IG*, IX, 2, *addenda*, p. x = *FDelphes*, III, 4, 355. Cf. Daux, *ZPE*, 36 (1979): 139–144.

68. Cf., e.g., the arbitration of Hermione between Delphi and Locris (*FDelphes*, III, 4, 169—though this may refer to adjudication between individuals of the two states rather than between the states themselves) and of Demetrias between the Thessalians and Perrhaebians (*IG*, IX, 2, 1106), both ca. 130. Also of Cnossus between Lato and

kings generally held aloof. But not altogether: an official of Philip V passed judgment on a dispute between Heracleum and Gonnoi perhaps ca. 200.[69] And Eumenes II settled differences between Teos and the Dionysian guild.[70] Finally, Greek states still framed treaties with one another that provided for the hearing of controversies by neutral tribunals.[71] How effective or enduring were these rulings and agreements none can say. But the Hellenic traditions of diplomacy held firm.[72]

A summation is called for. The use of third parties to arbitrate interstate quarrels had a long history in the Greek experience. Rome, on the other hand, showed little interest, and even less inclination, toward it. She paid lip service to arbitration in the war against Philip, an idea brought to her attention by the Greeks, but not seriously embraced by the westerner. Philip, Antiochus, and Aetolia in turn struck no responsive chords in Rome when they proposed recourse to arbitration. Only the Roman senate would dictate the terms of a settlement. Once her foes were beaten, however, Rome's posture altered. Impartial arbitration was a convenient principle for the power who wished to turn her attention to the West and let the Greeks settle their own differences. Thus it found place in the treaty of Apamea as yet another example of Rome's acknowledgment of a Hellenic convention. The Greeks themselves did not fully comprehend the victor's posture. They sought out the senate again and again to exercise jurisdiction and to resolve controversy. Rome, for her part, far from capitalizing on the situation to extend authority or tighten control, shunned the role of arbiter. The *patres* adjudicated with reluctance, made half-hearted gestures, endorsed Greek rulings, or referred matters to Greek tribunals. Insofar as there was any Roman "policy" on the principle, it was to promote the idea of Hellenic arbitration. So, they embodied it in the peace of Apamea, a Roman legate made reference to the κοινοδίκιον in Crete, and the senate upheld the jurisdiction of the

Olus, a decision endorsed without change by the Romans ca. 113: *REA* 44 (1942): 34–36.

69. B. Helly, *Gonnoi, II: Les Inscriptions* (Amsterdam, 1973), no. 93, pp. 100–105.

70. *IvPergamon*, 163 = Welles, *RC*, no. 53.

71. E.g., between Hierapytna and Prianous, early second century: *IC*, III, 3, 4, lines 47–71; cf. Gauthier, *Symbola*, 316–323; between Heraclea and Miletus, early second century: *Syll.*[3] 633, lines 36–39; between Temnos and Clazomenae, early second century; Herrmann *IstMitt*: 29 (1979): 253–254; between the Thessalians and Perrhaebians before 130: *IG*, IX, 2, 1106; between Lato and Olus, ca. 116: *Syll.*[3] 712 = *IC*, I, 16, 4, lines 9–11; between Sardis and Ephesus in the 90s: *OGIS*, 437, lines 73–76.

72. There is no reason to believe that arbitral decisions in this era were any less effective than those of earlier periods in Greek history. Lack of success did not prevent recourse to arbitration and adherence to the principle in fifth- and fourth-century Greece; see Martin, *La vie internationale*, 487–576; Calabi, *Ricerche sui rapporti*, 91–124.

Achaean confederacy. Indeed, Rome could become most exasperated when the Greeks refused recourse to their own procedures.[73] Not surprisingly, therefore, the Hellenic practice resumed and thrived. Interstate arbitration reached its heyday in late Hellenistic Greece. Roman statesmen had not usurped it, but advanced and abetted it.[74]

Mediation

Requests for arbitration of a judicial or quasi-judicial sort constitute but a small proportion of the Hellenic missions to Rome. By far the greater majority were political in nature: appeals for Roman assistance by one city or nation against another. That the senate cared little for petty boundary disputes or wrangles over possessory rights can readily be understood. Those were tedious matters, best dealt with by encouraging the Greeks to fall back on their own institutions. Requests for military aid or for the demonstration of Roman authority, on the other hand, belong in a different category. The pages of Polybius and Livy are filled with such petitions.[75] Here lay the ideal means whereby to place Hellas in a condition of increasing dependency upon Rome. And analysis of the occasions provides the best test of how far Rome encouraged the process or grasped the opportunities it presented.

What kind of response did the senate typically make to foreign embassies soliciting military or moral support? The answer, on any objective assessment, can hardly be in doubt. Rome, in the overwhelming majority of instances, refrained from taking sides and advocated instead a reconciliation of the contending parties.

A very large number of Roman missions seeking pacific solutions stand on record. Already in 200, during the preliminaries of the Second Macedonian War, senatorial envoys to the East carried

73. Observe, for example, the indignation of Rome when her envoys, seeking to end the war between Prusias and Attalus in 154 and requiring Prusias to submit to arbitration, found the Bithynian recalcitrant: Polyb. 33.7.3–4, 33.12.4–9.

74. A useful summary of modern opinions on the Greek and Roman attitudes toward arbitration may be found now in Marshall *ANRW* II:13 (1980), 626–661. Marshall rightly argues that Rome adapted rather than undermined the Greek system. But his view that Roman concepts like *fides*, *amicitia*, and *clientela* were difficult to reconcile with the Greek system and altered its frame of reference is unsubstantiated and unwarranted.

75. It is not, of course, always easy to draw a sharp line between applications for support and requests for arbitration. And several of the instances noted in the first part of this chapter have political implications that go beyond mere territorial squabbles, just as some in the later parts involve adjudication rather than direct assistance. But the general distinction remains valid.

instructions to resolve conflict between Antiochus III and Egypt.[76] The purpose at that time may have been primarily to keep the eastern sector of the world quiet while Rome prepared for hostilities with Philip. The picture had changed four years later; yet when pleas came again from Egypt to halt the aggressions of Antiochus, Rome took the same position: her ambassadors were charged with settling the quarrels of Syria and Egypt.[77] Antiochus outmaneuvered the Romans here, at the conference of Lysimacheia, announcing that he had already contracted a marriage alliance with Ptolemy.[78] For Rome, however, the news was welcome enough. She need not concern herself about Egypt.

The senate repeatedly took a similar line with regard to the affairs of Asia Minor. In 184 war raged between Eumenes and Prusias of Bithynia.[79] The complaints of Eumenes were heard in Rome, especially with reference to the assistance that Prusias obtained from his father-in-law Philip of Macedonia.[80] The senate paid enough heed to send Flamininus to the court of Prusias, but only after Eumenes had gained a decisive victory on his own.[81] In the course of that embassy occurred the mysterious end of Hannibal, now an adviser to the king of Bithynia. But, despite rumors and innuendo, the senate had not dispatched its envoy principally to deal with Hannibal. Flamininus went to reconcile Prusias to Eumenes.[82] When peace came, the belligerents concluded it; extant evidence suggests no Roman role in the

76. Polyb. 16.27.5 cf. Appian, Mac. 4. This probably came in response to a Ptolemaic request for support. Polybius reports an earlier Egyptian mission to Rome: Polyb. 15.25.14. An overblown account in Justin, 30.2.8–30.3.3. Livy, 31.2.3–4, gives a different purpose to the Roman embassy, but his narrative is dubious on various grounds; cf. Walbank, Philip V, 313–317; Briscoe, Commentary, 39–47, with good bibliography; T. J. Luce, Livy: The Composition of his History (Princeton, 1977), 62–73. Livy also records an Egyptian delegation in Rome in 200 catering to the senate and expressing willingness to defend Athens against Philip only if the Romans desired it: Livy, 31.9.1–5; cf. Paus. 1.36.5. The embassy need not be rejected, even if the offer can hardly have been seriously meant. It was another means of soliciting Rome's good will.

77. Polyb. 18.49.3: πρέσβεις ἐπὶ τὰς διαλύσεις ἐξαπεσταλμένοι τὰς Ἀντιόχου καὶ Πτολεμαίου; Livy, 33.39.1. The pleas of Italy are registered by Appian, Syr. 2, plainly a reference to these events—despite the doubts of Holleaux, Rome, la Grèce, 50, n. 3, 72, n. 2. Cf. Schmitt, Untersuchungen, 258, n. 2.

78. Polyb. 18.51.10; Livy, 33.40.3; Appian, Syr. 3.

79. Cf. Nepos, Hann. 10–11; Justin, 32.4.2–7.

80. Polyb. 23.1.4, 23.3.1; Livy, 39.46.9.

81. Eumenes' triumph: RivFilol 60 (1932): 446–447; cf. Nepos, Hann. 10; Justin, 32.4.6; OGIS, 298. The mission of Flamininus: Polyb. 23.5.1; Livy, 39.51.1; Appian, Syr. 11; Plut. Flam. 20.3; Zon. 9.21. On the chronology, see Habicht, Hermes 84 (1956): 96–100.

82. Justin, 32.4.8: missi a senatu legati sunt, qui utrumque regem in pacem cogerent; cf. Livy, 39.51.1; Appian, Syr. 11; Plut. Flam. 20.3. So, rightly, Habicht, Hermes 84 (1956): 96–97. Contra: Bredehorn, Senatsakten, 175–177.

settlement.[83] The official posture, in any case, continued to be promotion of peace rather than assistance in war. Hostilities broke out between Pergamum and the Pontic monarchy of Pharnaces in 183. Eumenes again sought Roman backing and got a friendly response but no offer of aid. Different sets of senatorial envoys visited Asia Minor over a period of two years, pronouncing Eumenes' cause just and taking no further action.[84] The Pergamene king eventually deputized his brother Attalus to urge upon Rome the need for some punishment of Pharnaces' contumacy. Still another Roman delegation went out in 180, this one more active than its predecessors, but the envoys confined themselves strictly to the task of bringing about peace.[85] Once their efforts proved fruitless, they simply withdrew to let matters take their course. Eumenes and his allies pressed the war to conclusion and compelled Pharnaces to accept terms of peace favorable to themselves, without Roman involvement.[86]

Periodic conflicts among the states of Anatolia recurred with frequency in the generation after Pydna as well. The Roman attitude showed little change. Requests for intervention were routinely met by the dispatch of legates who sought pacific solutions but rarely pressed the matter. In response to a Pergamene appeal of 167 to protect that kingdom against incursion by the Galatians, Rome's representatives sought to bring the belligerents to an accord. The mission came to naught and Eumenes was again left to finish off the war himself.[87] When hostilities resumed, the king went so far as to make a personal trip to Italy in 167/6. But the senate would not even consent to see him, constructing an ad hoc pretext to put him off. They preferred to avoid further embarrassments.[88] The pattern persists. In 163 it was the Galatians who endeavored to stir Roman anger against Ariarathes of Cappadocia. The *patres* sent a delegation, however, commissioned to smooth over differences between the hostile parties.[89] Nothing

83. Polyb. 22.20.8; Strabo, 12.4.3 (C 564).

84. Polyb. 23.9.1–3, 24.1.1–3; Livy, 40.2.6–8, 40.20.1.

85. Attalus' plea: Polyb. 24.5.1–7; Diod. 29.22. The instructions of the envoys: Polyb. 24.5.8: ἡ δὲ σύγκλητος διακούσασα φιλανθρώπως ἀπεκρίθη διότι πέμψει πρεσβευτὰς τοὺς κατὰ πάντα τρόπον λύσοντας τὸν πόλεμον; Diod. 29.22. Their actions in Asia Minor: Polyb. 24.14.10–24.15.10.

86. Polyb. 24.15.11–13, 25.2.

87. Polyb. 30.1.1–3, 30.2.8, 30.3.2, 30.3.7–8; Livy, 45.19.1–3, 45.19.12, 45.20.1–2, 45.34.10–14; Diod. 31.12–14; cf. *OGIS*, 305 = FDelphes, III, 3, 241–242; IvPergamon, 165.

88. Polyb. 30.19; cf. 29.6.4; Livy, 45.44.21; *Per.* 46; Justin, 38.6.4. Polybius' interpretation, that Rome deliberately humiliated Eumenes in order to encourage the Gauls, is not compelling. It was the Gauls who had sabotaged Rome's peace efforts: Livy, 45.34.12–14.

89. Polyb. 31.8; cf. Strabo, 12.2.8 (C 538–539).

tangible, it seems, was accomplished; another Roman embassy appeared in Asia the following year with the same task.[90] In the next decade, Attalus II and Prusias II rekindled the conflict that had once divided their predecessors on the thrones of Pergamum and Bithynia. The customary charges and counter-charges were heard in Rome—and the customary Roman embassies set forth for Asia. In this affair, three separate delegations went between the years 156 and 154, with increasingly stiffer instructions as Prusias proved intractable. Their efforts to deter the Bithynian and to incline him toward arbitration encountered resistance and hostility.[91] At last Rome took stronger measures. But even then not an intervention by force; rather an encouragement of Pergamum and other states of Asia Minor to make Prusias see reason, then still another Roman embassy to bring about a treaty of peace.[92] A few years later, the situation reversed itself. Prusias came under attack by forces in support of his son Nicomedes and abetted by Attalus. The Bithynian made application to Rome this time.[93] The senate responded in characteristic fashion: in 149 an embassy went with orders to halt the war and check the aggressions of Nicomedes and his Pergamene patrons. The outcome was equally characteristic. Rome's legates dawdled and dithered, war proceeded, and the Greek coalition against Prusias put his reign to an end on its own. Cato had forecast the result with pungent wit: by the time the senate's ill-chosen envoys could accomplish anything, not only would Prusias have perished but even Nicomedes would die of old age.[94] An apt description of Rome's sluggish diplomacy.

A more forceful diplomatic act had occurred in 168, when Roman authorities received word of Pydna: the celebrated "day of Eleusis" on which C. Popillius Laenas brusquely ordered Antiochus IV out of Egypt. Yet, even here—the *locus classicus* for Roman arrogance in eastern affairs—the position is quite consistent with what we have seen elsewhere and at other times. The background needs to be recalled. Antiochus had protested in Rome of Ptolemaic aggression in 170; and, after the fortunes of war shifted, a mission from Ptolemy in 169/8 pleaded with the senate to deter Antiochus from subjecting all

90. Polyb. 31.15.10.

91. Polyb. 32.16, 33.1.1–2, 33.7, 33.12.1–4; Appian, *Mithr.* 3.

92. Polyb. 33.12.5–9, 33.13.4–10; cf. Appian, *Mithr.* 3; *OGIS*, 327. Observe also that Rome made some representations to Attalus during this time to discourage his assault on Priene: *OGIS*, 351 = Sherk, *RDGE*, no. 6. But the representations, not untypically, were half-hearted and ineffectual: Polyb. 33.6.

93. Appian, *Mithr.* 4–6; Strabo, 13.4.2 (C 624).

94. Polyb. 36.14; Appian, *Mithr.* 6–7; Diod. 32.20–21; Livy, *Per.* 50; Plut. *Cato*, 9; Zon. 9.28; Justin, 35.4.2–5; cf. *OGIS*, 327.

of Egypt.[95] Rome's attitude throughout this time was to promote an amicable settlement, though she could take no decisive action while her hands were full with the conflict against Perseus. She not only sent a peace mission of her own, but encouraged both Achaea and Rhodes to mediate the Syrian war.[96] Antiochus resumed his aggressions in the spring of 168 and soon seemed on the point of reducing Egypt to subjection.[97] The news of Pydna, however, altered the situation dramatically: Popillius could now proceed to deliver his ultimatum with impunity. But, it should be observed, his instructions derived from an unchanged senatorial policy: he was to put an end to war between Antiochus and the Ptolemaic regime.[98] With this accomplished, Rome drew back once more.[99]

Other embassies announcing Roman interest in the peaceful resolution of conflicts may be briefly registered. Roman envoys on their way to Antioch in 164 sent a message to the Jews declaring their approval of arrangements made between that people and the Seleucid kingdom, arrangements which promised a settlement of their quarrel.[100] Twice, in 164/3 and again in 162, the senate dispatched ambassadors with the task of reconciling the warring brothers, Ptolemy Philometor and Ptolemy Euergetes, who contended for power in Egypt and her possessions.[101] In neither case was the Roman intervention decisive in effecting an accord. Philometor imposed his own terms.[102]

95. The embassy of 170: Polyb. 27.19, 28.1. The embassy of 168: Livy, 44.19.6–12; Justin, 34.2.8. Antiochus' victories in the interim: Polyb. 28.18, 28.19.1, 28.20.1; Diod. 30.14, 30.18; Livy, 44.19.9; Justin, 34.2.7–8. In general, on the Sixth Syrian War, see W. Otto, *AbhMünch* 11 (1934): 23–81; acutely criticized in many particulars by J. W. Swain, *CP* 39 (1944): 80–94. More briefly, with useful bibliographical references, Briscoe, *JRS* 54 (1964): 71–73; Walbank, *Commentary* III: 321–324.

96. Polyb. 28.17.4–15, 28.23, 29.25.1–6; see, e.g., 29.25.2: τῇ Ῥωμαίων προαιρέσει πειρᾶσθαι διαλύειν τοὺς βασιλεῖς.

97. Livy, 45.11.1–45.12.2; Polyb. 29.2.2, 29.26.1–29.27.1; Diod. 31.1; Zon. 9.25.

98. Polyb. 29.2.2–3: κατέστησε πρεσβευτὰς τοὺς περὶ Γαῖον Ποπίλιον, τόν τε πόλεμον λύσοντας; 29.27.7: ἦν δὲ τὰ γεγραμμένα λύειν ἐξ αὐτῆς τὸν πρὸς Πτολεμαῖον πόλεμον; Diod. 31.2.2; Livy, 44.19.13, 45.10.2–3, 45.12.3–7, 45.13.1; Appian, *Syr.* 66; Justin, 34.3.1; Zon. 9.25. Cf. the discussion in Walbank, *Commentary* III: 361–363.

99. Cf. Gruen, *Chiron* 6 (1976): 73–95.

100. 2 Macc. 11:34–38; cf. 11:16–21. Despite Mørkholm, *Antiochos IV*, 162–165, the letter's authenticity seems clear; cf. J. Bunge, *Untersuchungen zum zweiten Makkabäerbuch* (Bonn, 1971), 392–395.

101. The embassy of 164/3: Polyb. 31.2.14: αὐτοῖς ἐπαπεστάλη γράμματα παρὰ τῆς συγκλήτου καὶ τοὺς ἐν Ἀλεξανδρείᾳ βασιλεῖς διαλῦσαι κατὰ δύναμιν. The embassy of 162: Polyb. 31.10.9–10: δόντες ἐντολὰς διαλῦσαι τοὺς ἀδελφοὺς καὶ κατασκευάσαι τῷ νεωτέρῳ τὴν Κύπρον χωρὶς πολέμου; 31.17.4, 31.18.1.

102. Only Zon. 9.25 and Trogus, *Prol.* 34 imply that Rome brought about reconciliation, evidently after the first mission; but their accounts are much abbreviated and not of much help. The partition of territory in 163 stemmed from agreement between

Rhodes solicited Roman assistance in her war on the Cretans in 153; the senate instead sent a commission to terminate the conflict. That decision, a plain disappointment to the Rhodians, induced them to go elsewhere for help, namely to the Achaean Confederacy.[103] Rome's preference for pacific solutions rather than military engagement continued to frustrate appellants. This was true even in the preliminaries to what would become the Achaean War. The seemingly eternal conflict between Sparta and the Achaeans set events in motion. Sparta challenged Achaea's authority and the League sought to coerce her contumacious member. A famous Roman embassy in 147 issued threats, in the hope of bringing Achaea to her senses—without tangible result. Less famous, but more characteristic, were two further Roman missions in subsequent months which endeavored to smooth over differences and prevent an outbreak of war.[104] Only miscalculation and mischance brought Achaea to her knees. Rome's proposals for concord had been rejected once too often.[105] We need not go beyond 146. Yet examples of Roman efforts to resolve rather than exacerbate disputes can be found after that time as well. To mention but one: the baffling and long-term contention between Itanus and Hierapytna in Crete, already noted in another context. During the course of thirty years from 141 to 112, the senate twice sent delegations to bring warfare on the island to an end, once sent an embassy to investigate the claims and counter-claims, and twice more gave the case to impartial arbiters in Magnesia for decision.[106]

---

the brothers, with Philometor holding the upper hand: Polyb. 31.10.1–5; cf. Livy, *Per.* 46, 47. The claims of Euergetes on Cyprus were approved by the senate in dispatching the second embassy. But the *legati* could make no headway with Philometor and returned without an agreement: Polyb. 31.17–19. Rome took a harder line in 161: Polyb. 31.20; Diod. 31.23. Yet, even then, the settlement seems to have been imposed by Philometor, not by the Romans: Zon. 9.25; cf. Polyb. 39.7.6. A similar confrontation and a similar outcome in 154: Polyb. 33.11, 39.7.6; Diod. 31.33; *OGIS*, 116 = *I de Delos*, 1518. Cf. the analysis of Winkler, *Rom und Aegypten*, 41–61. Otto, *AbhMünch* 11 (1934): 90–119, exaggerates the Roman role. See also Manni, *RivFilol* 28 (1950): 237–252; Walbank, *Commentary* III:468, 474–477, 553. A fuller discussion below, pp. 694–708.

103. Polyb. 33.15.3–4, 33.16.1–8. Observe also that when Andriscus' revolution in Macedonia a few years later threatened Thessaly, the Thessalians did not even bother to apply to Rome, but sought the aid of Achaea: Polyb. 36.10.5; cf. Livy, *Per.* 50.

104. The first embassy: Polyb. 38.9.6–8; Paus. 7.14.1; cf. Dio, 21.72.1; Livy, *Per.* 51; Florus, 1.32.2; Justin, 34.1.5. The second: Polyb. 38.9.3–5, 38.10.1–5; Dio, 21.72.2; cf. Paus. 7.14.3. The third: Polyb. 38.12.1–3; cf. Paus. 7.15.1.

105. See the full discussion in Gruen, *JHS* 96 (1976): 53–69. Cf. now Walbank, *Commentary* III:698–709. Similarly, the initial Roman response to the uprising of Andriscus in 150 was to send a representative in hopes of finding a peaceful solution: Zon. 9.28.

106. Ser. Sulpicius Galba, as legate in 141, induced the parties to end hostilities:

The evidence is clear and abundant. Rome had opportunities aplenty for forceful intervention: calls for military aid or moral support, summons to overawe aggressors or back the cause of friends and allies. She neither initiated those appeals nor took much advantage of them. Diplomatic missions rather than armed companies almost invariably constituted the response. Again and again the senate's representatives avoided lending authority to one side or the other, argued for amicable means to end dissension or war, and frequently left without seeing the matter through. It is difficult to escape the impression that many of these delegations conducted *pro forma* inquiries, made appropriate noises, and returned home leaving the conflicts to be sorted out by Greeks. Rome plainly did not solicit appeals in order to extend and entrench her influence abroad. She preferred agreeable solutions to direct interference. And, though she treated appellants with courtesy, she showed little inclination to impose settlements.

Nor was Rome averse to the mediation of Greeks even in conflicts in which she was herself directly involved.[107] This is discernible already in the First Macedonian War, when neutral states like Egypt, Rhodes, Athens, Byzantium, Chios, Mytilene, and Athamania sought on at least three occasions to bring the belligerents to terms. The efforts proved abortive as in each instance either Rome, Aetolia, or Philip preferred to fight on. There is no suggestion, however, that Romans regarded the intermediacy of Greeks as illegitimate or unacceptable on principle.[108] And in 205, when Epirus took the initiative in peace negotiations, the Romans readily consented to make a settlement.[109]

Willingness to accept Hellenic intervention can be illustrated from several later episodes. In 196 Flamininus was on the point of a major campaign against Boeotia, to punish her people for harassment and murder of Roman soldiers and for refusal to submit to a heavy fine. Representatives from Athens and Achaea stepped in to dissuade the Roman commander and to arrange a settlement under which

*Syll.*³ 685 = *IC*, III, 4, 9, lines 49–50. In 115 and 114 Rome directed the cessation of another war on the island: *IC*, III, 4, 10 = Sherk, *RDGE*, no. 14, lines 10–13. And ca. 113 an embassy headed by Q. Fabius investigated the rights and wrongs of the dispute: *Syll.*³ 685 = *IC*, III, 4, 9, lines 75–84. On the references to a Magnesian tribunal, once ca. 140 and once in 112, see above n. 54.

107. The assertion of Matthaei, *CQ* 2 (1908): 262, that "from the outset she had a vehement dislike to submit to arbitration or mediation herself" simply ignores a great deal of evidence.

108. Livy, 27.30.4–15; Polyb. 10.25 (209); Livy, 28.5.13, 28.7.13–15; Appian, *Mac.* 3 (208); Polyb. 11.4–6; Appian, *Mac.* 3 (207).

109. Livy, 29.12.8–14.

Boeotia would pay a modest sum in compensation. Flamininus called off his invasion.[110] Four years later, Aetolian enmity toward Rome brought matters to the brink of war. Flamininus, not ready for it or desirous of it, asked Athenian spokesmen to put Rome's case before the Aetolian assembly and to prevent an outbreak of hostilities.[111] When Scipio Africanus arrived in Greece in 190, he welcomed with eagerness an Athenian offer to mediate differences between Rome and Aetolia.[112] Negotiations broke down because the Roman terms were too harsh. Then Athenian and Rhodian envoys intervened again the following year, a mediation which proved instrumental in softening the Roman position and terminating the war with Aetolia.[113]

Rome's attitude on this score shows little change even at the time of the Third Macedonian War. Rhodes, to be sure, had attempted to interpose her good offices between Rome and Perseus and got severe chastisement after the war for taking that liberty.[114] But Rome had other reasons for humbling independent powers in the immediate aftermath of Perseus' fall. Rhodes' actions served as mere pretext. The charge against her, in any case, was that she had interceded at a time unsuitable to Roman interests, not the fact of mediation itself.[115] Rome had had no objection to neutral states interposing themselves in the past and had none now.[116] Prusias of Bithynia offered his services as mediator in the war in 169, and a Ptolemaic embassy came to the senate intending to make the same proposal.[117] Yet both Bithynia and

110. Livy, 33.29.

111. Livy, 35.32.

112. Polyb. 21.4.1–6; Livy, 37.6.4–6.

113. Polyb. 21.29.1, 21.29.9, 21.30.6, 21.31.5–16; Livy, 38.3.7–8, 38.9.3, 38.9.6, 38.10.2–6. D. Golan, *RivStorAnt* 6–7 (1977): 324–327, misconstrues this as mere abject supplication. Polybius, however, uses the term ὁμιλοῦντες only with regard to appeals to the Roman commander in camp: 21.29.9—not on the mediation with the senate.

114. Polyb. 29.10.1–4, 29.11.1–6, 29.19; Livy, 44.14.8–44.15.7, 44.29.6–8, 44.35.4–6, 45.3.3–8; Zon. 9.23; Diod. 30.24. Polybius elsewhere gives the impression that the consul Q. Marcius Philippus himself advised the Rhodians upon this course: Polyb. 28.16.3–7, 28.17.1–9. But Philippus' suggestion, very probably, was that Rhodes mediate in the Syrian war, not in the Macedonian war; see Gruen, *CQ* 25 (1975): 71–74, with references to modern literature. Cf. Walbank, *Commentary* III: 350–351.

115. Polyb. 29.19.5–9: προφανὲς εἶναι τοῖς ὀρθῶς σκοπουμένοις διότι τὰς πρεσβείας ἐξέπεμψαν οὐ διαλύειν ἐθέλοντες τὸν πόλεμον, ἀλλ' ἐξελέσθαι τὸν Περσέα καὶ σῶσαι; Livy, 45.3.6–8.

116. The fact is proved, if proof be needed, by the Rhodians' open assertion of their intent before the Roman senate: Polyb. 29.19.3; Livy, 45.3.4–5; Diod. 30.24. On the whole matter of Rhodian behavior and the reasons for Rome's reaction, see Gruen, *CQ* 25 (1975): 74–81.

117. Prusias: Livy, 44.14.5–7. Ptolemy: Polyb. 28.1.7–9. The Ptolemaic envoys, in fact, were advised by the *princeps senatus* M. Lepidus not to propose mediation—it

Egypt continued to enjoy Roman favor after Pydna.[118] The western power had not arrogated to herself the position of sole arbiter of international affairs. Very far from it.

Indecision and Imprecision

The persistence with which Greeks applied to Rome in the first half of the second century tells more about Hellenic attitudes than about Roman. The applicants continued to hope that they could mobilize and manipulate Rome's authority to serve their own ends, to provide protection, outmaneuver their rivals, and enhance their position in local struggles for power. Roman might could make Hellenic right. Yet if one looks with care at senatorial responses, it becomes increasingly clear how disinclined the westerner was to assume the role which appellants thrust upon her.

A remarkable number of pronouncements issued from the *curia* which were ambiguous in tone and meaning, noncommittal in character, and ultimately indifferent to the issues addressed. The recurring controversy over Sparta's position in the Achaean League provides the best case in point. Achaea, under the leadership of Philopoemen, had absorbed the city into her federation in 192, seizing the moment of confusion after the tyrant Nabis' assassination.[119] Rome, so far as is known, expressed no concern—despite the fact that she had left Sparta independent after her own war on Nabis in 195.[120] Resentment among the Lacedaemonians, however, provided a perpetual source of friction.[121] A Spartan embassy to Rome, probably in winter 191/0, came with several requests: return of hostages, recovery of control over the coastal towns of Laconia, and restoration of exiles. The *patres* began by equivocating: they would instruct their legates on the matter of the villages, and they needed more time to think about the hostages. As for the exiles, Rome's reply was especially revealing: since Sparta was a free city, why didn't she bring them home herself?[122] No

was wiser to stress loyalty to Rome at a time when Antiochus IV's envoys were denouncing Ptolemaic aggression.

118. Polyb. 29.27, 30.18; Livy, 45.12, 45.44; Diod. 31.2, 31.15; Zon. 9.25.

119. Livy, 35.37.1–2; Plut. *Phil.* 15.2; Paus. 8.50.10–8.51.1.

120. Livy, 34.35, 34.41; Plut. *Flam.* 13.1.

121. There was defection already in the spring of 191 and Sparta had to be coerced back into the League: Plut. *Phil.* 16.1–2; Paus. 8.51.1.

122. Polyb. 21.1.1–3: περὶ δὲ τῶν φυγάδων τῶν ἀρχαίων θαυμάζειν ἔφησαν, πῶς οὐ κατάγουσιν αὐτοὺς εἰς τὴν οἰκείαν, ἠλευθερωμένης τῆς Σπάρτης. The hostages involved were evidently those taken by Rome after the war in 195: Livy, 34.35.11. She

need to dissect that statement and discern hidden and devious policy therein. It was a quip and a shrug. Sparta was at liberty to restore her exiles if she could; the senate would not help her.[123]

The response set a pattern for Roman attitudes toward the Peloponnesian tangle. Sparta broke with the League again in 189, seeking to regain the coastal villages and to take advantage of the presence of the Roman commander, Fulvius Nobilior, who was in Greece to conclude the Aetolian war. Violence and murder ensued; Achaea readied herself to mobilize against the rebels. The Lacedaemonians now played what they expected to be a trump card; they surrendered their city to Fulvius, pleading that it be taken *in fidem dicionemque populi Romani*.[124] Subsequent behavior by the consul and by the senate bears notice. Fulvius, to all intents and purposes, simply ignored the *deditio*. Instead he urged a summoning of the League assembly to consider the whole Spartan issue, an action entirely in line with so many other examples of Rome shifting responsibility to Greek political or judicial organs. Feeling ran high in the assembly and the meeting threatened to degenerate into violence. Fulvius' speech took a moderate line, of nebulous import, favoring neither side and arguing for prevention of war—again a typical Roman posture. To avert the outbreak of hostilities he suggested a cooling-off period, in which the contending principals would send representatives to Rome.[125] The sequel shows the Roman disposition quite plainly. After hearing the Spartan complaints and speeches from two sets of Achaean envoys, the *patres* delivered a verdict, if such it can be called: the Spartan situation is to remain *status quo*.[126] The statement was so baffling that the Lacedaemonians read it in their interests, the Achaeans in theirs.[127] In a word, it accomplished nothing but to take Rome off the hook. And

did, in fact, subsequently restore them in 190: Polyb. 21.3.4. The coastal towns had been put under Achaean authority at the same time; cf. Livy, 35.13.2, 38.31.2. The identity of the exiles, a much discussed subject, can happily be left aside here; cf. Aymard, *Premiers rapports*, 356–366; Errington, *Philopoemen*, 133–135; B. Shimron, *Late Sparta* (Buffalo, 1972), 137–150; Walbank, *Commentary* III:88–89.

123. Flamininus expressed an interest in the exiles at an Achaean meeting about this time, as did the consul M'. Acilius Glabrio: Plut. *Phil.* 17.4; Livy, 36.35.7; cf. Paus. 8.51.4. But that did not represent senatorial policy, as Philopoemen knew—he successfully blocked them.

124. Livy, 38.30.6–38.32.2.

125. Livy, 38.32.3–4: *altercatio fuit, cui consul, cum alia satis ambitiose partem utramque fovendo incerta respondisset, una denuntiatione ut bello abstinerent, donec Romam ad senatum legatos misissent, finem imposuit.*

126. Livy, 38.32.5–9: *novari tamen nihil de Lacedaemoniis placebat.*

127. Livy, 38.32.9–10: *responsum ita perplexum fuit ut et Achaei sibi de Lacedaemone permissum acciperent, et Lacedaemonii non omnia concessa iis interpretarentur.*

that is doubtless what the senate wanted. Achaean forces went on to crush Lacedaemon, destroy her walls, restructure her system, and coerce her citizenry.[128] Rome turned her back on the whole situation.

Roman ambiguity, however, did not prevent repeated embassies from the Peloponnese. No settlement in that area ever seemed permanent. Spartan delegates pestered the senate again some months later with complaints about the actions of Achaea. This time they managed to get a slightly more favorable reaction and even a letter from the consul of 187 to the Confederacy delivering a mild rebuke and expressing Roman displeasure with the harshness of Achaean behavior. But the message issued no demand for change and no threat of Roman interference. The Achaeans could safely ignore it—which they did.[129]

This is not the place for detailed scrutiny of the missions that continued to shuttle back and forth between Italy and the Peloponnese.[130] Only once in all the comings and goings, the complaints, appeals, and demands, did the senate consent to deliver something approximating a decision. In 184, when delegates from Achaea and no fewer than four separate groups of Spartan envoys were in Rome, the dispute was turned over to a commission of Roman senators with some prior experience in the Peloponnese. Their deliberations resulted in a compromise set of pronouncements, with something for everyone: exiles were to be restored and the walls of Sparta rebuilt, but the city was to remain part of the Achaean federation; the amount of compensation for property lost had still to be determined, for the commissioners could not decide among themselves; and all future disputes were to be heard not by Rome but by the League itself or, in the case of capital crimes, by impartial jurors drawn from outside

128. Livy, 38.33–34, 39.36.9–39.37.8; Plut. *Phil.* 16.3–5, 17.4; Paus. 8.51.3; cf. Polyb. 21.32c.3, 22.11.7.

129. Polyb. 22.3, 22.7.1–7; cf. Diod. 29.17. The chronological problems here need not detain us; see Aymard, *REA* 30 (1928): 30–42; Errington, *Philopoemen*, 255–261; Walbank, *Commentary* III:177–178.

130. Q. Metellus delivered a stern reprimand to Achaea in 185, but he acted without senatorial instructions and was denied a formal hearing by the League: Polyb. 22.10; Paus. 7.9.1; Livy, 39.33.1, 39.33.5–7. When Spartans complained again of mistreatment by Achaea, Metellus joined in their chorus. But the senate did no more than send another commission and ask for more courtesy to Roman envoys in the future: Polyb. 22.12; Livy, 39.33; Paus. 7.9.1. The bluster of Rome's envoy Ap. Claudius in 184 was also a personal outburst dictated by the exigencies of the altercation and not necessarily reflecting senatorial sympathies: Livy, 39.37.18–20; cf. Paus. 7.9.3–4; *contra*: Lehmann, *Untersuchungen*, 278–279; a better interpretation in Errington, *Philopoemen*, 174–178. The actual message of the senate which Appius delivered simply said that the *patres* disapproved of Achaean treatment of Sparta; Livy, 39.36.3–4; Diod. 29.17. That had been Rome's official posture for the last four years.

states.[131] The thrust of those rulings, far from asserting Rome's prerogatives as arbiter, aimed at washing her hands of the sticky mess.[132]

Not that this halted the stream of appellants from the Peloponnese. Sparta had nowhere else to go. And Achaea kept sending observers to make sure the Lacedaemonians could not mobilize Roman backing. The senate resorted once more to ambiguity and indifference. Two further groups of Spartan exiles applied to Rome in 183. The *patres* gave vent to annoyance: they had done enough already and the matter no longer concerned them.[133] As if it ever had. Sparta broke with the League still again and was reabsorbed still again in 182/1. The inevitable results followed: two separate missions from Sparta and one from the League to explain matters in Rome. The senate wearily heard them all out and criticized nobody; they would take no sides.[134] The most that could be wrung out of Roman officials was a letter to Achaea asking for repatriation of Lacedaemonian exiles. Achaea's own envoy reported that the *patres* had done this not out of any genuine enthusiasm but only to avoid listening to any more Spartan speeches.[135] A most perceptive assessment of the Roman attitude. Achaea proceeded with confidence to disregard the letter.[136]

131. Polyb. 23.4; Paus. 7.9.5; Livy, 39.48.2–4.

132. Achaean leaders seem to have read the message correctly. They went about their business and ignored the advice of individual Romans, Flamininus and Q. Philippus, which was unaccompanied by specific senatorial directives: Polyb. 23.5.14–18, 23.9.8, 24.9.12.

133. Polyb. 23.6.1–3, 23.9.1, 23.9.5, 23.9.11: διότι πάντα πεποιήκασιν αὐτοῖς τὰ δυνατά, κατὰ δὲ τὸ παρὸν οὐ νομίζουσιν εἶναι τοῦτο τὸ πρᾶγμα πρὸς αὐτούς; 23.17.7: ἀποκεκρίσθαι γὰρ αὐτοὺς νῦν μηθὲν εἶναι τῶν κατὰ Λακεδαίμονα πραγμάτων πρὸς αὐτούς. Similarly, the senate brushed aside an Achaean request for assistance in stamping out the Messenian revolt: Polyb. 23.9.12–13. They also refrained from giving any aid to the rebels: Polyb. 23.9.14, 23.17.3, 24.1.6–7; Livy, 40.20.2. Messenian exiles appealed to Rome for judgment on their grievances after the revolt, but obviously got no satisfaction: Polyb. 24.9.12–13, 24.10.13.

134. Polyb. 23.18.3–5, 24.1.1, 24.1.4, 24.1.6–7: οὐθενὶ δυσαρεστήσασα περὶ τῶν οἰκονομουμένων ἡ σύγκλητος ἀπεδέξατο φιλανθρώπως τοὺς πρεσβευτάς. On the readmission of Sparta to the League, Polyb. 23.17.5–23.18.2.

135. Polyb. 24.1.5, 24.2.1, 24.2.4: τῶν δὲ περὶ τὸν Βίππον παραγενομένων ἐκ τῆς Ῥώμης καὶ διασαφούντων γραφῆναι τὰ γράμματα περὶ τῶν φυγάδων οὐ διὰ τὴν τῆς συγκλήτου σπουδήν, ἀλλὰ διὰ τὴν τῶν φυγάδων φιλοτιμίαν; cf. Livy, 40.20.2.

136. Polyb. 24.2.5, 24.9.14. The issue of the Spartan exiles and Rome's letter was raised again in 181/0 by the Achaean faction of Hyperbatus and Callicrates: Polyb. 24.8.1–6—this surely refers to the same Roman missive, not a new request; cf. Aymard, REA, 30 (1928), 59–61; contra: Walbank, Commentary III:18–19. Here it became embroiled in Achaean internal politics. Rome was quite happy to give encouragement tò Callicrates, who eventually brought back the restoration of the exiles: Polyb. 24.8–10; Paus. 7.9.6–7; Syll.³ 634. It was a plain case of Greek politicians utilizing Roman pronouncements for their own ends—not an example of Rome exerting pressure; cf. Gruen, AJAH 1 (1976): 32–33.

In the next generation, when we gain another glimpse at it, the mood of the senate was unchanged. Spartan separatism caused a new crisis in the Peloponnese and her leaders hastened to Rome in 150/49 for support. The *patres* reiterated their old position: the Achaean League should have jurisdiction on all disputes, save capital cases.[137] The customary indifference still held. This strengthened Achaea's hand and brought Lacedaemon to the brink of despair. A year later, Spartan and Achaean envoys were both in Rome to clarify their positions. The senate had recourse to another old device, the ambiguous response that each party could interpret as it wished. A commission was promised to look into the dispute, its departure, however, delayed for a year and a half—doubtless in hopes that the matter would be settled by the Greeks. In the meanwhile, Spartan and Achaean authorities did indeed place their own constructions upon the senate's posture, each in accordance with his own intent. Rome preferred to stay out of it.[138]

The long record of indifference and indecision can hardly be more obvious. We have no evidence comparable in extent to that on Peloponnesian affairs in this period. Yet it is easy enough to find parallel examples of Roman aloofness elsewhere. The senate made a virtual science of ambiguity.

The *decem legati* whose task was to settle Asian matters after the Antiochene war in 188 addressed the claims of Rhodes and Lycia by trying to keep both sides happy. Their pronouncement was fuzzy enough to allow the Lycians to think they had been granted independence and the Rhodians to believe they had a free hand in controlling the area.[139] A decade passed during which Rome paid no attention to intermittent conflict between Lycia and Rhodes. Only when a desperate Lycian delegation came to plead for succor against Rhodian coercion in 177 did the senate stir itself. A commission to Rhodes asserted that Lycia had not been awarded to the island as a gift but should be treated as a friend and ally. Rhodes sent envoys to Italy in turn, explaining her case. The senate, as so often, equivocated and delayed. For how long we do not know, but long enough for Rhodes to bring the Lycians to heel, while the Romans relapsed into unconcern.[140]

Analogous behavior can be documented over the next half century. Word reached Rome in 175 that Perseus was instigating conflict

137. Paus. 7.12.4; cf. 7.9.5.
138. Paus. 7.12.5–9; cf. Gruen, *JHS* 96 (1976): 55–56.
139. Polyb. 22.5.1–7; cf. Schmitt, *Rom und Rhodos*, 81–128; Gruen, *CQ* 25 (1975): 64–65.
140. Polyb. 25.4.1–25.6.1; cf. Livy, 41.6.8–12, 41.25.8. Discussion, with bibliography, in Gruen, *CQ* 25 (1975): 66–67; see further, Walbank, *Commentary* III: 277–281.

between Bastarnae and Dardanians to his own advantage. Macedonian envoys came to Italy and denied the charge. The senate abjured praise or blame, asking only that Perseus avoid the appearance of violating his accord with Rome—a minimalist response, if ever there was one.[141] In 167 Prusias made a celebrated appearance before the senate, flattering the *patres* to the point of abject servility, offering to show his loyalty in a host of ways, and making but one concrete request: that Rome assign him land presently occupied by the Galatians. The senators gave him every courtesy and hospitality, but on the matter of Galatia they issued a long-winded and casuistic reply that amounted to indefinite postponement.[142] Two years later, Prusias' envoys were back in Rome, together with others, to complain of Pergamene meddling in Galatia and even aggression in Bithynia. The *patres* engaged in their usual dodge: they took the complaints under advisement and ventured no opinion.[143] The Bithynian monarch tried again in 164/3 and still once more in 160/59. He sent delegates along with the Galatians to Rome in order to arouse hostility against Eumenes and Attalus. The *patres* on both occasions coolly dismissed the charges and sat on their hands.[144] In 158 rival claimants to the throne of Cappadocia, Ariarathes V, now an exile, and Orophernes, who had usurped the crown, made representations to the senate. What response they got is uncertain: at best, a suggestion that they rule the land jointly. But Rome had no intention of insisting on any change of the *status quo*. The contending princes would have to fight their own battles and seek Hellenic allies.[145] The Epirote politician Charops crossed the Adriatic ca. 157 asking for endorsement of his domestic policies. He got a cold shoulder from individual Romans and a characteristically vague answer from the *curia*—which he, like so many others, felt free to interpret to his own advantage.[146] Even when the senate gave an encouraging reply to an appellant, it was not always what it seemed. The offer to "assist" young Alexander Balas in 153 in capturing the realm of Syria from Demetrius I never translated itself into concrete action. Balas had to find assistance elsewhere, from Hellenistic monarchs, not Roman officials.[147]

141. Livy, 41.19.4–6; cf. Appian, *Mac.* 11.1.

142. Livy, 45.44.4–21, especially 45.44.10–12; cf. Polyb. 30.18; Diod. 31.15.

143. Polyb. 30.30.2–7; Livy, *Per.* 46.

144. 164/3: Polyb. 31.1.2–6; Diod. 31.7.2. 160/159: Polyb. 31.32.1, 32.1.5–6.

145. Polyb. 32.10; Appian, *Syr.* 47; Zon. 9.24; cf. Gruen, *Chiron* 6 (1976): 89–90.

146. Polyb. 32.6.3–9.

147. Balas' appeal and Rome's response: Polyb. 33.15.1–2, 33.18.6–14. Real assistance came from Ptolemy, Attalus, and Ariarathes: Polyb. 3.5.3; Justin, 35.1.6–9; Appian, *Syr.* 67; Strabo, 13.4.2 (C 624); cf. Gruen, *Chiron* 6 (1976): 91–93.

By contrast with this host of evasions, blurred responses, side-steppings, and equivocations, decisive rulings of the senate on eastern affairs were rare indeed. Rome did consent to hear a multitude of complaints by Eumenes, the Thessalians, Perrhaebians, and Athamanians about Philip's aggrandizements after the Antiochene war. Roman commissioners in 186/5 instructed the Macedonian king to evacuate his garrisons from Aenus and Maronea and withdraw from cities in dispute with Thessaly and Perrhaebia. The senate backed up those pronouncements in 184. Philip ultimately abandoned the Thracian towns in 183. An example of forceful exercise of Roman authority? If so, it shows only how halting and sluggish that exercise was. For two and a half years passed between the initial demand and Philip's compliance; the compliance itself was incomplete and partial; senatorial envoys had hemmed and hawed, their adjudication ambivalent and tentative; and the *patres* proved more interested in appeasing all sides than in ramming through a settlement.[148] Similarly, as we have seen, the judgments delivered by a special board of senators on the Achaean-Spartan imbroglio in 184 derived more from exasperation than zeal, and issued in bland compromises.[149] On those few occasions when Rome did vigorously endorse the claims of certain appellants, she preferred to arouse Greek states in support of them rather than to bother about enforcement herself, as in the case of a pro-Roman Boeotian in 187/6, Callicrates and the Lacedaemonian exiles in 180, Ptolemy Euergetes in 154, Attalus in 154, and Alexander Balas in 153.[150] The senate acknowledged the autonomy of the Galatians in 166; of Timarchus the satrap of Media in 162/1; of the Jews, with whom they even made alliance, in 161. Empty gestures in each instance; Rome did little to implement those pronouncements and generally allowed matters to take their own course.[151] The senate, in fact, proved more assertive in meeting Greek complaints about Roman officials abroad than in paying heed to their grievances against one another.[152] At the level of state policy meddlesomeness was frowned

148. Polyb. 22.6, 22.11.1–4, 22.13–14, 23.1–3, 23.7–8, 23.9.4–7; Livy, 39.24.1–39.29.3, 39.33.1–4, 39.34.1–39.35.4, 39.46.6–39.47.11, 39.5.3, 40.3; Diod. 29.16; Appian, *Mac.* 9.6. A more extensive discussion, with references to the scholarship, in Gruen, *GRBS* 15 (1974): 226–239.

149. See above pp. 121–122.

150. The Boeotian: Polyb. 22.4.9; Callicrates and the exiles: Polyb. 24.10.6–7; Paus. 7.9.6; Ptolemy Euergetes: Polyb. 33.11.5–7; Attalus: Polyb. 33.12.7–9; Alexander Balas: Polyb. 33.18.11–14.

151. The Galatians: Polyb. 30.28, 30.30.6; Timarchus: Diod. 31.27a; Appian, *Syr.* 47; the Jews: 1 Macc. 8:17–32; Jos. *Ant.* 12.415–419. On the latter two examples, see Gruen, *Chiron* 6 (1976): 85–87.

152. As is illustrated by the protests of Hellenic states against depredations by

upon. Even when the *curia* or its representatives did emit decisions of some clarity, they were tardy, jejune, or left for others to execute.

Investigation

The number of Roman missions to the East would itself seem to be a fact of some significance. Hardly a year went by without some delegation, occasionally more than one, appearing in Hellas, Macedonia, or Hellenic Asia. Roman envoys became a familiar sight at the courts of kings and the assemblies of republics or federations. To what end? Did the practice serve to hold Greeks in check, entrench Roman dominance, and dictate the orders of the western power?

In fact, as has been observed in example after example, these visits came at the behest of Greek applicants, not as part of a Roman design. And what needs further to be observed is how frequently the task of the *legati* amounted to nothing more than an inquiry into the state of affairs, with no directives to deliver and no results to show.

Time and again Romans were asked to intervene but went only to investigate. The conflict between Eumenes and Pharnaces may be taken as typical. After hearing grievances on both sides in 183/2, the senate dispatched an embassy to "look into" the situation. Its report favored Eumenes, but the *patres* declined to act; instead, a new embassy in 182/1 went to "look into the controversy more diligently." Meanwhile hostilities continued and expanded, followed by additional appeals and still another Roman mission in 181/0 to urge a reconciliation. This one was no more effective than its predecessors, gave it all up, and came home. Three years of ambassadorial visits and a record of futility: the senate had merely gone through the motions.[153] No different was the delegation sent to Macedonia ca. 175 at request of the Thessalians and Dardanians to "see for themselves." They duly reported a war in Dardania, but the senate heard Perseus' explanation and dropped the matter.[154] The next year another set of envoys traveled to Macedonia in order to investigate rumors that Perseus was intriguing with Carthage; they never got to see the king and came back with nothing accomplished.[155] In 165 Ti. Gracchus toured the East as the senate's envoy, stopping in at the courts of Pergamum

---

Rome's commanders during the Third Macedonian War. The *patres* reacted strongly to check those abuses: Livy, 43.4, 43.6.1–3, 43.7.5–43.8.10. A similar response to complaints from Alpine peoples: Livy, 43.5.

153. Polyb. 23.9.1–3, 24.1.2–3, 24.5, 24.14–15; Livy, 40.2.6–8, 40.20.1; Diod. 29.22.

154. Polyb. 25.6.2–6; Livy, 41.19.3–6; Appian, *Mac.* 11.1.

155. Livy, 41.22.1–3, 42.2.1.

and Cappadocia, in the Seleucid realm, and in the island of Rhodes. Everyone proved most affable and Gracchus returned with cheerful reports on all concerned. Thus the senate had, in advance, cut the ground out from several complainants who had hoped for Roman intervention.[156]

The presentation of claims continued, however, especially from Prusias of Bithynia, relentless in his efforts to steal a march on Eumenes by prodding Rome into action. In 164, the embassy of C. Sulpicius Gallus and M'. Sergius left for the East—if Polybius' language is accurate—with an unusual task: they were to "meddle" in the affairs of Pergamum and Syria.[157] Does this represent a change of tone and a more vigorous Roman interference abroad? Sulpicius indeed established himself at Sardis and invited everyone with grievances against Eumenes to beat a path to his door.[158] But the episode need not betoken a new thrust toward Roman domineering in Asia. The procedure itself had precedents. In 186/5 the senate's representatives called upon all those who had a bill of particulars against Philip to meet them at Tempe.[159] Sulpicius' bullying tactics may be more a matter of personality than state policy. Polybius found him an objectionable and obnoxious character, a man who consorted with the historian's *bête noir* Callicrates.[160] The Polybian account is slanted and colored: Sulpicius eagerly embraced any malicious slander against the king to advance his own private quarrel.[161] That assessment does not warrant implicit confidence. The legate, in fact, appointed a specific date by which complaints had to be brought. After that, no other charge would be admitted. Sulpicius did not plan a long stay: for ten days he heard applicants and then left.[162] He set up no permanent office and intended no fostering of recurrent accusations. On the contrary. Announcement of a deadline and the brief visit indicate a desire to get all the complaints over with at a shot, thus not to be bothered with them again. Nothing suggests that Rome ever acted on any of these indictments. Sulpicius' demeanor at Sardis seems more intent upon clearing the book of charges than of seeing them through. As for "meddling" in Syria, we do not even know that the embassy got that far, let alone that it achieved anything.

A mission to the East in 163, headed by Cn. Octavius, appears to

---

156. Polyb. 30.27, 30.30, 30.31.19–20, 31.3; Diod. 31.17, 31.28; cf. Livy, *Per.* 46.

157. Polyb. 31.1.6–8: μάλιστα δὲ πολυπραγμονήσοντας τὰ κατὰ τὸν Ἀντίοχον καὶ τὰ κατὰ τὸν Εὐμένη.

158. Polyb. 31.6.1–5.   159. Polyb. 22.6.5.   160. Cf. Paus. 7.11.1–3.

161. Polyb. 31.6.4–5: πᾶσαν ἐπιδεχόμενος αἰσχρολογίαν καὶ λοιδορίαν κατὰ τοῦ βασιλέως καὶ καθόλου πᾶν ἕλκων πρᾶγμα καὶ κατηγορίαν, ἅτε παρεστηκὼς ἄνθρωπος τῇ διανοίᾳ καὶ φιλοδοξῶν ἐν τῇ πρὸς Εὐμένην διαφορᾷ.

162. Polyb. 31.6.2–3.

have had a broader mandate. It was instructed to "examine" the *stasis* in Macedonia, to "look into" the situations in Galatia and Cappadocia, and to "reconcile" the rival kings in Alexandria—all quite conventional orders that committed Rome to nothing and, in fact, brought no discernible changes.[163] But the senate also directed these *legati* to "arrange" the affairs of Syria in accordance with senatorial wishes.[164] The commission included burning of the Seleucid navy, crippling of the elephants, and a general impairment of the regime's authority.[165] What is one to make of it? The facts cannot be explained away. Yet to regard the behavior as exemplary of Roman policy in the East is way off the mark. In fact, it is a unique exception, unparalleled at this time, perhaps due to a temporary outburst by angry senators or by the legates themselves. More to the point is the outcome of this episode. The Syrians reacted with violence: Octavius himself was slain. No one made any secret of the deed and some praised it openly. When envoys reached Rome to explain matters, the senate showed not the slightest concern. Even the murderer appeared before the *curia* to justify his actions and got off scot-free. Octavius had been buried and forgotten; his behavior received not even a posthumous defense.[166] Business as usual resumed in the diplomatic sphere. The ubiquitous Ti. Gracchus was off to the East again in 162 on another mission of "inquiry," visiting various kings and states of Greece and Asia Minor. He could be relied on to find no trouble and to justify the *status quo*—which he did.[167] That is what the *patres* wanted to hear.

The practice of dispatching envoys to inquire, investigate, and observe became standard procedure.[168] It gave the appearance of interest without the drawback of involvement. Trips abroad assumed the regularity of an annual ritual. Greeks took comfort in the fact that their claims received attention and took hope in the possibility that the very presence of Roman officials might advance their individual causes. The senate, for its part, could ignore belligerent reports, dis-

---

163. Polyb. 31.2.12–14: τὰ κατὰ τὴν Μακεδονίαν ἐπισκέψασθαι . . . τὰ περὶ τοὺς Γαλάτας καὶ τὰ κατὰ τὴν Ἀριαράθου βασιλείαν ἐποπτεῦσαι . . . καὶ τοὺς ἐν Ἀλεξανδρείᾳ βασιλεῖς διαλῦσαι κατὰ δύναμιν; 31.8.4–8.

164. Polyb. 31.2.9–10: τοὺς διοικήσοντας τὰ κατὰ τὴν βασιλείαν ὡς αὐτὴ προῃρεῖτο.

165. Polyb. 31.2.11; Appian, *Syr.* 46; Zon. 9.25.

166. Polyb. 31.11.1–3, 31.33.5, 32.2.1–32.3.11; Diod. 31.29; Appian, *Syr.* 46–47; Zon. 9.25; cf. the discussion in Gruen, *Chiron* 6 (1976): 81–84.

167. Polyb. 31.15.9–10, 31.32.3, 31.33.1–4; Diod. 31.28.

168. Other instances could readily be cited. Cf. the mission to Epirus in 158, Polyb. 32.6.8: ἐπισκέψασθαι περὶ τῶν γεγονότων. And another to Asia Minor in 156/5, Polyb. 32.16.5: τοὺς ἐπισκεψομένους πῶς ἔχει τὰ κατὰ τοὺς προειρημένους βασιλεῖς (Attalus and Prusias).

claim embarrassing behavior by its legates, and welcome endorsements of the *status quo*. "Investigatory" commissions proved eminently convenient: a courtesy to appellants without a commitment for Rome.

V

An unmistakable pattern emerges from this survey. The great wars against Philip, Antiochus, and Perseus gave Rome untrammeled authority to prescribe the fate of the East. The Greeks, at least, drew that conclusion or fostered that understanding. Issues once decided by Hellenistic princes and neutral tribunals were regularly dumped in the lap of the Roman senate. A wearisome procession of embassies unburdened grievances in Rome, forcing attention upon Hellenic feuds, territorial rivalries, and border warfare. Rome could adjudicate at will, as the supreme court of the Mediterranean world, if so she chose.

She did not so choose. Greeks sought out the senate to render decisions and sit in judgment; Roman legates they described as judges, the senate as a court of appeal.[169] But Romans cast off the judicial robes. While the Greeks endeavored to set her in the center of their own system of interstate arbitration, Rome cultivated the system while removing herself. Just as she adopted Hellenic treaty forms, diplomatic discourse, and propaganda, so she embraced the principle of arbitration. But she would not be the arbiter. The *patres* heard grievances politely, rendered verdicts only rarely. Roman representatives made token appearances in the East, senatorial rulings were hesitant or innocuous, leaving matters unresolved, following the lead of Greek arbiters, or placing decisions in their hands. Romans found the Hellenic institution congenial and took it at face value. Disputes arising out of territorial claims, property rights, boundary demarcations, and repayment of damages should be settled by Hellenic tribunals. The Republic inscribed that principle into the peace of Apamea, promoted

169. Cf. the Pergamene request to Roman envoys in Asia Minor in 180 to be "fair and impartial judges", Polyb. 24.15.3: αὐτοὺς γενέσθαι κριτὰς τῶν πραγμάτων ἴσους καὶ δικαίους. The envoys, however, had instructions only to make peace and, when that proved impossible, abandoned their mission: Polyb. 24.15.1, 24.15.5, 24.15.9–12. The Dolopians in 174 looked to Rome as a court of appeal to adjudicate their differences with Perseus: Livy, 41.22.4: *de quibus ambigebatur rebus disceptationem ab rege ad Romanos revocabant*; 41.23.13. But the senate paid no heed and Perseus went on to crush the Dolopians with impunity: Livy, 41.22.4, 41.23.13, 41.24.8, 42.13.8, 42.41.13; Appian, *Mac.* 11.6. The Romans do not even cite this among the complaints against Perseus in their letter to Delphi of 171 or 170; *Syll.*[3] 643 = Sherk, *RDGE*, no. 40. Pomtow restored Δόλοπες in line 19, but Colin, more prudently, omits them; see Sherk, *loc. cit.*

the authority of Greek courts, and repeatedly consigned appeals to Greek jurisdiction. Hence international arbitration entered into its most flourishing period, with Roman encouragement and without Roman control.

Of greater consequence were issues that went beyond mere disagreements over boundaries or rights of possession: the attempts to engage Roman power in order to overawe rivals, take sides in armed conflict, and compel adherence or submission. A continuous parade of applicants delivered their petitions to the senate, subjecting the *patres* to plaintive pleas or subtle rhetoric. Yet Rome stubbornly resisted the role which Greeks foisted upon her. The senate found means to keep faith with allies and friends, while keeping involvement and commitments to a minimum. Roman envoys made repeated trips abroad, giving the appearance of interest and paying lip service to Hellenic complaints. Seldom could they boast of tangible accomplishments. The legates generally promoted reconciliation rather than forcible intervention; if efforts proved unavailing, the matter was dropped. Or else they went simply to inquire and investigate—a mode of postponement and an excuse for inaction. When their representatives hectored or bullied, the senate could always disclaim responsibility or send gentler successors; when they brought favorable reports, the *patres* adopted them with alacrity. Senatorial resolutions showed a decided preference for compromise, mild reproof, and ambiguities that left the Greeks to find their own solutions.[170]

170. A close parallel exists in Rome's treatment of the recurrent and troublesome disputes between Numidia and Carthage in the first half of the second century. Again and again the senate chose to leave matters hanging rather than to impose a settlement. Roman envoys were in Carthage to adjudicate differences between Massinissa and the Carthaginians in 195; no decision is recorded: Livy, 33.47.8; cf. 33.49.1–4; Nepos, *Hann.* 7.6–7; Justin, 31.2.1–8. Both sides brought renewed complaints to Rome in 193 and the senate responded with an embassy that included Scipio Africanus; but the envoys ventured no opinion and left the issue undecided: Livy, 34.62.4–18; Zon. 9.18; Appian, *Lib.* 67; cf. Polyb. 31.21.1–5. Roman representatives visited Africa again in 182 to hear the rival claims over possession of disputed land; they found for neither side, simply accepted the *status quo*, and referred the question back to the senate: Livy, 40.17.1–6; Appian, *Lib.* 68. The senate's policy was to keep the peace: Livy, 40.34.14; Appian, *Lib.* 68. More aggression by Numidia followed in the next decade and Carthaginian envoys in Rome begged the senate in 172 to establish firm frontiers once and for all. The *patres* again opted for evasion, endorsing the claims of neither side, and announcing that they "would not set new boundaries but adhere to the old"—whatever they were: Livy, 42.23–24; cf. Appian, *Lib.* 68. Even in the years leading to the Third Punic War Roman investigative embassies went back and forth between Italy and Africa, advocating peaceful solutions and bringing back alarming reports, while the senate debated and procrastinated: Livy, *Per.* 47–49; Appian, *Lib.* 69–72; Zon. 9.26; cf. Plut. *Cato*, 26–27. Polybius' opinion, 31.21.5–6, that Roman decisions always favored Massinissa during this period, does not meet all the facts. Rome rarely rendered decisions. And his asser-

Victory in war bestowed the privilege of domination. Rome neither seized nor capitalized upon it. Despite endless appeals, requests, and prodding, the western power paid scant attention to the interstate conflicts of Hellas. Her attitudes toward them were scarcely different ca. 150 from what they had been a half-century earlier. She would observe when asked, occasionally rebuke, take a stand—if at all—only in vague and noncommittal language, and propose conciliation. She did not deliver dictates or enforce pronouncements. She sustained rather than manipulated or subverted Greek institutions. And she preferred that Greeks compose their own quarrels. It was less a matter of altruism or philhellenism than of disinclination. Rome did not aspire to be arbiter and judge of Greek affairs.

---

tion that Rome awaited only a pretext to bring war on Carthage, 36.2.1, is a retrospective judgment; cf. Appian, *Lib.* 69. Modern literature is too much influenced by the Polybian opinion; cf. P. G. Walsh, *JRS* 55 (1965): 149–160. The argument of M. Lemosse, *Gedachtnisschrift für Rudolf Schmidt* (1966), 341–348, that Rome's handling of the African dispute contrasted with her recognition of impartial arbitration in the Greek world, misses all the parallels.

• Chapter 4 •

Slogans and Propaganda:
The "Freedom of the Greeks"

The Isthmian Games of 196 served as setting for a dramatic announcement that stunned the Greek world into disbelief and then joyous celebration. Rome's proconsul T. Flamininus, the conqueror of Philip V, read out a momentous proclamation: the Greeks were to be free, ungarrisoned, subject to no tribute, and at liberty to govern themselves in accordance with their own ancestral laws.[1] A spectacular scene ensued and the echoes of this report reverberated through Greece and Asia. The "freedom of the Greeks" became a repeated slogan in the diplomacy of subsequent years. Wherein lay its origins? Was this another cunning Roman device, a contrived pose formed to lend an air of legitimacy to the assumption of a *patrocinium*?

Lengthy modern debate focuses on the proclamation. Greek precedents have been discerned and a Hellenic background recognized as paramount.[2] But the argument rests primarily on distant models: the King's Peace of 386 and the ἐλευθερία propaganda of Alexander's successors in the late fourth century. Hence, it is easy to puncture that theory: how well versed would Roman statesmen have been in the obscurities of remote Greek history? And how likely that they would utilize long discredited models as a foundation for their foreign policy in 196?[3] The rhetorical questions have obvious answers. The alternative hypothesis, that this approach grew directly out of Ro-

---

1. Polyb. 18.46.5: ἐλευθέρους, ἀφρουρήτους, ἀφορολογήτους, νόμοις χρωμένους τοῖς πατρίοις; 18.46.15; Livy, 33.32.5: *liberos, immunes, suis legibus esse*; 33.33.5–7, 34.41.3, 39.37.10; Plut. *Flam.* 10.4, 12.2; Appian, *Mac.* 9.4.

2. E.g., Täubler, *Imperium Romanum* I:434–436; Sherwin-White, *Roman Citizenship*, 175–176; Petzold, *Die Eröffnung*, 37.

3. Cf. Heuss, *Völkerrechtliche Grundlagen*, 95–96, n. 1; Badian, *Foreign Clientelae*, 73–75.

man practice and experience, depends, however, on surmise and speculation. No comparable proclamation is discoverable in Rome's history.

A different and more thorough investigation would be helpful. It can be shown that declarations of "freedom," in one form or another, play a persistent role in international affairs through the whole of the Hellenistic era.[4] When Rome first moved into Greece such declarations were common and frequent—far from a distant memory or an obsolete archaism.

The Hellenistic Background

The prevalence of this practice in the late third century is remarked on by Polybius. For the historian, it is a sham and a mockery, a screen to disarm the unsuspecting and permit monarchs to solidify their rule. The actions of Philip V served as target for Polybius' cynicism. But his comments are generalized and bitter: all kings mouth platitudes about "freedom" at the beginning of their reigns, but later tyrannize over those who believed them.[5] Similar remarks are put by Polybius into the mouth of an Aetolian seeking Sparta's aid against Macedonia in 211: a vehement mocking of Antigonus Doson's professed "freeing" of Sparta a decade earlier.[6] In his own voice the historian challenges the idea that Thessaly is permitted to govern itself under its own laws; in fact, the Thessalians are as subject to the Macedonian monarchy as are the Macedonians themselves.[7] Any state, so another Polybian speaker asserted, that summons rescue from an outside power may escape danger from its enemies but falls into the power of its "liberator."[8] The validity of these generalizations need not here be subjected to scrutiny.[9] They attest in any case to the

4. Most useful discussion, with some but not all the evidence, in Heuss, *Stadt und Herrscher*, 216–244. Cf. also Bernhardt, *Imperium und Eleutheria*, 4–18. More briefly, Magie, *RRAM* II:825–829; A. H. M. Jones, *The Greek City* (Oxford, 1940), 95–102; A. Mastrocinque, *AttiIstVeneto* 135 (1976–77):1–23.

5. Polyb. 15.24.4: πάντες οἱ βασιλεῖς κατὰ τὰς πρώτας ἀρχὰς πᾶσι προτείνουσι τὸ τῆς ἐλευθερίας ὄνομα . . . καθικόμενοι δὲ τῶν πράξεων παρὰ πόδας οὐ συμμαχικῶς, ἀλλὰ δεσποτικῶς χρῶνται τοῖς πιστεύσασι; see K.-W. Welwei, *Könige und Königtum im Urteil des Polybios* (Köln, 1963), 45–47. Cf. the even broader cynicism, much later, of Tacitus: the specious pretext of bringing *libertas* is common coin for those who seek to enslave and dominate others, *Hist.* 4.73.3: *ceterum libertas et speciosa nomina praetexuntur, nec quisquam alienum servitium et dominationem sibi concupivit, ut non eadem ista vocabula usurparet*—with regard to the Germans!

6. Polyb. 9.31.4: τῆς πολυθρυλήτου ταύτης ἐλευθερίας καὶ σωτηρίας, ἣν οὗτοι παρ' ἕκαστον ὑμῖν ὀνειδίζουσι.

7. Polyb. 4.76.2

8. Polyb. 9.37.9.

9. Cf. Heuss, *Stadt und Herrscher*, 235–236.

widespread professions of "liberators" in Greece in the years just prior to Rome's appearance in that theater.

Announcements of freedom for Greek states were particularly prominent in the generation that followed the death of Alexander the Great. They supplied convenient propaganda for various leaders and princes in the bewildering struggles for power that marked that turbulent era.[10] The round of proclamations began apparently in 319/318. Polyperchon, regent for the young Macedonian kings, recognized the value of Greek support in his contest with Cassander and Antigonus Monophthalmus. In the name of the kings, Polyperchon issued an edict to be distributed throughout Greece. The decree restored to all Greeks the constitutions which they had enjoyed in the days of Philip II and Alexander. In practical terms, that meant the overthrow of oligarchies instituted by Antipater. For Polyperchon and his propagandists, it was equivalent to "liberation" and "autonomy."[11] The policy had immediate effects. Polyperchon's decree found reflection in Athens, a temporary beneficiary, in reference to the city's escape from oligarchy and return to "the laws and democracy."[12]

Three years later a greater man than Polyperchon took up the principle and extended it with dramatic impact. Antigonus Monophthalmus, previously an opponent of Polyperchon, came to accord with him and created a new coalition against Cassander. In 315 Antigonus took a leaf from his erstwhile enemy's book: all Greeks were to be free, ungarrisoned, and autonomous.[13] The purpose was clear, set forth in undisguised candor by Diodorus: an effort to win Greek support, in expectation of ἐλευθερία, for his military efforts.[14] Personal motives aside, the logic of his propaganda induced Antigonus to carry the banner of Greek freedom through the next several years. Alexander, son of Polyperchon and now ally of Antigonus, traveled through the Peloponnese and assaulted the strongholds of Cassander in the name of freedom.[15] The same slogan was advanced by Antigo-

10. Cf. H. Braunert, *Historia* 13 (1964):82–91.

11. Diod. 18.55–57. See, especially, Diod. 18.55.2: τὰς μὲν κατὰ τὴν Ἑλλάδα πόλεις ἐλευθεροῦν τὰς δ'ἐν αὐταῖς ὀλιγαρχίας καθεσταμένας ὑπ' Ἀντιπάτρου καταλύειν. And cf. Diod. 18.69.3: ἐξέπεμψε [Polyperchon] δὲ καὶ πρὸς τὰς πόλεις πρεσβευτάς, προστάττων τοὺς μὲν δι᾽Ἀντιπάτρου καθεσταμένους ἄρχοντας ἐπὶ τῆς ὀλιγαρχίας θανατῶσαι, τοῖς δὲ δήμοις ἀποδοῦναι τὴν αὐτονομίαν. That Polyperchon had no genuine zeal for Greek liberty need hardly be argued; cf. C. Wehrli, *Antigone et Démétrios* (Geneva, 1968), 107–108.

12. *Syll.*³ 317, lines 25–31. Athens had been uppermost in Polyperchon's mind: Diod. 18.56.6–7.

13. Diod. 19.61.3: τοὺς Ἕλληνας ἅπαντας ἐλευθέρους, ἀφρουρητούς, αὐτονόμους.

14. Diod. 19.61.4: τοὺς μὲν γὰρ Ἕλληνας ὑπελάμβανε διὰ τὴν ἐλπίδα τῆς ἐλευθερίας προθύμους ἕξειν συναγωνιστὰς εἰς τὸν πόλεμον.

15. Diod. 19.64.2.

nus' generals in their Greek campaigns of 314 to 312.[16] Antigonus utilized it as well in Asia Minor. The Carian dynast Asander agreed to terms that included leaving the Greek cities autonomous. When he reneged on those terms Antigonus took firm action, culminated by the liberation of Miletus.[17] Judgment on his sincerity is beside the point; the policy was comprehensive and effective.[18] Imitation is the best mirror of success. The shrewd Ptolemy I copied Antigonus' design in 315, issuing a proclamation of his own on Greek freedom, lest it be thought that he was any less zealous in the matter than Antigonus.[19]

The famed pact of 311 set the seal on this development. The major contenders of the past decade, Antigonus, Ptolemy, Cassander, and Lysimachus, publicly laid aside enmities, announced peace, agreement, and the division of Alexander's empire. Enshrined in the covenant was a joint announcement that the Greeks be free and autonomous. Its chief perpetrator Antigonus made certain to underline the message in personal letters to Greek cities everywhere.[20] Precise definition of "freedom" and "autonomy" was, of course, avoided. Few rational men would have regarded this move as betokening genuine independence for the smaller states of Greece. The agreement

16. Diod. 19.66.3, 19.74.1, 19.77.2, 19.78.2, 19.78.5, 19.87.3. Cf. *AthMitt* 67 (1942):258–260 = *ISE*, no. 71. Athens too was induced to send private messages to Antigonus urging him to free the city: Diod. 19.78.4. The indiscriminate use of the terms ἐλευθερία and αὐτονομία shows that there is little point in the modern effort to discern fine and precise differences in their meanings here; a recent effort by Mastrocinque, *AttiIstVeneto* 135 (1976–77):3–5, 9–11. Cf. Diod. 19.74.1: τὰς πόλεις ἐλευθεροῦν ἐνετείλατο· τοῦτο γὰρ πράξας ἤλπιζε πίστιν κατασκευάζειν παρὰ τοῖς Ἕλλησιν ὅτι πρὸς ἀλήθειαν φροντίζει τῆς αὐτονομίας αὐτῶν.

17. Diod. 19.75.1, 19.75.3–4; *Milet* I:123 = *Syll.*[3] 322, lines 2–4: ἡ πόλις ἐλευθέρα καὶ αὐτόνομος ἐγένετο ὑπὸ Ἀντιγόνου καὶ ἡ δημοκρατία ἀπεδόθη.

18. On Antigonus' policy, generally, the literature is extensive and requires no recapitulation here. Cf., e.g., Heuss, *Hermes* 73 (1938):133–194, R. H. Simpson, *Historia* 8 (1959):385–409; Wehrli, *Antigone et Démétrios*, 110–113; O. Müller, *Antigonos Monophthalmos und "das Jahr der Könige"* (Bonn, 1973), 32–39.

19. Diod. 19.62.1: περὶ τῆς τῶν Ἑλλήνων ἐλευθερίας ἔγραψε καὶ αὐτὸς τὰ παραπλήσια, βουλόμενος εἰδέναι τοὺς Ἕλληνας ὅτι φροντίζει τῆς αὐτονομίας αὐτῶν οὐχ ἧττον Ἀντιγόνου. The posture is suggested by the image of Athena Promachos on Ptolemaic coinage between 315 and 310, in the opinion of C. M. Havelock, *AJA* 84 (1980):41–50—a far-fetched hypothesis.

20. One such letter is preserved, to the city of Scepsis: *OGIS*, 5 = Welles, *RC*, no. 1 = Schmitt, *Staatsverträge*, no. 428, lines 1–2, 53–61. But Antigonus wrote everywhere, as the letter makes clear: lines 24–26. Note again the juxtaposition, without clear differentiation, of ἐλευθερία and αὐτονομία: lines 54–56. Diodorus twice refers to the pact, once in terms of αὐτονομία, once of ἐλευθερία: Diod. 19.105.1, 20.19.3. Most important bibliography on the peace of 311 is cited by Schmitt, *Staatsverträge*, no. 44; add Müller, *Antigonos*, 39–44. A decree of Scepsis acknowledges the freedom and autonomy guaranteed by the peace and sets up cult honors for Antigonus: *OGIS*, 6, lines 9–10, 15–17; cf. Habicht, *Gottmenschentum und griechische Städte* (2nd ed., Munich, 1970), 42–44.

itself was short-lived, shattered by the ambitions of the dynasts. Nonetheless, each of them continued to employ the conventional catchwords in order to outbid rivals and pose as a liberator of Greece. So Ptolemy and Demetrius Poliorcetes, son of Antigonus, agreed to a φιλία and a defensive alliance, possibly in 309/8, for the purpose of "liberating all of Greece."[21] Ptolemy maintained the posture in 308, trumpeting his designs in order to gain Greek good will; but, when resistance emerged to his empty promises, he dropped the mask, linked himself with Cassander, and installed garrisons in the Peloponnese.[22] Demetrius, carrying on the propaganda of his father, milked it for all it was worth. The renewed and lengthy conflict against Cassander saw its use again and again. Demetrius set sail in 307 with instructions from Antigonus to liberate all Greek cities. The pronouncement was implemented at, among other places, Athens, Megara, Chalcis, Sicyon, Corinth, Bura in Achaea, Larisa, and Pherae in the next several years.[23]

Of course, liberation of towns from Cassander's garrisons was perfectly consistent with the installation of Demetrius' own garrisons for the "protection" of the liberated. That practice in no way compromised the propaganda—whatever the "freed" communities may have thought.[24] Demetrius' lifting of the siege of Rhodes in 304 was also accompanied by acknowledgment that the city be autonomous, ungarrisoned, and in control of its own revenues.[25] Even his temporary truce with Cassander in 302 included the by now conventional phrase that "all Hellenic cities are to be free," not only in Greece proper but in Asia as well.[26] Antigonus, in control of Asia during these years, could

---

21. Suda, s.v. Δημήτριος: ἐπ᾽ ἐλευθερώσει τῆς πάσης Ἑλλάδος; cf. Schmitt, *Staatsverträge*, no. 433. Note the recently published inscriptions from Iasus, probably from these years, giving Ptolemaic guarantees that Iasus is to be free, autonomous, ungarrisoned, and untaxed—the full formula. G. P. Caratelli, *Annuario* 45–46 (1967–68):438–439, 1A, lines 30–31, 50–51; 1B, lines 8–9, 18–19, 29. Republished with new readings by Y. Garlan, *ZPE* 18 (1975):193–198.

22. Diod. 20.37.2.

23. Diod. 20.45.1, 20.46.1–3; Plut. *Dem.* 8.5; *Hesperia* 17 (1948):114–136 = *ISE*, no. 5, lines 5–9; *Syll.*[3] 342, lines 14–16 (Athens); Diod. 20.46.3 (Megara); 20.100.6 (Chalcis); 20.102.2 (Sicyon); 20.103.3 (Corinth); 20.103.4 (Bura); 20.110.2 (Larisa); 20.110.6 (Pherae). General declarations of autonomy by Demetrius: Diod. 20.45.1, 20.93.7, 20.100.6, 20.102.1. On his campaigns and pronouncements, see also Plut. *Dem.* 8–9.

24. Cf. Diod. 20.103.3. As to what they did think, cf. the voluntary withdrawals of garrisons at Chalcis and Eretria in 308, celebrated by inhabitants as ἐλευθερία: *Syll.*[3] 328, lines 3–7; *Syll.*[3] 323, lines 3–5. On the date and circumstances, Holleaux, *Études* I:41–73. Other evidence on garrisons collected in Jones, *The Greek City*, 316, n. 13.

25. Diod. 20.99.3.

26. Diod. 20.111.2; cf. 20.110.6.

securely mouth the phrases in his dealings with individual communities. He was recognized as master but continued to speak in terms of ἐλευθερία, as is clear, for example, from a decree of Colophon, ca. 311–306, and from his own letter to Teos, ca. 306–302.[27] The lesson was not lost on Lysimachus who, while contending with Antigonus for supremacy in Asia in 302, exploited the same slogans. Major cities that fell into his hands, like Lampsacus, Priene, and Ephesus, were "left free."[28] There is no doubt that when Antigonus and Demetrius created a new Hellenic League under their own leadership in 302 they included solemn guarantees of Greek autonomy.[29] That line was well established by the end of the fourth century.

Our information falls off sharply after 301, with the loss of Diodorus' continuous narrative. But enough evidence survives from epigraphic sources, however sporadic, to show that pronouncements of "freedom" continued through the third century.

The plight of cities, bounced about like footballs from one dynast to another in the era of the *epigonoi*, is well known. With each transfer of power, however, the new status is customarily and hypocritically referred to as ἐλευθερία. Athens is an obvious example. She was freed from Cassander's stranglehold by Demetrius and Antigonus in 307 and welcomed her liberators with elaborate honors.[30] Loyalty, however, endured only as long as Demetrius' power. After the battle of Ipsus in 301 the Athenians broke with their "liberator"; the new regime was backed by Lysimachus, who could later be described as promoting Athens' "freedom."[31] That too did not last long. Internal dissension in Athens gave Demetrius another opportunity. In the mid-290s he assaulted the city, once again in the guise of liberator.[32] Athens resisted stubbornly but to no avail. When rescue failed to

27. Colophon: *AJP* 56 (1935):361, no. 1, lines 6–8; cf. Robert, *RPh* 10 (1936): 158–161. Teos: *Syll.*³ 344 = Welles, *RC*, no. 3, lines 88–90. Cf. also a decree of the *synedroi* of the Troad federation ca. 306; *Syll.*³ 330, lines 24–25. And see *IG*, XII, Suppl. 168, lines 2–4 (Ios, perhaps 306–301).

28. Diod. 20.107.2, 20.107.4. Others who resisted, like Sigeum, of course got garrisons: Diod. 20.107.2.

29. Such phrases do not appear in the lengthy decree from Epidaurus setting forth the regulations of the League. But much is missing from the preserved fragments and there can be little question that references to freedom and autonomy were in the original text—if only to contrast Antigonid policy with that of Cassander: *IG*, IV², 1, 68 = *ISE*, no. 44 = Schmitt, *Staatsverträge*, no. 446; cf. Plut. *Dem*. 25.4. Modern bibliography in Schmitt, *op. cit.*, 80.

30. Diod. 20.46.1–3; Plut. *Dem*. 8–9; cf. Habicht, *Gottmenschentum*, 44–48.

31. *Syll.*³ 374, lines 10–14, 30–35—a decree of 283/2 honoring the poet Philippides, a favorite of Lysimachus, for, among other things, persuading the king to assist Athens after Ipsus.

32. Cf. Polyaen. 4.7.5.

materialize Demetrius reestablished control, with little concern for Athenian autonomy or democracy; he nevertheless received fawning adulation.[33] Turnabout came once more ca. 287 as Demetrius' power waned in the Mediterranean and Athens released herself from his grip. One Athenian general, honored later for the event, gained credit for giving his successors a city "free, under democratic government, autonomous, and with its laws intact."[34] The *demos* similarly paid tribute to Audoleon, king of the Paeonians, who had furnished assistance leading to the "freedom" of the city.[35] The Athenian experience, by no means unique, demonstrates the ease with which this terminology was thrown about. Removal of one overlord through the assistance of another was conventionally greeted as the restoration of liberty.[36] A commonplace, but a persistent one.

Monarchs and princes of the mid-third century propounded this verbiage with monotonous regularity. Ptolemy II Philadelphus gained control of the Nesiotic League after the fall of Demetrius in the 280s. In a celebrated decree to the islanders he reaffirmed his father's generosity. The latter had been a great benefactor, so it is claimed: he freed Greek cities and restored to them their laws and ancestral constitutions.[37] Fifteen years later, Philadelphus backed the coalition of Sparta and Athens in their revolt against Antigonus Gonatas, the so-called Chremonidean War. Once more the same slogans applied: the effort was on behalf of Greek liberty, to restore rightful laws and constitutions.[38] In Crete the Ptolemies dressed up their suzerainty with simi-

33. Plut. *Dem.* 34.1–5. Cf. *AthMitt* 66 (1941): 221–227 = *ISE*, no. 7, an Athenian decree, perhaps of 294, honoring Demetrius for freeing Athens and the rest of Greece—if the restorations be correct: lines 3–4, 9–10. This may, however, belong to 303/2.

34. *Syll.*[3] 409, lines 38–39: τὴν πόλιν ἐλευθέραν καὶ δημοκρατουμένην αὐτόνομον παρέδωκεν καὶ τοὺς νόμους κυρίους. The decree honors Phaedrus, on whom see J. K. Davies, *Athenian Propertied Families* (Oxford, 1971), 526–527. On the circumstances, see now Habicht, *Untersuchungen zur politischen Geschichte Athens im 3. Jahrhundert v. Chr.* (Munich, 1979), 52–62, as against T. L. Shear, Jr., *Kallias of Sphettos and the Revolt of Athens in 286 B.C.* (*Hesperia*, Supplement 17, 1978), 65–73. Cf. also M. J. Osborne, *ZPE* 35 (1979): 181–194.

35. *Syll.*[3] 371, line 15. On Athenian history between Ipsus and 287, see W. S. Ferguson, *Hellenistic Athens* (London, 1911), 122–151; Habicht, *Untersuchungen*, 1–67.

36. Cf. the third-century decree of Troezen alluding to the recovery of her "ancient laws": *SEG*, XIII, 341 = *ISE*, no. 62, lines 5–6. The precise occasion is unknown.

37. *Syll.*[3] 390, lines 12–15: τάς τε πόλεις ἐλευθερώσας καὶ τοὺς νόμους ἀποδοὺς [κ]αὶ τὴμ πάτριαμ πολιτείαμ πᾶσιν καταστήσα[ς].

38. *Syll.*[3] 434 = Schmitt, *Staatsverträge*, no. 476, lines 13–18: καὶ νῦν δὲ κ[α]ιρῶν καθειληφότων ὁμοίων τὴν Ἑλλάδα πᾶσαν διὰ το[ὺς κ]αταλύειν ἐπιχειροῦντας τούς τε νόμους καὶ τὰς πατρίους ἑκάστοις πολιτείας ὅ τε βασιλεὺς Πτολεμαῖος ἀκολούθως τεῖ τῶν προγόνων καὶ τεῖ τῆς ἀδελφῆς προ[α]ιρέσει φανερός ἐστιν σπουδάζων ὑπὲρ τῆς κοινῆς τ[ῶ]ν Ἑλλήνων ἐλευθερίας. Confirmed now in the decree of the Greeks at Plataea honoring Glaucon the Athenian: *AthAnnArch* 6 (1973): 375–377; *BCH* 99 (1975):

lar pronouncements. A general of Philadelphus is praised by Itanus ca. 265 for helping the city to live under its own laws. And Philadelphus' successor Ptolemy III receives honors in analogous terms from Itanus twenty years later.[39]

The Seleucid house of Syria adopted comparable formulas, duly reiterated from reign to reign. Under Seleucus I the island of Lemnos was liberated from Lysimachus, as is affirmed by an Athenian inscription of 280/79.[40] A decree of the Ionians ca. 265 recorded honors for Antiochus I and called upon him to maintain vigilance over the liberties, democratic constitutions, and ancestral laws of Ionian cities. "Democracy," like freedom and autonomy, had by now become a traditional catchword, not necessarily denoting the form of government.[41] At perhaps this same time Antiochus I, in a letter to Erythrae, reaffirmed the city's autonomy and freedom from tribute, proclaiming to follow the lines set out by Alexander the Great and Antigonus Monophthalmus.[42] The stress on continuity is thus common to both the Ptolemies and the Seleucids. Antiochus II expelled a tyrannical regime in Miletus ca. 259 and was thanked by the Milesians for restoring ἐλευθερία and δημοκρατία.[43] In the following reign, that of Seleucus II, Smyrna received similar guarantees. The king pledged himself to uphold her freedom, variously described as ἐλευθερία, αὐτονομία, δημοκρατία, and ἀφορολογία. In this too he seems simply to have reaffirmed privileges awarded by his predecessor Antiochus II.[44]

51–53, lines 20–24: τὸν ἀγῶνα ὃν τιθέασιν οἱ Ἕλληνες ἐπὶ τοῖς ἀνδράσιν τοῖς ἀγαθοῖς καὶ ἀγωνισαμένοις πρὸς τοὺς βαρβάρους ὑπὲρ τῆς τῶν Ἑλλήνων ἐλευθερίας.

39. OGIS, 45 = IC, III, 4, 2, lines 13–15; Syll.³ 463 = IC, III, 4, 4, lines 5–6.

40. IG, II², 672, lines 18, 28, 41; cf. FGH, 81, fr. 29; Habicht, Gottmenschentum, 89–90; W. Orth, Königlicher Machtanspruch und städtische Freiheit (Munich, 1977), 36–39.

41. OGIS, aaa – IvErythrai und Klazomenai, II, no. 504, lines 15–18: [πᾶσαν ἐπι-μ]έλειαν ποιεῖσθαι τῶμ πόλε[ων τῶν Ἰάδων ὅπως ἂν τὸ λοιπὸ]ν ἐλεύθεραι οὖσαι καὶ δημο[κρατούμεναι βεβαίως ἤδη πολι]τεύωνται κατὰ τοὺς πατρί[ους νόμους]. Cf. Syll.³ 442 = IvErythrai und Klazomenai, I, no. 29, an Erythraean decree of a few years later, in which the city praises its own generals for preserving δημοκρατία and ἐλευθερία: lines 12–13. The combination of freedom and democracy may be seen already in an Eretrian decree of 308: Syll.³ 323, lines 3–5. The view of Holleaux, Études I:43–44, that this must mean a democratic constitution, is unnecessary. F. Quass, Chiron 9 (1979): 37–52, surprisingly takes all such references to δημοκρατία as accurate designation of the constitutional system.

42. OGIS, 223 = Welles, RC, no. 15 = IvErythrai u. Klazomenai, I, no. 31, lines 21–28; cf. ZPE 4 (1969): 151–156 = IvErythrai und Klazomenai, I, no. 30. The letter is sometimes ascribed to Antiochus II, but a strong case can be made for the reign of his predecessor; see Habicht, Gottmenschentum, 95–99. A good discussion by Orth, Königlicher Machtanspruch, 78–97.

43. OGIS, 226, lines 5–7; cf. Appian, Syr. 65.

44. OGIS, 228, lines 7–9; cf. Magie, RRAM II:934, n. 29; Robert, REG 71 (1958): 304, no. 418; OGIS, 229 = Schmitt, Staatsverträge, no. 492, lines 7–12, 67–68; cf. Habicht,

Seleucus' practice may be illustrated further in recently discovered documents attesting his acknowledgment of "freedom" and "democracy" for Mylasa.[45]

The evidence is fragmentary and scattered—but sufficient to demonstrate the repeated use of "autonomy" formulas by the major powers to assure the good will and cooperation of lesser states.[46] If literary sources were available in any abundance for the first three quarters of the third century, we should doubtless have additional instances aplenty.[47] The catchwords had become platitudinous by repetition, but no less expected for that: "freedom," "autonomy," "democracy," "ancestral constitution," "government by one's own laws."

The tradition was as strong as ever in the generation immediately preceding Rome's declaration of 196. Availability of Polybius' text permits a multiplication of examples. Inscriptional testimony confirms the picture.

Polybius reports that it had been the policy of the Achaean League throughout the third century to extend ἰσηγορία and παρρησία, to wage war against kings and tyrants who endeavored to enslave Greeks, and to uphold ἐλευθερία everywhere.[48] A partisan judgment, to be sure, and a conscious whitewash. Yet there is no reason to doubt that Aratus and other Achaean leaders utilized this sort of propaganda in detaching cities from the grip of Antigonus Gonatas' adherents and in expanding the membership of the League.[49] So federal organs could usurp the sloganeering of Hellenistic monarchs and turn it against them. The island of Rhodes used it too: she claimed to be guarantor of the freedom and autonomy of Iasus.[50]

The Macedonian kings themselves continued to employ the

Gottmenschentum, 99–100. On δημοκρατία in Seleucid inscriptions, see D. Musti, *StudClassOrient* 15 (1966): 138–145.

45. J. Crampa, *Labraunda* (Lund, 1969), III, 1, no. 3, lines 8, 30; no. 5, line 34; no. 7, lines 9–10; no. 8, lines 14–15; cf. Heuss, *Le monde grec*, 404–415. On the policy of the early Seleucids in western Asia Minor, see now Orth, *Königlicher Machtanspruch*, *passim*—unrelievedly skeptical about the value of freedom declarations.

46. And not just the major powers. Cf., e.g., Athens' honoring of Aristomachus, the Argive tyrant, in the mid-third century for preserving the ἐλευθερία of the demos: *IG*, II², 774 = *ISE*, no. 23, lines 34–35. Also the epigram of the early third century honoring Rhodes as a beacon of liberty on land and sea: *Anth. Pal.* 6.171.

47. Cf., e.g., Pyrrhus' assertion that he would liberate Greek cities from the control of Antigonus Gonatas in 272: Plut. *Pyrrh.* 26.10.

48. Polyb. 2.42.3–6.

49. Cf. Polyb. 2.43.3–8: τυραννουμένην δ᾽ ἐλευθερώσας [Aratus] τὴν πατρίδα . . . προσένειμε πρὸς τὴν τῶν Ἀχαιῶν πολιτείαν . . . καὶ πράξεις πρὸς ἕν τέλος ἀναφέρων. τοῦτο δ᾽ ἦν τὸ Μακεδόνας μὲν ἐκβαλεῖν ἐκ Πελοποννήσου, τὰς δὲ μοναρχίας καταλῦσαι, βεβαιῶσαι δ᾽ ἑκάστοις τὴν κοινὴν καὶ πάτριον ἐλευθερίαν.

50. Holleaux, *REA* 5 (1903): 224 = *Études* IV: 147–148, line 10: [ὅπ]ως ἅ τε πόλις

same overworked terminology in this period. Antigonus Doson, after expulsion of the tyrant Cleomenes in the late 220s, claimed to return to Sparta and then to Tegea their νόμοι, πάτριον πολίτευμα, and ἐλευθερία.[51] The rallying cry was taken up by Doson's successor Philip V in 220, at the head of a Greek coalition against Aetolia. The allies adopted a ringing declaration at the outset of this so-called "Social War"; they vowed that communities under Aetolian control would recover their νόμοι and πάτρια πολιτεύματα and would henceforth be ἀφρούρητοι, ἀφορολόγητοι, and ἐλεύθεροι.[52] The similarity to Rome's declaration a quarter-century later, is striking and unmistakable. Senatorial diplomats did not have to research distant history.

Philip proceeded to use these convenient mottos again and again. Near the outset of his reign he confirmed the freedom of Mylasa, which had been awarded her by Seleucus II.[53] In 218 he attempted to win the allegiance of Elis by promising that her citizens would be free, without garrisons, without tribute, and in control of their own institutions.[54] Fifteen years later he made the identical commitment to Thasos after that city had fallen into his hands.[55] The propaganda was evidently employed also in Philip's restoration of "liberty" to Dyme during the First Macedonian War.[56] In 201, or thereabouts, he dispatched a letter to the island of Nisyros, pledging that she would live under her ancestral laws.[57]

In these same years Antiochus III indulged in like pronouncements to communities under his authority. To Teos he granted freedom from tribute ca. 204, a tribute that had been exacted by the Attalids.[58] To Alabanda about the same time he promised to preserve the "democracy," as his ancestors had done.[59] And to Iasos in the 190s he gave a guarantee of δημοκρατία and αὐτονομία.[60] That stance

αὐτῶν ἐλευθέρα καὶ αὐτόνομος [διαμέ]νηι. More recent discussion in Crampa, Labraunda, III, 1, 93–96.

51. Polyb. 2.70.1, 2.70.4, 4.22.4, 5.9.9, 9.31.4, 9.36.4; Paus. 2.9.2; Plut. Cleom. 30.1.

52. Polyb. 4.25.6–8.

53. Crampa, Labraunda, III, 1, no. 5, line 34; no. 7, lines 9–10.

54. Polyb. 4.84.4–5.

55. Polyb. 15.24.1–3: συγχωρεῖν τὸν βασιλέα Θασίους ἀφρουρήτους, ἀφορολογήτους, ἀνεπισταθμεύτους νόμοις χρῆσθαι τοῖς ἰδίοις.

56. Livy, 32.22.10.

57. Syll.[3] 572, lines 16–20: δεδώκεν βασιλῆ ἁμὶν νόμοις τοῖς πατρίοις καὶ ὑπάρχουσιν χρῆσθαι.

58. Herrmann, Anatolia 9 (1965): 34–35, lines 18–20, 33–34, 47–49; 38, lines 50–53.

59. OGIS, 234 = F Delphes, III, 4, 163, lines 21–22.

60. OGIS, 237, line 3. See now the recently discovered letter of Laodice and decree of Iasus for Antiochus: Carratelli, Annuario 45–46 (1967–68): 445–453, 2I, lines

appears also in his pronouncements on the Jews, now under Seleucid authority as consequence of the Fifth Syrian War: they were to live in accordance with their ancestral laws.[61]

The foregoing survey has brought us to the eve of the Second Macedonian War. It can hardly be plainer that the practice of declaring Greek communities, whether in general or in particular, as free, autonomous, and democratic, as at liberty to live under their own laws and ancestral government, as free of tribute and of garrisons, extended in time and space through the Hellenistic era and through the Hellenistic world. It served as a convenient instrument for rival dynasts to use against one another in the decades after Alexander's death. It became commonplace language in the dealings between monarchs, whether Ptolemaic, Seleucid, or Antigonid, and the cities which they claimed to protect and defend in the third century, as it had been in the period of the *diadochoi*.[62] It legitimized wars, the overthrow of regimes, and the exercise of suzerainty. Indeed, one would be most surprised if any Greek state, in conducting a campaign against Philip V after 200, *failed* to speak in terms of ἐλευθερία.[63] So a whole collection of Greek envoys to the senate in 197 announced that unless Macedonian garrisons were removed from Chalcis, Corinth, and Demetrias, there could be no ἐλευθερία.[64] The point was reiterated at a peace conference later in the year by an Aetolian speaker: leaving Philip on the throne would never bring ἐλευθερία to the Greeks.[65] And Polybius' obituary for Attalus I asserted that he perished in the war on Philip while fighting for the freedom of the Greeks.[66] The slogan was a thoroughly Hellenic one.

8–10, 43–48; *BE* (1971), no. 621, 502–509; Garlan, *ZPE* 13 (1974): 197–198. Iasus had, a few years earlier, received similar guarantees from Rhodes: *REA* 5 (1903): 224, line 10; see above, n. 50. On Antiochus' policy generally, see the remark of Plut. *Mor.* 183f: Ἀντίοχος ὁ τρίτος ἔγραψε ταῖς πόλεσιν, ἄν τι γράφῃ παρὰ τοὺς νόμους κελεύων γενέσθαι, μὴ προσέχειν ὡς ἠγνοηκότι.

61. Jos. *Ant.* 12.142, 12.150. The authenticity of these documents continues to be debated. See especially Bickermann, *REJ* 100 (1935): 4–35; A. Schalit, *JQR* 50 (1959–60): 289–318; Gauger, *Beiträge*, 23–151.

62. Philopoemen, after his victory at Mantinea, was greeted at the Nemean games as the man who brought freedom to Hellas: Plut. *Phil.* 11.2. It is unfortunate that, in the latest contribution to this subject, Seager, *CQ* 31 (1981): 106–107, again leaps directly from the *diadochoi* to the Second Macedonian War, taking no notice of the usage of this concept in the third century.

63. Notice, for example, that in Aetolia in 200 a Macedonian spokesman had to deal with charges of Philip's interference with Aetolian *libertas*: Livy, 31.29.13.

64. Polyb. 18.11.4, 18.11.11.

65. Polyb. 18.36.6–7.

66. Polyb. 18.41.9: ἀγωνιζόμενος ὑπὲρ τῆς τῶν Ἑλλήνων ἐλευθερίας.

The Roman Background

By contrast, it had played virtually no role at all in Rome's history to that date. During the Pyrrhic war Pyrrhus' representative offered peace terms on the condition, among other things, that Rome leave the Greek communities of Italy "free and autonomous."[67] That was standard Greek propaganda, a useful message to establish Pyrrhus' credentials in the West. Rome, of course, gave the proposal no serious consideration. Nor did she ever, before 196, issue any general proclamations about the defense of liberty for all the states within her or anyone else's realm.

References to *libertas* with regard to external affairs occur but rarely and only in particular circumstances, in connection with particular communities. In 305, we are told, the Hernici had "their own laws restored" by Rome. This connotes no overall, not even a specific, policy on Rome's part. As Livy's account makes clear, the request came from the Hernici: they preferred *suas leges* and *conubium* among themselves to Roman citizenship.[68] So the phrase "their own laws" is simply used in contrast with the exercise of Roman citizenship. No further meaning is implied and no symptom of a Roman policy. The same holds for the senate's decision on the subdued Campanians in 210. The *patres* ordered them "to be free"; i.e. that none would obtain Roman citizenship or Latin privileges.[69] Obviously the expression is here not even a slogan, just an announcement of clemency, to be distinguished from the status of closer connection with Rome that other states enjoyed. Elsewhere, comparable announcements were made when Rome deposed an oppressive regime. So *libertas* and *leges* were restored to the people of Rhegium ca. 270.[70] And the same language served with reference to Locri in 204.[71] In both instances, however, Rome was simply making amends for the misbehavior of her own officials or garrisons. From Rhegium she expelled the forces which she

67. Appian, *Samn.* 10.1: τοὺς δ' ἄλλους Ἕλληνας τοὺς ἐν Ἰταλίᾳ κατοικοῦντας ἐλευθέρους καὶ αὐτονόμους ἐῶμεν; *Ined. Vat.* 2, quoted in Schmitt, *Staatsverträge*, 107.

68. Livy, 9.43.23: *Hernicorum tribus populis, Aletrinati, Verulano, Ferentinati quia maluerunt quam civitatem, suae leges redditae, conubiumque inter ipsos, quod aliquamdiu soli Hernicorum habuerunt, permissum.*

69. Livy, 26.34.6–13: *Campanos omnes . . . extraquam qui eorum aut ipsi aut parentes eorum apud hostes essent, liberos esse iusserunt ita, ut nemo eorum civis Romanus aut Latini nominis esset.*

70. Polyb. 1.7.10–13; Livy, 31.31.7: *urbem agros suaque omnia cum libertate legibusque Reginis reddidimus.*

71. Livy, 29.21.7: *iis libertatem legesque suas populum Romanum senatumque restituere dixit.*

herself had installed at the time of the Pyrrhic war, but which had acted with tyrannical license since that time. At Locri she acted to relieve the citizens of the oppressive burdens and savagery imposed by her own commander Q. Pleminius. Neither case corresponds to any strategy of liberating cities from foreign control. The nearest parallel occurs in connection with the siege of Syracuse during the Hannibalic war. Rome offered a peaceful solution in 214 on condition that her sympathizers be reinstated, her opponents surrendered, and *libertas legesque* be restored to the city.[72] The same terms were discussed two years later. When Syracuse fell, her conqueror Marcellus magnanimously awarded her ἐλευθερίαν and τοὺς νόμους, a decision ratified by the senate.[73] Here again special circumstances prevailed. Rome was underlining her generosity to a state whose future support would be eminently valuable in Sicily. *Libertas* had not become a watchword to designate or disguise any general policy.[74] Finally, the peace treaty with Carthage in 201 stipulated that the Carthaginians would be governed by their own laws and subject to no Roman garrison.[75] That, however, was simply a statement that Rome did not intend to convert Carthaginian Africa into a province. It is in no way comparable to the propaganda campaigns familiar in Hellenistic Greece.

More striking—and decisive—is the absence of any such propaganda during Rome's first military ventures in the eastern world. There were no claims of defending freedom, no grandiose pronouncements about liberating communities during the Illyrian wars. Rome collected a number of *amici*; she did not profess to have brought them ἐλευθερία.[76] In the First Macedonian War she was quite unconcerned with Greek "freedom." Indeed the reverse. Rome's alliance with the Aetolians explicitly and unashamedly specified that the cities and land captured or surrendered would be at the disposal of Aetolia.[77]

72. Livy, 24.33.6.

73. Plut. *Marc.* 23.7; Livy, 25.23.4, 25.28.2–3; cf. 31.29.6, 31.31.8.

74. This sort of language during the Second Punic War was by no means exclusively Roman. Cf. the same phraseology in Carthaginian negotiations with the Campanians and Lucanians: Livy, 23.7.1, 25.16.7; and with the Gauls: Livy, 29.5.4.

75. Polyb. 15.18.2: ἔθεσι καὶ νόμοις χρῆσθαι τοῖς ἰδίοις, ἀφρουρήτους ὄντας. The Polybian text makes no explicit mention of ἐλευθερία, though that is inferred and added by Livy, 30.37.1: *ut liberi legibus suis viverent*; 37.54.26: *Carthago libera cum suis legibus est*. On this treaty, see, most recently, F. Gschnitzer, *WS* 79 (1966): 276–289, with bibliography.

76. Appian's statement, *Ill.* 8, that, after the First Illyrian War, Rome left Corcyra and Apollonia free refers, no doubt, only to the withdrawal of Roman troops. The phrase possesses no technical significance; see Bernhardt, *Imperium und Eleutheria*, 28–29, as against Kienast, *ZSS* 85 (1968): 355–356.

77. *SEG*, XIII, 382 = *IG*, IX, 1², 241 = Schmitt, *Staatsverträge*, no. 536 = *ISE*, no. 87; Livy, 26.24.11; cf. Polyb. 9.39.2, 11.5.5, 18.38.7; Livy, 33.13.10.

Neither practice nor propaganda paid any heed to the concept of liberation.

"Freedom" as Slogan and Propaganda

There can be little doubt that the Isthmian declaration of 196 is a product of Greek formulation. Nothing comparable had been utilized by Rome before.[78] Nor indeed did she even adopt it at the outset of the war with Philip or for some time thereafter. The senate had no clear intentions about the fate of Greece when Rome entered the war. The initial demands on Philip in 200 were simply that he refrain from warring on any Greeks.[79] Two years later, the terms were harsher: Philip was asked to evacuate all of Greece. But still no propaganda about ἐλευθερία.[80] Not until after Cynoscephalae did Rome begin to adopt that posture.[81] It was unquestionably suggested to her as appropriate by the Greeks themselves. In light of the above discussion this conclusion should cause no surprise. It is unnecessary to postulate Roman acquaintance with the precedents of a century earlier, equally unnecessary to talk of Flamininus' familiarity with Hellenic history,—and still less to imagine Rome's twisting of Greek institutions to her own purposes. The practice of "autonomy declarations," as we have seen, was persistent and continuous down to the eve of the Second Macedonian War. Rome fought in collaboration with the Greeks for four years before the Isthmus proclamation: there was plenty of time and opportunity for Rome to be advised of the proper stance to take. If she did not know it before 197, the message came through clearly when Greek envoys to the senate in that year spoke of ἐλευθερία as the only acceptable outcome of the war.[82] Only after this

78. The thesis of Badian, *Foreign Clientelae*, 33–43, that the *civitas libera* was an institution developed by Rome through her experience in Sicily lacks any hard evidence; cf. the criticism of Bleicken, *Gnomon* 36 (1964): 178–180. See now Dahlheim, *Gewalt und Herrschaft*, 186–190. And Badian's conclusion that the idea of the freedom of the Greeks "is thoroughly Roman" is most implausible: *op. cit.*, 73–74.

79. Polyb. 16.27.1–2, 16.34.2–5.

80. Polyb. 18.1.13, 18.2.6, 18.5.5, 18.9.1; Livy, 32.33.3; Appian, *Mac.* 5; Plut. *Flam.* 5.6. Livy's statement about *civitates liberandae* refers only to the withdrawal of Philip's garrisons: 32.10.3–7. The formulation in Diod. 28.11, that Greece is to be ἀφρούρητος καὶ αὐτόνομος, is clearly anticipatory; cf. Seager, *CQ* 31 (1981): 108.

81. The steps in this slow development are duly noted by Badian, *Foreign Clientelae*, 66–75. Cf. M.-L. Heidemann, *Die Freiheitsparole in der griechisch-römischen Auseinandersetzung (200–188 v. Chr.)* (Bonn, 1966), 21–36.

82. Polyb. 18.11.4, 18.11.11; cf. 18.36.6. Note particularly the envoys' insistence that Greece cannot be free, so long as Philip holds the "Three Fetters": Polyb. 18.11.4—a rallying cry that Romans then took up, word for word: Livy, 34.23.8–9. Seager, *CQ* 31

Greek enunciation did the senate dispatch its commissioners with instructions that the Greeks of Europe and Asia were to be free and governed by their own laws.[83] And only then did Flamininus stage his ringing announcement at the Isthmus. If there was stunned surprise and elation among those who heard the announcement, it was not because the formula was new and unfamiliar to Greeks; rather, because the prior reputation of Rome, often maligned in Greek circles and sullied by Roman behavior in the First Macedonian War, made it so unexpected to hear the Hellenic slogans from the mouth of a Roman.[84]

From the senate's standpoint this Greek convention was entirely welcome and suitable: not a cynical distortion in order to advance imperialistic aims, but a convenient mode of expressing magnanimity and evading direct commitments. The Roman declaration carried no precise legal meaning, any more than did the Hellenic pronouncements on which it was modeled.[85] Like the long string of Hellenic pronouncements, "freedom" was not to be taken as meaning atomistic independence for each community. Ἐλευθερία had for a long time been quite consistent with the suzerainty of larger powers over smaller. The Romans were perfectly content to adopt that understanding. After the Isthmian games, they declared several states free,

---

(1981): 108–109, rightly recognizes the role played by Greek pressure in the articulation of this slogan in 197, but asserts without evidence or argument that Romans knew the virtues of *libertas* as slogan and administrative convenience before any involvement with Greece: *op. cit.*, 107.

83. Polyb. 18.44.2: ἐλευθέρους ὑπάρχειν καὶ νόμοις χρῆσθαι τοῖς ἰδίοις; Livy, 33.30.1–2; cf. Polyb. 18.42.5.

84. On Rome's negative reputation in Greece before 199, see material and discussion in Heidemann, *Freiheitsparole*, 14–21; J. Deininger, *Der politische Widerstand gegen Rom in Griechenland, 217–86 v. Chr.* (Berlin, 1971), 23–37. The surprise at Flamininus' proclamation: Polyb. 18.46.6–15; Livy, 33.32.6–33.33.8; Appian, *Mac.* 9.4; Plut. *Flam.* 10.4–11.4.

85. It is pointless to discern fine distinctions in the status of states that were "originally free" and those handed over by Philip, or to contrast those freed by the peace treaty with those specified in the Isthmian announcement. On this controversy, see the discussions of Täubler, *Imperium Romanum* I:436–440; Heuss, *Völkerrechtliche Grundlagen*, 94–99; Dahlheim, *Struktur und Entwicklung*, 83–98; and cf. the sober remarks of Badian, *Foreign Clientelae*, 73–74. There was, of course, debate between Flamininus and the senatorial commissioners as to whether Roman troops should be evacuated entirely or remain in certain strongholds. But the issue centered upon how best to show Rome's sincerity while still protecting against the potential threat of Antiochus: Polyb. 18.45.7–12; Livy, 33.31.1–11. Nor is there much point to the modern argument over whether the award of freedom was "precarious" and could be withdrawn at will. The judicial question resolves itself into a political one—for Rome as for Hellenistic powers before her. Bibliography and discussion in Dahlheim, *Gewalt und Herrschaft*, 247–254. The cynical view of the decree as a vehicle for further extending Roman power in Greece is conveyed again most recently by W. V. Harris, *War and Imperialism in Republican Rome, 327–70 B.C.* (Oxford, 1979), 142.

such as the Thessalians, the Perrhaebians, Dolopians, Magnesians, and Orestae; also Chalcis, Bargylia, Thasos, and cities in Thrace.[86] At the same time they handed other communities over to larger entities: Phthiotic Achaea to Thessaly; Phocis and Locris to Aetolia; Corinth, Triphylia, and Heraea to the Achaean League; Lychnis and Parthus to Pleuratus; certain towns to Amynander; and there was talk even of giving Oreus and Eretria to Eumenes.[87] Some complaints surfaced, as individual ambitions were thwarted, but no argument with the principle. "Freedom" and attachment to a stronger power could go hand in hand, as they always had in the Hellenistic era. The Greeks, with perfect sincerity—and within the traditional understanding of the term—celebrated Rome's victory as a liberation.[88] The Aetolians, to be sure, demurred. Angered by failure to obtain some of the territory they coveted, they denounced the ἐλευθερία as a sham, for Roman forces were still occupying the "fetters of Greece."[89] Those troops, however, were removed in 194, and the argument evaporated. Greece, as Flamininus now repeated, was free, ungarrisoned, and self-governing.[90]

Once the motif was adopted it found use again and again: an ideal fit for the image that Rome sought to project. In 195 the "liberation" of Argos became the slogan to legitimize a war on Nabis of Sparta. Rome's *decem legati* returned from Greece to malign Nabis' tyranny and argue that Greek freedom was incompatible with Nabis' hold over Argos.[91] In fact, the war was chiefly to the interest of Achaea. The senate cared little and left the matter to Flamininus, who gained an opportunity to reemphasize his propaganda line.[92] Before a council of Greeks Flamininus asserted that the oppression of one city compromised the liberty of all Greece and would diminish Rome's own achievement.[93] To Nabis himself he reiterated the message that Rome had delivered Hellas from despotism, would free Argos, and would restore Sparta *in antiquam libertatem atque in leges suas*.[94] That is familiar

86. Polyb. 18.47.6–7, 18.48.1–2; Livy, 33.34.6–7, 33.35.1–2; Plut. *Flam.* 12.1–3. On Thessaly, see also Livy, 34.51.4, 39.25.11; Euseb. *Chron.* 1.243.

87. Polyb. 18.47.7–13; Livy, 33.34.7–11. The status of Phthiotic Thebes and Pharsalus is not quite certain; but see Livy, 34.23.7–8, 36.10.9, 39.25.8–9, and the argument of Dahlheim, *Struktur und Entwicklung*, 92, n. 37.

88. E.g., the poem of Alcaeus contrasting Xerxes who came to enslave Greeks and Flamininus who came to end slavery: *Anth. Pal.* 16.5; cf. Plut. *Flam.* 12.5–6. Note too the sentiment of the Rhodians, as characterized by Livy, 33.20.3: *Romanis liberantibus Graeciam*. Cf. also the request of the Lampsacenes to be included in the peace treaty with Philip which would preserve their δημοκρατία and αὐτονομία: *Syll.*³ 591, lines 33–34.

89. Polyb. 18.45.3–5; Livy, 33.31.1–5, 34.23.8–10.

90. Diod. 28.13; Livy, 34.49.4–6, 34.50.8–9.

91. Livy, 33.44.8–9.   92. Livy, 33.45.3–5, 34.24.1–4.

93. Livy, 34.22.11–12.

94. Livy, 34.32.3–5, 34.32.8, 34.32.13.

Hellenic terminology. And the Greeks echoed it: the defeat of Nabis was welcomed as a feat worthy of the "liberators."[95] The withdrawal of Rome's forces followed—but not without a last flourish by Flamininus. Freedom, he affirmed, had been won by Roman valor; its preservation was now entrusted to the Greeks themselves.[96]

Rome maintained the posture. As is well known, she utilized it to best advantage in confrontation with Antiochus the Great. The *senatus consultum* of 196 had declared the Greeks of Asia, as well as those of Europe, free.[97] After the Isthmian Games Rome's representatives asked Antiochus to stay away from the "autonomous" cities of Asia.[98] That gesture served merely to maintain consistency in the public pronouncements. Rome certainly did not anticipate taking up arms on behalf of the Asian Greeks. The pronouncements themselves were becoming routine in Rome's diplomatic language. An exchange with Antiochus' envoys in Rome in 193 concluded with, by now, typical bluster: Rome would champion Greek freedom in Asia as she had in Europe.[99] The role of this encounter in the context of a coming war is not our concern here. It would be erroneous to see the Roman stance as plain militancy and deliberate provocation. More interesting, for our purposes, it provides illustration of how ready Rome was to embrace the Hellenistic terminology in her interchange with Greeks.

Striking confirmation comes from a Roman letter to the city of Teos in this very year. Tean representatives had sought a guarantee of *asylia* from the senate, as they had from states throughout the Greek world. In this instance their spokesman was none other than Antiochus' own agent Menippus. The same man to whom the senate announced its insistence on *libertas* for Asian Greeks is here treated with every courtesy and respect. Not only was the Tean request granted, but Rome's letter affirmed that the city was to be "inviolate and free from taxation by the Roman people."[100] The phrase has revealing implications. Rome, of course, had never exacted taxes from Teos and

95. Livy, 34.33.6, 34.41.3. There was disappointment, however, that Nabis himself was not removed—and some wondered whether that was consistent with Greek freedom: Livy, 34.48.5–6.

96. Livy, 34.49.6–11, 34.50.9.

97. Polyb. 18.44.2; Livy, 33.30.2.

98. Polyb. 18.47.1, 18.50.7; Livy, 33.34.3; Plut. *Flam.* 12.1; Appian, *Syr.* 3.

99. Livy, 34.58.8–12, 34.59.4–5; Diod. 28.15.4; Appian, *Syr.* 6. Badian's view that Flamininus offered a more cynical deal to Antiochus behind closed doors is without support in the evidence: *Studies*, 126–127. The sources know no distinction between terms offered in the private parley and those proclaimed in public. Cf. Balsdon, *Phoenix* 21 (1967): 187–189. A different interpretation in Desideri, *StudClassOrient* 19–20 (1970–71): 506–510.

100. *Syll.*³ 601 = Sherk, *RDGE*, no. 34, lines 20–21: ἄσυλον καὶ ἀφορολόγητον ἀπὸ τοῦ δήμου τοῦ Ῥωμαίων.

therefore had none to exempt her from. Nor was this a device to extend Roman influence in Asia at the expense of Antiochus.[101] The gesture, in fact, came at the request of Antiochus' envoy. A simpler explanation proves more satisfactory. The Romans merely adopted the conventional language of Hellenistic decrees: Teos would be ἄσυλος and ἀφορολόγητος.[102] No sinister meanings need be imputed. Rome found the terminology of the Greek world suitable and comfortable.

The adoption of such terminology, however, had not become an exclusive Roman preserve. Hellenistic states which had utilized it for generations naturally continued to do so. The Rhodians in 197, for example, claimed to protect the *libertas* of Asian communities against the designs of Antiochus.[103] Athens honored her statesman Cephisodorus ca. 196 for preserving the city's αὐτονομία, without a mention of Rome.[104] Antiochus himself described his aim as "the freedom of the Greeks."[105] The posture was in no way novel for that monarch, whatever its practical import. As we have seen, preserved letters to individual cities in the late third century guaranteed their autonomy or awarded privileges, a convention long practiced by his Seleucid forebears. Antiochus carried it on in the 190s.[106] Even when he besieged the recalcitrant cities of Smyrna and Lampsacus in 196, Antiochus announced that they would have their freedom—but only as his gift. A typical stance for a Hellenistic monarch.[107] So, when Roman envoys in that year asked him to leave the autonomous cities alone, Antiochus immediately replied that the ἐλευθερία of Asian Greeks was not a *beneficium* to be bestowed by Romans but one that fell under his own auspices.[108] That was no mere debater's point to gain a diplomatic

101. As is suggested by Accame, *Il dominio*, 51–52; cf. Magie, *Buckler Studies* (1939): 168–169; Errington, *ZPE* 39 (1980): 279–284.

102. See the same response to Teos by King Theodorus and Amynander of Athamania: Welles, *RC*, no. 35, lines 5–6: τὴν τε πόλιν καὶ τὴν χώραν ἱε[ρ]ὰν τῶι Διονύσωι καὶ ἄσυλον καὶ ἀφορολόγητον. Cf. also the Delphian award to Teos: *Syll.*³ 566, lines 2–5: [Δελφοὶ ἔ]δωκαν . . . ἀσυλίαν, ἀτέλειαν πάντων.

103. Livy, 33.20.11–12; cf. Polyb. 18.41a.1.

104. *Hesperia* 5 (1936): 419–428 = *ISE*, no. 33, lines 29–30.

105. Polyb. 20.8.1: τήν τε τῶν Ἑλλήνων ἐλευθέρωσιν, ὡς αὐτὸς ἐπηγγέλλετο.

106. *OGIS*, 237, line 3, for Iasus. See also Caratelli, *Annuario* 45–46 (1967–68): 445–453, 2I, lines 8–10, 43–48. Cf. the contemporary letter to Ilium which grants ancestral privileges to the demos: Welles, *RC*, no. 42 = *Ivllion*, no. 37, lines 3–5: πειρασόμεθα γὰ[ρ οὐ μόνον τὰ δι]ὰ προγόνων προυπηργμ[ένα πρὸς τὸν δῆ]μον συντηρεῖν. And the recently discovered treaty between Antiochus and Lysimacheia which gives promise of "democracy," freedom from garrisons and tribute, and—doubtless—autonomy: *ZPE* 17 (1975): 101–102, lines 12–15 = *Ivllion*, no. 45; cf. Polyb. 18.51.7; Livy, 33.38.10–14; Appian, *Syr.* 1.

107. Livy, 33.38.5–7: *ab rege impetratam eos libertatem, non per occasionem raptam habere.*

108. Polyb. 18.51.9: τὰς δ' αὐτονόμους τῶν κατὰ τὴν Ἀσίαν πόλεων οὐ διὰ τῆς

advantage, as it is often described. It was assertion of longstanding tradition within the realm of the Seleucids.

The familiar tale of propaganda and counter-propaganda between Rome and Antiochus on the eve of their conflict need not be retold *in extenso*. Both, of course, laid heavy stress upon their claims as liberators. Neither party actively sought war, an undesirable outcome for all concerned.[109] Antiochus' man at Ephesus labeled as specious the Roman pretext of freeing Greek states.[110] All over Greece in 192 and 191 his spokesmen and allies trumpeted the king's mission and sole aim as that of a champion of *libertas*.[111] As Cato sniffed, "Antiochus wages war with letters and fights with pen and ink."[112] Yet the Romans took on the same propaganda mission.[113] A mixed response from the Greeks greeted these protestations. The sincerity of their "liberators" did not go unquestioned. The Magnetes were divided in opinion, some relying on Rome's professions, others skeptical of her duplicity. Ultimately they rejected the advances and, with a pointed remark, stated that they preferred *libertas* to a Roman alliance, so puncturing the balloon.[114] The reverse situation held at Chalcis. Her leaders said they had no need of *libertas* at Antiochus' hands; they were already free, a freedom won through Roman aid.[115] It was, in any case, quite clear that communities made their decisions not on the basis of how much stock they placed in the sincerity of the major powers but how much advantage they saw in attachment to one or

---

Ῥωμαίων ἐπιταγῆς δέον εἶναι τυγχάνειν τῆς ἐλευθερίας, ἀλλὰ διὰ τῆς αὐτοῦ χάριτος; Appian, *Syr.* 3: τὰς δ᾽ ἐν Ἀσίᾳ πόλεις αὐτονόμους ἐάσειν, εἰ τὴν χάριν οὐ Ῥωμαίοις ἀλλ᾽ ἑαυτῷ μέλλοιεν ἕξειν. Cf. the similar response of Antiochus' envoys at Rome in 193: Livy, 34.57.10. The discussion of Bickermann, *Hermes* 67 (1932): 56–66, is excessively legalistic.

109. See the analysis of Badian, *Studies*, 112–139. On the propaganda, see now the thorough and intelligent discussion of Mastrocinque, *AttIstVeneto* 136 (1977–78): 1–17. Unfortunately, however, he pays almost no attention to antecedents in earlier Hellenistic history.

110. Livy, 35.16.2; cf. Appian, *Syr.* 12.

111. E.g., Polyb. 3.7.3; Plut. *Cato*, 12.2; Livy, 35.32.10–11, 35.33.8, 35.38.9, 35.44.6, 35.46.6, 36.9.4.

112. Cato, *ORF*, fr. 20: *Antiochus epistulis bellum gerit, calamo et atramento militat.*

113. Cf. Livy, 35.31.8–10. It is quite erroneous to assert that Antiochus got the idea for his propaganda *from the Romans*; as J. L. Ferrary, in C. Nicolet, *Rome et la conquête du monde méditerranéen* II (Paris, 1978), 745–746.

114. Livy, 35.31.8–15, 35.39.6: *abstineret portu et sineret Magnetas in concordia et libertate esse.*

115. Livy, 35.46.9–11: *Micythio, unus ex principibus, mirari se dixit ad quos liberandos Antiochus relicto regno suo in Europam traiecisset . . . Chalcidenses neque vindice libertatis ullo egere, cum liberi sint, neque praesidio, cum pacem eiusdem populi Romani beneficio et libertatem habeant.* Cf. Livy, 35.39.3.

the other.[116] So the conflict evolved, though unwanted by its participants. It arose through the clash of rival and overlapping claims. Antiochus projected the traditional posture of a Hellenistic suzerain. And the Romans, who had adopted a similar tactic out of convenience, found themselves propelled on a collision course.

Little is heard of the sloganeering while the war itself was in progress.[117] But it was not forgotten. For Greek politicians it was a commonplace, to be trotted out wherever suitable—or even unsuitable. So, the Achaean leader Philopoemen, after forcibly bringing Sparta into the Achaean League in 192, was described by his supporters as a guardian of Spartan ἐλευθερία![118] Messenia, not long thereafter, sought independence from the League and turned to Flamininus as her *auctor libertatis*.[119] The stock phrases were not simply retailed by the major powers.

"Freedom" as Convention

For Roman diplomats the Hellenistic propaganda line had now become standard terminology. When Antiochus was ready to talk peace in 190, the Scipios announced that he must liberate the cities of Aeolis and Ionia and renounce all possessions on that side of the Taurus.[120] The praetor Aemilius Regillus, after taking Phocaea, declared that he restored *suas leges* to her citizens, a decision later confirmed by the final settlement in 188: Phocaea got her πάτριον πολίτευμα.[121] To the Asian cities that joined Rome's cause Scipio sent reassuring letters. One example is extant, the missive to Heraclea by Latmus, a famous and revealing document. The language of Hellenistic chancelleries is appropriated with exactness: Heraclea receives assurance of ἐλευθερία and of the right of self-government under her own laws.[122]

116. Livy, 35.17.8–9: *si non libertas servitute potior sit, tamen omni praesenti statu spem cuique novandi res suas blandiorem esse*; cf. 36.7.2–5.

117. Indeed in Asia Rome had to counter a rather different type of propaganda: Antiochus' allegation that the Romans were out to topple all kings. A letter of the Scipios to Prusias calmed his fears on this score: Polyb. 21.11; Livy, 37.35.4–15. Of course, the recognition of legitimate rulers was not inconsistent with "liberty."

118. Plut, *Phil.* 15.3.

119. Livy, 36.31.4–6.

120. Polyb. 21.14.8. Rather more elaborately stated by Livy, 37.35.9–10: *sicut Graecia omnis liberata esset, ita quae in Asia sint omnes liberari urbes*.

121. Regillus' decision: Livy, 37.32.14; the final settlement: Polyb. 21.45.7; Livy, 38.39.12.

122. *Syll.*³ 618 = Sherk, *RDGE*, no. 35, lines 10–12: συγχωροῦμεν δὲ ὑμῖν τήν τε ἐλευθερίαν καθότι καὶ [ταῖς ἄ]λλαις πόλεσιν ὅσαι ἡμῖν τὴν ἐπιτροπὴν ἔδωκαν, ἔχουσιν

In European Greece the same applied. Acilius Glabrio's letter to Delphi in early 190 promised αὐτονομία and the safeguarding of ancestral privileges.[123] That ruling was reaffirmed by senatorial decree in 189: the Delphians were free, autonomous, without tribute, and self-governing.[124] "Freedom" was now as ready a slogan for the Romans as ever it had been for Hellenistic rulers.[125]

Ambiguity and elasticity had long been a feature of this term in Greek diplomatic affairs.[126] After the defeat of Antiochus, Rome's ally Eumenes was apprehensive lest the senate apply too strict a meaning to ἐλευθερία. A rigid interpretation would deprive him of coveted territorial gains as reward for his services and possibly even of areas previously under his control. Eumenes pleaded his case before the senate in 189: Rome should not be misled by the words "freedom and autonomy"; for Asian states fully liberated will just fall under the control of Rhodes.[127] As Eumenes predicted—or already knew—the Rhodians did indeed urge the stricter interpretation on Rome. Their spokesmen played upon Rome's reputation and record as the liberator of the Greeks.[128] Eumenes should indeed receive his just deserts, they acknowledged: the areas wrested involuntarily from the control of Anti-

---

ὑ[φ' αὐτοὺς πά]ντα τὰ αὐτῶν πολιτεύεσθαι κατὰ τοὺς ὑμετέρους νόμους. Cf. Tac. *Ann.* 3.62.

123. *Syll.*³ 609 = Sherk, *RDGE*, no. 37A, lines 9–10: ἵνα ὑμῖν κατάμονα ἦι τὰ ἐξ ἀρχῆς ὑπάρχοντα πάτρ[ια . . .] τῆς πόλεως καὶ τοῦ ἱεροῦ αὐτονομίας.

124. *Syll.*³ 612 = Sherk, *RDGE*, nos. 1A and B, lines 5–7: αὐτονόμους καὶ ἐλευθέρους κ[αὶ ἀνεισφόρους, οἰκοῦν]τας καὶ πολιτεύοντας αὐτοὺς καθ' αὑ[τοὺς καὶ] κυριευό[ν]τας τῆς τε ἱερᾶς χώρ[ας καὶ τοῦ ἱεροῦ λι]μένος καθὼς πάτριον αὐτοῖς ἐξ ἀρχῆς [ἦν]. Badian, *Foreign Clientelae*, 87–89, holds that Rome here for the first time became aware that Greek states could be "free" while paying tribute and therefore had to spell out Delphi's immunity. But, as we have seen, immunity from tribute was acknowledged in a Roman decree for Teos in 193: above n. 100.

125. Cf. Livy, 37.60.7—the removal of Antiochus' garrisons from Aenus and Maronea *ut in libertate eae civitates essent*. And note the language of L. Aemilius Paullus' decree after a successful campaign in Spain in 189: *ILLRP*, II, no. 514, lines 2–6: *utei quei Hastensium servii in turri Lascutana habitarent leiberei essent*. Dahlheim, *Gewalt und Herrschaft*, 193–198, recognizes the Greek influence on Rome's terminology, but strains mightily—and unsuccessfully—to detect a difference. His notion, that "freedom" was simply a tool for power struggles among Hellenistic states but became an element in organizing foreign arrangements for Rome, is oversubtle and unsubstantiated.

126. Cf. the decree of Gortyn for the island of Kaudos, clearly treated as a dependency, with conditions, even tribute, imposed by the stronger power. Yet the people of Kaudos are described as ἐλευθέρους καὶ αὐτονόμους καὶ αὐτοδίκους . . . χρημένους νόμοις τοῖς ἰδίοις; *IC*, IV, 184, lines 5–8—probably of the early second century.

127. Polyb. 21.19.5–10: τὸ γὰρ τῆς ἐλευθερίας ὄνομα καὶ τῆς αὐτονομίας ἡμῖν μὲν ἄρδην ἀποσπάσει πάντας οὐ μόνον τοὺς νῦν ἐλευθερωθησομένους, ἀλλὰ καὶ τοὺς πρότερον ἡμῖν ὑποταττομένους . . . τούτοις [the Rhodians] δὲ προσθήσει πάντας; Livy, 37.53.3–6; cf. Polyb. 21.21.10–11; Livy, 37.53.28.

128. Polyb. 21.22.10–11, 21.23.7, 21.23.10; Livy, 37.54.9, 37.54.13–17.

ochus. The "autonomous" cities of Asia, by contrast, should remain entirely free.[129] Rome had no need for these lectures. She was by now well acquainted with Greek diplomatic practices and with the elastic character of ἐλευθερία. A senatorial decree followed, alloting to Eumenes and to Rhodes much of western Asia Minor that had been in the dominions of Antiochus.[130] Rome's *decem legati* sharpened the terms at Apamea in 188: autonomous towns previously tributary to Antiochus that had abandoned him were now free of tribute, those who stuck with him would now pay it to Eumenes; the towns traditionally subject to the Attalids would remain so; in addition, large chunks of territory were turned over to Eumenes, others to Rhodes; but still other cities and communities obtained freedom.[131] The mixed character of the arrangements corresponded to Rhodian advice, while at the same time awarding to Eumenes all he could have hoped to acquire. They were suitable also to the categories of Hellenistic diplomacy. Rome's principal allies secured the overlordship of key territories. Yet it is quite erroneous to assert that "the claim to be fighting for the freedom of the Greeks was completely abandoned."[132] Numerous communities in Asia Minor were independent of the major suzerains and no serious restructuring took place in Greece. That areas were assigned to Pergamum and Rhodes marks no new departure in principle. As we saw, assignments of the same type were made in 196, after the Isthmian declaration, and reckoned as entirely consistent with ἐλευθερία. The flexibility of the concept still held—not by any means a Roman invention. The fall of Antiochus was hailed as a "liberation."[133]

After 188 no major power loomed on the horizon to challenge Rome's military might. Roman use of ἐλευθερία as a general rallying cry to mobilize forces and support was no longer necessary. The war against Perseus was fought on different pretexts and with different propaganda. It does not follow, however, that the conventional phrases, so long prevalent in the Hellenistic world, had passed out of

129. Polyb. 21.22.10–15; Livy, 37.54.6–13, 37.54.24–27. On these speeches, cf. Schmitt, *Rom und Rhodos*, 81–84.

130. Polyb. 21.24.7–8; Livy, 37.56.1–6.

131. Polyb. 21.46.2–10; Livy, 38.39.7–16; Diod. 29.11; Appian, *Syr.* 44. Identity of the free cities is, in many cases, uncertain. See Bickermann, *REG* 50 (1937): 235–239; Magie, *RRAM* II:958, n. 75; H. Seyrig, *RevNum* 5 (1963): 19–22; Schmitt, *Untersuchungen*, 278–290; Walbank, *Commentary* III:164–168; Mastrocinque, *La Carie e la Ionia meridionale in epoca ellenistica* (Rome, 1979), 201–203; and, especially, the thorough discussion of Bernhardt, *Imperium und Eleutheria*, 52–71.

132. As Badian, *Foreign Clientelae*, 80.

133. Cf. Polyb. 21.40.2; Strabo, 12.8.14 (C 577). The Thessalians continued to speak of the Romans as *libertatis auctores*: Livy, 39.25.11 (185 B.C.); 42.38.6 (172 B.C.). See also the decree of the Delphic Amphictyony in 186 with its reference to the Greeks who have chosen ἐλευθερία and δημοκρατία: *Syll.*³ 613, lines 18–19.

the diplomatic vocabulary. The senate periodically employed them on suitable occasions after Apamea. So, in 187 a *senatus consultum* on Ambracia declared that her citizens should live in freedom and enjoy their own *leges*, so long as they exempted Romans and Latins from port dues.[134] Lycia was handed over to the suzerainty of Rhodes; and Rome did not directly interfere with that suzerainty. Appeals to Rome on Lycia's behalf in 188 and 178, however, drew some guarded and platitudinous responses about Lycian ἐλευθερία, though the senate had no intention of doing anything about it.[135] During the Third Macedonian War, when complaints came from Abdera about the misbehavior of Roman officials, the senate sent envoys to restore the city *in libertatem*.[136] Perhaps at this same time another *senatus consultum*, upon request from Alabanda, confirmed that city's freedom from tribute.[137] Acknowledgment of such privileges, when summoned, was still forthcoming, with the standard phraseology. The more general propaganda retained its usefulness as well. In response to envoys from Chalcis in 170, the senate characterized the war on Perseus as one *pro libertate Graeciae*.[138]

In the wake of the Third Macedonian War Rome exploited the technique to drive home a lesson, to weaken states that might be a menace to the new settlement. So, a senatorial decree set the Lycians and Carians free of Rhodian control.[139] Another "liberated" Aenus and Maronea from Eumenes, and still another declared the Galatians "autonomous," a message to Eumenes and the Galatians alike.[140] Roman victories in Greece were still described by partisans as liberation. The defeat of Perseus and the abolition of monarchy in Macedonia and Illyria received characterization in a senatorial announcement as a "setting free" of those peoples. The Macedonians indeed were still

---

134. Livy, 38.44.4: *in libertate essent ac legibus suis uterentur.*

135. Lycian supporters certainly interpreted the response as affirming ἐλευθερία in 188: Polyb. 22.5.6. And the senatorial reply in 178, whatever its intention, inspired the Lycians to contend for their ἐλευθερία and αὐτονομία: Polyb. 25.5.3. For that reply see Polyb. 25.4.5; somewhat overblown by Livy, 41.6.11–12: *nec Lycios Rhodiis nec ullos alii cuiquam qui nati liberi sint in servitutem dari placere.* In general on this, see Schmitt, *Rom und Rhodos,* 81–128; and cf. Gruen, *CQ* 25 (1975): 64–68.

136. Livy, 43.4.12. This act of restitution, of course, stands in a long Roman tradition, as illustrated in the third century at Rhegium and at Locri; see above pp. 143–144.

137. *BCH* 10 (1886): 299–306 = Holleaux, *REG* 11 (1898): 258–266, lines 25–32: δόγμα περὶ τῆς ἀφορολογησίας; see below, Appendix I.

138. Livy, 43.8.6. Cf. *FDelphes,* III, 4, 367, line 3: πᾶσι τοῖς δημοκρατουμένοις τῶν Ἑλλήνων. Perseus, of course, saw it differently: he was fighting to liberate the world from Roman rule: Livy, 42.50.9, 42.52.15–16.

139. Polyb. 30.5.12; cf. Livy, 45.25.6; *IGUR,* no. 5 = *ILLRP,* I, no. 174.

140. Aenus and Maronea: Polyb. 30.3.7; Galatia: Polyb. 30.28: αὐτονομία; 30.30.6: ἐλευθερία.

to "use their own laws."[141] Individual peoples, formerly under Illyrian rule, were granted not only freedom but tax exemption for supporting the cause of Rome; others who failed to do so would remain tributary, a settlement on principles parallel to those applied at Apamea twenty years earlier.[142] The Romans plundered, pillaged, and destroyed in Epirus—after announcing that garrisons were to be removed so that "the Epirotes might be as free as the Macedonians." The irony is transmitted in straight-faced fashion by Livy.[143]

Even after the Achaean war in 146 when Greece had been crushed by Roman force, Rome declared all Greek cities (except Corinth) "free and autonomous." The traditional terminology persisted.[144] The terms had become debased, so it is customarily said, and empty of content. Clearly true, if by that is meant that real independence became circumscribed after 167 and more severely so after 146. Yet it is misconception to imagine that Rome deliberately distorted the language to screen her acquisitiveness and deceive her dependents. There is no deception here, nor any sham conceived to delude. The terms carried no less and no more meaning than they had in the third century: a rallying cry to win support and defame opponents, or an expression of *beneficia* bestowed by the greater power upon the weaker. Rome had reproduced the traditional phraseology; she had not devalued it. In the second century it became as common a parlance for her as it had long been for Hellenistic communities.[145]

Traditions died hard in the ancient world. The fact that Rome availed herself of the "freedom and autonomy" formula did not mean that Greek states had abandoned it as meaningless. Even in the era

141. Livy, 45.18.1–2, 45.26.12, 45.29.4. *liberos esse iubere Macedonas . . . utentes legibus suis*; cf. Polyb. 36.17.13.

142. Livy, 45.26.13–14.

143. Livy, 45.34.2–7.

144. Zon. 9.31.6: ἐλευθέρους πάντας καὶ αὐτονόμους . . . ἀφῆκε. Cf. the Delphic decree for Postumius Albinus, probably a member of the senatorial commission to settle Greece after the war; *SEG*, I, 152: ὑπὲρ τᾶς τῶν Ἑλλ[άνων ἐλευθερ]ίας. The terminology is confirmed by a document, the letter of a Roman governor to Dyme, perhaps in 115, referring to [τ]ῆς ἀποδεδομένης κατὰ [κ]οινὸν τοῖς Ἑλλη[σιν ἐ]λευθερίας: *Syll.*³ 684 = Sherk, *RDGE*, no. 43, lines 15–16; cf. Appian, *Mithr.* 58.

145. Cf., e.g., Rome's acknowledgment of *libertas* for the Jews in 164: Justin, 36.3.9. Also in 149, during negotiations with Carthage, the senate promised ἐλευθερίαν καὶ τοὺς νόμους; Polyb. 36.4.4. During the 90s the *patres* awarded freedom to Cappadocia and Paphlagonia—a freedom the Cappadocians declined, preferring submission to a monarch: Strabo, 12.2.11 (C 540); Justin, 38.2.6–8. And even as late as the 80s Sulla rewarded the Asian cities that fought against Mithridates by declaring them ἐλευθέρους: Appian, *Mithr.* 61; *Syll.*³ 742, lines 12–18; *OGIS*, 441 = Sherk, *RDGE*, no. 18, lines 49–50, 91–92; *FIRA*, 1, no. 11, lines 5–10. For discussion of *civitates liberae*, as a status within Roman provinces, an issue not relevant here, see Accame, *Il Dominio*, 46–74; Bernhardt, *Imperium und Eleutheria*, 88–176.

when Rome's military might was supreme the formula retained its currency in diplomatic relations among the Hellenes. The fragmentary character of Polybius' text and the Rome-centered orientation of Livy do not disclose many examples, but it is clear enough that Rome had usurped no monopoly on the convention after Apamea. Perseus flattered the Rhodians by calling them the persistent champions of freedom for all Greeks.[146] A Pergamene *strategos* of the Hellespontine area, probably in the reign of Eumenes II, urged upon the king recognition of the "ancestral constitution and laws" of a Greek city under his authority.[147] The peace treaty of 180/179 among several monarchs in Asia Minor also included as signatories various autonomous Greek communities.[148] The last testament of Attalus III, as is well known, willed his kingdom to Rome, but it also affirmed the freedom of Pergamum itself.[149] At about the same time, in the 130s, Antiochus Sidetes came to an agreement with the Jews which secured for them "their ancestral constitution."[150] And as late as 109/8 Antiochus VIII or IX, whose kingdom was but a shell, still solemnly authorized for the citizens of Seleucia in Pieria "freedom for all time."[151] The standard practices prevailed, even through the end of the second century.

V

To sum up. Declarations of freedom and autonomy, restoration of ancestral constitutions and laws, liberation from garrisons or tribute, had a long and continuous history throughout the Hellenistic period. Such pronouncements served as repeated slogans during the struggles among Alexander's successors. They continued as expressions to define cordial relations between monarchs and cities, as mottos to justify military action or topple hostile regimes, as polite terminology to indicate the suzerainty of greater over lesser powers. Rome did not concoct these formulas, nor did she ever employ them, in

146. Polyb. 27.4.7: διατελοῦσι προστατοῦντες οὐ μόνον τῆς αὐτῶν ἀλλὰ καὶ τῆς τῶν ἄλλων Ἑλλήνων ἐλευθερίας—pointedly omitted by Livy, 42.46.4.

147. BCH, 48 (1924), 2–3 = SEG, II, 663, lines 9–10: ἠξίωσεν τὸν βασιλέα ἀποδοθῆναι τοὺς τε νόμους καὶ τὴν πατρίον πολιτείαν. Discussion in Holleaux, Études II:73–125; cf. Magie, RRAM II:1012–1013, n. 55.

148. Polyb. 25.2.13.

149. OGIS, 338, line 5: ἀπολέλοιπεν τὴ[μ πατρί]δα ἡμῶν ἐλευθέραν. Cf. OGIS, 337, lines 4–5: ὁ δῆμος κατεστάθη εἰς τὴν πάτριον δημοκρατίαν. Most recent discussion by J. Hopp, Untersuchungen zur Geschichte der letzten Attaliden (Munich, 1977), 121–131, with bibliography.

150. Jos. Ant. 13.245: ἀξιῶν τὴν πάτριον αὐτοῖς πολιτείαν ἀποδοῦναι.

151. OGIS, 257 = Welles, RC, no. 71, lines 13–14: [ἐκρίναμεν εἰ]ς τὸν ἄπαντα χρόνον ἐλευθέρους [εἶναι].

their Hellenistic meaning, until the Second Macedonian War. And then the idea was brought naturally to her attention by her Greek allies for whom it was traditional—and who stood to gain by it. To the senate it was convenient and welcome; it draped Rome in the garb of benefactor and made the more splendid the withdrawal which she intended anyway.

When friction developed with Antiochus these same conventions allowed Rome to appeal for Greek support in terms familiar to the Hellenes. Thereafter they furnished a normal mode of discourse for Roman diplomats, as they had long done for Greeks. Propaganda, to be sure, but not fraudulence. Everyone knew the meaning. Interstate relations among Greeks continued to exercise that terminology in the second century, without resigning it to a Roman monopoly. As with φιλία, so with ἐλευθερία and αὐτονομία; not a duplicitous artifice of Rome, but a natural adaptation to Hellenic categories.

· Chapter 5 ·

Patrocinium and *Clientela*

Patron-client relationships pervaded the Roman political and social structure. As an integral part of the system on the domestic scene, they swayed the operations of state and governed associations among individuals and families at all levels of society. The facts are well known and long established.[1] In more recent years, however, scholarship has placed increasing emphasis upon extension of the patron-client formula to foreign affairs. Private relations of *fides*, *hospitium*, and *clientela* saw a natural transformation, so it is argued, into the bonds that tied external communities to Rome. Hence, we read of a Roman *patrocinium* abroad, of client states and client kings, the pattern of personal obligations and *officia* converted into an international system, an explanation for Rome's evolving ascendancy over dependent principalities.[2] The subject merits a detailed assessment. In particular, one must avoid the anachronism of reading back the developed standards of the late Republic into the era of Rome's early contacts with the Hellenistic world. Did the senate indeed apply the *clientela* model to overseas arrangements during the third and second centuries?

1. See the important exposition of M. Gelzer, *The Roman Nobility*, tr. by R. Seager (New York, 1969), 62–86; drawing on concepts first formulated by Fustel de Coulanges. See also A. von Premerstein, *RE* IV:23–55, "*clientes*."

2. Cf. Sands, *Client Princes, passim*; Gelzer, *Roman Nobility*, 86–101; H. Volkmann, *Hermes*, 82 (1954), 465–476; Badian, *Foreign Clientelae, passim*; especially, 1–13, 154–167; H. Drexler, *RhM* 102 (1959): 119–122; D. Timpe, *Hermes* 90 (1962), 334–375; R. M. Errington, *The Dawn of Empire: Rome's Rise to World Power* (London, 1971), *passim*; I. E. M. Edlund, *Klio*, 59 (1977), 129–136. Apt criticisms of this approach are delivered by J. Bleicken, *Gnomon* 36 (1964): 176–183, though only in general terms. Similarly, Harris, *War and Imperialism*, 135, n. 2.

Anachronisms

A noteworthy item needs to be underlined. The terms *cliens* and *clientela* are almost never used with regard to interstate relations between Rome and the Greek East during the long period under scrutiny here.[3] When they do appear, they occur in late contexts and with reference to the West. Cicero puts into the mouth of Scipio Aemilianus a passing allusion to the Massiliotes as *nostri clientes*.[4] No elaboration is given and none called for. Massilia's *amicitia* with Rome was of great antiquity by that time. But whether Scipio would have employed the phrase even as late as 129 must remain uncertain. We can be sure only that Cicero used it.

Much later still, Florus refers to Numidia at the time of Jugurtha as *in fide et in clientela* of the Roman senate and people.[5] But that explicit formulation is not to be found even in Sallust's monograph on the Jugurthine war.[6] Sallust does, to be sure, have the Numidian prince Adherbal, in a plea to the senate for aid, express an affiliation that amounts to clientship: his rule of Numidia is a mere *procuratio*; the *ius* and *imperium* belong to Rome; the kingdom is a Roman gift.[7] A similar formulation occurs in Livy's account of Masgaba's mission to Rome in 168: Massinissa's son affirms that he has but the *usus* of his *regnum*; Rome possesses the *dominium* and *ius*.[8] But general principles ought not to be extrapolated from these passages. The house of Massinissa was in a special category, its dominion over Numidia secured by Scipio Africanus for services in the Hannibalic war and ratified by the senate as a counter-balance to Carthage.[9] Dependence on Roman favor and the importance of Roman interest in the area sharply distinguish Massinissa and his family from states in the Hellenistic East. Furthermore, the circumstances of Masgaba's embassy and of

3. On Livy, 37.54.17, see below pp. 176–177.

4. Cic. *De Rep.* 1.43—part of his remarks on the failings of various constitutional forms, not a discussion of interstate relations.

5. Florus, 1.36.3.

6. The nearest approximation is Sallust, *Iug.* 33.4: *in fide et clementia populi Romani*. Public documents were more forthright. The *lex repetundarum* of 123 refers to external nations as *in arbitratu dicione potestate amicitiav[e populi Romani]*; *FIRA*, I, no. 7, line 1.

7. Sallust, *Iug.* 14.1, 14.8, 14.11, 14.25, 24.7, 24.10.

8. Livy, 45.13.15. The Roman response is courteous and parallel, Livy, 45.14.2: *illum favente populo Romano regnum adeptum*. This need not imply a misunderstanding or contrasting views of *clientela*, as Badian, *Foreign Clientelae*, 129. See the remarks of Timpe, *Hermes* 90 (1962): 341–343.

9. Livy, 30.15.11, 30.17.7–12, 30.44.12, 37.25.9; Sallust, *Iug.* 5.4; Val. Max. 5.2.ext.4.

Adherbal's plea need to be considered. Massinissa's generous assistance to Rome during the Third Macedonian War had his own designs on Carthage in view, designs which he hoped to implement after the war; hence, the fulsome phrases of Masgaba.[10] A half-century later Adherbal, of course, came in despair and fear of Jugurtha. It is no wonder that he laid stress on Roman *beneficia*, and called upon the *patres* to vindicate Rome's *maiestas* by protecting her friends against aggression.[11] Nor should one overlook Sallust's own purposes in contrasting an idealized Roman tutelage in the past with sordid senatorial behavior at the time of Jugurtha.[12] It will be prudent to avoid using the Numidian situation as exemplary of senatorial attitudes toward foreign *clientelae*.

Idealization of the past was standard fare in late Republican literature, as in most periods of Roman history. It has left its mark on the image of Rome's external policy. A celebrated and oft-cited comment of Cicero belongs under this heading: the Roman *imperium* was held together by *beneficia*, wars were waged and provinces defended on behalf of allies, the senate was a refuge for kings, peoples, and nations, justice and *fides* predominated, Rome exercised a *patrocinium orbis terrae*.[13] To take this as serious analysis of the senate's practice or even as description of its posture would be misguided. Cicero's aim is to highlight the evils of post-Sullan oppression, the exploitation of *socii*, the degeneracy of Roman foreign policy into injustice and tyranny. For those purposes it was convenient to project a righteous *patrocinium* into the unspecified past.[14] Cicero's contemporary Diodorus gives expression to comparable sentiments: the Romans acquired hegemony by treating even conquered peoples as beneficiaries and friends, thereby winning the voluntary allegiance of kings, cities, and nations, but later gave way to terrorism and destruction.[15] Sallust's

10. See, especially, Livy, 43.3 6–7, 43.6.11–14. Rome withheld concurrence to Massinissa's requests: Livy, 45.14.4–5.

11. Sallust, *Iug.* 14.3, 14.7–8, 14.12, 14.16, 14.18–19, 14.25, 24.10. Cf. the analysis of W. Suerbaum, *Hermes* 92 (1964): 85–106. Detailed commentary on the speech, with bibliography, in E. Koestermann, *C. Sallustius Crispus, Bellum Iugurthinum* (Heidelberg, 1971), 66–81.

12. On this, see the astute remarks of Timpe, *Hermes* 90 (1962): 334–375.

13. Cic. *De Off.* 2.26–27. On Cicero's attitude toward the Roman *patrocinium* generally, see the references and discussion in H. Meyer, *Cicero und das Reich* (Köln, 1957), 211–239. A recent collection of testimony also by P. A. Brunt, in P. D. A. Garnsey and C. R. Whittaker, *Imperialism in the Ancient World* (Cambridge, 1978), 162–172.

14. Cic. *De Off.* 2.26–29. An example in Cic. *Pro Sest.* 57.

15. Diod. 32.4.4–5. The statement is customarily supposed to have been copied from Polybius; e.g., Gelzer, *Philologus* 86 (1931): 290–291; Walbank, *JRS* 55 (1965): 10–11. But it comes from Diodorus' preface to Book 32 (cf. 32.2), and Diodorus was

strictures on Roman behavior after the fall of Carthage are too well known to require rehearsal: justice and integrity yielded to the worst sorts of cruelty visited upon the vanquished; the exercise of empire became equivalent to the infliction of injury.[16] With deliberate irony Sallust has Sulla himself proclaim the theoretical principles of a bygone era, that Rome preferred *amici* to *servi*, voluntary compliance to constraint.[17] In this spirit Cicero calls upon his brother, as governor of Asia, to redress grievances, promote the welfare of provincials, earn the appellation of *parens Asiae*.[18] Such statements reflect the aspirations of late Republican thinkers and their discontent with contemporary practices. The standards of an earlier age appeared the more admirable by contrast. But that literary device ought not to be confused with the actual principles of Roman policy makers in the third and second centuries.

Another confusion needs to be cleared away: the *post eventum* justifications of Rome's overseas rule. Vergil supplied the classic formulation: Rome's mission was to spare the subdued and humble the haughty.[19] For Cicero, Rome was the *arx regum ac nationum exterrarum*.[20] The orator goes further still in a famous pronouncement: Rome gained her dominion over all lands by defending allies; her *imperium* is not only just but natural, for superior peoples will govern their inferiors to the advantage of the latter.[21] The idea derives from Greek ethical theory, ultimately from Plato and Aristotle. Whether it was mediated by Panaetius or Posidonius is debatable and not of concern here.[22] Application of the theory to Roman rule, however,

---

capable of composing his own prefaces. Cf. his remarks elsewhere on Roman harshness toward allies after 146: 34/5.33.5; and on decline in Roman character after acquisition of empire: 37.3.1–6.

16. Sallust, *Cat.* 9–12; note 12.5: *proinde quasi iniuriam facere id demum esset imperio uti.*

17. Sallust, *Iug.* 102.6: *a principio imperi melius visum amicos quam servos quaerere, tutiusque rati volentibus quam coactis imperitare.*

18. Cic. *Ad Q. Frat.* 1.1.3; cf. *De Leg.* 3.9.

19. Vergil *Aen.* 6.853.

20. Cic. *Pro Sulla*, 33; cf. *De Leg. Agrar.* 1.18; *P. Red. in Sen.* 2; *Pro Mil.* 90. See also his description of the *lex repetundarum* as *patrona* of Rome's friends and allies: Cic. *Div. in Caec.* 65; cf. 18. A somewhat more realistic assessment in *Ad Herenn.* 4.9.13: *cui imperio omnes gentes, reges, nationes, partim vi, partim voluntate consenserunt, cum aut armis aut liberalitate a populo Romano superati essent.*

21. Cic. *De Rep.* 3.35–37.

22. The Greek philosophical background is admirably elucidated by W. Capelle, *Klio* 25 (1932): 86–113. The view that Panaetius lies behind Cicero's statement has won general acceptance; e.g., Capelle, *op. cit.*, 93–95; Walbank, *JRS* 55 (1965): 13–14; strongly controverted by H. Strasburger, *JRS* 55 (1965): 44–45, n. 50. The fragments of Posidonius enunciate similar attitudes; see references and discussion in Capelle, *op. cit.*,

belongs to the late Republic. Livy alleges that Italian communities in the Hannibalic war remained unmoved in loyalty to a just and moderate regime, fixed by the bond of "obeying their betters."[23] And Diodorus has a senatorial spokesman in 201 argue that the crushing of Carthage, like the extirpation of wild beasts, will make Rome a κοινὸς εὐεργέτης.[24] As subsequent rationalizations—at a time when Roman supremacy in the Mediterranean had long been a fact—these pronouncements are intelligible. But they shed no light on the period when that supremacy was in process of accomplishment. It is noteworthy and revealing that Polybius proved unable to formulate a theory of Roman imperialism. And nowhere, even among these later affirmations, do we find a clear acknowledgment that Rome modeled her international dealings on the private relations of a patron to his client.[25]

Personal Patronage, Homage, and Gratitude

A somewhat different item demands attention: the patronage of individual Romans and their families over foreign communities and principalities. Evidence does exist for this type of relationship.[26] But

---

98–105; cf. Walbank, *op. cit.*, 14–15. But he was no mere apologist for Roman imperialism: Strasburger, *op. cit.*, 46–53. Cf. A. Momigliano, *Alien Wisdom: The Limits of Hellenization* (Cambridge, 1975), 30–36. The fragments of Posidonius are collected now in L. Edelstein and I. G. Kidd, *Posidonius: Volume I. The Fragments* (Cambridge, 1972).

23. Livy, 22.13.11: *quia iusto et moderato regebantur imperio nec abnuebant, quod unum vinculum fidei est, melioribus parere.*

24. Diod. 27.18.2. The passage is rightly called attention to by H. Volkmann, *Hermes* 82 (1954): 465–476. But his view, accepted by Strasburger, *op. cit.*, 45, that this authentically represents Roman attitudes at the turn of the third century, is quite unconvincing.

25. The closest such statement is in Dion. Hal. 2.11.1, who sees them as simultaneous institutions extant already at the time of Romulus! He refers, of course, to Italian communities, not to overseas dependencies. The parallel between individual clients and client states is drawn in the early Principate by the jurist Proculus, *Dig.* 49.15.7.1: *quemadmodum clientes nostros intellegimus liberos esse, etiamsi neque auctoritate neque dignitate neque viribus nobis pares sunt, sic eos, qui maiestatem nostram comiter conservare debent, liberos esse intellegendum est.* Proculus' point, however, is that interstate relations between superior and inferior powers need not compromise the *libertas* of the latter. Patron-client associations on the personal level are summoned up as an analogy—not as an explanation. There is no inference that external relations patterned themselves on private *clientela*.

26. E.g., Cic. *Ad Fam.* 13.64.2. See examples cited by Gelzer, *Roman Nobility*, 86–101; Badian, *Foreign Clientelae*, 154–167; L. Harmand, *Le patronat sur les collectivités publiques des origines au Bas-Empire* (Paris, 1957), 13–23, 27–48. In a rather different cate-

again one must be wary of building too much on late Republican instances. Early examples are few—and, in some cases, disputable. More important is a question rarely, if ever, asked: was this practice generated from a specifically Roman institution?

Cicero remarks that *imperatores* who receive conquered peoples into *fides* become their *patroni* by ancestral tradition.[27] How firm and how old was the *mos maiorum* on this matter we cannot know. The Samnites in 325 allegedly surrendered and entrusted their cause to the *fides* and *virtus* of the Roman dictator L. Papirius Cursor.[28] But no subsequent patronage over Samnium by the Papirii stands on record. A half-century later, we are told, C. Fabricius Luscinus had all the Samnites in his *clientela*; a patent exaggeration, if not an invention.[29] The first clear case, and a most notorious one, is that of M. Marcellus, conqueror of Syracuse and later patron of the city. The hereditary connections of Marcellus' house to Sicily endured for generations thereafter, as Cicero's *Verrines* make plain.[30] But the origins of that association need to be underscored. It came on the initiative of the Syracusans, not on invitation of Marcellus. In 212, with the city on its knees, representatives approached the Roman and raised the possibility of a *clientela* and *tutela* by the Marcellan clan over Syracuse.[31] Marcellus, of course, went on to plunder the city anyway. And in 210, when Syracusan envoys failed to receive satisfaction from the senate, they once again desperately implored Marcellus to accept Syracuse *in fidem clientelamque*, a request he then acceded to.[32] The story distinctly places Greek initiative in the forefront.

Scipio Africanus' victory at New Carthage in 209 brought

---

gory are patrons of colonial foundations in Italy. The institution is mentioned but once for the early Republic: Livy, 9.20.10. Other examples in the first century B.C.: Cic. *Pro Sulla*, 60–61; *CIL*, I², 594 = *ILS*, 6087; Harmand, *Le patronat*, 23–26.

27. Cic. *De Off.* 1.35. By contrast, Dionysius asserts that conquered states chose their own patrons from among the Romans, 2.11.1: τῶν ἐκ πολέμου κεκρατημένων ἑκάστη φύλακας εἶχε καὶ προστάτας οὓς ἐβούλετο Ῥωμαίων.

28. Livy, 8.36.12.

29. Val. Max. 4.3.6; cf. Gellius, 1.14. See the arguments of G. Forni, *Athenaeum* 21 (1953): 176–179. Still another century later, the Samnites are called clients of the elder Cato: Cic. *De Rep.* 3.40.

30. Cic. *Div. in Caec.* 13; *Verr.* 2.3.45, 2.4.89–90; Ps.-Ascon. 187, 190, Stangl. The hypothesis of Harmand, *Le patronat*, 27, 108–109, that the patronage of the Claudii Pulchri over Messana (Cic. *Verr.* 2.4.6) derives from the First Punic War, is refuted by Cic. *Verr.* 2.3.45, 2.4.90.

31. Livy, 25.29.6: *incolumesque Syracusas familiae vestrae sub clientela nominis Marcellorum tutelaque habendas tradas.*

32. Livy, 26.32.8: *obsecrantes ut . . . veniam eis daret, et in fidem clientelamque se urbemque Syracusas acciperet; pollicens hoc consul clementer appellatos eos dimisit;* Val. Max. 4.1.7.

Spanish chieftains and tribes scurrying to be accepted as his friends and offering assistance in the war.[33] His relationship with Massinissa too began when the Numidian prince volunteered his services.[34] After Scipio sanctioned Massinissa's claim to the throne, bonds between the two houses became especially close.[35] As conqueror of Carthage and benefactor of Massinissa, Africanus naturally had a hand in adjudicating disputes between the two, as in 193.[136] Nearly half a century later Scipio Aemilianus, capitalizing on the ancestral links, arrived in Africa to obtain elephants. He also sought—in vain—to mediate a quarrel between Massinissa and Carthage.[37] And, as is well known, Massinissa's death-bed request authorized Aemilianus to settle affairs in the kingdom and divide its holdings among the king's sons.[38] But it was plainly in Massinissa's interest to maintain and enhance those ties.[39] They did not define and rarely influenced state policy in Rome. Despite Scipionic patronage, Massinissa again and again met with frustration at senatorial hands.[40] In a comparable instance, the Macedonians sought out Aemilianus, son of their conqueror L. Aemilius Paullus, to arbitrate civil strife in 151. Aemilianus brushed aside the request, preferring military service in Spain.[41] It seems clear that foreign states or leaders called upon these prior connections when it suited their purposes. Roman *patroni* seldom commenced the actions or brought results. And senatorial policy was largely unaffected by the personal ties of individual members.[42]

The pattern remains consistent prior to the late Republic, so far as our evidence goes. War and conquest need not be the only methods whereby to inaugurate relations between a Roman family and a foreign community.[43] Hellenistic states would curry favor on any available grounds. So, the Sicilians in 195 sent grain to Rome in honor of the aedile C. Flaminius, whose father had once governed the province.[44] Aetolian envoys, hoping for lenient terms in 189, sought the

33. Polyb. 10.34.1–10.35.3; Livy, 27.17.1–3, 37.6.6, 37.25.9.

34. Appian, *Iber.* 37.

35. Livy, 30.15.11, 30.17.7–12, 30.44.12, 37.25.9; Sallust, *Iug.* 5.4; Val. Max. 5.2.ext.4.

36. Livy, 34.62.15–18; Zon. 9.18; cf. Appian, *Lib.* 67.

37. Appian, *Lib.* 71–72; Val. Max. 10.2.4.

38. Polyb. 36.16.10; Appian, *Lib.* 105–106; Zon. 9.27; Livy, *Per.* 50.

39. Cf. also Jugurtha's efforts to play up to Aemilianus: Sallust, *Iug.* 7.4, 8.2–9.2, 22.2.

40. Cf. Livy, 40.17.5, 40.34.14, 42.24.6–9, 42.29.9–10, 45.14.5; Appian, *Lib.* 94.

41. Polyb. 35.4.10–12. On Paullus' *beneficia* for the Macedonians, see Plut. *Aem. Paull.* 39.4–5.

42. The elder Cato's service in Spain induced him later to act as protector of Spanish interests but created serious opposition among his peers: Cic. *Div. in Caec.* 66.

43. As is rightly pointed out by Badian, *Foreign Clientelae*, 157–159.

44. Livy, 33.42.8. A parallel case has now turned up in a new inscription from

assistance of C. Valerius Laevinus, for his father had negotiated the original treaty with Aetolia.[45] We may note, however, that this recourse had to be suggested to the Aetolians by others, and that Laevinus' relationship with the consul was at least as important an element in their application to him.[46] Aetolia's claims were challenged by Philip V of Macedonia, who applied to his "friends" in the Roman senate.[47] Yet the senate's eventual decision was swayed by Greek advocates of Aetolia—not by Laevinus or by Philip.[48]

In the later 180s Deinocrates of Messene hoped to exploit his personal friendship with Flamininus for schemes in the Peloponnese; and Demetrius, the younger son of Philip V, took encouragement from his handsome treatment by Flamininus. But the Roman's support for Deinocrates came to naught. And his association with Demetrius inadvertently issued in the young man's destruction.[49] At the same time Eumenes solicited Roman assistance against Pharnaces by sending his brothers to make contact with his own friends and *hospites* in Rome.[50] They received warm welcome and full courtesies. But Rome's public policy was simply to make peace between Eumenes and Pharnaces.[51] In 172 Perseus endeavored to prevent war with Rome in a parley with Q. Marcius Philippus, alluding to a *hospitium* between the two houses.[52] The fruitlessness of that appeal was, of course, dramatically demonstrated by what followed: the Third Macedonian War. Antiochus IV ingratiated himself with members of the senate and young aristocrats during his stay as hostage at Rome in the 180s and 170s, an experience that enhanced his later representations to the *patres*.[53] But his Roman friends did not prevent the "day of Eleusis." The Epirote politician Charops consciously cultivated Roman acquaintances during a long stay in Italy. Again without immediate

---

Larisa announced at the 1982 Epigraphical Congress in Athens by K. J. Gallis. The Thessalians honor the wishes of the Roman aedile Q. Caecilius Metellus, Q.F. to send grain in relief of a Roman food shortage, citing their gratitude for his benefactions and those of his πρόγονοι (lines 16–20). Gallis identifies Q. Metellus as Macedonicus, aedile ca. 150 B.C. More plausibly, he is Balearicus, aedile ca. 130 B.C., with Macedonicus among his πρόγονοι. Cf. also *ArchEph* (1910): 374–375 = *ISE*, no. 101. See below, n. 79.

45. Polyb. 21.29.10–12; Livy, 38.9.8; cf. Livy, 26.24.
46. Polyb. 21.29.10–11; Livy, 38.9.8.
47. Polyb. 21.31.3–4—not repeated by Livy, 38.10.3, who speaks only of *principes*.
48. Polyb. 21.31.5–16; Livy, 38.10.
49. On Deinocrates: Polyb. 23.5.1–3, 23.5.13–18; on Demetrius: Polyb. 23.3.7–8; Livy, 40.11.1–3, 40.12.17, 40.20.3, 40.23–24; Appian, *Mac.* 9.6, etc.; a detailed discussion in Gruen, *GRBS* 15 (1974): 221–246.
50. Polyb. 24.5.1–7.
51. Polyb. 24.5.8, 24.14.10–11, 24.15.
52. Livy, 42.38.8–9, 42.40.11.
53. Livy, 42.6.6–12; cf. Asconius, 13, Clark.

effect. It took the events of the Third Macedonian War to bring Charops political ascendancy in Epirus. The ascendancy did not endure.
A reign of terror at home eroded his position and a later trip to Rome
gained him nothing but snubs from Roman senators.[54] Rhodian envoys in 167 addressed pitiful appeals to their Roman "friends" to escape a declaration of war. That much they obtained, but no more. The
island suffered grievously at Rome's hands in the aftermath of the
Third Macedonian War.[55]

In short, assistance by *patroni* throughout this period had little
impact.[56] Insofar as such patronage existed at all, it came almost invariably at the behest of foreigners advancing personal aims or hoping to avoid ruin. There is no testimony that Romans employed overseas clients for their own ends prior to the late Republic.[57] The practice
can hardly be reckoned a Roman institution in origin—or indeed
an institution at all before the conquest of the Mediterranean was
complete.[58]

Greek communities also bestowed honors upon individual Romans in increasing numbers during the second century. Proxeny decrees, tributes of various kinds, and expressions of gratitude abound.
Such practices were, of course, typically Hellenic. Grants of *proxenia*
for favors performed, testimonials to benefactors, or cultivation of pro-

54. Polyb. 27.15, 32.5–6.

55. The appeal to friends: Polyb. 30.4.5–9; cf. Livy, 45.20.10. The severe treat-
ment: Polyb. 30.19–21, 30.23, 30.31; Livy, 45.25; Dio, 20.68.2–3; Zon. 9.24. An earlier
Rhodian embassy, before the war, is recorded by Livy. The envoys came to denounce
Eumenes and obtained audience in the senate through their *patroni*: Livy, 42.14.5–10.
Even if the story is authentic, which is doubtful, it shows only that the *patroni* of
Rhodes were unable to avert a hostile attitude against them.

56. Cf. also the Tean embassy which solicited Roman *patroni* on behalf of Abdera: *Syll.*[3] 656, lines 20–24. The inscription pointedly omits any reference to the mission's success; cf. Robert, *BCH* 59 (1935): 507–513. Its date is customarily given as 167;
so, most recently, E. Condurachi, *Latomus* 29 (1970): 581–594. But there is no firm evidence, and it may come much later. See now G. Chiranky, *Athenaeum* 60 (1982): 470–481.

57. The tutelage of Egyptian princes by M. Aemilius Lepidus, reflected on a coin
by Lepidus the triumvir (M. Crawford, *Roman Republican Coinage* [Cambridge, 1974],
419.2) is plainly a late Republican fiction; see below pp. 680–682. The only second-
century evidence that exists on this is advice given by Lepidus to Egyptian envoys in
169, suggesting that they not offer themselves as peace mediators before the Roman
senate: Polyb. 28.1.8. But nothing is said about patronage here. Lepidus' position as a
senior consular, *pontifex maximus*, and, especially, *princeps senatus* is more than adequate to explain his role.

58. In this regard we might notice the procedure involved when Spanish envoys
complained of Roman rapacity in 171. The senate authorized them to select *patroni* to
take up their case: Livy, 43.2.4–5. The term refers here to advocates in a judicial hearing; it does not denote a more general patronage—as erroneously assumed by Gelzer,
Roman Nobility, 86–87; also, Badian, *Foreign Clientelae*, 161. What the affair suggests, in
fact, is that provincials did not possess established patrons but had to choose them on
an *ad hoc* basis. Cf. Dion. Hal. 2.11.1.

spective benefactors are found throughout Greek history and throughout the Greek world. Homage paid to particular Romans who earned
such tributes falls naturally within that pattern. It bears no relation to
any Roman assertions of patronage.[59]

T. Flamininus, as is well known, received such official compliments in bulk. His victory over Philip V and his supervision of the
subsequent settlement inescapably called forth lavish tokens of esteem.[60] Festivals were established, with priests and sacrifices, in his
honor at Chalcis and Argos.[61] In true Hellenistic style, Flamininus is
hailed as *soter* and *euergetes*, or reference is made to his *euergesia*, his
arete, and his *eunoia* in honorific decrees from Chalcis, Cos, Gytheum,
Corinth, Scotussa in Thessaly, and probably Phanotia in Phocis.[62] An
equestrian statue of Flamininus was dedicated at Delphi.[63] Such expressions of gratitude may represent genuine enthusiasm—or efforts
to curry favor. But the motive matters little. There is no reason to imagine that Flamininus deliberately prompted them, any more than he did
the gold coins bearing his image, which surely came on Greek initiative.[64] Flamininus did offer his own dedications at the great Greek
shrines in Delphi and Delos. This, however, was the standard Greek
practice of conquerors and benefactors, congenial to but hardly an invention of the Roman.[65]

59. Notice the Aetolian proxeny list of ca. 260 which includes a L. L.f. Olcaius
(or Volceius?); *IG*, IX,1 ², 17, line 51. Plainly this comes well before Roman state involvement in the East. Another Roman, in fact, enjoyed the patronage of Ptolemy IV, served
him as officer of the Ptolemaic garrison in Itanus, and dedicated buildings to him and
his queen: *IC*, III, 4, 18. We have record of still another Roman who participated in the
games at Lebadeia in Boeotia in the time of Ptolemy Philopator: *BCH* 25 (1901): 367–
368. Huss, *Untersuchungen*, 121–125, identifies the king with Ptolemy IV; more probably he is Ptolemy VII or Ptolemy XII; see Holleaux, *Études* I: 99–120.

60. Most, but not all, are collected by H. Gundel, *RE* XXIV: 1075–1076, "Quinctius," n. 45.

61. Chalcis: Plut. *Flam*. 16.4; Argos: G. Daux, *BCH* 88 (1964): 569–576, cf. Livy,
34.41.1–3. Perhaps also at Eretria: *IG*, XII, 9, 233.

62. Chalcis: *IG*, XII, 9, 931; cf. Livy, 35.49.6; Cos: *IGRR*, IV, 1049; Gytheum: *Syll*.³
592; Corinth: *SEG*, XI, 73 = Moretti, *ISE*, no. 37; Scotussa: E. Mastrokostas, *REA* 66
(1964): 309–310 = *ISE*, no. 98; cf. Daux, *BCH* 89 (1965): 301–303; Phanotea: G. Klaffenbach, *Chiron* 1 (1971): 167–168; cf. Livy, 32.18.6.

63. *Syll*.³ 616. He appears also in a lengthy proxeny list at Delphi under the year
189/8; *Syll*.³ 585, line 46. Whether certain portrait busts at Delphi are representations of
Flamininus must remain conjectural: F. Chamoux, *BCH* 89 (1965): 214–224. More hypothetical still is the identification of a bronze statue by a Greek artist as a portrait of
Flamininus: J. C. Balty, *MEFRA* 90 (1978): 669–686.

64. On the coinage, see Crawford, *RRC*, I, no. 548. Cf. also the poem of the Messenian Alcaeus in praise of Flamininus: *Anth. Pal*. 16.5.

65. The dedication at Delphi: Plut. *Flam*. 12.6–7. At Delos Flamininus' dedications are recorded in long inventories, where he appears among many dedicants, some
Roman but mostly Greek: *IdeDélos*, 439A, lines 77–78; 442B, lines 85–86; 1429A, lines
21–22; 1441A, lines 105–106; 1446, line 15.

Similar documents commemorated the deeds of the Scipios. P. Scipio Africanus, as early as 206/5, sent gifts to Delphi from Carthaginian spoils in Spain.[66] Numerous dedications by the brothers stand in the Delian records and apparently one at Delphi, in consequence of the victory over Antiochus.[67] Proxeny decrees, in turn, from Delos and from Aptera in Crete, honor the Scipios as *euergetes*—in conventional Hellenistic language.[68] But the Scipios had no monopoly and no special relationship to the pan-Hellenic sites. Various commanders, praetors, and promagistrates who served in the Asian campaigns of 191–189 made offerings at Delos, thereby to take their place in the register of dedicants: A. Atilius Serranus, C. Livius Salinator, L. Aemilius Regillus, Cn. Manlius Vulso, Q. Fabius Labeo.[69] Delphi naturally paid its respects to M.' Acilius Glabrio, who drove Antiochus out of Greece in 191 and liberated the sacred city from Aetolian control. The Delphians erected an equestrian statue and bestowed numerous privileges upon the victor.[70] Obscure Romans and Italians too received the thanks of Greek communities for services performed in the Aetolian war: like Sex. Orfidienus, who protected Chyretiae from depredations by garrison soldiers.[71]

None of this established any *clientela* relations. The Delian inventories contain lengthy rolls of benefactors, including not only Roman generals who served in the East, but private citizens, Romans

66. Livy, 28.45.12.

67. Delphi: *SEG*, I, 144; cf. Daux, *Delphes*, 599–600; Delos: *IdeDélos*, 427, lines 12–13; 428, lines 13–14; 439A, line 81; 442B, lines 85–86, 90–91, 102; 1429A, col. I, lines 23, 26–28; 1429A, col. II, line 16; 1441A, line 106; 1443, line 94; 1450A, lines 67–68, 90; 1458, lines 14–15. It has been argued that some of these dedications belong to L. Scipio's praetorship and a purported trip to the East by P. Scipio in 193: Zon. 9.18; Holleaux, *Études* V: 184–207; cf. H. H. Scullard, *Scipio Africanus: Soldier and Politician* (Ithaca, 1970), 285–286, n. 163. But that presumes more precision than should be accorded to the terms στρατηγὸς and στρατηγὸς ὕπατος; see U. Schlag, *Regnum in Senatu* (Stuttgart, 1968), 132–138.

68. Delos (P. Scipio): *Syll.*³ 617; Aptera (the Scipios): *IC*, II, 3, 5. Cf. *IC*, II, 23, 13, from Polyrrhenia, which honors Cn. Scipio "Hispanus," probably Hispallus, the future consul of 176 and also named in the Aptera decree. All these date most likely to 189, during the Scipios' return from Asia; cf. M. Guarducci, *RivFilol* 7 (1929): 60–85.

69. Serranus, *IdeDélos*, 442B, line 86; 1429A, col. I, line 20; 1450A, line 66; Salinator: *IdeDélos*, 439A, line 78; 442, lines 78, 80; 1429A, col. I, lines 20, 30; Regillus: *IdeDélos*, 442B, line 104; Vulso: *IdeDélos*, 442B, line 100; 1429A, col. I, lines 24–25; 1441A, line 107; 1450A, line 67; Labeo: *IdeDélos*, 442B, line 103; 1429A, col. I, line 19; 1441A, line 104; 1443, line 92; 1450A, line 66; 1458, line 11. Regillus is also given proxeny honors, together with the Scipios, by Aptera: *IC*, II, 3, 5—if the restoration be correct.

70. *Syll.*³ 607–608.

71. *ArchEph* (1917), 1–7 = *ISE*, no. 95. Cf. also the decree of Larisa for "Quintus, son of Titus": *ArchEph* (1910), 344–349; and that of Gonnoi for C. Flavius Apollonius and C. Flavius Bucco: Helly, *Gonnoi*, II, no. 42.

and Italians, otherwise unknown, who made offerings to the shrine, their names intermingled with numerous Hellenic kings, dynasts, and quite obscure individuals.[72] Delphi was also generous with its awards of *proxenia*. A long catalogue of those so honored contains 135 names stretching over the first half of the second century. A few are recognizable as Romans who had earned Delphic gratitude and received honorific decrees after the Aetolian war in 190–188, including Flamininus. Others are mere names to us, private individuals, businessmen, or visitors whose services to Delphi can hardly have been of international significance. Here again they are heavily outnumbered by the Greeks who obtained such honors, and are interspersed among them without any special distinction.[73] It is plain that offerings at Delos and proxeny awards from Delphi did not signify patronage in any extended sense.

The anxieties of war and the relief felt by states that were spared naturally called forth honorific decrees for Romans engaged in the struggle. The Third Macedonian War produced several examples. So, the Achaean League erected a statue in Olympia for Q. Marcius Philippus, consul and head of the Roman forces in 169.[74] And Philippus made his own dedications at Delos.[75] L. Hortensius, praetor and commander of the fleet in 170, earned a reputation for harshness and brutality in various Greek cities. Yet the Athenians awarded him *proxenia* and the Delians dedicated a crown for him. That was elementary prudence and a means of self-preservation.[76] Junior officers too could obtain similar dignities: Acraephia in Boeotia bestowed *proxenia* upon P. Cornelius Lentulus, a mere military tribune, though one who had temporarily conducted the siege of Haliartus in 171.[77] Even an envoy could secure benefits for a Greek state: the Achaeans showed

72. E.g., *IdeDélos*, 427, line 11; 442B, line 148; 1429A, col. III, lines 5, 17–24; 1450A, lines 72–73.

73. *Syll.*³ 585. For the Romans honored in 190–188, see numbers 32–36, 46–48, with Dittenberger's notes; cf. *SEG*, I, 147 = *FDelphes*, III, 4, 427, on M. Aemilius Lepidus. All the Romans contained in the catalogue, plus a few others in individual decrees, are conveniently listed by Daux, *Delphes*, 587–589, who finds a total of thirty-seven in the second and first centuries.

74. *Syll.*³ 649.

75. *IdeDélos*, 1429A, lines 31–32; 1450A, line 69.

76. The Athenian proxeny decree: *IG*, II², 907, lines 3–10; the Delian crown: *IdeDélos*, 461Aa, lines 82–83. On Hortensius' savagery at Abdera and Chalcis, see Livy, 43.4.8–13, 43.7.5–43.8.7. Similarly, C. Lucretius Gallus, brutal in his treatment of Greeks as commander of the fleet in 171, but nonetheless honored by the Delians afterward: Livy, 43.4.5–7; *IdeDélos*, 460E, lines 18–19.

77. M. Feyel, *BCH* 79 (1955): 419–422; *SEG*, XV, 331; republished in *ISE*, no. 70. On Lentulus' rank and service, see Livy, 42.49.9, 42.56.3. He may also be the envoy of 172 and 168; Livy, 42.47.12, 45.4.7.

gratitude to Cn. Octavius with a proxeny decree for his mission in the winter of 170/69.[78] The Cn. Domitius Ahenobarbus honored as εὐεργέτης by Amphipolis may be the man who served among the *decem legati* in 167, arranging the postwar settlement.[79] The Romans left their own memorials: Philippus and Octavius inscribed gifts to Delos; and L. Aemilius Paullus, the conqueror of Perseus, ordered the setting of his own statue on a column at Delphi that had been meant for Perseus.[80] No question of *clientela* relationships here. The exigencies of war impelled Greeks to cultivate the favor of military men and ambassadors temporarily in their midst. And the Romans were eager to leave testimonials to their virtues.

Naturally the number of Romans who visited the East, either on state missions or on private business, increased substantially in the middle of the second century. The individuals, most of them otherwise unknown, turn up on documents as recipients of distinctions voted by Greek states. Their services are undesignated, the circumstances that called them forth unrecorded. They might derive from a diplomatic embassy, as attested by two decrees of the Phocian *koinon* authorizing statues for Roman commissioners, but providing no details. Or from private benefactions, the nature of which eludes our grasp, but sufficient to stimulate proxeny decrees.[81] Such awards represent token acts of gratitude, long conventional among Hellenes,

78. P. Charneux, *BCH* 81 (1957): 181–202 = *SEG*, XVI, 255 = *ISE*, I, no. 42. Cf. Polyb. 28.3; Livy, 43.17.2–4. Other services performed by Octavius are also suggested by the decree; lines 2–5; cf. E. Lanzillotta, *Sesta miscellanea greca e romana* (1978), 233–247. The Elians voted him a statue: *Syll.*[3] 650; but this doubtless came after his service as praetor in 168, when he was instrumental in obtaining Perseus' surrender: Livy, 45.5.1, 45.6.7–12. So too the statue erected by Echinus in Thessaly in his honor: *ArchDelt* 22 (1967), Chron. 247 = *SEG*, XXV, 642 = *ISE*, no. 93; cf. now L. Bliquez, *Hesperia* 44 (1975): 431–434. Cf. also Octavius' donation at Delos: *IdeDélos*, 1429A, lines 11–12—a man fluent in Greek: Livy, 45.29.3.

79. *SEG*, XXIV, 580; see C. Schuler, *CP*, 55 (1960), 94–96. One might note here the decree of the Thessalians in honor of M. Caecilius L.f. Metellus: *ArchEph* (1910), 374–375 = *ISE*, no. 101. Date and identity of the man are uncertain. He is normally considered to be the praetor of 206 and conjectured as member of the senatorial commission to bring peace terms in 196: Münzer, *RE*, Supplb., 3.222; Broughton, *MRR* I: 337. But no Roman, save Flamininus, is known to have received such honors as early as this. Other candidates deserve consideration: e.g., M. Caecilius Denter, among the envoys sent to Macedonia in 173 on the eve of the war with Perseus: Livy, 42.6.5. Denter was a *cognomen* in use by the Metelli; cf. the consul of 284. The question should be left open.

80. Plut. *Aem. Paull.* 28.2; Polyb. 30.10; Livy, 45.27.7. The marble inscription is preserved: *Syll.*[3] 652a = *ILLRP*, I, no. 323.

81. Phocian Decrees: *SEG*, I, 149, 151. Private benefactions: e.g., *IG*, IX, 1[2], 208 (two Acilii honored by the Acarnanians); *IG*, VII, 4128 (C. Octavius by Acraephia in Boeotia); *IG*, IX, 2, 258 (M. Perperna, M. Popillius, Q. Pactomeius, and others by Kierion in Thessaly); *SEG*, I, 148 = *FDelphes*, III, 4, 427 (L. Hortensius of Brundisium by

neither confined to Roman honorants nor indicative of any special relationship created by Rome.

Military intervention in the early 140s, of course, generated a new outpouring of honors to those responsible for victory or for the postwar settlement. Q. Metellus Macedonicus, conqueror of Andriscus, received statues and inscribed memorials from various places in Greece and Macedonia. The customary language prevails: Metellus is *euergetes*, honored for his *arete* and *eunoia*.[82] Similar distinctions came to L. Mummius, who had suppressed the Achaean insurrection in 146.[83] Mummius, following the practice of his predecessors, left dedications in numerous Greek cities to remind men of his achievements.[84] And the Hellenes, eager to put their gratitude, real or simulated, on display, erected monuments not only to Mummius but to the ten senatorial commissioners who had come to arrange affairs after the war.[85] They went further still. Polybius himself, left behind in Greece to clean up details in the new settlement, obtained lavish honors from his countrymen.[86] Marks of distinction were freely bestowed upon those who represented the victors—an old Hellenic custom.

No need to follow this practice into the late second century: the pattern is plain enough. Individual Romans appear in increasing numbers on late Hellenistic documents, as recipients or donors of commemorative tokens. Identifiable personages, naturally enough,

---

the Delphians); *SGDI*, 1339 = *ISE*, no. 119 (C. Rennius of Brundisium by the Epirotes). None of these can be dated with any precision beyond some time in the second century. Other examples and discussion in Harmand, *Le patronat*, 55–73. There is no reason to follow him, however, in the view that proxeny decrees for Roman officials altered the character of the convention and signified a state of dependency.

82. *IG*, VII, 3490 (Megara); *IG*, IX, 2, 37 = *ISE*, no. 92 (Hypata in Thessaly); *SEG*, III, 414 (Hyampolis); *IG*, X, 2, 134 (Thessalonica); *IG*, X, 2, 1031 = *Syll.*[3] 680 (Olympia).

83. As in an Elean decree set up to him in Olympia: *Syll.*[3] 676.

84. *IvOlympia*, 278–281 (Olympia); *IG*, V, 2, 77 (Tegea); *IG*, VII, 433 (Oropus); *IG*, VII, 1808 (Thespiae); *IG*, VII, 2478, 2478a (Thebes); *IG*, IV[2], 306; W. Peek, *AbhLeipzig* 63.5 (1972): 30–31, no. 47 (Epidaurus); *BCH* 83 (1959): 683 (Tanagra); and, in general, Polyb. 39.6.1–2; cf. Walbank, *Commentary* III:735–736. Most recent discussion of Mummius and the monuments by H. Philipp and W. Koenigs, *AthMitt* 94 (1979): 193–216.

85. *IvOlympia*, 320–324; cf. D. Bradeen, *Hesperia* 35 (1966): 326–329, no. 7. A statue at Corinth to one of them, A. Postumius Albinus, is recorded by Cic. *Ad Att.* 13.32.3. He may also be the recipient of a Delphian decree, *SEG*, I, 152: ἁ πόλις τῶν Δελφῶν Πο[στόμιον ᾿Αλ]βεῖνον τὸν ἑαυτᾶς πάτρω[να καὶ εὐ]εργέταν ὑπὲρ τᾶς τῶν ῾Ελλάνων ἐλευθερ]ίας. Use of the term πάτρων was, of course, a borrowing from the Latin. But it merely replaced the conventional πρόξενος in the standard πρόξενος καὶ εὐεργέτης formula. Cf. also the Phocian decree for a Roman envoy, *SEG*, I, 149: τὸ κοινὸν τῶν Φωκ[έων . . .]ον, Μάρκου υἱόν πρεσβευ[τὰν ῾Ρωμαίων, τὸν αὐτοῦ] πάτρωνα καὶ εὐεργέταν. For Harmand, *Le patronat*, 73–78, Greek adoption of the Latin word implies conforming to the Roman concept of protection—an unwarranted conclusion.

86. Polyb. 39.5.2–4. An example in *Syll.*[3] 686.

tend to cluster about the periods of Rome's wars in the East. Greek communities were swift to declare public approbation of Roman generals, envoys, and commissioners, just as they had for Hellenistic kings, their agents, and their representatives. It was a matter of self-protection and an investment for the future. But most of the Romans attested in Greek documents are mere names to us, cited in proxeny decrees or as dedicants at shrines. Few institutions were more common in the Greek world than *proxenia*, and few means of advertisement more characteristic than religious dedications. Romans fitted themselves into the traditional framework.

Interstate Loyalties and Obligations

We must now approach a larger and more central set of questions. To what extent did the concept of *clientela* underlie Roman state policy during its formative years in the East? How far does the idea of interstate relationships based on mutual benefits and moral obligations represent a distinctively Roman contribution? Were the Greeks confronted with a patronage system which they failed to comprehend and to which they were compelled to adapt?

There can be little doubt that by the late second century Greek principalities were client states in fact. But the ultimate results must not be allowed to cloud our vision of attitudes and purposes that prevailed at the outset. The initial process requires investigation, in particular the years of active Roman presence and involvement between 200 and 188. Therein lies much of the evidence that has stimulated modern theories about the *clientela* relationship. That evidence needs to be subjected to scrutiny.

The Romans, of course, expected gratitude for favors bestowed. And they could become duly indignant when beneficiaries failed to show the proper appreciation. As early as 219, when Demetrius of Pharus violated an agreement, he is described by Polybius as "forgetful of prior benefits granted by the Romans."[87] Rome determined to punish Demetrius for his "ingratitude."[88] The theme of Roman paternalism is central to Flamininus' declarations after the Second Macedonian War. In his letter to Chyretiae, consenting to restoration of property, the proconsul insists that Rome seeks only good will and honor.[89] When announcement was made of evacuation of the "Three

87. Polyb. 3.16.2.

88. Polyb. 3.16.4: κολάσαντες τὴν ἀχαριστίαν.

89. Syll.³ 593 = Sherk, *RDGE*, no. 33, line 13: περὶ πλείστου ποιούμενοι χάριτα καὶ φιλοδοξίαν.

Fetters" in 194, Flamininus referred to it as a *munus*. The scene receives embellishment from Livy: Flamininus spoke "like a father," bringing tears of joy from his audience; and, at his request, the Achaeans sought out and released Roman citizens who had been held in servitude, thereby performing a *pium officium*.[90] Two years later, when one of the "Fetters," Demetrias, contemplated siding with Antiochus III, Flamininus reminded her leaders that all of Greece owed *libertas* to a Roman *beneficium* and called the gods as witnesses to this wilful ingratitude.[91] M.' Acilius Glabrio in 191 upbraided the Boeotians for erecting a statue to Antiochus: an ungrateful return for Rome's *beneficia*.[92]

Flamininus, as is well known, had a flair for the dramatic. And he regarded himself as the special benefactor of the Greeks.[93] But he was not alone among Romans in conferring favors and emphasizing expressions of paternalistic good will. A letter of the praetor M. Valerius Messalla in 193, acknowleding ἀσυλία for Teos, makes the point with clarity: the kindness is granted because of Roman εὔνοια and further kindnesses can be expected—so long as the Teans maintain their εὔνοια toward Rome.[94] The Scipios' missive to Heraclea-by-Latmus in 190 affirmed the city's freedom and proclaimed readiness to perform additional services: none would surpass them in the returning of favors.[95] Similar sentiments are found in C. Livius Salinator's response to a Delphian request in 189: the Romans will not only grant it but will forever be benefactors of Delphi.[96]

90. Livy, 34.49.11–34.50.4.

91. Livy, 35.31.8: *totam Graeciam beneficio libertatis obnoxiam Romanis esse*; 35.31.13: *Quinctius quidem adeo exarsit ira, ut manus ad caelum tendens deos testes ingrati ac perfidi animi Magnetum invocaret*; 35.39.7: *ingratos increparet Magnetas*. Cf. the effort of a Boeotian faction to play up to Flamininus in 196 by denouncing the ἀχαριστία of the people who supported their political foes: Polyb. 18.43.8; cf. Livy, 33.27.7.

92. Livy, 36.20.4; cf. 36.22.2. The Aetolians too, of course, were blamed for lack of gratitude to Rome in 189—a speech which Polybius puts in the mouth of an Athenian: Polyb. 21.31.7.

93. Cf. Plut. *Flam.* 15–16.

94. *Syll.*[3] 601 = Sherk, *RDGE*, no. 34, line 18: διὰ τὴν πρὸς ὑμᾶς εὔνοιαν; lines 22–24: τὰ εἰς ὑμᾶς φιλάνθρωπα πειρασόμεθα συνεπαύξειν, διατηρούντων ὑμῶν καὶ εἰς τὸ μετὰ ταῦτα τὴν πρὸς ἡμᾶς εὔνοιαν. This is much overinterpreted by Errington, *ZPE* 39 (1980): 279–284, who believes that Antiochus induced the Romans to guarantee Tean ἀσυλία, thus to brand them as criminals should they begin a war in Asia. The senate, in Errington's view, saw through this trick and added the last clause as announcement of Rome's own standing in Asia and preparation for her expansion into that area. The idea wrings far too much out of this brief text.

95. *Syll.*[3] 618 = Sherk, *RDGE*, no. 35, line 15: πειρασόμεθα μηδενὸς λείπεσθαι ἐγ χάριτος ἀποδόσει.

96. *Syll.*[3] 611 = Sherk, *RDGE*, no. 38, lines 22–23: καὶ εἰς τὸ λοιπὸν δὲ πειρασόμεθα ἀεί τινος ἀγαθοῦ [παρ]αίτιοι τοῖς Δελφοῖς γίνεσθαι.

What does all this amount to? That Rome had come as bountiful patron, dispensing gifts and good will and expecting dutiful subservience from *clientes*? In fact, there is nothing unique or novel in the Roman attitude. Bestowal of favors, anticipation of gratitude, and annoyance at its absence were hardly features peculiar to the Roman character. The Greeks had ample experience along these lines.

Hellenistic monarchs regularly postured as patrons and took great pride in that stance. The fact does not require documentation.[97] But the language of royal epistles on this score is worthy of note. They form a clear precedent for the missives of Roman magistrates. So Antiochus I awarded autonomy to Erythrae in the early third century, promised further advantages, and pointedly summoned the Erythraeans to remember the author of those advantages.[98] The same reminder was given to Miletus by Ptolemy II ca. 262: future benefactions by the monarch will depend on continued loyalty by the city.[99] A decree from Smyrna ca. 240 refers to favors performed by Seleucus II and declares the allegiance incumbent upon recipients of those favors.[100] The kings expected beneficiaries to be mindful of their benefits, so it was plainly hinted to Magnesia by Attalus I near the end of the third century.[101] And the beneficiaries understood their duties very well.[102]

97. As an early example, observe the list of *beneficia* for Cyzicus by the Pergamene dynast Philetaerus, stretching over a number of years and duly recorded on stone: *OGIS*, 748. In the 230s or 220s, the Aetolian League expressed warm gratitude to Ptolemy III and his family in the form of a statue group that signaled his services τὰς εἰς τὸ ἔθν[ος] καὶ τοὺς ἄλλους Ἕλληνας; *IG*, IX, 1², 56; see, most recently, W. Huss, *ChronEg* 50 (1975): 312–320.

98. *OGIS*, 223 = Welles, *RC*, no. 15 = *IvErythrai u. Klazomenai*, I, no. 31, lines 30–34: παρακαλοῦμεν δὲ καὶ ὑμᾶς μνημονεύον[τας ἡμῶν . . . τ]ὴν ἐκτενεστάτην πεῖραν εἰληφότων . . . [ὑφ᾿ ὧν ε]ὐεργέτησθε μνημονεύσειν ἀξίως. Cf. *OGIS*, 221 = Welles, *RC*, no. 10–13 = *Ivllion*, no. 33, lines 13–17, for a similar broad hint to the Ilians.

99. *Milet*, I, 3, 139 = Welles, *RC*, no. 14, lines 12–14: παρακαλοῦμεν δὲ καὶ εἰς τὸν λοιπὸν χρόνον τὴν αὐτὴν ἔχειν αἵρεσιν πρὸς ἡμᾶς, ἵνα καὶ ἡμεῖς τοιούτων ὑμῶν ὄντων ἐπὶ πλέον τὴν ἐπιμέλειαν τῆς πόλεως ποιώμεθα.

100. *OGIS*, 229 = Schmitt, *Staatsverträge*, no. 492, lines 6–8: μεγαλόψυχος ὢν καὶ ἐπιστάμενος χάριτας ἀποδιδόναι τοῖς ἑαυτὸν εὐεργετοῦσιν ἐτίμησεν τὴμ πόλιν ἡμῶν διά τε τὴν τοῦ δήμου εὔνοιαν; cf. lines 17–18, 89–93.

101. *OGIS*, 282 = Welles, *RC*, no. 34, lines 13–16: θεωρῶ[ν δὲ] τὸν δῆμον μεμνημένον τῶν [ὑπ᾿ ἐ]μοῦ γεγενημένων εἰς αὐτὸν εὐ[εργε]σιῶν. Similar phraseology reappears in a purported letter of Antiochus IV to the Jews in 164, as transmitted by 2 Macc. 9:26: παρακαλῶ οὖν ὑμᾶς καὶ ἀξιῶ, μεμνημένους τῶν εὐεργεσιῶν κοινῇ καὶ κατ᾿ ἰδίαν, ἕκαστον συντηρεῖν τὴν οὖσαν εὔνοιαν εἰς ἐμὲ καὶ τὸν υἱόν.

102. Note the Rhodian eagerness to lavish honors on Ptolemy I for his relief of their siege in 304, Diod. 20.100.3: τὸν δὲ Πτολεμαῖον ἐν ἀνταποδόσει μείζονος χάριτος ὑπερβάλλεσθαι βουλόμενοι. The language affords an instructive parallel to that of the Scipios' letter to Heraclea more than a century later, quoted above, n. 95.

The Greeks did not need Rome to explain such matters to them. Paternalistic pronouncements, protection of the lesser powers by the greater, expressions of mutual loyalty, the whole matrix of extralegal obligations—none of this was foreign to the Hellenistic world. Antigonus Doson placed heavy stress on his benefits to the Greeks after Sellasia, and handsome honors were paid him in return.[103] Much of the famous debate at Sparta in 210 hinged upon rival Aetolian and Macedonian claims on gratitude for their protection of Greek freedom against barbarians.[104] The Antigonids had particularly close relations with certain cities in Achaea, Doson with Megalopolis, Philip V with Dyme and Argos. In 198 representatives of those cities refused to abandon the Macedonian alliance although the League voted to join Rome. Their actions were tolerated and sanctioned by the League: a recognition of the ties created by a Greek patron's *beneficia*.[105]

Nor were the Romans alone in feeling resentment at unilateral rupture of such relationships. One need point only to the justifiable ire of Philip V at the Achaeans in 197. The king rehearsed a lengthy list of favors performed by Macedonian rulers for Achaea and branded her defection to Rome as crass ingratitude.[106] It was a violation of those bonds that had been cemented by longstanding *beneficia*.[107] Achaean statesmen expressed similar outrage in 185/4 at former Spartan exiles: they had been restored to their homeland through Achaean favor and had turned on their benefactors, an unpardonable offense that led to capital condemnation.[108] As should now be obvious, the acknowledgment of moral obligations on the international scene did not await the coming of Rome.

Confrontation with Philip V and Antiochus III brought Roman power and prestige to the forefront. Did the Republic now lay claim to a general protectorate, a *patrocinium*, over the Hellenes? That

---

103. Polyb. 5.9.9–10, 9 36 5; *IG*, IV², 589 = *ISE*, no. 46; *IG*, V, 1, 1122; *IG*, V, 2, 299.

104. See, especially, Polyb. 9.30.3–4, 9.31.4, 9.33.6–7, 9.34.2–3, 9.35.1–4.

105. Livy, 32.22.9–12: *reliquerunt concilium neque mirante ullo nec improbante . . . veniaque iis huius secessionis fuit et magnis et recentibus obligatis beneficiis.* Polybius lays stress on Philip's benefactions to a whole range of Greek states early in his reign which won him widespread affection, especially among the Cretans: Polyb. 7.11.7–9, 7.14.4; Plut. *Arat.* 48.3, 50.5–6.

106. Polyb. 18.6.5–7: ἀχαριστίαν.

107. Cf. Livy, 32.19.7: *Macedonum beneficiis et veteribus et recentibus obligati erant.*

108. Polyb. 22.11.7–8; Livy, 39.35.7–8; Paus. 7.9.2. The charge of ingratitude was also levelled by the Aetolians—against Rome: Livy, 35.48.11–12. The peculiar view of Edlund, *Talanta* 8–9 (1977): 56–57, that Greeks expressed only "disappointment" while Romans underlined "ingratitude," needs no discussion. Cf. also, *idem, Klio* 59 (1977): 131–136.

assumption, often made, is quite baseless. The evidence on which it is founded is not only flimsy in the extreme but turns out, upon examination, to be altogether nugatory.

The term *patrocinium*, with reference to international relations, appears but twice in all of Livy's extant text. Both occurrences come in speeches—and the phraseology is almost certainly that of the historian. The first appears in Flamininus' reply to Antiochus' envoys in 193: the Roman people will not abandon their *susceptum patrocinium libertatis Graecorum*.[109] A good rhetorical manifesto. But the interview of which it formed part took place *in camera*.[110] So neither Livy nor Polybius had access to the *ipsissima verba*. Polybius' version of these events is unfortunately lost, but Livy would have felt no obligation to reproduce it with exactitude anyway. The fact is demonstrable from the second and even more interesting passage. Rhodian spokesmen, for their own ends, flatter the Roman senate in 189. It is proper, so they maintain, that Rome preserve forever her *patrocinium* of an entire people *receptae in fidem et clientelam vestram*.[111] Ostensibly a most telling statement; not merely *patrocinium* here, but *clientela*—the sole reference to that term in Roman-Greek relations. But it dissolves on inspection. This time the Polybian original is extant; and nothing therein to warrant such language. The world is under Roman authority, ἐξουσία; and the obligation of Rome, as the Rhodians represent it, was simply to leave it free.[112] Livy has taken liberties. So he doubtless did with Flamininus' speech as well. And these are not the only such occasions.[113] The language is anachronistic, the language of the late Republic. At the beginning of the second century Rome was not prepared to undertake, nor concerned to exercise, an enduring protectorate. Nor did all the Greeks expect any such patronage. Already in 197, after Cynoscephalae, Amynander of Athamania called upon fellow Hellenes to promise him protection against Macedonia, in anticipation of the Roman departure.[114] The prognostication was accurate. When Flamininus withdrew the last garrisons in 194 and described Greek liberty as a Roman gift, he affirmed that that liberty was now

---

109. Livy, 34.58.11.

110. Cf. Livy, 34.57.5.

111. Livy, 37.54.17. Cf. on this passage, H. Tränkle, *Livius und Polybios* (Basel and Stuttgart, 1977), 125–126.

112. Polyb. 21.23.4, 21.23.7, 21.23.10–12.

113. Cf. the argument of the *decem legati* in 196 on the maintenance of Roman forces in the Fetters, as rendered by Livy; the Greek cities should remain for a time *sub tutela praesidii Romani*: Livy, 33.31.10. The corresponding passage in Polybius has nothing like this euphemism: Polyb. 18.45.10.

114. Polyb. 18.36.4; a somewhat exaggerated rendition in Livy, 33.12.2.

entrusted to the care of the Greeks themselves.[115] So much for a Roman *patrocinium*.

Of course various Hellenic states paid homage to Rome in this period, professing their loyalty for purposes of self-advantage or in hope of assistance against other foes. The display of Roman military power in the defeat of Philip adequately accounts for such behavior. Antiochus III ran into resistance from cities who claimed to rely on Rome as a counterweight. The Lampsacenes in 196 rejected Antiochus' advances, asserting that those driven to desperation will fly to the Romans and put themselves in their hands.[116] Four years later Chalcis also turned her back on the king with the remark that her liberty was Rome's *beneficium* and that she would enter into no alliance without Roman consent.[117] Subsequent Chalcidian gratitude, after Antiochus' flight, manifested itself in handsome honors for Flamininus and a hymn to Roman *fides*.[118] For the war against Aetolia, we are told, both Philip and Ptolemy offered substantial aid; and the Macedonian king dedicated a crown to Jupiter Capitolinus in celebration of the victory.[119] He wanted the return of his son Demetrius, a hostage in Rome. The hope of reaping personal advantage also inspired the fawning language of Eumenes to the senate in 189,[120] and Sparta's desperate plea to escape Achaean overlordship.[121] In none of these instances did any prompting come from Rome. The Greeks had their own reasons for summoning aid, citing Roman power, or honoring the victor. The Romans were not setting out the ground rules of clientship.[122]

Comparable motives lay behind a more striking development:

115. Livy, 34.49.11: *redditam libertatem sua cura custodirent servarentque.* An unwarranted interpretation by D. Golan, *RivStorAnt* 6–7 (1977): 316–317: "The Greeks were to become the implementers and keepers of *Roman* order within their own territories." Cf. the statement of Philopoemen in 189 that Flamininus had placed the villages and forts of the Laconian coast *in fidem Achaeorum tutelamque*: Livy, 38.31.2. Sparta, of course, would have preferred, but did not receive, direct Roman supervision: Livy, 38.31.6.

116. Polyb. 18.49.1; see Walbank, *Commentary* II:620–621.

117. Livy, 35.36.11–13.

118. Plut. *Flam.* 16.3–4.

119. Livy, 36.4.1–2, on the offers of assistance. Not an altogether reliable tale; cf. Walbank, *Philip V*, 200–201. On the dedication: Zon. 9.9.18.

120. Polyb. 21.18.6: ἄριστον εἶναι νομίζει τὸ διδόναι τὴν ἐπιτροπὴν ἐκείνοις καὶ περὶ αὑτοῦ καὶ περὶ τῶν ἀδελφῶν.

121. Livy, 38.31.5–6: *orarentque eum, ut veniret in Peloponnesum ad urbem Lacedaemonem in fidem dicionemque populi Romani accipiendam.*

122. The story that Ptolemy's envoys as early as 200 requested Roman authorization before answering an Athenian appeal for aid is fictitious: Livy, 31.9.2; see Winkler, *Rom und Aegypten*, 19–20.

the creation of cults to the goddess Roma. The practice began in the East, a symbolic deification. Roma represented and personified the *res publica Romana*. So the Greeks not only hailed the western power but conducted official worship in her honor. The city of Smyrna, so it is reported by Tacitus, was the first to erect a temple to *urbs Roma* in 195.[123] If that date be correct, it is plain that the shadow of Antiochus again loomed in the background. Smyrna was looking to the West for rescue.[124] The cult spread elsewhere in subsequent years. The chronology of its progress cannot be charted with certitude, but the first half of the second century saw a number of Hellenic states embrace the worship of Roma. Games and sacrifices were instituted at Delphi in 189 and, as a recent find discloses, similar honors at Athens by 184.[125] Other dates are largely a matter of guesswork. But we know of festivals organized for Roma by corporate bodies, the Euboean *koinon*, the Lycian confederacy, and the Ionian League, in the first few decades of the second century.[126] At least one other existed in this period, at Chios.[127] The goddess was becoming a familiar feature in mainland Greece, the Aegean, and Asia Minor.

But there can be no question of Roman initiative here. The worship of Roma, hitherto unknown in the West or to the Romans themselves, originated among the Greeks. An obvious model stands out: Hellenistic ruler cult, dating back to the late fourth century and long since flourishing all over the Greek world.[128] The accoutre-

123. Tac. *Ann.* 4.56.1.

124. Cf. R. Mellor, *ΘΕΑ ΡΩΜΗ: The Worship of the Goddess Roma in the Greek World* (Göttingen, 1975), 14–16; C. Fayer, *Il culto della dea Roma* (Pescara, 1976), 31–32.

125. Delphi: *Syll.*³ 611 = Sherk, *RDGE*, no. 38, lines 6–7; Athens: J. Traill, *Hesperia* 40 (1971): 308, lines 11–12.

126. Euboea: *IG*, XII, 9, 898–899; see the discussion of Robert, *ArchEph* (1969): 44–49. Lycia: *SEG*, XVIII, 570; much debate on this, with most scholars preferring a date of 189/8; cf., especially, Robert, *REG* 63 (1950): no. 183, 185–197; Moretti, *RivFilol* 78 (1950): 326–350; Larsen, *CP* 51 (1956): 161–169. Ionia: F. Sokolowski, *Lois sacreés de l'Asie Mineure* (Paris, 1955), no. 26 = *IvErythrai u. Klazomenai*, II, no. 207; cf. Habicht, *Gottmenschentum*, 93. Mellor consistently opts for the earliest possible date: *ΘΕΑ ΡΩΜΗ*, 37–38, 51, 99; *ANRW*, II: 17 (1981), 958–959. See also Fayer, *Il culto*, 32–42, 46–47. A recently discovered catalogue of victors in games honoring Roma at Xanthus further attests to this festival of the Lycian League: Robert, *RA* (1978): 277–278.

127. Noticed in *SEG*, XVI, 486; *BE* (1965), no. 305, with further bibliography in Mellor, *ΘΕΑ ΡΩΜΗ*, 60–61. An accessible text has at last been published by Moretti, *RivFilol* 108 (1980): 36–37, with translation and commentary. See also *BE* (1980), no. 353. Although the letter forms would be consistent with a third-century date, reference to Rome's κατὰ τὸμ πόλεμον ἐπιφανείας (line 3) must put the inscription shortly after the Antiochene war; see Moretti, *op. cit.*, 34.

128. Its origins go back at least to the divine honors paid to Antigonus and Demetrius by Athens in 307: Diod. 20.46.2; Plut. *Demetr.* 10.3–4. Subsequent history

ments of Roma-worship—statues, temples, altars, sacrifices, religious festivals—all find clear precedents in the devotions paid to Hellenistic kings.[129] If further antecedents be sought for the veneration of a personified state, they can easily be found in cults of the Demos of various cities, such as Athens or Rhodes.[130]

Formal worship of this character, after more than a century of Hellenic usage, had itself become a convention. It need not imply suzerainty or political control by the recipient of divine honors. To mention but a few examples from these very years: Ptolemy V was hailed as a god in a Lydian inscription—set up by an Aetolian—in the late third century; the city of Argos added Philip V's name to that of the gods in public prayers; and Sicyon erected a colossal statue and instituted sacrifices to Attalus I in 198.[131] The creation of a cult to Roma designated a typically Greek means of showing gratitude and hope for favor. It bore no relationship to the Roman idea of *clientela*. The practice was thoroughly Hellenic. Any impression left on Rome was altogether minimal.[132]

Greek cities, long accustomed to rendering official respect to Hellenistic kings, quite easily adopted the same demeanor toward Rome. The formulas were ready to hand and substitution was simple. A particular example suffices: certain proxeny decrees of the second century grant to the recipient, among other privileges, the right of immediate access to the city's council and assembly, precedence to be given only to sacred matters and to business brought up by the Romans: μετὰ τὰ ἱερὰ καὶ ʿΡωμαίους.[133] Does this mean then that Romans were regularly presenting items to Greek political meetings or that Rome insisted upon special prerogatives to insure her influence in Greek deliberations? Plainly not. The formula is a pure convention.

---

treated *in extenso* by Habicht, *Gottmenschentum*, 42–126, and F. Taeger, *Charisma* (Stuttgart, 1957), I:234–415. J. R. Fears, *Mnemosyne* 31 (1978): 274–286, argues that the worship of Roma was not alien or contemptible to the Roman mind, citing the cult of the Genius Publicus which began in 218/7: Livy, 21.62.9. But that cult too, as he concedes, owed its form to Hellenistic influences.

129. Evidence for these features with regard to Roma is fully set out by Mellor, ΘΕΑ ΡΩΜΗ, 134–180.

130. So, rightly, Mellor, ΘΕΑ ΡΩΜΗ, 22–25.

131. Ptolemy V: *OGIS*, 91; Philip V: Livy, 32.25.2; Attalus I: Polyb. 18.16.

132. The cult receives no mention at all in the literary sources until a brief reference by Livy on Alabanda's erection of a temple to Urbs Roma in 170: Livy, 43.6.5. Otherwise the only Roman allusion to it in this period comes in the letter politely acknowledging Delphi's creation of games and sacrifices in 189—and that letter dealt primarily with other matters; *Syll.*³ 611 = Sherk, *RDGE*, no. 38.

133. *Syll.*³ 587, lines 27–28 (Peparethus); *IG*, XII, 9, 898 (Euboea); *IG*, VII, 20, lines 16–18 (Tanagra); cf. Robert, *ArchEph* (1969): 45.

It appears with great frequency in earlier proxeny decrees, where the identical privilege is accorded to Hellenistic monarchs—who made as little use of it as did Rome: μετὰ τὰ ἱερὰ καὶ Βασιλικά.[134] Nothing is involved here but the merest replacement of a word in the standard phraseology. Such features are common fare in Hellenistic documents, polite banalities which Rome neither imposed nor availed herself of.

In similar fashion one finds professions of loyalty to Rome in agreements among Greek states. A pact that linked King Pharnaces of Pontus and Chersonesus in the early second century contained the provision that both maintain their φιλία with Rome.[135] A Samian decree on relations with Antiochia on the Maeander underlined the favor and good will that were due to Rome. And the agreement relating Aphrodisias, Cibyra, and Tabae that recently came to light pledges restraint from any action in opposition to the Romans.[136] To postulate Roman machinations lurking behind such contracts, however, would be erroneous presumption. Hellenistic parallels are discoverable, to provide adequate precedent. Notice the *sympoliteia* between Smyrna and Magnesia in the later third century, which repeatedly alludes to the benefits and εὔνοια of Seleucus II.[137] Rhodes guaranteed safety and security for the people of Iasus ca. 220, adding that this conformed to her cordial relationship with Philip V.[138] And the treaty joining Miletus and Heraclea-by-Latmus in the early second century bids both to observe their allegiance to the island of Rhodes.[139] Once more the Hellenic practice predominates.

The context of Greek courtesies and tributes to Roman power is now clear enough. They follow patterns of the East, fitting the westerner into their schemata rather than succumbing to a foreign system. There had been no importation of a Roman patronate.

134. E.g., *OGIS*, 81, line 21 (Oropus); *Syll.*³ 333, lines 24–25 (Samos); *Syll.*³ 426, line 26 (Bargylia); *Clara Rhodos* 10 (1941); 27, n.1, line 11 (Samos); *Öst. Jahreshefte* (1961–63), Beiblatt 20, line 13 (Ephesus); *AthMitt* 9 (1884): 195–196 (Samos).

135. *IPE*, I², 402, lines 3–5, 25–28. Cf. the decree of Tanagra for the Megarians: *IG*, VII, 20, lines 16–18. But this depends on substantial restoration: [πλὴν εἴ τινα ἄλλως] προστέτ[ακται ἡμῖν ἐν ταῖς σ]υν[θήκαις τ]αῖ[ς γενομέναις πρὸς] ᾿Ρωμαίους.

136. Samos and Antiocheia: Habicht, *AthMitt* 72 (1957): 242–244, no. 65, lines 5–6, 20–25. Aphrodisias, Cibyra, and Tabae: Reynolds, *Aphrodisias and Rome*, 6–7, no. 1, lines 10–11. Cf. also *Syll.*³ 692, lines 61–62.

137. *OGIS*, 229 = Schmitt, *Staatsverträge*, no. 492, lines 3, 13–19, 22–24, 37–39, 61–69, 89–98. Cf. the similar effusions by Bargylia in honoring a Tean juror while reiterating her gratitude to Antiochus: *Syll.*³ 426, lines 3–4, 9–11, 18–22, 41–49; see Orth, *Königlicher Machtanspruch*, 116–123.

138. Holleaux, *REA* 5 (1903): 226 = *Études* IV:152, lines 88–93.

139. *Syll.*³ 633, lines 34–36.

One can go further. Rome's military successes obtained due acknowlegments. But she was still just one amidst a concert of powers. Greeks continued to exchange courtesies with one another, and the lesser states to show deference to the greater. The Attalid kingdom of Pergamum grew markedly in stature during the last years of the third century and only enhanced that stature by a position on the winning side in the Second Macedonian War. Something akin to divine honors were paid to Attalus I by Aegina after that island had come under his aegis in 209; similar allegiance was affirmed by Andros, which Attalus obtained as reward for his efforts against Philip in 199.[140] Plaudits came also from distant places not directly under Pergamene authority: from Athens, from Sicyon in the Peloponnese, and from Aptera in Crete.[141] The practice manifests itself elsewhere as well. Delos, always swift to invest in the future, awarded an honorific decree to Nabis of Sparta in the 190s as *proxenos* and *euergetes*.[142] Even the royal family of Cappadocia had far-flung connections, attested in manifestos from Athens and from Cos, probably in the 180s.[143] The Greeks had multiple benefactors in the wars of the early second century, and Hellenistic propriety enjoined the acknowledgment of gratitude. Roman power may have been chiefly responsible for the crushing of Nabis. But other Greeks had a hand in it too and received appreciative honors, including the Gortynian who helped rescue Mycenaean ephebes from Nabis, and the commander of Cretan auxiliaries who fought against Nabis with the Achaeans and to whom the Achaeans erected a bronze statue.[144] Eumenes took due credit as well in dedications to celebrate the victory over Nabis.[145] A complex network of allegiances and shifting alliances permeated the Greek world. Rome's dramatic display of martial prowess did not eradicate that network nor direct all allegiances to herself. The fragmentation of loyalties persisted.

Patronage as extended by the mightier to the weaker constituted a well-known practice in Hellas. Aratus expressed it clearly enough to

140. Aegina: *IG*, II², 885; see R. E. Allen, *BSA* 66 (1971): 6–9; cf. Polyb. 22.8.10; *OGIS*, 281; *ISE*, I, no. 36; Andros: Th. Sauciuc, *Andros* (Vienna, 1914), 134–138; cf. Livy, 31.45.7; Holleaux, *Études* V:42. See also the award of *isopoliteia* by Lilaea in Phocis to the Pergamene garrison stationed there by Attalus ca. 208: *FDelphes*, III, 4, 132–135 = *ISE*, no. 81.

141. Athens: Polyb. 16.25.8–9; Livy, 31.15.6; Paus. 1.5.5, 1.8.1; Sicyon: Polyb. 18.16; Aptera: *OGIS*, 270 = *IC*, II, 3, 4C. Cf. also the dedication by Achaeans to the Attalid house for its collaboration against Antiochus in 190: *Syll.*³ 606.

142. *Syll.*³ 584.

143. Athens: *OGIS*, 350; Cos: M. Segre, *PP* 27 (1972): 182.

144. The Mycenaean decree: *Syll.*³ 594; cf. *SEG*, III, 313; the bronze statue: *IG*, IV², 1, 244 = *ISE*, no. 49; cf. Polyb. 33.16; Livy, 35.28.8, 35.29.1.

145. *Syll.*³ 595.

Philip V in the later third century: nothing more firmly shores up the power of a king than the trust and gratitude of states beholden to him.[146] The notion that Rome carried that principle to the East, where Greeks encountered it for the first time—and failed to comprehend it!—violates all the facts known to us.

The institution is readily illustrated. Hellenistic kings interceded for cities that sought recognition of privileges on the international scene. The right of *asylia* supplies an obvious example. Seleucus II around 240 exerted himself to write to kings, dynasts, cities, and peoples of the Greek world on behalf of *asylia* for Smyrna.[147] The same was done near the end of the third century by Antiochus III for Teos. Record exists of visits by the king's agent to three cities in Crete where he advocated the Tean cause.[148] Not to be outdone, Philip V sent his own representative to Crete, to no fewer than eight cities, thereby to demonstrate that he too could be a patron to Teos.[149] The competition for foreign *clientelae* seems plain.[150] Especially noteworthy is the visit of another envoy of Antiochus in 193, again to secure recognition of Teos' *asylia*, this time from the Roman senate itself. The cordial letter of Rome's praetor to Teos grants all that is requested—and makes it clear that the favor is obtained through the intermediacy of Antiochus.[151] The significance of that letter ought not to be overlooked. It is Rome who acknowledges the Hellenic act of patronage! Small wonder

146. Plut. *Arat.* 50.5–6: βασιλεῖ δὲ πίστεως καὶ χάριτος ἰσχυρότερον οὐδὲν οὐδὲ ὀχυρώτερον.

147. *OGIS*, 229 = Schmitt, *Staatsverträge*, no. 492, lines 11–12: ἔγραψεν δὲ καὶ πρὸς τοὺς βασιλεῖς καὶ τοὺς δυνάστας καὶ τὰς πόλεις καὶ τὰ ἔθνη ἀξιώσας ἀποδέξασθαι τό τε ἱερὸν τῆς Στρατονικίδος Ἀφροδίτης ἄσυλον εἶναι καὶ τὴμ πόλιν ἡμῶν ἱερὰν καὶ ἄσυλον. See also *OGIS*, 228, lines 2–5.

148. *IC*, I, 27, 1, lines 8–10 (Rhaucus); *IC*, II, 12, 21, lines 13–19 (Eleutherna); *IC*, II, 16, 3, lines 7–9 (Lappa); cf. the recently discovered Tean decree which makes reference to Antiochus' guarantee of *asylia*: Herrmann, *Anatolia* 9 (1965): 34, lines 16–19. Antiochus' agent even helped in bringing a Cretan war to a close: *IC*, II, 12, 21, line 14.

149. *IC*, I, 5, 52, lines 18–20 (Arcades); *IC*, I, 14, 1, lines 17–19 (Istron); *IC*, I, 16, 2, lines 21–22; *IC*, I, 16, 15, lines 17–19 (Lato); *IC*, II, 1, 1, lines 14–17 (Allaria); *IC*, II, 5, 17, lines 11–13 (Axos); *IC*, II, 26, 1 (Sybrita). The agents of both monarchs were at Eleutherna: *IC*, II, 12, 21, lines 13–19.

150. There is no reason to believe that Philip's actions here imply a suzerainty over Teos, as Holleaux, *Études* IV:178–203. It was his influence in Crete that gave him access in this affair; cf. Polyb. 7.11.9, 7.14.4. Exact chronology remains disputed; cf. Holleaux, *loc. cit.*; Herrmann, *Anatolia*, 9 (1965), 118–138. The recent effort of H. Rawlings, *AJAH* 1 (1976): 17–19, to date these decrees to the 190s is unconvincing. He does not address the question of how Philip could have possessed authority in Crete at that time.

151. *Syll.*³ 601 = Sherk, *RDGE*, no. 34, lines 4–8, 18–21: καὶ διὰ τὴν πρὸς ὑμᾶς εὔνοιαν καὶ διὰ τὸν ἠξιω[μέν]ον πρεσβευτὴν κρίνομεν εἶναι τὴν πόλιν καὶ τὴν χώραν ἱεράν, καθὼς καὶ νῦν ἐστιν, καὶ ἄσυλον καὶ ἀφορολόγητον.

then that Antiochus could insist that, if the Greeks of Asia are to be free, the freedom is his gift to bestow.[152] *Patrocinium* was not a Roman invention.[153]

Nor were the kings alone in exercising this kind of paternalism. Rivalry between Philopoemen and Flamininus supplies illustration. The Achaean statesman strove to steal a march on the Roman by restoring Spartan exiles—who would then owe their gratitude to him.[154] The island of Rhodes stepped easily into a patron's role. She heard the plea of the Iasians and promised to defend their security ca. 220.[155] In 197 she professed to be protector of Asian cities allied to Ptolemy against the menace of Antiochus and to be champion of their *libertas*.[156] A year later the Rhodians were instrumental in ending a war between Miletus and Magnesia. Conclusion of the peace treaty came under their auspices; Rhodes would be guarantor of the new settlement.[157] The moral obligations of the patron state were duly discharged. In 188 Rhodes argued the claims of the Cilician city of Soli before the Roman senate: it was a fulfillment of duties incumbent upon her position.[158] In similar fashion Massilia took up the cause of her kinsmen in Lampsacus when the latter desired inclusion in the Roman peace treaty with Philip.[159] The city of Stymphalus interceded for Elatea both with the Achaean League and with the Roman commander in 191 to permit the Elateans to recover their homeland.[160] And Eumenes quite properly assumed in 189 that if Rome liberated the cities of Asia at Rhodian behest those cities would feel themselves bound in obligation to Rhodes.[161] Nearly two decades later Perseus—

---

152. Polyb. 18.51.9; Livy, 33.38.5–7, 34.57.10; Appian, *Syr.* 3. See above pp. 149–150.

153. Note too Eumenes' successful intervention with Manlius Vulso on behalf of his father-in-law Ariarathes in 188. The reduction of Ariarathes' indemnity payment by one-half was due to Eumenes' *beneficium*: Livy, 38.39.6.

154. Plut. *Phil.* 17.4: βουλόμενος δι αὐτοῦ καὶ τῶν Ἀχαιῶν ἀλλὰ μὴ Τίτου μηδὲ Ῥωμαίων χάριτι τοῦτο πραχθῆναι. Cf. the speech of Lycortas to the Messenians who had entrusted themselves to his πίστις: Polyb. 23.16.11.

155. Holleaux, *REA* 5 (1903): 223–228 = *Études* IV:147–152.

156. Livy, 33.20.11–12; cf. Polyb. 18.41a.1. The posture may conceal Rhodian control of the states named; cf. Holleaux, *Etudes* IV:303–305; Schmitt, *Rom und Rhodos*, 76; Rawlings, *AJAH* 1 (1976): 9–13.

157. *Syll.*³ 588; especially lines 4–5, 68–69, 92–94.

158. Polyb. 21.24.10–15: ἔφασαν καθήκειν αὐτοῖς προνοεῖσθαι τῆς πόλεως ταύτης; Livy, 37.56.7–10.

159. *Syll.*³ 591, lines 44–64.

160. Elatean gratitude expressed in a decree of ca. 189; *SEG*, XI, 1107 = *ISE*, no. 55, lines 9–18. The Elateans had been expelled probably by the Aetolians some time after 196: Passerini, *Athenaeum* 26 (1948): 83–95.

161. Polyb. 21.19.5–10; Livy, 37.53.3–4.

for his own purposes—could still refer to the Rhodians as patrons of Greek freedom.[162]

The advocacy of one state's rights by another, the mutual responsibilities of greater and lesser powers, the bestowal of favors and expectation of gratitude, intercessions to secure advantages for dependent cities tied through kinship or protection—in a word, the system of patronage on an interstate level—were all part of the Hellenic scene. If Rome behaved in similar fashion in the East it was because she found the model already there, not because she transformed her private *clientela* into an international system.

The Continuities After Apamea

After Apamea the superiority of Roman arms was no longer in question. But the Republic withdrew her forces once again from the East and avoided any visible presence there. Did she expect the Greeks to behave as humble and loyal clients thereafter, awaiting her instructions and heeding her will? Such a presumption finds little support in our evidence.

Peace treaties with Aetolia and Antiochus, as we have seen, followed Hellenic patterns for the most part and instituted no *clientela* relations that were subsequently appealed to.[163] One would be hard pressed to discern Roman insistence upon prerogatives of any significance in the Greek world.[164] An Achaean law, to be sure, provided for summoning of the League's assembly upon written request from the Roman senate.[165] But, as noted earlier, Macedonian kings had exercised that prerogative in the past; and its reconstitution now placed a restraint upon individual Roman officials rather than expanding the influence of the Roman state.[166] The provision plainly came at Achaean insistence, not Roman. Q. Marcius Philippus, rebuffed by Achaea while on a diplomatic mission in 183, complained bitterly that

162. Polyb. 27.4.7: διατελοῦσι προστατοῦντες οὐ μόνον τῆς αὐτῶν ἀλλὰ καὶ τῆς τῶν ἄλλων Ἑλλήνων ἐλευθερίας.

163. See above pp. 31–33.

164. A senatorial decree of 187 provided that Roman and Latin merchants be exempt from port dues at Ambracia; Livy, 38.44.4. That is the only example of its kind known to us. No suggestion that the stipulation applied to arrangements with any other state. And the favor shown to Italian traders—which may indeed have been to Ambracia's advantage in stimulating commerce—hardly amounts to a *clientela* relationship with Rome. See below pp. 310–311.

165. Polyb. 22.10.10–12, 22.12.5–7, 23.5.14–17; Paus. 7.9.1; Livy, 39.33.7.

166. See above p. 37.

the Achaeans were unwilling to refer any matters to Rome.[167] It hardly follows that the senate *expected* Achaea to seek their advice on all Peloponnesian issues. Philippus' demand, in fact, that the Achaeans take no action against Messenia without Roman consent, was pointedly ignored; the senate maintained a hands-off policy.[168] Polybius paused to insert an analysis: Rome felt annoyance if foreign states conducted diplomacy without reference to her judgment and approval.[169] But that analysis, which bears no relation to the events and is contradicted by Polybius' own narrative, is an obvious *post eventum* interpretation. From Apamea to the Third Macedonian War, Rome's attitude was most conspicuous for its passivity. Her judgments, when sought, tended to affirm the status quo and maintain her distance. Observe, for example, the response to a Delphian request, perhaps in 186: nothing is to be given and nothing to be taken away![170] If Rome reckoned herself as patron of Hellas she was most restrained in implementing any privileges attaching to that role.

The Hellenes, of course, when it suited their interests, hailed the western power for victories won and benefits conferred. Various kings and states, it was reported, supplied cash to pay for L. Scipio's lavish games in 186.[171] The Thessalians, urging senatorial sanctions against Philip V, alluded to Roman *beneficia* and described the Romans as *libertatis auctores*.[172] A Delphian decree of 182 went further still: Eumenes II is praised for his loyalty to Rome and the Romans appear as "public benefactors," κοινοὶ εὐεργέται.[173] That laudatory

167. Polyb. 23.9.8: τῶν Ἀχαιῶν οὐ βουλομένων ἀναφέρειν οὐδὲν ἐπὶ τὴν σύγκλητον; cf. 24.9.12.

168. Polyb. 24.9.12–13; cf. 23.17.3.

169. Polyb. 23.17.4.

170. *Syll.*³ 826k = Sherk, *RDGE*, no. 39, lines 10–11: [περ]ὶ τούτων ἔδοξεν οὕτως ἀποκριθῆναι ὅτ[ι οὔ]τε ἀφαιρεῖσθαι οὔτε διδόναι νομίζομε[ν δεῖν]. On the date, see the discussion of Daux, *Delphes*, 675–678. Cf. the Amphictyonic decree for Nicostratus, an envoy to Rome on unspecified business, who reported on his trip at Delphi and exhorted the Delphians to abide by the prior resolutions of the *Greeks*: *Syll.*³ 613A, lines 24–29: διελέγη περὶ ὧν ἔχων τὰς ἐντολὰς ἐπεπρέσβευκεν πρός τε τὴν σύγκλητον τῶν Ῥωμαίων καὶ τοὺς στρατηγοὺς καὶ δημάρχους καὶ παρεκάλεσεν Δελφούς, διατηρεῖν τὴν εὔνοιαν πρὸς ἄπαντας τοὺς Ἕλληνας καὶ μηθὲν αὐτοὺς ὑπεναντίον πράττειν τοῖς πρότερον ὑπὸ τῶν Ἑλλήνων ἐψηφισμένοις. Not a word here about obedience to any Roman directives. The senate evidently rubber-stamped Nicostratus' announcement of the Amphictyony's reconstitution; cf. lines 8–11, and *Syll.*³ 613B. The decree presents other difficulties, not relevant here; see Daux, *Delphes*, 280–292; Giovannini, *Ancient Macedonia* 1 (1970): 147–154.

171. Livy, 39.22.8—from Valerius Antias.

172. Livy, 39.25.11; cf. 42.38.6.

173. *Syll.*³ 630 = *FDelphes*, III, 3, 261, especially lines 17–18: ὅσοι διατηροῦντες τὴν πρὸς Ῥωμ[αί]ους τοὺς κοινοὺς [εὐεργέτας φιλία]ν; cf. lines 6–10.

phraseology comes to be applied more regularly in subsequent years.[174] But the commendations carry no special significance and certainly do not betoken reception of a Roman-style clientship. Nothing is more conventional in Hellenistic documents than acknowledgment of εὐεργεσία. And the exact terminology, κοινὸς εὐεργέτης, is applied to Eumenes himself by the Ionians ca. 167.[175] Once again the Greeks fitted Rome into their own categories of homage.

As one would expect, the crisis of the Third Macedonian War engendered effusions of loyalty in greater volume and in exaggerated mode. Antiochus IV sent a deputation to Rome in 173, with tribute, gifts, a request for renewal of *amicitia*, and a declaration that he was prepared to abide by any instructions suitable to a loyal ally.[176] Antiochus, it seems, anticipated a coming clash between Rome and Perseus, and he had his own designs on Egypt.[177] A Roman mission in the following year, if Livy's source is to be trusted, obtained further protestations of loyalty from Antiochus, from Eumenes, and from Ptolemy: they had promised to carry out all of Rome's commands.[178] Ariarathes of Cappadocia hurried to show his good will, even dispatching his son to be raised in Rome.[179] Smaller states too, during the course of the war, expressed their fidelity in conspicuous fashion. The Delians dedicated gold crowns to the senate and people of Rome.[180] The same gesture was made by Thisbae in Boeotia; or at least gold was collected for the purpose.[181] Envoys from Lampsacus and Alabanda brought massive crowns to be placed on the Capitol; the latter even announced erection of a temple to Urbs Roma.[182] Representatives of the Ptolemaic family came to Rome, unkempt and bedraggled, underlined their *amicitia*, and pleaded for assistance against

174. See below pp. 196–197.

175. *OGIS*, 763 = Welles, *RC*, no. 52, lines 7–8: κοινόν ἀναδείξας ἐμαυτὸν εὐεργέτην τῶν Ἑλλήνων. For the date and circumstances, see Holleaux, *Études* II:153–178. The view of Robert, *CRAI* (1969): 59, that the Ionians deliberately applied the phrase to Eumenes in imitation of its use for the Romans, is unconvincing. See the Tean decree for Antiochus III: Herrmann, *Anatolia* 9 (1965): 34, lines 6–9: κοινὸς [εὐεργέτης πρ]οείρηται γίνεσθαι τῶν τε ἄλλων Ἑλληνίδωμ. Cf. also Polyb. 7.11.8: κοινός τις [Philip V] οἷον ἐρώμενος ἐγένετο τῶν Ἑλλήνων διὰ τὸ τῆς αἱρέσεως εὐεργετικόν.

176. Livy, 42.6.8: *imperaretque sibi populus Romanus, quae bono fidelique socio regi essent imperanda.*

177. Cf. Livy, 42.29.5–6.

178. Livy, 42.26.7–8; cf. 42.29.7. The account, however, is a questionable doublet and probably fictitious. An accurate version of this embassy in Polyb. 27.3.1–5, followed by Livy elsewhere: 42.45.1–7.

179. Livy, 42.19.3–5; cf. 42.29.4.

180. *IdeDélos*, 465C.

181. *Syll.*³ 646 = Sherk, *RDGE*, no. 2, lines 31–35.

182. Livy, 43.6.5–8.

Antiochus.[183] These actions are all intelligible and predictable. So too is the rush to pay respects after Pydna, especially by those who stood to profit by it—or those who otherwise stood to lose. Fulsome praise and flattery of Rome became rapidly fashionable in the aftermath of Pydna. The envoys of Antiochus and Ptolemy outbid one another in excessive adulation: the orders of Roman legates were compared to divine commands, the debt owed to Rome adjudged as greater than that to the gods themselves.[184] Rhodes too trembled in the wake of Rome's victory, with good reason. Not coincidentally, she chose this occasion to vote a crown of ten thousand gold pieces to Roma.[185] The Bithynian king Prusias excelled all others in abject sycophancy, taking on the garb of a freedman, prostrating himself, and hailing Roman senators as θεοί σωτῆρες: a performance that left Polybius nauseated.[186]

None of this causes any surprise. Nor does the proliferation of cults to the goddess Roma in subsequent years, all over the East: at Athens, Delos, Antiochia on the Maeander, Caunus, Cibyra, Petres in Macedonia, Lycia, Rhodes, Stratonicea, Aphrodisias, Teos, Melos, and elsewhere.[187] The anxieties of war stimulated profuse claims of fidelity and the opportunities brought by peace generated even more extravagant deference to the conqueror. It was all familiar Greek behavior. What right have we to say that any of this conformed to Roman dictates or represented an embracing of Roman ideas?

It will be recalled that the senate took pains to drum up support against Perseus of Macedonia; its envoys and commissioners scattered over the Greek world to test attitudes, strengthen resolve, and encourage the wavering. Yet nowhere, in our testimony, did they draw attention to moral commitments or the obligations of clientship. Instead Rome had recourse to dubious propaganda, exaggerated

183. Livy, 44.19.6–12.

184. Livy, 45.13.2–5. Cf. Antiochus' reception of Roman envoys in 166; Polyb. 30.27.2–3.

185. Polyb. 30.5.4.

186. Polyb. 30.18; cf. Livy, 45.44.4–20; Diod. 31.15.

187. Athens: IG, II², 1938; Delos: IdeDélos, 1950; cf. 2484; Antiochia: Habicht, AthMitt 72 (1957): 242–244; Caunus: SEG, XII, 466; Cibyra: OGIS, 762; Petres: Edson, HSCP 51 (1940): 131, n. 6; Mellor, ΘΕΑ ΡΩΜΗ, 107–108; Lycia: RA (1970): 321; Rhodes: Polyb. 31.4.4; IG, XII, 1, 46; XII, 1, 730 = Syll.³ 724; Stratonicea: IGRR, IV, 247; Aphrodisias: Reynolds, Aphrodisias and Rome, 6–7, no. 1; Teos: IGRR, IV, 1556; Melos: IG, XII, 3, 1097. Some of the dedications by Greek states on the Capitol—from Laodicea, the Lycian League, Mithridates, Tabae, and Ephesus—may stem from this period; IGUR, no. 5 = ILLRP, I, no. 174 (Lycia); IGUR, no. 6 = ILLRP, I, no. 177 (Laodicea); IGUR, no. 9 (Mithridates); no. 10 (Tabae); ILS, 34 (Ephesus). But the dates remain in dispute; bibliography and most recent discussion in Mellor, op. cit., 203–206; Chiron 8 (1978): 319–330; Lintott, ZPE 30 (1978): 137–144.

denunciations of Perseus, a recapitulation of Eumenes' slanders.[188] If she possessed claims on loyalty from past benefits, she was markedly mute about them.[189] Roman *legati* to Asia, in fact, made a point of seeking aid from the wealthier states, with the expectation that lesser communities would follow the lead of the greater—a Hellenic *clientela* system.[190] Those Greeks who proffered assistance did so out of self-interest and self-preservation, not because Rome insisted on fulfillment of any duties toward a patron.[191]

More important and more revealing still is the fact that even after Apamea Rome was by no means reckoned as the sole power to whom Greeks should tender their respects. Indeed the western nation makes remarkably few appearances in the epigraphical record. The Greek world settled back into a familiar mold. Hellenistic princes claimed the bulk of honorific compliments. Their esteem remained high, their influence wide—and not just within their own immediate realms. This fact needs stress for it is easily overlooked by a conventional Rome-centered approach to the period. To regard honors for Greek rulers as a reflection of their standing with Rome or potential opposition to Rome—a persistent tendency in modern works—constitutes *a priori* reasoning and *post eventum* interpretation.

Eumenes II's holdings had received considerable augmentation as consequence of his alliance with Rome and the terms of Apamea. The association is duly reflected in a decree of the Delphian Amphictyony in 182: the Amphictyons tie Eumenes' prestige closely to his friendship with the Romans, κοινοὶ εὐεργέται of Greece.[192] But that

188. *FDelphes*, III, 4, 75 : *Syll.*³ 643 = Sherk, *RDGE*, no. 40; *FDelphes*, III, 4, 367— with new restoration by J. Bousquet, *BCH* 105 (1981): 407–416; Polyb. 22.18; Livy, 42.40. Eumenes' charges: Livy, 42.11–13; Appian, *Mac.* 11.1–2. See above pp. 91–93.

189. Notice, for example, that in Thessaly it was the Thessalians who affirmed that their *libertas* has been Rome's *munus*; the Roman envoys expressed gratitude for Thessaly's aid in prior wars and hope for its continuation; Livy, 42.38.6.

190. Livy, 42.45.2: *quo quaeque opulentior civitas erat eo accuratius agebant, quia minores secuturae maiorum auctoritatem erant*—a Polybian passage; cf. Polyb. 27.3.

191. The Roman decision on elevating supporters in Thisbae to authority in 170, after the city surrendered, came as consequence of an embassy from that party who sought the upper hand over their opponents. The senate was happy to oblige: *Syll.*³ 646 = Sherk, *RDGE*, no. 2. Sherk's analysis, *op. cit.*, 29, that the Thisbaean envoys became *clientes* of the Roman praetor and the senatorial commission, has no foundation in the text. On several matters the senate deferred any judgment: lines 35–56. And in one, at least, they denied a request: line 31. It was again the reaction rather than the initiative of Rome which produced the senate's statement in 168 that Egypt regard its chief protection as the *fides* of the Roman people: Livy, 45.13.7. That was a polite reply to the fawning compliments of Ptolemy's envoys, not an assertion of senatorial policy on patronage; cf. Livy, 45.13.4–5.

192. *Syll.*³ 630 = *FDelphes*, II, 3, 261, lines 3–10, 16–18; cf. Holleaux, *Études* II:63–72; Daux, *Delphes*, 293–298.

was not his sole claim on allegiance. The city of Telmessus, which had come under Pergamene authority at Apamea, heaped praise upon Eumenes in 184 for victories against Prusias and against the Gauls.[193] Eumenes' eminence obtained recognition elsewhere in subsequent years, from areas outside his immediate control, in particular from Aetolia and from Athens, as attested in several documents, none of which makes the barest mention of Rome.[194] Most notable is the famous Athenian decree lauding Eumenes and his family for their successful installation of Antiochus IV on the throne of Syria in 175.[195] There were parties in both Aenus and Maronea who looked to Eumenes as their champion.[196] He grasped very well indeed the concept of dispensing patronage, as exemplified by his offer of monetary favors to the Achaean League in the early 180s. The Achaeans grasped it too: they preferred to decline the offer, lest they find their decisions dictated by Pergamene interests.[197] If Livy is to be believed, all the states of Greece and many of her *principes* as well had come under obligation to the king by the late 170s.[198] When Greeks felt threatened by Perseus, the one person to whom they hastily sent word was Eumenes.[199] The Pergamene monarch enjoyed international repute in his own right, not the reflected glory of Roman authority.[200] Well might the Ionian League depict Eumenes as κοινὸς εὐεργέτης.[201]

The influence of Antiochus IV also extended well beyond his holdings. Athenian joy at Antiochus' accession, through Pergamene aid, represents genuine emotion. Bonds that linked the Seleucid house to Athens and Delos in this period are amply attested.[202] Antiochus

193. M. Segre, *RivFilol* 60 (1932): 446–447, lines 5–14. On the acquisition of Telmessus, see Polyb. 21.46.10; Livy, 38.39.16.

194. Aetolia: *Syll.*³ 628; *Syll.*³ 629 = *IG*, IX, 1², 179 (182 B.C.). Athens: W. Dinsmoor, *AJA* 24 (1920): 83 (178 B.C.); *Syll.*³ 641 (ca. 174 B.C.); *IG*, II², 1, 905 (ca. 174 B.C.); *Syll.*³ 651 (168 B.C.). In addition, of course, numerous decrees from Asian cities inside the Pergamene sphere honoring the royal house or its agents and making no allusion to Rome, e.g., *OGIS*, 308 (Hieropolis); Herrmann, *AnzAkadWien* 107 (1970): 98–100 (Mysia); H. Vetters, *AnzAkadWien*, 108 (1971): 90 (Ephesus); *OGIS*, 301–304 (Panium in Thrace).

195. *OGIS*, 248; cf. Appian, *Syr.* 45. For attribution of the decree to Athens, see Holleaux, *Études* II:127–147. Good relations between Eumenes and Antiochus are further affirmed by a Milesian decree of this period: Herrmann, *IstMitt* 15 (1965): 71–90.

196. Polyb. 22.6.7, 22.13.9; Livy, 39.34.4.

197. Polyb. 22.7.3–22.8.13.   198. Livy, 42.5.3   199. Livy, 41.22.5.

200. Cf. the alliance between Eumenes and thirty Cretan cities in 183: *Syll.*³ 627 = *IC*, IV, 179.

201. *OGIS*, 763 = Welles, *RC*, no. 52, lines 7–8. See above n. 175. Hopp, *Untersuchungen*, 55–58, unfortunately, continues to see Eumenes as a watchdog for Roman interests in Anatolia.

202. Cf. *OGIS*, 247; *Syll.*³ 639 = Dürrbach, *Choix*, no. 70; *IG*, XI, 4, 1112 = Dürrbach, *Choix*, no. 71; *SEG*, XVI, 94 = *ISE*, no. 34; *SEG*, XXIV, 135; cf. Robert, *ArchEph*

took special pride in his reputation for generosity to Athens and to Delian Apollo.[203] But they were not all. The policy of Antiochus IV featured far-flung connections. His agent Eudemus of Seleucia moved through much of Hellas to distribute the favors of his king. The well-traveled courtier collected tokens of gratitude, proxeny decrees, from a remarkable assortment of Greek states: Argos, Boeotia, Rhodes, Byzantium, Chalcedon, and Cyzicus.[204] Further testimony stems from Dyme in Achaea, where statues were erected to Antiochus and his family by an Achaean with close connections to the Seleucid court; and from Delphi, which honored another of the king's ministers for his services to the city's embassies.[205] Tangible reminders of Antiochus' beneficence stood in Tegea, in Megalopolis, in Cyzicus—and they doubtless do not exhaust the list.[206] In projecting a paternalistic image none was more assiduous than Antiochus IV.[207]

Hellenic states, eager as ever to cement ties with the powerful, did not limit themselves to single patrons. The Aetolians erected equestrian statues both to Eumenes and to Prusias II of Bithynia in the late 180s.[208] Athens, in addition to her close links with Eumenes and with Antiochus IV, paid homage also to Pharnaces of Pontus, now married to a Seleucid princess.[209] Delos' association with the Seleucids brought her within the orbit of Perseus as well.[210] And in 175 the island voted the dedication of crowns to Perseus, Eumenes, and Prusias of Bithynia![211] The sanctuary of Delphi, which conferred dignities upon Rome and upon the kings of Pergamum and Syria, did not neglect matters closer to home: a bronze statue for the *strategos* of

---

(1969): 1–6; OGIS, 249; OGIS, 250 = Dürrbach, Choix, no. 87; cf. OGIS, 251. See also Hesperia 26 (1957): 47–51; and see now Hesperia 51 (1982): 61–62.

203. Polyb. 26.1.11; Livy, 41.20.8–9; Strabo, 9.1.17 (C 396); Vitruv. 7, praef. 15; Paus. 5.12.4.

204. Syll.³ 644–645. For Rhodes and Cyzicus, see also Livy, 41.20.7.

205. Dyme: OGIS, 252 = ISE, no. 56; cf. Habicht, Historia 7 (1958): 376–378. Delphi: OGIS, 241; cf. Daux, Delphes, 511–514.

206. Livy, 41.20.6–7.

207. Cf. Polyb. 29.24.13: ἡ τοῦ τότε βασιλεύοντος μεγαλοψυχία διάδηλος ἐγένετο τοῖς Ἕλλησιν; Livy, 41.20.5: in duabus tamen magnis honestisque rebus vere regius erat animus, in urbium donis et deorum cultu. On Antiochus' policy toward the Greeks, see Mørkholm, Antiochos IV, 51–63. Cf. Walbank, Commentary III: 287–288.

208. On Eumenes, see above n. 194; on Prusias, Syll.³ 632 = FDelphes, III, 4, 76.

209. OGIS, 771 = Dürrbach, Choix, no. 73 = IdeDélos, 1497. The date is 160/59; see Hopp, Untersuchungen, 4, n. 8. Mørkholm's view, Antiochos IV, 60, that Athens simply shifted her loyalty to Antiochus' daughter after his death, ignores the text of the decree, which speaks of benefits conferred by the ancestors of Pharnaces and of prior agreements made with the Pontic monarch: lines 8–10, 19–20.

210. Syll.³ 639 = Dürrbach, Choix, no. 70.

211. IdeDélos, 449A, lines 14–23.

the Aetolians.[212] Hellenistic rulers, of course, welcomed and encouraged attentions from smaller states, as they always had. The publicity was gratifying, especially when adulation came from distant places, however loose the connection: as in a Lycian decree for Ptolemy V in the 180s, or one from Aptera for Prusias in the same period.[213] Nor were they averse to generating the publicity themselves. Perseus opened his reign with a conspicuous recall of exiles, posting the lists of his beneficiaries at Delos, Delphi, and the sanctuary of Itonian Athena. And when he framed an alliance with Boeotia, the treaty was also put on public view at three major sites in Greece.[214]

Cultivation of manifold diplomatic bonds was traditional Hellenistic practice.[215] The overlapping of entanglements provided some security for vulnerable communities and supplied marks of prestige for rulers and dynasts.[216] Roman entrance upon the scene, and then retreat, had left the old structure basically intact. Patrons and clients there were aplenty. So there had always been. The western power had not altered that pattern nor created a new one.

The Continuities After Pydna

Rome's victory over Perseus, it might be assumed, changed everything. Faithless clients were to be put in their place, obligations to Rome spelled out with decisiveness, the dependency of Greece made plain and unambiguous. Henceforth there would be deference and docility, to avoid the risk of retaliation. A genuine enforcement of clientage.[217] Is it so?

The immediate aftermath of Pydna would seem to confirm it. Vigorous enunciations of Roman authority rang across the Mediterranean. Not just that the Macedonian monarchy was abolished and its alleged collaborators in Greece deported to Italy. Some of Rome's erstwhile friends who had been lukewarm, neutral, or suspect during the

212. *Syll.*³ 621.

213. Ptolemy: *OGIS*, 99; Prusias: *OGIS*, 341 = *IC*, II, 3, 4A.

214. Recall of exiles: Polyb. 25.3.1–2; treaty with Boeotia: Livy, 42.12.5–6. Cf. the newly published donation of the Ptolemaic rulers, together with Cypriote cities, to Argos in the early 160s; P. Aupert, *BCH* 106 (1982): 263–277.

215. Notice, e.g., Athenian eagerness in the later third century to win favor by honoring all the kings with adulatory pronouncements: Polyb. 5.106.6–8.

216. Cf. Livy, 35.46.7—Chalcis is urged to embrace the friendship of both Rome and Antiochus in 192: *ita enim ab utriusque iniuria tutas alterius semper praesidio et fiducia fore.*

217. So, e.g., Badian, *Foreign Clientelae*, 100–115; Errington, *Dawn of Empire*, 229–256.

war suffered humiliation and even emasculation. The facts are well known. Rhodes was stripped of Lycia and Caria, and later ordered out of Caunus and Stratonicea; Delos became a free port, with serious economic repercussions for Rhodes; the island was even threatened with war by the Romans; she was to be made an example of.[218] Eumenes fared little better. He was snubbed by the senate, his Asian rivals embraced, the Galatians declared autonomous, and the king's authority undermined.[219] The humbling of Antiochus IV was more dramatic still. A Roman legate ordered him out of Egypt with a pointed display of arrogance.[220] A few years later, so Polybius claims, the senate sent representatives to take in hand the affairs of the Syrian kingdom.[221] Others were to carry out a partition of Egyptian holdings.[222] The conferral of benefits was a mere pretense, according to the Greek historian: Rome arranged matters to enhance her own dominion.[223]

It was plainly in Rome's interest to make a firm display of power after the Third Macedonian War. That conflict had sorely taxed the Republic's energies, surprising her in its length and difficulty, alerting her to the danger of upset in the power balance of the East. What Perseus had almost accomplished, no other state should be permitted to contemplate.

The pragmatic purposes suffice as explanation. We hear nothing of any Roman resentment at clients' failure to discharge moral duties.[224] Even the pretexts employed took different forms. Rhodian efforts at mediation were described as advancing Perseus' interests.[225] And slanderous reports about Eumenes alleged that he had engaged in private negotiations with the Macedonian.[226] Such were the ex-

218. Polyb. 29.19, 30.4–5, 30.20–21, 30.23, 30.31; Livy, 45.3.3–8, 45.10.4–15, 45.20–25; Diod. 31.5; Dio, 20.68.1–3; Zon. 9.24.

219. Polyb. 30.1–3, 30.18–19, 30.30, 31.6; Livy, Per. 46; Diod. 31.7.2.

220. Polyb. 29.27.1–8; Livy, 45.12.1–6; Diod. 31.2; Appian, Syr. 66; Zon. 9.25; Justin, 34.3.1–4.

221. Polyb. 31.2.9–11; cf. Appian, Syr. 46; Zon. 9.25; Cic. Phil. 9.4.

222. Polyb. 31.10.6.

223. Polyb. 31.10.7: αὔξουσι καὶ κατασκευάζονται τὴν ἰδίαν ἀρχὴν πραγματικ- ῶς, ἅμα χαριζόμενοι καὶ δοκοῦντες εὐεργετεῖν τοὺς ἁμαρτάνοντας.

224. Polybius does feel the need to meet a potential charge of ἀχαριστία against those who leaned toward Perseus: 27.10.5: ἵνα μὴ τις ἀκρίτως εἰς ἀχαριστίαν ὀνειδίζῃ τοῖς Ἕλλησι τὴν τότε διάθεσιν. But that is the sort of reproach leveled by Greek against Greek in the scramble for political ascendancy during and after the war—not an accusation emanating from Rome. Note the exact language employed by Polybius in describing accusations hurled in an interparty dispute in Aetolia, 28.4.11: τὰ δ' ὀνειδίσας εἰς ἀχαριστίαν αὐτῷ. And cf. generally Polyb. 27.15.8–16, 28.4.3–12, 28.5.1–5, 30.1.5– 8, 30.13; Livy, 45.31.5–11; Paus. 7.10.7–11.

225. Polyb. 29.19.5–11; Livy, 45.3.6–8.

226. Polyb. 29.5–9; Livy, 44.13.12–14.

cuses for Roman displeasure. As for Antiochus, his rebuke stemmed simply from the senate's desire to halt conflict between Syria and Egypt and to forestall Seleucid aggrandizement.[227] Violation of a client's *officia* played no role as motive or pretext. Rome's posture in the wake of Pydna had a clear and straightforward purpose: to discourage any imitators of Perseus.

The Greeks did not mistake that message. As we have seen, deputations from various principalities hastened to congratulate the Republic, to flatter her leaders, to solicit her indulgence. That flurry of activity is intelligible, even inevitable, in view of the conqueror's stern visage after Pydna. The cajolery continued, however, in subsequent years, as new rulers or those shaky on their thrones curried senatorial favor in hopes of strengthening their own positions. So, young Ariarathes V, nervous about his hold on the Cappadocian kingdom, dispatched missions to obtain Roman recognition, expressed readiness to help in any endeavors, and presented the senate with a crown of ten thousand gold pieces.[228] He had good reason for concern. Ariarathes' foe Demetrius of Syria also gained Rome's acknowledgment, punctuated again with the conveyance of a gold crown.[229] Demetrius later expelled Ariarathes from Cappadocia and replaced him with Orophernes, who then went through the same ritual at Rome.[230] Intense rivalries in the Hellenistic East impelled more than one pretender to seek some token of Roman support.[231] No example is more striking than the publication by Ptolemy Euergetes of his will in 155, leaving all his possessions to Rome. His bequest was neither philanthropy nor the fulfillment of a client's duties, but a transparent move to gain the political upper hand over his brother Philometor.[232]

These transactions need to be understood for what they were. On the surface, they appeared as acts of deference to the great power, a stream of sycophantic demonstrations that marked the era from Pydna to 146. Conventional wisdom has it that Hellenistic kingdoms became mere dependencies, that a new international structure took shape under the extended protective wing of Rome. But that image misconceives context and circumstances. The instances noted above

227. Polyb. 29.2.1–3, 29.27.7; Livy, 44.19.3, 45.10.2–3, 45.12.3–7; Diod. 31.2.2; Appian, *Syr.* 66; Zon. 9.25; Justin, 34.3.1.

228. Polyb. 31.3, 31.7–8, 31.32, 32.1.1–3; Diod. 31.19.8, 31.28; Zon. 9.24.

229. Polyb. 31.33, 32.2.1, 32.3.13; Diod. 31.29–30; Appian, *Syr.* 47.

230. Polyb. 32.10; cf. Appian, *Syr.* 47; Zon. 9.24.

231. Cf. Diod. 31.27a; Polyb. 33.15, 33.18. On the circumstances generally in Syria and Cappadocia during this period, see Gruen, *Chiron* 6 (1976): 73–95.

232. *SEG*, IX, 7, with bibliography cited there. On the political and personal motivations of Euergetes see, especially, Winkler, *Rom und Aegypten*, 47–60; Otto, *Abh-Münch* 11 (1934): 97–116. A more recent discussion in Liebmann-Frankfort, *RIDA* 13 (1966): 73–94. And see below pp. 702–705.

point in a different direction. Hellenistic rulers and states endeavored to mold, even to manipulate, Roman opinion to their own advantage. Appearances before the senate, presentation of gifts, requests for some manifestations of favor aimed at enhancing the stature of those who had to confront rivals and opposition at home. Men like Ptolemy Euergetes, Ariarathes V, Orophernes, Demetrius I, Timarchus, and Alexander Balas were engaged in dynastic competition and struggles to acquire or retain control of their dominions against domestic foes and neighbors. Endorsement by the victor of Pydna could be a valuable weapon to discourage competitors and to entrench dynasts who obtained (and magnified) that endorsement. This is a far cry from international patronage orchestrated by Rome. The initiative persistently comes from Greeks. Rome is a passive recipient. And, as we shall see, senatorial blessing is generally empty of substantive content, its beneficiaries left to wage their battles without expectation of rescue should they fail.[233] The importance of those endorsements lies in the use to which they were put by Greek leaders and principalities who had called them forth in the first place. Theirs was the initiative, theirs the ends that were served.

Seen in this light, deference to Rome is more intelligible. Consider that practice often reckoned as the surest acknowledgment of a client relationship: the kings' sending of their sons to Rome for education and political nourishment. A means of assuring succession to the desired heir under the umbrella of Roman protection? Not so. In fact, only two examples are known in the entire period under scrutiny, one just before and one just after the Third Macedonian War.[234] In the account of Livy, the kings could hardly have been more obsequious, or the senate more accommodating. Ariarathes IV had his young son delivered to Rome in 172 with the request that he come under the care of the state and imbibe the customs of Rome. Five years later Prusias II came in person with his boy Nicomedes and entrusted him to the tutelage of the senate. In both cases, the *patres* gave gracious welcome and accepted the princes. So far Livy.[235] He restricts himself to the scenes in Rome, a plausible enough recounting of the formal occasions. The darker side, however, emerges from other evidence. Two supposed sons of Ariarathes IV were in fact sent abroad, one to Rome

233. Cf. Gruen, *Chiron* 6 (1976): 84–93.

234. In a different category, of course, are Greek princes held in Rome as hostages: Demetrius, son of Philip V, Antiochus IV, and Demetrius I of Syria. Brizzi, *I sistemi informativi*, 217–219, combines both categories as mere instruments of Roman policy.

235. Livy, 42.19.3–6, 45.44.4, 45.44.9, 45.44.13. Only the Livian passages are cited by Sands, *Client Princes*, 198, 201, and Badian, *Foreign Clientelae*, 105–106.

and one to Ionia. But the purpose was not to groom them for the throne; rather to clear them out of the way for the eventual succession of the favored heir, Ariarathes V.[236] The case of Prusias is analogous. The Bithynian king distrusted his older son; Nicomedes was sent to Rome because Prusias preferred his other heirs.[237] Acquiescence in clientage is not at issue here. The monarchs simply fastened on a convenient device. They exploited Roman hospitality by depositing unwanted sons to advance their personal dynastic schemes.

The acquisition of Rome's good will carried useful publicity value, even when Rome's basic indifference limited any tangible benefits. Association (or claims of association) with the conqueror of Perseus supplied to the Greeks a means for self-advertisement and an instrument for aggrandizement at home. After Rhodes secured a Roman alliance in 164, she erected a colossal statue to the Roman people in the temple of Athena. Not out of mere gratitude: it was a sign to neighbors that Rhodes was back on her feet again. The island shortly thereafter absorbed Calynda.[238] And, perhaps about this time also, her assistance and alliance were sought by Ceramus.[239] Rhodes evidently paraded reconciliation with Rome to recover standing in Caria. Attalus also made shrewd use of the Roman name when it suited his purposes. He sent his young nephew to the senate in 154/3 for introduction to the friends and sympathizers of Pergamum in that body. The boy's return journey was marked by warm greetings from the Greek cities through which he passed, an obvious publicity move.[240] Attalus was looking ahead to a final reckoning with Prusias of Bithynia. And when Prusias fell in 149, Attalus commemorated his victory with an inscription that again invoked Rome: justification for the war rested on Prusias' supposed violation of a treaty sanctioned by the Romans.[241] But the Pergamene king could also make allusion to Rome when he wished to avoid conflict. His letter to the priest at

236. Diod. 31.19.7; cf. Zon. 9.24. The son deposited in Rome is never heard from again.

237. Appian, *Mithr.* 4; Justin, 34.4.1; Zon. 9.28. This may refer to a second and later dispatch of Nicomedes. The maneuver, of course, eventually backfired on Prusias, who was turned on by his son.

238. Polyb. 31.4.4–31.5.5.

239. Michel, *Recueil*, no. 458, lines 13–18; cf. Robert, *Villes d'Asie Mineure*, 60–61; P. M. Fraser and G. E. Bean, *The Rhodian Peraea* (Oxford, 1954), 110–111; Schmitt, *Rom und Rhodos*, 176–177.

240. Polyb. 33.18.1–4. The *amici* and *hospites* in Rome had been cultivated by Eumenes a generation earlier when he sent his brothers on a mission to the senate: Polyb. 24.5.1–7. Demetrius of Syria employed the same technique in 154/3, but his son—too young to make an impact—was snubbed: Polyb. 33.18.5.

241. *OGIS*, 327, line 4: παραβάντα τὰς διὰ Ῥωμαίων γε[νομένας συνθήκας].

Pessinus perhaps in 156 declined a request for armed assistance, on the pretext that Rome might disapprove.[242] Actual exertion of Roman pressure is an unnecessary inference. Attalus adverted to it for his own ends. An analogous posture was adopted by Ptolemy Philometor in the mid-150s. Senatorial opinion at Rome had expressed itself in favor of Philometor's brother Euergetes, and had directed the latter's restoration to Cyprus. Philometor pointedly ignored the decision, captured his brother, and confined his holdings to Cyrene—a most unclientlike behavior.[243] Yet an honorary decree for Philometor, set up at Delos by his Cretan auxiliaries and obviously reflecting the king's public stance, made reference to his special devotion to Rome.[244]

Smaller states and groups also found advantage in claiming Roman friendship or ingratiating themselves with the western power. The city of Oropus, while giving thanks to an Achaean for support in her dispute with Athens during the 150s, made sure to describe herself as being in the *amicitia* and *fides* of Rome. The Roman role in this dispute had been distant and minor, but it was plainly desirable to be associated with it.[245] Flattering epithets for the Romans become more common in the documents, even when they have little to do with the issue at stake. A decree from Olympia describes them as guardians of Greek order and concord.[246] And the period after Pydna sees increasing numbers of references to the Romans as κοινοὶ εὐεργέται. They are so depicted by Athenians on Lemnos celebrating the island's reincorporation by Athens; by the Samians in a decree recording treaty relations with Antiochia on the Maeander; by Delphi in honoring a historian from Troezen who gave recitations lauding the Romans; by the corporation of Dionysian artists from Ionia and the Hellespont in praise of Iasus; by Chalcis in an honorary decree for one of her cit-

242. *OGIS*, 315 = Welles, *RC*, no. 61. Cf. the same maneuver utilized by Callicrates to avoid Achaean involvement in a war between Rhodes and Crete at about this time: Polyb. 33.16.2–8; cf. also Polyb. 29.23.10.

243. Polyb. 33.11, 39.7.6; Diod. 31.33.

244. *OGIS*, 116 = *IdeDélos*, 1518, lines 9–11: προαι[ρούμε]νος ἐν οἷς μάλιστα χαρίζεσθαι καὶ ʼΡωμ[αίοι]ς. Authors of the document discernible by comparison with Dürrbach, *Choix*, no. 92 = *IdeDélos*, 1517.

245. *Syll.*[3] 675, lines 11–12, 21–22: ἐν τεῖ ʼΡωμαίων φιλίαι καὶ πίστει διατελοῦμεν ὑπάρχοντες. Cf. the discussion in Gruen, *JHS* 96 (1976): 51–53. Note also the recently published inscription from Lydia honoring a certain Mogetes as πρόκριτον πάτρας καὶ ὑπέρμαχον ἀε[ὶ] ʼΡώμας κυδίσταις θῆκατ ἐν ἀγεμόσι—perhaps of the later second century; G. Petzl, *ZPE* 30 (1978); 269–273.

246. *Syll.*[3] 665, lines 43–44: ʼΡωμαίους τοὺς προεστατακότας τὰς τῶν Ἑλλάν[ων εὐνομίας καὶ ὁμο]νοίας. The decree concerns an arbitral dispute between Megalopolis and Sparta actually decided by the Achaeans; cf. Gruen, *JHS* 96 (1976): 50–51. Similar restoration in a decree from Priene is quite unverifiable: *OGIS*, 351 = Sherk, *RDGE* no. 6A, lines 5–6. The stone has only καὶ ʼΡωμαίων τῶν [. . .]τῶν. And this may be a Roman letter anyway.

izens.[247] As is evident, the phrase itself became a convention employed by Greeks in various contexts and dealings with one another. And it could be assigned to Hellenistic kings as well.[248] Yet nowhere to be found is active Roman interest in fostering such homage. The backing of Rome would be sought by Greek appellants and the name of Rome invoked by Greeks when it seemed useful. But the issues at stake were matters within and among Hellenic communities—rarely of concern to the senate.[249] Demands did not issue from the West. The notion of *clientela* is quite inappropriate.[250]

Nor did all eyes look to Rome, even in the post-Pydna generation. Hellas was still far from a collection of Roman dependencies. Epigraphic testimony on the Attalid kings, for example, shows little change in their reputation among fellow Greeks before and after the Third Macedonian War. Cults, games, festivals, statues, and honors of various kinds accrued to Eumenes II and his successor Attalus II in the 160s and 150s from the Greek cities of Asia Minor and the islands within their orbit: Sardis, Tralles, Magnesia, Miletus, Teos, Apamea, Sestus, Cos, Aegina.[251] Formalities and conventions, for the most part. But not altogether. There was some genuine gratitude paid for tangible benefits: the Attalids were saluted as patrons and protectors.[252] And their connections abroad, with places like Athens, Delos,

247. Lemnos: *IG*, II², 1224, line 9; cf. Polyb. 30.20; Robert, *CRAI* (1969), 60 (ca. 165 B.C.); Samos: Habicht, *AthMitt* 72 (1957): 242–244, lines 20–21 (ca. 165 B.C.); Delphi: *Syll.*³ 702 = *FDelphes*, III, 3, 124, lines 6–7 (157 B.C.); Dionysiac *technites*: Michel, *Recueil*, no. 1014, with corrections by Robert, *Études Anatoliennes* (Paris, 1937), 445–450; Chalcis: *IG*, XII, 9, 899, lines 1–2; cf. Robert, *ArchEph* (1969): 44–49 (mid-second century?). Further and later examples in Robert, *Études Anat.*, 448, n. 3; *REG* 62 (1949): 123–124; Volkmann, *Hermes*, 82 (1954): 467–468.

248. *OGIS*, 763 = Welles, *RC*, no. 52, lines 7–8; see above n. 175.

249. Cf. the senate's confirming of Delphic privileges, perhaps in 165—on request of the Delphians; *Syll.*³ 612C = Sherk, *RDGE*, no. 1C; cf. *Syll.*³ 612D = Sherk, *RDGE*, no. 1D. Also the *senatus consultum* of later date instructing the Athenians to allow a priest of Delos to maintain control of his sanctuary; again it was mere reaffirmation of the status quo: *Syll.*³ 664 = *IdeDélos*, 1510 = Sherk, *RDGE*, no. 5, lines 32–36: καθὼς τὸ πρότερον ἐθεράπευεν, ἕνεκεν ἡμῶν θεραπεύειν ἔξεστιν τοῦ μή τι ὑπεναντίον τῶι τῆς συγκλήτου δόγματι γίνηται.

250. Roman envoys, enraged by Prusias' behavior in 154, did seek to stir opposition to him among Greek cities in Ionia and the Hellespont—but without any appeal to obligations, whether formal or moral. And, more noteworthy, upon the envoys' return to Rome, their hot-headed policy was promptly reversed by the senate: Polyb. 33.12.2–33.13.5.

251. Sardis: *OGIS*, 305 = *FDelphes*, III, 3, 241–242; Tralles: Robert, *RevPhil* 60 (1934): 279–291; Magnesia: *OGIS*, 319; Miletus: *OGIS*, 320–321; Herrmann, *IstMitt* 15 (1965) 71–117; Teos: *OGIS*, 309, 325; Apamea: W. H. Buckler, *JHS* 55 (1935): 71–75; Sestus: *OGIS*, 339; Cos: *Syll.*³ 1028; Aegina: *OGIS*, 329.

252. E.g., *OGIS*, 305 = *FDelphes*, III, 3, 241–242, lines 10–11: Εὐ]μένη Σαρδιανοὶ διαφυγόντες [τὸν μέγιστον] κίνδυνον μετὰ τ[ε τᾶς τ]ῶν [θεῶν] εὐν[ο]ίας καὶ [μετὰ τᾶς

and Delphi, persisted.[253] Other kings too appear in the documents, honored by Greek states, corporations, or individuals: Ariarathes V, Demetrius I, Pharnaces I, Ptolemy Philometor.[254] The exercise of patronage as a feature of Hellenistic diplomacy remained firmly entrenched—and unhindered by Rome. Greek rulers spread their wealth and competed with one another for the gratitude of beneficiaries. Political advantage lay therein, as it always had. Eumenes II, so Polybius remarks, outstripped all other kings in bestowing benefits upon Greek cities: it was a means of elevating his reputation.[255] And not cities alone. Eumenes financed individual foreign clients who would serve his interests abroad, a practice also followed by others.[256] The shrewder states knew how to capitalize on this bounty. Rhodes virtually had kings dance attendance upon her, offering calculated flattery and distinctions while they outbid one another with gifts to win the island's adherence.[257] In the time of Ptolemy VI the *koinon* of the Cretans could refer officially to that monarch's προστασία.[258] Rome, when she chose, was, of course, the most potent dispenser of favors. But even in tapping that fount the Greeks made application in their own way and through their own patrons. So, Abdera had her requests conveyed through representatives of her patron city Teos, just as Lampsacus had done through her patron city Massilia a generation earlier.[259] The Hellenic institutions subsisted intact.

τοῦ β]ασιλέος Εὐμένεος ἀρετᾶς. Herrmann, *IstMitt* 15 (1965), 73, lines 12–13: ὥστε τὴν μὲν τοῦ πλήθους εἰς τοὺς εὐεργέτας εὐχαριστίαν φανερὰν πᾶσιν καταστῆσας.

253. Athens: *IG*, II², 953; Delos: *IdeDélos*, 1554; Delphi: *Syll.*³ 670–672; *FDelphes*, III, 3, 121; III, 3, 237–239.

254. *OGIS*, 352: a decree of the Dionysian *technites* at Athens for Ariarathes; cf. *ArchEph* (1950): 5–9; *IdeDélos*, 1543 = Dürrbach, *Choix*, no. 88: a Delian dedication honoring a secretary of Demetrius I; *IdeDélos*, 1555: a Delian dedication for the daughter of Pharnaces; *IdeDélos*, 1525 = Dürrbach, *Choix*, no. 90: statue erected by an Athenian for one of Ptolemy's chief ministers; Dürrbach, *Choix*, no. 91: a Theran dedication for another Ptolemaic minister.

255. Polyb. 32.8.5: φιλοδοξότατος ἐγενήθη καὶ πλείστας μὲν τῶν καθ' αὑτὸν βασιλέων πόλεις Ἑλληνίδας εὐεργέτησε.

256. Polyb. 32.8.5: πλείστους δὲ κατ' ἰδίαν ἀνθρώπους ἐσωματοποίησε. One particular example known: a Boeotian politician whose career was fostered by Eumenes and Philetaerus, Polyb. 38.14.2: δι' Εὐμένους καὶ Φιλεταίρου σεσωματοποιημένος.

257. Diod. 31.36: ἐπιδεξίοις γὰρ θωπεύμασι καὶ ψηφίσμασι τιμῶντες τοὺς ἐν ἐξουσίαις ὄντας, καὶ τοῦτο πράττοντες βεβαίως καὶ μετὰ πολλῆς προνοίας, πολλαπλασίους χάριτας κομίζονται καὶ δωρεὰς λαμβάνουσι παρὰ τῶν βασιλέων . . . πολλοὺς ἔσχον ἁμιλλωμένους τῶν δυναστῶν εἰς τὰς τῆς πόλεως εὐεργεσίας. Demetrius and Eumenes receive specific mention. The fact is confirmed by Polyb. 31.31.1. This was an old practice on the part of the Rhodians, dramatically illustrated in the aftermath of an earthquake in the 220s, when kings and princes fell all over themselves to bring gifts and earn gratitude: Polyb. 5.88–90.

258. *Syll.*³ 685 = *IC*, III, 4, 9, line 107.

259. Abdera: *Syll.*³ 656; Lampsacus: *Syll.*³ 591. One could go back further still for

V

The *clientela* model as explanation of Rome's evolving ascendancy in the East is a modern creation, unsuited to the facts as we know them. Relations between patron and client were imbedded in the social and political life of ancient Italy. But international affairs stood on a different level. Tight bonds characterized personal connections in Roman society. But foreign entanglements on that scale of intimacy were precisely what the state wished to avoid.

By the time Rome took any significant part in eastern affairs, the Hellenistic world could look back on more than a century of complex interstate diplomacy. Exercise of foreign patronage by rulers and major powers, the sheltering of smaller principalities under the greater, competition among kings for the loyalty of Greek communities, the informal obligations attaching to bestowal of favors and repayment in faithful compliance, the extension of the paternalistic embrace—all of this was contained in the Hellenistic diplomatic experience.

The Greeks freely conferred distinctions and professed fidelity to conquerors and to successful powers. Self-preservation and future expectations depended on it. That conventional liberality they naturally applied to the western conqueror as well. Honors came to Roman leaders and generals operating in the East, and they, in turn, left dedications in the Greek manner as testimony to their achievements. Affirmations of loyalty to the Roman government were also forthcoming, even worship of the goddess Roma, an extension of traditional Greek practice. The instances of homage are especially prominent in the wake of Rome's wars, as eastern states attempted to deflect senatorial ire or engender senatorial favor. The logic is plain enough. Delegations from Greek kings and communities solicited Roman backing for their own schemes and sought Roman endorsement to confound domestic foes and outstrip contending rivals. In a word, the Hellenes persistently treated Rome within categories familiar to themselves: they endeavored to exploit her power in the quite specific framework of the Greek experience. The Romans, of course, took pleasure in flattery, accepted adulation, and extended courtesies. But they preferred to avoid encumbrances. For the most part, it was Rome who drew back from Greek advances. The idea that Rome transplanted her *clientela* system to the East misconceives both the direction and the structure of Graeco-Roman relations.

---

examples. Cf. the request by Heraclea that the Aetolians take up their cause with Ptolemy ca. 256; *IG*, IX, 1², 173 = *SEG*, II, 257 = *FDelphes*, III, 3, 144 = *ISE*, no. 77; cf. Robert, *BCH* 102 (1978): 477–490.

The Hellenistic order did not crumble at the approach of Rome. In fact, the old practices—of deference paid to the kings from abroad, of overlapping interstate associations among the Greeks, of competition for and accumulation of foreign *clientelae*—endured after Apamea and even after Pydna. The Romans neither fashioned nor dismantled that structure; rather they became part of it. Only in the age of Cicero did they look back on this era and discern (or imagine) a *patrocinium* exercised for the benefit of their inferiors.

· *Part* II ·

Attitudes and Motivation

Chapter 6

"Eastern Experts"
and Attitudes toward Hellas

Rome had nothing resembling a diplomatic corps. She did not station representatives abroad nor set up offices for foreign area specialists at home. She avoided too the installation of occupying forces in the East prior to the late second century (if then). Commanders and officers carried out overseas tours of duty when called upon, but did not stay to form a permanent establishment. The government had neither professional diplomats nor professional soldiers. There was no place for them in an aristocratic society of men who prided themselves upon management of public affairs across a broad spectrum of varied activities. Under such a system it is difficult to conceive the mechanism for creation and maintenance of a "foreign policy."

Yet the conception persists. Moderns continue to speak of an "eastern lobby" or "eastern experts" who guided the senate in formulating attitudes toward and influencing actions in the Hellenic world.[1] The idea possesses superficial attraction and plausibility. P. Sulpicius Galba is a prime exhibit: six years in command of Roman forces during the first war against Philip, elected again to the consulship of 200 as "expert" in Greek affairs, and successful advocate of the Second Macedonian War. More dramatic still is the career of T. Quinctius Flamininus, victor over Philip, prorogued again and again, chief Roman spokesman on eastern matters through the 190s and occasionally in the 180s. Then senatorial embassies proliferated and further military intervention followed. A growing body of Romans could

---

1. Cf., e.g., W. G. Forrest, *JRS* 46 (1956): 170; Badian, *Foreign Clientelae*, 63–66, 90; *Titus Quinctius Flamininus* (Cincinnati, 1970), 31–32, 46; Dell, *Ancient Macedonia* 2 (1977): 308, n. 15; and, especially, G. Clemente, *Athenaeum* 54 (1976): 319–352. See now also Brizzi, *I sistemi informativi*, 166–169, 262–267.

claim familiarity with the East, their experience valuable and their opinions weighty. The accumulation of knowledge and of knowledge-able men would seem to constitute a logical force for drawing Rome ever more deeply into the world of the Greeks. Rome could call upon increasing numbers of citizens who had served in the East to head her armies or form her legations abroad. The ranks of the senate soon swelled with those who had fought against Greeks, visited Hellenic states, or negotiated with Hellenistic princes. Whether or not one can speak of formulated "policy," the momentum itself of these develop-ments could intensify Rome's concerns for and entrench her involve-ment in the East.

How much truth does this picture contain? Impressions will not suffice. There is need to inject some precision into the analysis. Terms like "eastern experts" are too frequently tossed about; the assumption that men received assignments in the East on the basis of prior experi-ence there is too readily made. Did Rome customarily appoint gener-als and officers to sectors with which they were familiar? Did she compose legations of diplomats already seasoned in the affairs of Hellas? Did her decisions rest on the advice of lobbyists schooled by experience in the East?

The Military Appointments

We begin with an issue of the highest importance: the choice of commanders to conduct military operations across the Adriatic. To what extent was that choice determined by previous eastern service?

P. Sulpicius Galba is the obvious example, so often pointed to as the paradigm for Roman reliance on men with a knowledge of the East. Galba had taken charge of Rome's armies against Philip as pro-consul in 210. The senate prorogued him continuously until 205: six long years in the East, with campaigns in central and northern Greece and in the islands.[2] Then in the winter of 201/0, with the prospect of a new Macedonian war hovering, Galba obtained election to a second consulship, went on to present the war motion and argue for it with vigor and eloquence.[3] The province of Macedonia fell to his lot. Galba undertook recruitment and prepared to conduct the initial campaigns of the fateful Second Macedonian War.[4] On the face of it, coincidence

2. Sources in Broughton, *MRR* I:280, 287, 292, 296, 300.
3. The election: Polyb. 16.24.1; Livy, 31.4.4; the war motion: Livy, 31.5.9–31.6.1; the speech: Livy, 31.7—plainly a Livian composition, but no reason to doubt that Galba did urge the war.
4. Livy, 31.6.1, 31.8, 31.14,1–3, 31.22.4.

seems unthinkable. Scholars, even of the most varied opinions on the origins of the war, concur in regarding Galba's elevation as a telling pointer of policy: his eastern "expertise" fitted him for the role, his anti-Macedonian posture determined the election, his provincial allotment was "managed."[5]

Yet it may be salutary to insert some caution. The *communis opinio* on this subject, assumed and never argued, sidesteps certain troublesome obstacles. Nothing in our evidence declares or implies that Sulpicius Galba owed election to prior service in the eastern sector. Nor to his attitudes toward Macedonia. As for the lot, Livy breathes no hint of chicanery. The senate determined that whichever consul drew Macedonia would present the war motion to the assembly; it happened to be Galba.[6] Is this all a cover-up? Galba had indeed headed Roman operations for six years in the First Macedonian War. But his concrete accomplishments were small, his successes minimal. Rome, in fact, seems to have reduced her commitment when sending Galba to the East.[7] In 210 he took the island of Aegina but failed ignominiously to lift the siege of Echinus.[8] Indecisive operations followed in 209: the Romans lent supplementary aid to Aetolia at Lamia and prevented Philip from taking Elis, while a Roman raiding party in the Corinthiad was routed by the Macedonians.[9] The year 208 saw similarly dubious results: Galba's fleet cooperated with Attalus against various islands and cities, he secured Oreum through treachery and sacked Dyme, but miscalculated and had to withdraw from Chalcis. Most of the year's gains belonged to Philip.[10] For the next two years Galba stayed on in Greece but conducted no campaigns, as Rome neglected the eastern front, and in 205 he was replaced.[11] That was hardly a record of sterling accomplishment. Galba had indeed

5. Cf., e.g., Holleaux, *Rome, la Grèce*, 294; Passerini, *Athenaeum* 9 (1931): 551–552; McDonald and Walbank, *JRS* 27 (1937): 185, n. 39, 189; Petzold, *Die Eröffnung*, 36; Scullard, *Roman Politics, 220–150 B.C.* (2nd ed., Oxford, 1973), 92–93; Ferro, *Le origini*, 96–97; Balsdon, *JRS* 44 (1954): 38; Dahlheim, *Struktur und Entwicklung*, 242; Briscoe, *Historia* 18 (1969): 65; Badian, *Flamininus*, 31–32. Doubts expressed only by A. M. Eckstein, *Phoenix* 30 (1976): 125, who considers coincidence "at least a possibility."

6. Livy, 31.5.9–31.6.1: *responderi placere cum consules provincias sortiti essent atque is consul cui Macedonia provincia evenisset ad populum tulisset, ut Philippo, regi Macedonum, indiceretur bellum. P. Sulpicio provincia Macedonia sorti evenit, isque rogationem promulgavit.*

7. Livy, 26.28.9; cf. 26.28.1–2—though Galba apparently retained a legion, as well as the fleet: Livy, 27.7.15; cf. 27.32.2.

8. Polyb. 9.42.

9. Livy, 27.30.1–2, 27.31.1–2, 27.32.1–8.

10. Livy, 28.5–8; Dio, fr. 57.57–58; Zon. 9.11. The Polybian fragments make no mention of Roman activities: Polyb. 10.41–42. On the sacking of Dyme, see Paus. 7.17.5; cf. Livy, 32.21.28, 32.22.10—probably in 208.

11. Livy, 29.12.1–2; cf. 31.31.19.

developed a reputation for ruthlessness: the plundering of Aegina, Oreum, and Dyme by Roman soldiers earned him widespread unpopularity in Greece.[12] Of military achievement, however, he had little to show. If Rome sought a general for 200 who had earned plaudits in war or who could win the confidence of Greeks, Sulpicius Galba would not seem the most likely choice.

Political prestige and connections counted for more in the Roman system. Galba was a patrician of distinguished family. He secured his first consulship in 211 despite having held no previous curule magistracy. Even in the dark days of the Hannibalic war that was a striking elevation, worthy of remark by Livy.[13] In 203 Galba held the dictatorship, employing his office not only to conduct elections but (it is reported) to issue peremptory orders to the consul of that year, who had designs of crossing over to Africa.[14] This was a man of authority in Roman politics. Election to a second consulship just when the ten-year gap had expired proves it. Galba wished to be consul and the time had arrived. Eastern "expertise" need not be the explanation.

One can go further. When Galba presented a war motion to the assembly at the beginning of the consular year 200, nearly all the voting centuries rejected his proposal.[15] Astonishingly enough, almost no one has seen fit to remark on the fact with regard to the matter at hand. Yet these are the self-same centuries which—just a short time before—had elected Sulpicius Galba to the consulship. The idea that his action signaled a Roman receptivity to intervention in Greece is difficult to square with the vote of the *comitia* a few weeks later. Additional difficulties arise. Galba got his year of campaigning abroad— but only one year.[16] Macedonia was allotted to the new consul, P. Villius Tappulus, already in March of 199, and, though Villius did not take over until late in the year so that Galba could have a full season, it is plain that the senate never considered an extended command for its eastern "expert."[17] Galba's year produced mixed results: some indeci-

12. Appian, *Mac.* 3.1, 7; cf. Paus. 7.17.5; Polyb. 9.42.5–8; 11.5.6–8; Livy, 28.7.4, 32.22.10.

13. Livy, 25.41.11.

14. Livy, 30.24.1–4, 30.26.12. Though the tale may involve some constitutional misunderstanding, there is no good reason to reject it altogether; *contra*; J. Jahn, *Interregnum und Wahldiktatur* (Kallmünz, 1970), 142–144.

15. Livy, 31.6.3: *rogatio de bello Macedonico primis comitiis ab omnibus ferme centuriis antiquata est*.

16. He was, of course, prorogued for 199, but had only arrived in Epirus late in the campaigning season of 200, in time to enter winter quarters and conduct no more than minor operations: Livy, 31.18.9, 31.22.4, 31.27.1–6. The real campaign took place in 199.

17. Livy, 32.1.2–3, 32.3.2, 32.6.1; cf. Plut. *Flam.* 3.1.

sive battles, much plundering and brutality, and a mutinous soldiery. Philip more than held his own. The Aetolians, to be sure, had come over to Rome's side and prospects might seem brighter for the coming season.[18] But Galba's term was up and home he came. There would be no prorogation for a second campaigning year. And who was P. Villius Tappulus? A man who, so far as is known, never set foot in Greece. Two years as praetor and propraetor in Sicily constituted his experience of command. He had charge of a fleet instructed to protect the coasts as the Hannibalic war drew to a close in 203 and 202, an appointment that involved him in no known fighting. Few would contend that the lot was manipulated in this instance.[19] The Roman armies of the East did not have to be entrusted to men with exposure to that theater of the world.

So even the prize *exemplum* of P. Sulpicius Galba turns out to be, at the very least, questionable. We can make a fresh start, without preconceptions. The appointment of Villius Tappulus, as will become clear, is more representative and illuminating than that of Sulpicius Galba.

Villius himself never got the opportunity to conduct a campaign against Philip. He succeeded Galba late in the year, had to quell a mutiny, and then retired into winter quarters. In the spring of 198 he was promptly superseded by T. Quinctius Flamininus.[20] Villius had certainly expected to engage the Macedonian king. He was in the midst of preparations when his successor arrived. The supersession came as a surprise.[21] Villius' appointment had not been intended as a mere holding operation.

The literature on Flamininus' election and acquisition of the Macedonian command is immense. We can happily refrain from adding to its bulk. Much of the speculation has its origin precisely in the assumption that generals in the East must have had special qualifications for the task: hence, Flamininus must have had knowledge of or sympathy with the Greeks; his selection must represent a policy of some sort; the allotment of provinces must have been rigged. Banish that assumption and the ground is clear. The fact is that Flamininus'

18. Discussion in Hammond, *JRS* 56 (1966): 42–45; cf. Eckstein, *Phoenix* 30 (1976): 126–127.

19. Villius' praetorship and promagistracy: Livy, 30.2.2, 30.27.8, 30.41.6. Villius' colleague in the consulate of 199, L. Cornelius Lentulus, had had long experience in Spain, including the last six years with *imperium pro consule*; see Broughton, *MRR* I, under the relevant years. Acutely pointed out by Eckstein, *Phoenix*, 30 (1976): 125.

20. Livy, 32.3.2–7, 32.6.1–4, 32.9.6, 32.28.5; Plut. *Flam.* 3.1–2; cf. Livy, 32.21.19–20.

21. Livy, 32.6.3–4; so, rightly, Eckstein, *Phoenix* 30 (1976): 127–128. An alternative tradition, recorded by Valerius Antias and rejected by Livy, gives Villius some successes: Livy, 32.6.5–8; Paus. 7.7.8–9—clearly overblown and probably worthless.

previous encounters with Greeks (so far as is known) had been limited to two years as a garrison commander at Tarentum, a city where Romans had pillaged and murdered indiscriminately.[22] Far from making a claim on the consulate by virtue of prior experience and demonstrated ability, Flamininus found his candidacy heavily criticized on just those grounds: he was jumping from quaestorship to consulship, avoiding intermediate offices, and thus had yet to show his wares.[23] The evidence fails to sustain hypotheses about his "philhellenism," "bold strategy," or "new image" as explaining Flamininus' elevation. We may follow where the sources lead. Flamininus reached high office through membership of a socially prominent family, with support by veterans and colonists whom he had benefited as a land commissioner and colonial administrator, and by powerful backing in the ranks of the senate.[24] His fellow consul, Sex. Aelius Paetus, had no more military background than he. As for the provincial assignment, the senate permitted the consuls to arrange it between themselves or to leave it to the luck of the draw. It was a matter of indifference. As it happened, the lot decided.[25] The Roman system did not demand credentials of specific competence.

22. Plut. *Flam.* 1.4; Livy, 29.13.6. For the looting of Tarentum in 209, four years before Flamininus' command, see Livy, 27.16.6–9; Plut. *Fab.* 22.4–6.

23. Livy, 32.7.8–10: *iam aedilitatem praeturamque fastidiri, nec per honorum gradus, documentum sui dantes, nobiles homines tendere ad consulatum, sed transcendendo media summa imis continuare;* Plut. *Flam.* 2.1.

24. Prominence of the family is demonstrated by Badian, *JRS* 61 (1971): 102–111. On the land commissions and the enthusiasm they inspired for his electoral ambitions, see Plut. *Flam.* 1.4–2.1; Livy, 31.4.1–3; cf. Plut. *Flam.* 3.3; Livy, 32.9.1. Support in the senate emerges clearly when the *patres* overrode objection to Flamininus' candidacy: Livy, 32.7.11–12; cf. Plut. *Flam.* 2.2; note also his φίλοι in the senate in 198/7: Polyb. 18.10.7; Plut. *Flam.* 7.2. Just which families or factions backed him evades conjecture—though this has not prevented a parade of scholarly conjectures. We know only of a connection with the Fabii Buteones: Polyb. 18.10.8; Livy, 32.36.10. This hardly warrants making Flamininus a "Fabian"; as F. Münzer, *Römische Adelsparteien und Adelsfamilien* (Stuttgart, 1920), 117–118. Relations with the Scipios remain obscure and unhelpful despite many modern attempts; e.g., Scullard, *Roman Politics*, 97–100; Cassola, *Labeo* 6 (1960): 105–130; Dorey, *Klio* 39 (1961): 191–198. Badian's effort to see P. Galba as a promoter of Flamininus rests on a string of unsupported hypotheses: *Flamininus*, 34–35. We gain little from notions about "Philhellenism" (Mommsen, *Römische Geschichte* I [Berlin, 1903], 707–708), "definite policy" and "bold strategy" (Briscoe, *Commentary*, 32), or "new image" (Badian, *Flamininus*, 37). No need to register the long bibliography here. Most of the relevant evidence can be found in H. Gundel, *RE* XXIV : 1047–1054, "Quinctius," n. 45. By far the best analysis, at last injecting a note of common sense and adhering to the sources, is Eckstein, *Phoenix* 30 (1976): 119–126, whose conclusions are adopted here.

25. Livy, 32.8.1: *decreverunt patres, ut provincias Macedoniam atque Italiam consules compararent inter se sortirenturve;* 32.8.4: *sortiti consules provincias; Aelio Italia, Quinctio Macedonia evenit.* Plut. *Flam.* 2.2 emphasizes the good fortune of the sortition. Cf. Eck-

Decisive confirmation of that inference comes when one looks to subsequent wars in the East. Unusually heated canvassing marked the electoral campaign for 192: a contest between Rome's most illustrious figures, T. Flamininus and P. Scipio Africanus, each in the lists by proxy, supporting a relative for the consulship. Flamininus argued a stronger claim: that he backed a brother not a cousin and that his brother had shared with him leadership in the previous war on Philip. With such arguments, says Livy, L. Flamininus gained election over P. Scipio Nasica.[26] A preference for the experienced soldier? Not so. Nasica had impressive martial deeds to his credit in Spain, victories more recent and more substantial than those of L. Flamininus, and conducted under his sole command.[27] War with Antiochus was being discussed but not yet certain, and no preparations had been made. The senate declared Italy as province for both consuls of 192; if need should be found for an overseas invasion, the *patres* once again left to the consuls decision as to who should go, whether by arrangement or by lot.[28] And, it should be observed, L. Flamininus' colleague was Cn. Domitius Ahenobarbus, a *novus homo* with no prior taste of command.[29] Only in late 192 did a war in Greece loom as ever more certain, and the Romans at last began to prepare for it. Nasica got his consulship this time, for 191—a matter of politics rather than prowess.[30] The lot operated with cool impartiality. Command in the East eluded Nasica and fell instead to another *novus homo*, M'. Acilius Glabrio, a man whose credentials could not compare with those of his colleague and whose generalship had been tested only by a slave rebellion in Etruria.[31]

The successes of Rome's marshals in the great contests against Antiochus and the Aetolians decorate the annals of the city's historians. It is easy to forget but essential to remember that none had held command in the East before. The appointment of Glabrio was characteristic rather than exceptional. L. Scipio, brother of Africanus, and C. Laelius, Africanus' bosom friend, secured the consulships for 190.

---

stein, *Phoenix* 30 (1976): 124–125. Sex. Aelius Paetus had gone no further than the aedileship: Livy, 31.50.1–2.

26. Livy, 35.10.1–9.

27. Livy, 35.1.3–12, 35.10.2: *ex Hispania provincia nuper decesserat magnis rebus gestis.*

28. Livy, 35.20.1–3.

29. He had been *praetor urbanus* in 194; Livy, 34.43.7; Pliny, *NH*, 14.90.

30. Livy, 35.24.5: *P. Scipioni, ut dilatum viro tali, non negatum honorem appararet, consulatus datus est.* The preparations for war: Livy, 35.24.1–35.25.1, 35.41.1–7.

31. *Novitas*: Livy, 37.57.10–12; slave rebellion: Livy, 33.36.1–3. Nasica, in fact, brought the war motion to the people in 191, but the provincial allotment, indisputably objective, gave Greece to Glabrio: Livy, 36.1.5–36.2.1.

Both had seen long service in the Second Punic War under Hannibal's conqueror, but neither one, in all probability, had fought in Greece.[32] Eastern experience was immaterial. Each of the consuls coveted the command against Antiochus and openly sought it. The senate, as was customary, had left them to decide or to submit to sortition. Scipio and Laelius, in turn, dropped the matter back into the lap of the *patres*, an extraordinary if not unprecedented procedure; no one could remember when last it had been done. Africanus came to the rescue and announced himself ready to serve on his brother's staff. That settled the issue: the senate appointed L. Scipio to Greece.[33] The episode is remarkable, in ways not often appreciated. Its exceptional character underscores the normal reluctance of the *patres* to interfere in provincial allotments. When given the chance for once, they ignored the experience of the consuls and considered only the identity of the legate.[34] Africanus' role proved decisive. The senate had an eye to the fact that Hannibal now resided at the court of Antiochus. Exposure to the East remained irrelevant. Africanus had had none.[35]

There would be a divided command for 189, one consul to take

32. For service in the Hannibalic war, see Broughton, *MRR* I, under the years 209–202. The story in Livy, 36.21.7–8, that L. Scipio had been sent to Rome by Glabrio in 191 to announce the victory at Thermopylae would imply some service under the consul in Greece. But he is mentioned nowhere in the narrative of the war, and the tale—of separate missions by L. Scipio and Cato, unbeknownst to one another, to bring the same news—is, at best, dubious. Why should Glabrio send two independent envoys? Cf. H. Nissen, *Kritische Untersuchungen über die Quellen der vierten und fünften Dekade des Livius* (Berlin, 1863), 183–184. Livy's story is by no means proved by *IdeDélos*, 442B, lines 89–90—which probably refers to L. Scipio's consulship. The double mission is accepted by Briscoe, *Commentary*, II, 252–253.

33. Livy, 37.1.7–10.

34. Livy, 36.45.9, 37.1.9–10. Less plausible is the version of Cicero, *Phil.* 11.17, that L. Scipio had obtained the province by lot but would have lost it to Laelius by senatorial decree had not Africanus intervened and offered his services as legate to his brother; cf. Cic. *Mur.* 32; Val. Max. 5.5.1; Appian, *Syr.* 100. The senate would not likely overturn the decision of the lot. This aspect is ignored by those who prefer Cicero's account; e.g. Briscoe, *Latomus* 31 (1972): 51. The idea that all this had been arranged clandestinely in advance—as, e.g., Münzer, *RE* XII:403–404, "Laelius," n. 2; Scullard, *Roman Politics*, 128–129—is pure speculation and unnecessary. Balsdon, *Historia* 21 (1972): 224–234, seeks to give L. Scipio greater stature, but cannot explain away this narrative.

35. Unless one credits the tale of Africanus' mission to Ephesus in 193, where he debated Hannibal on the identity of the world's greatest general: Livy, 35.14.5–12; Appian, *Syr.* 9–11; Plut. *Flam.* 21.3; *Pyrrh.* 8.2; Zon. 9.18. That is patent invention. Scipio gets no mention in the Polybian account of this embassy; Polyb. 3.11–12; Livy, 34.59.4–8, 35.14.1–4, 35.15.1–35.17.2; cf. Walbank, *Commentary* I:314–315; Schlag, *Regnum in Senatu*, 132–139. To reject the story but retain an eastern trip for Scipio is unsound; as, e.g., Holleaux, *Études* V:184–207; Scullard, *Scipio Africanus: Soldier and Politician* (London, 1970), 285–286, n. 163. See now Briscoe, *Commentary*, II, 165–166.

Aetolia, the other Asia. Rome now concentrated her energies on the eastern front. An intense electoral campaign ensued, as both victors could look to *gloria* abroad. The results conformed to pattern. The electorate returned M. Fulvius Nobilior and Cn. Manlius Vulso, men who lacked prior acquaintance with the East. The one candidate who could boast of some familiarity with Hellenic affairs, M. Aemilius Lepidus, once legate on the critical embassy of 200 and deliverer of the ultimatum to Philip V, was resoundingly defeated.[36]

By the time of the Third Macedonian War many more Romans had been to the East on campaign, in diplomatic missions, or as visitors. A large pool of knowledgeable men could be called upon to supply military leadership. Who in fact headed the armies from 171 to 168? P. Licinius Crassus conducted the opening campaign, a startling choice and an embarrassment to any theory that the voters examined specific qualifications. Not only had Crassus gained no eastern laurels. Five years earlier, as praetor, when assigned the province of Hispania Citerior, he had found the excuse of some sacrificial duties to beg off going at all![37] His behavior came in for heavy sarcasm in 171 as Crassus' consular colleague, C. Cassius Longinus, eager for the Macedonian command, argued that Crassus had disqualified himself and that he (Cassius) should obtain Macedonia by senatorial decree without recourse to the lot. A plausible enough (if self-interested) proposal. The *patres*' response is significant—and entirely in accord with past procedure: since the *populus* did not deny Crassus a consulship, they would not deny him a province; let the lot fall where it may.[38] And fall it did, upon the pusillanimous Crassus, while C. Cassius departed to take out his anger on innocent tribes in the north.[39] Neither senate nor people was moved by consideration of proven ability. The appointment for the following year reinforces that conclusion. A. Hostilius Mancinus succeeded Crassus in 170, a new man whose praetorship had come a decade before and had been spent in Rome. Hostilius proved to be a poor choice, as it turned out; he made no more headway against Perseus than his predecessor had, and came within a hair of being kidnapped by Epirotes. Passed over for the command was Hostilius' consular colleague, A. Atilius Serranus, who carried a long record of involvement in eastern affairs: commander

36. Livy, 37.47.6–7. Manlius had previously served in Sicily, Fulvius in Spain: Livy, 33.43.5, 34.55.6, 35.7.8, 35.22.6–8; Orosius, 4.20.16, 4.20.19. On Lepidus' embassy in 200, see Polyb. 16.34; Livy, 31.2.1–4, 31.18.1–5.

37. Livy, 41.15.9–10.

38. Livy, 42.32.1–4: *consulti patres, cui consulatum populus Romanus non negasset, ei ab se provinciam negari superbum rati, sortiri consules iusserunt.*

39. Livy, 42.32.4, 43.1.4–12, 43.5.1–9.

of the fleet in Greece as praetor and propraetor in 192 and 191, a dedicant at Delos, among the envoys designed to stir up support for Rome's cause in central Greece and the Peloponnese in 172, and engaged in some of the preliminary operations of the Third Macedonian War in 171. Here, if ever, there was a clear choice between an experienced and an inexperienced commander at a critical time in the war. The inexperienced man got the job.[40]

The individual and cumulative force of this testimony makes a compelling case. As a consequence, it is singularly pointless to ransack the sources for evidence of a man's earlier service on delegations to explain his appointment to command of the eastern forces. Q. Marcius Philippus headed the army against Perseus in 169 and L. Aemilius Paullus succeeded him in 168. For the former one can find a prior embassy to Greece and Macedonia in 183 and a famous mission to solicit Hellenic backing and keep Perseus off guard in 172/1; for the latter, an assignment (twenty years before!) among the *decem legati* who arranged the settlement of the Antiochene war.[41] Only blind adherence to a preconceived theory will reckon those tours of duty as determining the appointments of 169 and 168. The lot ruled. Arrangement or manipulation would offend the gods. The senate, in fact, took pains in 169 to avoid even the appearance of partiality in the allotment.[42] And the same in 168: Paullus received Macedonia through sortition, leaving Italy to his colleague C. Crassus, a man who (unlike Paullus) had actually served against Perseus, in command of the right wing of his brother's forces in 171.[43] Rome retained confidence in the traditional system. The outcome would justify it.

The same attitude prevailed a generation later, when Rome crushed the final insurrections of Greeks and Macedonians. No prior eastern experience dictated the dispatch of P. Iuventius Thalna and then Q. Metellus Macedonicus to deal with the rebellion of Andriscus

40. Hostilius' operations in 170: Broughton, *MRR* I:420; Serranus' background and experience: Broughton, *MRR* I:350, 353, 412, 413, 418.

41. Broughton, *MRR* I:363, 379, 413.

42. Livy, 43.12.2: *priusquam id sors cerneret, in incertum, ne quid gratia momenti faceret, in utramque provinciam quod res desideraret supplementi decerni.*

43. Crassus' service in 171: Livy, 42.58.12. The sortition in 168: Livy, 44.17.7–10; Val. Max. 1.5.3. Plutarch's story, *Aem. Paull.* 10.1–3, that the people sought out Paullus, elected him, and appointed him to Macedonia, without sortition, is plainly false, *ad maiorem gloriam Paulli*; similarly, Justin, 33.1.6. As Plutarch himself indicates elsewhere, Paullus desired a second consulship: Plut. *Aem. Paull.* 6.4. Nor does the *elogium* of Paullus prove that he was specially appointed for the war, *CIL,* I, 194: *iterum cos. ut cum rege [Per]se bellum gereret ap[. . . . f]actus est. Contra*: Meloni, *Perseo*, 319, n. 4; E. Meissner, *Lucius Aemilius Paullus Macedonicus und seine Bedeutung für das römische Reich (229–160 v. Chr.)* (Bischberg/Oberfranken, 1974), 67–71. The question is left open by Scullard, *Roman Politics*, 207, n. 2.

in 149 and 148, nor of L. Mummius to quell the Achaean war in 146. A succession of consuls went to Asia between 131 and 129 to dispose of Aristonicus and to pacify western Anatolia, P. Crassus Mucianus, M. Perperna, and M'. Aquillius, none of whom, so far as is known, had served in that theater before.[44] Our evidence for the period is, of course, defective. But the principles and practices of the past half-century preclude superfluous hypotheses. Romans did not select their generals by applying geographic tests.[45]

If one looks at a slightly lower level of officer, praetors and legates with relatively independent spheres of command, a different picture might be expected. Perhaps here knowledgable men could provide the expertise lacking in consuls who owed election to politics and prestige? Ancient testimony soon disabuses that expectation. The commanders of the fleet during the Second Macedonian War, L. Apustius, Livius, and L. Flamininus, were all new to eastern warfare, the last no doubt sent to assure close cooperation with his brother.[46] A similar pattern holds for the Syrian and Aetolian wars. Significant responsibilities fell to men without training in the East: A. Atilius Serranus had charge of naval operations in 192 and 191; M. Baebius Tamphilus commanded Roman forces in northern Greece and Macedonia in 191, concerting his campaigns with Philip V until the arrival of the consul; the praetor L. Aemilius Regillus headed the navy in 190, victor in the decisive sea battle of the war at Myonessus; A. Cornelius Mammula brought a fresh army to Greece in 190, with instructions to take full command when the proconsul returned to Rome; and Q. Fabius Labeo took over the fleet in 189, earning a naval triumph, depositing dedications at Delos to commemorate his stay, and even fixing the boundary between the kingdom of Macedonia and Thrace.[47] None of them owed his success to any previous sojourns in Greece.

44. Of all these men only Q. Metellus Macedonicus had any attested time in Greece to his credit, a subordinate commission as a very young man in Paullus' army of 168: Livy, 44.45.3, 45.1.1–5. Not even the boldest hypothesis will find in this a reason for his appointment against Andriscus twenty years later!

45. It is quite irrelevant, for example, that the consuls of 156 and 155, C. Marcius Figulus and P. Scipio Nasica, who led Roman forces in Dalmatia, had both served in the Third Macedonian War thirteen years before: Broughton, *MRR* I:424, 429, 434, 447, 448. If Polybius is to be believed, Rome decided upon a Dalmatian invasion in part because her armies had not set foot in that area for almost three-quarters of a century: Polyb. 32.13.5–6.

46. Cf. Plut. *Flam.* 3.3—according to whom T. Flamininus specifically asked the senate to appoint his brother to the fleet.

47. Evidence in Broughton, *MRR* I, under the relevant years. Only two possible exceptions to this rule and both are, at least, questionable. C. Livius Salinator had command of the fleet against Antiochus as praetor in 191 and propraetor in 190: Broughton,

Twenty years later, circumstances altered the pattern somewhat. So many Roman missions to the East had occurred in the meantime that it would have been difficult to limit selection of officers for the Third Macedonian War to men altogether innocent of Hellas. So, A. Atilius Serranus, the praetorian commander of the fleet in 192 and 191, obtained a second praetorship in 173 and saw service in the East during the war's preliminary operations; Ap. Claudius Centho, an envoy to Perseus in 172, became a legate exercising an independent command in Illyria and Epirus from 170 to 168; and Cn. Octavius, who had rallied Greek support for the Roman cause as envoy in 169, went on to command the fleet as praetor in 168, a man whose knowledge of Greek made him useful in the peace negotiations of 167.[48] Yet we can hardly conclude that they received their appointments *because* of their previous appearances in Greece. The inference is refuted decisively by the number of men with praetorian and independent commands in the war who had *not* seen service across the Adriatic before: Cn. Sicinius, C. Lucretius Gallus, L. Hortensius, L. Coelius, C. Marcius Figulus, and L. Anicius Gallus.[49] The evidence is overwhelming and inescapable. Rome never held eastern experience as a requirement for her commanders in the Hellenic wars.

To be sure, prorogation might get round the problem—if problem it were. Generals who lacked previous familiarity with Greece could be kept at the task, thereby gaining the needed expertise in the course of duty. The senate certainly did have resort to long-term commands. M. Valerius Laevinus, first of the Roman generals against Philip, stayed at his post for five years between 215 and 211, his successor Galba for another six between 211 and 206. Flamininus, of course, is the supreme example: prorogued four times for two wars,

---

MRR I:353, 357. It is just possible that he had had a similar task in 199 and 198; Münzer, RE XIII:888, "Livius," n. 29, assumes it without argument. But the evidence reports only a "Livius," succeeded as admiral in 198 by L. Flamininus: Livy, 32.16.2–4. Nothing is heard of his activities; Livy elsewhere has Apustius in charge of the fleet (31.44.1, 31.47.2, 32.16.5); and "Livius" need not, in any case, be identical with the praetor of 191. The other exception is more dubious still. L. Flamininus' service as legate to his brother from 198 to 194 is amply attested. Yet only a single notice asserts that the senate appointed him as legate to Glabrio in 191: Livy, 36.1.8. And he appears nowhere in the campaign narratives for that year. Gundel, RE XXIV:1045, "Quinctius," n. 43, ignores the problem. Confusion by Livy is a distinct possibility: T. Flamininus did serve abroad and cooperate with Glabrio in that year. Broughton, MRR I:354; see especially Plut. Flam. 15.2.

48. On Atilius Serranus, see Livy, 42.27.4, 42.37–38, 42.47.10–11—but, significantly, as consul in 170 he was allotted Gaul as his province, not Greece; see above pp. 211–212. As for Ap. Claudius Centho, his legation to Perseus is reported only in a questionable annalistic account: Livy, 42.25.1–13. On Cn. Octavius, Broughton, MRR I:426, 428, 434.

49. Broughton, MRR I:411, 416, 417, 420, 422, 424, 428.

the second war on Philip and the conflict with Nabis, in the mid-190s. The consuls of 189, Fulvius and Manlius, in charge of the Greek and Asian spheres respectively, continued as promagistrates for more than a year to finish off the Roman victories and settlements. Was prorogation then a device to provide commanders with on-the-job training?

That conclusion would be hasty. Other factors come into play. The successive renewals for Valerius Laevinus and Sulpicius Galba carry no special significance. They form part of a general pattern during the Hannibalic war. The inordinate length of that conflict and the concomitant loss of life in Rome's upper echelons obliged the government to keep men in command for long periods, especially in areas where the Republic could avoid direct confrontation with Hannibal. Repeated prorogations occurred in Spain, in Sicily, in Sardinia, and in the supervision of the fleets.[50] The problem of manpower in the leadership, not the development of expertise, dictated those decisions.

Flamininus, of course, is another matter. But Flamininus, one needs to be reminded, is an exception, hardly a representative example. And even he had no assurance of prorogation. Far from it. Flamininus had serious anxieties in 198 lest he be superseded, with victory as yet unaccomplished. He bent all his energies to prevent the dispatch of a successor, communicating with his friends in the senate to that purpose, and sending home some of his more illustrious legates and even Amynander, the king of Athamania, to espouse his cause before the *patres*.[51] In the event, Flamininus got his continuance. If Polybius is to be believed, however, the senate's decision to keep both consuls of 197 in Italy came out of concern for the Gallic uprising—not out of positive desire to prorogue Flamininus![52]

50. So, e.g., the Scipio brothers held charge in Spain from 217 to their deaths in 211, Africanus and M. Junius Silanus followed them for another five years until 206, and then L. Cornelius Lentulus and L. Manlius Acidinus through the end of the war and beyond in 200; T. Otacilius Crassus commanded the fleet off Sicily for seven successive years between 217 and 211; M. Claudius Marcellus headed military operations in Sicily from 214 until the fall of Syracuse in 211; Q. Mucius Scaevola was four years in Sardinia between 215 and 212, and Cn. Octavius protected that island with the fleet from 205 to 201; C. Terentius Varro, despite his defeat at Cannae, went on to serve in Picenum for three years between 215 and 213; P. Sempronius Tuditanus spent three years in Cisalpine Gaul, 213 to 211, Q. Fulvius Flaccus five years in Campania, 212–208, and C. Hostilius Tubulus four years in Campania, 207–204.

51. Polyb. 18.10.3–8; Livy, 32.32.6–8; Plut. *Flam.* 7.1. Balsdon's cavalier dismissal of these and other passages regarding Flamininus' anxiety about prorogation, *Phoenix* 21 (1967): 179, is rash and unfounded.

52. Polyb. 18.11.1–2: πεπεισμένων δὲ τῶν τοῦ Τίτου φίλων μένειν τοὺς ὑπάτους ἀμφοτέρους κατὰ τὴν Ἰταλίαν διὰ τὸν ἀπὸ τῶν Κελτῶν φόβον, εἰσελθόντες εἰς τὴν σύγκλητον πάντες κατηγόρουν ἀποτόμως τοῦ Φιλίππου; cf. 18.12.1; Livy, 32.28.3–9, 32.37.1–6; Plut. *Flam.* 7.2.

That fact, generally passed over in the countless modern discussions of the episode, bears emphasis. Pragmatic considerations guided the senate, a direct and present danger, rather than any policy on Macedonia.[53]

Cynoscephalae followed in 197 and then the capitulation of Philip. The issue of a peace settlement would now exercise the Roman senate. Flamininus, despite the laurels of victory, still felt insecure about his position. Prorogation was anything but automatic in the Roman system.[54] The proconsul speeded on negotiations as the year drew to a close, nervous lest Philip catch hope from the movements of Antiochus and prolong the war, thus calling forth another commander in Greece to rob the present one of his glory.[55] Flamininus had good reason for concern. The new consul for 196, M. Claudius Marcellus, endeavored to torpedo peace negotiations and urged that Macedonia be allotted as a province in order to carry on the war. Only a vote of the people, eager for peace, prevented a renewal of hostilities. Flamininus, having earned his *gloria*, remained in Greece to help conclude a settlement. But it was a near miss.[56]

The conqueror of Philip and author of the Isthmian declaration was prorogued once again for 195. It would be perverse to deny that this was done because the *patres* had confidence in his judgment and in his knowledge of the Greek situation. Rumors circulated about a potential menace from Antiochus, about restlessness among the Aetolians, and, more immediately, about the ambitions of Nabis of Sparta. In the wake of those reports Flamininus received an extension of his promagistracy.[57] When the issue of actual war with Nabis arose, the senate went so far as to curtail debate and decree that the decision

53. This is not, of course, to deny that Flamininus' friends and supporters lobbied on his behalf. The debate on prolonging his command recorded in Livy, 32.28.3–9, has no counterpart in Polybius. Even if it be accepted, however, the argument for prorogation rested on the ineffectiveness of two previous annual commands and the need to capitalize on preparations already made for the coming summer's campaign: Livy, 32.28.4–7. The issue of an "experienced" commander does not arise. For bibliography on these events, see Briscoe, *Commentary*, 22–26.

54. Note that even when proroguing him for 197 the senate indicated that he might yet get a successor: Livy, 32.28.9: *prorogarunt imperium donec successor ex senatus consulta venisset.*

55. Polyb. 18.39.4: διόπερ ἠγωνία μὴ ταύτης ὁ Φίλιππος τῆς ἐλπίδος ἀντιλαμβανόμενος ἐπὶ τὸ πολιοφυλακεῖν ὁρμήσῃ καὶ τρίβειν τὸν πόλεμον, εἶθ᾽ ἑτέρου παραγενηθέντος ὑπάτου τὸ κεφάλαιον τῶν πράξεων εἰς ἐκεῖνον ἀνακλασθῇ.

56. Polyb. 18.42.3–4; Livy, 33.24.7, 33.25.5–8, 33.25.11. Note Livy, 33.25.6: *et forsitan obtinuisset consul, ni . . . tribuni plebis se intercessuros dixissent, ni prius ipsi ad plebem tulissent.* Schlag, *Regnum in Senatu*, 89–91, argues, unconvincingly and without direct evidence, that Flamininus was prorogued partly in anticipation of a possible war with Antiochus. This is plainly refuted by Livy, 33.20.8–9.

57. Livy, 33.43.6, 33.44.6–9.

be left to Flamininus himself.[58] A resounding vote of confidence, so it would appear. Yet we should pay heed to the reason for this senatorial action. The *patres* consigned responsibility to Flamininus because the conflict with Nabis was of no great importance to the state! Their attention focused on Hannibal and Antiochus, and if hostilities should break out from that direction (so it is implied and so it happened), Rome would turn to other generals.[59] Flamininus never lost sight of the fact that long service and a series of successes guaranteed nothing in the competitive world of Roman politics. As the siege of Sparta loomed before him in 195, the old nagging worries returned: a drawn-out struggle could bring another consul to Greece and eventual triumph might fall to the successor.[60] The proconsul pressed for peace and soon terminated the contest, even risking the ire of his allies, so as to assure that credit would be his.[61] He could then safely return to Rome in uncontested triumph. So, even in the case of Flamininus, the eastern "expert" *par excellence*, prorogation could never be counted on. The general persistently looked over his shoulder at prospective successors, plagued by anxiety that his accomplishments would be incomplete and eclipsed. Senatorial politics, pragmatism, convenience, and, to some extent, indifference allowed him to finish the task uninterrupted. Rome had not committed herself to a system of experts.

Politics played a part also in the extension of commands for M. Fulvius Nobilior and Cn. Manlius Vulso. The battle of Magnesia in 190 had already sealed the fate of Antiochus; and the capitulation of Aetolia was only a matter of time. A prorogation for L. Scipio, however, did not even receive consideration. Aetolia and Asia were allotted to Fulvius and Manlius, the new consuls for 189.[62] The news of Magnesia reached Rome shortly thereafter. By announcing the cessation of hostilities, L. Scipio could expect to head off the appointment

58. Livy, 33.45.3; cf. Justin, 31.1.6–7. This is clearly to be preferred to Livy's later implication that war had been declared by the senate: Livy, 34.22.5; cf. Briscoe, *Commentary*, 334, with bibliography.

59. Livy, 33.45.4–5: *eam rem esse rati, quae maturata dilatave non ita magni momenti ad summam rem publicam esset; magis id animadvertendum esse, quid Hannibal et Carthaginienses, si cum Antiocho bellum motum foret, acturi essent.*

60. Livy, 34.33.14: *illa tacita suberat cura, ne novus consul Graeciam provinciam sortiretur et incohata belli victoria successori tradenda esset*; cf. also Plut. *Flam.* 13.1.

61. Livy, 34.34–41; Plut. *Flam.* 13.1. Schlag, *Regnum in Senatu*, 95–98, conjectures that Flamininus actually pressed for another prorogation and was turned down, for which no evidence exists in the sources. Discussion on provincial assignments for 194, in fact, did not take place until after peace with Nabis was ratified: Livy, 34.43. Schlag's general view, that Flamininus remained in authority through these years by misleading the senate with deceitful messages, is overdrawn and unsatisfactory.

62. Livy, 37.50.1–8.

of a successor and thus be permitted, like Flamininus, to cap his victory by presiding over the settlement. The *patres*, however, pressed ahead with the original plan: Manlius would go to Asia Minor (there were Galatians to fight); and the *decem legati* would be sent to effect a settlement in conjunction with the new commander.[63] It is hard not to see in this a political defeat for the Scipios, who failed to get the same privilege that had been accorded to Flamininus. One may observe further that the bitterly fought censorial elections of that same year returned Flamininus as patrician victor, defeating in the process P. Scipio Nasica, the cousin of Africanus.[64]

Manlius determined to make his year a memorable one, provoking war with the Galatians, and conducting a ruthless campaign punctuated with greed and treachery until the foe submitted. Fulvius, in the meanwhile, was engaged in stamping out the last resistance in Greece and negotiating the terms for Aetolian surrender.[65] At the end of 189 there was little left to do. Yet Manlius and Fulvius got the prorogation for 188 that had been denied L. Scipio the year before— when a better case might have been made out for it. There can be little doubt that politics rather than policy lurked behind the decision.[66] The consuls for 188, it appears, had expected an allotment of eastern provinces, and were disappointed.[67] The promagistrates stayed abroad another year, and took their time in coming home. M. Aemilius Lepidus, an old *inimicus* of Fulvius, objected vehemently that the consuls of 187 (himself being one) were fobbed off with Liguria once again, while Fulvius and Manlius still nominally held charge of all the East: let the senate allocate Greece and Asia to the consuls if there was still work to be done there. Annual commands, Lepidus argued with some justice (and self-interest), had been the rule and should continue to be so. The *patres* recognized the force of that claim. They made no change in the provincial distribution but ordered the promagistrates home forthwith.[68] The political character of this whole

---

63. Livy, 37.51.8–10, 37.55.4–7.

64. Livy, 37.57.9–37.58.2; cf. 35.10.2–10.

65. Broughton, *MRR* I:360.

66. Livy, 38.35.1–3. Fulvius, it is true, may have been engaged in the siege of Same when he returned to conduct elections and was prorogued to complete it—if the chronological reconstruction of Holleaux, *Études* V:249–281, is correct. But no such explanation holds for the reappointment of Manlius. Observe also that L. Scipio, though he obtained his triumph, was subject to carping from political foes that the real victory over Antiochus had come at Thermopylae: Scipio had merely reaped the benefits; Livy, 37.58.7.

67. Such is the implication of Livy, 38.35.7–8: *M. Valerius Messala inde et C. Livius Salinator consulatum idibus Martiis cum inissent, de re publica deque provinciis et exercitibus senatum consuluerunt; de Aetolia et Asia nihil mutatum est.*

68. Livy, 38.42.8–13; cf. 38.46.14.

train of events stands out with clarity: a fierce competition among senatorial leaders and factions to grasp the glory of overseas triumph and the credit of an enduring settlement.[69] The fact is demonstrated beyond question by the heavy criticism leveled at Fulvius and Manlius after their return and the notorious trials of the Scipios that followed in retaliation.[70] Nowhere in the evidence is there a hint that a prolonging of command was justified to train generals in the ways of the East.

So, even the exceptions are explicable. And exceptions they were. The normal practice, unchallenged and regular, terminated commanders after but one campaigning season: Galba in 200, Villius in 199 (who did not even get a full season), Glabrio in 191, and L. Scipio in 190. The same in the Third Macedonian War: Crassus in 171, Hostilius in 170, and Philippus in 169.[71] Praetorian officers and legates more often got extensions: a matter of convenience, long traditional in Roman practice and by no means confined to the East. Their victories did not carry the same political clout. M. Lepidus expressed the standard principle properly in 187: Roman consuls should have one year abroad to exercise their skills and earn their honors.[72] Command was the natural prerogative of the ruling class, so the Roman assumption went. *Nobiles* had no need for on-the-job training.

The Uses of Military Experience

One may approach the issue from a slightly different angle and with a slightly different question: To what use was the experience of eastern command put afterwards? How often did the senate reach into its stock of former generals and legates in Hellas for later appointments to the East? In theory, such reappointments would seem logical and desirable, even perhaps imperative. So, all the more striking is

69. Cf. L. Scipio's insistence on the *cognomen* Asiaticus after his return from abroad: Livy, 37.58.6.

70. The attacks on Fulvius and Manlius: Livy, 38.43–50, 39.4–5. The considerable and confused evidence on the trials of the Scipios need not here be registered.

71. L. Aemilius Paullus was prorogued for 167 after his consulship of 168, but the fighting was over and only the organization of peace remained: Livy, 45.16.2. Yet even Paullus' prestige did not prevent a serious challenge to his triumph later in the year: Livy, 45.35–39; Plut. *Aem. Paull.* 30–32.

72. Livy, 38.42.11–12: *si eas provincias exercitibus obtinere opus esset, sicut M'. Acilio L. Scipio consul, L. Scipioni M. Fulvius et Cn. Manlius successissent consules, ita Fulvio Manlioque C. Livium et M. Valerium consules debuisse succedere . . . aut consules ad exercitus consulares mitti aut reportari legiones inde reddique tandem rei publicae debere.* Cf. the conversation between Flamininus and Glabrio in 191, in which it is taken for granted that Glabrio would have only a year of command: Livy, 36.34.8–36.35.1.

their comparative rarity. Romans did not feel bound by the same logic that occurs to us.

Flamininus, of course, can be held up as argument for the cause. Victor over Philip in the Second Macedonian War, he took charge of Roman forces again in the war on Nabis in 195. Yet Flamininus' position contains its own ambiguities. He owed the command against Nabis not to senatorial conviction but to a bland unconcern toward that Peloponnesian quarrel. He received a new commission in 192 and 191, shuttled about to various Greek assemblies, reminded them of Roman *beneficia*, and steeled their resolve for resistance against Antiochus. He threw his weight around effectively with the Hellenes, but he commanded no troops and engaged in no battles, confining himself to some unsolicited advice for the consul Glabrio.[73] During the great campaigns of 190 and 189, Flamininus was back in Rome. He never again led an army. The jealousy of the *nobilitas* insisted on the parceling out of military *gloria*.

In the diplomatic sphere, however, Flamininus possessed exceptional ability and held unparalleled esteem. In 193 the senate entrusted to him the conduct of private negotiations with Antiochus' ministers in Rome and then allowed him to announce Rome's public posture to a gathering of envoys from all over Greece and Asia.[74] He had nearly a free hand in his roving mission of 192 and 191, exploiting his prestige among Greek leaders, bullying some Hellenic gatherings, and manipulating opinion at others.[75] He issued peremptory instructions to Greek commanders and communities.[76] And, though he had no express military authority, he took it upon himself to provide counsel to Glabrio, counsel which the general found it prudent to heed.[77] Flamininus' meddlesomeness, official and unofficial, continued in the 180s. He ingratiated himself with Demetrius, younger son of Philip V, and promoted his reputation among the Macedonians.[78] He advocated the interest of his partisans Zeuxippus in Boeotia and Deinocrates in Messenia.[79] The senate turned again to Flamininus and others to adjudicate the tangled Achaean-Spartan

73. Broughton, *MRR* I: 351, 354.

74. Livy, 34.57–59; Diod. 28.15; cf. Appian, *Syr.* 6. Not that Flamininus was accorded sole responsibility. The *decem legati* were included in the parley: Livy, 34.57.5, 34.59.1; Diod. 28.15.1.

75. Cf., e.g., Livy, 35.25.5, 35.31.13, 35.32.6–14, 35.33.2–6, 35.49, 36.31.6–10, 36.32.4–9; Plut. *Flam.* 17.2; Phil. 16.2.

76. Livy, 35.39.1–4, 35.39.8, 35.50.3, 35.50.10, 36.31.8–10.

77. Livy, 36.34.6–36.35.2; Plut. *Flam.* 15.4–16.2.

78. Polyb. 23.3.7–8; Livy, 40.11.1–3, 40.12.17, 40.20.3, 40.23.7–9, 40.24.1, 40.54.9; cf. Gruen, *GRBS* 15 (1974): 234–245.

79. Zeuxippus: Polyb. 22.4.4; cf. 18.43; Livy, 33.27–29; Deinocrates: Polyb. 23.5.

dispute in 184/3.[80] Finally, in 183 he got his last commission, an embassy to the court of Prusias, the fateful embassy that ended with the suicide of Hannibal. How far Flamininus bore responsibility for that deed and how far he exceeded senatorial instructions in the matter was debated in antiquity and remains uncertain now.[81] The pertinent fact is that many found it entirely consistent with Flamininus' character and behavior that he had intrigued privately to achieve his ends abroad. And so it was.

Flamininus had had a remarkable career. He capitalized upon his prestige and connections to advance personal aims while ostensibly acting in the service of state. The schemes, to be sure, sometimes backfired. Machinations on behalf of Zeuxippus and Deinocrates came to naught, the Demetrian escapade resulted in the young man's death, and the suicide of Hannibal brought odium and discredit to Flamininus' last years. Yet the *patres* had rarely interfered, partly because his associations abroad were useful to the Republic and partly out of indifference. Better than anyone, Flamininus knew how to exploit his authority in the East while maintaining repute among his peers in Rome. He got away with arrogance abroad through influence at home and gained standing at home through success abroad.[82] It was precisely his skill at blending private interest and public service that outmatched all contemporaries, as Polybius shrewdly observed.[83]

The extraordinary character of Flamininus' ability and achievements itself forbids citation of his career as representative of a Roman policy. That career itself, in fact, may have engendered a reaction. The nobility was sensitive to the political implications of so much prestige commanded by a single individual. How many other commanders in the East enjoyed a comparable run of reappointments? Or any reappointments of significance and relevance?

A few examples can be cited. Rome certainly did not *exclude* former generals from later missions to Greece. The question is whether the prior service dictated or influenced the appointment. No clear claims along these lines can be made for the commanders of the First

80. Polyb. 23.4.7–16; cf. Paus. 7.9.5; Livy, 39.48.2–4.

81. On the ancient controversy, see, especially, Plut. *Flam.* 20–21. Livy, 39.51.1–3, suggests that the *patres* desired Hannibal's removal; cf. 39.56.7; Zon. 9.21. Others attributed the idea to Flamininus: Appian, *Syr.* 11; Plut. *Flam.* 20.3. Additional sources in Broughton, *MRR* I: 380.

82. There were limits, however, to what Flamininus could achieve on his own. He could not always count on senatorial backing for his endeavors abroad; see below pp. 463–472.

83. Polyb. 18.12.3–4: πάνυ γὰρ ἀγχίνους, εἰ καί τις ἕτερος 'Ρωμαίων, ὁ προειρημένος ἀνὴρ γέγονεν· οὕτως γὰρ εὐστόχως ἐχείριζε καὶ νουνεχῶς οὐ μόνον τὰς κοινὰς ἐπιβολάς, ἀλλὰ καὶ τὰς κατ' ἰδίαν ἐντεύξεις, ὥσθ' ὑπερβολὴν μὴ καταλιπεῖν.

Macedonian War. M. Valerius Laevinus had headed the Roman effort across the Adriatic from 214 to 211. Six years later, a promising oracle induced the senate to send envoys to Attalus of Pergamum and bring back the sacred stone of Pessinus, emblematic of the Great Mother of the gods. Laevinus was among those on the mission.[84] As a senior consular he had worthy credentials. But "eastern experience" is irrelevant. None of Laevinus' fellow envoys had any. Attalus' cooperation with Rome in the First Macedonian War, which gave confidence in his compliance here, had begun in 209, well after Laevinus' command had terminated.[85] Of the Romans who may have come to know him during that contest, none participated in the embassy. So, the appointments obviously proceeded on other grounds.[86] The same holds for P. Sempronius Tuditanus, proconsul in Macedonia in 205 and then one of three envoys to the East in 200 on the eve of war with Philip.[87] The other two had seen no eastern service, and one of them, M. Lepidus who actually delivered the ultimatum to Philip, was but a youth without public experience of any kind.[88] As for the consulship and command of P. Sulpicius Galba, that has already received full discussion. Reasons other than his previous commission can and probably should explain the appointment.[89]

During the 190s different circumstances prevailed. Rome had become engaged in Hellenic affairs more swiftly and more deeply than anticipated. The counsel of those on the scene and those who had been on the scene became the more valuable—not because the senate had developed a policy of reliance on "experts" but because a "policy" toward the East had yet to be developed. The broad scope of Flamininus' activities in those years illustrates the absence, rather than the presence, of clear directives. His predecessors in the Mac-

84. Livy, 29.10.4–29.11.8.

85. Livy, 27.29.10. Overlooked, e.g., by Clemente, *Athenaeum* 54 (1976): 325–326.

86. Laevinus may have been appointed in late 201 to take a fleet across the Adriatic and observe the activities of Philip V—if one believes Livy, 31.3.2–6, 31.5.5–9; cf. Paus. 7.7.7. But this is imbedded in a dubious annalistic account, grossly inflating the transgressions of Philip. Its authenticity is too fragile to support any hypotheses; see, e.g., Holleaux, *CAH* VIII:156, n. 1; Petzold, *Die Eröffnung*, 77–80; Walbank, *Philip V*, 127, n. 7; *contra*: Briscoe, *Commentary*, 60. Nothing more is heard of this venture. Sulpicius Galba in 200 made no use of that fleet, getting his ships from elsewhere: Livy, 31.14.2. Laevinus, in fact, died in 200: Livy, 31.50.4.

87. Named only by Livy, 31.2.3. Tuditanus had but limited fighting in 205 anyway; the peace of Phoenice followed closely upon his arrival: Livy, 29.12.

88. Polyb. 16.34.6: νέος ἐστὶ καὶ πραγμάτων ἄπειρος; Livy, 31.18.1–3. The most recent discussion of Lepidus' embassy, J. W. Rich, *Declaring War in the Roman Republic in the Period of Transmarine Expansion* (Brussels, 1976), 128–137, argues that he was about thirty and already a senator by 200 B.C. But Rich fails to come to grips with the Polybian passage.

89. See above pp. 204–207.

edonian command, Sulpicius Galba and Villius Tappulus, found themselves similarly busy during the decade. Both received appointment to Flamininus' staff as legates in 197.[90] Both returned again among the *decem legati* in 196 and 195 to help arrange the peace settlement. In the course of that mission, Villius at least and Galba probably entered into negotiations with Antiochus at Lysimacheia.[91] When the king's envoys came to Rome for a parley in 193, the *decem legati* were once more called upon to deal with them, together with Flamininus; and Galba, the senior member, made his presence felt with some sharp questioning.[92] A new embassy went abroad in the wake of that encounter, an embassy that included both Galba and Villius, who visited Eumenes, conversed with Hannibal, and held further meetings with Antiochus.[93] Still one more mission came in 192: Villius, among others, joined Flamininus to win Hellenic hearts to Rome's cause for the coming conflict.[94]

Surely here, if anywhere, experience and "expertise" determined the repeated appointments?[95] Perhaps. Yet that may not tell the whole story. Galba had had only a single campaigning season in 199, Villius did not get even that. His command was aborted by Flamininus before it could properly begin. How much "expertise" could here be brought into play? And how did fighting in Illyria and western Macedonia fit one for delicate diplomacy with Antiochus the Great?[96] The circumstances of Galba's and Villius' appointments need to be recalled. Flamininus, after some anxious weeks, at last obtained prorogation, a privilege withheld from his predecessors. The matter had been hotly debated, with, if Livy be believed, some critical remarks about the previous commanders. Assignment of Galba and Villius as legates could soften jealousies and permit a smoother execution of the war. Political considerations must be given their due.[97]

90. Livy, 32.28.12.

91. The appointment of the *decem legati*: Livy, 33.24.7. Galba is not mentioned among the envoys to Antiochus in Polyb. 18.48.3, 18.50.3; Livy, 33.35.3, 33.39.2, 34.33.12; Plut. *Flam.* 12.1. But a later notice affirms his presence: Livy, 34.59.8.

92. Livy, 34.57.4–5, 34.59.1–2; Diod. 28.15.1.

93. Livy, 34.59.8, 35.13.6–35.14.4, 35.15.1–35.17.2. Villius alone met Hannibal, since Galba was ill: Livy, 35.14.1–4.

94. Livy, 35.23.5, 35.39.4–7.

95. Cf. Balsdon, *Phoenix* 21 (1967): 185–186; Clemente, *Athenaeum* 54 (1976): 333–340.

96. Galba had engaged in negotiations with the Aetolians—but quite without success: Livy, 31.28.3, 31.29–32. The Aetolian decision was not determined by diplomacy: Livy, 31.40.7–10.

97. Livy, 32.28.3–12. It does not follow that Flamininus, Galba, and Villius represented separate political factions, let alone that they had differing policies on the war and on eastern affairs. Elaborate conjectures on their affiliations may be set aside. For some hypotheses, all without firm support in the evidence, see Scullard, *Roman Poli-*

In similar fashion, the senate's selection of *decem legati* in 196 placed explicit emphasis on Villius and Galba as former commanders in Macedonia. The reference may be less to their special expertise than to their claims on a due meed of credit.[98] *Legati* of stature and seniority would assure that Flamininus did not (and did not appear to) run a one-man show, thereby defusing potential political controversy. Indeed, some differences of opinion on the peace arrangements did surface between the proconsul and the ten commissioners, requiring settlement by compromise.[99] Roman *nobiles* looked with disfavor upon the undue elevation of one of their peers. Diplomatic confrontation with Antiochus at Lysimacheia no doubt played a part in the choice of Galba and Villius to confront him again in 193. But, for all their "expertise," the new round of talks left them bewildered, their reports to the senate contained no firm recommendations on Antiochus, and their investigations turned up more rumor than fact. The senate found "expert" opinion an inadequate guide on which to act.[100] One may observe too that Villius and Galba had company on these delegations; their colleagues in 196, 193, and 192, so far as is known, carried no eastern credentials.[101] Politics, it seems, had as much—if not more—to do with the missions of Galba and Villius as did knowledge of the East.[102] They catered to the sensitivities of the nobility rather than to the principles of a diplomatic service.

What of the consuls, promagistrates, and major legates of the Syrian and Aetolian wars? A determined search will produce instances in which they make later appearances in the East. The relevance of their prior experience to their subsequent appointments, however, needs to be questioned.

The case of M. Baebius Tamphilus, at first sight, does appear to

---

tics, 96, 105–109; Schlag, *Regnum in Senatu*, 100–110; Briscoe, *Latomus* 31 (1972) 40–48. But there can be no doubt that Villius, at least, who had planned a campaign and had been cut off before implementing it, would find Flamininus' prorogation especially irritating: Livy, 32.6.3–4.

98. Livy, 33.24.7: *decem legati more maiorum . . . decreti, adiectumque ut in eo numero legatorum P. Sulpicius et P. Villius essent, qui consules provinciam Macedoniam obtinuissent.*

99. Polyb. 18.45.7–12, 18.47.10–11; Livy, 33.31.7–11, 33.34.10; Plut. *Flam.* 10.1–2. Balsdon's picture of a happy unanimity (*Phoenix* 21 [1967]: 185–186) is too rosy.

100. Livy, 35.17.2: *itaque nec remissa ulla re nec impetrata, aeque ac venerant, omnium incerti legati Romam redierunt;* 35.22.1–2, 35.23.2: *nam etsi per legatos identidem omnia explorabantur, tamen rumores temere sine ullis auctoribus orti multa falsa veris miscebant.*

101. The names, some of them uncertain, in Broughton, *MRR* I: 337–338, 348, 351. Of the other envoys only P. Aelius Paetus may have served on more than one of these missions: Livy, 34.59.8.

102. Neither man receives subsequent mention in the record, their diplomatic and military "skills" evidently not called on again. Galba, of course, was full of years by 192 and may have died soon after. He had been ill, though recovered, in 193: Livy,

have relevance. As propraetor in the winter of 192/1, he commanded Rome's forces in Greece until the arrival of the consul Glabrio. The occasion brought him into contact with Philip V. Baebius consulted with the king and concerted operations with him in the spring of 191 in Thessaly and Perrhaebia.[103] So, it would seem no coincidence that six years later, when Thessalians, Perrhaebians, and others brought complaint against Philip for holding towns taken in that war, Baebius should be among the envoys sent to investigate.[104] Since the issue at stake was Philip's right to captured towns based on battlefield arrangements with Roman generals, Baebius ought to have been able to deliver a decisive opinion.[105] All the more revealing, therefore, that the commissioners shrank from decision and claimed uncertainty on the appropriate procedures for adjudication.[106] Baebius' "experience" never came into play.

Other instances lead to similar conclusions. C. Livius Salinator headed the fleet in 191 and 190, with a mixed record of success and failure. The operations included a certain amount of diplomatic dealings with Hellenic allies and negotiations with towns and communities.[107] This may help explain the fact that, shortly after his return home in 190, Livius was sent straight back to the East, this time on a mission to persuade Prusias of Bithynia to break with Antiochus.[108] Yet, when Livius reached the consulship two years later he was denied a chance to cast lots for the eastern *provinciae*. And, though he lived for nearly two decades more, he never again appeared on a diplomatic legation.[109] His "experience" went untapped. Twenty years separated the services of A. Atilius Serranus as admiral against Antiochus and as envoy to Greece in the preliminaries to the Third Macedonian War. The same chronological gap divided Q. Fabius Labeo's naval command in the Syrian war and his inclusion among the *decem legati* after Pydna in 167.[110] It will hardly be maintained that the later appointments grew out of the earlier in those cases. No other

---

35.14.1, 35.16.1. But the disappearance of Villius, a younger man, is not so easily explained.

103. Livy, 36.8.6, 36.10.10, 36.13; Appian, *Syr.* 16; cf. Zon. 9.19.

104. Polyb. 22.6.2–6; Livy, 39.24.10–13.

105. Especially Livy, 39.25.5, 39.26.11.

106. Livy, 39.26.14.

107. Cf. Livy, 37.8.6–7, 37.9.7–11, 37.12.2–3, 37.16.1–3.

108. Polyb. 21.11.11–12; Livy, 37.25.13–14.

109. Provincial allocation in 188: Livy, 38.35.7–8. Livius' death in 170: Livy, 43.11.13.

110. On Atilius' two commissions: Broughton, *MRR* I: 350, 353, 413. He also had a minor military post in 171: Livy, 42.47.10–11. On Fabius, Broughton, *MRR* I: 361, 366, 435, 436, n. 3.

commander of forces against Antiochus or Aetolia seems to have represented his government again in the East.[111]

As the second century progressed and the occasions for official contacts between Rome and the East multiplied enormously, an increased number of men who had fought Greeks in war found themselves on later missions to Hellas in peace. The process was inevitable in a society that utilized the same elite to head its armies and to conduct its diplomacy. It does not follow—and this distinction must be reemphasized—that wartime experience across the Adriatic fitted one (or was thought to fit one) for future eastern service. Of the examples known, almost all show no ostensible connection between the initial military operations and the later appearances abroad.

Certainly commands in the eastern wars by M. Junius Brutus and C. Claudius Pulcher, consuls in 178 and 177 respectively, had not the slightest bearing on participation in an embassy to Asia and the islands in 172 for the one and membership of the *decem legati* in 167 for the other.[112] Of all the commanders in the Third Macedonian War only one, C. Marcius Figulus who led the fleet in 169, headed forces again in the East, in the Dalmatian campaign of 156, plainly a very different and unrelated operation.[113] A few others saw later service of a diplomatic nature, which had little or no connection with their wartime experience: P. Licinius Crassus, consul in 171 who fought Perseus in Thessaly, later envoy to Asia Minor to settle differences between Gala-

111. Two dubious tales about L. Scipio Asiaticus after the war with Antiochus should be noted but carry little weight. Both derive from Valerius Antias. Asiaticus allegedly served as mediator between Eumenes and Antiochus ca. 187 or 186, collecting money from kings and cities to celebrate his games: Livy, 39.22.8–10. A questionable story, not endorsed by Livy or mentioned elsewhere: Antias puts it after Asiaticus' condemnation! And he ignores the fact that Antiochus died on an eastern expedition in 187. The other tale puts Asiaticus (and P. Scipio Nasica) on the mission to Prusias, together with Flamininus, which issued in Hannibal's death: Livy, 39.56.7; Plut. *Flam.* 21.8. That is another variant by Antias, omitted by the rest of our (very considerable) evidence on the affair.

112. The consulships and Istrian campaigns: Broughton, *MRR* I:395, 397–399. The embassies: Broughton, *MRR* I:413, 435. Whether Brutus is also the M. Junius who went to mediate a quarrel between Galatia and Cappadocia in 163 is uncertain: Polyb. 31.8.1–3. Broughton prefers Brutus over M. Junius Pennus, consul 167, on grounds that the former "had had experience in the East": *MRR* I:441, n. 2; so also Walbank, *Commentary* III:472. The argument carries no weight. C. Claudius had one more military venture abroad after the Istrian war, as *tribunus militum* on the staff of P. Crassus in 171. But "eastern experience" was irrelevant here as well. The object was to lend prestige to Crassus' staff. Q. Mucius Scaevola, another ex-consul, also went along as *tribunus militum*, a man without previous service in the East, and *tres illustres iuvenes*: Livy, 42.49.9.

113. Broughton, *MRR* I:424, 447. See, especially, Polyb. 32.13.5–6, who makes it clear that no one had had previous exposure to Dalmatia.

tians and Eumenes in 167; Cn. Sicinius, praetor and propraetor in 172 and 171 to establish Rome's position across the Adriatic, later ambassador to the Istrians in 170 to express senatorial apologies for unnecessary pillaging; L. Hortensius, admiral in the Aegean in 170, later on an embassy to Bithynia in 155; L. Anicius Gallus, victor over Genthius in Illyria in 168 and 167, later an envoy to Asia Minor in 154 to bring Prusias' war on Attalus to an end. In each instance the subsequent service came in an area and for a purpose quite different from the previous. In each instance also the ex-commander took but one part in an embassy that included several men who lacked military background in the East. As these cases suggest, the senate did not look for special diplomatic skills in dispatching envoys. Savage campaigns in Greece, marked by extortionate demands upon allies, had been conducted by Crassus and by Hortensius, calling forth a host of complaints by the Hellenes. Yet the senate had no qualms about sending these men on later missions that required tact and diplomacy. To regard their former experience as qualification for their subsequent duties is plainly absurd.[114] If any legates to the East in the mid-second century had held earlier commands which proved of some use, that was accidental—and exceptional.[115]

Apparent exceptions and questionable examples have occupied us long enough. A singular fact springs into view: the roster of successful generals who made their reputations and earned their triumphs in the East—and did *not* return. The consuls of 229, L.

114. Crassus: Broughton, *MRR* I:416, 435; Sicinius: Broughton *MRR* I:411, 417, 421; Hortensius: Broughton, *MRR* I:420, 449; Anicius: Broughton, *MRR* I:428, 434, 450. The depredations of Crassus and Hortensius and the charges leveled against them: Livy, 43.4.5–13, 43.6.1–3, 43.7.5–43.8.8; *Per.* 43; Zon. 9.22.

115. Two possible instances may be cited. Cn. Octavius, praetor and commander of the fleet in 168 and 167, accomplished the surrender of Perseus: Broughton, *MRR* I:428, 434. His fluency in Greek (Livy, 45.29.3) had proved serviceable in presenting the senate's messages to various Greek communities in 169: Broughton, *MRR* I:426. And it may have been a factor in his appointment as part of an embassy to Syria in 163: Broughton, *MRR* I:441. But naval warfare against Perseus has little relevance for supervising the affairs of the Seleucid kingdom. Octavius' heavy-handed behavior in Syria, moreover, was anything but diplomatic, and his murder at the hands of the Syrians went unavenged by Rome: Broughton, *MRR* I:443. The other instance is that of P. Scipio Nasica Corculum, consul and victor in the Dalmatian war of 155: Broughton, *MRR* I:448. Whether that experience had any bearing on his mission to Greece in 150 to check on the activities of Andriscus (Zon. 9.28) must remain uncertain—and doubtful. No need here to explore the lists of subordinate officers, legates, and military tribunes who served in eastern wars and later turn up in the East in a military or diplomatic capacity. Naturally there are many more of them. The limited personnel of Rome's ruling class made that inevitable. Once more the connection between prior experience and later duty is rarely discernible. And there are approximately twice as many such subordinate officers who never again make an eastern appearance in our records.

Postumius Albinus and Cn. Fulvius Centumalus, routed the Illyrians in a single season, Rome's first invasion across the Adriatic. A decade later, another lightning campaign wiped out Illyrian resistance, gaining plaudits and triumphs for the commanders L. Aemilius Paullus and M. Livius Salinator. Success also attended the expedition of P. Scipio Asina and M. Minucius Rufus in 221: a subjugation of the troublesome Istrian tribes. Rome had made her power felt across the Adriatic. Yet she called on none of these victorious and "experienced" generals again, as commanders, advisers, or officers when Philip's alliance with Hannibal drew her forces once more to Greece. Untimely deaths removed some from consideration. But not the dour and embittered Livius, who moped for years after being convicted of peculation, unkempt and bedraggled to remind his countrymen of their injustice, and coaxed out of retirement only to face the crisis of Hasdrubal's march across the Alps in 207. Not the eminent patrician Scipio Asina, later an *interrex* but never again sent to war. And not Fulvius who gained the official credit for crushing the Illyrians in 229 and is unheard from later.[116]

A still greater revelation comes from pondering the fate of triumphant commanders in the Antiochene and Aetolian wars. Did they take their rightful places thereafter as senior counselors in affairs of the East? Far from it. They ran straight into harsh criticism. Political opposition blocked or even ruined their careers. M'. Acilius Glabrio, the hero of Thermopylae who sent Antiochus scampering back to Asia and arrogantly rattled chains at the Aetolians, returned to Rome for a lavish triumph in 190. He expected to cap the success with election to the censorship in the following year. It was not to be. Tribunes emerged to accuse him of pocketing some of the booty, his former legates and junior officers gave damaging testimony, the *nobiles* turned their backs, and Glabrio sourly withdrew his candidacy. Thereafter he vanishes from the record.[117] The Scipio brothers had humbled the mightiest of Seleucid kings at Magnesia, left tokens of their generosity and beneficence at various shrines of the Greek world, and L. Scipio paraded the spoils of Asia before his countrymen's awed gaze, riches, it was said, equivalent to ten triumphs. Yet they did not long enjoy their glory. Accusations flew about in both senate and assembly, tarnishing their reputations with hints of embezzlement and corruption. Africanus brazenly tore up his account books in full view of the senate, rebuking his accusers for quibbling about three thou-

116. The other three all perished before the First Macedonian War. Paullus and Minucius fell at Cannae, Postumius died in Gaul in 215. On Livius Salinator, see especially Livy, 27.34.3–15; cf. 22.35.3; Val. Max. 4.2.2.

117. The triumph: Livy, 37.46.2–6; the abortive censorial campaign: Livy, 37.57.9–15.

sand talents when he had deposited fifteen thousand into the treasury. Further displays of arrogance followed or preceded, dazzling audiences with reminders of his conquests that brought freedom and salvation to the state. But the harsh political realities could not be gainsaid. Whether formal trials took place and how many are matters of dispute, hopelessly muddled in the sources. The results, however, are clear. Prominence and power slipped from L. Scipio's grasp. And P. Scipio retired to his country estates, never again to serve the *res publica*.[118]

What of M. Fulvius Nobilior, who finally subdued the recalcitrant Aetolians and brought the war in Greece to a successful close? By all rights, a triumph awarded by grateful fellow citizens should have been a foregone conclusion. But spite and envy intervened. The *inimici* of Fulvius solicited testimony from Ambraciote envoys who delivered their prepared lines to good effect: Fulvius had attacked Ambracia unprovoked, had plundered, murdered, and destroyed with wanton disregard for justice or humanity. A tribune rose to block or delay triumphal honors, providing Fulvius' enemies with more opportunity to build a case against him. In the end opposition was overborne and the consul got his triumph in 187.[119] His reputation, however, had suffered severe damage. A candidacy for the censorship of 184 fell through, and when Fulvius at last achieved that post in 179 it required political machinations and a public reconciliation with his senatorial foes. Even then he was lambasted by the redoubtable Cato, who raked up old charges of misconduct in the Aetolian war and added denunciations of the censorship.[120] Consul, proconsul, *triumphator*, and censor, a controversial political figure, a patron of the arts and literature, M. Fulvius Nobilior had a long and conspicuous career. Yet not once after his return from Greece (so far as our evidence goes) did he receive a summons to speak on or engage in affairs of the East.

A similar fate awaited his colleague in the consulship of 189, Cn.

118. No need to cite all the confused evidence on the trials of the Scipios. For a recent discussion, see G. Bandelli, *Index* 3 (1972): 304–342; idem, *Index* 4 (1974–75): 93–126. A summary of scholarship in Walbank, *Commentary* III: 242–247. On L. Scipio's triumph: Broughton, *MRR* I: 362. Africanus' arrogant speeches and dramatic displays: Polyb. 23.14; Livy, 38.50–51, 38.55.10–13; Gellius, 4.18; Val. Max. 3.7.1d–e; Diod. 29.21; *Vir. Ill.* 49.17; Plut. *Cato*, 15.1–2; Appian, *Syr.* 40. The retirement of Africanus: Livy, 38.52.1–3; *Vir. Ill.* 49.17–18; Zon. 9.20. L. Scipio later offered his candidacy for the censorship of 184, but failed—and then drops from sight: Livy, 39.40.2.

119. Livy, 38.43–44, 39.4–5.

120. Failure in the censorial elections for 184: Livy, 39.40.3. Political reconciliation and success in 179: Livy, 40.45.6–40.46.16; Cic. *Prov. Cons.* 20; Val. Max. 4.2.1; Gellius, 12.8.5–6; on this, see now M. Martina, *Quaderni di filologia classica* 2 (1979): 21–37. Cato's attacks: *ORF*, fr. 148–151.

Manlius Vulso. Manlius had wrapped up the Syrian war and presided over the peace of Apamea. He had also conducted brutal campaigns against the Galatians, campaigns marked by greed and treachery, with heavy sufferings inflicted on the inhabitants of Asia Minor, and slack military discipline which encouraged every form of license. Victory followed, and booty flowed into Rome of unprecedented scale and luxury.[121] Naturally, Manlius' request for a triumph in 187 met with fierce resistance, not least from some of the *decem legati* who had witnessed his unscrupulous conduct. They fired a hail of charges: Manlius had fought a private and undeclared war, requisitioning cash and loot everywhere, causing needless loss of life through folly and avarice. Sharp debates ensued in Rome before Manlius obtained his triumph. Senators, willing enough to entertain a variety of accusations, proved reluctant to deny a triumph lest this set a precedent that would rob them of similar distinctions in the future. The parade of plunder conveyed through the city made Manlius' triumph proverbial for the introduction of insidious eastern opulence.[122] His political career, however, saw no further progress. Manlius too was among the failed censorial candidates for 184. Nothing more is heard from him.[123] So, all the commanders and victors of the greater eastern wars of 191–188, laden with spoils and distinctions, stayed at home thereafter, never again recorded in our sources with regard to Roman "policy" on Hellas.[124] Expertise did not count in the world of Roman politics. Blind jealousy disparaged achievements and degraded the prizes of victory.[125]

The pattern holds for the next generation as well. Rome saw no special advantage in posting her ex-commanders to areas where once they had fought. Several of the generals and admirals of the Third Macedonian War found that to be their last assignment in the East: C. Lucretius Gallus, the naval commander of 171, A. Hostilius Mancinus, consul in Greece in 170, and his successor, the devious and resourceful Q. Marcius Philippus in 169.[126] Finally, the heroes of Rome's

121. The campaigns: Broughton, *MRR* I:360. On the booty, see especially Livy, 39.6.7–39.7.5.

122. Opposition to Manlius: Livy, 38.44.9–38.50.3, 38.54.7, 38.58.11–12, 39.1.4, 39.6.3–6, 39.7.3; Florus, 1.27.3; *Vir. Ill.* 55.1. The triumph and its later reputation: Livy, 39.6.7–39.7.5; Pliny, *NH*, 34.14, 37.12; Augustine, *CD*, 3.21.

123. Livy, 39.40.2.

124. One may add to this list L. Aemilius Regillus, admiral of the fleet that crippled the Syrian navy at Myonessus in 190, and A. Cornelius Mamulla, the propraetor who commanded Rome's forces in Aetolia before arrival of the Scipios in the same year: Broughton, *MRR* I:356–357. Neither one served again in Greece.

125. Livy, 38.49.5 (the speech of Manlius): *caeca invidia est, patres conscripti, nec quicquam aliud scit quam detractare virtutes, corrumpere honores ac praemia earum.*

126. Note also A. Manlius Vulso who fought the Istri, outside his allotted province, in 178: Livy, 41.1–5. And C. Cassius Longinus who attempted, without authoriza-

crushing and decisive victories of the 140s. Q. Metellus Macedonicus, with swift efficiency, snuffed out the revolt of Andriscus and subjugated Macedonia in 148. An illustrious career followed, but no further concern with the East. And L. Mummius, who reduced Achaea to humble submission in 146, turned Corinth into rubble, distributed the spoils as his gifts to Rome, Italy, and the provinces, deposited his monuments all over the Greek world, celebrated his triumph and took the *cognomen* Achaicus, but returned to politics in Rome and left the care of Hellas to others.[127]

The results of this survey leave little room for doubt. Rome's commanders and principal officers gained their posts through election to magistracies: a matter of politics, prestige, and familial connections. Familiarity with a theater of war and knowledge of a foreign people received but slight attention and only on rare occasions. When exceptions occur, political considerations normally provide the reason. The aristocratic corporation reckoned that membership in its ranks and attainment of high office sufficed to authorize command. The prudent general would, of course, seek the counsel of men skilled in military matters. Such skills belonged to the staff; they were not a prerequisite for the *imperator*.[128] The lot could fall where it may upon those who had risen to the top. Even prorogation was unusual, for the prizes of military glory brought a plethora of competitors, each of whom could claim his due. The generals of the Hellenic wars, however successful and triumphant, seldom looked eastward again. Some fell afoul of envious *inimici* at home, others overcame opposition to proceed through the hierarchy. Few were tapped for renewed service in the East, few gave further attention to Hellas. The senate spawned no "eastern lobby" of veteran officers and never considered itself dependent on the "expertise" of former generals.

The Diplomatic Appointments

Diplomacy, it could be argued, falls in a separate category. Granted that military command remained the prerogative of an elite

---

tion, to lead an army into Macedonia during his consulship of 171: Livy, 42.32.1–5, 43.1.4–8. Both came under heavy fire in Rome and neither served across the Adriatic again: Livy, 41.6.1–3, 41.7.4–10, 43.1.9–12, 43.5.1–10. The insertion of Q. Marcius Philippus among the *decem legati* of 167 is entirely baseless. Livy, 45.17.2, does not name him and the conjecture about "previous experience" is here, as elsewhere, hollow; cf. Broughton, *MRR* I:436, n. 4. The later missions by other generals in the Third Macedonian War have, at best, only the most tenuous connection with their service in that conflict; see above pp. 226–227.

127. Sources in Broughton, *MRR* I:461, 465–467, 470.

128. Livy, 44.22.12: *a prudentibus et proprie rei militaris peritis et usu doctis monendi*

who competed for political prominence, without regard to specialist knowledge. Granted also that victors and conquerors in Hellas need not thereby become suited for or interested in an "eastern policy." Nevertheless, the multiple and multifarious ambassadorial activities of the second century (it might be supposed) created a bloc of skilled negotiators whose talents were indispensable and whose counsel guided the deliberations of the *res publica*.[129] That supposition requires some detailed scrutiny.

How often, in fact, did Rome avail herself of the services of individual diplomats on more than a single occasion? An obvious question once it is posed, yet never asked—and ignored by those who reckon a few instances to be exemplary.

The circumstances of the mid-190s, as we have seen, were unusual and unrepresentative. Rome groped about for a satisfactory settlement with Philip and for some means short of war, if possible, to check the activities of Antiochus the Great. In those years, Flamininus' connections in Greece and his influence in Rome gave him a unique position. The senate proved willing also to give multiple assignments to Sulpicius Galba and Villius Tappulus, partly in trust of their judgment, partly as political compensation.[130] Yet even here no policy of reliance on experts had taken hold. Parallel examples are difficult to discover. P. Aelius Paetus, a man distinguished for judicial learning, served with Galba and Villius on the decemviral commission of 196, treated with Antiochus at Lysimacheia, and was dispatched to the king again in 193. On that last occasion, as the cold war with Antiochus began to heat up, the senate clearly did want men who had negotiated with the Seleucid before.[131] The mission once accomplished however, Paetus returned to a long career as jurist and augur, surviving until struck down by a plague in 174, and never again an envoy to the East.[132] One other personage can be cited: P. Cornelius Lentulus, member of the *decem legati* to administer peace

---

imperatores sunt. Naturally, the senate or a consul might on occasion appoint senior leggates to assure a trusted and capable general staff. Note, e.g., the distinguished *legati* who served with Glabrio in 191: Broughton, *MRR*, I:355; those with L. Scipio in 190: Broughton, *MRR*, I:358–359; and the officers of P. Crassus in 171: Livy, 42.49.9.

129. Assumed in most modern accounts, and most recently spelled out by Clemente, *Athenaeum* 54 (1976): 319–352. By contrast, absence of continuity in the decision-making process is correctly discerned by A. E. Astin, *Politics and Policies in the Roman Republic* (Belfast, 1968), 14–17; *Cato the Censor* (Oxford, 1978), 282–283. But even he accepts the view that the senate paid special attention to those with expertise in certain fields.

130. See above pp. 222–224.

131. Livy, 34.59.8: *legatos mitti ad regem eosdem qui Lysimachiae apud eum fuerant placuit, P. Sulpicium, P. Villium, P. Aelium.*

132. Livy, 41.21.8. His judicial learning: *Dig.* 1.2.2.38.

in both 196 and in 189/8. Since he was also among those who negotiated with Antiochus at Lysimacheia in his first assignment, the experience may have influenced his nomination to the second.[133] Perhaps. But it is important to observe that Lentulus was the *only* man to appear on both decemviral commissions. The board of 189/8 contained none other with demonstrated negotiating talents, not Villius, not Galba, not even Flamininus.[134] Rome obviously selected her peace commissions without regard to diplomatic aptitude.

In the years after Apamea embassies sallied forth to Greece with monotonous regularity. The senate could hardly avoid some duplication of personnel even if the choices were entirely random. A few notable individuals went more than once—but remarkably few.

Ap. Claudius Pulcher stands out, a repeated visitor to the East. Extensive service under Flamininus in the 190s gave him military experience in Greece. Flamininus evidently trusted him alone, as *tribunus militum*, to accompany him in private negotiations with Philip V in 198, an early taste of diplomacy. There followed campaigns as legate in Boeotia and in the Peloponnese from 196 to 194; then a new tour of duty in the Aetolian war of 191.[135] After his consulship in 185 the senate turned to Ap. Claudius again the following year to head a legation to the East, with dual purpose: to check on Philip, thus hastening his evacuation of Thessaly and the Thracian coast, and to look into charges of Achaean maltreatment of Sparta. Appius relished the task. The haughty patrician showed eagerness to throw his weight about in Hellas. He delivered a stern lecture to Philip for the massacre in Maronea and demanded that those responsible be delivered up to Rome. In Achaea he bullied a gathering of the League assembly, issuing advice laced with threats. Ap. Claudius was not to be trifled with.[136] Before returning home, the delegation also stopped in

133. The assignment in 196: Polyb. 18.48.2, 18.50.2; Livy, 33.35.2, 33.39.2; Plut. *Flam.* 12.1; the assignment in 189: Livy, 37.55.7.

134. Only two members had fought before in the East, both in subordinate capacities and both in the Macedonian war, not in the Syrian war: L. Furius Purpureo, a legate under Galba in 199 (Livy, 31.29–32), and Ap. Claudius Nero, legate under Flamininus in 198 (Polyb. 18.10.8; Livy, 32.36.10). Purpureo had been used by Galba to induce the Aetolians over to Rome's side—but his rhetoric proved unavailing and the experience bears no relevance to the later appointment. Ap. Claudius Nero must be distinguished from the Ap. Claudius (probably Pulcher) who, as military tribune, joined Flamininus in private talks with Philip: Polyb. 18.8.6; Livy, 32.35.7; so, rightly, Badian, *Flamininus*, 44–45; denied, without argument, by Briscoe, *Commentary*, 288.

135. The secret parley with Philip: see previous note. The service in 196 to 194: Livy, 33.29.9, 34.28.10, 34.50.10. The Aetolian war: Livy, 36.10.10–14, 36.13.1, 36.22.8, 36.30.2; Appian, *Syr.* 16.

136. The visit to Philip: Polyb. 22.11.3–4, 22.12.4, 22.13.8–22.14.6: τῶν περὶ τὸν Ἄππιον . . . πικρῶς τῷ Φιλίππῳ μεμψιμοιρούντων . . . οὐ φασκόντων προσδεῖσθαι δικαιολογίας, σαφῶς γὰρ εἰδέναι, τὰ γεγονότα καὶ τὸν αἴτιον τούτων; Livy, 39.33.3,

Crete where it arbitrated quarrels, issued directives, and turned remaining matters over to a common tribunal.[137] A year later, the senate professed itself baffled by bewildering claims from the Peloponnese and delegated the decision to a committee of men who had been to the area, among whom doubtless was Ap. Claudius.[138] A decade passed, and Appius, now a senior consular, again represented Rome abroad. Twice more, in fact: to settle fierce internal disputes arising from debt problems in Aetolia in 174, and a similar mission the next year to Thessaly. Nothing much got accomplished in Aetolia; Thessaly had a compromise settlement imposed on her. Ap. Claudius was his old self. He returned from the first legation fuming about the lunacy of the Aetolians; and in Thessaly he gave sharp rebuke to both quarreling factions.[139]

If anyone qualifies as "eastern expert," it is surely Ap. Claudius. The facts are clear, but their meaning can too easily be exaggerated. It is hard to detect, even in this ostensibly best of examples, any consistent policy toward affairs of the East. Appius engaged in bluster and hectoring with certain people: Philip, the Achaeans, the Aetolians; elsewhere, he offered reasonable solutions to disputes: in Crete and in Thessaly—a man who tolerated no back-talk from Greeks, but who showed moderation when they were submissive. And how far did the senate follow his advice? They eschewed firm action against Philip and against the Achaean League, despite Appius' negative reports, and they took no sides in the Aetolian dispute. By delegating the thorny Peloponnesian problem to Appius and others, they expressed more indifference than dependence on "expertise." Ap. Claudius was a useful agent in badgering Hellenes. But the *patres* kept their own counsel.

None other in the post-Apamea period saw comparable service. Q. Metellus, a senior *consularis* in 185 (consul two decades before) but without prior experience in Greece, led an embassy to investigate complaints about Philip by Eumenes, the Thessalians, and others. A plethora of charges and counter-charges came before the legates. At Tempe, Metellus and his colleagues directed that Philip withdraw to the "ancient bounds of Macedonia," a studiously vague pronouncement, and claimed uncertainty on appropriate procedures to handle

---

39.34.3–5. The visit to Achaea: Polyb. 22.12.4, 22.12.9–10; Livy, 39.33.5, 39.35.8–39.37.21: *tum Appius suadere se magnopere Achaeis dixit ut, dum liceret voluntate suo facere, gratiam inirent, ne mox inviti et coacti facerent;* cf. Paus. 7.9.3–4.

137. Polyb. 22.15.

138. A three-man committee, says Polybius; but the third name has dropped out of the text. Büttner-Wobst's insertion of Ap. Claudius is almost certainly right: Polyb. 23.4.7; cf. Paus. 7.9.5; Livy, 39.48.2–4.

139. Aetolia: Livy, 41.25.5–6, 41.27.4: *legati . . . renuntiarunt coerceri rabiem gentis non posse;* cf. 42.2.2. Thessaly: Livy, 42.5.8–10: *utriusque partis principibus castigatis.*

detailed claims. At Thessalonica, their pronouncement was more uncertain still: they professed ignorance even of the terms of Apamea.[140]
So, Metellus was either unprepared or unwilling to pass clear judgment. The irresolute conclusion may have prompted another visit: an
unscheduled stop in Achaea where Metellus could show some decisiveness worthy of a Roman *nobilis*. There he censured Achaean
magistrates in strong language for mistreatment of Lacedaemonians.
An inadequate reply came back, so Metellus insisted on a summoning
of the assembly, only to be refused again on grounds that he had
no official commission from the senate. The Roman legate made an
abrupt and indignant departure.[141] He received little satisfaction from
the *patres* as well when he returned to denounce the Achaeans and
lodge bitter protest about his impolite reception. The senate restricted
itself to sending another legation and asking for greater courtesy to
Roman envoys.[142] Metellus' ruffled feelings may have been somewhat
soothed by appointment to the arbitral board in 183 that offered settlement for Achaean-Spartan claims.[143] But he went no more to the
East and his "expertise," based on one abortive and frustrated visit, is
a chimera.

Scarcely better credentials were carried by the notorious Q. Marcius Philippus. Third in the series of Roman ambassadors to Macedonia and Greece, following Metellus and Ap. Claudius in 183, he
saw to Philip's evacuation of his Thracian holdings and delivered senatorial messages in Achaea.[144] How much did he actually accomplish?
Agreement on the withdrawal from Thrace had, in effect, been secured in the senate before Philippus' departure.[145] In Achaea, the
legate's insistence that the League refrain from war in Messenia received cold rebuff. So he too, like Metellus, came back to Rome in a
black mood. Philippus urged the senate to ignore Achaean requests
for aid and to encourage revolts in the Peloponnese. If Polybius is to
be believed, the *patres* went along with that advice. Their official response, however, was rather more moderate and noncommittal.[146]
The results, in any case, did not materialize as Philippus predicted.
Achaea crushed the Messenian uprising, leaving the senate to cover
its tracks in awkward fashion.[147] The "expert" counsel proved far from

140. Polyb. 22.6.6; Livy, 39.24.13–39.29.2.
141. Polyb. 22.10; Paus. 7.8.6, 7.9.1; cf. Livy, 39.33.5.
142. Polyb. 22.12.8–10; Livy, 39.33.6–8; Paus. 7.9.1–3.
143. Polyb. 23.4.7.
144. Polyb. 23.4.16, 23.8.1; Livy, 39.47.11, 39.48.5–6, 39.53.11.
145. Polyb. 23.1–3, 23.7; Livy, 39.47; cf. Gruen, *GRBS* 15 (1974): 231–238; Walbank, *Commentary* III: 215–216.
146. Polyb. 23.9.4–14, 24.9.12; Livy, 40.2.6–8.
147. Polyb. 23.9.14, 23.17.3.

wise. And the senate's appointment of Philippus more than a decade later to the famed mission of 172 can hardly be based on any demonstrated diplomatic proficiency.[148]

Rare indeed are the occasions when a man with special connections in an eastern area was summoned to duty for that reason. C. Valerius Laevinus qualifies as such a person. Son of the consul of 210 who conducted the campaigns of the First Macedonian War and concluded the treaty of alliance with Aetolia, he fought as legate in the Aetolian war of 189. There he was contacted by Aetolian envoys seeking a peace and took up their cause, a personal duty he felt obliged to discharge and a προστασία he could exercise.[149] Hence, it appears no coincidence that fifteen years later, when civil strife erupted in Aetolia, Laevinus headed a legation to resolve the conflict.[150] Yet the outcome of that mission should be underscored. Whatever influence Laevinus once possessed among Aetolians had dissipated. The embassy returned empty-handed and with some vitriolic comments about Aetolians gone berserk.[151] When a Roman legate did make settlement the following year, he was not Valerius Laevinus.[152] Laevinus went instead on a mission to various eastern parts to gauge Perseus' activities and shore up support for Rome.[153] Diplomatic failures did not preclude further appointments. Laevinus was by then an eminent *consularis*. Special expertise was plainly irrelevant. An analogous example strengthens the conclusion. C. Cicereius, junior member of a group sent in 172 to keep King Genthius of Illyria loyal or neutral, turns up again as one of the commissioners to impose a settlement on Illyria after the Third Macedonian War.[154] His earlier venture, however, had been a signal failure. Genthius had proceeded to war on Rome as ally of Perseus. Cicereius' subsequent appointment can have had nothing to do with any competence shown in Illyrian matters.

Several other personages appear on the numerous embassies of the 170s and reappear on later diplomatic legations. Yet one would be hard pressed to discover any connections among their multiple services (usually two, at the most, for a single individual anyway). The eminent A. Postumius Albinus Luscus, consul in 180 and member of a powerful political house, led a group of envoys to investigate charges of Perseus' stirring up the Bastarnae in 176; four years later, he headed a mission to Crete to assure support for Rome's initial cam-

148. The missions of 172: Broughton, *MRR* I:413.

149. Polyb. 21.29.10–12: νομίσας ἴδιον εἶναι τὸ πρᾶγμα καὶ καθήκειν αὐτῷ τὸ προστατῆσαι τῶν Αἰτωλῶν; 21.31.2; Livy, 38.9.8, 38.10.2.

150. Livy, 41.25.5–6.

151. Livy, 41.27.4; cf. 42.2.2; see above, n. 139.

152. Livy, 42.4.5, 42.5.10–12.   153. Livy, 42.6.4–5, 42.17.1–9.

154. Livy, 42.26.6–7, 45.17.4.

paigning season in the Third Macedonian War; and he was the first named to the decemviral commission after conclusion of the war.[155] The influence and *dignitas* of the man must have earned these appointments: ex-consul, the stern and exacting censor of 174, a *princeps* within the *curia*.[156] The ambassadorial posts (leadership of the delegation each time) derived from his political status rather than from a pattern of eastern involvement.

Nor does any pattern form itself in the other cases of repeated assignments: M. Junius Brutus, a junior member of the *decem legati* in 189/8, an envoy to places in the Aegean and Asia in 172 to rally backing for Rome's cause, and perhaps in Asia Minor a decade later to cool down a controversy between Ariarathes and the Galatians; L. Canuleius Dives, on missions to Aetolia in 174 and to Alexandria in 163; Ap. Claudius Centho, one of those who delivered Roman terms to Perseus in 172, and who put an end to hostilities between Attalus and Prusias in 154; P. Cornelius Lentulus, commissioned to the Peloponnese to confirm loyalties in 172, and a senatorial representative in Asia Minor in 156; A. Terentius Varro, among the envoys to Genthius in 172, and among the *decem legati* for Macedonia in 167; M. Caninius Rebilus, dispatched by the senate to investigate conditions in the Roman army of the East in 170, and to escort Thracian hostages back to King Cotys in 167; and Sex. Julius Caesar, posted to Abdera to make amends to that city in 170, and head of a delegation to Achaea twenty-three years later on the eve of the Achaean war. Not all these identifications are certain and some of the missions depend on tainted evidence. Even if all be accepted, however, it is plain beyond dispute that assignments diverged in time, place, and character. They were *ad hoc* duties without follow-through. Their cumulative experience did not make these men specialists in the affairs of Hellas.[157] And when

155. The investigatory mission of 176: Polyb. 25.6.2–6; Livy, 41.19.4; Appian, *Mac.* 11.1; cf. Walbank, *Commentary* III:282–283. The trip to Crete: Livy, 42.35.7. Service among the *decem legati*: Livy, 45.17.2. Postumius may also have been a subordinate officer as a young man in the Aetolian war of 191; Livy, 36.12.9. But the identification is uncertain and the relevance dubious anyway.

156. On the censorship, cf. Livy, 41.27, 42.10; Vell. Pat. 1.10.6: *aspera . . . censura Fulvii Flacci et Postumii Albini fuit.*

157. On M. Junius Brutus as member of the *decem legati*: Livy, 37.55.7; as envoy in 172: Livy, 42.45—the name missing in Polyb. 27.3.1; cf. Walbank, *Commentary* III: 294–295; that he did mediate between Galatia and Ariarathes in 163 is uncertain, for the M. Junius of Polyb. 31.8.1–3 could be M. Junius Pennus, cos. 167. On L. Canuleius Dives' mission to Aetolia in 174: Livy, 41.25.5–6; on the mission to Alexandria in 163: Polyb. 31.10.1–5, giving only the *nomen* Canuleius. On Ap. Claudius Centho's embassy to Perseus in 172: Livy, 42.25.1–13—possibly annalistic invention; on his assignment to Asia Minor in 154: Polyb. 33.13.4–10; he had fought also as legate and with independent command in the Third Macedonian War: Broughton, *MRR* I:422, 425, 428. On P. Lentulus as ambassador to the Peloponnese in 172: Polyb. 27.2.12; Livy,

Rome undertook a major settlement after the Third Macedonian War, appointing ten commissioners for Macedonia and five for Illyria, the makeup of those boards tells the tale unambiguously: almost all the *legati* were—so far as negotiating skills in the East are concerned—rank amateurs.[158]

The picture for the post-Pydna generation shows no perceptible change. Roman embassies came thick and fast to the East. How many seasoned diplomats were there?

Most prominent and celebrated by far was Ti. Sempronius Gracchus, son-in-law of Africanus, father of the Gracchi, twice consul, twice *triumphator*, censor, and the one Roman general in Spain who earned both the loyalty of his troops and the enduring affection of the Spaniards. He held almost every office within the gift of his state; no sinecures, each became a showcase for his energies and intelligence. Gracchus commanded respect and admiration, a man second to none among the *principes* of the *res publica*.[159] Already as a young man in 190

42.37.1–3, 42.37.7–9; as envoy to Asia Minor in 156: Polyb. 32.16.1, 33.1.1; he had probably been an officer in the war against Perseus in the meantime; Livy, 42.47.12, 42.49.9, 42.56.3–4, 45.4.7—though the identification is not secure. On A. Terentius Varro's legation to Genthius in 172: Livy, 42.26.6–7; as member of the *decem legati* in 167: Livy, 45.17.3; earlier service as junior officer in Greece in 190 is hardly relevant: Livy, 37.48.5, 37.49.8. On M. Caninius Rebilus' appointment in 170: Livy, 43.11.2, 43.11.9–10—more an investigation of the Roman army than a visit to Greeks; on his escorting of Thracian hostages in 167: Livy, 45.42.11. On Sex. Julius Caesar as envoy to Abdera in 170: Livy, 43.4.12–13—essentially to implement a senatorial decision rather than to engage in negotiations; on his embassy to Achaea in 147: Polyb. 38.9–11.

158. Only a few exceptions to this: A. Postumius Albinus Luscus, chief of the Macedonian legation, whose appointment, as we have seen, surely owed more to his political *auctoritas* than to his diplomatic talent (see above pp. 236–237); C. Cicereius, appointed to the Illyrian board, despite his earlier failure on a mission there (see above p. 236); A. Terentius Varro, also a member of the abortive mission to Genthius (see above p. 237); T. Numisius Tarquiniensis, sent to Macedonia, although his previous effort to halt war between Antiochus and Ptolemy had been completely ineffectual (Polyb. 29.25.3–4). Their fruitless missions hardly qualified them as eastern experts. None of the others had had any known diplomatic experience, though a few had fought as subordinate officers in the East. Cn. Domitius Ahenobarbus' trip to Macedonia in 169 was an inspection of the military situation, not a matter of diplomacy (Livy, 44.18.1–5, 44.20.1–7). And the inclusion of Q. Marcius Philippus among the *decem legati* for Macedonia is pure conjecture, without a trace of evidence: Broughton, *MRR* I:436, n. 4. The facts, here as elsewhere, refute the efforts of B. Schleussner, *Die Legaten der römischen Republik* (Munich, 1978), 91–92, n. 311, to regard *decem legati* as consisting primarily of "Fachleute" and "Sachkenner."

159. A summary of his career in Münzer, *RE* IIA:1403–1409, "Sempronius," n. 54; also, A. H. Bernstein, *Tiberius Sempronius Gracchus. Tradition and Apostasy* (Ithaca, 1978), 26–42. Cf. especially, the famous anecdote of the betrothal to Cornelia which, whatever truth it contains, attests to his preeminent reputation: Livy, 38.57.5–8; cf. Val. Max. 4.2.3; Gellius, 12.8.1–4; Dio, 19, fr. 65. And see Polyb. 31.27.16 (on Gracchus and Scipio Nasica): ὄντες οὐδενὸς δεύτεροι Ῥωμαίων.

he was entrusted by the Scipios with the delicate task of sounding out Philip V to secure a route through Thrace into Asia, a task successfully accomplished.[160] In the years after Pydna, when Gracchus was already *consularis*, *triumphator*, and *censorius*, he undertook two extensive journeys to the East as representative of the senate. The trip in 165 brought him to the courts of Eumenes, Antiochus IV, and Ariarathes, and to the island of Rhodes, in each place hosted with the ceremony and respect due his *dignitas*.[161] In 162, after his second consulship, he traveled again to Greece and Asia, looking in on Demetrius of Syria, Ariarathes, and various princes of Anatolia.[162] A specialist in eastern affairs, trusted for his knowledge of the area and its leaders? Polybius does remark that his second assignment came because he had been an eyewitness in the first.[163] Yet Gracchus was hardly an intense student of Hellenic affairs. A quarter-century elapsed between his assignment by the Scipios and his embassy to the Hellenistic kings, a quarter-century marked by a full and vigorous political career in Rome, service as a colonial commissioner in Italy, extensive campaigns in Spain and in Sardinia.[164] More important, a remarkable consistency characterizes the reports which Gracchus brought back from his meetings with monarchs in the Greek world: they were uniformly favorable to the kings, finding no fault with any, and recommending acceptance of the status quo everywhere.[165] Was this mere affability or gullibility? A different conclusion seems more reasonable. Gracchus set out to provide the very testimony that the senate desired and to justify a policy already determined: noninterference in the squabbles of the East. Gracchus' political prestige would assure acceptance of his message both at home and abroad. He did not go as an eastern expert.

A real student of Greece was A. Postumius Albinus, consul in 151. Schooled in the language and literature of that land, Postumius wrote poetry and a history in Greek and affected Hellenic mannerisms,

---

160. Livy, 37.7.11–14.

161. Broughton, *MRR* I:438. Obscure operations, perhaps partly military, against the Cammani in Cappadocia formed part of his activities: Polyb. 31.1.1; Walbank, *Commentary* III:463.

162. Broughton, *MRR* I:443.

163. Polyb. 31.15.11: διὸ τὸν Τεβέριον κατεστήσαντο . . . πάντων αὐτόπτην γεγονέναι.

164. That Gracchus was among the envoys to hear complaints against Philip in 185 is, at the very least, dubious. Polybius records a Ti. Claudius; 22.6.6. The name in Livy is Ti. Sempronius; 39.24.13, 39.33.1. Even if the latter be correct, it need not be Gracchus; cf. R. M. Geer, *TAPA* 69 (1938): 385–386, n. 10; Walbank, *Commentary* III:186.

165. Polyb. 30.27.1–4, 30.30.7–8, 30.31.19–20, 31.3.4, 31.33.1–4, 32.1.1–2; Diod. 31.17, 31.28. Polybius goes so far as to suggest that Gracchus was seduced by the warmth of his receptions: 30.27.1–2, 30.30.7–8.

drawing the scorn of Cato and the disdain of Polybius. The historian had a personal grudge: Postumius had presided as praetor over a senatorial hearing on restoring exiles (including Polybius) to Achaea in 155; his presentation of the motion—according to Polybius—helped insure its defeat. Nevertheless, Postumius was a learned man, a writer and orator, and a genuine philhellene.[166] To what extent did Rome make use of his talents in formulating Greek policy? Not much should be made of Postumius' putting the question on Achaean exiles in 155. He simply discharged the duty of presiding officer of the senate, as urban praetor with both consuls abroad. Polybius blames him for asking just for yea or nay rather than offering the alternative of postponement.[167] But postponement was the effect. The Achaeans received a negative answer at least five times between 166 and 154; the senate had long been firm on the matter, neither awaiting nor influenced by the opinion of Postumius.[168] An A. Postumius Albinus had served as legate under L. Paullus in 168 and 167, sent by his commander to arrange Perseus' surrender and later commissioned to keep the Macedonian king under guard.[169] And an A. Postumius took part in the Roman embassy to Asia in 154, effecting a peace between Prusias and Attalus.[170] Amalgamation of these individuals and identification with the philhellenic consul of 151 seems a logical inference— and universally assumed.[171] Yet the evidence of Polybius undermines that *communis opinio*. He places Postumius, his *bête noir*, in Greece in 146 when he allegedly feigned illness to avoid battle and then wrote the senate to announce victory as if he had himself engaged in the fighting. And, says Polybius, that was his first appearance in Hellenic parts.[172] Postumius stayed—or returned shortly—to participate in the decemviral commission after the Achaean war.[173] Despite all his Greek learning and admiration for things Hellenic, however, he had had no demonstrable history of eastern service.[174]

166. A favorable assessment by Cic. *Acad. Prior.* 2.137; *Brutus*, 81. For Polybius' judgment, not without bias, see 33.1.3–8, 39.1; cf. Walbank, *JRS* 52 (1962): 5.

167. Polyb. 33.1.3–8.

168. Polyb. 30.29.1, 30.30.1, 30.32.1–9, 32.3.14–17, 33.1.3–8, 33.3.1–2, 33.14.

169. Livy, 45.4.7, 45.28.11.

170. Polyb. 33.13.4–10.

171. E.g., Münzer, *RE* XXII:1,903–904, "Postumius," n. 31; Broughton, *MRR* I:430, 434, 450; Walbank, *Commentary* III:556, 726.

172. Polyb. 39.1.11–12: ὃς πρῶτος παρὼν ἐν τοῖς κατὰ τὴν Ἑλλάδα τόποις. It is less plausible to take this as "being first to enter Greece," for Polybius does not appear to be discussing Postumius in relation to others in this context.

173. Cic. *Ad Att.* 13.30.2, 13.32.3. Honors paid him by the Greeks: Cic. *Ad Att.* 13.32.3; *SEG*, I, 152.

174. Just who was the officer of 168/7 and the envoy of 154 must remain unknown. Hardly the senior and distinguished A. Postumius Luscinus, cos. 180. An otherwise unrecorded cousin of the consul of 151 remains possible.

Remaining examples of men with multiple assignments in the East are sparse indeed. Only one is known to have gone twice to the same area and with a similar purpose. The *patres* commissioned Cn. Cornelius Merula, among others, in 162 to reconcile the feuding Ptolemies and to establish Euergetes in Cyprus. The venture failed to achieve its aim, as Philometor dragged his feet, Merula accomplished nothing in Alexandria, and Euergetes fell afoul of a revolt in Cyrene.[175] Eight years later, Merula went again with instructions to restore Euergetes to Cyprus and to intimidate Philometor; the endeavor proved equally ineffectual.[176] So Merula may have gained some acquaintance with Egyptian affairs, but only enough to learn frustration. Further, Merula who, so far as the record shows, failed to reach curule office, could hardly have been a major voice in senatorial counsels.[177] The other Romans who appeared more than once on eastern embassies in this generation had unrelated duties: L. Aurelius Orestes, sent with a group to investigate conditions in various Hellenistic realms in 163, and head of a delegation to Corinth in 147 to cow the Achaeans into good behavior—from which he beat an ignominious retreat, bringing exaggerated complaints to Rome about his reception; and C. Fannius Strabo, an envoy to look into the doings of the Dalmatians in 158, whence he was rudely rebuffed, and member of an embassy to halt war between Pergamum and Bithynia in 154, which met with recalcitrance from Prusias.[178] These cases reinforce what we have observed again and again. Successful experience did not qualify, nor did fruitless missions disqualify, a man for reappointment.

So far the repeaters. Precious few of them exist anyway and they are quite adequately explained by the finite numbers of the Roman ruling class. All the more extraordinary then to compare them with the lists of those who held but one ambassadorial post and got no further assignments in the East: between three and four times their total! The repeaters were in a decided minority.

Quantity alone does not tell the tale. The roster of one-time

175. Polyb. 31.10.9–10, 31.17–19.
176. Polyb. 33.11.6–7, 39.7.6; Diod. 31.33; *OGIS*, 116 = *IdeDélos*, 1518.
177. One additional individual might fall in this category: L. Minucius Thermus was with Merula on the embassy of 154: Polyb. 33.11.6. He may be the Thermus recorded as an envoy in Alexandria in 145, for unknown purpose: Jos. *Contra Apionem*, 2.50; cf. Justin, 38.8.2–4. But absence of a *praenomen* leaves the identification uncertain. The bold conjectures of Otto, *AbhMünch* 11 (1934): 118–119, are unwarranted; so, rightly, Manni, *RivFilol* 28 (1950): 249–250, n. 2.
178. Orestes' mission of 163: Polyb. 31.2.9–14; the mission of 147: Polyb. 38.9.1–2, 38.9.6, 38.10.2; Paus. 7.14.1–3; cf. Livy, *Per.* 51; Strabo, 8.6.23 (C 381); Dio, 21.72.2; Cic. *Imp. Pomp.* 11; Florus, 1.32.3; Justin, 34.1.9. Orestes returned to Greece as legate of Mummius in 146; Paus. 7.16.1. But no evidence for the view that he was among the *decem legati*: Broughton, *MRR* I: 469, n. 5. Fannius' embassy in 158: Polyb. 32.9, 32.13.1–3; cf. Appian, *Ill.* 11; Zon. 9.25; the embassy in 154; Polyb. 33.7, 33.12.2–33.13.4.

ministers includes some of the most illustrious of names and some of the most celebrated of missions.

Q. Fabius Pictor, first of the Roman annalists, author of his city's history in Greek, went on solemn assignment to Delphi for divine comfort to his state in its darkest hour after Cannae.[179] The brash young M. Aemilius Lepidus, comeliest of the Romans, delivered terms to Philip V and engaged in a sharp interchange with the king that led to the Second Macedonian War. Lepidus proceeded to a brilliant career: twice consul, censor, *pontifex maximus*, and *princeps senatus*. He was probably the most distinguished man of his day, but never again returned to the East.[180] Two Cornelii Lentuli, brothers and ex-consuls, played key roles in the negotiating that followed the Second Macedonian War in 196: Cn. Lentulus in talks with Philip and the Aetolians, and L. Lentulus as Roman spokesman for the meeting with Antiochus at Lysimacheia.[181] The gruff M. Cato, most notorious of Greek-baiters, was once—and once only—posted to the East on a diplomatic assignment: to assist M. Fulvius Nobilior in reaching an accord with the Aetolians in 189.[182] C. Laelius, the intimate friend and companion of Africanus from boyhood, a lover of learning, the *novus homo* who enjoyed a full public career, also had but one eastern voyage: to look into Prusias' dealings with Carthage in 174.[183] M. Claudius Marcellus accomplished that most difficult of tasks, a reasonable settlement of the Aetolian civil strife in 173, an accomplishment that had eluded and frustrated previous Roman negotiators; yet his diplomatic talents were not utilized again in the East.[184]

Examples multiply. The irascible and obdurate C. Popillius Laenas conducted perhaps the best known of Roman missions to the East: the blunt directive to Antiochus IV to evacuate Egypt in 168, bullying the king with word and deed until he withdrew in humble retreat, the "day of Eleusis." Popillius returned to further laurels including a second consulship ten years later, but no other eastern appointments.[185] A similar reputation for arrogance attaches to C. Sul-

179. Livy, 22.57.5, 23.11.1–6; Plut. *Fab.* 18.6; Appian, *Hann.* 27.

180. The confrontation with Philip: Polyb. 16.34.1–7; Livy, 31.2.1–4, 31.18.1–7; Diod. 28.6. Similarly, Lepidus' senior colleagues on that critical embassy, C. Claudius Nero and P. Sempronius Tuditanus, received no other diplomatic appointments.

181. Cn. Lentulus: Polyb. 18.48.3–9; Livy, 33.35.2–12. L. Lentulus: Polyb. 18.49.2, 18.50.5–9, 18.52; Livy, 33.39, 33.41.1–2.

182. Cato, *ORF*, fr. 130 = Festus, 196, L: *M. Fulvio consuli legatus sum in Aetoliam, propterea quod ex Aetolia complures venerant: Aetolos pacem velle: de ea re oratores Romam profectos.*

183. Livy, 41.22.3; cf. 42.2.1–2. Laelius' learning: *Ad Herenn.* 4.19; Cic. *Top.* 78.

184. Livy, 42.5.10–12. Marcellus also addressed a meeting of the Achaean League on that trip: Livy, 42.5.1–3.

185. The "day of Eleusis": Polyb. 29.2, 29.27; Livy, 44.19.13–14, 45.10–12; Val.

picius Gallus. Learned in matters Greek and a specialist in astronomical calculations, Gallus nevertheless, it is reported, treated Hellenes with scorn and insolence on a mission to the Peloponnese in 164 and welcomed every kind of abusive insinuation against Eumenes when he reached Sardis on that same trip. It was Gallus' first and last diplomatic assignment to the East.[186] T. Quinctius Flamininus, son (or possibly nephew) of the great Flamininus, did not inherit his father's commitment and connections to Hellas. He received but a single nomination abroad, an embassy to escort Thracian hostages to Cotys in 167.[187] So much for the idea of enduring continuity in eastern associations. The erudite and distinguished T. Manlius Torquatus, a man skilled in civil law and pontifical rites and a major figure in the senate, also had just a single ambassadorial post, to reconcile the Ptolemies and support Euergetes' claims on Cyprus in 162, a trip that ended in failure.[188] P. Crassus Mucianus, eminent jurist and scholar, not only knew Greek but was fluent in five Hellenic dialects. His one known posting to the East, however, came late in his career, while consul in 131, to subdue the rebellious armies of Aristonicus.[189] Finally, the renowned embassy of Rome's most renowned personality, P. Scipio Aemilianus: a splendid tour and review of eastern lands ca. 140 that took Aemilianus to Alexandria, Cyprus, Syria, Pergamum, Rhodes, and elsewhere for visits with kings and republics and to lavish welcome at each stop. The glamor of Scipio Aemilianus, conqueror of Carthage, dazzled all. It is easy to forget that he made no official trips to the East before—or after.[190]

Max. 6.4.3; Cic. Phil. 8.23; Vell. Pat. 1.10.1–2; Justin, 34.3.1–4; Diod. 31.2; Zon. 9.25; Appian, Syr. 66; Plut. Mor. 202F. Popillius' personality: Livy, 45.10.8, 45.12.5. He had appeared at various Greek assemblies the year before, but this was as legate of the proconsul, not on a senatorial embassy: Polyb. 28.3–5; Livy, 43.17.

186. Gallus' behavior in the Peloponnese: Paus. 7.11.1–3; cf. Polyb. 31.1.6–7, 31.6.1; the behavior in Sardis: Polyb. 31.1.8, 31.6.1–5; cf. Diod. 31.7.2; his scholarly reputation: Cic. De Rep. 1.21, 1.23–24, 1.30; Pro Mur. 66; Brutus, 78; De Sen. 49; De Amicit. 21; De Off. 1.19; Val. Max. 8.11.1; Livy, 44.37.5–9; Pliny, NH, 2.53, 2.83; Quint. Inst. Orat. 1.10.47.

187. Livy, 45.42.11.

188. Polyb. 31.10.9–10, 31.17–19: ἀπέλυσε δὲ κατὰ τὸν αὐτὸν καιρὸν καὶ τοὺς περὶ Τίτον ἀπράκτους ὁ πρεσβύτερος Πτολεμαῖος; 31.20.1–2. On Torquatus' reputation, see Val. Max. 5.8.3

189. Crassus' command: Broughton, MRR I:500. His control of Greek dialects: Val. Max. 8.7.6; Quint. Inst. Orat. 11.2.50.

190. Evidence on the embassy in Broughton, MRR I:481. On the date, see Astin, CP 54 (1959): 221–227. He had, of course, been with his father as a youth in Macedonia and stayed for a time, engaged in hunting, after Pydna: Polyb. 31.29.3–7; Livy, 44.44.1–3; Plut. Aem. Paull. 22.2–4; Diod. 30.22; Cic. De Rep. 1.23; Vir. Ill. 58.1. When the Macedonians later requested his presence to help resolve internal disputes in 151, he turned them down: Polyb. 35.4.10–12.

Many more instances could be cited, a superfluous exercise at this point. The numbers of those who had just one ambassadorial assignment in Hellas far exceed the few who went twice and the mere handful who were there more often. The contrast leaps to our attention when once it is discerned. Preeminent figures carried Roman instructions and displayed Roman authority abroad—and failed to get recurrent appointments. Envoys who negotiated successful settlements stayed home thereafter, while some of those whose missions miscarried abysmally were sent out again. When second assignments did come, they were rarely to the same area and almost never of the same sort. It is clear as can be that Rome consciously avoided the creation of anything resembling a professional diplomatic service. With good reason did Cato mock the Roman embassy to Asia Minor in 149, a group of three inexperienced and inept men, one afflicted with gout, one with head injuries, and one with serious character deficiencies: an embassy that lacked legs, head, and heart.[191] The characterization would not, of course, fit many embassies; but it affords just commentary on the principle of selection. Three-quarters of a century after Roman legations began going to the East there was no body of trained personnel from which to choose.

Attitudes and Policy

Roman *nobiles* focused their attention on politics: on the accumulation of offices, the assertion of *dignitas*, the enhancement of influence within the senate, the acquisition of *gloria* in war. That is not to say they lacked principle, shunned ideology, or avoided positions on issues. But prominence and power were independent of diplomatic skills and unrelated to knowledge obtained in foreign lands. The *principes* of Rome never "specialized" in Hellenic affairs or developed a commitment to an eastern policy.[192]

Of course, occasional debate took place on appropriate public posture and behavior toward affairs of the East. Differences of opin-

---

191. Polyb. 36.14; Appian, *Mithr.* 6; Diod. 32.20; Livy, *Per.* 50; Plut. *Cato*, 9.

192. Even Flamininus, as we have seen, rose to consular rank before he had eastern "experience." And when he translated his foreign accomplishments into further political influence at home—in the successful backing of his brother to the consulship of 192—the success was due not his eastern "expertise" but to his military victories: Livy, 35.10.4–9: *Ceterum ante omnia certamen accendebant fratres candidatorum, duo clarissimi aetatis suae imperatores. Maior gloria Scipionis, et quo maior, eo propior invidiam; Quincti recentior, ut qui eo anno triumphasset . . . Pro fratre germano, non patrueli se petere aiebat, pro legato et participe administrandi belli; se terra fratrem mari rem gessisse. His obtinuit ut praeferretur candidato quem Africanus frater ducebat.*

ion divided Flamininus and the *decem legati* in 196 with regard to retention of forces in Greece.[193] When Philippus in 172/1 reported proudly on his subterfuge, which lulled Perseus into inactivity and allowed Rome to prepare war, he received approval from a majority of the *patres* but evoked displeasure from those who frowned on the *nova sapientia*.[194] Sharp verbal conflict, at least on the surface, arose on the issue of making war on Rhodes in 167, a clash between two tribunes and a praetor, and impassioned pleas before the *curia* on both sides of the question.[195] Rivalry in Egypt between the brothers Ptolemy Philometor and Ptolemy Euergetes found echoes in Rome, with some spokesmen for the one and some for the other.[196] And when young Alexander Balas appeared before the senate in 152 with requests for support, he got an encouraging decree sponsored by a senatorial majority but opposed, according to Polybius, by the μέτριοι in that body.[197]

Nonetheless, it is distortion and error to postulate party lines in the senate, divided on attitudes toward "eastern policy": a harsh and unfeeling group pitted against those with a more generous outlook, the devious diplomats striving to weaken and emasculate Hellenistic states against the principled *nobiles* who opposed duplicity and aggressiveness.[198] Individuals took stands on particular issues, *ad hoc* positions that generated debate and controversy. There were no enduring alignments that can identify groups wedded to consistent policies.

A few examples suffice to make the point. M'. Juventius Thalna, as praetor in 167, led the movement to declare war upon the helpless and probably innocent Rhodians; he had to be dragged down from the rostra by tribunes, lest he goad the populace into a rash belligerency.[199] Yet this same Juventius, in his tribunate of 170, had taken up the cause of Greeks lamenting the rapacity of Roman officers and initiated prosecution for their misconduct.[200] Among the chief offenders in this regard was the consul of 171, P. Licinius Crassus, who had

193. See above, n. 99.

194. Livy, 42.47.1–9: *haec ut summa ratione acta magna pars senatus approbabat, veteres et moris antiqui memores negabant se in ea legatione Romanas agnoscere artes . . . Haec seniores, quibus nova ac nimis callida minus placebat sapientia;* Diod. 30.7.1.

195. Polyb. 30.4.1–9; Livy, 45.20.4–45.21.8, 45.24.3, 45.25.1–4; Diod. 31.5; Cato, *ORF*, fr. 163–171.

196. Polyb. 31.10.1–4, 31.20.1–3, 33.11.5–7; Cato, *ORF*, fr. 177–181.

197. Polyb. 33.18.6–13.

198. So, Briscoe, *JRS* 54 (1964): 73–77; *Historia* 18 (1969): 60–70. Cf. Scullard, *Roman Politics*, 194–219, on the "violence and rapacity" of the "new, plebeian leaders" of the late 170s and 160s.

199. Polyb. 30.4.4–6; Livy, 45.21.1–8; Diod. 31.5.

200. Livy, 43.4.6, 43.8.2–10.

come under sharp censure for his brutality and pillaging during the Third Macedonian War.[201] Four years later, however, Crassus headed an embassy to Asia Minor assigned to bring peaceful reconciliation between Eumenes and the Galatians, and he behaved with restraint and tact.[202] Cn. Octavius, whose ferocity in Syria in 163 led to his assassination, had treated the king of Cappadocia in cordial and amicable fashion, following the line of Ti. Gracchus, allegedly of the mild, generous faction.[203] Even C. Popillius Laenas, who bullied Antiochus IV into submission, behaved with generosity in Egypt.[204] The men most conspicuous in urging war on Rhodes in 167, according to Livy, were those who had fought against Perseus as consuls, praetors, or legates. That particular common experience formed the connecting link, not any factional unity.[205] A host of missions went to Asia Minor between 156 and 154 to bring peace between Pergamum and Bithynia, with different personnel each time, a total of ten known individuals; the policy was clearly that of the senate, rather than of a particular group therein.[206]

The indefatigable M. Cato cannot be pinned down to a senatorial faction or a consistent foreign policy. His eloquent speech of 167 denouncing plans for war on the unoffending Rhodians is justly famous. So also, of course, is his repeated advocacy of war on another unoffending state: the city of Carthage.[207] When Prusias made appeal to Rome in 151/0 for remission of his indemnity payments to Attalus, Cato spoke up, doubtless in opposition. A year later, however, he castigated the embassy to Asia Minor chosen by a supporter of Attalus, thus showing equal scorn for the other protagonist.[208] Cato's positions

201. Livy, 43.4.5; *Per.* 43.

202. Polyb. 30.3.7–8; Livy, 45.34.10–14.

203. Polyb. 31.3, 31.8.4–8.

204. Polyb. 30.16.2

205. Livy, 45.25.2. One of the ex-consuls was P. Crassus, here in concord with M. Juventius Thalna on the issue of a Rhodian war. Yet Crassus had been among those assailed by Juventius in 170 for misbehavior in Greece: Livy, 43.4.5–6, 43.8.1–2.

206. Polyb. 32.16.1, 33.1.1–2, 33.7.3–4, 33.13.4. Among the envoys, for example, was Q. Fabius Maximus Aemilianus, son of Aemilius Paullus and brother of Scipio Aemilianus. Another was A. Postumius Albinus, sharply attacked by Polybius, and evidently no friend of the Scipios; cf. Polyb. 39.1. One may note too that the embassy that included Fabius took a hard line and encouraged a coalition against Prusias: Polyb. 33.12.5–9—despite the modern notion that the Scipionic faction represented a milder policy toward the East.

207. The Rhodian speech: *ORF*, fr. 163–171; the speeches against Carthage: *ORF*, fr. 191–195.

208. The speech in 151/0: *ORF*, fr. 190; cf. Scullard, *Roman Politics*, 271; the criticisms of the embassy in 149: Appian, *Mithr.* 6. Astin, *Cato the Censor*, 271–272, rightly denies that Cato followed any "balance of power policy." But the evidence is inadequate to conclude that he simply "judged the cases on their merits." Cato's sarcasm on the Bithynian embassy suggests a more aloof stance.

depended on the individual matter at hand, rather than pursuit of a party line on Hellas. Indeed, the very frequency of his asseverations on eastern affairs is worthy of mark. They occur through most of his career and in a variety of contexts: attacks on Glabrio, Fulvius Nobilior, and the Scipios at different times for mismanagement of booty and misbehavior in Greece; criticism of the Istrian campaign ca. 178; a caustic characterization of Eumenes; the Rhodian oration of 167; an argument in that same year that Macedonia be left free; participation in the debate on Aemilius Paullus' triumph after Pydna; accusation of Thermus regarding his embassy to restore Ptolemy Euergetes; speeches on the clash between Attalus and Prusias; and a famous quip on release of the Achaean exiles in 151.[209] Cato's outspoken views were heard often—and listened to.[210] Yet Cato had served in just one campaign in the East, as *tribunus militum* in 191 at Thermopylae, and on one diplomatic voyage, as *legatus* to the consul in 189. Neither experience in Hellas nor a systematic policy gave weight to his words. The sheer *auctoritas* of the man was decisive.

V

Conclusions can now be offered with some confidence. The Roman social and political order guaranteed the ascendancy of an elite: the land-owning, office-holding class whose members swayed the electorate, sat in the senate, and reached the upper magistracies. With the magistracies came command in war. The system assumed competence in those who attained political success. Generals in the Hellenic wars were men elected to high office and posted abroad by the lot. Legates and officers too came from leading families and served a turn as part of their political careers. The opportunity to achieve martial *gloria*, to lay claim to a triumph, to add distinction to the *gens* were perquisites belonging to the political class. They did not train themselves as area specialists nor receive advancement through familiarity with the East.

Specific credentials were unsought and unneeded. Indeed, they would go against the grain of an aristocratic society whose leaders asserted capacity in every aspect of public life. The commanders of armies in the East went to acquire personal laurels and wealth, not to carve out a realm of expertise. Tours of duty normally occupied only a single campaigning season. The senate seldom consented to

209. For the fragments of these orations, see *ORF*, fr. 66–67, 147–149, 161–172, 177–181, 187–190. The remark on Eumenes in Plut. *Cato*, 8.7–8.

210. Cf. Plut. *Cato*, 9.2–3—on the Achaean exiles. Astin, *Cato the Censor*, 267–288, is properly cautious about any discernible foreign policy on the part of Cato. But he minimizes too much Cato's influence on individual decisions.

prorogation. The advantages of continuity were overwhelmed by the clamor of aspirants to fame. When prorogations came, they more often reflected political circumstances than the claims of experience. Successes abroad heightened prestige at home but also fostered envy and stimulated rivalry. The men who led forces in one Hellenic conflict almost never did so again. A few returned to the East on ambassadorial service but to territories and on missions for which their previous stints gave no special competence. Several of the most successful generals came home to face political opposition that obstructed their careers; others turned to pursuits remote from any concern for the East. The ex-officers formed no corporation of Hellenic lobbyists.

The same aversion to professionalism holds in the sphere of diplomacy. A multitude of missions crossed the Adriatic in the second century. Given the limited numbers of the ruling elite, some duplication was inescapable. Hence, it is the rarity, not the existence, of that duplication which carries significance. Rome spread out the personnel of her legations to an extent so remarkable that chance seems excluded. The vast majority of envoys had but one diplomatic journey to Hellas. And the repeaters usually went on assignments unconnected with one another. Flamininus stands out as exceptional, if not unique. Indeed, it was precisely the power accumulated by Flamininus through his experience abroad that helped fix the *patres'* determination not to encourage another such career. The plural commissions for men like Ap. Claudius, A. Postumius Luscus, and Ti. Gracchus derived more from their *auctoritas* in Rome than their knowledge of Greece. Several of Rome's most prominent figures went once to the East and not again. Some *nobiles* negotiated with skill and got no reappointment; others showed little talent or success but got posted abroad once more. The actions of envoys overseas seldom dictated the decisions of senators in Rome. The *patres* could and did shelve the messages of their legates and diassociate themselves from the behavior of individual representatives. Debates in the *curia* were guided by men of prestige and influence, whether or not they had ever visited the capitals of the East.

The Roman senate, proud of its corporate identity and jealous of individual accomplishment, deterred the emergence of a corps of experts. They would not have their hands tied by dependence on a narrow circle with specialized knowledge and particular commitments.[211] On the occasions when decisions were delegated to persons of relevant competence, like Flamininus in the war with Nabis or three former envoys to the Peloponnese in the Achaea-Sparta dispute, the del-

---

211. The problem is recognized by Brizzi, *I sistemi informativi*, 258–267. But he misconceives its solution as an increase in the number of "experts."

egation reflected senatorial indifference or inattention. Concern with Greece was intermittent and often of secondary importance. Individuals could differ on *ad hoc* issues, but no group formed to advocate policy over the long term.

The absence of eastern factions or eastern experts carries significant implications. Roman attitudes toward Hellas lacked continuity or systematic formulation. The large numbers of men who served the *res publica* in Greek lands over three-quarters of a century did so—with rare exceptions—only for a short time and with limited exposure. Fragmentary impressions prevailed. Even Romans who imbibed Hellenic culture did not translate this into state policy on Hellas. Senatorial aristocrats had little incentive to identify themselves with eastern issues or develop coherent positions around which a party could coalesce. Their concentration centered on politics in Rome. The East offered opportunities for individuals to attain distinction in war, receive honors from allies, and display authority while abroad. But they returned home without enduring obligations or a psychological engagement. The political system saw to that. Eastern matters were marginal to the affairs of state, arising to prominence only briefly and occasionally, not a demand that captured the continuous attention of the *res publica* or its leadership.

Chapter 7

Philhellenism: Culture and Policy

The collective attitudes and ideas of a nation evade sharp definition. Even the most diligent inquiry can hope only to sketch the outlines of common beliefs when glimpsed through the actions and expressions of a select few. In the case of middle Republican Rome a major obstacle blocks investigation. The remains of Latin writers from the third and second centuries, with very few exceptions, exist in mere fragments. Deeds rather than words must supply the basis for any reconstruction of Roman attitudes toward Hellas. From the Roman vantage-point, however, that is the most appropriate kind of evidence. The Greeks claim precedence in teaching, the Romans in action.[1]

Philhellenism is a fact. Numerous Roman aristocrats of the third and second centuries B.C. are certifiable philhellenes—if by that is meant that they spoke and wrote Greek, that they admired Greek culture and came under its influence, that they emulated it or envied it. So much is indisputable.[2] A different set of questions concerns us here. To what extent did admiration for things Hellenic translate itself into national policy toward Hellas? Did the lure of Greek culture play

1. See, e.g., Quint. *Inst. Orat.* 12.2.30: *quantum enim Graeci praeceptis valent, tantum Romani, quod est maius, exemplis.*

2. A useful collection of evidence in N. Petrochilos, *Roman Attitudes to the Greeks* (Athens, 1974), *passim*; especially 23–33, 141–162. Some value still resides in the verbose discussion of A. Besancon, *Les adversaires de l'hellénisme à Rome pendant la période republicaine* (Paris-Lausanne, 1910), 1–182. See also T. J. Haarhoff, *The Stranger at the Gate* (Oxford, 1948), 169–215; Balsdon, *Romans and Aliens* (Chapel Hill, 1979), 30–52. The work of A. Wardman, *Rome's Debt to Greece* (London, 1976), has little to offer on this period.

a role in drawing Romans across the Adriatic? Did increasing acquaintance with Greeks, their language, literature, and civilization, provide a lever whereby Romans could establish their superiority and control over the Hellenic world? In short, what connection held between cultural dialogue and political interaction?

The Allure of Hellenism

Exposure to Hellenic influence came early in Rome's history. How far back and how deep were the initial impressions cannot be determined. Legend has it that the Sibylline Books were introduced into Rome at the time of Tarquinius Superbus. Too early, no doubt. Yet several notices attest to consultation of those texts in the fifth and fourth centuries.[3] Romans avidly embraced the association of their origins with the tales of Aeneas and Troy, tales of Greek derivation. When? We cannot tell. No later than the fourth century surely, but the legends may have reached Rome through the Etruscans or through traditions in Latium rather than through direct contact with Greeks.[4] Direct contact, however, came with certainty in the later fourth century, as Rome encountered Alexander the Molossian and extended her influence into Campania. Roman consuls begin to turn up with Greek *cognomina*: Philo, Sophus, Philippus, Philus. The infiltration of Hellenic culture had commenced.[5]

Roman aristocrats—or some of them at least—undertook to familiarize themselves with the Greek language. Initial results were less than fully satisfactory. L. Postumius Megellus carried senatorial demands for reparations to the Tarentines in 282, speaking to them in their own tongue. He got only jeers for his faulty Greek, then outright insult in so degrading a fashion that, as the story goes, the incident provoked war.[6] Rome would take steps to assure that similar

3. Dion. Hal. 4.62, 6.17, 10.2; Zon. 7.11.1; Livy, 3.10.7, 4.25.3, 5.13.5, 5.50.2; Pliny, *NH*, 13.88.

4. A recent discussion, with bibliography, by Cornell, *PCPS* 201 (1975): 11–16. But he goes too far in pushing the arrival of the Aeneas legend in Italy down to the third century: *LCM* 2 (1977): 77–83.

5. There is likely to be some truth to the tales of Roman interest in Pythagoreanism in the fourth century. Note, for example, the "Pythagorean *carmen*" composed by Ap. Claudius Caecus, censor in 312, admired by Panaetius and possibly even written in Greek: Cic. *Tusc. Disp.* 4.4. On Rome and Pythagoreanism, see G. Garbarino, *Roma e la filosofia greca dalle origini alla fine del II secolo a.C.* (Turin, 1973), II: 221–244; H .D. Jocelyn, *BRL* 59 (1977): 324, 328–330. Whether an actual statue of Pythagoras was erected in the city during the Samnite wars remains questionable: Pliny, *NH*, 34.26; Plut. *Numa*, 8.10.

6. Dion. Hal. 19.5; Appian, *Samn.* 7.2.

embarrassment was not to occur again. No problem in communication arose during Roman negotiations with Pyrrhus. Nor in dealings with Greek cities across the Straits of Otranto during the First Illyrian War. After that conflict, legates visited the Aetolian and Achaean Leagues to explain terms of the treaty and entered into parleys at Athens and Corinth, even receiving admittance to the Isthmian Games.[7] That they spoke Greek is possible but improbable. More likely, they took along an interpreter; or simply delivered their messages in Latin and let Greek translators do the work. Romans would not subject themselves to ridicule again.[8]

Their interest and taste for Hellenic culture nevertheless increased during the later third century, demonstrably so. Livius Andronicus translated Homer for Roman intellectuals and taught in both Greek and Latin.[9] Hellenic art began to be prized. It came to Rome as war booty, to be sure, but its presence among the spoils implies at least that the victors valued it. Statues and paintings were carted to Rome and paraded among captured objects as early as the 270s, after the fall of Tarentum.[10] More celebrated or notorious were the spoils of Syracuse. M. Marcellus took the city in 211, a major turning point in the Hannibalic war, and carried off, among other things, silver and bronze work, a collection of statuary and a host of paintings.[11] Items taken from private homes went to decorate the dwellings of individual Romans; those from public buildings became state property. A genuine interest in Greek art manifests itself here, not just desire for a lavish triumphal display.[12] Two years later Q. Fabius Maximus captured Tarentum and had its treasures at his mercy. Sources draw a famous contrast with Marcellus. Fabius, so it was said, scorned to remove the colossal statues of the gods: "let us leave the angry gods to

7. Polyb. 2.12.4–8.

8. For Roman insistence on Latin in official parlance, see below pp. 267–268. A Greek freedman, Cn. Publilius Menander, accompanied Roman delegates as interpreter on a mission to his native land: Cic. *Pro Balbo*, 28; *Dig*. 49.15.5.3. The sources provide no date or context for the embassy; are they perhaps to be associated with the visits following the First Illyrian War?

9. Suet. *De Gramm*. 1.2. Cf. also the *elogium* of L. Scipio, consul 259, which shows the influence of Hellenic poetry or a Hellenic education: *ILLRP*, I, no. 310; bibliography and most recent discussion by M. Martina, *Quaderni di storia* 12 (1980): 149–170. And one might notice as well the consul of 244 and 241, A. Manlius Torquatus, who took on the second cognomen "Atticus."

10. Florus, 1.13.27.

11. Livy, 25.40.1–3, 26.21.6–8, 34.4.4; Cic. *Verr*. 2.1.55, 2.4.120–123; Plut. *Marc*. 21.1–3.

12. Polyb. 9.10.13: Ῥωμαῖοι δὲ μετακομίσαντες τὰ προειρημένα ταῖς μὲν ἰδιωτικαῖς κατασκευαῖς τοὺς αὑτῶν ἐκόσμησαν βίους, ταῖς δὲ δημοσίαις τὰ κοινὰ τῆς πόλεως.

the Tarentines."[13] But he was not over-scrupulous on that score. One enormous statue of Hercules did find its way to Rome and another one, of Jupiter attributed to Lysippus, stayed in Tarentum only because Fabius was unable to remove it! Other statues and pictures Fabius brought home without qualms, of a richness to rival the booty of Syracuse.[14]

Greek gods were, of course, well known in Rome and had been for a long time. Apollo had his cult in the city since 431.[15] A temple to Demeter had been dedicated as early as 493. The Hellenic ceremonial was practiced there with Greek priestesses in charge, from Naples or Velia, presumably after the establishment of *foedera* with those cities in the late fourth and early third centuries.[16] A famine in 292 prompted a Roman delegation to Epidaurus to fetch the serpent of Aesculapius and to establish the cult of the god.[17] Delphic Apollo was quite familiar to the Romans by the later third century. They presented a golden bowl at Delphi in 222 in gratitude to Apollo for a victory over the Gauls. The disaster at Cannae sent Roman officials scurrying to the Sibylline Books and provoked the dispatch of a commission to Delphi whose responses provided guidelines for worship and propitiation of the gods. When victory and salvation came, the Romans plucked rich gifts from the Carthaginian spoils and delivered them to Delphi in 205. Q. Fabius Pictor headed the commission after Cannae. He knew his Greek and he knew it well. Pictor came back with instructions from Delphi which he had evidently translated from Greek verse into Latin.[18]

Fabius Pictor it was, of course, who first composed the annals of

13. Livy, 27.16.8; Plut. *Fab.* 22.5; *Marc.* 21.3–4.

14. Statue of Hercules: Plut. *Fab.* 22.6; statue of Jupiter: Pliny, *NH*, 34.40; other statues and pictures: Livy, 27.16.7: *signa tabulae, prope ut Syracusarum ornamenta aequaverint.*

15. Livy, 4.25.3, 4.29.7; cf. J. Gagé, *L'Apollon romain* (Paris, 1955), 19–113.

16. Dion. Hal. 6.17.2; Cic. *Pro Balbo*, 55; Pliny, *NH*, 35.154. Cf. Cic. *Verr.* 2.4.115. On the intermingling of Greek and Roman religious institutions and practices generally, see the survey of K. Latte, *Römische Religionsgeschichte* (Munich, 1960), 213–263. And on cultural contacts in the fourth century, particularly with Italian Greeks, see Hoffman, *Rom und die griechische Welt*, 68–103.

17. Val. Max. 1.8.2; *Vir. Ill.* 22.1; cf. Livy, 10.47.6–7.

18. The golden bowl in 222: Plut. *Marc.* 8.6. The mission of Fabius Pictor: Livy, 22.57.4–5, 23.11.1–6; Plut. *Fab.* 18.3; Appian, *Hann.* 27. Carthaginian spoils in 205: Livy, 28.45.12. The Sibylline Books, reinforced by advice from Delphi, also guided Romans in obtaining the sacred stone of Magna Mater from Pessinus in 205: Livy, 29.10.4–29.11.8; other sources in Broughton, *MRR* I:304. More dubious is a supposed trip to Delphi a century earlier, during the Samnite wars; Pliny, *NH*, 34.26. On Fabius' life and family, see, most recently, B. W. Frier, *Libri Annales Pontificum Maximorum: The Origins of the Annalistic Tradition* (Rome, 1979), 227–253; G. F. Verbrugghe, *Miscellanea Manni* (1980), VI:2160–2164.

his nation's history—in Greek.[19] What prompted that pioneering enterprise? A desire to explain Roman policies and institutions to the Greeks, it is customarily said.[20] But which Greeks? Roman contact with overseas Greeks had been distant, sporadic, and brief prior to the beginning of the second century. Whether Pictor wrote after the turn of the century is indeterminable, but nothing suggests that Romans felt a need to explain themselves to Hellenic audiences even then. As usual, deeds rather than words would carry the message. Certainly no apologia would be directed toward the Greeks of southern Italy or Sicily. And how many Greeks would become avid readers of a Roman history, especially since some of it was already available in Greek writers like Timaeus?[21] Fabius wrote in Greek simply because there was no tradition of Latin historiography. The models, the genre, the techniques were all Greek. It was a natural idea and swiftly found imitators: L. Cincius Alimentus, a close contemporary of Fabius', also wrote Roman annals in Greek, as did C. Acilius and A. Postumius Albinus a half-century or so later.[22] Did Roman policy need to be justified to Greeks again and again? The readership surely was to be a Roman readership, at least in the main, a cultivated intelligentsia

19. Dion. Hal. 1.6.2; Cic. *De Div.* 1.43: *Graeci annales*. The ingenious but misguided attempt by H. B. Mattingly, *LCM* 1 (1976): 3–7, to deny most of the ancient testimony and argue that Fabius wrote in Latin was refuted in advance by publication of a document that gives secure identification: G. Manganaro, *PP* 29 (1974): 394–397. See further N. Horsfall, *LCM* 1 (1976): 18; Badian, *LCM* 1 (1976): 97–98.

20. So, e.g., Gelzer, *Kleine Schriften* (Wiesbaden, 1964), III:51, 102, 107–109; Badian, in T. A. Dorey, *Latin Historians* (London, 1966), 2–6.

21. Fabius did, of course, challenge the pro-Carthaginian interpretations of the First Punic War, as retailed by Philinus: Polyb. 1.14–15; perhaps also the analyses of the Second Punic War delivered by Greek writers like Chaereas, Sosylus, and Silenus: Polyb. 3.20.5; Nepos, *Hann.* 13.3. For many, this explains the genesis of Fabius' work; e.g., K. Hanell, *EntrFondHardt* 4 (1956): 163–169; Alföldi, *Early Rome and the Latins*, 169–172; Gabba, *EntrFondHardt* 13 (1967): 142. A more moderate statement in Momigliano, *RendAccadLinc* 15 (1960): 316–319 = *Terzo contributo alla storia degli studi classici e del mondo antico* (Rome, 1966), I:55–68. But the theory is quite inadequate. Pictor began his history with the origins of Rome and dwelt at length upon the city's earliest period—hardly designed as an answer to Greek apologists for Carthage.

22. Cincius: Münzer and Cichorius, *RE* III:2556–2557, "Cincius," n. 5; Acilius: Livy, *Per.* 53; Cic. *De Off.* 3.115; Dion. Hal. 3.67; Postumius: Cic. *Brutus*, 81; *Acad. Prior.* 2.137; Polyb. 39.1; Gellius, 11.8. The debt to Greek historiography is stressed by Momigliano, *RendAccadLinc* 15 (1960): 310–320. Timpe expands on the theme in *ANRW* I:2 (1972), 928–948—with a full and valuable bibliographic survey. See further Verbrugghe, *Miscellanea Manni* (1980), VI:2165–2167. Latin *annales*, ascribed to Fabius Pictor, also circulated; Quint. *Inst. Orat.* 1.6.12; Gellius, 5.4.3; cf. Cic. *De Orat.* 2.51, 2.53. Nothing suggests, however, that this was a Latin edition prepared by the author of the *Graeci annales* himself. More likely, it represents a later translation or even a separate work by a descendant; cf. Frier, *Libri Annales*, 246–252, with bibliography.

familiar with the Hellenic language already in the time of Fabius Pictor.[23]

The allure of Hellenic civilization attracted many in the aristocracy of Rome. The great Scipio Africanus succumbed. At Syracuse in 205, while commander of the Republic's army, he was seen sauntering about the gymnasium, clad in Greek garb and sandals, indulging in Greek forms of exercise and reading Greek books.[24] Tales were told even of the redoubtable M. Cato: he sat at the feet of a Pythagorean philosopher while at Tarentum in 209, or he received instruction in Greek letters from Ennius, whom he had brought to Rome in 203.[25] Whatever truth lies in these particular stories is of secondary importance. They reflect a cultural scene of the late third century wherein Hellenism already exercised a strong pull upon some of the more sophisticated among Rome's leadership.[26]

A flood tide came in the second century.[27] Ennius' arrival in Rome, under Cato's auspices, heralded an era of the commingling of the cultures and the critical impact of Hellenism on Latin literature. It also signified the increasing attachment of Roman senators to Greek learning. Cato had effected the poet's migration. Ennius subsequently enjoyed the patronage of M. Fulvius Nobilior, who included him in his entourage during the Aetolian war of 189. The poet had access to other aristocratic circles as well, as a friend of P. Scipio Africanus, of Ser. Sulpicius Galba, and of P. Scipio Nasica.[28]

23. For doubts that Fabius directed his work toward Greeks, cf., e.g., F. Bömer, *SO* 29 (1952): 42–43; *Historia* 2 (1953 4): 201–203. Timpe, *ANRW* I:2 (1972), 928–969, argues, with good reason, that Fabius had no single purpose or unified conception in composing his history. A variety of motives is canvassed also by Frier, *Libri Annales*, 280–284—though it is difficult to adopt the suggestion that Pictor wrote in Greek as reaction to inaccuracies found in Greek historians.

24. Livy, 29.19.12: *cum pallio crepidisque inambulare in gymnasio*; Val. Max. 3.6.1. Notice Africanus' letter to Philip V a few years later, doubtless in Greek: Polyb. 10.9.3.

25. The Pythagorean Nearchus: Cic. *De Sen.* 41; Plut. *Cato*, 2.3. Ennius and Cato: *Vir. Ill.* 47.1. The authenticity of the stories is properly in doubt; see Garbarino, *Roma e la filosofia greca* II: 326–329; Astin, *Cato the Censor*, 7, 16, 160, with bibliography.

26. Cf. Gellius, 1.24.2, who professes to quote Naevius and may reflect the prevalence of Greek in third-century Rome. Another attestation of Roman philhellenism in this period in Plut. *Marc.* 1.2.

27. Cic. *De Rep.* 2.34: *influxit enim non tenuis quidam e Graecia rivulus in hanc urbem, sed abundantissimus amnis illarum disciplinarum et artium*—not with explicit reference to the second century.

28. Cato's patronage of Ennius: Nepos, *Cato*, 1.4—denied by Badian, *EntrFond-Hardt* 17 (1972): 155–163, on the grounds of Cicero's silence, an indecisive argument. J. S. Ruebel, *LCM* 2 (1977): 155–157, stresses the silence of Plutarch, which is equally indecisive. Cicero, in any case, refers to Ennius as Cato's *familiaris*: *De Sen.* 10. He reports Ennius' lavish praise of the Roman: *Pro Arch.* 22. The association with Fulvius

Nor was this mere conspicuous cultural consumption. Notable Romans in increasing numbers possessed a fluency in Greek and used it to good purpose. Flamininus, of course, stands out, "a veritable Greek in sound and language."[29] He conversed readily with Hellenes, engaged in subtle negotiations, and traded banter, with never a call for an interpreter.[30] And when he dedicated offerings at Delphi he provided them with inscriptions in Greek verse, probably of his own composition.[31] A feeble constitution prevented the son of Scipio Africanus from emulating his father's military and political career, but he had some talent in letters and produced a historical work in Greek.[32] L. Aemilius Paullus, victor at Pydna, addressed the humbled Perseus in his own language, then switched to Latin in turning to his staff, completely at ease in both tongues.[33] And Paullus' officer corps in Macedonia was by no means innocent of Hellenism. The praetor Cn. Octavius, commander of the fleet and captor of Perseus, apparently served as translator when the *senatus consultum* on terms of peace was read out to the Macedonians.[34] Of all Roman *nobiles* in the mid-second century C. Sulpicius Gallus was the most accomplished Greek scholar: a scientist, writer, and orator whose explanation of the lunar eclipse in 168 cheered panicky Roman soldiers in Macedonia.[35]

Students of Hellenic culture multiplied. Ti. Gracchus the elder delivered a polished and eloquent oration in Greek to the Rhodians in the 160s.[36] His son received thorough training in Greek studies from boyhood, whether through the example of his father or, as we are told, through the insistence of his mother, the daughter of Africanus. The philosopher Blossius of Cumae and the rhetorician Diophanes of

Nobilior: Cic. *Tusc. Disp.* 1.3; *Brutus,* 79; with Africanus: Cic. *Pro Arch.* 22; Livy, 38.56.4; with Galba: Cic. *Acad. Prior.* 2.51; with Nasica: Cic. *De Orat.* 2.276. On these and other connections, see Badian, *op. cit.,* 168–195. Martina, *Quaderni di filologia classica* 2 (1979): 15–74, goes too far in tying Ennius' fortunes almost exclusively to the patronage of Fulvius Nobilior. For literature on Ennius generally, see H. D. Jocelyn, *ANRW* I:2 (1972), 987–1026.

29. Plut. *Flam.* 5.5: φωνήν τε καὶ διάλεκτων ῞Ελλησι.

30. See, e.g., Polyb. 18.1, 18.4–9, 18.36–37; Plut. *Flam.* 6.1–3.

31. Plut. *Flam.* 12.6–7. A bronze statue of Flamininus stood in Rome, its inscription in Greek: Plut. *Flam.* 1.1.

32. Cic. *Brutus,* 77; cf. *De Sen.* 35; *De Off.* 1.121. A harsher verdict in Vell. Pat. 1.10.3.

33. Livy, 45.8.1–7; cf: Val. Max. 5.1.8.

34. Livy, 45.29.3.

35. Cic. *Brutus,* 78: *maxime omnium nobilium Graecis litteris studuit; De Rep.* 1.21, 1.23–24, 1.30; *Pro Mur.* 66; *De Sen.* 49; *De Off.* 1.19; Val. Max. 8.11.1; Livy, 44.37.5–9; Pliny, *NH,* 2.53, 2.83; Quint. *Inst. Orat.* 1.10.47.

36. Cic. *Brutus,* 79.

Mitylene stayed with the younger Ti. Gracchus to the end.[37] In similar fashion Aemilius Paullus took pains to assure the Hellenic education of his sons. He had them surrounded from an early age by Greek teachers, philosophers, rhetoricians, even sculptors, painters, and animal trainers, with Paullus himself attending the sessions as often as possible. After Pydna he grasped the occasion to elevate their learning. The distribution of booty included an invitation to his sons to take for their own use the well-endowed library of Perseus, an invitation they avidly availed themselves of. Paullus even called upon Athens to supply a philosopher to teach his sons and a painter to decorate his triumph. The Athenians shrewdly produced a man who could do double duty, Metrodorus. How much impact he had cannot be guessed. But another Greek transported to Italy after Pydna did indeed become the close friend and informal mentor of Scipio Aemilianus: Polybius himself.[38] Cato too, of all people, can be cited in this connection. Everyone recalls the tale that Cato took his son's education out of the hands of a talented Greek slave and schoolmaster, Chilon: Cato would see to his intellectual upbringing personally. The most interesting feature of that story, however, is easily overlooked: the fact that a Greek teacher was attached to the Catonian household in the first place![39] Hellenic education had taken a secure place in the homes of the Roman upper classes.

A similar conclusion derives from another well-known episode. Cato was instrumental in having Carneades and the Athenian philosophic embassy of 155 hurried out of Rome back to their native land. He scored the cynicism and lack of principle inherent in the philosophers' public lectures. And he expressed concern lest Rome's impressionable youth be led astray from laws and institutions by the tricks of Greek rhetoric.[40] Again what attracts attention here—or should attract attention—is not so much Cato's strictures as the impressions made on the impressionable youth. Our sources make the point with unmistakable clarity: Carneades' speeches wove a magic spell, enticing the city's young men in droves and delighting other Romans also, as they encouraged their sons' fascination for Hellenic culture. There may be embellishment and exaggeration here. But some basis for the

37. Cic. *Brutus*, 104: *fuit Gracchus diligentia Corneliae matris a puero doctus et Graecis litteris eruditus*; cf. Plut. *Ti. Gr.* 8.4–5, 20.3–4; Cic. *De Amicit.* 37; Val. Max. 4.7.1; Strabo, 13.2.3 (C 617). On Cornelia's own cultivation of Greeks and intellectuals, see Plut. *C. Gr.* 19.2.

38. The early education of Paullus' sons: Plut. *Aem. Paull.* 6.4–5. Cf. Cic. *De Rep.* 1.36. The library of Perseus: Plut. *Aem. Paull.* 28.6. Metrodorus: Pliny, *NH*, 35.135. Polybius and Aemilianus: Polyb. 31.23.3–31.25.1; cf. Vell. Pat. 1.13.3.

39. Plut. *Cato*, 20.3–5. Noted by Petrochilos, *Roman Attitudes*, 167.

40. Plut. *Cato*, 22.4–5; Pliny, *NH*, 7.112; Cic. *De Rep.* 3.9; Quint. *Inst. Orat.* 12.1.35.

tale must exist. Romans flocked to the lectures of Carneades, relished the philosophy and the rhetoric—and, evidently, had no problem understanding the Greek.[41]

Familiarity with Hellenic language, literature, and philosophy among Rome's intelligentsia in the later second century is beyond question.[42] Cato himself, no stranger to things Hellenic even at an early stage, became, we are told, a zealous student of Greek literature in his older years.[43] The Stoic philosopher Panaetius found welcome in numerous homes of the aristocracy, from men who were part patrons and part disciples: Scipio Aemilianus in particular, but other luminaries as well, including C. Laelius, Q. Mucius Scaevola, C. Fannius, Q. Aelius Tubero, and P. Rutilius Rufus.[44] Near the end of the century, the distinguished orator L. Crassus sought out all the eminent sages of the philosophical schools in Athens for study and interchange.[45] Despite Cato's censures and his *Origines*, some Romans, like Rutilius Rufus, even continued to compose historical works in Greek.[46] Skill in the use of the Greek tongue reached stunning levels

41. See, especially, Cic. *De Orat.* 2.155; Plut. *Cato*, 22.2–3. Other references to the embassy in Cic. *Acad. Prior.* 2.137; Tusc. *Disp.* 4.5; *Ad Att.* 12.23.2; Gellius, 17.21.48. The point is missed by Astin, *Cato the Censor*, 174–178, in an otherwise most sensible discussion of Cato's attitude. Observe also the lectures and seminars offered to eager audiences by the Pergamene grammarian Crates in the first half of the second century—an envoy of Attalus who stayed in Rome while his broken leg healed: Suet. *De Gramm.* 2.1; cf. Garbarino, *Roma e la filosofia greca* II: 356–362.

42. Cf. Cic. *Pro Arch.* 5: *erat Italia tum plena Graecarum artium ac disciplinarum.*

43. Cic. *De Sen.* 3: *litteris Graecis, quarum constat eum perstudiosum fuisse in senectute; ibid.* 26; *Acad. Prior.* 2.5; Val. Max. 8.7.1; Nepos, *Cato*, 3.2; Quint. *Inst. Orat.* 12.11.23; Plut. *Cato*, 2.4. Astin, *Cato the Censor*, 159–168, casts doubt on the tradition. It is certainly misleading as it stands: Cato was familiar with Greeks and Greek learning well before his old age. But nothing in Astin's argument disproves the idea that the Censor took a more avid interest in Hellenic literature late in life.

44. See, e.g., Cic. *De Fin.* 4.23; *Brutus*, 101, 114; *De Off.* 1.90, 3.10; *De Rep.* 1.34; *Pro Mur.* 66; *De Orat.* 1.75; *Tusc. Disp.* 1.81; *Ad Att.* 9.12.2; *Acad. Prior.* 2.5; Vell. Pat. 1.13.3. Astin, *Scipio Aemilianus* (Oxford, 1967), 296–299, is skeptical about how much philosophic influence Panaetius actually exercised on Roman *nobiles.* More recently, K. Abel, *Antike und Abendland* 17 (1971): 119–143, reaffirms Panaetius' impact upon the "Scipionic circle." Fullest discussion, with restrained and cautious conclusions, by Garbarino, *Roma e la filosofia greca* I: 14–36; II: 390–445. Other philosophers too had access to the Roman nobility. Note the philosophic correspondence between Clitomachus the Academic and L. Marcius Censorinus, consul in 149; Cic. *Acad. Prior.* 2.102. And cf. Cic. *De Orat.* 2.154; *De Rep.* 3.5. Jocelyn, *BRL*, 59 (1977), 323–366, unduly minimizes Roman familiarity with Greek philosophy.

45. Cic. *De Orat.* 1.45–47; cf. 1.82, 1.93, 2.365. And he was not alone; cf. Cic. *De Orat.* 1.57, 3.68, 3.78; *Brutus*, 94, 131.

46. Athenaeus, 4.168e. Other Romans who wrote history in Greek: Cn. Aufidius (Cic. *Tusc. Disp.* 5.112); L. Lucullus (Cic. *Ad Att.* 1.19.10; Plut. *Luc.* 1.5); Cicero (Cic. *Ad Att.* 1.20.6).

of refinement. P. Crassus Mucianus, consul in 131, mastered five Hellenic dialects and administered justice in Asia by responding to astonished Greeks each in his own subtle shade of the language.[47] Q. Catulus' command of Greek impressed the Greeks themselves, who acknowledged the fineness and elegant grace of his style.[48] L. Crassus spoke Greek so well that one imagined he knew no other tongue.[49] By the end of the second century Roman intellectuals were regularly bilingual.[50]

Material objects from the Hellenic world flowed west as well during that century. Victorious generals and armies hauled off the art treasures of the East. Flamininus himself had no scruples on this score, carting a splendid statue of Zeus from Macedonia for placement on the Capitoline.[51] M. Fulvius Nobilior, consul in 189, stripped the sacred shrines of Ambracia of all bronze and marble statuary and all paintings for transferral to Rome, leaving the Ambraciotes nothing but bare walls and door posts to which to pray.[52] Ancient writers recounted in loving detail the even more luxurious items of furniture and adornments that graced the triumph of Cn. Manlius Vulso in 187.[53] C. Lucretius Gallus, a praetorian commander during the Third Macedonian War, looted temples in Greece and used the captured paintings to decorate the shrine of Aesculapius at Antium.[54] Q. Metellus Macedonicus showed enough taste to take what were reputed to be equestrian statues fashioned by Lysippus on commission from Alexander the Great.[55] And, of course, from Corinth after the Achaean war came a stream of artistic masterpieces. Corinth's conqueror, L. Mummius, could boast that he had adorned much of Italy with these treasures.[56]

47. Quint. *Inst. Orat.* 11.2.50; Val. Max. 8.7.6

48. Cic. *De Orat.* 2.28: *etiam Graeci ipsi solent suae linguae subtilitatem elegantiamque concedere.*

49. Cic. *De Orat.* 2.2: *Graece sic loqui, nullam ut nosse aliam linguam videretur.*

50. The development of Romans' command of Greek is traced by P. Boyancé, *REL* 34 (1956): 111–131.

51. Cic. *Verr.* 2.4.129.

52. Livy, 38.9.13, 38.43.2–5, 39.5.15. Nobilior's spoils included statues of the Muses, which he dedicated at Rome in the new temple of Hercules of the Muses—further testimony to his cultural interests: Pliny, *NH*, 35.66; *Pan. Lat.* 9.7. Martina, *Dial-Arch* (1981): 49–68, overemphasizes the political motivation.

53. Livy, 39.6.7–39.7.4; Pliny, *NH*, 34.14.

54. Livy, 43.4.7, 43.7.10.

55. Vell. Pat. 1.11.3–4; cf. Pliny, *NH*, 34.31.

56. Strabo, 8.6.23 (C 381); Cic. *De Off.* 2.76; Vell. Pat. 1.13.4; Pliny, *NH*, 35.24; Livy, *Per.* 52; Paus. 7.16.8. By contrast, Scipio Aemilianus, after the capture of Carthage in 146, restored to the Sicilians much of the artistic work that had been seized from them by Carthage—or so, at least, Cicero would have it: *Verr.* 2.2.86–87, 2.4.72–93;

Other elements of Hellenism migrated to Rome also, together with returning commanders of the Republic's forces. L. Scipio, like his brother before him, took a liking to the Greek cloak and sandals, apparel in which he was clad even on the statue erected in his honor on the Capitoline.[57] The lavish games of M. Fulvius Nobilior in 186 to celebrate victory in the Aetolian war for the first time introduced athletic contests into a Roman festival.[58] Nobilior also brought numerous actors from Greece for his games, as did L. Scipio for his in the same year, or so it is reported.[59] After the Third Macedonian War, L. Aemilius Paullus organized a great festival at Amphipolis, having gathered athletes, actors, and entertainers of all sorts, to demonstrate that a Roman could give Greek games better than any Greek.[60] L. Anicius, victor over Genthius the Illyrian, went a step further. He took the performance to Rome, producing a display of dancers, flute players, and boxers in a hodge-podge variety show enlivened by fisticuffs.[61]

The Stigma of Hellenism

The fascination for things Greek is plain and powerful. Cultural fervor, however, stands in ambiguous relationship to Rome's political and military penetration of the East. To assume a connection is to skirt central difficulties. The appeal of Hellenism had its reverse counterpart: an aversion to and contempt for Greeks. A strange paradox, and yet inescapable. The complexities of Roman attitudes baffle modern efforts to translate them into policy.

Cato exemplifies the paradox in extreme form. His acquaintance with the intellectual products of Hellas has already been noted. Yet his image as anti-Hellenist dominates the evidence. Posturing may account for some of it. Cato had a fondness for sweeping statements. He denounced all Greek doctors, heaped scorn on philosophers, and ad-

Ps.-Ascon. 187, Stangl. A valuable survey of all the evidence on Roman transport of Greek art treasures to Italy during the Republic, conveniently organized and presented, by M. Pape, *Griechische Kunstwerke aus Kriegsbeute und ihre öffentliche Anstellung in Rom* (Hamburg, 1975), *passim*—who, however, stresses the political and economic value of these objects, giving little credence to Roman appreciation of their artistic quality. A more balanced view in H. Jucker, *Vom Verhältnis der Römer zu bildenden Kunst der Griechen* (Frankfurt, 1950), 46–86.

57. Cic. *Pro Rab. Post.* 27; Val. Max. 3.6.2.

58. Livy, 39.22.2.

59. Livy, 39.22.2. 39.22.10. The notice on L. Scipio comes only from Valerius Antias.

60. Livy, 45.32.8–11.

61. Polyb. 30.22. A further step in the presentation of dancing entertainers came in L. Mummius' triumph of 145; Tac. *Ann.* 14.21.

vised his son that the infection of Greek learning could be the ruin of Rome. The venom of these assertions hardly reflects representative Roman thinking. Cato affected fury that Greeks reckoned Romans as ignorant barbarians, he branded the Hellenic race as vile and ungovernable, and he maintained that Greek physicians had pledged themselves to poison all Romans with their medicine.[62] Even if it be posturing, however, that itself discloses an important fact: the presence of anti-Greek prejudice in Rome.

In that regard, Cato was by no means alone. Plautus' plays catered to the prejudice. The comic dramatist regularly used the term *pergraecari* as synonymous with loose living and dissipation.[63] When the antics of slaves in comedy become especially outrageous, Plautus reminds his Roman audience: "that sort of thing is permitted in Athens."[64] Philosophizing too comes in for some barbs from Plautus, an activity preeminently associated with Greeks.[65] Attacks on false philosophers who rely on verbal trickery rather than genuine understanding can be found in the lines of the younger dramatist Pacuvius. And a little later still L. Afranius adumbrates what would become standard contrast between Roman practical wisdom and Greek theoretical wisdom.[66] The contempt for vacuous Hellenic theorizing appears in the tale of the pompous professor Phormio, who had never seen a battlefield but ventured to lecture Hannibal on military strategy![67] Greek stereotypes as conceived by the Romans and reflected in late Republican or imperial writers must go back to this period or earlier: the notions of Greek loquaciousness, untrustworthiness, irresponsibility, excessive luxury, and lack of courage.[68] It comes as no

62. Plut. *Cato*, 23.1–3; Pliny, *NH*, 7.113, 29.13–14; for discussion of these passages, see Astin, *Cato the Censor*, 169–174. Add also Gellius, 18.7.3.

63. Plautus, *Most.* 20–24: *nunc, dum tibi lubet licetque, pota, perde rem, / corrumpe erilem adulescentem optumum; / dies noctesque bibite, pergraecamini, / amicas emite liberate, pascite / parasitos, obsonate pollucibiliter*; also 64–65, 958–960; *Bacch.* 742–743, 812–813; *Truc.* 86–87; *Poen.* 600–603; cf. Macrob. *Sat.* 3.14.9.

64. Plaut. *Stich.* 446–448: *licet haec Athenis*.

65. Plaut. *Capt.* 284; *Pseud.* 687, 974; *Curc.* 288–295. Note also an oft-quoted line from Ennius, in which a Greek frowns on excessive *philosophari*; Cic. *Tusc. Disp.* 2.1; *De Rep.* 1.30; *De Orat.* 2.156; Gellius, 5.15.9, 5.16.5.

66. Gellius, 13.8.1–5.

67. Cic. *De Orat.* 2.75–76.

68. See Petrochilos, *Roman Attitudes*, 35–53; Balsdon, *Romans and Aliens*, 30–40—although most of the evidence there cited comes from later periods. Note, however, Livy, 8.22.8, with reference to the year 325 and the Greeks in Palaeopolis: *a Graecis, gente lingua magis strenua quam factis*. Similarly, the pointed contrast reportedly made by Cato, that Greeks speak with their tongues, Romans from the heart: Plut. *Cato*, 12.5: τὰ ῥήματα τοῖς μὲν Ἕλλησιν ἀπὸ χειλέων, τοῖς δὲ Ῥωμαίοις ἀπὸ καρδίας φέρεσθαι. And observe Livy, 42.47.7, from Polybius: reference to Roman senators in 172 who spoke of *calliditas Graeca*.

surprise that when the Aetolian Phaeneas objected to Roman demands in 191 as not being in accord with Greek custom, M'. Acilius Glabrio snapped back with a sarcastic retort about "playing the Greek." [69]

Random examples from the second century further illustrate Roman antipathy for Hellenic practices and character—or what they took to be Hellenic practices and character. Cato deplored the custom of nude bathing, adopted by the Romans from the Greeks, and then transformed for the worse into mixed bathing, in which version the Romans then taught the Greeks! [70] The building of a theater authorized by the censors of 154 was halted in its tracks through a senatorial decree moved by the eminent ex-consul P. Scipio Nasica on the grounds that Romans should not become addicted to Greek pleasures. [71] Later, Cicero represents even the philhellene L. Crassus as sharply critical of the Greeks' *ineptia*, a fault they possess in abundance. [72] And he quotes a bitter jibe of his own grandfather: "the better one gets to know Greek, the worse scoundrel one becomes." [73] Are these merely isolated and idiosyncratic attitudes? Polybius proves the contrary. He notes a growing corruption of morals among Roman youth, an excess of sexual affairs, luxury, and extravagance, all stemming from their encounters with Greek licentiousness. [74] Quite plainly, Polybius did not derive that analysis from Greek informants. It arose from interchange with Roman aristocrats.

The attitudes could also translate themselves into action. In 186 the senate took firm steps to control and curtail the burgeoning Bacchanalian cult in Italy, branding its members as subversive conspirators. [75] Five years later, a bizarre episode prompted the *patres* to authorize the burning of volumes freshly discovered but allegedly deposited by Numa Pompilius. Some were composed in Greek, purportedly delivering Pythagorean doctrines, and denounced by the praetor as undermining Roman religion. [76] Within a decade, in 173,

69. Polyb. 20.10.6–7: ἔτι γὰρ ὑμεῖς ἑλληνοκοπεῖτε; cf. Livy, 36.28.4–5.

70. Plut. *Cato*, 20.5–6.

71. Appian, *BC*, 1.28—who misplaces the event chronologically; see Gabba, *Appiani Bellorum Civilium Liber Primus* (2nd ed., Florence, 1967), 96–97. Further evidence: Livy, *Per.* 48; Val. Max. 2.4.2; Vell. Pat. 1.15.3; Oros. 4.21.4.

72. Cic. *De Orat.* 2.17–18; cf. 1.221: *ineptum et Graeculum; Tusc. Disp.* 1.86.

73. Cic. *De Orat.* 2.265: *ut quisque optime Graece sciret, ita esse nequissimum.*

74. Polyb. 31.25.4; cf. Diod. 31.26.7, 37.3.1–6. Recall also Polybius' famous contrast between Greek faithlessness and Roman incorruptibility: Polyb. 6.56.13–15.

75. Livy, 39.8–18; *ILLRP*, II, no. 511. Recent discussions, with reference to earlier literature, by P. V. Cova, *Athenaeum* 52 (1974): 82–109; J. A. North, *PCPS* 25 (1979): 85–103.

76. Livy, 40.29.3–14; Val. Max. 1.1.12; Pliny, *NH*, 13.84–88; Plut. *Numa*, 22.2–5;

the government expelled two Epicurean philosophers from Rome, for reasons unknown but on the pretext, it seems, of corrupting the young or teaching atheistic doctrine.[77] A *senatus consultum* followed in 161 banning philosophers and rhetoricians from Rome.[78] That striking sequence of decisions furnishes the background for Cato's insistence upon the immediate shipment of Carneades and his colleagues back to Athens in 155. Whether any or all of these moves possessed a specifically anti-Greek character remains subject for speculation. The evidence contains too many deficiencies. But the series of measures attests at least to an official stand against cults and philosophies that might undermine traditional Roman values—cults and philosophies that in every case had a strong, if not exclusive, Hellenic component.

A still more striking fact needs to be accentuated. Despite the prevalence of Greek learning among the senatorial aristocracy, it was never quite respectable to be identified as a philhellene.

Some Romans may have chafed under the suggestion that they were uncultivated and ignorant of the finer things in life. Greeks, of course, reckoned the westerner as among the *barbaroi*, an attitude playfully reflected by Plautus.[79] Cato returned the charge and characterized Hellenes as thoroughly wicked and unruly. M. Antonius professed lack of concern; he found Greek snobbishness more amusing than annoying.[80] Yet it would be worse still to emulate the Greeks. Poets and artists might do so with impunity, but a Roman senator ran the risk of censure by friends and colleagues.[81]

A. Postumius Albinus, consul in 151, offers a suitable instance. A learned man and devoted to Hellenic culture, he composed poetry and a history in Greek. The preface to his history included an apology to readers who might find his command of the language less than perfect. That preface drew the withering disdain of M. Cato: if Postumius had to apologize for his Greek, why use it in the first place? Polybius, who retailed the story, added that men like Postumius, with

---

Aug. *CD*, 7.34. The matter was apparently much discussed by historians and scholars in the late Republic: Piso, Antias, Hemina, Tuditanus, Varro. See also Garbarino, *Roma e la filosofia greca* II:244–258.

77. Athenaeus, 12.547a; Aelian, *VH*, 9.12; Garbarino, *Roma e la filosofia greca* II:372–378.

78. Suet. *Rhet.* 1.2; Gellius, 15.11.1.

79. Plautus, *Asin.* 11; *Capt.* 492, 884; *Miles*, 211; *Most.* 828.

80. Cato: Pliny, *NH*, 29.14; Antonius: Cic. *De Orat.* 2.77.

81. So, e.g., Fabius Pictor, ancestor of the historian, took up painting in the late fourth century but did not find favor with his peers: Val. Max. 8.14.6. Public esteem for Roman painters was still wanting at the end of the Republic, according to Cic. *Tusc. Disp.* 1.4. Pliny, *NH*, 35.19–20, wrongly takes the example of Pictor as evidence for an early appreciation of art by the Roman public.

excessive attachment to Greek culture and language, gave Hellenism a bad name among older and more distinguished Romans.[82] A generation later, T. Albucius presented an even more inviting target. He trained himself in all things Greek, indeed nearly was a Greek or liked to be regarded as such.[83] He came in for some heavy sarcasm from contemporaries, especially Q. Mucius Scaevola, whose mockery of Albucius' affectations was recorded with glee by the poet Lucilius.[84]

The foppishness of Albucius carried Hellenic dandyism rather too far. In the negative reaction he stirred up, however, Roman attitudes come more clearly to light. Other *nobiles* with an interest in Hellenic culture denied it or played it down as much as possible.[85] Identification with philhellenism could be a liability for a Roman senator. The rival orators of the late second century, L. Crassus and M. Antonius, found the label most uncomfortable. Crassus, despite his considerable intellectual attainments, affected contempt for Greek learning; Antonius sought to give the impression that he was entirely untutored by formal study. Both expected to gain in reputation, the one by belittling Greeks, the other by pretending he knew nothing of them.[86] As Antonius reportedly said, to converse openly with Greeks can only damage one's influence among fellow-citizens; hence he recommended eavesdropping![87] Marius made a point of insisting that he studied no Greek literature: why bother with the learning of a subject people? He evidently knew Greek, but, says Plutarch, he would not use it for anything serious.[88] L. Lucullus actually composed a his-

82. Polyb. 39.1.1–10; esp. 39.1.3: ἐπιθυμήσας δ᾽ εὐθέως ἐκ παίδων τῆς Ἑλληνικῆς ἀγωγῆς καὶ διαλέκτου πολὺς μὲν ἦν ἐν τούτοις καὶ κατακορής, ὥστε δι᾽ ἐκεῖνον καὶ τὴν αἵρεσιν τὴν Ἑλληνικὴν προσκόψαι τοῖς πρεσβυτέροις καὶ τοῖς ἀξιολογωτάτοις τῶν Ῥωμαίων. Cato's contemptuous remarks are recorded also in Plut. *Cato*, 12.5; Gellius, 11.8; Macrob. *Sat*. 1, praef. 13–16. The apology itself was probably a literary convention; cf. Walbank, *Commentary* III:727. On Postumius' learning, see Cic. *Brutus*, 81; *Acad. Prior*. 2.137. Note further Cato's attacks on a certain M. Caelius who, among other things, *Graecos versus agit*: Macrob. *Sat*. 3.14.9 = *ORF*, fr. 115.

83. Cic. *Brutus*, 131: *doctus etiam Graecis T. Albucius vel potius plane Graecus; De Fin*. 1.8: *qui se plane Graecum dici velit*.

84. Lucilius, 84–94, Marx = Cic. *De Orat*. 3.171; *Orat*. 149; *De Fin*. 1.9. See also Cic. *Tusc. Disp*. 5.108, and Cicero's own verdict; *De Prov. Cons*. 15: *Graecum hominem ac levem*.

85. Cic. *Acad. Prior*. 2.5: *reliqui qui etiam si haec non improbent tamen earum rerum disputationem principibus civitatis non ita decoram putent*.

86. Cic. *De Orat*. 2.4: *atque ita se uterque graviorem fore, si alter contemnere, alter ne nosse quidem Graecos videretur*. Cf. Cic. *De Orat*. 1.82, 1.102, 1.105. Crassus did, however, have praise for certain skilled and eloquent Greeks: Cic. *De Orat*. 1.62.

87. Cic. *De Orat*. 2.153: *si palam audire eos non auderes, ne minueres apud tuos cives auctoritatem tuam, subauscultando tamen excipere voces eorum et procul quid narrarent attendere*.

88. Plut. *Mar*. 2.2: λέγεται δὲ μήτε γράμματα μαθεῖν Ἑλληνικὰ μήτε γλώττῃ πρὸς μηδὲν Ἑλληνίδι χρῆσθαι τῶν σπουδῆς ἐχομένων, ὡς γελοῖον γράμματα μανθάνειν ὧν οἱ διδάσκαλοι δουλεύοειν ἑτέροις; Sallust, *Iug*. 85.32.

tory in Greek but made certain to sprinkle it with Latin barbarisms, thereby to underscore the fact that a true Roman was the author.[89]

The prejudice persisted well into the late Republic. Cicero felt it. L. Metellus rebuked him sharply for addressing the Syracusan council in Greek.[90] Hence he had to walk a fine line in the fourth *Verrine*. The orator lambasted Verres mercilessly for plundering the art treasures of Sicily. At the same time, however, Cicero needed to avoid the impression that he regarded Greek art as anything worth troubling over. A neat trick—which he managed with some deft side-stepping. He was unctuously condescending to the Greeks: Romans know that artifacts, statues, and paintings are of negligible importance, but poor benighted Greeks place a high value on them; thus, the wickedness of Verres in depriving them of their fancies.[91] And when discussing certain individual statues the orator put up a front of not recalling the names of the sculptors—with a stooge placed in the audience to prompt him.[92] Indeed, he could be downright contemptuous of Romans who laid a claim to Hellenic culture while lacking the elements of civility: they were *Graeculi*.[93] Not that he could escape the same charge himself. *Inimici* fastened the label on Cicero as well.[94] Political aspirants did well to avoid the stigma of aesthete or intellectual.[95]

The foregoing evidence sheds a different light on that notorious Roman cultural boor, L. Mummius. His sack of Corinth gave rise to stories remembered long afterwards: Mummius epitomized the worst sort of philistinism. His soldiers rolled dice on priceless Corinthian paintings. He had pictures and sculpture packed up indiscriminately for shipment to Italy, a man so oblivious to value that he instructed those responsible to replace any works lost by supplying new ones.

89. Cic. *Ad Att.* 1.19.10.

90. Cic. *Verr.* 2.4.147—Cicero had no reply to the point of the criticism.

91. Cic. *Verr.* 2.4.132: *deinde hic ornatus, haec opera atque artificia, signa, tabulae pictae, Graecos homines nimio opere delectant; itaque ex illorum querimoniis intellegere possumus haec illis acerbissima videri quae forsitan nobis levia et contemnanda esse videantur;* 2.4.134: *etenim mirandum in modum Graeci rebus istis quas nos contemnimus delectantur;* cf. 2.4.124.

92. Cic. *Verr.* 2.4.4–5. Further on Cicero's disclaimers of interest in Greek art: *Verr.* 2.4.13, 2.4.94. In a more candid moment and a less public pronouncement, Cicero admitted to his brother his considerable debt to Hellenic culture: *Ad Q. Frat.* 1.1.28; cf. *Ad Att.* 1.15.1; *Pro Flacco*, 9. He was himself an avid collector of Greek art later—for which he also suffered criticism: *Ad Att.* 1.8.2; cf. 1.1.5, 1.3.2, 1.4.3, 1.6.1, 1.9.2, 1.10.3, 1.11.3. A thorough gathering of Ciceronian comments on Greek matters, both negative and positive, by M. A. Trouard, *Cicero's Attitude towards the Greeks* (Chicago, 1942), passim; especially, 3–32, 60–71; more briefly and pointedly, H. Guite, *Greece and Rome* 31 (1962): 142–159.

93. Cic. *Verr.* 2.4.127; *Pro Sest.* 110; *De Orat.* 1.22.1; *De Fin.* 1.9; *De Off.* 1.11.

94. Cf. Dio, 46.18.1; Plut. *Cic.* 5.2.

95. This is not simply a matter of Roman "inferiority complex" in the face of Greek culture, as argued by M. Dubuisson, *LEC* 49 (1981): 27–45.

He could not tell a statue of Zeus from one of Poseidon. And he was content to auction off Corinthian masterpieces with no idea of their worth, withdrawing one particular painting only when an especially handsome offer came: if it could fetch that much money perhaps it was worth keeping. Mummius qualified as a prize oaf.[96] Yet other evidence presents a wholly different and much more favorable image. Polybius gives ungrudging praise: Mummius' generosity adorned shrines at Delphi, Olympia, and elsewhere in Greece. Epigraphic testimony bears out the statement. Mummius won repute also for personal austerity. He decorated Italy with eastern treasures, but none of the spoils found their way into his own home. Indeed he showed enough taste and respect to leave consecrated statues intact, removing as booty only the unconsecrated ones.[97] Was Mummius then an uncultivated philistine or not? Which characterization by the sources is credible and which tainted by bias and distortion? The question itself perhaps misleads. A different approach is possible which takes both versions into account. Mummius knew enough about the value of Hellenic art objects (or had knowledgeable people tell him) to arrange for auctions and to ship precious items to Italy for public display. He could advertise his magnanimity by dedications in Greek shrines and his prestige by bringing the spoils back home. But it would not do to profess a personal interest, let alone an expertise, in Hellenic art. Better to affect indifference or even ignorance. Strabo most closely reflects the image Mummius endeavored to project: generosity rather than taste for art prompted his distribution of Greek treasures in Italy.[98] The victorious commander could receive adulation in Greece but would not be thought a philhellene at Rome.

This tension runs throughout the evidence. Appreciation for Greek culture moved alongside professed scorn for it and disclaimers of interest in it. Individual Romans might savor philosophy, collect statues and paintings, and master the Greek tongue. But most shrank from a close identification with Hellenism. The incongruities of attitude predominate. And they scuttle schemes that relate them to the collective posture of the polity.

96. Soldiers playing dice: Strabo, 8.6.23 (C381); instructions for replacing paintings: Vell. Pat. 1.13.4; Zeus and Poseidon: Dio Chrys. 37.42; the auction: Pliny, *NH*, 35.24; cf. Paus. 7.16.8.

97. Mummius' generosity: Polyb. 39.6.1–2; Paus. 5.10.5, 5.24.4; for the epigraphical testimony, see above p. 171; personal austerity: Cic. *De Off.* 2.76; *Verr.* 2.1.55; Livy, *Per.* 52; consecrated statues: Cic. *Verr.* 2.4.4.

98. Strabo, 8.6.23 (C381): μεγαλόφρων γὰρ ὢν μᾶλλον ἢ φιλότεχνος ὁ Μόμμιος, ὥς φασι, μετεδίδου ῥᾳδίως τοῖς δεηθεῖσι. Philipp, *AthMitt* 94 (1979): 204, misinterprets Mummius' displays in Rome and Italy as the *novus homo*'s attempt to show his cultivation and his sensitivity to Hellenic civilization.

Personal Predilection and Public Policy

Clearing of the path leads now to the central point. Romans drew a firm line between private predilection and official demeanor. They did not confuse philhellenism (or antihellenism for that matter) with state policy. The distinction is vital—and demonstrable.

When L. Aemilius Paullus announced the terms of the *senatus consultum* at Amphipolis after conclusion of the Third Macedonian War, he delivered the address in Latin, although his Greek was fully up to the occasion. He then had the message repeated in Greek translation—but not by himself. He could converse freely with Perseus in Greek, but in official capacity as Roman proconsul and *imperator* only Latin was appropriate.[99] It was a matter of principle. Rome's *auctoritas* demanded use of Latin. The allure and charm of Hellenic culture could not be allowed to demean the weight and authority of Roman power.[100] Cato, of course, adhered to that principle. At Athens in 191, he spoke to a gathering of Athenians in his native tongue, disdaining to use Greek, a language he already controlled.[101] And more than a century later, when L. Metellus rebuked Cicero for speaking Greek in Sicily, it was not so much the orator's philhellenism that came under attack as the unworthy deed of a formal address in Greek by a Roman senator at an official gathering of Greeks.[102]

Similarly, Roman practice forbade an address to the senate in any language but Latin. Greeks who wished a hearing would have to find an interpreter.[103] So, the distinguished senator and historian C. Acilius performed that function for Athens' philosophic embassy in 155.[104] It was not until the Sullan era that Rome for the first time permitted a Greek, the rhetorician Molo, to use his native tongue, without translator, at a senatorial meeting.[105] And, even in subsequent years, any member of the senate had the right to demand an

---

99. Livy, 45.29.3. Notice also that Paullus had the base of his statue at Delphi inscribed with commendation of his victory as *imperator*—in Latin: *Syll.*[3] 652a = *ILLRP*, I, no. 323.

100. Val. Max. 2.2.2: *ne Graecis umquam nisi latine responsa darent . . . indignum esse existimantes inlecebris et suavitati litterarum imperii pondus et auctoritatem donari.*

101. So, at least, Plutarch affirms: *Cato*, 12.4—perhaps on Cato's own authority; cf. Astin, *Cato the Censor*, 160.

102. Cic. *Verr.* 2.4.147: *ait indignum facinus esse quod ego in senatu Graeco verba fecissem; quod quidem apud Graecos Graece locutus essem, id ferri nullo modo posse.*

103. Val. Max. 2.2.2; cf. John Lydus, *Mag.* 3.68.

104. Gellius, 6.14.9; Plut. *Cato*, 22.4; cf. Macrob. *Sat.* 1.5.16.

105. Val. Max. 2.2.3. The evidence is not refuted by Plut. *Pyrrh.* 18.2–4. Cineas' speech on Pyrrhus' behalf no doubt had the services of a translator.

interpreter when a representative from abroad spoke in the *curia*.[106] The *patres* may have understood their Greek perfectly well, but its use would sully the dignity of the House.

The lesson seems clear. Romans kept private admiration for (or aversion to) Hellenic culture quite separate and distinct from the affairs of state. And one can go further. The divide stood not only between individual inclination and collective policy, but between sentiment and behavior. Even for individuals themselves feelings toward Hellenism stayed on a plane entirely apart from dealings with Hellenes.

T. Flamininus, the philhellene *par excellence*, never permitted any cultural attachments to interfere with decisions based on national goals or self-interest. His own prorogation took precedence over both Hellenic aims and Roman policies during the Second Macedonian War. Flamininus manipulated the Achaeans, faced down the Aetolians, intrigued in Boeotia, reshaped the constitution of Thessaly, overrode allied wishes in the war on Nabis, issued threats at Demetrias, and gave peremptory orders to Greek commanders and communities. Not a hint exists anywhere that his familiarity with Greek language and civilization put the slightest restraint upon his behavior.[107] M. Fulvius Nobilior may have shown interest in the life of the mind by having Ennius accompany him in the Aetolian war; that did not prevent him from assaulting the helpless state of Ambracia and creating widespread devastation, slaughter, and rapine.[108] The eminently cultivated L. Aemilius Paullus made respectful visits to Greek shrines everywhere, moved about the land as an awe-struck tourist, sought out philosophers, and urged his sons to avail themselves of the library of Perseus. Yet the same Paullus at Delphi, when he saw marble columns erected for statues of Perseus, commanded the Delphians to place his own statues upon the pedestals.[109] The conqueror's *dignitas* overrode any sensitivity to Greek feelings. And the interests of state rendered "philhellenism" irrelevant: Paullus issued the commands which resulted in the sacking of seventy Epirote towns and the sale of 150 thousand men into slavery.[110] Nor is there much sign that the Hellenic education given to his son Scipio Aemilianus and the Greek

106. Cic. *De Fin.* 5.89; *De Div.* 2.131.

107. Flamininus and prorogation: see above pp. 215–217. Achaea: Polyb. 18.13.8; Livy, 32.21.7, 32.21.33–37; cf. 41.24.13–14. Aetolia: Polyb. 18.37–38; Livy, 33.12–13. Boeotia: Polyb. 18.43; Livy, 33.27.5–33.29.1. Thessaly: Livy, 34.51.4–6. The war on Nabis: Livy, 34.26.4–8. Demetrias: Livy, 35.31.13–16. Ordering of Greek commanders and communities: Livy, 35.39.1–4, 35.39.8, 35.50.3, 35.50.10, 36.31.8–10.

108. Livy, 38.9.9–13, 38.43.

109. Polyb. 30.10.2; Livy, 45.27.7; Plut. *Aem. Paull.* 28.2.

110. Polyb. 30.15; Livy, 45.34.1–6; Plut. *Aem. Paull.* 29.1–3.

scholars and literary figures with whom he associated affected Aemilianus' public behavior. Certainly his actions in Spain and his punishment of deserters after the fall of Carthage disclose a powerful strain of vindictiveness and ferocity.[111]

Further examples nail down the point. The noted scientist and most erudite of Romans in Hellenic matters, C. Sulpicius Gallus, browbeat Spartans and other Peloponnesians with tactless severity while arbitrating a dispute in 164, and, according to Polybius, encouraged shameful and libelous accusations against Eumenes of Pergamum out of personal pique.[112] Cn. Octavius spoke fluent Greek, rendered the senate's decrees into that language after Pydna, received proxeny honors from the Achaeans and statues voted him by Elis and Echinus, and made dedications at Delos. Yet the same Cn. Octavius, as leader of an embassy to Syria in 163, destroyed Seleucid ships and crippled the elephants, rousing the fury of the Greeks to such a pitch as to provoke his own assassination.[113] P. Crassus Mucianus spoke five Hellenic dialects and won the admiration of all who pleaded at his court in Asia Minor. But Mucianus also ordered the stripping and beating of a Greek official who—on good grounds—disobeyed his instructions. Pleas and reasoning alike were ignored. Mucianus insisted upon a display of his own *dignitas* by making an example of the unwitting miscreant.[114] One last illustration. L. Licinius Crassus, an authentic philhellene, who used his quaestorship in Asia ca. 109 to search out philosophers, rhetoricians, and scholars, had his boorish side as well. Crassus arrived in Athens two days late for the celebration of the Mysteries. Junior officer though he was, he railed at Athenian officials for declining to repeat the Mysteries for his personal benefit![115] The petulance of the Roman magistrate took precedence over civility to the Greeks.

Compartmentalization was complete. The most cultivated Romans, however well-versed in Hellenic literature, philosophy, and

111. Spain: Appian, *Iber.* 94–98; Val. Max. 2.7.1; Florus, 1.34.12–17; deserters: Livy, *Per.* 51; Val. Max. 2.7.13—on the example of Paullus: Val. Max. 2.7.14; Livy, *Per.* 51.

112. The arbitration: Paus. 7.11.1–3; Eumenes and Gallus: Polyb. 31.6.1–5.

113. Honors for Octavius: *SEG*, XVI, 255 = *ISE*, no. 42; *Syll.*³ 650; *SEG*, XXV, 642 = *ISE*, no. 93. Dedication at Delos: *IdeDélos*, 1429A, lines 11–12. The mission to Syria and the assassination: Polyb. 31.2.7–14, 31.11.1; Zon. 9.25; Appian, *Syr.* 46; Cic. *Phil.* 9.4. On Octavius' philhellenism, see now E. Lanzillotta, *Sesta miscellanea greca e romana* (1978), 233–247—who brushes past the Syrian affair without comment.

114. Gellius, 1.13.9–13.

115. Cic. *De Orat.* 3.75. Cf. the demeanor of L. Gellius Publicola who, as proconsul in the East in 93, summoned the heads of the philosophical schools to him in Athens and declared his readiness to help resolve their intellectual disputes: Cic. *De Leg.* 1.53.

art, insulated those interests from performance as servants of the Republic. They might evince appreciation for the cultural traditions of the Hellenes—but that appreciation did not dictate their treatment of the Hellenes themselves. The intellectual attainments of Roman senators bore little relevance to their activities as public officials abroad.

V

We are in a position now to offer some answers to the questions posed earlier. Cultural attractions and state policies rode very different tracks. Inquiry turns up apparent tension and paradox everywhere in the evidence on Roman attitudes. Ambivalence, it is often called, or a complex range of dispositions. But perhaps not so ambivalent, and the paradox may lie more in the eye of the inquirer than in the attitudes of the Romans. Our inconsistencies were not theirs; the tensions we discern they tolerated quite unperturbed.

Romans distinguished between Hellenism and Hellenes. Their acquaintance with the literature, mythology, and art of the Greeks began no later than the fourth century, expanded through contact with Campania and southern Italy, increased markedly by the end of the third century, and reached high levels of sophistication in the second century. Control of the Greek language, exposure to the doctrines of the philosophic schools, and insistence upon a Hellenic education for their sons became characteristic in many circles of the Roman aristocracy. Purloined art objects from the East were set up in Roman temples and public sites. Greek artists, intellectuals, even athletes, actors, and entertainers found their way to Italy in increasing numbers. At the same time, however, there was disparagement of Greek character, ridicule of Greek loquaciousness and philosophizing, even occasional state action against Greek cults, philosophers, and rhetoricians. Roman intellectuals absorbed and benefited from Hellenic culture, but felt free to belittle and defame its representatives. They saw no contradiction.

Indeed most of them shrank from too close an association with Hellenism. The flaunting of one's cultural and intellectual attainments could provoke sharp reproof or derision. Attachment to Greek learning and fascination for Greek art might be a political and social liability for a Roman aristocrat. Some professed ignorance even when they were knowledgeable, indifference even when they had expertise. They preferred to soft-pedal such predilections and avoid the blemish of a philhellenic reputation.

It should follow that the Hellenic pretensions of Romans had no relation to public policy toward the Hellenes. The available evidence confirms it. Roman practice demanded that magistrates and promagistrates, however competent in foreign tongues, employ only Latin in official declarations and negotiations; and it demanded, at least until the first century B.C., that Greeks present any formal communications to Roman representatives or to the senate in Latin through translators. A heavy emphasis lay on the *maiestas* of the state and the *dignitas* of its officials. There would be no catering to Greeks. Indeed the very same persons who were certifiable philhellenes, in the sense of enthusiasm for Greek learning, often behaved with arrogance, incivility, and even ruthlessness toward Greeks.

The divorce between cultural leanings and matters of state was sharp. The very idea of philhellenism as national policy would be unintelligible to a Roman. Similarly, the modern construct of Rome's political factions as divided between groups favorable to the Greeks and those committed to a hard-line attitude falls to the ground.[116] Nor is there any discernible connection between Roman zeal for learning Greek and the subordination of the East to the western power.[117] Greek intellectuals found welcome in the homes of many Roman *nobiles*; but nothing indicates that their influence went beyond the cultural into the political or diplomatic sphere.[118]

Appreciation for the Hellenic achievement and for what it could teach the Romans went side by side with condescension toward Greeks and contempt for those who aped them. This is not the stuff from which foreign policy is made. The tide of Hellenism ran strong in the time of Fabius Pictor, when Rome had only a minimal interest across the Adriatic. Two generations later, state involvement abroad had expanded enormously, but its connection with intellectual enterprise was no closer. Sulpicius Gallus was not dependent on Roman expansion for his researches into astronomy; and Crassus Mucianus had become an expert in Greek dialects well before he served in any official capacity in the East or ever expected to. The most ardent advocate of Greek culture, Aemilius Paullus, acted with unrestrained severity against the Epirotes, while its sharpest critic, M. Cato, defended Rhodes against those senators who proposed a declaration of war on the island.

Attempts to find interaction between personal sentiments

116. As, e.g., Briscoe, *JRS* 54 (1964): 73–77; *Historia* 18 (1969): 60–70. Cf. Scullard, *Roman Politics*, 194–219. And see above pp. 245–247.

117. As is tentatively hinted at by Momigliano, *Alien Wisdom*, 18–21.

118. As is suggested by M. H. Crawford, in Garnsey and Whittaker, *Imperialism*, 193–207—who, in any case, cites evidence only for the first century B.C.

toward Hellas and interstate relations are doomed to failure. The Romans segregated their private and public *personae* on this score. Individuals could partake of Hellenic culture or affect to despise it (or both). The senate's decisions on foreign affairs turned on other considerations: the perceived interests of state.

Chapter 8

The Roman Concept of Empire in the Age of Expansion

"Empire" is a slippery concept. Definitions tend to satisfy only the definer. Should the term be restricted only to direct control by a state over other states and peoples through annexation, occupation, and exploitation? Or can it be applied more widely to indirect suzerainty or "hegemony," in which ultimate authority rather than active rule belongs to the imperial power?[1] In the context of Rome and the Greek world during the period under scrutiny, that distinction may be irrelevant. Roman behavior in the East seems too erratic, unsystematic, and unpredictable to apply any neat label. Romans threw their weight around in certain places and at certain times; on occasion they exercised firm authority, barked commands, carried off the wealth of a state. On other occasions and under other circumstances, they shunned involvement or decision, showed little interest in tangible gain, and shrank even from anything that can be characterized as "hegemony." A term for such behavior and attitude has yet to be concocted.

Terminology need not detain us. A different set of questions may be more illuminating. Did Romans of the Middle Republic rationalize overseas expansion? Were they indeed even self-conscious about expansionism as a process that required apologia or explanation? To put it more bluntly, did they have a concept of empire at all? Or of "hegemony" for that matter?

---

1. The distinction is elaborated at length by Werner, *ANRW* I:1 (1972), 501–563; see also Veyne, *MEFRA* 87 (1975): 793–855. A briefer statement in Badian, *Roman Imperialism in the Late Republic* (Oxford, 1968), 1–15. For M. I. Finley, *Greece and Rome* 25 (1978): 1–6, the idea of empire must involve "exploitation and gain," whether the imperial state annexed territory or not.

Retrospective Judgments

By the age of Cicero, empire was a fact—acknowledged, lauded, celebrated. A writer in the 80s, with no trace of embarrassment, asserted Rome's *imperium orbis terrae*, an *imperium* submitted to by all peoples, kings, and nations, some of their own accord, others through compulsion by superior force.[2] For Cicero, the *orbis terrarum imperium* is Rome's *gloria*. The orator unabashedly singled out military power as having compelled all the world to obey the Republic's dictates.[3] Speech after speech adverts to the theme: Rome is a beacon to the world and a citadel for every nation and people.[4] Numismatic evidence conveys the image with equal clarity; the globe appears repeatedly on coinage as emblematic of Roman rule over the known world.[5] *Maiestas* and *imperium* can now be invoked side by side.[6]

In the era of Augustus the chorus of praise for Rome's empire rings out in bold tones. Jupiter in the *Aeneid* promises the Romans unlimited empire, no territorial bounds or temporal restrictions to confine it. They will rule all.[7] The poet has Anchises deliver a similar prognostication: Augustus will extend Roman sway to the most distant peoples, his awesome power striking from everywhere.[8] Horace sings his own refrain: Italy's strength and renown increase, the *maiestas* of the *imperium* extends from one end of the world to the other.[9] Variations on this theme are sprinkled through much of the lengthy

2. *Ad Herenn.* 4.13: *imperium orbis terrae, cui imperio omnes gentes, reges, nationes partim vi, partim voluntate consenserunt, cum aut armis aut liberalitate a populo Romano superati essent.*

3. Cic. *De Imp. Pomp.* 53: *hanc gloriam atque hoc orbis terrae imperium*; *Pro Mur.* 22: *militaris virtus . . . orbem terrarum parere huic imperio coegit.*

4. Cic. *Cat.* 4.11: *hanc urbem, lucem orbis terrarum atque arcem omnium gentium*; *Pro Sulla*, 33: *arcem regum ac nationum exterarum*; cf. *De Lege agrar.* 1.18; *P. red. in sen.* 2; *Pro Mil.* 90; *De Off.* 2.26; *Phil.* 6.19. Other references in J. Vogt, *Orbis Romanus* (Tübingen, 1929), reprinted in *Orbis* (Freiburg, 1960), 151–160; Werner, *ANRW* I:1 (1972), 531–532; Brunt, in Garnsey and Whittaker, *Imperialism in the Ancient World*, 162–172.

5. See, e.g., Crawford, *RRC*, nos. 393, 397, 403, 409.2, 426.4, 449.4, 464.3, 465.8, 480.3, 480.6, 480.15–17, 494.5, 494.39, 520; cf. Vogt, *Orbis*, 157–159; S. Weinstock, *Divus Julius* (Oxford, 1971), 42–43.

6. Cic. *Pro Rab. Perd.* 2. On Roman attitudes toward world conquest in the first century B.C., see M. G. Morgan, "*Imperium sine finibus*: Romans and World Conquest in the First Century B.C.," in S. M. Burstein and L. A. Okin, *Panhellenica: Essays in Ancient History and Historiography in Honor of Truesdell S. Brown* (Lawrence, Kansas, 1980), 143–154.

7. Verg. *Aen.* 1.278–282: *his ego nec metas rerum nec tempora pono; imperium sine fine dedi . . . Romanos rerum dominos.*

8. Verg. *Aen.* 6.791–807.

9. Horace, *Carm.* 4.15.13–16; cf. 4.3.13, 4.14.43–44.

text of Livy. Rome is the *caput orbis terrarum*, her citizens the *princeps orbis terrarum populus*.[10] Into the mouths of her generals Livy places boasts that Rome's dominion will stretch from Gades to the Red Sea, that Greece and Asia are in her *iure ac dicione*, that enemies are compelled to atone for their offenses against the *dignitas* of her empire, that her power embraces the entire globe.[11] Greeks themselves are made to acknowledge that the Republic's citizens are *domini orbis terrarum* and that all people of the world come under her *dicio*.[12] This is the language of Livy's era, a reflection of late Republican and Augustan thinking.[13] The concept finds expression in still another contemporary, the architect and engineer Vitruvius, who attributes to a divine plan the location of Rome, an ideal site for holding sovereignty over the world.[14]

Justification and rationalization make their appearance in the Ciceronian age. Cicero gives voice to that most celebrated apologia: Rome gained mastery over all lands simply by coming to the defense of her allies.[15] Neither avarice nor lust for power, therefore, motivated the expansion, just the noble aim of defending the defenseless. If the acquisition of empire is explicable, so also is its retention. Rome maintained hers, says Cicero, by providing *beneficia*, by serving as a bulwark for those who need protection, by taking on more the character of a *patrocinium* than an *imperium*.[16] The altruistic mission is not only laudable but natural: nature ordains that the strong will govern the weak to the advantage of the latter.[17] A small step only from this to

10. Livy, praef. 3; 1.16.7, 21.30.10, 34.58.8, 42.39.3.

11. Livy, 36.17.15 (Glabrio in 191); 38.48.3, 38.48.11 (Manlius in 187); 44.1.12 (Philippus in 169).

12. Livy, 36.41.5, 37.45.8 (Antiochus in 191 and 190); 37.54.15–16 (Rhodians in 189). Cf. 38.51.4.

13. Note the almost identical language in Glabrio's speech and that of the Rhodians, Livy, 36.17.15: *omne humanum genus secundum deos nomen Romanum veneretur*; 37.54.16: *omne humanum genus quod vestrum nomen imperiumque iuxta ac deos immortales iam pridem intuetur*. For such thinking, *maiestas imperii* belonged in a speech of Fabius Maximus, and the Hannibalic war would be depicted as a contest for empire, with worldwide dominion at stake: Livy, 22.58.3, 28.19.6–7, 28.42.21, 29.17.6, 30.32.2.

14. Vitruvius, 6.1.10–11: *uti orbis terrarum imperio potiretur*; cf. Pliny, *NH*, 3.39.

15. Cic. *De Rep.* 3.35: *noster autem populus sociis defendendis terrarum iam omnium potitus est*; cf. *De Imp. Pomp.* 6, 14; Caes. *BG*, 1.43.

16. Cic. *De Off.* 2.26–27; on the notion of *patrocinium*, see above pp. 160–162. From the perspective of the 40s B.C. the praiseworthy ends of empire had given way to oppression of allies and exploitation of subjects—with the age of Sulla as turning point: Cic. *De Off.* 2.27–29; Sallust, *Cat.* 9.5, 10.6, 11.5, 12.5, 52.21–22; cf. Cic. *De Rep.* 3.41; and see Gabba, *RendAccadLinc* 34 (1979): 132–134.

17. Cic. *De Rep.* 3.37: *an non cernimus optimo cuique dominatum ab ipsa natura cum summa utilitate infirmorum datum?* Cf. *Ad Q. Fr.* 1.1.27; Vogt, *Ciceros Glaube an Rom* (Stuttgart, 1935), 89–92; Meyer, *Cicero und das Reich*, 103–162; and see above pp. 160–162.

the famed formulation of Vergil: Rome's mandate is to govern, to spare the humbled and humble the haughty, and to supplement peace with law.[18]

The foregoing precepts, familiar and flattering, belong to the late Republic. They surface at a time when Rome's mastery of the Mediterranean had swept away all challengers and stimulated the retrospective analysis of intellectuals. That any such ratiocination took place a century or more earlier cannot be inferred on the basis of this testimony. In fact, how much serious thinking about the nature of empire and imperialism is suggested even by the remarks cited above?

As a collection, they amount to nothing like a systematic elucidation of Roman expansion. Nor were they meant to provide one. The Ciceronian comments, scattered in speeches, addressed particular situations without drawing a larger picture. His political treatises, De Republica and De Legibus, directed themselves to the principles of government, and only marginally and incidentally spared attention to relations with overseas states and dependencies. The philosophical works touch on those subjects as occasional illustration, not as organized treatment.[19] Republican intellectuals, it appears, never elaborated the theoretical underpinnings of empire.

Cicero, in any case, felt no compulsion to develop a consistent rationale on the matter. Protection of allies generated imperial power, so he observed.[20] But that was not the whole story. In the same passage which contrasts patrocinium with imperium, he pronounces that Roman wars are waged either pro sociis or de imperio.[21] So, power or dominion can be an end in itself. The idea arises in a different form and different context elsewhere in the De Officiis. Cicero distinguishes between two types of war, the one fought with deadly enemies when survival itself is at stake, the other a contest de imperio. In the latter category fall the conflicts with Latins, Sabines, Samnites, Pyrrhus, and even Carthaginians. In the former Cicero sets wars with the Celtiberians and Cimbri. The very existence of the state depended upon defeat of the barbarians. For the rest, the prize was imperium.[22] The

18. Verg. Aen. 6.851–853: tu regere imperio populos, Romane, memento—hae tibi erunt artes—pacique imponere morem, parcere subiectis et debellare superbos. Cf. Livy, 30.42.17: plus paene parcendo victis quam vincendo imperium auxisse.

19. Cf. S. E. Smethurst, TAPA 84 (1953): 216–226.

20. See above, n. 15.

21. Cic. De Off. 2.26: bella aut pro sociis aut de imperio. Werner, ANRW I:1 (1972), 528–530, attempts unsuccessfully to explain this passage away. And he overlooks the Ciceronian statements cited below, nn. 22–25.

22. Cic. De Off. 1.38: sic cum Celtiberis, cum Cimbris bellum ut cum inimicis gerebatur, uter esset, non uter imperaret, cum Latinis, Sabinis . . . de imperio dimicabatur. A similar formulation in Livy, 28.19.6–7.

term, of course, is not equivalent to "empire" here; more like "ascendancy" or "dominance" over the conquered nation. But the germ of empire is there. Cicero, it would appear, finds it a perfectly legitimate object of warfare. And he declaimed with equal forthrightness in the *Eighth Philippic*: our ancestors took up arms not only to win their freedom—but to rule.[23] No mention of defending allies or protecting dependencies here. Cicero overlooked the inconsistency.

How to explain it? A grasping for dominance and a championing of the weak could, to be sure, coincide. Did Cicero then reconcile the ideas and justify expansionism? Nothing suggests that he saw the need for reconciliation. It is a goal of the statesman, so he affirms in the *De Officiis*, to swell the Republic's power, territory, and revenues; the same treatise, however, also contains as clear a condemnation of imperialism as one could wish: nature prohibits us from augmenting our own assets, wealth, and resources from the spoils of others.[24] That generalization names no specific culprits. But Cicero knew which power derived its prosperity from foreign revenues. Just how then did he account for Roman expansionism? In the speech for Pompey's command against Mithridates he set all the motives in juxtaposition: the Romans, stung by injury, have every reason to preserve the safety of their allies, while at the same time protecting the *dignitas* of their empire, especially since their greatest revenues are in jeopardy.[25] The reasons are not mutually exclusive. Nor, however, do they easily march together. When does the exaction of revenues mean the despoiling of others, a deed contrary to nature, and when does it constitute legitimate protection of the *dignitas imperii*? A fine line to draw. Cicero never draws it. He has simply not thought the problem through. At one point in the *De Officiis* he condemns Rome for the destruction of Corinth, an act undertaken under the phony cover of expediency.[26] At another he reckons the decision regrettable but responsible: the location of the city made it a perpetual danger that needed to be eliminated.[27]

The incongruities and discrepancies lead to a noteworthy conclusion. Cicero never attempted a methodical evaluation of Roman

23. Cic. *Phil.* 8.12: *maiores quidem nostri non modo ut liberi essent sed etiam ut imperarent*; cf. *Verr.* 2.2.2–3.

24. Cic. *De Off.* 2.85: *rem publicam augeant imperio, agris, vectigalibus*. Ibid. 3.22: *illud natura non patitur, ut aliorum spoliis nostras facultates, copias, opes augeamus*.

25. Cic. *De Imp. Pomp.* 6, 14: *quanto vos studio convenit iniuriis provocatos sociorum salutem una cum imperii vestri dignitate defendere, praesertim cum de maximis vestris vectigalibus agatur*.

26. Cic. *De Off.* 3.46: *sed utilitatis specie in re publica saepissime peccatur, ut in Corinthi disturbatione nostri*; cf. Florus, 1.32.1.

27. Cic. *De Off.* 1.35.

expansionism. Nor, so far as we can tell, did any of his contemporary countrymen. The acquisition of empire had been accomplished by the Ciceronian age. Late Republican and Augustan writers acknowledged the fact and boasted of it. Martial prowess had made Rome the *caput orbis terrarum*, her people the world's *principes*, her power such that it encircled the globe. The achievement seemed its own justification. No one felt the need for a thoroughgoing analysis of goals and rationale. A few scattered remarks about protection of allies, *patrocinium*, or bringing down the proud do not constitute a philosophy. Cicero's own incidental comments range from pride in imperial power to criticism of foreign exploitation, from overseas rule as altruistic protectorate to the attainment of ascendancy as an end in itself.

Greek thinkers like Polybius and Posidonius at least made an attempt at a general assessment of Roman imperialism, even if an abortive one. Romans did not even try. The upshot of this bears notice. If the Ciceronian and Augustan periods generated no comprehensive thinking on the subject, at a time when the fact of empire should have stimulated reflection, then we ought not to expect it from the Middle Republic, when the process itself was begun, haltingly, ill-defined, and perhaps beyond the grasp of its own participants.

Contemporary Attitudes

Did Romans during the great outburst of overseas expansion, from the late third to the late second century, evince any notion of empire?

Polybius awards such prescience to Scipio Africanus. The great general's exhortation to his troops before Zama includes the prognostication that victory will bring the victor undisputed leadership and dominion not only in Africa but in the rest of the world.[28] That this is authentic representation of Africanus' sentiments, however, none can say with confidence. The hyperbole of pre-battle speeches is not confined to reality anyway. And this particular sentiment coincides too neatly with Polybius' own view of the Hannibalic war as determining the future of the Mediterranean world.[29] Similarly hyperbolic is Africanus' rhetorical eruption at those who charged him with embezzlement in 187: he reminded them pointedly that his accomplishments had made Romans masters of Asia, Africa, and Spain.[30] The words again derive from Polybius. And the bravado again suit-

---

28. Polyb. 15.10.2: τῆς ἄλλης οἰκουμένης τὴν ἡγεμονίαν καὶ δυναστείαν ἀδήριτον.
29. Cf. Polyb. 1.3.7, 15.9.2–5.
30. Polyb. 23.14.10.

ably coheres with Polybius' repeated assertion that the Antiochene war settled the fate of Asia.[31] The historian's reflections intervene here. They cannot be reckoned as interchangeable with the words and thoughts of Scipio Africanus—let alone of his generation as a whole.

The Roman peace treaty with Aetolia in 189 possessed a heading which, in Livy's report, obliged the Aetolians to adhere faithfully to the *imperium maiestatemque populi Romani*. Whether that phraseology actually stood in the text of the treaty is not quite certain. Livy follows Polybius here. The Achaean historian gives τὴν ἀρχὴν καὶ τὴν δυναστείαν, either his own translation of the original or a rendition of the official Greek version. Cicero's transmission of the comparable clause in the treaty with Gades, interestingly enough, gives simply *maiestatem populi Romani comiter conservanto*. No mention of *imperium*.[32] The combination of *imperium* and *maiestas* may owe more to literary influence than to official terminology.[33] Even if the word belongs, however, what does it establish? The Aetolian treaty, as we have seen, was most unusual and quite probably unique among Rome's compacts with eastern states. For none other is a similar clause attested or suggested. Rome had a special lesson to administer to the Aetolians.[34] Further, the term *imperium*, as noted earlier and as is well known, does not always—or even usually—carry the meaning of "empire." In this circumstance, it almost certainly has a different connotation: Aetolia is required to respect the "power" or "supremacy" of Rome, not the Roman "empire."[35] Cato used the word in that sense when delivering his speech on the Rhodians in 167: they were frightened, he said, lest, when there was no one left whom we feared, they would *sub solo*

31. Cf. Polyb. 3.3.5, 21.4.4–5, 21.16.8, 21.23.4.

32. The Aetolian treaty: Polyb. 21.32.2; Livy, 38.11.2. The Gaditane treaty: Cic. *Pro Balbo*, 35; and see Proculus, *Dig.* 49.15.7.

33. Cf., e.g., Horace, *Carm.* 4.15.14–15; Livy, 28.42.21; Cic. *Pro Rab. Perd.* 20; *Ad Fam.* 12.15.2. The combination appears in an Augustan document: *ILS*, 5050, lines 93, 127.

34. See above pp. 29–30.

35. Cf., on the earlier relations between Rome and Aetolia in 211, Livy, 26.24.7: *cum fide vim maiestatemque populi Romani extollentes*. The treaty of Apamea in 188, in Livy's transmission, employs the term *imperium* only once—and then with regard to Antiochus, Livy, 38.38.3: *iis qui sub imperio eius*. The Polybian equivalent is τοὺς ὑπ' ἐκεῖνον ταττομένους: 21.43.3. One later clause of that treaty forbids Antiochus to recruit mercenaries ἐκ τῆς ὑπὸ Ῥωμαίους ταττομένης: Polyb. 21.43.15. Harris, *War and Imperialism*, 106, takes it as a reference to "the concept of empire as extending far beyond the provinces." But the clause can hardly apply to Roman ascendancy in the East. The Hellenistic states who combined with Rome against Antiochus are consistently identified in the treaty as "allies": Polyb. 21.43.2–3, 21.43.9–10; Livy, 38.38.2–3, 38.38.7, 38.38.16. One notes that Livy renders the phrase in question not *sub imperio* but *sub dicione*: 38.38.10. The reference must be to states in Italy and the West.

imperio nostro in servitute nostra essent. Being "in our power alone" was equivalent to "being in servitude." Cato, it is plain, was not speaking of a Roman "empire."[36]

In short, no evidence exists that points unambiguously to a time before 146 and attests Roman consciousness of anything that can be termed "empire." When then do we get a sign of it? The celebrated mission of Scipio Aemilianus traversed many of the lands of the eastern Mediterranean ca. 140; Diodorus even says "most of the world." The legates visited kings and republics, we are told, adjudicated and arbitrated, resolved some quarrels, coerced recalcitrants, renewed friendships, and fortified Roman ἡγεμονία.[37] Was this a survey of "empire" or "hegemony"? Diodorus' language and his interpretation need not represent Roman thinking at the time of the embassy. Scipio's assignment, as other sources put it, was to visit "allies," "allied kingdoms," and "foreign peoples"—not subjects, clients, or dependencies.[38] It was an extraordinary journey on any reckoning. The purpose or purposes still baffle investigation. To characterize it as a tidying up of the empire, however, falls into anachronism. The *legati* went in for a lot of sight-seeing, but no trace survives of any tangible political, diplomatic, or economic results.

Ti. Gracchus junior, it is reported, spoke with eloquence on behalf of his agrarian bill in 133. Roman commanders, he said, exhort their troops to fight for hearth and home; yet, though they are called "masters of the world," most have nary a hearth nor a home.[39] Did Tiberius in fact utter those words, and what do they mean? The notice appears in Plutarch's biography, the source unknown and a matter of guesswork. Appian paraphrases what may be the same or a similar speech. In his account, the tribune asserted that Romans acquired most of the land they possessed through success in war, and that they had hopes of obtaining "the rest of the world."[40] The two versions are awkward in juxtaposition. The first reckons Romans as masters of the world, the other has that station still in prospect. Both sources, of course, are late. More important, they are Greek, and perhaps dependent on Greek outlooks. Hellenes—or some of them at least—as we know did adjudge Rome as ruler of the Mediterranean.

36. Gellius, 6.3.16 = Cato, *ORF*, fr. 164. G. Calboli, *Marci Porci Catonis Oratio Pro Rhodiensibus* (Bologna, 1978), 292–293, wrongly sees this as prefiguring the idea of an empire over all peoples and Cato's point as "anti-imperialistic."

37. Diod. 33.28b.

38. Cf. Val. Max. 4.3.13: *per socios et exteras gentes*; Justin, 38.8.8: *ad inspicienda sociorum regna veniebant*. Additional sources in Broughton, *MRR* I:481.

39. Plut. *Ti. Gr.* 9.5: κύριοι τῆς οἰκουμένης εἶναι λεγόμενοι; cf. Florus, 2.2.3.

40. Appian, *BC*, 1.11: πλείστης γῆς ἐκ πολέμου βίᾳ κατέχοντες καὶ τὴν λοιπὴν τῆς οἰκουμένης χώραν ἐν ἐλπίδι ἔχοντες.

That disposition, rather than any Roman attitude, may lie at the root of Plutarch's presentation. Let the words be Tiberius' however, for sake of argument. Romans were termed masters of the world. By whom? Other Romans, one usually imagines. But no authority for that lies in the text. Those who hold the Romans as κύριοι may well be Greeks. Tiberius had a sound Hellenic education; he perhaps reflects here or indeed reacts to a Hellenic vantage-point. So, the testimony affords no guarantee of second-century *Roman* attitudes.[41]

Evidence for the late second century is sparse in the extreme. In the funeral speech for Scipio Aemilianus in 129, Laelius wrote that we must thank the immortal gods that such a man was born in Rome; for, of necessity, wherever he was there was *terrarum imperium*.[42] Allowance should perhaps be made for the rhetoric of funerary laudation. And Scipio's conquests, in any case, belonged to the West, not the East. But the phrase *terrarum imperium* can only be understood as some form of allusion to world dominion, openly enunciated by a Roman senator in 129. A few years later, the beginning of the *repetundae* law preserved on bronze refers to allies, Latins, and foreign nations, all those held in Rome's authority, governance, power, or friendship: *arbitratu dicione potestate amicitiave*.[43] The term *imperium*, oddly and interestingly, stays out of the public document. Varied phraseology encompasses a range of relationships rather than a unified entity identifiable as empire. Those diverse relationships, however, constitute a scale of dependencies, publicly and officially acknowledged. That marks a change, at least in the extant evidence. A generation passes with nothing more to the point. Then we get the first unequivocal assertion by a Roman that his state holds *imperium orbis terrae*.[44] The steps which made up this transition to acknowledgment of empire cannot be traced in any detail. But the transitional period falls in those very years from the Gracchi to Sulla—well after the eclipse of Hellenistic states by Roman power. Self-consciousness about the acquisition of hegemony trailed the acquisition itself, by a noticeable margin.

None of this implies that Rome had an aversion to expansionism prior to the late Republic. A city which extended its power and influence from the banks of the Tiber throughout the Italian peninsula can hardly have shrunk in horror from the very idea of territorial growth.

41. On Greek attitudes, see below pp. 336–343. Harris, *War and Imperialism*, 126–127, assumes without argument that Plutarch refers to other Romans.

42. Cic. *Pro Mur.* 75: *necesse enim fuisse ibi esse terrarum imperium ubi ille esset.* The speech was delivered by Scipio's nephew Fabius Maximus, but composed by Laelius: Schol. Bob. 118, Stangl.

43. *FIRA*, I, no. 7, line 1.

44. *Ad Herenn.* 4.9.13; see above, n. 2. Cf. Werner, *ANRW* I:1 (1972), 531–533.

The proposition that all Rome's wars were defensive or fought on behalf of allies is not to be taken seriously. Cicero retailed it but knew it to be untrue. His ancestors contended *de imperio* and *ut imperarent*. Such, at least, was the retrospective formulation.[45] And there is further evidence that can take the stimulus to expansion well back into Roman history.[46] The question we need to confront, however, takes a somewhat different direction. What role, if any, did the growth of national power as a concept and goal play in Roman involvement with the eastern Mediterranean?

The evidence demands caution and care. Rome lived with war throughout the history of the Republic, expected it and exploited it, developed a social and military system that assumed it, occasionally at least welcomed and even provoked it.[47] That, nevertheless, leaves the question unanswered. However aggressive and bellicose Rome may have been in her Italian wars, it does not follow that she actively sought overseas expansion, grasped after power across the Adriatic, and strove to extend her sway over the East. The distinctions need to be brought to the fore. A commitment to dominance of one's neighbors differs from a drive for territorial aggrandizement on a large scale. Aggressiveness in the national character still falls short of explaining imperialism.

Vestiges of antique formulas survived to the late Republic, giving a glimpse of Roman mentality from the distant and indeterminate past. A solemn prayer accompanied the censor's closing of the *lustrum*, at least down to the mid-second century. It asked of the gods that they improve and augment the condition of the Roman people.[48] The tale in which the prayer's text is reported raises a host of difficulties and commands little faith. The text itself, however, has every claim on authenticity.[49] But what does it mean? Valerius Maximus,

45. See above pp. 276–277.

46. See, e.g., Vogt, *Ciceros Glaube an Rom*, 72–76; F. Hampl, *HZ* 188 (1959), 521–523; Harris, *War and Imperialism*, 117–130.

47. On Roman attitudes toward war, see now the excellent treatment by Harris, *War and Imperialism*, 9–53, which supplants all previous discussions.

48. Val. Max. 4.1.10: *quo di immortales ut populi Romani res meliores amplioresque facerent rogabantur*. The text of the prayer is preserved as part of an anecdote in Valerius Maximus who reports that the prayer was altered by Scipio Aemilianus in his censorship of 142/1: since Roman affairs were now *satis bonae et magnae*, the gods would henceforth only be asked *ut eas perpetuo incolumes servent*.

49. For arguments against the story in Val. Max. 4.1.10, see, especially, F. Marx, *RhM* 39 (1884): 65–68; Aymard, *Études*, 396–408; Astin, *Scipio Aemilianus*, 325–331. It is defended, unconvincingly, by Werner *ANRW* I: 1 (1972), 537, n. 119. Nevertheless, the story, even as an invention, has no point unless some such prayer was once part of the censorial ritual and was subsequently altered.

who conveys it, took *res ampliores* as territorial increase: the censors prayed for the expansion of Rome's possessions. A possible though by no means inevitable interpretation. The phrase could have a broader and vaguer meaning: increased resources or wellbeing.[50] One cannot tell. Take it, however, that territorial growth is meant. What does that prove about overseas aggrandizement? The censorial ritual may have an ancient pedigree, its words originally designed to win divine favor for contests in Latium and Italy. The formula then simply persisted.

That possibility gains greater force when one considers another apparently archaic formula. Augustus reinstituted the *ludi saeculares* in 17 B.C., the centennial festival celebrated in 249 B.C. and perhaps as early as 348. The Augustan prayer asked for increase of the *imperium* and *maiestas* of the Roman people in war and at home, and for enduring obeisance by the Latin.[51] How much of the wording goes back to the early Republic is indeterminable. One may justifiably suspect the combination *imperium maiestatemque* as an Augustan addition. Nevertheless, the phrase *utique semper Latinus obtemperassit* points unmistakably to the distant past when Rome struggled for control of Latium and put down the great Latin revolt.[52] Expansion outside the confines of Italy is not envisioned.[53]

These prayers provide a key for understanding some otherwise baffling evidence, also on the convergence of religion and politics: a remarkable set of responses by the *haruspices* predicting Rome's success in war and the increase of her territory. Livy supplies the

50. So, P. Frei, *MH* 32 (1975): 74; cf. Astin, *Scipio Aemilianus*, 328–329—though his argument that a prayer for territorial expansion would conflict with fetial law is rightly rejected by Harris, *War and Imperialism*, 119–120. Harris, however, does not consider the possibility that the prayer might connote anything but territorial expansion. Observe, e.g., Livy, 23.11.2: *si ita faxitis, Romani, vestrae res meliores facilioresque erunt.*

51. *ILS*, 5050, lines 93–94: [*uti imperium maiestatemque p. R.*] *Quiritium duelli domique au*[*xitis, utique semper Latinus obtemperassit*]. Text and commentary in G. B. Pighi, *De ludis saecularibus* (2nd. ed., Amsterdam, 1965), 107–130.

52. Cf. Livy, 8.13.16: *certe id firmissimum longe imperium est quo oboedientes gaudent* [*Latini*]. See further E. Diehl, *RhM* 83 (1934): 268–270, 356–370; L. R. Taylor, *AJP* 55 (1934): 101–120; Harris, *War and Imperialism*, 120–122, 265–266.

53. Increase of Roman power in the peninsula is also the point of Ennius' lines in the early second century: 465–466, Vahlen: *audire est operae pretium procedere recte qui rem Romanam Latiumque augescere vultis*. The words of Accius, *pulcherrume auguratum est rem Romanam publicam summan fore* (Cic. *De Div.* 1.45), do not have the connotation of territorial aggrandizement: *pace* Vogt, *Ciceros Glaube an Rom*, 74; Harris, *War and Imperialism*, 126. Harris, *op. cit.*, 122–123, also cites the oath sworn by Italian insurgents for Livius Drusus in 91, as recorded by Diod. 37.11: a vow to the demigods who founded Rome and the heroes who increased her ἡγεμονία. Even if the oath be authentic, however, it plainly refers not to an overseas empire but to Rome's ἡγεμονία in Italy.

testimony. Four times he has the state consult the Etruscan priests as to the likely outcome of imminent struggles: the wars with Philip, Antiochus, and (twice) Perseus. And four times they produced essentially the same answer: Rome will attain victory, triumph, and the extension of her boundaries.[54] The purport seems unambiguous. As part of state ceremonial, the *haruspices*—who themselves, of course, did not make or conceive policy—announced that the outcome of war would bring not only military triumph but national expansion. Yet a puzzling incongruity supervenes. The very wars for which these predictions were made resulted in no territorial acquisition. Nor is there the slightest hint that Rome intended any. How to explain the discrepancy? Livy invented the prayers, it has been suggested, as reflection of Augustus' interest in expanding boundaries; or else Roman annalists made them up, thus the better to emphasize Rome's restraint even in the face of divine sanction for imperialism. Far-fetched hypotheses.[55] A far easier and more plausible solution lies at hand. The *haruspices* delivered ritual pronouncements that date back to the early Republic, at a time when *prolatio finium* and *terminos propagari* meant quite literally the advance of frontiers. Their responses prior to the wars with Philip, Antiochus, and Perseus amount to nothing more than mechanical repetition of the old formulas.[56] They can hardly represent impetus or sanction for territorial aggrandizement in the eastern wars—which Rome manifestly shunned.

Pride in acquisition of territory makes no appearance in the era of Rome's great victories over the Hellenistic powers. Cicero asserts that the Republic's great commanders have their monuments inscribed with the words "he extended the borders of the empire."[57] When did that practice begin? Cicero puts the assertion in the mouth of L. Furius Philus, an interlocutor in the *De Republica*, set in the year 129 B.C. The possibility of anachronism, however, has to be considered. Cicero's statement gets no confirmation from extant *elogia*. Roman *nobiles* of the Middle Republic celebrated their accomplishments on stone and boasted of their martial exploits but never (in the pre-

54. Livy, 31.5.7: *prolationem finium victoriamque et triumphum portendi*; 36.1.3: *eo bello terminos populi Romani propagari, victoriam ac triumphum ostendi*; 42.20.4: *prolationemque finium et interitum perduellium portendi*; 42.30.9: *victoriam, triumphum propagationem* [*finium?*].

55. Augustan propaganda: Briscoe, *Commentary*, 69. Annalistic invention: Frei, *MH* 32 (1975): 76–78. Harris, *War and Imperialism*, 122, accepts the genuineness of the testimony but does not address the problem of how to reconcile the priests' prophecies with Roman actions.

56. Cf. Hampl, *HZ* 188 (1959): 523.

57. Cic. *De Rep.* 3.24: *finis imperii propagavit*.

served inscriptions) laid claim to advancing the boundaries or adding to the size of the Roman empire.[58] The first such inscribed boast is known to us through a literary source. Diodorus transmits Pompey's dedication of ca. 61 which commemorated his achievements in Asia: a long list of nations and peoples humbled by him and then the proud declaration that he had pushed the frontiers of the empire to the boundaries of the earth.[59] The increase of empire had certainly become an open vaunt in the last generation of the Republic. A law of the people in 58 b.c. proclaimed it boldly for all to see: Rome had augmented her empire and secured peace for the world.[60] Her commanders and their flatterers hailed the spread of Roman power and the expansion of Roman borders.[61] Cicero, it may be deduced, transferred what was a commonplace in his own day to the age of Scipio Aemilianus. The boasts of second-century generals did not include territorial gains.

V

A meager harvest of information remains, made the more meager by careful winnowing. But the residue allows for some tentative propositions. Roman attitudes, like Roman institutions, show a clear divide between the experience in Italy and the expectations in the eastern Mediterranean.[62] Bellicosity and aggrandizement characterized

58. For Harris, *War and Imperialism*, 125, the surviving inscriptions are too few in number to serve as a check on Cicero. See, however, *ILLRP*, I, nos. 309, 310, 319, 321, 321a, 322, 323 (= *Syll.*³ 652a), 326, 327, 328, 331, 335, 337—all of which call attention to victory and conquest without a mention of expanding Roman territory.

59. Diod. 40.4: τὰ ὅρια τῆς ἡγεμονίας τοῖς ὅροις τῆς γῆς προσβιβάσας; cf. Pliny, *NH*, 7.97. Cicero had made an even bolder claim for Pompey: *Cat.* 3.26: *finis vestri imperii non terrae sed caeli regionibus terminaret*; *Pro Sest.* 67. Similar hyperbole in describing Caesar's Gallic conquests: Cic. *Pro Balbo*, 64; cf. *Prov. Cons.* 33.

60. *CIL*, I,2,2500 = *SEG*, I, 335, lines 19–20: *imperio am[pli]ficato [p]ace per orbe[m terrarum parta]*.

61. E.g., Cic. *Pro Rosc. Amer.* 50; *De Imp. Pomp.* 49; *Prov. Cons.* 29; *De Rep.* 6.13; *Phil.* 13.14; Harris, *War and Imperialism*, 129–130. Only from the time of Sulla was the privilege of extending the *pomerium* accorded to those who had advanced Rome's overseas frontiers: Seneca, *De Brev. Vitae*, 13.8; Tac. *Ann.* 12.23; Gellius, 13.14.2–4; *SHA*, "Aurelian," 21.9–10; cf. Frei, *MH* 32 (1975): 75–76. The assertion in Val. Max. 2.8.4, followed by Amm. Marc. 25.9.9–10, that triumphs were awarded only *pro aucto imperio*, is demonstrably false; cf. Cic. *In Pis.* 58; *Ad Att.* 4.18.4; see, most recently, the arguments of Frei, *op. cit.*, 78–79.

62. Cf. the excellent discussion—with different purposes—by P. Catalano, *Atti-AccadTorino* 96 (1961–62): 198–228, who demonstrates that Romans drew a sharp distinction between *Italia*, as both a juridical and a political concept, and all *externae gentes* as early as the third century and certainly in the second.

Rome's role in Italy from the start. Struggles against neighbors in Latium and Etruria set a pattern featured during the first two and a half centuries of the Republic. Romans may have worried about having an appropriate pretext for war, but they never showed moral anguish about stripping defeated foes of their possessions and moving from conquest to occupation. Items from the sphere where religion and politics intersect bring the attitudes to light. Censors regularly called on the gods for improved and increased national resources—which perhaps encompassed territorial acquisitions. The prayer at the *ludi saeculares* asked for augmentation of Roman power and continued submission to it by the Latin. Prewar prognostications by the *haruspices* promised the advance of Roman borders. The drive toward supremacy in the peninsula was relentless. Avarice for annexation, however, did not spill over into relations with the East. Prayers for increase in resources and power continued in mechanical fashion, and priests predicted expanse of boundaries, repeating old formulas. Those formulas no longer fitted the circumstances. Rome eschewed annexation, her commanders exulted in conquest but not in extension of frontiers. Only in the late Republic did a self-conscious imperialism and a sense of Mediterranean hegemony take hold. The collapse of the Hellenistic powers in the later second century placed Rome in a role unanticipated and uncalculated but at last embraced both materially and intellectually. Conception of herself as mistress of the *orbis terrarum* evolved in the Gracchan and Sullan eras, well after the fact. And in the age of Cicero, the idea of expanding national boundaries, an idea once confined to advance toward suzerainty in Italy, became incorporated in the proud claims of Roman conquerors abroad— claims unheard in the third and second centuries.

Analysis and rationalization came late. One errs in assuming that the momentum from conquest carried over irresistibly to eastern imperialism. In a sense, the importance attached to the submission of Latins and Italians and to the security of the peninsula may have deterred any schemes of aggrandizement across the Adriatic, where Rome had no interests of consequence. Overseas empire as an articulated concept gained formulation only after Rome had achieved it as a fact. Worldwide supremacy appears first not as a goal but as an accomplishment. Hence it can hardly be reckoned an impetus to expansion. In Cicero's view, the very absence of avarice for others' possessions enabled his forefathers to build the empire and reputation of the Roman people by acquiring land, cities, and nations.[63] The inter-

63. Cic. *Pro Rosc. Amer.* 50: *non alienos cupide adpetebant; quibus rebus et agris et urbibus et nationibus rem publicam atque hoc imperium et populi Romani nomen auxerunt.*

pretation is paradoxical and partisan. Yet it catches the echoes of an era that witnessed the dramatic expansion of Roman power without the self-consciousness of creating an empire.[64]

64. Reluctance to transform conquered eastern nations into annexed provinces is rightly stressed by Badian, *Roman Imperialism*, 1–15. Cf. Veyne, *MEFRA* 87 (1975): 804–817. A lengthy challenge to that view now in Harris, *War and Imperialism*, 131–162; see his excellent bibliography on the subject at 131, n. 1; further, Brunt, in Garnsey and Whittaker, *Imperialism in the Ancient World*, 172–175, which adds little. Yet Harris cannot deny the fact, only attempt to explain it away. He offers sound reasons for the Republic's unwillingness to annex Carthage, Macedonia, Illyria, and Asia Minor after Roman victories in those areas during the first half of the second century. But the need to supply putative reasons follows only on the premise that Rome would otherwise consider provincialization. That stands the whole question on its head. Even in the case of Sicily, Rome's earliest "province," the process of provincialization was extremely slow, halting, and partial, a fact obscured by Harris' brief treatment, *op. cit.*, 63–64, 136; see now Dahlheim, *Gewalt und Herrschaft*, 19–53, 59–73. As for the East, where Rome's concerns were considerably less urgent, the very idea of provincialization did not arise before the middle of the second century—if then. What Harris has established—and quite properly—is the absence of a "non-annexationist principle." Indeed. There was also, however, no "annexationist principle."

Chapter 9

The Tangible Benefits of Empire

Conquest brought tangible benefits. The laws of war in antiquity assured and legitimized them. Expropriation of land, seizure of movable goods, imposition of monetary penalties, enslavement of the enemy went unquestioned as the earned emoluments of the victor. Romans certainly never questioned them. A society persistently primed for war, most of whose adult males could expect to see active military duty, appreciated both the risks and the rewards of battle. Only the naive or myopic will deny that Romans perceived, indeed welcomed, the economic advantages of conquest. The proposition seems self-evident. But what does it tell us? Does the desire for gain entail a drive for empire? To what extent did the acquisition of material benefits depend upon the practice of imperialism, i.e. the deliberate and systematic exploitation of other states' resources and the control of their policies and personnel?

A growing body of scholarly literature finds war and greed tantamount to imperialism.[1] The equation may be too simple. Distinctions need to be made and emphasized. The prospect of loot could entice generals and stimulate recruiting—which is not the same as de-

---

1. See, e.g., L. Perelli, *Imperialismo, capitalismo e rivoluzione culturale nella prima meta del IIe secolo a.C.* I (Turin, 1975), 130–153; Harris, *AHR* 76 (1971): 1371–1385; *idem*, *War and Imperialism*, 54–104; Crawford, *Economic History Review* 30 (1977): 42–52; K. Hopkins, *Conquerors and Slaves* (Cambridge, 1978), 25–47; D. Musti, *Polibio e l'imperialismo romano* (Naples, 1978), 88–124. Finley, *Greece and Rome* 25 (1978): 6, rightly draws the proper distinction: "particular wars and single campaigns often produced much booty without leading to a permanent exploitation of the defeated, and without the latter there is no empire." But Finley's brief and general treatment passes from the conquest of Italy to the "rise of the provincial system," thus begging the question on Roman attitudes and aspirations in the middle Republic.

termining a senatorial decision to make war. The carrying off of spoils and the exaction of indemnity might enrich the state, but would not necessarily impel it toward an enduring system of regulation and exploitation. Enslavement or sale of defeated enemies helped stock the plantations of rural Italy; yet nothing shows that this either inspired Roman expansion or dictated imperial control. The leaps of logic too easily distort and mislead.

The Revenues of Conquest

Romans had concrete expectations from war. Soldiers enrolled eagerly for the first conflict with Carthage, says Polybius, when commanders pointed out the prospects for plunder. A century later, the same enticements seduced recruits for the Third Macedonian War: they glimpsed the wealthy life-styles of veterans of previous eastern wars and swiftly filled up the ranks.[2] In neither case, however, did the motives of *milites* coincide with the reasons of state.[3] The alliance with Aetolia in 212 or 211 specified distribution of the fruits of victory: Aetolians to get all conquered territory, farms, fields, and buildings, the Romans to get all movable booty. A clue to Rome's motivation? Hardly. Aetolia held the upper hand in that alliance and the terms were probably hers, leaving to Rome what (for the Aetolians) was of secondary interest. Indeed, an earlier Roman treaty with Carthage conceded to the Punic power all booty from captured towns in Latium, so long as the towns would be yielded up. Plunder did not occupy a central place in the making of policy.[4]

War meant booty. The conjunction was taken for granted, unquestioned and undebated. The Roman army even had routine, established procedures for the collection and distribution of loot.[5] The prayer of Scipio Africanus before embarking for Africa in 204 asked

2. The First Punic War: Polyb. 1.11.2; cf. 1.20.1, 1.49.5. The Third Macedonian War: Livy, 42.32.6.

3. They are afterthoughts, useful for recruiting but not determinants of war-declarations which had already taken place. Observe the circumstances prior to the outbreak of the Second Macedonian War. The *comitia centuriata* first rejected, then accepted, war. A consular speech helped reverse the verdict, according to Livy: in his composition, that speech contained not a word about plunder and gain: Livy, 31.6.1–31.8.1.

4. On the Aetolian treaty, see above pp. 17–20. The treaty with Carthage: Polyb. 3.24.5. How much truth lies in the claim, fostered by Cato, that some Roman leaders wished to war on Rhodes in 167 in order to seize her wealth cannot be known: Gellius, 6.3.7. The war, in any case, was never undertaken.

5. Polyb. 10.16.2–9.

for punishment of the enemy, safe return, triumph—and plunder.[6] The contemporary comedies of Plautus regularly link warfare with enrichment, the greed of the soldier a common theme and the connection of victory and spoils an automatic one.[7] Eastern victories, of course, produced spoils in spectacular quantities. The triumphs of T. Flamininus, M'. Acilius Glabrio, L. Scipio, M. Fulvius Nobilior, and Cn. Manlius Vulso in the period 194–187 dazzled Rome with their brilliance, vast treasures on display, statues of marble and bronze, coined and uncoined gold and silver, precious art objects, and captured prizes of every description.[8] Equally majestic was the triumph of L. Aemilius Paullus twenty years later, rivaling theirs in splendor and fortune.[9] The repute of the generals soared at such demonstrations; the more so when they utilized the cash to finance lavish games, make dedications at shrines, build public monuments and bestow handsome gifts.

The public coffers benefited, to be sure. But not in any regular or predictable way. The state economy can hardly have depended upon transmission of plunder. Commanders, in fact, had considerable leeway in the matter of booty. Distribution to the soldiers was essential; morale and politics demanded it. Occasionally all the loot was disposed of in this fashion. Otherwise, the *imperator* had broad scope; no laws compelled him to deliver specific sums or percentages to the *aerarium*. He made his own determination, often enriching friends and officers to put his generosity on show. Cato sternly stood above the practice: he would pocket no loot and play no favorites with his disbursements. Aemilius Paullus too, we are told, refrained from touching the booty of Pydna; and his son Scipio Aemilianus was equally conscientious after the fall of Carthage. The cases are, of course, exceptional, that very fact preserving the tales for posterity. They point up by contrast what the norm was or was expected to be. And even Cato did not take the position that plunder from war belonged exclusively to the treasury: the men who had first claim on the

6. Livy, 29.27.1–4: *salvos incolumesque victis perduellibus victores, spoliis decoratos, praeda onustos triumphantesque mecum domos reduces sistatis.* C. Duilius' column proudly detailed the spoils taken from Carthage after the First Punic War: *CIL*, I², 25 = *ILLRP*, I, no. 319. The acquisition of booty from Sardinia was inscribed on Ti. Gracchus' dedication in 174: Livy, 41.28.8–9.

7. Plautus, *Epid.* 158–160; *Amph.* 193–194; *Bacch.* 1068–1071; *Poen.* 802–803; *Pseud.* 583–589; *Truc.* 508; *Most.* 312. Rightly noted by Harris, *War and Imperialism*, 102–103.

8. Sources in Broughton, *MRR* I:344, 357, 362, 369.

9. Broughton, *MRR* I:433–434; cf. also the triumph of L. Anicius, lesser in character because earned against Illyrians, but Anicius turned it into a memorable event: *MRR* I:434.

booty were the soldiers who captured it.[10] That principle was axiomatic. It also has certain interesting implications. The spoils of war belonged to the warriors; the men who issued commands also issued the proceeds. Material rewards, as well as renown and an opportunity for beneficence, accrued to victorious generals. The state got a share sometimes, though not always. It did not receive first consideration in the matter of *praeda*. Even when, as in the case of the eastern victories, the spoils were of colossal magnitude, that principle held. The practice underscores Roman avarice; who could ever have denied that characteristic? But far from providing a link between the prizes of conquest and a policy of imperialism, it points in the opposite direction. The profits of plunder meant private gains for officers and men, but did not and were not meant to supply steady income for the treasury or provide a basis on which to build the state economy.

Indemnity payments would bring in higher sums and more regular ones.[11] Eastern kings and states that fell to Roman might had to pay dearly for their failures. The Illyrians were first to experience it across the Adriatic: Queen Teuta agreed to any exaction the Romans demanded in 228 and the Republic was still collecting cash from her successor Pinnes more than a decade later.[12] A *senatus consultum* in 196 demanded 1,000 talents from Philip V, 500 of it on the spot, the rest to be paid in ten annual installments.[13] Nabis' defeat in 195 cost him 500 talents, one fifth of it immediately, the remainder at a rate of 50 *per annum*.[14] The vanquished Aetolians in 189 were saddled with a 200-talent indemnity, plus another 300 due over a six-year period.[15] From Antiochus the Great Rome exacted a far larger sum in 188: a down payment of 500 talents, 2,500 more upon ratification of the peace, then twelve annual payments of 1,000 talents each.[16] Manlius Vulso

10. On the whole question of the general's authority in distribution of spoils, see I. Shatzman, *Historia* 21 (1972): 177–205, with extensive references. Cato's speeches on the subject: Plut. *Cato*, 10.4; Cato, *ORF*, fr. 98, 173, 203, 224–226. See, especially, fr. 173: *numquam ego praedam neque quod de hostibus captum esset neque manubias inter pauculos amicos meos divisi, ut illis eriperem qui cepissent.* Aemilius Paullus: Polyb. 18.35.4–5, 31.22. Scipio Aemilianus: Polyb. 18.35.9–12; cf. Val. Max. 4.3.13.

11. Much but not all the evidence in T. Frank, *An Economic Survey of Ancient Rome* I (Baltimore, 1933), 127–138, who combines testimony on both booty and indemnities.

12. Polyb. 2.12.3; Livy, 22.33.5. The sum is not reported.

13. Polyb. 18.44.7; Livy, 33.30.7; Plut. *Flam.* 9.5; Appian, *Mac.* 9.3. Alternative and less reliable figures reported by Valerius Antias and Claudius Quadrigarius: Livy, 33.30.8.

14. Livy, 34.35.11.

15. Polyb. 21.32.8–9; Livy, 38.11.8.

16. Polyb. 21.17.4–5, 21.41.8, 21.43.19; Livy, 37.45.14, 38.37.9, 38.38.13; Appian, *Syr.* 38; Diod. 29.10.

demanded 600 talents from Ariarathes of Cappadocia, who had collaborated with Antiochus and now showed himself belatedly repentant.[17] After Perseus' defeat in 168, Rome presented a hefty bill to the Macedonians: they would have to pay to the Republic half the taxes normally paid to the monarchy. A similar burden fell upon the former subjects of Genthius in Illyria.[18]

The combined revenues from these sources added up to an impressive sum. Enough to constitute a motive? One cannot readily put price tags on motives. Approach from that direction may be altogether erroneous anyway. A closer look at these exactions suggests that economic considerations do not supply the principal ingredient.

Longstanding Roman policy held that the costs of war should be reimbursed by the defeated foe.[19] The principle is implicit in every insistence upon indemnity. It becomes explicit in negotiations with Antiochus the Great. The Seleucid king offered to pay half the expenses incurred by Rome in the course of her war with him. L. Scipio the consul and his *consilium* dismissed that proposal out of hand: Antiochus would pay it all. He had started the war and he was liable for its costs.[20] Roman negotiators operated with consistency on that principle. Which is not to say that figures were calculated precisely to cover the outlays of the previous conflict. The round sums belie any rigid bookkeeping of that sort. Indemnities penalized as well as reimbursed. They underlined the power of the victor and the submission of the vanquished.[21]

Politics rather than economics took central place. The senate canceled Philip's reparation payments in 190 when he proved cooperative and valuable—just as they had done, under like circumstances, with Hiero II of Syracuse more than a half-century earlier.[22] The use of

17. Polyb. 21.41.7; Livy, 38.37.5–6.

18. Livy, 45.18.7, 45.26.14, 45.29.4; Diod. 31.18.3; Plut. *Aem. Paull.* 28.3.

19. Cf. Livy, 10.46.12—293 B.C.

20. Polyb. 21.14.1–7: ἔδοξε τῷ συνεδρίῳ τὸν στρατηγὸν ἀποκριθῆναι διότι τῆς μὲν δαπάνης οὐ τὴν ἡμίσειαν, ἀλλὰ πᾶσαν δίκαιόν ἐστιν Ἀντίοχον ἀποδοῦναι· φῦναι γὰρ τὸν πόλεμον ἐξ ἀρχῆς οὐ δι' αὑτούς, ἀλλὰ δι' ἐκεῖνον; Livy, 37.35.1–10; Appian, *Syr.* 29. And see Polyb. 21.17.4.

21. Cic. *Verr.* 2.3.12: *quasi victoriae praemium ac poena belli.* Cf. the thirty talents demanded of Boeotia in 196, after the murder of Roman soldiers: a "fine," says Livy, 33.29.12: *multae nomine triginta conferre talenta.*

22. On the cancellation of Philip's indemnity: Polyb. 21.3.3, 21.11.9; Livy, 37.25.12; Appian, *Mac.* 9.5; *Syr.* 23; Plut. *Flam.* 14.2. The treaty with Hiero in 263 imposed a payment of one hundred talents, according to Polyb. 1.16.9. Late Latin writers preserve a figure of two hundred talents, a less likely sum: Eutrop. 2.19.1; Oros. 4.7.3. Diodorus, 23.4.1, gives (the equivalent of) twenty-five talents, which may be a down payment; so Berve, *König Hieron II*, 36. The obligation, in any case, was cancelled in 248 when Rome framed a φιλία αἴδιος with Hiero: Zon. 8.16. Nothing in the evidence sanctions Harris'

monetary demands as a diplomatic posture gets clear illustration in Roman dealings with Aetolia in 191–189. Again and again, the Republic's representatives demanded unconditional surrender and a staggering indemnity of 1,000 talents, unyielding in their severity—until the Aetolians submitted. Then the consul suddenly proved amenable to persuasion: the indemnity demand was reduced by fifty percent.[23] Cash as enrichment of the public coffers evidently did not hold first importance for the Romans. In similar fashion, Manlius Vulso bullied Ariarathes of Cappadocia, stipulating 600 talents as price for a peaceful settlement with Rome. It took only the intervention of Eumenes, however, to get that fine also cut in half.[24] The Galatians, against whom Manlius had waged ruthless warfare and from whom he carried off considerable plunder, escaped any indemnity. The *aerarium* would get no steady income from that source.

The political character of these payments stands out. Rome looked to her prestige and her international position. In the midst of the Hannibalic war, the senate gave pointed reminder to Pinnes of Illyria about an overdue bill. The act served as a clear demonstration: Rome still held sway in the Adriatic, a message to Hannibal and the Illyrians alike. It was surely not the cash that mattered.[25] More than forty years later, the *patres* were unperturbed when Antiochus IV failed to meet the deadline for his indemnity payment.[26] An incident outside the eastern context shines the brightest light on Roman attitudes. Carthaginian envoys in 191 proposed to pay off their entire indemnity. Terms of the treaty after the Hannibalic war had obliged them to remit 10,000 talents in a payment schedule that stretched over fifty years. Now, only a decade or so after the agreement, Carthage showed herself ready to discharge her obligation in a single lump sum. The *patres*, however, rejected the offer with alacrity. They would accept not a coin before the date it fell due.[27] There can be but one explanation for that sharp retort. Continuous, long-term payments emphasized the submission of the former enemy and gave repeated reminder of her defeat, a lesson to other powers who might be recalcitrant or belligerent. The economic benefit was incidental.

To be sure, Rome welcomed the revenue. The first two-thirds of

---

assertion, *War and Imperialism*, 64, that Hiero paid an annual tax in addition to an indemnity.

23. Polyb. 21.2.3–6, 21.4–5, 21.29.9–21.30.2, 21.32.8–9; Livy, 37.1.5–6, 37.6.4–37.7.6, 37.49, 38.8.1–38.9.2, 38.9.8–38.11.1, 38.11.8.

24. Polyb. 21.41.7, 21.45; Livy, 38.37.5–6, 38.39.5–6; cf. Strabo, 13.4.2 (C624).

25. In fact, Rome offered the alternative of a further postponement of the indemnity, if Pinnes were willing to provide hostages; Livy, 22.33.5.

26. Livy, 42.6.6–11; cf. 2 Macc. 8:10.

27. Livy, 36.4.5–9: *de pecunia item responsum, nullam ante diem accepturos.*

the second century witnessed large-scale expenditures, major build-ing projects and public works, construction of the great highways in Italy.[28] Pliny reports a vast surplus in the *aerarium* for the year 157 B.C., one of its best-stocked years, of over 100 million HS.[29] Sub-stantial public wealth marks this era; and the connection with receipts from overseas is undeniable. But a pattern of planned and deliberate exploitation aimed at public enrichment is missing. Windfall prof-its were utilized, of course. Booty from Manlius Vulso's triumph in 187 wiped out the arrears of a public debt.[30] The loot that Aemilius Paullus deposited with the treasury after Pydna was so sizable that the government could dispense with direct taxation of Roman citi-zens.[31] A national budget, however, could hardly depend on the pro-ceeds of occasional plunder, even when spectacular. And indemnity payments were subject to the vagaries of international politics, re-tained, reduced, or cancelled in accordance with the diplomatic cir-cumstances, not the public economy. Insofar as regular, steady, and long-term income flowed from abroad, the West rather than the East supplied it. The fifty-year indemnity from Carthage was only a part. Receipts from the Spanish mines brought in about 36 million HS an-nually, so Polybius attests.[32]

Nothing like this regularity featured the profits that came out of the East, though the gains from particular conflicts could be phenom-enal. The senate refrained for a remarkably long time from institut-ing a permanent tribute in any Hellenic state. Even the assessments levied upon the Macedonians in 167 seem to represent an arrange-ment whereby the new republics could pay reparations for a war provoked (from the Roman point of view) by the now deposed mon-archy.[33] Systematic impositions in Macedonia began no earlier than 148, after the fall of Andriscus, when Rome at last accepted responsi-

28. Most of the references conveniently collected in Frank, *ESAR* I:183–187; cf. Crawford, *RRC* II:633–637, with table at 696–707; and see F. Coarelli, *AbhGött*, 97.1 (1976), 21–32; *PBSR* 32 (1977): 1–23.

29. Pliny, *NH*, 33.55–56; cf. Crawford, *RRC* II:635.

30. Livy, 39.7.5.

31. Cic. *De Off.* 2.76; Pliny, *NH*, 33.56; Plut. *Aem. Paull.* 38.1; Val. Max. 4.3.8. This did not mean that the state could count on a permanent abolition of *tributum*; see Nico-let, *Tributum* (Bonn, 1976), 1–5, 79–80.

32. Polyb. 34.9.9—as reported by Strabo, 3.2.10 (C148). Revenues from the Spanish mines have received considerable recent discussion: Badian, *Publicans and Sin-ners* (Ithaca, 1972), 31–34; J. S. Richardson, *JRS* 66 (1976): 140–147; R. C. Knapp, *As-pects of the Roman Experience in Iberia* (Vitoria, 1977), 171–173; Calboli, *Catonis, Oratio Pro Rhodiensibus*, 156–165.

33. Livy, 45.18.7, 45.26.13–14, 45.29.4; Diod. 31.8.3; Plut. *Aem. Paull.* 28.3; see Frank, *Roman Imperialism*, 209–210; Badian, *Roman Imperialism*, 18–19; Dahlheim, *Ge-walt und Herrschaft*, 259–261; and see below pp. 427–429.

bility for military supervision of the area, a supervision that needed to be paid for.[34] The Macedonian mines too were treated differently from those in Spain. Rome shut them down after the fall of Perseus, unwilling to let *publicani* reap the profits and distrustful of Macedonian management.[35] The rich revenues of Asia Minor came on the initiative of Attalus III, not on the prompting of Roman policy; and installation of a tax system waited still a decade after Attalus III's death, until the tribunate of C. Gracchus.[36] In the case of Greece proper, Rome probably fixed no tribute for yet another century, in the era of Augustus.[37] Of course, neither abstinence nor altruism guided this restraint. The Republic, its leaders and its representatives had rewarded themselves handsomely with spoils from the Greek East. But until they were ready to accept the chore of policing and administering that area, they never regarded it as a steady resource for the state economy.

Slavery and Policy

The spoils of war included the grimmest of commodities: human beings. The influx of slaves into Italy reached massive proportions in the third and second centuries. Total figures are impossible to come by, but there is no question that the era of the Punic Wars witnessed a sharp jump in numbers of slaves imported; war and the activities of the slave mart kept the process going throughout most of the second century.[38] The largest portion in the third century naturally came from the West, as war captives from Sicily, Spain, Africa, and Gaul. Fighting in the East, however, produced an increasingly large share during the second century. So, for example, Flamininus took five thousand prisoners in 197, sold some of them, and gave the rest to his soldiers as booty.[39] For the sale of Istrian captives in 177 we have surprisingly precise figures: 5,632.[40] Twenty-five hundred Boeotians at Haliartus went on the auction block after the city was taken in 171.[41] Then, at a

34. Porphyry, *FGH*, 2B, 260, F3, 19; Eusebius, *Chron.* 424c (Helm): Ῥωμαῖοι Μακεδόνας ὑποφόρους ἐποίησαντο ἀναιρεθέντος τοῦ Ψευδοφιλίππου; Jerome, *Chron.* 143 (Helm): *Romani interfecto Pseudophilippo Macedonas tributarios faciunt.*

35. Livy, 45.18.3–5; Diod 31.8.7; Cassiodorus, *Chron.* s. ann. 158 B.C. See below pp. 426–427.

36. See below pp. 605–608.

37. Cf. H. Hill, *CP* 41 (1946): 35–42; and see below pp. 525–526.

38. See W. L. Westermann, *The Slave Systems of Greek and Roman Antiquity* (Philadelphia, 1955), 60–63; H. Volkmann, *Die Massenversklavungen der Einwohner eroberter Städte in hellenistisch-römischen Zeit* (Mainz, 1961), 14–71, 110–118. A convenient summary in A. J. Toynbee, *Hannibal's Legacy* (Oxford, 1965), II:171–172.

39. Livy, 33.10.7, 33.11.2.   40. Livy, 41.11.8.   41. Livy, 42.63.10–11.

very different order of magnitude, after Pydna, Aemilius Paullus, on senatorial instructions, ordered the pillaging of seventy Epirote towns and the sale of 150 thousand souls into servitude.[42] No numbers survive for the aftermath of Andriscus' revolt, the Achaean war, and the suppression of Aristonicus in Asia Minor. That those conflicts brought substantial additions to the slave totals in Italy, however, we can take for granted.

This same era, the first half of the second century, witnessed a major shift in Italian land ownership. Wealth became concentrated in fewer hands, many peasant proprietors sold out to the capitalist farmer, and larger holdings stimulated the growth of ranches and plantations, as well as increased emphasis upon cash crops like the olive and the vine. For such operations, slave labor proved especially attractive and efficient. The small farmer had by no means vanished, but the trend is significant: a drop in numbers of free peasants, heavier investment in cash-crop farming and in pasturage, and a major expansion of the servile work force.[43] It seems compelling, therefore, to postulate a connection between the importation of slaves through overseas conquest and servile markets and the spread of capitalist agriculture in Italy—thus a potent economic element in Roman imperialism.[44]

Yet a reconsideration gives pause. Enslavement of war prisoners or their sale into slavery had a long history in the Roman experience and in antiquity generally. The practice stands on record again and again during the Republic's fight for control of Italy in the fifth and fourth centuries, well before the emergence of slave-based agriculture on any scale. As examples: seven thousand Samnites, so Livy states, were put on auction in 306; and the sale of Samnite captives in 293

42. Polyb. 30.15; Livy, 45.34.1–6; Plut. *Aem. Paull.* 29.1–3.

43. The trend is plain enough in Cato, *RR*, *passim*. A law to curb the ownership of excess public land by individuals was already on the books by 167: Cato, *ORF*, fr. 167. Cf. Livy, 42.1.6; Appian, *BC*, 1.7–8. Among numerous discussions, see G. Tibiletti, *Athenaeum* 26 (1948): 173–236; 27 (1949): 3–42; Toynbee, *Hannibal's Legacy* II: 155–189, 286–312, 554–561; Calboli, *Catonis Oratio Pro Rhodiensibus*, 200–214; Hopkins, *Conquerors and Slaves*, 48–64, 99–115.

44. So, e.g., Crawford, *Economic History Review* 30 (1977): 49–50. The connection finds acceptance in much but by no means all Marxist literature; see the summary of opinions in E. M. Štaerman, *Die Blütezeit der Sklavenwirtschaft in der römischen Republik* (Wiesbaden, 1969), 10–14. Štaerman herself questions the connection, stressing the importance of slave-breeding and enslavement for debt as principal sources for the servile population: *op. cit.* 36–70. But most of the information discussed refers to the late Republic; and she concedes that in the earlier period of Roman expansion war captives played a much larger role: *op. cit.*, 69. A balanced view in Harris, *War and Imperialism*, 80–85, who believes that Romans reckoned overseas war as a highly desirable means of obtaining slaves, though he denies that it is "the root of Roman imperialism."

brought in an enormous profit.[45] Romans naturally pursued this form of plunder when they engaged across the Adriatic as well. They were hardly alone in such activity. Indeed, Romans and Italians who fell into the hands of the enemy found themselves marketed as slaves. The land of Achaea alone held twelve hundred Italians in servitude in 194, and many more were scattered throughout Hellas, victims of the Hannibalic war.[46] Others languished as slaves in Crete, recorded under the year 189, sold as captives either by the Carthaginians or as a result of warfare in the Aegean and Asia Minor.[47] A clause in the peace of Apamea directed Antiochus to release all citizens and allies of Rome held as prisoners of war, deserters, captives, and slaves.[48]

Economics alone does not explain enslavement. Wrath and retaliation come into play: severe punishment as an object lesson. So, three towns of the Hirpini who betrayed Rome and joined Hannibal had their leaders executed and five thousand men sold into captivity in 215.[49] The defection of Capua incited fierce rage in Rome and issued, after its capture, in the nearly wholesale disposal of its population at the mart.[50] Scipio Africanus inflicted the same penalty upon the Turdetani because they were judged responsible for embroiling Saguntum with the Carthaginians and thus provoking the war.[51] The city of Same defected abruptly from the Roman cause and stirred up all Cephallenia in 189, a miscalculation that soon led to defeat and the sale of all those who surrendered.[52] Scipio Nasica administered similar punishments to the Dalmatians in 156; they had insulted Roman envoys and now suffered for it.[53] Other instances can readily be cited.[54] Retribution and reprisal dictated the harshness—and the need to make an example.

Where such purposes were absent, the senate could pursue a very different line. Undue ruthlessness featured the behavior of several Roman commanders in Greece during the Third Macedonian War. The consul of 171, P. Crassus, and the praetor, C. Lucretius

---

45. Livy, 9.42.8, 10.46.5. M. I. Finley argues cogently for an extensive growth of slavery in Italy by the third century B.C.; *Ancient Slavery and Modern Ideology* (New York, 1980), 83–86.

46. Livy, 34.50.3–7.

47. Livy, 37.60.3.

48. Polyb. 21.43.10; Livy, 38.38.7. Enslavement of the conquered foe was standard Hellenistic practice; Livy, 31.30.1–3.

49. Livy, 23.37.12–13.

50. Livy, 26.16.6, 26.34.1–3, 26.34.11.

51. Livy, 24.42.9–11.

52. Livy, 38.28.7, 38.29.11.

53. Zon. 9.25; cf. Polyb. 32.13.1–3, 32.13.9; Appian, *Ill.* 11.

54. Cf. Štaerman, *Blütezeit*, 38–40.

Gallus, assaulted the pro-Macedonian cities of Boeotia, plundered brutally, and sold captives directly into slavery. Sharp complaints were later heard in the senate about their reckless depredations. Envoys from Abdera and Chalcis delivered similar charges against Lucretius and also against L. Hortensius, praetor in Greece in 170, who had sacked those cities and indiscriminately enslaved their citizens. Senatorial action came swiftly and without equivocation: a stern censure of the offending generals and immediate orders that all those placed in bondage be sought out and emancipated.[55] Indeed, the peace treaty with Nabis in 195, a treaty whose terms were dictated by the Romans, asserted that no public or private slaves should be taken from the defeated Spartans and any already removed were to be returned to their owners.[56]

The facts plainly militate against any Roman policy of hunting slaves in the East to stock the farms of Italy. Inclusion of captives among the booty and sale of the vanquished foe accompanied Roman victories well before eastern expansion and well before the emergence of Italian capitalist agriculture. And it was by no means an invariable practice even in the age of expansion. Circumstances dictated particular decisions. Betrayal or defection would bring severe retribution, including enslavement, after recapture. On other occasions, acquisition of slaves was simply foregone, or the sale of captives by Roman commanders was actually reversed by the senate. The demands of the situation normally determined the deed. Cn. Manlius Vulso's campaigns against Galatian tribes provide an illuminating instance. He inflicted heavy casualties upon the Tolistobagii in 188 and also took forty thousand of them prisoner. If retained for any length of time, while Manlius still conducted military operations, they would be more burden than benefit. The commander forthwith sold them all to neighboring tribes.[57] The economic advantages of agricultural slavery seem rarely, if ever, to have guided decisions in overseas warfare. Given the flexibility and variety of behavior in this matter, it would be altogether erroneous to take the enslavement of 150 thousand Epirotes in 167 as representative and routine: it was anything but. The numbers themselves are far out of proportion to the norm. Special

55. Crassus and Lucretius: Livy, 42.63.3–12, 43.4.5–11, 43.7.5–43.8.10; *Per.* 43; Zon. 9.22. Hortensius: Livy, 43.4.8–13, 43.7.5–43.8.8. Cf. also the senatorial response in 170 to complaints from representatives of Alpine tribes, thousands of whom, it was charged, had been forced into servitude by C. Cassius Longinus; Livy, 43.5. And the *patres'* action with regard to the Ligurian Stellates enslaved by M. Popillius Laenas in 173: they reversed the deed, ordering their liberation and the return of the purchase price; Livy, 42.8.

56. Livy, 34.35.3–4.

57. Appian, *Syr.* 42.

circumstances must have decided the move: outrage at Epirote withdrawal from the Roman camp, the near-abduction of a Roman consul, and, most important, the necessity of driving home a lesson to the state whose defection menaced the Roman line of communications across the Adriatic.[58] Retaliation and politics predominate, not a forced migration of Epirotes to rural Italy.

None of this should be taken to imply that Roman leaders turned a blind eye on the economic benefits of importing servile labor or that they failed to take advantage of the large numbers of human beings whom overseas conquest threw onto the slave mart. Of course they availed themselves of the prizes—with profound effects on Roman agriculture. One must, however, avoid confusion of results with motives. The island of Delos flourished as a center of the slave trade, and most of its customers were unquestionably wealthy Italian landowners. Rome had made Delos a free port in 166, a major opening toward the island's great era of prosperity. Yet the connection between these facts is incidental rather than deliberate. Piratical activities in the eastern Mediterranean, not Roman wars, deposited most of the slaves onto Delos' clearing-house. The real age of Delian prosperity followed the destruction of Corinth in 146, rather than the island's transformation into a free port.[59] The government in Rome at no time, in our evidence, issued a single decision aimed at the importation of slave labor or the protection of the slave supply.[60]

Private Gain and Public Interest

Groups hitherto unperceived begin to force their way into the limelight during this era. Our sources, as ever, focus on the upper stratum of society, the landed aristocracy and senatorial leadership. We can, however, catch a glimpse, occasional and inadvertent, of something else. Behind or to the side of that landed aristocracy, a business and financial community began to take shape. To what effect—if any—on Roman eastward expansion?

The glimpses, at first, are few and fleeting. *Publicani*, private businessmen who bid for government contracts on public works and

58. Cf. J. A. O. Larsen, *Greek Federal States* (Oxford, 1968), 481–482, and see below pp. 512–513, 516–517.

59. Strabo, 10.5.4 (C486), 14.5.2 (C668). The fact is implicit in H. Maróti's discussion, *Helikon* 9–10 (1969–1970): 24–42.

60. So, rightly, Hopkins, *Conquerors and Slaves*, 112–113: "although slaves were often a significant element in war booty for both soldiers and generals, there is no evidence that the capture of slaves was a primary objective of warfare. Slaves were an important but incidental product of empire."

services, pop up briefly but unforgettably in our evidence on the Hannibalic war. They generously offered to carry on the work at their own expense, allowing the state to operate on credit, and foregoing repayment until the treasury was solvent. It was not all patriotism and philanthropy. The *publicani* set their own conditions and some of their number subsequently engaged in inventive fraud to turn a profit at the government's cost. No need to retell the story; what matters is the existence of these contractors, already in full swing and well established by the later third century.[61] Their activities soon expanded and diversified. The censors let contracts for a salt tax beginning in 204. Harbor dues were collected by the *publicani* at least by 199. And they gained responsibility too for the *scriptura* or pasturage tax.[62] The contractors continued to manage the organization of supplies for Rome's armies during the second century, a task that grew in magnitude and augmented their influence.[63] More lucrative still was the operation of the Spanish mines, very probably in the hands of *publicani* since 195.[64]

Publicani were not alone among the rising tide of business interests. The *lex Claudia* of 218 forbade any senator or son of a senator from owning a seagoing vessel that could carry more than three hundred *amphorae*. Whatever the political meaning of this measure, it implies at least that there were men outside the senate who *did* engage

61. Livy, 23.48.4–23.49.4, 24.18.10–11, 25.3.8–25.5.1; Val. Max. 5.6.8; cf. Badian, *Publicans and Sinners*, 16–21. The government also borrowed money from a host of citizens outside the business community: Livy, 26.36, 29.16.1–3, 31.13, 33.42.2–4.

62. Salt tax: Livy, 29.37.3–4; Dio, 57.70–71; cf. Gellius, 2.22.29. Harbor dues: Livy, 32.7.3; extended after 179: Livy, 40.51.4; cf. S. J. De Laet, *Portorium* (Bruges, 1949), 55–63. Pasturage tax: Plautus, *Truc.* 143–151; cf. Appian, *BC*, 1.7; Pliny, *NH*, 18.11.

63. See, e.g., Livy, 44.16.4 (169 B.C.). Rightly, Badian, *Publicans and Sinners*, 27–29, against Frank, *ESAR* I:148–150, and Toynbee, *Hannibal's Legacy* II:356.

64. Livy, 34.21.7, affirms that Cato arranged for collection of revenues from the iron and silver mines in that year. The evidence of Polybius speaks to the handsome income derived from that source: twenty-five thousand *denarii* a day: Polyb. 34.9.8–11 = Strabo, 3.2.10 (C147–148). Frank's view, *ESAR* I:154–155, that the Roman government supervised the mines directly until 179, has been adequately refuted; see Brunt, in R. Seager, *The Crisis of the Roman Republic* (Cambridge, 1969), 104–107; Badian, *Publicans and Sinners*, 31–33; Cassola, *I gruppi politici*, 74–77. *Publicani* do not receive express mention. Hence, Richardson, *JRS* 66 (1976): 140–147, argues that the mines were let to small-scale lessees, rather than to the major companies of *publicani*—a suggestion buttressed by Diodorus' reference to a multitude of Italians who enriched themselves through the Spanish mines: 5.36.2: πλῆθος Ἰταλῶν ἐπεπόλασε τοῖς μετάλλοις, καὶ μεγάλους ἀνεφέροντο πλούτους διὰ τὴν φιλοκερδίαν; cf. Strabo, 3.2.10 (C147). However, these persons may well have been employees or agents for the *publicani*, rather than independent small contractors. Cf. Livy, 45.18.4, on the Macedonian mines in 167: *nam neque sine publicano exerceri posse*; and see Calboli, *Catonis Oratio Pro Rhodiensibus*, 156–165.

in maritime commerce on rather a handsome scale.[65] Moneylenders were much in evidence by the early second century—so much so that the government had to take action against usury and to close loopholes allowing for evasion of maximum interest rates.[66] Cato, with typical self-righteousness, unceremoniously expelled the moneylenders he found in Sardinia in 198.[67] The profession, however, certainly persisted. So long as loans for transactions, whether agricultural or commercial, were in demand, the *faenerator* would be around. The comedies of Plautus regularly mock bankers and loan sharks. Before the middle of the second century Scipio Aemilianus had his own personal banker to handle his financial obligations.[68] Merchants and profiteers followed the armies abroad in wartime, ready brokers of military spoils, who often made a nuisance of themselves.[69]

Business activities plainly proliferated in the late third and early

65. Livy, 21.63.3–4. Livy's assertion that all senators except C. Flaminius opposed the bill must be exaggerated. The assembly did pass it, and hardly over unanimous senatorial objection. Cf. A. Lippold, *Consules. Untersuchungen zur Geschichte des römischen Konsulates von 264 bis 201 v. Chr.* (Bonn, 1963), 93–95. Conventional opinion holds that the bill represents an effort by the commercial classes to exclude senators from maritime traffic. If so, it had little effect and could easily be skirted by using front men and agents; cf. Plut. *Cato*, 21.5–6; Cic. *Verr.* 2.5.45. A long register of scholarly viewpoints is summarized by Cassola, *I gruppi politici*, 216–217, who turns the theory on its head and argues that the *lex Claudia* was meant to exclude the commercial and business classes from the senate! That idea fails to account for the extensive senatorial opposition. Moralistic posturing rather than economic advantage may be the principal element. Cf. now Nicolet, *Annales, ESC* 5 (1980): 878–882; J. H. D'Arms, *Commerce and Social Standing in Ancient Rome* (Cambridge, Mass., 1981), 31–33.

66. Livy, 35.7.2–5, 35.41.9–10—very likely unenforceable. In any case, a *lex Junia de feneratione* was proposed not much later, containing provisions which did not find favor with M. Cato: *ORF*, fr. 56–57. The reasons for Cato's opposition have given rise to much conjecture, unverifiable and unimportant for our purposes; the most recent, with reference to previous discussions, by Astin, *Cato the Censor*, 321–323. Still another measure, the *lex Marcia*, perhaps in the 180s, endeavored to strengthen regulations against excessive interest charges: Gaius, *Inst.* 4.23.

67. Livy, 32.27.3–4. These *faeneratores* were surely Romans or Italians, not Carthaginians; as Frank, *ESAR* I: 208; see Briscoe, *Commentary*, 219–220. For Cato's attitude on usury, see further, Cato, *RR, praef.* 1; Cic. *De Off.* 2.89.

68. Polyb. 31.27. Among Plautine references to financiers and money lenders—surely not altogether limited to Greek experience—see *Curc.* 371–379, 480, 506–511, 558–559, 618, 679–685, 721–722; *Asin.* 438–440; *Persa*, 434–437; *Pseud.* 286–287; *Epid.* 53–54, 114–115, 252; *Most.* 532–540, 560–561, 621–631, 657–658, 916–917, 1140, 1160–1161; *Men.* 582–584; *Capt.* 192–193; *Aul.* 527–530; *Trin.* 425–426a; *Truc.* 66–73. See J. Andreau, *MEFRA* 80 (1968): 461–526—who endeavors to isolate the Greek and the Latin elements in Plautus' remarks on the subject.

69. Polyb. 14.7.2–3 (Scipio's African campaign in the Hannibalic war); Livy, 34.9.12 (Cato's campaign in Spain in 195); Appian, *Lib.* 115 (the Third Punic War). A much earlier example in Italy in Livy, 10.17.3.

second centuries. The *publicanus* makes appearance in the Plautine plays.[70] And from the activities of the *publicani*, many profited: censorial contracts for public works of every kind benefited shareholders, employees, agents, and a host of persons who capitalized on business arising out of the contracts.[71]

Most of the information gathered above, however, applies to Italy and the West. Activities of the *publicani* and their concomitant beneficiaries in the Hellenic world had to await the era of Rome's occupation and permanent installations. Lesser businessmen, on the other hand, *negotiatores* and *mercatores*, moved East much earlier. No need for them to hold back and calculate military conquest or annexation.

Scattered epigraphical and literary allusions disclose Italians in Hellenic lands even in the early and middle third century. A certain L. Folius (or Olius) made dedication to Athena on the Acropolis at Rhodian Lindos, a bilingual offering, some time in the first half of that century.[72] Not much later, an Aetolian proxeny decree named among its honorants a Roman, Olceus son of Lucius.[73] In 252, as it happens, an incidental notice in Plutarch's *Life of Aratus* makes reference to a Roman merchant vessel bound for Syria.[74] Before the end of the century we learn of a certain Lucius, son of Gaius, in the king's service, an official in the bureaucracy of Ptolemy IV Philopator.[75] The random character of our data makes it unlikely that these are isolated examples. But they are individual examples. Nothing in that evidence suggests that Rome, rather than particular Romans and Italians, enjoyed trade relations with Rhodes, Aetolia, Syria, or Egypt.[76]

Additional evidence, fragmentary but cumulative in effect, points to private dealings in the East by individuals or groups from Italy—a matter very different from interstate entanglements. Italian traders, doubtless south Italians, carried on regular commercial intercourse across the Adriatic and had done so for some time by 230.[77] Exiles from Italy had found refuge and were dwelling in Leucas by

70. Plautus, *Truc.* 143–151; cf. *Trin.* 794; *Men.* 117–118.

71. Polyb. 6.17.1–4: καὶ σχεδὸν ὡς ἔπος εἰπεῖν πάντας ἐνδεδέσθαι ταῖς ὠναῖς καὶ ταῖς ἐργασίαις ταῖς ἐκ τούτων. See the excellent discussion by Badian, *Publicans and Sinners*, 45–47. Add also Diod. 5.36.2, quoted above, n. 64.

72. *ILLRP*, I, no. 245; cf. Cassola, *PP* 15 (1960): 385–393.

73. *IG*, IX, 1², 17, line 51.

74. Plut. *Arat.* 12.4.

75. *IC*, III, 4, 18. Other individuals, Roman or Italian, receive mention on Delian inscriptions of the third century: *IG*, XI, 2, 115, line 25; *IG*, XI, 2, 287A, line 58; *IG*, XI, 4, 642. See further F. Cordano, *Settima miscellanea greca e romana* (1980), 255–270.

76. *Contra*: Cassola, *I gruppi politici*, 31–32—who offers only assertions and no arguments.

77. Polyb. 2.8.1–2.

197.[78] Frequent travel to the Peloponnese by Italians engaged in commerce is hinted at by a passage of Polybius with reference to the year 183.[79] Roman citizens and Latins in some numbers had settled in or were visiting Illyria where, it was alleged, they suffered indignities at the hands of Genthius and were held at Corcyra in 180.[80] D. Cossutius, a Roman citizen, got a commission from king Antiochus IV to complete the Athenian Olympeion ca. 174. He was the first known of a family that held prominence for several generations in architecture and the building-and-sculpture trade.[81]

The foregoing examples show just how varied and how random is our information.[82] In addition, numerous inscriptions attest the presence of individual Romans and Italians in the Greek East, most of them proxeny decrees revealing little about the persons except their presence. The vast majority, however, were clearly traders, financiers, or small businessmen. During the second century they are to be found primarily in Greece proper and in the Cyclades. Only toward the end of the century, as might be expected, do they begin to turn up in Asia Minor, and later still further east. The best evidence comes from the island of Delos, where communities of Ῥωμαῖοι appear in increasing numbers not long after Delos became a free port in 166, then considerably augmented by those who migrated there following the destruction of Corinth in 146. The settlers' provenance is often hard to make out. Earlier assumptions derived the largest number from southern Italy and Campania, many of them Italiote Greeks or of Oscan race, with few stemming from Rome, Latium, and central Italy—a logical hypothesis, but probably wrong. Identifiable names show, if anything, a majority of Romans and Latins.[83] The appeal of

78. Livy, 33.17.11—traders, according to Briscoe, *Commentary*, 280. That is conjecture.

79. Polyb. 23.9.12, cf. 23.17.3.

80. Livy, 40.42.4.

81. Vitruv. 7, praef. 15, 17; cf. *IG*, III, 1, 561. On the family, see E. Rawson, *PBSR* 43 (1975): 36–47.

82. One might add also Livy, 33.29.4—Roman soldiers after the Second Macedonian War traveling through Boeotia *negotiandi causa*. But they had not gone to Greece originally for that purpose.

83. Most of the evidence on the Italians at Delos is collected in the classic work of J. Hatzfeld, *BCH* 36 (1912): 5–218; see further P. Roussel, *Délos, colonie athénienne* (Paris, 1916), 75–84; W. A. Laidlaw, *A History of Delos* (Oxford, 1933), 201–210; cf. A. Donati, *Epigraphica* 27 (1965): 3–59, on Romans in the Aegean generally. Hatzfeld's broader study treats Italian traders and emigrants all over the East: *Les trafiquants italiens dans l'Orient hellénique* (Paris, 1919), *passim*, especially 17–51. His view, *op. cit.*, 238–256, that most of the emigrants were Italians from the south, with very few Roman citizens, held the field for a long time; accepted, e.g., without question by Toynbee, *Hannibal's Legacy* II: 363–369. The evidence, when reconsidered, however, seems to point in the opposite

the Hellenic East had worked its allure among steadily swelling numbers of 'Ρωμαῖοι, traders and tradesmen, bankers and pilgrims, visitors and settlers.[84]

A surge in business activities and a migration of Italians to the East in this era command attention. Yet the formidable question still confronts us: what reason is there to believe that increased commercial and banking activities and the movement of private individuals to Hellenic lands helped determine senatorial policy on the East?[85]

The influence of financiers and contractors on decisions of state would be most difficult to document. And some potent evidence to the contrary stands in the way. As noted already, the senate three times at least during the early second century sponsored enactments to crack down on usurious practices and to curb money lenders.[86] The aediles of 192 were so assiduous in imposing fines upon the *faeneratores* that they collected enough capital to set up rich dedications in the Capitol and finance the building of a portico.[87] The *lex Marcia*, probably of the 180s, in a stunning reversal of previous practice, even permitted debtors to seize upon the persons of their creditors and hold them until the excessive interest that had been exacted was repaid.[88]

More interesting still are the government's relations with the companies of *publicani*. Rome could not, of course, do without the contractors. Public services of all varieties, including military supplies, building projects, operation of the mines, and collection of indirect taxes, which the state was unwilling to manage itself, depended upon personnel and expertise provided by the *publicani*. It does not follow, however, that decisions reached in the senate adhered to the interests and goals of the contractors' community.

The insurance scandal engineered by two *publicani* during the dark days of the Hannibalic war hardly promoted cordiality between government and business. The pair had falsely claimed losses in their shipments to the armies in order to gain state compensation, indeed

---

direction; see A. J. N. Wilson, *Emigration from Italy in the Republican Age of Rome* (Manchester, 1966), 88–93, 105–111 (Delos); 152–155 (elsewhere in Greece—the evidence much thinner and most of it later than the second century). Cf. also Cassola, *DialArch* 4–5 (1970–1971): 317, who estimates an even larger proportion of Roman citizens.

84. Discussion of their activities, unfortunately marred by excessive speculation, in Hatzfeld, *Les trafiquants*, 193–237; briefer and more cautious is Wilson, *Emigration*, 156–164. Too little of the evidence on this matter, however, can be nailed down to the second century. As example note Sex. Orfidienus in Chyretiae in the late 190s: *ArchEph* (1917): 1–7 = *ISE*, no. 95.

85. As maintained, e.g., by Cassola, *I gruppi politici*, 56–71; Perelli, *Imperialismo*, 145–153.

86. See above p. 301.   87. Livy, 35.41.9–10.   88. Gaius, *Inst.* 4.23.

had deliberately put superannuated vessels to sea, thereby to rid themselves of worthless stock and obtain government subsidies on top of it. When the fraudulence came to light an explosive political battle erupted, ending in firm government action against the offending *publicani*.[89] This behavior may have been uncharacteristic of the contractors as a group. But the affair must have engendered an aura of suspicion and wariness in dealings between the state and business companies engaged in public services.

In the censorship of 184, M. Cato and L. Valerius Flaccus instituted major construction projects with the revenues acquired from recent wars in the East. They hoped to avoid lining the pockets of the *publicani*. Contracts were let at highest prices for the *vectigalia*, at lowest for goods and services. The *publicani* complained and got some support in the senate, mainly from political foes of Cato, like T. Flamininus. On senatorial instructions, the censors had to renegotiate the contracts. They did so in their own way: previous purchasers were excluded from the bidding and the new contracts differed little in price from the previous. *Publicani* had gained some temporary senatorial backing, but only as part of a factional fight in the *curia*. The censors prevailed in the end, with the *patres'* compliance. The contractors, obviously not a major political force, had to take what they could get.[90] Subsequent censors in 179 and 174 also had handsome contracts to let and rode out their terms without encountering friction from contractors, at least none on record. The *publicani*, it seems, were chastened.

Fireworks burst out again in the next censorship. For reasons unknown, the censors of 169 banned the companies that had obtained contracts under their predecessors from bidding in the auctions of that year and from any partnership with those which might win the bids. Complaints to the senate this time availed nothing. A tribune took up the cause of the aggrieved *publicani*, not out of sympathy for their claims but to pursue his own political grudge against the censors. The clash of censorial and tribunician authority heated passions and brought about criminal proceedings under which the assembly nearly convicted one of the censors. An acquittal terminated the contest; there followed political retaliation against the

89. Livy, 25.3.8–25.5.1. The analysis by Toynbee, *Hannibal's Legacy* II: 351–355, is unreliable. See Badian's discussion, *Publicans and Sinners*, 17–20.

90. Livy, 39.44.5–9; Plut. *Cato*, 19.1–2; *Flam.* 19.3. Cato plainly was not at variance with the senate here in any serious sense; rightly D. Kienast, *Cato der Zensor* (Heidelberg, 1954), 79–87; Calboli, *Catonis Oratio Pro Rhodiensibus*, 169–173. The relative impotence and lack of solidarity among the *publicani* is stressed by Badian, *Publicans and Sinners*, 35–38.

tribune. The aims of the contractors were thwarted. Indeed, they had been secondary from the outset, triggering a conflict which then revolved around other issues. None of the principals had the interests of the *publicani* at heart or was guided by them.[91] The storm aroused in that year, however, soured more *patres* on the activities of the business community. Resentment and annoyance received outlet in 167 when the senate refused to let contracts for the lucrative gold and silver mines and the royal estates of Macedonia, in order to keep those profits out of the hands of the *publicani*.[92] The mines were then shut down, to be reopened nearly a decade later—and then quite possibly turned over to the Macedonians rather than to the *publicani*.[93]

The upshot of this testimony is clear enough. Roman senators, far from making policy at the behest of the business communities, often found themselves in conflict with financiers, money lenders, and contractors. Those intermittent clashes should not be taken to imply a fundamental and consistent divergence of interests. But the *patres* plainly took their decisions on affairs of state for reasons other than the aims and profits of *negotiatores*. A noteworthy fact needs to be underscored: the absence of the Roman *denarius* as currency in Greek lands anywhere during the Republic.[94] The senate did not act to ripen Hellas for plucking by businessmen.

Businessmen apart, were not senators themselves interested in gain? They shunned the image, for certain, or, at least, historians and intellectuals shunned it for them. The *lex Claudia* of 218 was passed, so Livy claims, because all profit seemed unworthy of senators.[95] To increase one's patrimony, L. Crassus asserted in court, is simply not done by the *nobilitas*.[96] True *nobiles* despise money; their goal is *gloria*

91. Livy, 43.16.2–16.

92. Livy, 45.18.3–4: *metalli quoque Macedonici, quod ingens vectigal erat, locationes praediorumque rusticorum tolli placebat; nam neque sine publicano exerceri posse et, ubi publicanus esset, ibi aut ius publicum vanum aut libertatem sociis nullam esse*; cf. Diod. 31.8.7. In view of the episodes discussed above, there is no reason to regard Livy's language as reflecting only attitudes of the late Republic. Connection between the affairs of 169 and the senatorial decision of 167 is correctly affirmed by Badian, *Publicans and Sinners*, 40–43. But he goes too far in seeing the senate as frightened by a serious challenge to its authority on the part of the *publicani*. Nothing of this in the sources. The near conviction of one of the censors in 169 came on a very different issue: censorial interference with *tribunicia potestas*: Livy, 43.16.8–16.

93. Livy, 45.29.11; Cassiodorus, *Chron.* s.ann. 158 B.C. Who ran them subsequently is unknown. But no good reason exists to assume it was the *publicani*, as Badian, *Publicans and Sinners*, 44. Cf. L. Perelli, *RivFilol* 103 (1975): 408–409.

94. See, most recently, Giovannini, *Rome et la circulation monétaire en Grèce au IIe siecle avant Jésus-Christ* (Basel, 1978), 24–35, with reference to earlier literature.

95. Livy, 21.63.4: *quaestus omnis patribus indecorus visus.*

96. Cic. *De Orat.* 2.225: *patrimonione augendo? at id non est nobilitatis.*

and the affection of fellow citizens, as a Ciceronian oration declares.[97] The cultivation of simplicity and temperance, of self-restraint and self-sufficiency characterized the image as projected again and again in legends and literature.[98]

Restraint, however, was not tantamount to abstinence or asceticism. The very passage of the *lex Claudia* makes sense only if some senators had engaged in shipping on a fairly large scale; and the bill provoked substantial opposition in the *curia*. Moreover, it was honored more in the breach than in the observance.[99] The venerable Cato himself lent out cash for maritime enterprises and invested capital in various agricultural and business operations that brought in handsome profits.[100] Cato found no inconsistency here with his fulminations against usury and *faeneratores*. Rightly so: it was one thing to pursue the dubious profession as a livelihood, quite another—and entirely acceptable—for a landed aristocrat to add to his assets by lending cash on the side.[101] Cato, after all, wrote a book on capitalist agriculture, a venture he found perfectly in accord with the traditional virtues of a peasant farmer.[102] Avarice *per se*, of course, was deplorable, beneath the contempt of respectable *nobiles*. But the increase of wealth—so long as it was done in honorable and estimable fashion—could stand as a mark of prestige. The funeral *laudatio* delivered by Q. Metellus for his father in 221 listed among his proudest aspirations the aim to acquire great wealth *bono modo*.[103] Cato counseled his son in similar fashion: increase of property shows the measure of a man, indeed godlike qualities attach to him who added more to his holdings than he inherited.[104] Polybius observed the ethos and reported it: Romans condemn illicit gains with as much vehemence as they applaud honest money-making.[105] Sallust drew the same distinction a century later in commending Romans of an earlier day: glory and praise motivated them, but also "wealth acquired honorably."[106]

97. Cic. *Phil.* 1.29: *nobilis homines . . . non pecuniam . . . quae semper ab amplissimo quoque clarissimoque contempta est . . . sed caritatem civium et gloriam concupivisse.*

98. Some examples in Harris, *War and Imperialism*, 264–265.

99. See above pp. 300–301.

100. Plut. *Cato*, 21.5–6. Note also the activity of Cato's contemporary M. Aemilius Lepidus in 179; Livy, 40.51.2.

101. See the analysis by Astin, *Cato the Censor*, 319–320; cf. Calboli, *Catonis Oratio Pro Rhodiensibus*, 192–195, and n. 45.

102. Cf. Astin, *Cato the Censor*, 249–258.

103. Pliny, *NH*, 7.139–140 = *ORF*, no. 6, fr. 2: *pecuniam magnam bono modo invenire.*

104. Plut. *Cato*, 21.8. Cf. Cato, *ORF*, fr. 167.

105. Polyb. 6.56.3: καθ᾽ ὅσον γὰρ ἐν καλῷ τίθενται τὸν ἀπὸ τοῦ κρατίστου χρηματισμόν, κατὰ τοσοῦτο πάλιν ἐν ὀνείδει ποιοῦνται τὴν ἐκ τῶν ἀπειρημένων πλεονεξίαν.

106. Sallust, *Cat.* 7.6: *divitias honestas;* cf. Cic. *De Off.* 1.92.

The combined testimony forms a clear picture. Senatorial aristocrats might affect scorn for petty tradesmen and abhor business dealings as an occupation, but they had no disdain, in practice or principle, for the acquisition of capital.[107]

That many Roman senators had economic interests outside the possession of land in Italy ought never to have been doubted. It is a very long stride, however, from acknowledgment of this rather obvious fact to the speculative surmise that senators' economic enterprises determined or strongly influenced the decisions of state. The *patres* indeed seem to have been careful to avoid even the appearance of a conflict of interest along these lines. In the late Republic, senators were barred by law from membership or shareholding in the companies of contractors for public services, an exclusion that surely dates back to the third and second centuries.[108] Such scrupulousness in the official posture makes it most unlikely that any senator gave voice in *curia* or *contio* for economic considerations as grounds for determining foreign policy.[109] Those who reckon material advantages as a principal aim of empire get small comfort from the contemporary observations of Polybius. The Greek historian saw a connection but reversed it. In Polybius' view, accumulation of wealth had as its purpose the advance of imperialism.[110] It evidently never occurred to him that the means and ends might be the other way around.

Economics and the Decisions of State

Governmental decisions on matters of foreign policy had a host of elements to consider, political, diplomatic, strategic. Where did

107. The point is made, most recently, by Harris, *War and Imperialism*, 56–58, 65–67, 86–93; cf. Gabba, *MAAR* 36 (1980): 91–102; D'Arms, *Commerce and Social Standing*, 33–39. Obvious enough once stated, but too frequently unacknowledged. Even scorn for tradesmen, laborers, and merchants had its limitations. Petty operations earned little respect, but large-scale commerce, if one takes Cicero as guide, could win admiration, especially if profits were invested in land: Cic. *De Off.* 1.150–151; cf. Finley, *The Ancient Economy* (Berkeley and Los Angeles, 1973), 41–56; D'Arms, *op. cit.*, 20–31. Whether this same attitude held in the middle Republic is not demonstrable.

108. Paulus, Leyden fr. 3, in G. G. Archi, *Pauli sententiarum fragmentum leidense* (Leyden, 1965), 13; Asconius, 93, Clark; Dio, 55.10.4–5; cf. Badian, *Publicans and Sinners*, 120, n. 16; Harris, *War and Imperialism*, 90–91. Nicolet, *Annales*, ESC 5 (1980): 879–880, dates the ban, too confidently, to C. Gracchus' tribunate.

109. Cato alleged in 167 that advocates of war on Rhodes hoped to strip her of resources and make her wealth their own; Gellius, 6.3.7, 6.3.52. But no one surely argued for war openly on that basis. Indeed, if Sallust is right, the senate rejected war precisely to avoid the stigma of undertaking it for purpose of enrichment: Sallust, *Cat.* 51.5: *ne quis divitiarum magis quam iniuriae causa bellum inceptum diceret*.

110. Polyb. 9.10.11: τὸ μὲν οὖν τὸν χρυσὸν καὶ τὸν ἄργυρον ἀθροίζειν πρὸς

economic elements come into consideration? A few examples can be isolated. Assessment of their meaning and weight, however, encounters ambiguity. Only the audacious can claim confidence on this slippery terrain.

Did the state protect financial and commercial interests in its dealings with overseas powers? The evidence allows but a cautious answer: rarely, if at all, and without consistency. Roman mercantile activity gets mention in the second treaty with Carthage, probably ca. 348. The relevant clauses restrict it sharply. Rome was either unwilling or unable to promote it. Carthage obviously dictated those clauses in the compact.[111] The provisions, it appears, were renewed when the two cities concluded another agreement in 279. The state evidently did not extend itself to advance the interests of shippers and merchants.[112]

The Pyrrhic war put Rome in intimate contact with communities of southern Italy, especially Greek cities in the area, heavily engaged in traffic across the Adriatic. A heightening of the Republic's interest in such traffic would be logical enough, not in terms of direct involvement but to maintain the solidarity of Rome's new network of alliances. Associations in that area, particularly with Rhegium on the straits, led Messana to seek Roman aid against Syracuse and helped precipitate the First Punic War. Investigation of the reasons for that conflict lies outside our scope. As impetus for Rome's initial move, however, pressure from Greek allies in Campania and southern Italy might be taken into account. A threat to control the straits by either Syracuse or Carthage would give them good reason for alarm.[113] Rome herself had no commercial stake in that waterway; but her own suzerainty in Italy depended on compliance and cooperation of key cities in Magna Graecia. Considerations of that sort help to explain Roman threats and then action against the Illyrians in 230 and 229: Italian traders had been harassed, and the growing Illyrian power suddenly turned into a major menace in the Adriatic. Rome was by then well acquainted with the region. Envoys from Apollonia had sought her out after the Pyrrhic war, and the senate had dispatched a Latin colony to Brundisium in 244. Interconnections between Hellenic cities on both sides of the straits of Otranto had an impact. Rome sent her forces against Illyria, it might be noted, when Epidamnus was

αὐτοὺς ἴσως ἔχει τινὰ λόγον· οὐ γὰρ οἷόν τε τῶν καθόλου πραγμάτων ἀντιποιήσασθαι μὴ οὐ τοῖς μὲν ἄλλοις ἀδυναμίαν ἐνεργασαμένους, σφίσι δὲ τὴν τοιαύτην δύναμιν ἑτοιμάσαντας.

111. Polyb. 3.24.4, 3.24.8, 3.24.11–12.

112. Polyb. 3.25.2. The evidence discussed by Cassola, *I gruppi politici*, 27–33, nowhere supports his contention that the government backed commercial interests.

113. Observe Polyb. 1.20.14: ships supplied by Tarentum, Locris, Elea, and Naples to transport Rome's forces in the first crossing of the channel.

under assault.[114] The *patres* knew well the importance of commercial exchange in the Ionian Gulf, as they appreciated the crucial situation of the straits of Messina. Insofar as such matters played a role in decisions to intervene, however, they represented the claims of Rome's allies and *amici*, not the promotion of a Roman mercantile interest.[115] The political implications of maintaining a hold on the Italian "confederacy," rather than direct economic advantage, prevailed in those decisions.

One famous senatorial action would seem to support the economic hypothesis. In 187 the *patres* passed a decree awarding Ambracia the privilege of imposing whatever harbor dues she wished—so long as Romans and Latins were exempt from payment.[116] On the face of it, economic aims furthered by the government in this instance appear incontrovertible. Depending on one's viewpoint and argument, the episode is either a cornerstone or an embarrassment, either exemplary or exceptional.[117] The matter can benefit from closer scrutiny than it has received. No parallels exist, as is often pointed out, in other Roman treaties. One can go further. This provision is not contained in a treaty at all. The relevant pact with Aetolia had been concluded two years before. A *senatus consultum* is at issue here. Political circumstances called it forth, as Livy's account makes abundantly clear. Charges surfaced against M. Fulvius Nobilior for ruthless ravaging of Ambracia. Fulvius' embittered political foe, M. Lepidus, twice thwarted by him in consular elections, engineered the accusations and coached Ambraciote representatives in their testimony.[118]

114. Rome as advocating the cause of Italian traders: Polyb. 2.8.2–3. Dispatch of troops during the siege of Epidamnus: Polyb. 2.10.9–2.11.1. The visit from Apollonians: Livy, *Per.* 15; Zon. 8.7; Val. Max. 6.6.5. Colony at Brundisium: Vell. Pat. 1.14.8; Cic. *Ad Att.* 4.1.4; cf. Livy, *Per.* 19. And see below pp. 359–368. Similarly, Rome's decision to forge an alliance with Aetolia in 212 or 211 and enter the First Macedonian War probably came after Philip V's capture of Lissus, which made him a direct threat to the cities of the southern Adriatic: Polyb. 8.14; Livy, 26.24.8; and see below pp. 375–378.

115. The senate did take up the cause of traders from Italy captured by Carthage during the Mercenary War in the 230s. Swift negotiations secured their release: Polyb. 1.83.7–10, 3.28.3; cf. Zon. 8.17; Val. Max. 5.1.1a; Eutrop. 2.27. These merchants too were probably Italians for the most part, rather than Roman citizens. Cicero obscures the distinction: *Verr.* 2.5.149; *Imp. Pomp.* 11.

116. Livy, 38.44.4: *portoria quae vellent terra marique caperent, dum eorum immunes Romani ac socii nominis Latini essent.*

117. So, Frank, *Roman Imperialism,* 279–280: "an exceptional rather than a normal stipulation." By contrast, Harris, *War and Imperialism,* 94: "likely to have been extended later to some other places." Holleaux, *Études* V:430, n. 4, finds it irrelevant. Cassola, *I gruppi politici,* 63–64, takes it as proof of economic motivation. Badian, *Roman Imperialism,* 17, passes over the event hurriedly.

118. Livy, 38.43.1–2: *Inimicitiae inter M. Fulvium et M. Aemilium consulem erant, et super cetera Aemilius serius biennio se consulem factum M. Fulvii opera ducebat. Itaque ad invidiam ei faciendam legatos Ambracienses in senatum subornatos criminibus introduxit.*

Out of this acrimonious exchange came the senatorial resolution, a direct and deliberate slap at Fulvius. The decree declared Ambracia free and self-governing, authorized recovery of all property by her citizens, and ordered restoration of all art objects plundered from the land. The allowance of port dues was but one provision in that omnibus measure.[119] Its passage plainly directed a rebuke at Fulvius and sought to make amends to the Ambraciotes. Permission of unlimited harbor tolls showed senatorial favor in a gesture meant to rehabilitate the state's finances. It was only logical and proper for the benefactors to be exempt from paying the revenues authorized by their benefaction. The measure's purpose had nothing to do with enriching Rome's commercial classes.

The Ambracia incident is a special case. Hence, no surprise that similar provisions are absent in known treaties, and no reason to postulate their presence in unknown ones.[120] The peculiar circumstances operative here preclude its citation as symptomatic of a general Roman policy. If a parallel be sought, it might indeed be found in a precisely contemporary Roman treaty—but one not to the advantage of Roman traders. The peace of Apamea in 188 contained a clause allowing Rhodes to seek any reparations due her from the Seleucid kingdom, and which guaranteed that Rhodian goods would be free of duty.[121] We may be certain whence the initiative for that provision came. Rhodes had enjoyed the privilege before in Seleucid lands and wished to continue or revive it.[122] Rome simply indulged her ally.

Two decades later, when the Republic had reason to make an example of Rhodes, she emphasized economic means again. This time, in 166, she turned Delos into a free port and put the island under the authority of Athens. Rhodian revenues dropped precipitately, as the attractions of a toll-free harbor diverted commercial traffic to Delos.[123] Roman and Italian *negotiatores* gradually began to establish themselves in the island, a development that might not have been beyond the powers of the *patres* to foresee. Nonetheless, that motive can hardly serve as explanation. The advantages of the Delian mart were open equally to merchants of all nationalities. Greeks and easterners predominated, in fact, prior to 167 and might have been expected to become chief beneficiaries. Just when the Ῥωμαῖοι became a majority on Delos is undemonstrable; it certainly did not happen

119. Livy, 38.44.3–6.
120. As Frank, *Roman Imperialism*, 280, observed, the *lex Antonia de Termessibus* of 71 B.C. exempts *publicani* specifically from harbor tolls—thereby implying that others were not so privileged: *FIRA*, I, no. 11, *ad fin.*
121. Polyb. 18.43.16–17. The latter clause is omitted by Livy, 38.38.12.
122. Polyb. 5.88.7—in the 220s.
123. Polyb. 30.20.1–9, 30.31.9–12.

overnight. Strabo's evidence places the heyday of Delian prosperity after the destruction of Corinth.[124] The senate's decision in 166 must have had reasons other than filling the pocketbooks of Italian traders. The humiliation of Rhodes stood foremost as purpose. And, it might be noticed, delivery of Delos to Athenian overlordship came at the request of Athens; the island's prosperity would be a boon for Athens, still another opportunity for Rome to supply a *beneficium*. It is no accident that the Athenian *stephanephoros*, the so-called "New Style Attic coinage," now begins to reign supreme in the Aegean and gains widespread acceptance in Euboea, Thessaly, Macedonia, and the Thracian coast. Athens rather than Rome seems the principal economic beneficiary.[125]

So much for state action to promote private business enterprise in the East. No other instance can be cited down to the late second century. In wartime the government could indeed curtail such enter-

124. Strabo, 10.5.4 (C486). For Cassola, *I gruppi politici*, 62–63, Rome foresaw all the commercial consequences and future advantages for her trading classes. So also Schmitt, *Rom und Rhodos*, 166; Ferrary, in Nicolet, *Rome et la conquête* II: 783–784. Similarly, but more cautiously, Harris, *War and Imperialism*, 94. The idea is rejected by, e.g., Hatzfeld, *Les trafiquants*, 374; Frank, *Roman Imperialism*, 284–285; Wilson, *Emigration*, 102; Badian, *Roman Imperialism*, 17–18; Finley, *Greece and Rome* 25 (1978): 11–12.

125. The date proposed for the origin of New Style Attic coinage, ca. 196, by M. Thompson, *ANSMN* 5 (1952): 25–33, and *idem, The New Style Silver Coinage of Athens* (New York, 1961), *passim*, is now almost universally rejected. A time around 164, shortly after Delos came under Athenian control, seems preferable. See the arguments of D. M. Lewis, *NC* (1962): 275–300; followed and expanded by, e.g., Mattingly, *NC* (1969): 327–330; C. Boehringer, *Zur Chronologie mittelhellenistischer Münzserien, 220–160 v. Chr.* (Berlin, 1972), 22–38. Further bibliography in Habicht, *Chiron* 6 (1976): 130, n. 17. Note the famed Amphictyonic decree that directs all Greeks to accept the Athenian tetradrachm for four drachmas of silver: *Syll.*³ 729 = *FDelphes*, III, 2, 139. Giovannini, *Rome et la circulation monétaire*, 64–72, proposes a date of ca. 165 to coincide with the introduction of New Style coinage. Whether the date is right or wrong, his further conclusion that this came as a *Roman* directive and represents "a decisive step in the history of Roman imperialism," *op. cit.*, 95–102, lacks all foundation and plausibility. Giovannini argues that the disappearance of the Alexander and Lysimachus coinage in the Greek world after Pydna signals a Roman desire to wipe out the vestiges of Macedonian royal influence. An unnecessary hypothesis. The Antigonid monies quite naturally vanished in Greece after Pydna, as did the Seleucid coinage in Asia Minor after Magnesia. There is no reason to postulate Roman pressure, however popular Perseus may have been in Greece before, though a Hellenic desire to appease the victor may have influenced the hurrying of previous coinage out of circulation. Rome certainly did not adopt any general antimonarchical posture in the Greek world. It may be at this time that Eumenes began production of the Pergamene *cistophori*; cf. F. S. Kleiner-S. P. Noe, *The Early Cistophoric Coinage* (New York, 1977), 10–18. Even if its origins follow the defeat of Antiochus III in 190, however, as Boehringer, *op. cit.*, 40–46, the *cistophori* continue unaffected by the Roman victory at Pydna. More recent discussion by Mørkholm, *ANSMN* 24 (1979): 50–62, who opts for a date ca. 175; and a reply by Kleiner, *ANSMN* 25 (1980): 45–52. See also Robert, *REG* 94 (1981): 377–378.

prise.[126] Taken singly or together, the examples do little to buttress any idea of official protection or advancement of profit-making activity in the Hellenistic world.[127] Insofar as specific steps were taken, they seem directed to the advantage of other states and peoples, rather than of the Romans: south Italian traders, Rhodians, or Athenians, as circumstances determined. Of course, unselfish philanthropy did not provide the stimulus. Rome had her own ends very

126. As when the senate prevented shipment of goods and arms to the Messenians in the late 180s: Polyb. 23.9.12, 23.17.3. Note also the senate's control over Sicilian grain exports during the Third Macedonian War: Polyb. 28.2.2, 28.2.5; cf. Frank, *Roman Imperialism*, 281–282.

127. On the closing of the Macedonian mines to thwart the *publicani* in 167, see below pp. 426–427. When reopened they may well have been placed in Macedonian hands. The ban on importation of salt and cutting of ship timbers in Macedonia in the same year had political reasons, irrelevant to the Roman economy: Livy, 45.29.11, 45.29.14; see Frank, *Roman Imperialism*, 281. Harris' suggestion, *War and Imperialism*, 99, that the destruction of Corinth in 146 stemmed in part from hostility toward the city by businessmen in Delos, is implausible.

Economic considerations may—or may not—have played a larger role in Roman decisions in the West. The evidence is inadequate and requires no extended discussion here. The demolition of Carthage in 146 and the prohibition of any further settlement within ten miles of the sea obviously aimed to eliminate her as a maritime power: Livy, *Per.* 49; Appian, *Lib.* 81; Diod. 32.6.3; Zon. 9.26. Whether Italian businessmen were the intended beneficiaries, however, is beyond knowing. The fact that some Italians were in North Africa before the Third Punic War does not prove it: Polyb. 36.7.5; Appian, *Lib.* 92; cf. Plautus, *Poen.* 79–82; Frank, *ESAR* I:202–203. Cicero has no doubt that strategic and political reasons dictated the crushing of Corinth and Carthage: *De Leg. Agrar.* 2.87.

The notorious ban on vine and olive cultivation among Transalpine tribes continues to generate discussion. Cicero, *De Rep.* 3.16, claims it was designed to protect and enhance Italian agriculture. The dramatic date of the dialogue would set the measure some time before 129 B.C. Perhaps a reference to 154 when Romans last fought in Transalpine Gaul, at the behest of Massilia—thus an economic measure to benefit the Massiliotes rather than the Romans? So, Frank, *Roman Imperialism*, 280–281; followed by Badian, *Roman Imperialism*, 19–20; G. Clemente, *I romani nella Gallia meridionale* (Bologna, 1974), 18–19, 132–133. That is speculation and unverifiable. Aymard, *Études*, 585–600, set the measure late in the second century at the time of formation of the Roman province; similarly, B. Van Rinsveld, *Latomus* 40 (1981): 280–291. A first-century date too has been proposed by M. Clavel, *Béziers et son territoire dans l'Antiquité* (Paris, 1970), 310–316. J. Paterson, *CQ* 28 (1978): 452–458, offers the novel suggestion that Cicero refers to the Galli Transalpini who migrated to Italy and were expelled in 183; Livy, 39.22.6–7, 39.45.6–7, 39.54.2–13; L. Piso, in Peter, *HRR*, fr. 35. On this view, Cicero's language is metaphorical and no ban on cultivation existed. That is not the most obvious reading of the text. In any case, chronological uncertainty and the absence of known parallels forbid the building of any hypotheses about Roman economic policy on the basis of this passage. Clemente, *op. cit.*, 21–71, has compiled an impressive array of evidence for Italian commercial connections with southern Gaul, beginning in the third century. But none of it authorizes his claim, *op. cit.*, 75, that Roman senators took an interest in promoting this activity—at least not before the late Republic; cf. T. P. Wiseman, *LCM* 1 (1976): 21–22.

much in view: the loyalty of Italian states and the value of eastern allies in maintaining a stable order that could relieve the Republic of responsibility. The direct economic gains of Rome's business and commercial communities or, for that matter, of her senatorial order, find no clear reflection in the decisions of state.

V

Romans of all classes enjoyed the profits of empire. Whatever the image projected by poets and intellectuals, they were unrestrained by aversion to gain and commitment to rustic virtues. Foreign adventures meant indemnity for the state coffers, enrichment and prestige for commanders, booty for soldiers, financial and commercial opportunities for business enterprise. Yet the rewards of conquest ought not to be confused with the motives.[128] Decisions of state had to take account of matters other than economic. One may speculate about unspoken undercurrents that charged debate with the prospects of profit. But no single decision on eastern affairs exhibits an economic component demonstrable as central or primary.

With victory came spoils, whether material plunder or enslaved captives, an accepted consequence of war rather than its impulse. Victory also meant retribution, the humbled enemy to pay Rome's expenses as acknowledgment of his folly and failure, often a heavy indemnity to advertise punishment and prolong subjection. The lucrative proceeds stuffed state coffers, but their irregular character betrays political and diplomatic motivations. An economic boom resulted. Revenues paid for construction in Rome and Italy, employed countless hands, and put much cash in circulation; slaves imported through capture and purchase made possible the capitalist agriculture of the second century. Outcome, however, need not be identical with expectation. The closest Rome had to a steady income from abroad came out of the West rather than the East. Her budget was not predicated on exploitation of Hellas.

Business interests fattened on expansion, with or without official encouragement. Indeed the government occasionally set up roadblocks to capitalist enterprise, harassing some *publicani* and checking the profits of moneylenders. Migration of Roman and Italian *negotiatores* to the East increased in momentum, a feature of expanded contacts with the Hellenic world but independent of any governmental policy. Enrichment of the governing class was part of this whole process: the pocketing of plunder, accumulation of property, invest-

---

128. Cf. the brief and wise words of Nicolet, *Rome et la conquête,* 899–902.

ment in cash crops and business activity. The men who made policy knew the potential for gain; Romans were not immune from greed or blind to profit. Affairs of state, however, had their own determinants. The demands of international politics predominated in actions and decisions on the East. Material advantage was a welcome adjunct rather than a central ingredient.

Chapter 10

The Greek View of Roman Expansion

The Roman colossus stood astride the Greek world in the mid-second century B.C. A Greek poetess hailed her as supreme over land and sea, forever secure as ruler of the world.[1] For Polybius, Rome had subjected the whole *oikoumene* to her dominion: men everywhere acknowledged the necessity of heeding her dictates.[2] The author of 1 Maccabees summarized the march of Roman power: kings felled one by one, lands plundered and destroyed, enemies reduced to servitude.[3] To those writing after the fall of Carthage and Corinth, the succession of Roman victories emblazoned the historical landscape, all else cast into shadow. Surveyors of that landscape naturally focused on what appeared to be—for good or ill—relentless growth of an imperial power. Yet the vantage-point of the later second century provides a false angle. Inquiry must begin earlier. What image did Rome possess in Greek eyes prior to the collapse of the Hellenistic kingdoms? Did Greeks foresee, anticipate, or expect the western power to extend her dominion across the Adriatic? The process of expansion seems linear and logical in retrospect. But contemporary witnesses would serve as a better guide.

---

1. Melinno in Stobaeus, 3.7.12 = E. Diehl, *Anthologia Lyrica Graeca* (Leipzig, 1925), II: 315–316.
2. Polyb. 3.3.9: Ῥωμαῖοι πᾶσαν ἐποιήσαντο τὴν οἰκουμένην ὑπήκοον αὐτοῖς; 3.4.2–3; cf. 1.1.5, 3.1.4, etc., and see below pp. 344–346.
3. 1 Macc. 8:1–11.

Early Impressions

Contemporary witnesses, unfortunately, are hard to come by. What passes for information on Greek attitudes toward Rome prior to 200 B.C. dissolves into scattered and murky fragments. How much do they amount to?

The city had generated some interest among Greek intellectuals from an early date. Antiquarian matters piqued the imagination of some researchers. A lively discussion developed over the origins of Rome, their connection with the tale of Troy, the wanderings of Odysseus and Aeneas, and the legend of Romulus and Remus. Isolated reference to Aeneas' role as founder of Rome appears already in the fifth-century logographer Hellanicus of Lesbos.[4] A century later, Rome had entered into relations with the Greeks of Campania, and Alexander the Molossian had encountered the Romans in Italy. The investigations of Hellenic scholars received increased stimulus. Aristotle retailed a theory about Achaeans meandering after the fall of Troy and driven by storm to found a settlement in Latium. His pupil Heraclides Lembos fixed that settlement at Rome. Various versions of the city's beginnings found expression in such writers as Alcimus, Callias, and Xenagoras.[5] The sack of Rome by the Gauls excited some attention among Greek scholars. Heraclides Ponticus took note of it in the mid-fourth century, as did Theopompus, and the indefatigable Aristotle.[6] None of this adds up to anything like serious investigation. If Pliny is to be believed, Theophrastus was the first to take any care in writing about Roman affairs—and they certainly occupied no large place in his corpus of writings.[7] Antiquarianism, mild curiosity, and an occasional display of recondite erudition; nothing more can safely

4. Dion. Hal. 1.72.2. He was followed by Damastus of Sigeum, according to Dionysius, *loc. cit.* The skepticism of N. Horsfall, *CQ* 29 (1979): 376–383, who doubts that Hellanicus or Damastus connected Aeneas with Rome, is extreme. In another tale, Antiochus of Syracuse placed Rome's foundation prior to the Trojan War: Dion. Hal. 1.73.4–5.

5. Dion. Hal. 1.72.3–5; Festus, 326, 329 L; for discussion, see W. Hoffman, *Rom und die griechische Welt*, 108–115; also Bickermann, *CP* 47 (1952): 65–68, and, more recently, T. J. Cornell, *PCPS* 201 (1975): 16–27, with extensive bibliography. There may have been some interest among fourth-century writers from Magna Graecia or Sicily in the period of the Roman monarchy: Gabba, *EntrFondHardt* 13 (1967): 154–165. If so, however, it has left very little trace.

6. Plut. *Cam.* 22.2–3; Pliny, *NH*, 3.57.

7. Pliny, *NH*, 3.57: *Theophrastus qui primus externorum aliqua de Romanis diligentius scripsit.* Pliny refers to a single passage in Theophrastus' *History of Plants*—in which Rome receives but incidental mention: *Hist. Plant.* 5.8.3.

be inferred from the fragmentary allusions in writers of the fourth and early third centuries.[8]

One might add perhaps an ingredient of Hellenic literary imperialism. Heraclides Ponticus characterized Rome simply as a "Greek city."[9] Later tradition had it that Alexander the Great and, after him, Demetrius Poliorcetes asked Rome to check piratical activities based in Italy, appealing to a common kinship between Romans and Greeks.[10] In another story, Alexander wrote some sage advice to the Romans about how to deal with their enemies in Italy and received a gold crown from them on the eve of his Persian expedition.[11] Clitarchus, so Pliny informs us, recorded a Roman embassy to Alexander in Babylon. The truth of that statement remains in dispute, sometimes categorically denied, sometimes ingeniously defended. For our purposes it suffices to observe that one contemporary historian of Alexander saw fit to remark on (or invent) Romans dispatching a mission to the Macedonian monarch. But only one. Arrian found no mention of Roman envoys in his main sources and Diodorus, who recounts a host of embassies from all over the inhabited world, did not include one from Rome. The dramatic possibilities of an encounter between the western power and the greatest of Hellenic conquerors impressed themselves only upon writers of a much later era. So, in the subsequent tale, Alexander, like some philosopher or political scientist, is made to inquire after the nature of Rome's constitution, to comment on the demeanor and the independence of her representatives, and to predict her future greatness. Transparent invention, all of it—but not something a third-century writer would be moved to invent. Clitarchus' reference to Roman emissaries, fictitious or not, constitutes but an incidental item in the registry of distant peoples come to pay respect to Alexander the Great.[12] Rome as an intrinsic object of interest had not yet captured Hellenic fancy.

8. Cf. a fragment of Aristoxenus of Tarentum on the "Etruscanization or Romanization" of Paestum: Athen. 14. 632B. And one from Duris of Samos on Decius at the Battle of Sentinum: FGH 76 F 56.

9. Plut. Cam. 22.2.

10. Strabo, 5.3.5 (C232).

11. Memnon, FGH 3B, 434 F 18.2. The authenticity of this tale is defended, unconvincingly, by L. Braccesi, Alessandro e i romani (Bologna, 1975), 47–66, with references to the extensive literature.

12. The statement of Clitarchus in Pliny, NH, 3.57, a passage interminably discussed with regard to Clitarchus' date—which we may safely leave aside; cf. W. W. Tarn, Alexander the Great (Cambridge, 1948), II:21–26; T. S. Brown, AJP 71 (1950): 152, n. 131; L. Pearson, The Lost Histories of Alexander the Great (New York, 1960), 232–234; J. R. Hamilton, Historia 10 (1961): 452–455; Badian, PACA 8 (1965): 3–5; F. Schachermeyr, Alexander in Babylon (Vienna, 1970), 218–223. The statement, in any case, indicates no special awe for—or even special interest in—Rome. Diodorus' catalogue of

The Pyrrhic war sparked a new curiosity. Rome had humbled a major Hellenistic prince and ejected him from Italy; her authority in the peninsula was now unchallenged. Greek writers paid her a little more heed. Hieronymus of Cardia, so Dionysius affirms, first provided a sketch of early Roman history. This, however, was no more than a brief "run-through," unavoidable when Hieronymus dealt with Pyrrhus in his narrative of Alexander's successors.[13] Greater impact derived from the researches of Timaeus of Tauromenium. His Sicilian background naturally dictated the direction of his interests: despite a fifty-year residence in Athens, Timaeus concentrated on the West. A general history of Sicily incorporated extensive commentary on Rome. Ethnographic details, for the most part, emerge from the fragments and yet another inquiry into the foundation of the city.[14] But Timaeus went further: a separate composition on the Pyrrhic wars.[15] Its character and purpose escape detection. But Timaeus lived to witness the opening years of the First Punic War, and he divined the potential significance of that contest. Fond of synchronisms, he discovered (or fabricated) a striking one: simultaneous foundation dates for the cities of Rome and Carthage.[16] The literary device presaged that dramatic confrontation of the mid-third century. The victor, it could be forecast, would be arbiter of the West. Rome had risen to the level of Carthage as consequence of her victory over the Hellenistic invader. So, the Pyrrhic war, as Timaeus perceived, supplied the essential background for the future of the West.[17] Investigation into Roman history thereby found ample justification. Yet it would be rash to adjudge Timaeus as representative of Greek attitudes or as signalling Hellenic concern about Rome as an impending power in the

embassies omits the Romans: 17.113.1–4. Nor did they receive notice in the accounts of Aristobulus and Ptolemy. For the tale of a Roman mission warmly received by Alexander, who predicts the state's future power, Arrian cites Aristus and Asclepiades: 7.15.5–6. Their dates are unknown. A clue lies only in Strabo's allusion to Aristus as a writer much later than Aristobulus and Onesicritus: 14.6.3 (C682), 15.3.8 (C730). So, quite possibly beyond the third century, and at a time when it would be appropriate for a Greek writer to have Alexander forecast Roman greatness.

13. Dion. Hal. 1.6.1: τὴν Ῥωμαϊκὴν ἀρχαιολογίαν ἐπιδραμόντος Ἱερωνύμου.

14. Fragments collected in FGH, 3B, n. 566. Ethnographic curiosities and tales of wonder evidently were featured in the writings of the Rhegian Lycus as well: Agatharchides, De Mar. Rubr. 64. On Lycus, see now P. Fraser, Ptolemaic Alexandria (Oxford, 1972), I:771, II:1079–1080, nn. 383–384.

15. Polyb. 12.4b.1; Cic. Ad Fam. 5.12.2; Dion. Hal. 1.6.1; cf. Gellius, 11.1.1.

16. Dion. Hal. 1.74.1. According to Polybius, Timaeus took his history down to 264 B.C.: Polyb. 1.5.1; cf. 39.8.4.

17. See the incisive analysis of Momigliano, RivStorItal 71 (1959): 529–556 = Terzo contributo alla storia degli studi classici e del mondo antico (Rome, 1966), I:23–53, with bibliography.

eastern world. Timaeus' perspective betrays his Sicilian origins. The focus rests squarely upon the western Greeks, enmeshed in the history of their barbarian neighbors and rivals, their fate closely bound up with the future of those peoples. Nothing in his work suggests that Greeks of the mainland and the East noticed Rome's rise as potential menace or deliverance.[18]

Timaeus may have gathered more information in more systematic fashion than his predecessors. But Greek knowledge of and interest in Rome remained skimpy, a superficial collection of anecdotes and curiosities. Timaeus' work itself, hardly a history of Rome, seems to have dwelled on customs, ceremonies, myths, and ritual practices, a host of ethnographic matters to whet the appetite of a readership fascinated by foreign cultures. Legends and entertaining stories wended their way, whether via Timaeus or through other transmission, to the East, where they were picked up by Alexandrian scholars. So, Callimachus' *Aetia* includes the tale of "a Roman Gaius" shamed by his mother for lamenting a wound acquired in battle, a tale that owes more to Greek sources than to any direct acquaintance with Roman tradition.[19] Among the marvels recorded in the Alexandrian wonder book, *De Auscultationibus Mirabilibus*, was a poison that made limbs dissolve and all body hair fall out: two men, Aulus and Gaius, evidently Romans, had attempted to administer it to Cleonymus, the Spartan who brought a mercenary force to Italy.[20] Knowledge of Rome,

18. As is notorious, Lycophron in his *Alexandra* alluded to the Romans as masters of land and sea, lines 1226–1230: γῆς καὶ θαλάσσης σκῆπτρα καὶ μοναρχίαν λαβόντες; and evidently again in the more obscure fashion characteristic of that infuriating poem: lines 1446–1450. If the author of those lines is the Lycophron who wrote as court poet to Ptolemy II, this description of Rome would be quite extraordinary and unparalleled in the period. Much more satisfactory to date the description to the second century, no earlier than the defeat of Philip V by Flamininus, to whom lines 1446–1450 seem to refer. That solution is adopted after exhaustive analysis of the date by K. Ziegler, *RE* XIII:2, "Lykophron," 2354–2381. The alternative is to reckon Lycophron as adverting to Roman victory over Pyrrhus; so, with ingenious argumentation, Momigliano, *JRS* 32 (1942): 53–64 = *Secondo contributo alla storia degli studi classici* (Rome, 1960), 446–454; followed by P. Lévêque, *REA* 57 (1955): 36–56. But that victory was very far from elevating Rome to mastery over land and sea; and no matter how conventional that flattering formula may have been, allusion to Rome as a naval lord prior to the First Punic War is quite unthinkable; see Tarn, *Alexander* II:28–29, and now, in greater detail, S. Josifovíc, *RE*, Suppl.-Band, XI, "Lykophron," 925–930. The case for a third-century date has recently been revived by Fraser, *Ptolemaic Alexandria* II:1066–1067, n. 331, but only by relegating the passages in question to the status of later interpolations. They cannot, on any reckoning, serve as a reliable index for third-century Greek understanding of Rome.

19. Fr. 106–107, Pfeiffer; see the thorough discussion by Fraser, *Ptolemaic Alexandria* I:767–768, II:1073–1075.

20. Quoted in Fraser, *Ptolemaic Alexandria* II:1075, n. 365. On this work, see *op. cit.*, I:771–772.

if these examples bear any representative witness, had scarcely penetrated beneath the surface. The celebrated remark of Eratosthenes, that
men should not be praised as Greeks and damned as barbarians but
judged as good or evil, identifies the Romans as "refined barbarians,"
blessed with estimable institutions. But he did not single them out as
exemplary: Romans are here bracketed with Carthaginians, Indians,
and Aryans![21] None of this can count as evidence for serious and sustained study of Rome.

The harvest of data is meager indeed. Efforts to discern a Greek
"attitude" toward Rome before the end of the third century stand self-
condemned. No firm attitude existed for none was demanded. To
most Greeks, Rome was distant and remote, not of direct concern nor
an object of special attention.[22] What emerge from the fragmentary remains are discussions of Rome's origins, scattered items like the Gallic
sack that excited interest, legends and fables, fuzzy historical understanding, and a variety of ethnographic details. And whence comes
even this matter? Hellenistic scholarship dug it out, professorial disputes promoted it: a passion for recondite learning, for antique lore,
for arcane curiosities, for comparative anthropology.[23] Such testimony
does not carry us beyond a segment of the Greek intelligentsia. To

21. Strabo, 1.4.9 (C66).

22. The coinage of Locri that portrays 'Ρώμη and Πίστις, often cited in this connection, is irrelevant: BMC, "Italy," 365, no. 15. The Greeks of south Italy, well within
the shadow of Rome, shed no light on attitudes of Greeks across the Adriatic. Nor can
one extrapolate general Greek views from the anti-Roman posture of Punic War historians like Philinus, Chaereas, Sosylus, and Silenus. The hostility of Philinus, a native of
Agrigentum, doubtless derives from the plundering of that city by Rome in the First
Punic War—which Philinus probably witnessed; cf. Polyb. 1.14.1–3, 1.19.15. Sosylus
of Sparta and Silenus of Caleacte were both in Hannibal's retinue, the former his private tutor in Greek: Polyb. 3.20.5; Nepos, Hann. 13.3; cf. on Silenus, Walbank, Kokalos
14–15 (1968–69): 486–487, with bibliography. Plainly they do not speak for the Greeks
in general, who had no personal stake in the Punic Wars.

23. Reconstructions of Rome's origins and foundation continued to fascinate
Greek scholars. The Hellenic practice of composing κτίσεις lies behind that interest, an
academic pursuit; cf. in general Bickermann, CP 47 (1952): 65–81. Diocles of Peparethus, so it is reported, was the first Greek writer to present the canonical version of
Rome's origin, a version that linked the Aeneas and Romulus legends. Fabius Pictor
drew on his work, indeed followed him in essentials, if Plutarch is to be believed: Plut.
Rom. 3.1, 8.7. Where Diocles got his information we can only guess—quite possibly in
Rome itself. Too little is known of Diocles to indulge in conjecture; even his date remains elusive, obviously before Fabius, but probably not long before. The later third
century seems most likely: his death is noted by Demetrius of Scepsis (Athenaeus,
2.44e) who belongs in the early second century (Strabo, 13.1.27 [C594]). On Diocles, see
the pointed comments and bibliographical summary in Momigliano, Secondo contributo,
403; more recently, Fraser, Ptolemaic Alexandria II: 1076, n. 373; Timpe, ANRW I: 2 (1972),
941–948; Frier, Libri Annales, 260–262. After the Antiochene war, Chios honored Rome
by celebrating the founding of the city through a representation of Romulus and Remus: Moretti, RivFilol 108 (1980): 36–37, lines 24–27. But the impetus came from a

imagine that it betokens any broader Hellenic view of Rome as an ascending Mediterranean power is delusion.

That delusion, however, persists. Polybius supplies the prime exhibits: speeches put into the mouths of Greeks in the last years of the third century. First and foremost, an address delivered by the Aetolian leader Agelaus at Naupactus in 217. Agelaus undertook to dissuade Philip V from prolonging the Social War. Its continuance, so argued the Aetolian, carried grave consequences. A cloud loomed in the West. The momentous clash of Rome and Carthage overshadowed petty Hellenic squabbles. Whoever emerged victorious from that contest was bound to extend her ambitions to the East. The Greeks must heal their divisions forthwith, lest they be swept away by the western conqueror. Such was the urgent advice of Agelaus.[24] Philip took the suggestion to heart: the peace conference at Naupactus terminated the Social War—and all eyes were anxiously trained on the events in Italy.[25]

Seven years later, after the outbreak of the First Macedonian War, Polybius sets up a confrontation between Aetolian and Acarnanian spokesmen at Sparta. Each essayed to bring the Lacedaemonians into the war on his side. The Acarnanian arguments bear special relevance. They denounce Aetolia for her alliance with Rome, an alliance with barbarians, ruthless aliens who aim to enslave Hellas. Roman brutality in the war betokens aggressive designs. The cloud-image is invoked again: the western shadow will soon darken all of Greece.[26]

The same theme reappears in a Polybian fragment, part of a Macedonian speech in 209 designed to entice the Aetolians out of the war. The speaker affirms that Aetolians deceive themselves if they believe that a victory, with Rome as ally, will redound to their benefit. The Romans will simply proceed to bring Aetolia under subjection, just like the rest of Greece.[27]

Chian envoy who had just been in Rome—not testimony to widespread knowledge of the tale in Greece: lines 9–11; and see Moretti's discussion: *op. cit.*, 47–53.

24. Polyb. 5.104. Note, especially, 5.104.3: διότι κατ' οὐδένα τρόπον εἰκός ἐστι τοὺς κρατήσαντας ἐπὶ ταῖς Ἰταλιωτῶν καὶ Σικελιωτῶν μεῖναι δυναστείαις ἥξειν δὲ καὶ διατείνειν τὰς ἐπιβολὰς καὶ δυνάμεις αὐτῶν πέρα τοῦ δέοντος. For the cloud image, see 5.104.10.

25. Polyb. 5.105.1–5; cf. 5.33.4: πάντες δὲ ἠναγκάσθημεν πρὸς αὐτὸν ἀποβλέπειν διὰ τὸ μέγεθος, δεδιότες τὴν συντέλειαν τῶν ἀποβησομένων.

26. The paired orations are given in Polyb. 9.28–39. On the Acarnanian speech, note especially 9.37.6–10: νῦν δὲ περὶ δουλείας ἐνίσταται πόλεμος τοῖς Ἕλλησι πρὸς ἀλλοφύλους ἀνθρώπους . . . λελήθασιν αὐτοῖς ἐπισπασάμενοι τηλικοῦτο νέφος ἀπὸ τῆς ἑσπέρας, ὃ κατὰ μὲν τὸ παρὸν ἴσως πρώτοις ἐπισκοτήσει Μακεδόσι, κατὰ δὲ τὸ συνεχὲς πᾶσιν ἔσται τοῖς Ἕλλησι μεγάλων κακῶν αἴτιον; cf. 9.38.5–9, 9.39.1–3, 9.39.6.

27. Polyb. 10.25.1–5: νικησάντων δὲ τούτων, ὃ μὴ δόξειε τοῖς θεοῖς, ἅμα τούτοις καὶ τοὺς ἄλλους Ἕλληνας ὑφ' αὑτοὺς ἐκεῖνοι ποιήσονται.

The motif occurs once more in a peace endeavor of 207. A Greek, perhaps a Rhodian, mediator addresses still another appeal to the Aetolians: by bringing the Romans across the Adriatic they contribute to the enslavement and ruin of Hellas; once Rome washes her hands of the Hannibalic war, she will commit all her resources to the conquest of Greece.[28]

The several speeches coalesce to form a clear pattern. Taken together, they underscore Greek apprehension about the western power, a call for pan-Hellenic unity to thwart Roman ambitions, a conviction that the outcome of the Hannibalic war would furnish the victor with a springboard to dominance of the eastern world. For most scholars they represent accurate reflection of Hellenic opinion in the late third century.[29] Yet the very consistency of that pattern should generate suspicion rather than confidence. Polybius' own views cannot be left out of the reckoning. The historian assessed the Hannibalic war as a central turning point for his universal history. In his conception the struggle between Rome and Carthage determined the mastery of the world, a conception he transmits again and again.[30] Rome's victory gave decisive impetus toward universal dominion and engendered momentum for invasion of the East.[31] The speeches in question fit snugly into that schema. And it is no coincidence that the anxiety Polybius ascribes to the Greeks at the time of Agelaus' speech—they all looked to events in Italy—repeats the general observations he makes in an earlier historiographical excursus.[32] There can be little doubt that the historian's vision knits together the themes of these speeches.

Are the orations authentic? The question has generated scholarly debate. It can be pointed out that Polybius' methodological pronouncements demand fidelity to "what was really said," even though

28. Polyb. 11.4–6; especially, 11.5.1–2: πολεμεῖτε δ' ἐπ' ἐξανδραποδισμῷ καὶ καταφθορᾷ τῆς Ἑλλάδος; 11.5.7–9, 11.6.1–3: ἂν Ῥωμαῖοι τὸν ἐν Ἰταλίᾳ πόλεμον ἀποτρίψωνται . . . πάσῃ τῇ δυνάμει τὴν ὁρμὴν ἐπὶ τοὺς κατὰ τὴν Ἑλλάδα τόπους ποιήσονται . . . πᾶσαν ὑφ' ἑαυτοὺς ποιησόμενοι. Cf. Livy, 27.30.10; Appian, Mac. 3.1.

29. See, recently and especially, Deininger, Widerstand, 23–34, with bibliography.

30. Polyb. 1.3.7: τὰ πολιτεύματα τὰ περὶ τῆς τῶν ὅλων ἀρχῆς ἀμφισβητήσαντα; 15.9.2: περὶ τῆς τῶν ὅλων ἀρχῆς καὶ δυναστείας; 15.10.2: τῆς ἄλλης οἰκουμένης τὴν ἡγεμονίαν καὶ δυναστείαν ἀδήριτον; cf. Livy, 29.17.6: nunc humanum omne genus, utrum vos an Carthaginienses principes orbis terrarum videat; 30.32.2: orbem terrarum victoriae praemium fore.

31. Polyb. 1.3.6: νομίσαντες τὸ κυριώτατον καὶ μέγιστον μέρος αὐτοῖς ἠνύσθαι πρὸς τὴν τῶν ὅλων ἐπιβολήν, οὕτως καὶ τότε πρῶτον ἐθάρσησαν ἐπὶ τὰ λοιπὰ τὰς χεῖρας ἐκτείνειν καὶ περαιοῦσθαι μετὰ δυνάμεως εἴς τε τὴν Ἑλλάδα καὶ τοὺς κατὰ τὴν Ἀσίαν τόπους; 3.2.6: κρατήσαντας τῷ πολέμῳ Καρχηδονίων ἔννοιαν σχεῖν τῆς τῶν ὅλων ἐπιβολῆς; 8.1.3, 9.10.11.

32. Polyb. 5.33.4, quoted above, n. 25; 5.105.5: πάντες πρὸς τοὺς ἐν Ἰταλίᾳ σκοποὺς ἀπέβλεπον.

the historian has some leeway in the words he chooses.[33] For most moderns, that settles the issue: Polybius would not blatantly violate his own principles.[34] A recent assault on the *communis opinio*, however, particularly with regard to Agelaus' speech, finds it a free composition by Polybius and wholly fictitious.[35] But the polarity is too stark. Polybius need not be accused of deliberate deception and fabrication, of abandoning his own methodological precepts. He employed what sources he had, whether oral or written, sources that might well include speeches of this character. One can acknowledge even the possibility that such speeches (or something like them) were delivered. Critics of the Aetolian-Roman alliance would have reason to brand Rome as a menace, her people as barbarians, and her aim as aggrandizement. The rhetoric suggested itself easily enough. Nor is it unthinkable that Agelaus called attention to events in the West in order to reconcile warring Greek parties.

But when all that is conceded, what have we learned? Certainly not that Rome entertained imperialistic designs on the East. Nor even that any Greeks seriously believed that she did. The charges suited the speakers' purposes and fitted Polybius' conception. That they determined anyone's behavior, however, is illegitimate inference. The Acarnanian characterization of Rome carried no weight with the Spartans, who went on to become Roman allies. And, of course, the Aetolians were swayed not at all by the representations of Macedonian and Rhodian spokesmen. Aetolia pulled out of the conflict only when Rome failed to provide adequate assistance. Philip may have concluded the Social War after Agelaus' speech, but hardly for the reasons that Agelaus gave. Of Philip's views on Rome a contemporary document affords a glimpse: the renowned letter to Larisa, recommending an expanded citizen body and citing Roman practice of enfranchising slaves and promoting them to office.[36] No matter that his information was somewhat garbled. An important fact, rarely noted in this connection, stands out. Philip projects a benign image of Rome, an example (in this respect at least) to be imitated. Far from representing a barbaric menace to the Greeks, Rome possessed institutions which they could emulate with profit.[37] Agelaus' rhetoric

---

33. Polyb. 2.56.10, 12.25a.5, 29.12.10, 36.1.6–7.

34. Cf., especially, Walbank, *Commentary* I: 13–14; *JRS* 53 (1963): 8–11; *Speeches in Greek Historians* (Oxford, 1965), 7–18; *Polybius* (Berkeley, 1972) 69; Pedech, *La méthode historique de Polybe* (Paris, 1964), 259–276, 295–302; Heidemann, *Freiheitsparole*, 14–21; Lehmann, *Untersuchungen*, 135–149; Deininger, *Widerstand*, 23–34; *Chiron* 3 (1973): 103–108.

35. Mørkholm, *ClMed* 28 (1967): 240–253; *Chiron* 4 (1974): 127–132.

36. *Syll.*³ 543, lines 31–34.

37. Cf. Livy, 31.34.8: Philip's admiration for the Roman military camp. A similar

accorded well with the unfolding drama that Polybius could discern from the distance of more than half a century; Philip's sober suggestion spoke more directly to contemporary understanding of Rome.

To sum up to this point. The Hellenic perception of Rome remained nebulous and blurred to the end of the third century. Scholars and intellectuals had accumulated fragmentary items of interest, foundation legends, alien customs, geographic data, a few historical particulars, some ill-digested research into Roman institutions, as instanced by Philip's letter to Larisa. Even the most conscientious of investigators, the Sicilian Timaeus, directed his attention to the western Greeks, of minor relevance to those of the East. Scholarly learning did not, in any case, permeate the ranks of the average man in Hellas. Roman engagement in the First Macedonian War had been brutal, but abortive and brief. The orations highlighted in Polybius' pages owe more to rhetorical propaganda and to the historian's conception than to the realities of the third century. The future mistress of the Mediterranean was not yet foreseen. No distinct Hellenic image of Rome had taken shape.

The Reactions to Conquest

A new era dawned with the turn of the century. Or so it appeared. Roman armed might obtruded in Hellas with decisive impact. Philip of Macedonia proved unable to halt the juggernaut, the Aetolian confederacy was thoroughly whipped, the mighty Seleucid kingdom submitted to superior force. A mere dozen years sufficed to establish Roman military predominance over the eastern powers. No one could now ignore the presence or the achievements of the westerner. What form did the Greek conception of Rome take now?

The question presents no special difficulties. Hellenistic experience led the Greeks to a logical conclusion: the conqueror would rule—or exercise hegemony. Rome would succeed to the suzerainty vacated by the Antigonids and the Seleucids. Reaction, both positive and negative, operated on that assumption. The Macedonian spokesman who angled for an Aetolian alliance in 199 painted the Roman *imperium* in blackest colors, alleging that Greek cities in Italy and Sicily groaned under the weight of Rome's oppression: nothing less could be expected from a Roman victory in the East. The rhetoric followed lines already adumbrated in speeches of the late third century: Romans were barbarians, of an alien race, tongue, and character; if

---

tale, to be sure, was told of Pyrrhus: Plut. *Pyrrh*, 16.4–5. But that may be retrojection of Philip's experience; Briscoe, *Commentary*, 141.

the Greeks succumb, they will face a *dominus*.[38] The argument of the Achaean *strategos* Aristaenus in 198, urging cooperation with Rome, stressed not the advantage but the necessity of such a choice: the Romans control the sea and will rule any land they reach; opposition is impossible and even neutrality would be calamitous.[39] Embittered Aetolians, after the defeat of Philip, complained that Rome substituted herself for the Macedonian: Greece had simply exchanged masters.[40]

Nor did the declaration of Greek freedom at the Isthmian Games signal a sharp reversal, at least in Hellenic eyes. Surprise and pleasure resulted, for worse had been expected from the Romans. But freedom and autonomy, as we have seen, were conventional Greek slogans, consistent with and normally issuing from a hegemonial power. For the Greeks, continuation of Rome's hegemony was assumed.[41] Aetolians saw it in the worst light and charged Rome with making the Peloponnesian situation a pretext for retaining her garrisons in the Fetters.[42] Even two years after their evacuation, a representative of Antiochus could assert that all Greek affairs fell under the dominion and dictation of Rome.[43] The hostile statements exaggerate. But there is no doubt that Antiochus and the Aetolians reaped a harvest of discontent in those Hellenic circles which found irksome what they regarded as Roman overlordship.[44]

Hostile or not, the suggestion that the power which eclipsed Hellas in war would rule her in peace seemed obvious and logical. From this period, in all probability, date the lines of Lycophron, who describes Romans as holding scepter and monarchy over land and

38. Livy, 31.29.6–16: *iugum accipite . . . dominum Romanum habebitis*; cf. 31.30.4. The notion of Romans as barbarians appeared also in the Polybian speeches discussed above. Livy plainly adapted this speech from Polybius as well. But there is no reason to doubt that the propaganda circulated at the time; cf. Polyb. 18.22.8; Livy, 31.34.8; Plut. *Flam.* 5.5; in general, Schmitt, *Hellenen, Römer, und Barbaren* (Aschaffenburg, 1958).

39. Livy, 32.21.32–37: *mare in potestate habent; terras quascumque adeunt extemplo dicionis suae faciunt; quod rogant, cogere possunt . . . hos si socios aspernamini, vix mentis sanae estis; sed aut socios aut hostes habeatis oportet.*

40. Polyb. 18.45.6: γίνεται μεθάρμοσις δεσποτῶν; Livy, 33.31.1–3.

41. See above pp. 145–149.

42. Livy, 34.23.8–10.

43. Livy, 35.32.9: *omnia sub nutum dicionemque Romanam*; cf. 35.31.12.

44. Full references and extended discussion of Greek discontent—to be read with caution—in Deininger, *Widerstand*, 38–108. Polybius, however, shatters plausibility in affirming that almost all Greeks except the Achaeans were estranged from Rome in the Syrian war. But that is an apologia for Philopoemen, penned after 146: Polyb. 39.3.8–9. The allegation of Livy, 35.33.1, 35.34.3, that *principes* in each state leaned to Rome while the *multitudo* sought upheaval is gross oversimplification, if not altogether erroneous; cf. Gruen, *AJAH* 1 (1976): 31.

sea.[45] A prognostication ascribed to the Sibyl had announced the fall of Philip and collapse of Macedonia, ruined by men from the West.[46] Another oracular pronouncement forecast Roman triumph over the Carthaginians, to be followed by tremors beneath the sea, spectacular natural phenomena, and then further conquest. Seers interpreted the prognostication as reference to Philip's defeat at the hands of Romans and Aetolians; or, as a more majestic version had it, the rise of Rome's *imperium* to swallow up that of the Greeks and Macedonians.[47] As so often, oracles conveniently surfaced to flatter the conqueror and prove the prescience of priests.

Still greater drama could be imputed to the coming of Rome: nothing less than a cataclysmic confrontation of East and West. Such a vision underlies the singular tales of prophecy, distinctly anti-Roman and ominous, that stem from the Antiochene war and its aftermath.[48] The battlefield of Thermopylae in 191 provides the initial setting. A cavalry officer of Antiochus arises from among the corpses to deliver stern warning to the Roman victors: the wrath of Zeus will send an avenging force to Italy and strip Rome of her empire. A consultation of Delphi followed and additional threats of disaster if Rome fails to mend her ways. In the next episode, a demonic frenzy seized the Roman commander "Publius" who began to spew forth prophecy in prose and verse. The general gave accurate prediction of victory over Antiochus in Asia, details about the return home and the settlement of Apamea. But doom would follow: vengeance carried by the armies of the East, a coalition of kings and peoples to rain destruction upon Europe. The bizarre fable built to a climax. Publius forecast his own

45. Lycophron, *Alexandra*, 1226–1231; cf. 1446–1450; see above n. 18.

46. Appian, *Mac.* 2; Paus. 7.8.8–9.

47. The oracle and its interpretation in Plut. *Mor.* 399 C–D; cf. the discussion of H. W. Parke and D. E. W. Wormell, *The Delphic Oracle* (Oxford, 1956), I: 275–276; II: 144. Justin supplies the more dramatic formulation, 30.4.1–4: *oriens Romanorum imperium vetus Graecorum ac Macedonum voraturum*. That is *post eventum*, no doubt, but not much later. The interpretation, as conveyed by Plutarch, surely precedes the Antiochene war. Otherwise, the Aetolians would not have been coupled with Rome. Observe the epigram of Alcaeus ascribing Philip's defeat to Aetolians and Romans, composed shortly after the Second Macedonian War: Plut. *Flam.* 9.1–3. At a subsequent time the poet celebrates Rome alone—or, more specifically, Flamininus—as liberator of Hellas: *Anth. Pal.* 16.5. Of course, one cannot exclude the possibility that the seers' forecast as it appears in Justin may represent a later elaboration.

48. The stories are ascribed to Antisthenes the Peripatetic, preserved in the collection of wonder tales by Phlegon of Tralles at the time of the emperor Hadrian; *FGH*, 2B, 257 F 36, III. On the structure, cf. J. Mesk, *Philologus* 80 (1925): 298–311. Discussion in H. Fuchs, *Der geistige Widerstand gegen Rom in der antiken Welt* (Berlin, 1938), 5–7, 29–30. A full bibliography and extensive analysis now in J. D. Gauger, *Chiron* 10 (1980): 225–261.

fate, to be mangled by a huge red wolf; the wolf swiftly materialized, devoured the body, but spared the head which continued to spout prophetic utterances regarding certain invaders who would reduce Italy to rubble and make off with half its population as booty. An extraordinary narrative. The accuracy of historical details concentrated on events of the Antiochene war suggests that part of it at least derives from a time proximate to those events.[49] Vivid fantasy combines here with grim forebodings, a product of Greek circles that looked to a savior or saviors to smash Roman power and eradicate it.[50] There is no need to assume that the tale had a specific person in view.[51] A larger vision predominates, of the vengeance of East against West, Asia against Europe, a coming struggle for mastery. Italy would be crushed by those very Hellenes whom she had sought to subjugate. This amalgam of fact and invention, propaganda and prophecy, bitterness and absurdity draws to the surface Greek convictions that Rome's arrival in the East entailed a contest for world dominion.[52]

The hope of a successful eastern retaliation cannot have penetrated far or endured for long. Reveries about the avenging mission from Asia soon lost their luster after the submission of Antiochus III. Rome had humbled the two mightiest Hellenistic monarchs within a

49. This would be certain if the Peripatetic Antisthenes is identical with the Rhodian historian of that name, as usually assumed: Polyb. 16.14; cf. E. Schwartz, *RE* I, "Antisthenes," n. 9, 2537–2538; Jacoby, *FGH*, IIBD, 4, 844–846; Gabba, *Athenaeum* 53 (1975): 7–11. But this identification has little to recommend it; see Gauger, *Chiron* 10 (1980): 238–243. Others have dated the tales to the time of the Mithridatic wars, as E. Zeller, *SBBerlin* (1883), 1067–1083, or to the 170s, as A .J. Reinach, *BCH* 34 (1910): 277–282. See E. Gabba, *Athenaeum* 53 (1975): 7–11. Gauger's somewhat excessive dissection of the material sees various layers deriving from different times and put together in the period of Mithridates' conquests; *op. cit.*, 225–261. On the accuracy of details, see Holleaux, *RevPhil* 56 (1930): 305–309.

50. The origins may be Aetolian, as often conjectured; cf. Jacoby, *FGH*, IIBD, 4, 846; Gabba, *Athenaeum* 53 (1975): 9–10. Gauger, *Chiron* 10 (1980): 233–234, sees Aetolian influence only on part of the text. A Lycian origin for the last segment of the narrative is hypothesized by B. Forte, *Rome and the Romans as the Greeks Saw Them* (Rome, 1972): 41–43.

51. S. Mazzarino, *Il pensiero storico classico* II : 1 (Bari, 1968), 156–161, takes it to be Hannibal. For Momigliano, it is Hannibal or Antiochus: *AttiAccadTorino* 107 (1973): 703–704; similarly, Gabba, *Athenaeum* 53 (1975): 9. But specificity is not in point here. The prophecies speak once of a "king," later of "kings": a generalized hope, rather than an explicit individual. In any case, Antiochus was an unlikely prospect after Thermopylae; cf. Holleaux, *RevPhil* 56 (1930): 305. And the term "king" was inapplicable for Hannibal.

52. Gabba's notion, that Greek writers of the early second century who implicitly denied the Trojan migration to Italy were engaged in anti-Roman political propaganda, however, goes too far: *RivStorItal* 86 (1974): 630–634; *Contributi dell' Istituto di storia antica* 4 (1976): 84–93; similarly, Cornell, *PCPS* 201 (1975): 26–27. These were scholarly debates, antiquarian polemic, hardly the stuff of political propaganda.

decade. That stunning accomplishment brought to mind a different kind of prophecy: on the succession of world empires. Medes had succeeded Assyrians and Persians had supplanted Medes—a sequence that appears already in Herodotus and in Ctesias. Then the conquests of Alexander put Macedonians in the place of Persia as masters of the universe. But already in the late fourth century Demetrius of Phalerum foretold the demise of Macedonian dominion: Τύχη will deal with them as she had the Persians.[53] With the fall of Philip and Antiochus the prediction seemed fulfilled. Rome had stepped into the role of the new world empire, the heir of Assyria, Media, Persia, and Macedonia. The idea receives clear expression in a Roman writer not long after the Antiochene war but it reeks of eastern origins.[54] The *summa imperii* had now passed to the people of Rome. Greek experience and tradition made that inference logical, indeed inevitable. Collapse of Antigonid and Seleucid authority entailed the succession of a new suzerain, fifth in the sequence of universal empires.[55]

All of this exemplifies ingenuous Hellenic reaction. There are no theories of imperialism here. None was needed. Where the fact was taken for granted, theorizing would be superfluous. Greeks expected the conqueror to be sovereign, to take the position of hegemonial power.[56] The Chalcidians showered honors upon T. Flamininus in

53. Herod. 1.95, 1.130; Diod. 2.1–34. On Demetrius' prediction, see Polyb. 29.21.1–9. Earlier forms of the four-monarchy scheme derive from Persian sources; see now D. Flusser, *Israel Oriental Studies* 2 (1972): 148–175.

54. It appears in a gloss on Vell. Pat. 1.6.6 and is attributed to the otherwise unknown Aemilius Sura. Explicit reference to Roman conquest of Carthage, Philip, and Antiochus puts it after 189 but not much later and almost certainly before the Third Macedonian War, which goes unmentioned. The parade of kingdoms to which Rome succeeds betrays the eastern basis for the concept: *Assyrii principes omnium gentium rerum potiti sunt, deinde Medi, postea Persae, deinde Macedones; exinde duobus regibus Philippo et Antiocho, qui a Macedonibus oriundi erant, haud multo post Carthaginem subactam devictis summa imperii ad populum Romanum pervenit.* See the excellent account by J. W. Swain, *CP* 35 (1940): 1–12. Vague doubts on the chronology by F. Cassola, *I gruppi politici*, 65–66. D. Mendels, *AJP* 102 (1981): 331–332, dates the passage to the first century B.C. But Sallust, *Hist.* 1.55, Maur., which makes no reference to the sequence of empires or the acquisition of empire, is not a true parallel. Swain's hypothesis that Romans learned of the tradition from Persian colonies in Asia Minor, on the grounds that Orientals rather than Greeks promoted it, is unnecessary. Swain ignores the prediction of Demetrius, a *Greek* story transmitted by Polybius; see above, n. 53. And the passage from Aemilius Sura parallels the Greek oracular interpretation derived from this period and preserved in Justin, 30.4.1–4; see above, n. 47.

55. An indirect allusion to this in Polyb. 1.2.2–7. Cf. J.-L. Ferrary, *BCH* 100 (1976): 283–289. More explicit: Dion. Hal. 1.2.1–4, and Appian, *Praef.* 8–9. On the later tradition, see Swain, *CP* 35 (1940): 12–21; Flusser, *Israel Oriental Studies* 2 (1972): 159–162; cf. Gabba, *Athenaeum* 53 (1975): 11–12.

56. Polyb. 21.16.8 (speech of Antiochus' envoys to Scipio after Magnesia): ἐπείπερ

189, performed sacrifices, poured libations, chanted hymns. And the Chalcidian hymn expressed, above all, obeisance to the πίστις of the Romans.[57] Indignant Spartans appealed to the senate in 188 against Achaean actions, claiming that violation of the Peloponnesian settlement undermined the "power and dignity" of Rome.[58] That mission was among the earliest of a long series of Hellenic embassies in the years after Apamea seeking intervention, arbitration, or decision from Rome. The Greeks, as was natural, expected her to exercise authority.

Yet Rome did not behave like a conventional hegemonial power. The evacuation of her troops in 194 must itself have caused mystification and surprise, in addition to the rapture recorded in our favorable evidence.[59] Just how much dictation would come from Rome and how much control? Rhodian diplomats endeavored to exploit the ambiguities after defeat of Antiochus. They proclaimed—what all Greeks assumed—that the whole world was now under Roman dominion.[60] But they also elaborated on Roman proclamations, flattered the senate on its desire for fame rather than annexation or wealth, and prodded Romans to show devotion to liberty by leaving portions of Asia Minor free—and, by implication, beholden to Rhodes.[61] Perplexity doubtless increased as senatorial decisions issued forth with notable absence of clarity or resolve. So, for example, the *patres* gave but vague response to Spartan and Achaean appellants in Spring 188 allowing each party to make its own, even mutually exclusive, interpretations.[62] Not very different is the reply of senatorial commissioners in Asia to Rhodians and Ilians regarding the status of Lycia in 188; an effort to appease both sides led to divergent understandings and conflict, while Rome turned her back.[63] Puzzlement in Greece can readily

---

ἡ τύχη παρέδωκεν αὐτοῖς τὴν τῆς οἰκουμένης ἀρχὴν καὶ δυναστείαν; Livy, 37.45.8. Also Polyb. 21.31.7 (speech of Leon the Athenian to the senate in 189); εἰς μέγαν ἐνηνοχέναι κίνδυνον τὴν Ῥωμαίων ἡγεμονίαν.

57. Plut. *Flam.* 16.4: πίστιν δὲ Ῥωμαίων σέβομεν.

58. Polyb. 22.3.1: ἅμα τὴν δύναμιν καὶ τὴν προστασίαν καταλελύσθαι τὴν Ῥωμαίων. Wunderer emended to Λακεδαιμονίων, so printed in Büttner-Wobst—an unnecessary change. Cf. Walbank, *Commentary* III:177. Observe the anger of Achaeans against those Spartans who accused them πρὸς τοὺς κρατοῦντας (the Romans): Polyb. 22.11.8.

59. Livy, 34.49–50. Flamininus insisted that the Greeks be sentinels of their own liberty—but went on to restructure constitutions in Thessaly: Livy, 34.49.11, 34.51.4–6.

60. Polyb. 21.23.4: πάντα τὰ κατὰ τὴν οἰκουμένην τεθεικότες [μὲν] ὑπὸ τὴν ὑμετέραν ἐξουσίαν; Livy, 37.54.15: *cum orbis terrarum in dicione vestra sit.*

61. Polyb. 21.23.2–10; Livy, 37.54.15–27.

62. Livy, 38.32.9–10: *ceterum responsum ita perplexum fuit ut et Achaei sibi de Lacedaemone permissum acciperent, et Lacedaemonii non omnia concessa iis interpretarentur.*

63. Polyb. 22.5.1–10; cf. Gruen, *CQ* 25 (1975): 64–65, with bibliography cited there.

be imagined. Hellenes reckoned that the conqueror had achieved mastery of the Mediterranean. Yet that conqueror seemed reluctant to embrace the role. Not only had Rome withdrawn forces and abjured annexation but her pronouncements lacked both decisiveness and consistency.

Vivid portrayal of confusion in Greek circles springs from the pages of Polybius in his analysis of the contrasting policies of Aristaenus and Philopoemen.[64] That analysis has stimulated considerable discussion on the nature of Achaean politics and on the historian's own attitudes toward leading figures in his state. But it merits probing on a larger front, as reflection of genuine Hellenic uncertainty about the objectives of Rome.

Aristaenus, in the Polybian presentation, stands for a catering to Roman wishes, even an anticipation of them. He would save appearances by holding to Achaean law but yield readily when it seemed in conflict with Roman ordinances.[65] Philopoemen, by contrast, set a premium on Achaean laws and the terms of alliance with Rome. The senate's instructions would be carried out when consistent with those terms but objected to when not and complied with only under protest.[66] Into the mouth of Aristaenus Polybius sets a speech comparing τὸ καλόν and τὸ συμφέρον: states that lack the power to implement the former must content themselves with the latter; when obedience is obligatory, best to perform it with as good grace as possible.[67] Philopoemen conceded the discrepancy in power between Rome and Achaea and the eventual submission to Roman dictates: but to stand up for one's rights, he argued, would impress Romans who respected oaths, treaties, and justice; and thus Achaea could, at least, postpone rather than hasten the inevitable.[68]

Difficulty inheres in any explication of these passages. How much represents authentic discussion in Achaea and how much Polybian conceptualization remains uncertain. That a debate along these lines actually transpired at a particular time in history may well be doubted.[69] The reasoning is laced with generalizations, resembling more a summary of implicit argument than the record of a historical debate.[70] Abstractions play a central role: contrast between honor and advantage, the pragmatic and the noble, the possible and the

64. Polyb. 24.11–13.   65. Polyb. 24.11.4–5.   66. Polyb. 24.11.6–8.
67. Polyb. 24.12.1–4.   68. Polyb. 24.13.1–7.

69. Badian, *JRS* 42 (1952): 80, seeks to put it in 191; followed by Errington, *Philopoemen* 224–225. Holleaux, *REG* 34 (1921): 418–420 = *Études* V: 136–138, dates it before 188. All the arguments are quite inconclusive.

70. So, rightly, Aymard, *Premiers rapports*, 362; cf. Lehmann, *Untersuchungen*, 240–241; Walbank, *Commentary* III: 264–265.

impossible, sophisms that make the dialogue almost a dialectic. And the conviction expressed even in Philopoemen's speech, that Greeks will ultimately be under compulsion to perform all of Rome's bidding, is plainly anticipatory.[71] Polybius' own subsequent understanding sits at the basis of this reconstruction.[72]

But the account nonetheless carries echoes of a genuine Achaean —and Greek—dilemma in the early second century: how best to adjust to the puzzling hegemony of Rome. The hegemony itself goes unquestioned. And Polybius brackets his digression with explicit reference to Rome's position as it issued from the Macedonian and Antiochene wars. The set piece is framed at each end by that reference, both a chronological pointer and a diagnostic tool.[73] Rome had attained decisive superiority in Greek affairs, so says Polybius in his own voice, in the period of those wars.[74] Aristaenus underscores the fact by stressing Achaea's impotence in the face of the new superpower, and Philopoemen endorses it by acknowledging the gulf in authority that separated the two states.[75] So much for common ground. Aristaenus urged active cooperation with the westerner, ready compliance with Roman wishes, even when unexpressed. Obedience to all commands is the only prudent policy.[76] For Philopoemen Achaeans ought not prematurely to jettison their autonomy. The Romans treat sworn conventions with respect and honor loyalty to allies, an attitude that Achaeans can turn to their own benefit. Room for maneuvering exists; Achaea can avert—or postpone—oppression by calling upon the Roman sense of justice.[77] The principal point at issue here is not one between a "pro-Roman" and a "patriotic" party, modern formulations that miss Polybius' meaning.[78] Nor are these merely abstract musings from Polybius'

71. Polyb. 24.13.6: ὅτι μὲν γὰρ ἥξει ποτὲ τοῖς Ἕλλησιν ὁ καιρὸς οὗτος, ἐν ᾧ δεήσει ποιεῖν κατ᾽ ἀνάγκην πᾶν τὸ παραγγελλόμενον, σαφῶς ἔφη γινώσκειν.

72. For Pedech, La Méthode, 417–418, the speeches are pure fiction, a product of Polybius' psychologizing. K.-E. Petzold, Studien zur Methode des Polybios und zu ihrer historischen Auswertung (Munich, 1969), 43–49, argues that the ethical considerations contained in this dialogue demonstrate late composition: they are absent in Plut. Phil. 17.3, drawn from Polybius' biography of Philopoemen rather than his History. Doubts on this are expressed by Walbank, Polybius, 166–167 and in his contribution to Polybe, EntrFondHardt 20 (Geneva, 1974): 6–7. Nothing novel appears in the recent discussions of these passages by Deininger, Widerstand, 111–115, and Forte, Rome and the Romans, 34–36.

73. Polyb. 24.11.3, 24.13.9.

74. Polyb. 24.11.3: τῆς γὰρ Ῥωμαίων ὑπεροχῆς ἤδη τοῖς Ἑλληνικοῖς πράγμασιν ἐμπλεκομένης ὁλοσχερῶς κατά τε τοὺς Φιλιππικοὺς καὶ τοὺς Ἀντιοχικοὺς καιρούς.

75. Polyb. 24.12.1–24.13.1.

76. Polyb. 24.12.4: ὑπακουστέον ἑτοίμως εἶναι πᾶσι τοῖς παραγγελλομένοις.

77. Polyb. 24.13.3–5: περὶ πλείονος ποιουμένων Ῥωμαίων . . . τὸ τηρεῖν τοὺς ὅρκους καὶ τὰς συνθήκας καὶ τὴν πρὸς τοὺς συμμάχους πίστιν.

78. Polybius' sympathy for Philopoemen's position is clear. But the historian is

old age. They mirror legitimate differences of opinion that surfaced in the early second century among Hellenes confused about the posture of Rome and concerned about the limits of their own authority. Aristaenus had learned the hard lesson of Roman constraint in the emergency conditions of the Macedonian war when Achaean salvation depended upon compliance—and he never forgot it.[79] Philopoemen, on the other hand, latched onto Roman disclaimers of aggrandizement and accentuated a wider latitude for Achaean activity. Polybius appropriately penetrates to the core of this divergence.

The theme manifests itself again and again in the narrative of Achaean affairs. In the winter of 189/8 a double embassy from the League appeared in Rome to discuss the Spartan issue, motivated by characteristically ambiguous pronouncements from the Roman consul in Greece. Diophanes proposed that all matters of dispute be settled by the senate: the hegemon had decisive authority. By contrast, Lycortas, father of Polybius, held to the opinions of Philopoemen, urging that Rome leave to the Achaeans rights protected by treaty and laws and endorse that liberty of action of which she herself had been guarantor.[80] The senate once again avoided decision, thereby implicitly giving Achaean leaders a free hand to deal with Peloponnesian matters in their own way—as they proceeded to do.[81] So it was with genuine surprise a few years later in 184 that Lycortas confronted a Roman legate arrived in Greece to express the senate's strong displeasure with the fate of Sparta. Lycortas' speech, reconstructed by Polybius and transmitted by Livy, contains rhetorical flourish but an authentic substance. The wide disparity in power between Rome and Achaea is conceded, as usual. But Lycortas emphasizes the anomaly of allies on a technically equal footing pleading their case like slaves before masters who purported to be the wardens of liberty.[82] Roman bluster caused the Achaeans to cave in, but only qualifiedly so and with a token show of compliance.[83] No extensive interference followed. Behavior by senate and legates did not seem (at least to the

---

swift to defend Aristaenus as well: both men's policies were "safe" and both protected Achaean rights in the difficult times of war against Philip and Antiochus: Polyb. 24.13.8–10. A further defense of Aristaenus in Polyb. 18.13.8–10.

79. Polyb. 18.13.8: εἰ γὰρ μὴ σὺν καιρῷ τότε μετέρριψε τοὺς Ἀχαιοὺς Ἀρίσταινος ἀπὸ τῆς Φιλίππου συμμαχίας πρὸς τὴν Ῥωμαίων, φανερῶς ἄρδην ἀπολώλει τὸ ἔθνος; Livy, 32.21.32–37; see above, n. 39.

80. Livy, 38.32.3–8: Diophanes senatui disceptationem omnium rerum permittebat: eos optime controversias inter Achaeos ac Lacedaemonios finituros esse; Lycortas ex praeceptis Philopoemenis postulabat ut Achaeis ex foedere ac legibus suis quae decressent agere liceret, libertatemque sibi illibatam, cuius ipsi auctores essent, praestarent.

81. Livy, 38.32.9–10.

82. Livy, 39.37.9–17; cf. Paus. 7.9.3–4.

83. Livy, 39.37.18–21.

Greeks) to form any predictable pattern. The apparent inconsistencies prolonged divergent interpretations. Some Achaean politicians clung to the idea that eager submission to Rome's will brought not only safety to the state but political advancement for its advocates.[84] The faction of Lycortas, however, maintained its earlier stance, with sound reasoning based on nearly two decades of experience. Lycortas advised in 181 that unreasonable Roman requests can be resisted with impunity: the senate will not enforce demands in violation of Achaean vows, regulations, and inscribed ordinances.[85] That view is, of course, subscribed to by Polybius in retrospect: the Romans incline to assist appellants in difficulty but place highest value on the claims of justice.[86] Others, however, construed Roman objectives differently at the time. The uncertainty itself stands out above all. Contrasting opinions and conflicting interpretations dominate the first quarter, at least, of the second century. And no wonder. Hellas puzzled over how to adjust to a power who had earned the rights to suzerainty but seemed erratic, unpredictable, and even reluctant in exercising them.

The confusion is unmistakable—and understandable. Achaea supplies most of the information, for obvious reasons. But perplexities elsewhere in Greece about the westerner's behavior will have been little different.[87] Much scholarly energy has concentrated upon discerning pro- and anti-Roman elements in Hellenic groups and Hellenic attitudes.[88] The energy may be misplaced. Passionate feelings for or against Rome do not predominate in the first three decades of the second century. Surprise at Rome's aloofness and indifference would be closer to the mark, even annoyance in some circles at her failure to pronounce the judgments or implement the decisions expected of a hegemon, and bewilderment at her sporadic and inconsistent verbal interventions. Complex reactions, varied and diverse, belong to such circumstances, or perhaps, for the most part, no reactions at all as the westerner retired more and more from Hellenic affairs. A model that divides Greece into the friends and enemies of Rome simply will not do.[89]

84. The policy ascribed to Callicrates and Hyperbatus: Polyb. 24.8.6, 24.9.2. But the sycophancy is exaggerated and the portrait overdrawn; cf. Gruen, *AJAH* 1 (1976): 32–33.

85. Polyb. 24.8.2–5, 24.9.3.

86. Polyb. 24.10.11.

87. Cf. Roman attitudes and the reaction in Rhodes and Lycia during the 170s: Polyb. 25.4–6; Livy, 41.6.8–12, 41.25.8; Gruen, *CQ* 25 (1975): 66–68.

88. E.g. Deininger, *Widerstand, passim*; Forte, *Rome and the Romans, passim*.

89. Callicrates' claim in 180 that most Greeks were hostile to the friends of Rome and made a point of scorning Roman instructions is wild distortion: Polyb. 24.9.1–11. No more trustworthy is Polybius' statement that Rome henceforth had no true friends in Greece, only a collection of flatterers: 24.10.5. Cf. Gruen, *AJAH* 1 (1976): 30–31.

Expectations and Disillusionment

Passion erupts at last in the Third Macedonian War. Logic might tempt one to assume that subterranean anti-Romanism here exploded to the surface. The temptation should be resisted. A surge of sentiment for Perseus swept through Greece, we are told, after an initial victory in 171, a release of feelings long held in check.[90] The show of support is plausible enough. But allusion to secret sentiments now come to the fore represents conjecture.[91] The situation lends itself to a different interpretation. After nearly two decades of infuriating ambiguity the Romans had again arrived in Hellas with force. Greeks who had gradually ascertained Rome's disinclination to impose direct control suddenly confronted her armed might on their territory once more. Just as they had begun to count on indifference they encountered massive interference. Under the circumstances an outburst of indignation and resentment is quite comprehensible. Perseus' temporary triumph came as a shock; many hastily concluded that they had finally found a worthy adversary of Rome.[92] Support materialized for the Macedonian king in various quarters of Greece. So, at least, some general comments in our sources would suggest.[93] But more detailed scrutiny introduces qualifications. Commitment to Perseus nowhere ran deep. As Roman fortunes rose, it became expedient for cynical politicians to brand their foes as "pro-Macedonian." And that label gained increased use in postwar recriminations when individuals and factions besmirched their opponents in order to salvage their own positions. During the war itself there was little genuine sympathy in Greece for either side; rather, a widespread preference for neutrality and peace, anger at being drawn into an unwanted conflict, and conviction that any outcome would bring damaging consequences upon all Greeks.[94]

90. Polyb. 27.9.1; Livy, 42.63.1–2.

91. No weight should be placed on Perseus' claim that Rome wished to reduce Macedonia to servitude—an exhortation to his troops: Livy, 42.52.15 16; cf. 42.25.8, 42.50.9. Nor on his effort to win over Antiochus IV by implying that Rome aimed at toppling all kings: Polyb. 29.4.9–10. This is patent propaganda, not an authentic reflection of the image Rome possessed in Greece.

92. Polyb. 27.10.4.

93. Polyb. 30.6.5–8; Livy, 42.5.2, 42.30.1–7; Diod. 30.8. Eumenes' allegations about the popularity of Perseus had propagandistic ends in view: Livy, 42.12.1–8.

94. Detailed discussion with references in Gruen, *AJAH* 1 (1976): 29–60; on Rhodes, cf. Gruen, *CQ* 25 (1975): 68–76. The danger involved in taking sides is expressed by Lycortas: Polyb. 28.6.4: τὸ μὲν γὰρ συνεργεῖν ἀλυσιτελὲς ἐνόμιζε πᾶσιν εἶναι τοῖς Ἕλλησιν προορώμενος τὸ μέγεθος τῆς ἐσομένης ἐξουσίας περὶ τοὺς κρατήσαντας.

The damaging consequences duly followed. Rome's harsh retaliation after Pydna against foe and neutral alike cut deeply into Hellenic sensibilities. Puzzlement turned to bitterness, a bitterness compounded by impotence. The suzerain had at last acted the part, but in the most devastating and unwelcome manner. A brutal severity replaced the equivocation and lethargy of the past twenty years. Greece was in a state of shock. Adulations came pouring forth for the conqueror.[95] Sycophancy seemed the only proper course for states trembling under Roman displeasure, such as the Rhodians who, Polybius asserts, pleaded for clemency like slaves hoping to limit the number of blows from the lash.[96] One need not doubt that disillusionment and discontent were widespread. Popillius Laenas' tactless arrogance toward Antiochus IV exacerbated resentments.[97] The retention of Achaean hostages in Rome inflamed emotions against their political opponents and deepened a sense of emasculation in Greece.[98] Rage manifested itself in Syria where a Roman legate was assassinated in 162 and his murderer publicly boasted of the deed.[99]

Yet the power of the conqueror, once demonstrated, receded again. Rome continued to shrink from direct suzerainty. Affairs of Greece and Asia concerned her only marginally and sporadically. Hellenistic princes resumed traditional activities with but occasional glances at Rome, interstate relations in Greece proceeded without interference, communities and dynasts who appealed to the senate got more frustration than assistance.[100] The pattern that prevailed between Apamea and the Third Macedonian War repeated itself in the decades after Pydna with striking similitude. And parallel consequences can readily be surmised. Rome's image in Hellas became blurred again. The coercion that followed Perseus' demise gave way to Roman inertia, to ambivalence and uncertainty in Greece, then increased confidence as Rome withdrew attention, and finally indignant surprise when she reasserted authority. The last stage (which implies the others) emerges plainly from the Achaean imbroglio of the 140s. Achaea counted on a free hand against Sparta, a logical deduction from Rome's longstanding indifference and her absorption elsewhere.[101] Disillusionment was bitter. The unwelcome intervention of Roman legates triggered crowd reaction; a volley of abuse sent the

95. See above, pp. 193–197.   96. Polyb. 30.31.3.   97. Polyb. 29.27.4.
98. Polyb. 30.29, 30.32.10–11. The despair is exaggerated by Polybius—but is not altogether without foundation.
99. Polyb. 31.11.1, 32.2–3; Appian, *Syr.* 46; Zon. 9.25.
· 100. As exemplified by the events of Seleucid history after Pydna; see Gruen, *Chiron* 6 (1976): 73–95. For a similar view, with regard to Anatolia, see now A. N. Sherwin-White, *JRS* 67 (1977): 62–70.
101. Cf. Polyb. 38.10.10.

Romans packing.[102] That miscalculation, among others, brought even more cataclysmic consequences: the destruction of Corinth in 146.

For the Hellenes, Roman behavior must have been past understanding. Long periods of inaction punctuated by bursts of massive intrusion rendered it incomprehensible. The western power presented no coherent image and generated no consistent Greek reaction. Her passivity encouraged independence, her wavering and ambivalence caused frustration, her pronouncements created confusion, her invasions brought despair. To reckon Greece as divided into pro- and anti-Roman factions is gross oversimplification. Rather, there was a mixture of awe and hostility, of indifference and anxiety, of gratitude and dissatisfaction, of lengthy unconcern and sudden ire. Rome was a sovereign who shunned steady rule, who exercised authority sparingly but devastatingly, who spoke like a Hellenistic state and acted—rarely but capriciously—like a barbarian.

A range of dispositions can be illustrated. The Alexandrian historian and geographer Agatharchides gave vent to his bitterness in lines written probably not long after 146. He describes the wealth of the Sabaean Arabs, a wealth vouchsafed to them only because their location was remote from that power which turns her arms against all the world.[103] Reverence and admiration appear in the poem of Melinno: Rome is acclaimed as warrior goddess, sole ruler of men on land and sea, eternal sovereignty hers by decree of fate.[104] The awesome power here depicted and the stress on unchallenged dominance should date the poem after 168 and quite possibly after 146.[105] Comparable, though more prosaic, sentiments derive from the geographer Pseudo-Scymnus of the later second century who compares Rome to a constellation blanketing the world.[106] A hymn to Apollo by the Athenian Limenius

102. Polyb. 38.12.1–4.

103. Diod. 3.47.7–8. On Agatharchides, see Fraser, *Ptolemaic Alexandria* I:516–517, 539–550; S. Gozzoli, *Atheneum*, 66 (1978): 54–79.

104. Stobaeus, 3.7.12 = Diehl, *Anth. Lyr. Graec.* II:315–316. Best discussion of the poem: by C. M. Bowra, *JRS* 47 (1957): 21–28.

105. The chronology will forever remain uncertain, as will the provenance of the poetess. An early second-century date now seems fashionable among scholars; cf. F. Christ, *Die römische Weltherrschaft in der antiken Dichtung* (Stuttgart-Berlin, 1938), who ascribes it to a south Italian writer. The date is endorsed, without argument, by Momigliano, *Alien Wisdom*, 17, abandoning his own earlier view in *JRS* 32 (1942): 54–55, n. 12. So also Mellor, *ΘΕΑ ΡΩΜΗ*, 121–124, with useful bibliography. He rightly rejects an Italian origin for the poem. The view of H. Bengtson, *Gymnasium* 71 (1964): 153–154, that it must predate the 150s because of Rome's failure in Spain thereafter, carries no weight.

106. Ps. -Scymnus, lines 231–234, in Müller, *Geogr. Graec. Min.* I:205. In this period perhaps was invented the tale that Alexander the Great prophesied the future power of Rome: Arrian, 7.15.5; see above p. 318.

in the 120s also pays tribute to Rome's might and to her empire.[107] Double-edged connotation, however, may be contained in the lines of a certain Polystratus, penned after the destruction of Corinth. His epigram celebrates that deed as revenge by the descendants of Aeneas against the Achaeans who had sacked Troy and burned the house of Priam. The bones of the dead are thrust in a pile; the Achaeans, unmourned, are robbed of funeral obsequies.[108] The conqueror's power here receives its due—but also his pitilessness.

A similar ambivalence may be detected in 1 Maccabees, composed probably in the later second century. Evidence on Jewish attitudes toward Rome in this period, however scanty, serves to reinforce and expand the Greek material, testimony to parallel reactions in the eastern world. The text of 1 Maccabees contains a remarkable encomium to Roman power, including some good information with confused and garbled facts. Rome's military successes are registered with approval: subjugation of the Gauls and Spain, the successive victories over Philip, Antiochus, and Perseus, in each case Rome emerging triumphant against foes who had attacked her first. The Republic receives praise for keeping faith with friends and even for sound internal government, a senate dedicated to good order and an annual leader obeyed without rancor or jealousy.[109] The positive aspects stand out. But scholars have passed by the negative overtones which ought not to be missed. The passage records Rome's victory in the Achaean war of 146 and its baleful consequences: large-scale massacres, the placement of women and children in captivity, plunder of property, control of the land, and reduction of the populace to servitude.[110] Achaea is not alone in this; other kingdoms and islands that resisted Rome were destroyed and enslaved.[111] Repetition of the phrase "reduced to slavery" is harsh language indeed. And the author, though he pays homage to Rome's majesty, observes also that she installs or deposes kings at will. The very name of Rome injects fear into those who hear it.[112] The Roman image in the late second

107. Diehl, *Anth. Lyr. Graec.* II:306–309.

108. *Anth. Graec.* 7.297.

109. 1 Macc. 8:1–16. On the date of composition, cf. Abel, *Les livres des Maccabées*, xxviii–xxix. A slightly later date, in the reign of Alexander Jannaeus, most recently proposed by Goldstein, *I Maccabees*, 62–89.

110. 1 Macc. 8:10: καὶ ἔπεσον ἐξ αὐτῶν τραυματίαι πολλοί, καὶ ᾐχμαλώτισαν τὰς γυναῖκας αὐτῶν καὶ τὰ τέκνα αὐτῶν καὶ ἐπρονόμευσαν αὐτοὺς καὶ κατεκράτησαν τῆς γῆς αὐτῶν καὶ καθεῖλον τὰ ὀχυρώματα αὐτῶν καὶ κατεδουλώσαντο αὐτοὺς ἕως τῆς ἡμέρας ταύτης.

111. 1 Macc. 8:11: καὶ τὰς ἐπιλοίπους βασιλείας καὶ τὰς νήσους, ὅσοι ποτὲ ἀντέστησαν αὐτοῖς, κατέφθειραν καὶ ἐδούλωσαν αὐτούς.

112. 1 Macc. 8:12–13: ὅσοι ἤκουον τὸ ὄνομα αὐτῶν, ἐφοβοῦντο ἀπ᾿ αὐτῶν.

century has taken on darker hues. Plaudits for the conqueror mingle with terror of his ruthlessness.

Rome had acquired a well-earned reputation for deposing monarchs. Her spokesmen equated the abolition of monarchy in Macedonia and Illyria with the establishment of liberty.[113] But, like so much else noted already, this too generated a double-edged reaction. The passage in 1 Maccabees associated removal of kings with dread of the Roman name. It finds a close parallel in an excerpt from the Sibylline Oracles, also composed in the later second century and decidedly hostile: the empire from the western sea will rule over much territory, will topple many, and will instill fear in all kings thereafter.[114] This antimonarchist reputation had caused Rome some difficulty earlier. Antiochus III had endeavored to win the adherence of Prusias by alleging that the Romans were out to eliminate all kings, thus eliciting a lengthy apologia from the Scipios.[115] Perseus utilized the same propaganda in making appeal to Antiochus IV.[116] Hence, in Hellenic eyes, this took on an increasingly negative aspect, a means by which Rome cowed her enemies, as reflected by 1 Maccabees and the *Oracula Sibyllina*. It comes as no surprise that Pompeius Trogus later placed these precise sentiments in the mouth of Mithridates, as did even Sallust in the mouth of Jugurtha.[117] The antimonarchical stance could serve to discredit as well as to enhance the Roman name.

Analogous transformation took place in the vision of Rome as heir to the succession of world empires. At least one form of this oracular tradition, as we have seen, had already culminated the process with Rome earlier in the century, a natural inference from her smashing triumphs over Philip and Antiochus. In other eastern circles different versions found place. The most celebrated occurs, of course, in the Book of Daniel. Here cryptic prophecies foretell the rise and fall of four mighty kingdoms, the last to be shattered and replaced by a Kingdom of Heaven to endure forever.[118] Daniel, however, is little concerned with Rome. The work was composed or completed in the mid-160s, and the author's eye was trained on Jewish travails in the time of Antiochus IV. Destruction of the fourth kingdom plainly

113. Livy, 45.18.1–2; Polyb. 36.17.13.

114. *Orac. Sib.* 3.175–179: ἢ πολλῆς γαίης ἄρξει, πολλοὺς δὲ σαλεύσει καὶ πᾶσιν βασιλεῦσι φόβον μετόπισθε ποιήσει.

115. Polyb. 21.11.2–11; Livy, 37.25.4–12.

116. Polyb. 29.4.9–10; Livy, 44.24.2–6; cf. 42.52.16.

117. Justin, 38.6.7; Sallust, *Jug.* 81.1. In the hands of Livy, of course, the positive value is restored and given honorable place in the tale of the origins of the Republic; Livy, 2.2.5, 2.9.2. On all this, see L. Castiglioni, *RendIstLomb*, 61 (1928) 629–635, who, however, overlooks the important passages in 1 Maccabees and the *Sibylline Oracles*.

118. Daniel 2:31–45, 7:1–27.

refers to a future end to the Hellenistic monarchies and a triumph of the Jewish faithful.[119] The only allusions to Rome by Daniel are favorable but marginal: the foreign power that checked the advance of Antiochus III and sent ships to turn back Antiochus IV from Egypt.[120] From the Jewish vantage-point at this time Rome was benevolent yet distant, certainly not in the line of world empires to be feared or detested. But after 146 the perspective changed. The brutal exercise of armed might that spread terror left an evil impression in the East. In the third book of the Sibylline Oracles, much of it drafted around 140, Rome has become the successor empire of the eastern kingdoms, each worse than the last and Rome the most powerful and destructive of all.[121] She is the barbarian who lays Hellas waste, who ravages and plunders, who carries off women and children into slavery.[122]

It was but a short step from this to the apocalyptic predictions that forecast Rome's ruin. In the late Republic they take the form of oracles conjuring up an eastern avenger of the evils wrought by Rome: Asia will strip Italy of three times the wealth plundered from the East, twenty times the number of slaves, and will exact retribution a thousandfold.[123] Or else they prophesy internal corruption, civil strife, and destruction from within that will bring Rome down.[124] Similar prognostications, outside the Sibylline context, circulated under the name of the Persian magus Hystaspes, preserved in Lactantius.[125]

119. See the exhaustive but tedious review of modern interpretations of the four empires in Daniel by H. H. Rawley, *Darius the Mede and the Four World Empires in the Book of Daniel* (Cardiff, 1959; orig. pub. 1935), 67–173. More recently, M. Hengel, *Judaism and Hellenism* (2nd ed., London, 1974), 180–196. A new commentary on the relevant passages by L. F. Hartman and A. A. DiLella, *The Book of Daniel* (New York, 1978), 142–153, 208–220. And cf. the perceptive remarks of Momigliano, *Alien Wisdom*, 109–112; idem, *RendAccadLinc* 35 (1980): 157–162. An echo of the prophecies appears, it seems, in *Orac. Sib.* 3.388–400.

120. Daniel 11:18, 11:30.

121. *Orac. Sib.* 3.156–181. On the date, see A. Rzach, *RE* IIA:2118, 2122–2129; and cf. the discussion of Fuchs, *Geistige Widerstand*, 7–8, 30–31. A date in the later first century B.C. is proposed, but without decisive arguments, by V. Nikiprowetsky, *La troisième Sibylle* (Paris, 1970), 195–217. This same negative image of a long series of world empires, climaxed by Rome, is repeated in a later version, with explicit reference to the destruction of Corinth and Carthage: *Orac. Sib.* 4.49–114; see also Lactantius, *Inst.* 7.15; Clement Alex. *Strom.* 6.43.1. Cf., in general, Flusser, *Israel Oriental Studies* 2 (1972): 148–175.

122. *Orac. Sib.* 3.520–538; cf. 3.638–651.

123. *Orac. Sib.* 3.350–355; cf. 3.652–654; 4.145–148.

124. *Orac. Sib.* 3.182–191, 3.356–362, 3.464–469.

125. Lactantius, *Inst.* 7.15, 7.18; see H. Windisch, *Verhandlingen Akad. Amsterdam*, 28.3 (1929): 1–64; J. Bidez and F. Cumont, *Les mages hellénisés, Zoroastre, Ostanès et Hystaspe d'après la tradition grecque* (Paris, 1938), I:215–217; Fuchs, *Geistige Widerstand*, 31–35; S. Eddy, *The King is Dead* (Lincoln, Nebraska, 1961), 32–36.

Precise dates for these oracular pronouncements cannot be specified. Rumblings certainly began to be heard after the devastations in 146. By the early first century anti-Roman auguries proliferated, an underground current for the cause of Mithridates.[126]

The various streams of this apocalyptic literature here congealed in a new mold. Predictions of Rome's greatness had appeared in both friendly and hostile guises at the beginning of the second century: the Delphic forecasts of her successes against rivals and the bizarre tales of Antisthenes who saw her ravaged by eastern invaders. Theories on the sequence of world monarchies had also taken divergent paths. Some inserted Rome as climax of the process, others, like Daniel, had her to one side, a contributor to, but not a prime agent, in the divine scheme. By the later second century, however, Rome's arbitrary and destructive power had asserted itself in decisive fashion. Admiration and anxiety mingle in the lines that apply to Rome in 1 Maccabees. The darker side comes increasingly to the fore in the relevant portions of the Sibylline Oracles. Rome emerges as heir to, and the most baneful of, the world empires. But her own fate is sealed and her doom foretold.

The reactions followed no linear path. Rome, for the most part, provoked emotional response rather than contemplative reflection. Her victories brought esteem, her power apprehension, her benefits gratitude, her withdrawal bafflement, her reentry indignation, her savagery terror and odium. The very confusion created by this shifting image, the failure to exercise suzerainty in a consistent fashion, the unpredictable character of Roman behavior, all this impelled Hellenes to grope for some form of understanding but made it almost impossible to produce a coherent picture. The absence of pattern discouraged theoretical formulations. This was not a fertile field for philosophers and political scientists.

What of Carneades' celebrated speeches on justice, delivered at Rome in 155 and often cited in this connection? Mere fragments filter through at third or fourth hand via Cicero and later Lactantius. Carneades defended first justice, then injustice in equally compelling orations, an argument for the latter illustrated by pointing to the power of Rome's empire: if Romans wished to practice justice, they would have to yield up all acquisitions and retreat to a life of poverty and anguish.[127] That has been taken as an adaptation of Greek philosophy

126. Posidonius, *FGH*, 2A, 87 F 36 = Edelstein and Kidd, no. 253, lines 86–87: χρησμοὶ δὲ πάντοθεν τὸ κράτος τῆς οἰκουμένης θεσπιῳδοῦσι.

127. Cic. *De Rep.* 3.21 = Lactantius, *Inst.* 5.16.2–4: *omnibus populis qui florerent imperio et Romanis quoque ipsis, qui totius orbis potirentur, si iusti velint esse, hoc est si alieno restituant, ad casas esse redeundem et in egestate ac miseriis iacendum.*

to a theory of Roman imperialism,[128] and even as sharp criticism of Roman ideas of justice, an attack on the evils wrought by the western power's expansion.[129] But such analysis ignores the historical context and distorts the intent. Carneades was member of an Athenian embassy seeking favor from the senate. A deliberate insult to Roman character would be impolitic in the extreme.[130] The Athenian's speeches were showpieces, a dazzling display of rhetorical virtuosity, seductive and disarming, one of the reasons that Cato hurried him out of Italy. The verbal dexterity may have caused discomfort. But nothing suggests that Cato or anyone else took umbrage at an assault on Roman overseas policy.[131] Carneades' image of Romans relinquishing their holdings and retiring to poverty simply applied to various theories of justice a *reductio ad absurdum*. It neither challenged Rome nor stimulated any philosophy of empire.[132]

In the eyes of Greeks Roman actions did not readily lend themselves to conceptual treatment. The ruin of Corinth and Carthage left a deep impression and provoked efforts to place Roman motivation in some perspective. But opinions still diverged and results gained little in profundity. Polybius supplies a summary of Hellenic attitudes toward the destruction of Carthage. The passage has generated much speculation as to which view Polybius himself embraced, a matter we may put aside. He was evidently not eager to be explicit about it.[133]

128. W. Capelle, *Klio* 25 (1932): 86–89.

129. Fuchs, *Geistige Widerstand*, 2–5.

130. So, rightly, Forte, *Rome and the Romans*, 69–70. Nor is there any evidence that Carneades' formulations provoked a redefinition of Roman imperialism in favorable terms by Panaetius; as Capelle, *op. cit.*, 89–113; Walbank, *JRS* 55 (1965): 12–14; Garbarino, *Roma e la filosofia greca* I:37–43; II:362–370; properly criticized by Strasburger, *JRS* 55 (1965): 44–45.

131. Cic. *De Rep.* 3.8–12 = Lactantius, *Inst.* 5.14.3–5; Plut. *Cato*, 22; Pliny, *NH*, 7.112; Gellius, 6.14.8–10. Cicero elsewhere suggests that Carneades and his fellow envoys left a very good impression among Roman nobles: *De Orat.* 2.155. Reference to the embassy also in Cic. *Acad. Prior.* 2.137; *Tusc. Disp.* 4.5; *Ad Att.* 12.23; Gellius, 17.21.48. Most recently, Ferrary, *REL* 55 (1977): 152–156, has, with good reason, raised the question of whether the version of Carneades' arguments, as put into the mouth of L. Furius Philus by Cicero, accurately represents what was in fact said in 155. It may derive from a treatise of Clitomachus and the reference to Roman imperialism may indeed be an addition by Cicero himself.

132. There is no reason to believe that Lactantius' excerpt from the *De Republica*, which reproaches Rome for using fetial declarations to conceal aggressive wars and gain world supremacy, derives from Carneades' arguments: Cic. *De Rep.* 3.24, 3.28—which refers to the 130s and hence is plainly not from Carneades' speech.

133. Polyb. 36.9. Cf., especially, the discussions of W. Hoffman, *Historia* 9 (1960): 311–312; Walbank, *JRS* 55 (1965): 8–11; *Polybius*, 174–176; in *EntrFondHardt* 20 (Geneva, 1974): 14–17; *Commentary* III:663–668; Petzold, *Studien*, 62–63; Momigliano, *AttiAccadTorino* 107 (1973): 698–699; Harris, *War and Imperialism*, 271–272; Musti; *Polibio e l'imperialismo romano*, 54–57.

More to the point, it mirrors continued dissonance in the reactions evoked by Rome. Polybius conveys four different assessments: two sets of paired judgments favorable and critical, one concentrating on the Third Punic War, the other employing it as springboard for a more general verdict. Hostile observers castigated Rome for employing deception and trickery against Carthage, instead of beating her in a fair fight, an abandonment of former principles and more akin to despotic practice.[134] In her defense, others pulled out a legalistic argument (and one largely irrelevant to the criticism): that the Carthaginians had performed full surrender, so Rome had authority to deal with them as she wished.[135] The debate combines heightened anxiety about Rome's unprincipled behavior with desperate attempts to understand it in formalistic terms. The other paired comments operate on a somewhat broader plane. Unhappy Greeks saw the westerner forsake her earlier ways and pursue empire unabashedly, the process inaugurated by abolition of the Macedonian kingdom and now brought to fruition by the ruin of Carthage.[136] A different approach found justification in the need to remove a dangerous rival: the security of Roman rule demanded it, a wise and far-sighted decision.[137] This setting forth of varied opinions no doubt owes something to Polybius' own conception and perhaps even to debates in Rome.[138] But there is no reason to question his statement that Greeks themselves offered explanations along these lines after 146. They sought to find pattern where there was none, to detect principle in unprincipled action, to reduce apparently capricious behavior to intelligible system, whether in a favorable or a harsh light. But the diverse and inconsistent solutions show continued uncertainty in Hellas. After all this time the Roman image was still indistinct.

Polybius

Polybius himself tried to make sense of it. After Pydna he found himself an exile in Italy, his native land humbled, Roman ascendancy secure. For Polybius, as for most Greeks at that juncture, it appeared that the struggle for supremacy was over and Rome's firmness

134. Polyb. 36.9.9–11.
135. Polyb. 36.9.12–17.   136. Polyb. 36.9.5–8.   137. Polyb. 36.9.3–4.
138. The legalistic justification for the Third Punic War may well coincide with opinion in Roman circles: Polyb. 36.9.13; cf. 20.10.2–9. Even the criticism of Rome for engaging in deception and ambush rather than honest conduct of war (36.9.9–10) echoes statements supposedly made by some senators against their colleagues at the time of the Third Macedonian War: Livy, 42.47.4–5; Diod. 30.7.1. That evidence was plainly to be found in Polybius, who has a similar formulation in still another place; 13.3.1–8;

guaranteed that she would take seriously her role as hegemon. The circumstances inspired Polybius to embark on a general history to trace the rise of Rome and the consolidation of the Mediterranean under her sway. But for all the programmatic statements and reflections, no coherent picture emerges. Incongruities plague the analysis. Polybius did not produce a theory of imperialism.

Roman mastery of the world by 167 Polybius took as established fact.[139] The magnitude of the accomplishment filled him with admiration: Rome had far outstripped all previous conquerors and empires.[140] The historian announced as his task that of describing how, when, and to what purpose Rome achieved universal dominion.[141] A straightforward enough program—but the execution of that program leaves much to be desired.

In fact, Polybius never did address the question of why. The statement noted above marks the one time he even chose to raise it. Elsewhere he defines his aims more simply: to ascertain the means whereby Rome gained worldwide supremacy, not her reasons for seeking it.[142] Nor was he fully clear even on the means. Some Greeks ascribed the acquisition of empire to chance and unwilled circumstance. Polybius ostensibly rejected that approach and proposed a different explanation: the superiority of Roman institutions, training, and experience.[143] Yet he could not evade the power of Τύχη. She lurks behind Roman success in undefined fashion, her role central and significant, as Polybius acknowledges—a view never satisfactorily reconciled with his notion that Rome's accomplishment was due to national qualities.[144] So ambiguity inheres at the most fundamental level.

---

cf. Walbank, *Commentary* II:416–417. Whether Diodorus' remarks about hegemonial powers who employ courage and intelligence to gain empire, kindliness to extend it, and terror to hold it stem from Polybius must remain uncertain: Diod. 32.2, 32.4; cf. on this Gelzer, *Kleine Schriften* II:64–65; further bibliography in Walbank, *Polybius*, 179; more recently, J. Touloumakos, *Zum Geschichtsbewusstsein der Griechen in der Zeit der römischen Herrschaft* (Göttingen, 1971), 29 n. 22, and a revised view in Walbank, *EntrFondHardt* 20 (Geneva, 1974): 18–20.

139. Polyb. 3.4.2–3.

140. Polyb. 1.2.1–7, 3.59.3, 29.21.1–9; cf. Appian, *Praef.* 8–9; Dion. Hal. 1.2.1–4.

141. Polyb. 3.1.4: τοῦ πῶς καὶ πότε καὶ διὰ τί πάντα τὰ γνωριζόμενα μέρη τῆς οἰκουμένης ὑπὸ τὴν Ῥωμαίων δυναστείαν ἐγένετο.

142. Polyb. 1.1.5, 1.2.7–8, 1.3.9–10, 1.12.7, 3.3.9, 3.4.12, 6.2.3, 39.8.7.

143. Polyb. 1.63.9–1.64.2, 3.2.6, 3.118.8–9, 6.10.13–14, 6.50.3–6; cf. 18.28.5. That certain Greek writers did attribute Rome's success to mere chance is noted also by Dion. Hal. 1.4.2, 2.17.3.

144. Polyb. 8.2.3–6; cf. 1.1.4, 1.4.4–5, 21.16.8, 29.21.5–9; on Polybius and τύχη generally, see Pedech, *La méthode*, 331–354. Note too, with regard to the conquest of Italy, Polyb. 1.6.8: γενόμενοι δὲ παραδόξως ἁπάντων ἐγκρατεῖς.

Even the question of when Rome secured world empire receives more than one answer in Polybius' text. The Second Punic War seemed to him decisive: the two protagonists were contending for supremacy over all the known world.[145] Hellenes could only observe in helpless anxiety, awaiting its outcome.[146] But elsewhere Polybius finds that the definitive establishment of suzerainty over Greece came at the time of the wars with Philip and Antiochus.[147] Then again, he discerns its final achievement with the fall of Perseus, after which all must submit to Roman dictation.[148] Yet he altered his perspective still once more after witnessing the terrible events of the mid-140s. His history now had to be extended to cover that period as well, and his closing remarks imply that the process of acquiring unchallenged mastery concluded only with the fall of Carthage and Corinth.[149] The various statements are not self-contradictory or mutually exclusive. But they parallel the oscillating reactions of Greeks to Rome's alternate exercise of, and abdication from, sovereignty.

Was the acquisition of empire a conscious Roman objective? For the most part Polybius answers in the affirmative. He traces Rome's aggrandizement from the recovery of her strength after the Gallic sack of the city in an unbroken line through the conquest of Italy to the origins of the First Punic War.[150] The clashes with Carthage were part and parcel of a design for world dominion, the resources gathered in the course of them earmarked for fulfillment of that design.[151] Even here, however, there is some ambivalence. For Polybius at one point attributes the inception of a scheme for universal empire only to the time of victory over Carthage, not as something rooted in early Roman history.[152] And elsewhere the very idea of a conscious project seems to recede. The steps of expansion possess their own dynamic, the two Punic Wars and the conflicts with Philip and Antiochus

145. Polyb. 1.3.7, 15.9.2–5, 15.10.2; Livy, 29.17.6, 30.32.2.

146. Polyb. 5.33.4.

147. Polyb. 24.11.3; cf. 3.118.9; Livy, 36.17.14–15. The Antiochene war decided the mastery of Asia: Polyb. 3.3.5, 21.4.4–5, 21.16.8, 21.23.4, 23.14.10.

148. Polyb. 3.4.2–3; cf. 1.1.5, 3.1.9–10, 6.2.3.

149. Polyb. 39.8.7. On the decision to continue his history beyond 167, see Polyb. 3.4. By the Gracchan era the Romans could certainly be depicted as rulers of the world, Cic. De Rep. 3.24: cuius imperio iam orbis terrae tenetur; Plut. Ti. Gr. 9.5; cf. Appian, BC, 1.11; Gabba, Athenaeum 55 (1977): 49–62. J. S. Richardson, PBSR 47 (1979): 1–2, exaggerates the consistency and coherence of Polybius' views.

151. Polyb. 1.3.6, 8.1.3, 9.10.11; cf. 1.20.1–2, 3.4.9–11. Aspirations to world dominion, however, were not limited to Rome. Polybius ascribes them to Philip V as well; 5.101.9–5.102.1

152. Polyb. 3.2.6. The inconsistency is noted by Walbank, JRS 53 (1963): 5. For P. S. Derow, JRS 69 (1979): 2–4, it is "odd but . . . not inconsistent." He doubts that Polybius dated Roman designs on world empire any earlier than the Hannibalic war.

following upon one another with irresistible momentum.[153] So the historian falls back again on the ultimate authority of Τύχη.[154] This tension between deliberate purpose and an underlying kinetic also remains without resolution.

Further, Polybius' considered judgment of Rome follows no steady course. Admiration for her principles and constitution prevails, of course. It is to them (on most occasions) that he credits Roman imperial success. The Romans are men of noble temperament, with sympathy for those in misfortune but an even higher regard for law and justice.[155] They can be most uncompromising after defeat, but magnanimous and merciful after victory, an exemplary recipe for empire.[156] Yet those principles were not adhered to with consistency. Polybius acknowledges that the Romans as general practice relied upon force in all their endeavors.[157] Already in the early third century, the Gauls convinced themselves—not without reason—that Rome was bent on their total extermination.[158] Again the historian makes no effort to reconcile those impressions.

His understanding of Roman behavior was rudely shaken by the upheavals of the late 150s and early 140s, culminating in the subjugation of his native land. This shock induced Polybius to return to his writing table and to attach a whole new portion to his history, one that would take the story from Pydna down through 146. He gives as reason a desire to assess the character of Roman rule and to determine whether it merits praise or blame.[159] In fact, no general analysis does emerge from the text. But a long series of comments on Roman actions during these two decades are sprinkled through the last books of the history, all of them delivering a thrust very different from that which found expression in the earlier portions of his work. Polybius persistently draws attention to Roman cynicism and self-interest:

153. Polyb. 3.32.7; cf. Strabo, 6.4.2 (C287).

154. Polyb. 1.4.4–5, 8.2.3–6, 21.16.8, 21.23.4, 29.21.5–9. Cf. Walbank, *JRS* 53 (1963): 5–13.

155. Polyb. 24.8.2–5, 24.10.11–12, 24.13.3. An echo of this in Diod. 28.3; and cf. Plut. *Flam.* 11.2–4.

156. Polyb. 3.99.7, 10.36.2–5, 18.37.2–7, 27.8.8; cf. 15.4.8–12, 15.19.5, 38.18.12, 39.6.3. This theme too was picked up by Diod. 27.14–17, 30.8, 32.4.4—though not necessarily a direct borrowing from Polybius.

157. Polyb. 1.37.7.

158. Polyb. 2.21.9; cf. 2.19.11, 2.31.8. That reputation was one which Flamininus later had to abjure: Polyb. 18.37.2–4.

159. Polyb. 3.4; especially, 3.4.7: δῆλον γὰρ ὡς ἐκ τούτων φανερὸν ἔσται τοῖς μὲν νῦν οὖσι πότερα φευκτὴν ἢ τοὐναντίον αἱρετὴν εἶναι συμβαίνει τὴν Ῥωμαίων δυναστείαν, τοῖς δ' ἐπιγινομένοις πότερον ἐπαινετὴν καὶ ζηλωτὴν ἢ ψεκτὴν γεγονέναι νομιστέον τὴν ἀρχὴν αὐτῶν.

the encouragement of servility among some eastern princes, deliberate efforts to undermine others, both a readiness to manipulate and a susceptibility to manipulation, devious diplomacy in Asia Minor and Syria, specious pretexts for terrorizing Dalmatia and for bringing Carthage to her knees.[160] Rome adapts her policy for capitalizing on the faults of neighbors in order to augment her own dominions.[161] A remarkable assemblage of comments. As a group they constitute a stiff assessment. It does not follow that Polybius is here passing moral judgment, nor, to the contrary, that he is associating himself with Roman success.[162] The historian's verdict is tough-minded and realistic— but not altogether dispassionate. He had regarded Roman ascendancy in Greece as fixed beyond question by 167. There should have been smooth and untroubled acceptance of the fact thereafter. But upheavals shattered the peace again, lunatic and suicidal, heaping greater evils than ever before upon the Greek world.[163] Polybius determined to carry on his history, to throw a clear light on Roman behavior, to underline the cynicism and harshness, lest Greeks make the same mistake again.[164] But, whatever the impulse that brought

160. Polyb. 30.1.6–10, 30.3.5–7, 30.19.12–13 (Attalus and Eumenes); 30.18.1–7 (Prusias); 31.2.6–11, 32.3.11–13, 33.18.6–13 (the Seleucids); 32.10.1–2 (Ariarathes); 32.13.4–9 (Dalmatia); 31.21.5–6, 36.2.1–4; Appian, *Lib.* 69 (Carthage). Other examples in Walbank, *Polybius*, 68–71. Polybius' conclusions about Roman behavior find their way also into some earlier remarks: reference to the readiness with which Rome accepted false accusations against Greeks during and after the Third Macedonian War; e.g., Polyb. 27.15.10–16, 28.3–5, 30.13; and the allegation—quite outside the context in which it appears—that Rome was indignant if all affairs were not brought to her and done in accordance with her wishes: 23.17.4.

161. Polyb. 31.10.7: πολὺ γὰρ ἤδη τοῦτο τὸ γένος ἐστὶ τῶν διαβουλίων παρὰ Ῥωμαίοις, ἐν οἷς διὰ τῆς τῶν πέλας ἀγνοίας αὔξουσι καὶ κατασκευάζονται τὴν ἰδίαν ἀρχὴν πραγματικῶς. The comments are meant to apply generally, not just to Roman behavior after 167: Derow, *JRS* 69 (1979): 13–15.

162. The notion that Polybius takes on a moral posture in his writings after 146 is argued by Petzold, *Studien*, 53–64. For Walbank, Polybius identifies success with moral worth and has become spokesman for the Roman point of view: *JRS* 55 (1965): 2–11; *Polybius*, 166–181; *EntrFondHardt* 20 (Geneva, 1974) 11–29. More recently, Gabba maintains that Polybius' concern is with the effectiveness of Roman rule and the question of how far subjects found it acceptable: *Athenaeum* 55 (1977): 64–74. Musti, *Polibio e l'imperialismo romano*, 44–50, 75–88, gives more weight to Polybius' balanced moral judgment, his stress on Greek internal autonomy, and his reservations about Roman behavior that infringed upon it.

163. Polyb. 3.4.12–3.5.6, 36.10, 36.17.13–15, 38.1, 38.3.8–13, 38.12.5–7, 38.16.1, 38.16.7–9.

164. Cf. Gruen, *Chiron* 6 (1976): 74–75. A different suggestion for Polybius' reasons in adding to his history in Walbank, *Historiographia Antiqua: Commentationes Lovanienses in honorem W. Peremans septuagenarii editae* (Leuven, 1977), 139–162; rightly criticized by Shimron, *Scripta Classica Israelica* 5 (1979–80): 94–117.

continuation of his history, Polybius' observations on Rome after
Pydna do not march easily with the admiring attitudes he manifests
elsewhere or the encomium that underlies Book VI. Change in time
and circumstances altered and clouded the image.

Polybius caught a glimpse too of what seemed adulteration and
impairment of Roman character. The Aetolians misjudged Flamininus, he says, when they considered him susceptible to bribery; indeed, Romans of an earlier day, before expansion across the seas,
would never compromise principle for cash. But he could no longer
confidently make such assertion about Romans in his own time.[165]
When had matters taken a turn for the worse? Polybius has no precise
date. In retrospect he could go back even to the Hannibalic war and
the expropriation of Sicilian art treasures: Rome showed serious lack
of foresight, for the despoiling of Syracuse could engender only envy
and hatred, an impolitic act by the conqueror to introduce superfluous luxury and weaken the fiber of her society.[166] Elsewhere he lo-
cates a turning point at the time of conflict with Perseus, when acquaintance with slack Greek habits seduced Roman youths away from
their national virtues.[167] By 146 deterioration was evident in other
ways. The Romans who had once confiscated works of art from Syracuse now employed Corinthian paintings as dice boards.[168] Polybius
naturally exempts his friend and patron Scipio Aemilianus from such
indictment. But Scipio stands out as exceptional, a model of restraint
in an age when young men frittered away fortunes on immoral self-
gratifications, a gallant patriot at a time when Roman youths scrambled for excuses to evade military service.[169] The remarks are wistful
rather than hostile, stated more in sorrow than in anger. But the historian's disappointment is unmistakable. The character of Rome's
people, to which Polybius had attributed much of their success, no
longer conformed to earlier impressions and expectations.

Just when Polybius penned these comments is past knowing.
They need not all have come after the painful experiences of 146. Nor
were Greek sensibilities required to detect the changes in Roman society. The new practices had already come under fire from Roman

165. Polyb. 18.34.6–18.35.2: λέγω δὲ πρότερον ἢ τοῖς διαποντίοις αὐτοὺς ἐγχ-
ειρῆσαι πολέμοις, ἕως ἐπὶ τῶν ἰδίων ἐθῶν καὶ νομίμων ἔμενον. ἐν δὲ τοῖς νῦν καιροῖς
περὶ πάντων μὲν οὐκ ἂν τολμήσαιμι τοῦτ᾽ εἰπεῖν.

166. Polyb. 9.10; cf. Livy, 25.40.2.

167. Polyb. 31.25.4–6; Diod. 31.26.7, 37.3.1–6. Cf. Polyb. 30.22 on L. Anicius'
games celebrating victory over the Illyrians; a very different version in Livy, 45.43.

168. Polyb. 39.2.

169. Polyb. 31.25.2–8, 35.4; Diod. 31.26.5–6. On susceptibility to corruption,
Polybius also singles out Scipio and his father Aemilius Paullus as among the exceptions: 18.35.1–12.

critics.[170] M. Cato made a habit of railing against the insidious preoccupations of opulence, the mania for statuary, buildings, and ostentation, even Greek dancing, and, worse still, pederasty.[171] Polybius heard Cato, knew him, and quoted him.[172] In the circles of Rome's intelligentsia to which the Greek historian had access there was considerable grumbling about infiltration of luxury items and debilitating habits. Livy puts the origin of obsession with plush furnishings, female entertainers, and the culinary arts to the time of Manlius Vulso's triumph in 186.[173] Some of those items found mention in the work of Polybius' contemporary L. Piso, evidently objects of much discussion in mid-second century Rome.[174] Piso himself set the beginnings of Rome's degeneration in 154 and had some harsh words for the depravity of the city's youth.[175] Scipio Aemilianus, in a speech of 129, expressed shock at the existence of coeducational dancing schools.[176] Such was the milieu that both helped to shape, and gained some shape from, the attitudes of Polybius.

But it was not Polybius' purpose to moralize. His subject was empire: change in Roman character took on relevance as it related to empire. The historian sensed a connection but never worked it out and never elaborated it. Polybius persuaded himself that the inclination to excess came after the collapse of Macedonia, when Romans considered their world supremacy as unchallengeable.[177] Similar terminology is employed when he raises that principle to a general level: the state that attains unchallenged empire will enjoy prosperity but

170. Cf. the attacks on *nova sapientia* by certain Roman senators in 172: Livy, 42.47.9.

171. E.g., *ORF*, fr. 95–96, 114–116, 185. Cato's censorship of 184 was hailed in an inscription for stabilization of a slipping and collapsing state: Plut. *Cato*, 19.3. On Cato's views, see now Astin, *Cato the Censor*, 91–103.

172. Note, especially, his citation of Cato on Roman pederasty: Polyb. 31.25.5; Diod. 31.24, 37.3.6. On Polybius and Cato, see Kienast, *Cato der Zensor* (Heidelberg, 1954), 110–116; Nicolet, in *EntrFondHardt* 20 (Geneva, 1974) 246–255.

173. Livy, 39.6.7–9. On Livy's attitude toward these matters generally, see now T. J. Luce, *Livy: The Composition of his History* (Princeton, 1977), 250–275. L. Scipio's triumph is castigated in much the same terms: Pliny, *NH*, 33.148. For Val. Max. 9.1.3, the onset of luxury and its debilitating effects came after the wars with Hannibal and Philip.

174. Piso, in Peter, *HRR*, fr. 34 = Pliny, *NH*, 34.14; cf. 37.12.

175. Piso, in Peter, *HRR*, fr. 38 = Pliny, *NH*, 17.244; fr. 40 = Cic. *Ad Fam.* 8.22.2. On Piso, see K. Latte, *SBBerlin* (1960), 7:1–16.

176. *ORF*, no. 21, fr. 30. On second-century Roman discussions of moral decline, see Lintott, *Historia* 21 (1972): 626–638; K. Bringmann, *Antike und Abendland* 23 (1977): 28–36.

177. Polyb. 31.25.6: συνέβη δὲ τὴν παροῦσαν αἵρεσιν οἷον ἐκλάμψαι κατὰ τοὺς νῦν λεγομένους καιροὺς πρῶτον μὲν διὰ τὸ καταλυθείσης τῆς ἐν Μακεδονίᾳ βασιλείας δοκεῖν ἀδήριτον αὐτοῖς ὑπάρχειν τὴν περὶ τῶν ὅλων ἐξουσίαν.

yield to extravagance, its citizens absorbed in mutual rivalries; the struggle for office, wealth, and boastful ostentation will signal the beginnings of a change for the worse.[178] Whether those ruminations reflect disillusionment with Rome in Polybius' older years after 146 cannot be said with certainty.[179] But one celebrated tale does belong after 146: the moving account of Scipio's tears as flames rose over Carthage. Polybius was there with his friend and former pupil. The Roman commander wept, so he told Polybius, for he could foresee another conqueror some day issuing similar orders for the destruction of Rome—and punctuated the prophecy by quoting Homeric verses on the fate of Troy.[180] The scene left an impact on Polybius, who redrafted it later for his readers. And the form in which it is preserved recreates the eastern traditions of the succession of empires and the apocalyptic visions of the future: Rome will follow the path of Ilium, Assyria, Media, Persia, and Macedonia and will suffer their fate.[181] Such sentiments, as we have seen, would find expression again in the Sibylline Oracles which—with striking reminiscences of these statements—associate Roman collapse with the corruptions of wealth, male prostitution, and civil strife.[182]

Polybius' attitude, it bears repetition, was rueful but not rancorous. The institutions and character of Rome's people had gained her an empire. But once that empire was secured, the very qualities that made it possible showed signs of unraveling and would eventually place it in jeopardy. Polybius stood in awe of the achievement, yet ended with confusion rather than clarity. The vicissitudes of his own fortune produced greater respect for Τύχη. The advance of Roman arms by intermittent assault and withdrawal made it hard to discern critical turning points, impossible to outline a consistent rationale. Polybius was affected both by the milieu of Roman intellectuals

178. Polyb. 6.57.5–6.

179. They sit ill with Polybius' remarks on the strength of the mixed constitution, 6.18.1–8, and hence may represent a later stage of his thinking; so, most recently, Petzold, *Studien*, 84–90. But, it can be argued, the tension is not unresolvable, the inconsistency more apparent than real; see C. O. Brink and F. W. Walbank, *CQ* 4 (1954): 102–107; Walbank, *GRBS* 5 (1964): 244–256; Pedech, *La méthode*, 308–317; bibliography in Musti, *PP* 20 (1965): 388–396, and *ANRW* I:2 (1972), 1117–1122.

180. Polyb. 38.21–22; Diod. 32.24; Appian, *Lib.* 132. How large a role this may have played in Scipio's subsequent thinking is not our concern here. Scullard, *JRS* 50 (1960): 60–62, exaggerates it. On the other hand, much too prosaic an analysis is offered by Astin, *Scipio Aemilianus* (Oxford, 1967), 282–287. See, most recently, W. Schadewaldt, *ANRW* I:4 (1973), 52–58.

181. So Appian, *Lib.* 132, ultimately derived from Polybius. Mendels, *AJP* 102 (1981): 333–334, argues that the notion of "five empires" did not stand in Polybius' original text. Walbank, *Commentary* III:725, more properly, leaves the matter open.

182. *Orac. Sib.* 3.182–191; cf. 4.49–114.

and by Hellenic teachings on the *anacyclosis* of constitutions and the fate of empires. He experienced Rome's forceful authority in the aftermath of Pydna, detected cynicism and Machiavellian policy in the next two decades, and was stunned by the cataclysmic events of the 140s. It is no wonder that he failed to provide either a sharp image of Rome or a theory of imperialism.

Posidonius

To pursue Greek thinking into the period of Rome's full administration of overseas holdings is not our purpose here. Circumstances were very different when the erratic conqueror became a settled administrator. But it may be observed that the difficulties of framing a coherent philosophy of empire remained as formidable as ever. The one place where one should expect to find it is in the work of Posidonius, continuator of Polybius' history, pupil of the philosopher Panaetius, associate of the Roman statesman and thinker Rutilius Rufus, friend and protégé of Pompey the Great, whose settlement of the East he witnessed.[183] Yet, despite the efforts of modern scholars, a tidy and rounded portrait fails to emerge.

A Posidonian fragment asserts that many peoples, cognizant of their own incapacity and intellectual inferiority, voluntarily place themselves under the guidance of their superiors, offering as example the subjection by consent of the serfs called Mariandyni to the people of Heraclea.[184] Does this adumbrate justification for the Roman empire? Seneca later cites Posidonius on the golden age, a time when men committed themselves to the rule of their betters, the weaker yielded naturally to the stronger, a rule that holds in the animal as in the human world: the superior in power is the superior in wisdom and in moral worth.[185] The two fragments have been taken as philosophic rationalization for Roman dominion.[186] Certainly by the time of Augustus such rationalizations were common fare: a law of nature

183. On Posidonius' life and career, see K. Reinhardt, *RE* XXII: 1, "Posidonius," 558–826; a summary in Strasburger, *JRS* 55 (1965): 40–42. And see now K. von Fritz, *Historiographia Antiqua: Commentationes Lovanienses in honorem W. Peremans septuagenarii editae* (Leuven, 1977), 163–193.

184. *FGH*, 2A, 87 F 8 = Edelstein and Kidd, no. 60.

185. Seneca, *Ep.* 90.4–5.

186. So, most notably, Capelle, *Klio*, 25 (1932), 98–104. Capelle also regards as Posidonian various remarks of Strabo that praise Rome's bringing of peace to the barbarian chaos of Spain: Strabo, 3.2.5 (C144), 3.3.5 (C154), 3.3.8 (C156); 3.4.13 (C163)—accepted by Walbank, *JRS* 55 (1965): 14–15, and even by Strasburger, *JRS* 55 (1965): 46–47. But the attribution is unproved; cf. the doubts of Momigliano, *Alien Wisdom*, 32.

dictated that the superior rule the inferior.[187] But nothing compels us to trace this back to Posidonius. Rome appears in neither of the relevant fragments. The example of the Mariandyni and the Heracleotes would be a poor symbol for Roman governance of the world. And the voluntary submission of the weaker to their betters is explicitly put in the golden age before corruption set in and converted natural rule into tyranny.[188] This hardly serves to legitimize the Roman empire of Posidonius' own day.

In fact Posidonius lived through an age that witnessed the beginnings of Roman exploitation of the East on a systematic basis, the servile revolts in Sicily, the devastating conflict between Rome and her Italian *socii*, the eruption of the Mithridatic war, and the Roman brutality that followed it. Those events left a deep impression on the historian whose work encompassed them all. Insofar as he offered speculative explanation, it was anything but original or profound. Like Polybius, Posidonius pointed to the destruction of Carthage and Corinth as marking a significant dividing line in Roman history. He cited with concurrence Scipio Nasica's warning that Rome's internal harmony and successful external rule depended on the survival of Carthage. When that city was wiped off the map, the admonition seemed vindicated: Rome became engulfed in demagoguery and civil strife, a gentle rule gave way to ruthlessness, evoking hatred and revolution from subject peoples.[189] Polybius had had a foreboding; Posidonius had seen it happen. The Romans acquired untold wealth after the fall of Corinth and Carthage, so says Strabo, and applied it to the purchase of slaves, thus providing stimulus for a massive surge in both piracy and slavery. Posidonius' keen interest in each of these

187. Dion. Hal. 1.5.2: φύσεως γὰρ δὴ νόμος ἅπασι κοινός, ὃν οὐδεὶς καταλύσει χρόνος, ἄρχειν ἀεὶ τῶν ἡττόνων τοὺς κρείττονας—with explicit reference to Roman hegemony. Strabo consistently lauds the Romans for bringing government and civilization to the savages; see previous note and add also Strabo, 2.5.26 (C127); cf. Livy, 22.13.11. An equally common refrain in that period was stress on Roman clemency to the conquered: e.g. Diod. 27.18, 30.8, 31.3.2–3, 32.4, 33.28b.3–4; Livy, 30.42.17; Vergil, *Aen.* 6.853; Strabo, 17.3.24 (C839); Dion. Hal. 14.6.1.

188. Seneca, *Ep.* 90.4–6; so, rightly, O. Seel, *Römische Denker und römischer Staat* (Leipzig-Berlin, 1937), 78–78; Strasburger, *JRS* 55 (1965): 46–47. Posidonius does single out Marcellus as the first to show Greeks that Romans practiced justice as well as warfare: Plut. *Marc.* 20.1; cf. 20.7. But this too does not apply to his own age.

189. Diod. 34/5.33.5–6, quite certainly, as almost all scholars agree, from Posidonius. U. Hackl, *Gymnasium* 87 (1980): 151–166, goes too far, however, in seeing Nasica's argument as an invention of Posidonius. Cf. also Posidonius' lauding of the antique virtues of Romans in an earlier age: *FGH*, 2A, 87 F 59 = Edelstein and Kidd, no. 265–267. Bringmann's argument, that Posidonius dated Roman decline to the time of the Cimbric war, is unconvincing: *Antike und Abendland* 23 (1977): 37–40. He reads that interpretation into Diod. 37.1–2, where it does not exist.

subjects makes him the obvious candidate as original author of that analysis.[190] One hardly needs reminding that the notion of Rome's degeneracy as beginning with the elimination of her foreign foes in 146 became a commonplace in subsequent Latin literature.[191]

Posidonius observed with regret the character of Roman rule that bore a heavy burden of responsibility for the lamentable events of his time. C. Gracchus gave free rein to the *publicani*, whose ravenous exactions reaped a harvest of odium for Rome.[192] Their rapacity knew no bounds, even hauling defaulters into slavery from the principalities of Roman allies.[193] The servile uprisings in Sicily manifested reaction against a reckless abuse of power.[194] Italian revolt against Rome's overlordship came when Romans had allowed luxury and corruption to undermine the qualities that had won them an empire.[195] The origins of the Mithridatic war are put down to Marius' inordinate greed for the wealth of Asia.[196] A gloomy perspective appears dominant. Yet Posidonius did not compose his history, any more than Polybius did, to deliver a damning indictment of Rome. The strongest denunciations are put in the mouth of Athenion, Peripatetic philosopher and head of Mithridates' supporters in Athens. Yet Athenion himself is blackened beyond measure by the historian: an ostentatious social climber, effeminate, demagogic, and a charlatan.[197] Similarly, though

190. Strabo, 14.5.2 (C668); the argument of Strasburger, *JRS* 55 (1965): 42–43 and n. 34, is compelling.

191. E.g., Sallust, *Cat.* 10–13; *Iug.* 3.2, 41.1–5; *Hist.* 1.11–13, Maur.; cf. Livy, *Praef.* 11–12; Vell. Pat. 2.1.1; see W. Steidle, *Sallusts historische Monographien* (Wiesbaden, 1958), 16–21; D. C. Earl, *The Political Thought of Sallust* (Cambridge, 1961), 41–50.

192. Diod. 34/5.25.1.   193. Diod. 36.3.1.   194. Diod. 34/5.2.33.

195. Diod. 37.2.1; cf. 37.3.

196. Diod. 37.29.2; cf. 37.2.12, 37.30. See now, on all this,. P. Desideri, *Rend-IstLomb* 106 (1972): 481–493, though he goes too far in insisting that Posidonius' harshness was concentrated upon the Roman *equites*. Cf. also Rizzo, *Studi di storia antica offerti a E. Manni* (Rome, 1976): 259–293.

197. *FGH*, 2A, 87 F 36 = Edelstein and Kidd, no. 253. On the circumstances, see E. Candiloro, *StudClassOrient* 14 (1965): 145–171; Deininger, *Widerstand*, 245–261, with bibliography. Add Badian, *AJAH* 1 (1976): 105–128; Habicht, *Chiron* 6 (1976): 127–142. But the anti-Roman thrust is not delivered simply through Athenion. Posidonius offers a subtle barb of his own; see lines 37–43. Athenian attitudes toward Rome may be reflected in the fictitious letter of Hannibal to Athens announcing victory over the Romans and promoting a competition for the best poem on the subject; R. Merkelbach, *Griechische Papyri der Hamburger Staats-und Universitäts-Bibliothek* (Hamburg, 1954), 62–63. But the date of this invention is a matter of guesswork. Merkelbach, *op. cit.*, 51, puts it in the first century; Candiloro, *op. cit.*, 175–176, somewhere in the second century; Momigliano, *Alien Wisdom*, 41, without argument, ca. 185. Nor is it clear even that this is a piece of anti-Roman propaganda, as proposed by Candiloro, *op. cit.*, 171–175; cf. Momigliano, *op. cit.*, 41. The purpose may be irony, to set Hannibal's boastfulness

he deplored the conditions that inspired the Sicilian slave revolts, Posidonius had only contempt for their leaders.[198] The evils of Roman overseas administration, when in the wrong hands, is acknowledged. But Posidonius reserves high praise for other Roman administrators who carried out their responsibilities with scrupulousness, tact, and equity.[199] This was no anti-Roman tract.

Overt hostility toward Rome, to be sure, could be found in certain Greek writers of the first century. Metrodorus of Scepsis hated the very name of Rome and wrote fierce diatribes against her.[200] Timagenes issued vitriolic criticisms of the western power in his history, composed late in the century.[201] Others paid homage to Parthia, a comparison with Rome in which the latter came off very much second best.[202] Still others circulated petty tales about the founding of Rome, attributing it to vagabonds and barbarians.[203] Spiteful outbursts rather than reasoned critique. Posidonius rose above that level, his purpose perhaps to encourage Romans to follow the model of those few still among them who were men of integrity.[204] But, trained in philosophy and history though he was, not even Posidonius succeeded in putting the pieces of the Roman puzzle together. The upheavals of the late second and early first centuries gave him grave disquiet. Posidonius grasped at the conventional and unilluminating theory that corruption in character set in after the elimination of foreign rivals. Empire itself could be benevolent—but could also give rise to temptations that promoted avarice, arrogance, and exploitation. There were principled leaders, as well as rapacious administrators and financiers. Conditions that produced rebellion could be laid to Rome's charge, but the rebels proved to be worse even than their hegemon. So Posi-

---

against what readers knew to be his ultimate fate; so Merkelbach, op. cit., 55; Deininger, Widerstand, 246, n. 3.

198. Cf. Diod. 34/5.2.5–7, 34/5.2.22–23, 36.4.4.

199. Diod. 37.5, 37.8. Strasburger, JRS 55 (1965): 49; Desideri, RendIstLomb 106 (1972): 485–486; cf. also Plut. Pomp. 28.3–4, with Strasburger, op. cit., 50–51.

200. Ovid. Pont. 4.14.37–38; Pliny, NH, 34.34.

201. Seneca, Ep. 91.13; cf. G. W. Bowersock, Augustus and the Greek World (Oxford, 1965), 109–111, 125–126. Doubts about Timagenes' anti-Romanism recently expressed by G. B. Sunseri, Studi di storia antica offerti a E. Manni (Rome, 1976), 91–101— who does not, however, satisfactorily explain the Senecan passage. Cf. also Balsdon, Romans and Aliens, 183–185.

202. Livy, 9.18.6; cf. Dion. Hal. 1.4.3.

203. Dion. Hal. 1.4.2, 1.89.1, 7.70.1–2; cf. 1.5.1, 1.75.4; Justin, 28.2.8–10, 38.6.7; Castiglioni, RendIstLomb 61 (1928): 627–629. There were, of course, Greek flatterers of Rome in the first century as well; see Crawford, in Garnsey and Whittaker, Imperialism in the Ancient World, 199–207.

204. Strasburger, JRS, 55 (1965): 51–52; Momigliano, Alien Wisdom, 31–36.

donius too concluded with ambivalence and ambiguity. Roman behavior never quite fitted a mold.

V

Hellenic attitudes toward Rome over a period of two centuries fluctuated, varied, and wavered. The western power eluded clear definition for she persistently—if unwittingly—upset expectations.

Prior to 200 B.C. interest in Rome confined itself to narrow circles of the Greek intelligentsia and did not run deep even there. A fascination for the exotic piqued curiosity, engendering tales of an anthropological character; legends of Rome's origins connected with Aeneas and Troy provided material for learned disputation; facts about Roman history and institutions that drifted across the Adriatic were few and often garbled. There was but a small market for such information; the westerner still seemed remote. Rome obtruded herself upon the Greek world in a more visible way during the First Macedonian War, earning ill repute for ferocity. But her involvement was fragmentary and her departure sudden, leaving uncertain impressions in her wake. An image had yet to form.

The smashing victories over Philip, Aetolia, and Antiochus shook the balance of the East with dramatic force. Hellenistic experience could lead the Greeks to but one conclusion: that Rome had come to conquer and would stay to rule. Poets and oracles hailed her greatness as heir to a line of empires, or else they looked for vengeance and a savior from the domination that seemed inevitable. But the domination did not come, or at least not in the form that Greeks had learned to expect. Physical withdrawal had caused surprise, a surprise augmented by what seemed to be moral withdrawal as well. What kind of hegemon was this who shirked responsibility and had to be prodded to exercise any hegemony at all? Discussion and debate in Hellas reflect neither favor nor animosity so much as bafflement. For nearly two decades Rome retreated to aloofness from eastern affairs, a fact that began to engender new understanding, only to shatter it once again by a stunning reentry with even more devastating effects. The dismemberment of Macedonia and the humiliation of various eastern powers produced a spectrum of reactions from terror to despondency. Yet hardly had the air cleared when Roman coercion began to give way to inertia and indifference. The boundaries of Hellenistic autonomy evaporated just when they seemed to be receiving definition. Adjustment to unexpected latitude came in cautious and anxious steps. But when confidence was regained it issued in missteps—with the calamitous results of 146. Roman authority was anything but comprehensible: awesome and imposing, but capricious, arbitrary, and unpredictable. The traces of attitudes in mid- and late second century Greece fly in numerous directions: nervous celebration of Roman power, allusions to ruthlessness, apocalyptic visions of the new world empire that will follow the path and encounter the doom of its predecessors. A mixed brew of anxiety and admiration, hopes and disappointments, anger, frustration, and plain bafflement.

Efforts to rationalize were condemned to failure. Polybius commended the Roman accomplishment, framed his history around it, but proved unable to explain it. Or rather the explanation of its means fluctuated, while its end defied his understanding. Posidonius confronted the results rather than the acquisition of empire. But he came no closer to a systematic conception. Polybius took his history beyond its original terminus for the avowed purpose of assessing Roman overseas governance. But he never made that assessment. And Posidonius, who did make it, arrived at equivocal conclusions that involved moral corruption, avaricious Roman officials, lamentable social conditions, and noxious Greek rebels. The nature of Roman rule, like the reasons for attaining empire, remain elusive, even to the best-trained minds.

Division of Hellas into those who approved and those who despised Rome misses the point. Reactions were complex and diverse. Hatred there was—also admiration, fear, gratitude, anger, disappointment, and, above all, confusion. There was no image of Rome in Greece, rather a succession of images coming in and out of focus. The westerner kept breaking patterns and frustrating attempts at configuration. To those who had to come to terms with it Roman behavior was infuriatingly erratic, the combination of sluggishness and volatility unfathomable. The Romans did not articulate the process of empire. And each time the Greeks felt they had a grasp on it they found it slip through their fingers.